ܟܬܒܐ ܕܩܕܡ ܘܒܬܪ

THE BOOK OF
BEFORE & AFTER

The Liturgy of the Hours of the Church of the East

Eastern Catholic Studies and Texts

EDITOR
Yury P. Avvakumov
University of Notre Dame (Notre Dame, IN, USA)

ASSISTANT EDITOR
Charles C. Yost
Hillsdale College (Hillsdale, MI, USA)

EDITORIAL BOARD
Edward J. Alam
Notre Dame University (Beirut, Lebanon)

Katrin Boeckh
Ludwig Maximilian University (Munich, Germany)

Daniel Galadza
Pontifical Oriental Institute (Rome, Italy)

Thomas Kollamparampil
Christ University (Bangalore, India)

Mark Morozowich
The Catholic University of America (Washington DC, USA)

Thomas Mark Németh
University of Vienna (Vienna, Austria)

Laura Stanciu
University "1 Decembrie 1918" (Alba Iulia, Romania)

Oleh Turiy
Ukrainian Catholic University (Lviv, Ukraine)

THE BOOK OF BEFORE & AFTER

The Liturgy of the Hours
of the Church of the East

Edited and Translated
by
Fr. Andrew Younan

THE CATHOLIC UNIVERSITY OF AMERICA PRESS

WASHINGTON, D.C.

Copyright © 2024
The Catholic University of America Press
All rights reserved

The paper used in this publication meets the minimum requirements of American National Standards for Information Science—Permanence of Paper for Printed Library Materials, ANSI Z39.48-1992.

Cataloging-in-Publication Data is available from the Library of Congress

ISBN: 978-0-8132-3878-4
eISBN: 978-0-8132-3879-1

Table of Contents

Translator's Preface	vii
Psalm Numberings	xxxiii
Sunday and Feast Day Mass Readings	xxxv
Traditional *Ḥudhra* Introductions	
BrykhYsho', 13th Century	xxxix
Mar Putrus Eliya XII, 1887	xlii
Eugene Cardinal Tisserant, 1938	xlviii
Mar Thomas Darmo, 1960	l
Mar Eshai Shim'un XXIII, 1961	lix
PRAYER ORDINARIES	
Sunday Evening Prayer	1
Sunday Night Prayer	31
Sunday Morning Prayer	46
Weekday Evening Prayer	61
Cycle for Weekday Evening Prayer	69
Weekday Night Prayer	116
Weekday Morning Prayer	127
EMMANUEL PRAYERS	
Emmanuel Sunday Evening Prayer	141
Emmanuel Sunday Vigil	157
Seasonal Glorifications	159
Emmanuel Weekday Evening Prayer	167
Emmanuel Weekday Evening Prayer for Lent	175
Emmanuel Cycle for Weekday Evening Prayer	185
Emmanuel Weekday Morning Prayer	225
Shorter Prayers	243

PSALTER	257
MARTYR HYMNS	353

SELECTIONS FROM THE *ḤUDHRA*/SEASONAL PROPERS

Subara/Advent & Christmas	389
Dinḥa/Epiphany	408
Ba'utha of the Ninevites	423
Ṣawma/Lent	475
Holy Week	487
Resurrection & Ascension	501
Pentecost & Apostles	520
Summer/Repentance	534
Cross (with Elijah & Moses)	547
Sanctification of the Church	570

DEVOTIONS

Holy *Qurbana*/Eucharist	579
Blessed Virgin Mary	584
Way of the Cross	586
Ordering of the Month or Year	600
Novena to Mar Abba the Great	601
Various Blessings	603
Devotional Prayers	607
Funeral Rite Hymns	608
Confession	612

Translator's Preface

A Church's liturgy of the hours is its heartbeat: both a cause and an effect of its continued life from day to day and year to year. This volume is an attempt to render into English, for the first time in a form ready for the use of the faithful, the liturgy of the hours of the Church of the East (more precisely, the full repeated portion or "Ordinary" and selections of the seasonal "Propers").[1] I will therefore introduce this book by (1) delineating what is meant by the terms "Church of the East" and "liturgy of the hours." I will then outline the historical development of (2) the prayers and (3) the liturgical year presented in this book. After this historical sketch, I will discuss (4) some theological issues related to the Church of the East, (5) explain the rationale for the contents of this book and the manner of translation, and finally (6) present a glossary of terms with their translation equivalents in this volume.

I. The Church of the East and Her Prayer

"Church of the East" sounds like an imprecise term, but it is technically the most correct name for the Church that was founded, according to venerable tradition, by St. Thomas the Apostle and his companions Addai (popularly known as St. Jude Thaddeus) and Mari. "East," in this name, means "east of the Roman Empire," and *not* "the eastern part of the Roman Empire." This Church has also been called (in some cases imprecisely) "the Church of Persia," "the Church of the Martyrs," and "the Nestorian Church." This apostolic tradition, then, is one with its historical location farther east than any of the Greek Churches (Orthodox or otherwise), as well as the Syriac Churches who have their roots in Antioch.[2] The current branches of this Church are now named the Chaldean Catholic Church, the Assyrian Church of the East, the Ancient Apostolic Assyrian Church of the East, and the Malabar Catholic Church. Its liturgical language (from which this book was translated) is Aramaic, the language spoken by Jesus Christ, and more

---

[1] The last partial edition was Arthur John Maclean's *East Syrian Daily Offices* in 1894. Previous to this volume, there are also my *The Book of Before & After: Prayer in the AssyroChaldean Church of the East* (2008), *New Babylon Prayer Book* (2011), and *Emmanuel* (2013).

[2] See, for example, the Synod of Isaac in 410 AD, referring even to Antioch as "the Church of the West." *Syndicon*, 3, 27. See also Baby Varghese, *The Early History of the Syriac Liturgy*, 112–13.

precisely the scholastic dialect of Aramaic used in the ancient cities of Edessa and Nisibis called Syriac.[3] This is a Church that has faced various waves of brutal persecution and discrimination till today, but one which has also had periods of significant success in evangelization as far east as China, even boasting of a Mongolian Patriarch.[4] It claims the beautiful poetry of St. Ephrem (many of whose works are translated in this book), as well as that of other masterful poets like Narsai and Abba the Great, heirs of the great theological schools of Edessa and Nisibis.[5] It is a Church with a rich and ancient tradition of prayer, worthy of our closest attention.

There are many elements that make up the life and constitution of a Church: its creed, sacraments, life of charity and mission, leadership, history, and much more. But all of its various aspects point to its ultimate goal, which is the union with God we call prayer. There are, of course, many kinds of prayer, especially on the part of an individual member of a Church, but if one were to ask what is *the* prayer *of* any given apostolic Church taken collectively, the answer would in every case be its liturgy of the hours. Every evening, morning, and other times of the day, the Church officially and formally gathers and sings its praises to God in the tradition it has developed from its earliest beginnings. This book contains, then, the liturgy of the hours of the Church of the East: its heartbeat; the way it expresses its life from moment to moment.

Aristotle defines time as "the measuring of motion by before and after."[6] The title of this book is not, for better or worse, a reference to Aristotle, but an English translation of the traditional title given to a selection of the liturgy of the hours which contained the most-repeated elements of the various prayers (what is technically called the "Ordinary"). "Before and after" here refer to the selections of Psalms and Hymns which are prayed "before" and "after" the central repeating Psalms of Evening Prayer. I have kept this traditional title because, whatever its origin, it evokes the idea of the passing of time, which is precisely what the prayers contained in this book are designed for. There are

---

[3] See Holger Gzella, "The Syriac Language in the Context of the Semitic Languages," in Daniel King, ed., *The Syriac World,* 205–21, and Aaron Michael Butts, "The Classical Syriac Language," in the same volume, 222–42.

[4] See David Wilmshurst, *The Martyred Church*, 234–59, and Christoph Baumer, *The Church of the East*, 195–234.

[5] See Arthur Voobus, *History of the School of Nisibis,* and Adam Becker's *Fear of God and the Beginning of Wisdom* and *Sources for the Study of the School of Nisibis.*

[6] Aristotle, *Physics* IV.11, a25.

cycles that are repeated every day (like the repeated Psalms of each Morning and Evening Prayer); there are weekly cycles that overlap the daily cycles (like the Glorifications set for each night or morning); there are cycles for two or three weeks (like the "before" and "after" collections of Evening Prayer); there are cycles of seven weeks, corresponding to the weeks of the liturgical season. The overlapping and intermingling of these various repetitive cycles are like the gears of a clock, each turning and moving the other in a complex and beautiful unity.

There are, then, daily organizations of time, where the Church teaches us what we should sing to God, and indeed what we should feel, every day. Every single morning, the Church tells us to pray Psalm 100,[7] glorifying God and thanking him for creating the world and (according to the antiphon added) especially for giving us light: "Glorify the Lord, all the earth! *O Giver of Light, O Lord, we lift up praise to you!*" Every single evening, the Church tells us to pray Psalm 140, and to ask God to accept our prayer like the incense offered every evening in the Temple, and Psalm 118, which reminds us that, despite the setting of the sun and the encroaching darkness, God's word is a lamp for our feet and a light for our paths. These prayers, repeated (some would say *ad nauseam*) on a daily basis, are not meant to make us sick of them, but rather to form our souls. If we do not feel like thanking God for his creation in the morning or asking for his light in the evening, well, the Church says "too bad," because doing so is good for us, and she is our mother who teaches us to feel what we should feel, by example and by practice.

Similarly, the liturgical year cycles through salvation history over and over again, commemorating the angel's annunciation to Mary, the birth of Christ, his baptism, his battle with the devil in the desert, his passion, death, resurrection, and ascension, the descent of the Holy Spirit, the preaching of the Apostles, the repentance of the nations, the victory of the cross, and the final crowning of the Church in heavenly glory. Year after year, the Church invites us to be absorbed not only into our own lives and concerns, but more and more into the life of Christ, so that we can live with eyes open to a larger world, where God's salvation is the focus.

---

[7] In the numbering of the Pshytta. See chart on page xxxiii.

II. THE LITURGY OF THE HOURS

In the Church of the East, the new liturgical day begins not at midnight or in the morning but when the sun goes down in the evening. This ancient way of thinking about time hearkens back to Genesis 1:5: "there was evening and there was morning, one day."[8] Evening is named first here, and evening is consequentially the first part of the new day in the liturgy. There are still remnants of this understanding of the day in celebrations of Christmas Eve, and similar times. The first "hour" or "office" of the "liturgy of the hours" is therefore *Ramsha* or Evening Prayer. The other major "office" or "official prayer time" is *Ṣapra* or Morning Prayer. On Sundays and Feast Days, there is a Vigil Prayer, which is prayed late into the night.

These three prayer times, Evening, Vigil, and Morning, make up what is called the "Cathedral" set of prayers, which were designed for the life of everyday faithful to attend at their local parish church. Indeed, there is legislation requiring the faithful to attend these prayers as early as the first Synod of the Church of the East in 410 AD.[9] This is, in fact, one of the remarkable aspects of the liturgy of the hours of the Church of the East in particular, that to a great degree it is intended to be part of the life of all the members of the Church, not only clergy and monks.[10]

In addition to these "Cathedral" offices, there was also a set of "monastic" offices prayed more or less every three hours throughout the day. These "minor hours" were, to a great degree, lost or absorbed into the three major hours over the centuries, and indeed were never given the same kind of formal legislative attention given to the Cathedral hours. Different groups of monks prayed the entire Psalter (all 150 Psalms) at different intervals: some every two weeks, some weekly, some daily. Until very recently, with the publications of the *Ḥudhra* (the printed collection of the liturgy of the hours) there were many different distributions of the Psalter in the manuscripts.[11] In general, the Psalter was divided, first into a unit called a *Marmytha* (plural *Marmyatha*), which generally contains around 3 Psalms, and then later (historically

---

[8] Bible quotes in this volume are from the RSV, outside the Psalms and *Hulala* 21, which are translated directly from the Pshytta.

[9] See Jean-Baptiste Chabot, *Synodicon*, 28–29.

[10] See Robert Taft, *The Liturgy of the Hours in East and West*, 225–26.

[11] See Gabriele Winkler, "Das Offizium," 300–301; Robert Taft, *The Liturgy of the Hours in East and West*, 227; Juan Mateos, *Lelya-Sapra*, IV.2.

speaking) into larger sections called *Hulale* (singular *Hulala*), each of which contains 3 or so *Marmyatha*.[12] There is a table illustrating this division at the end of this Preface. In any case, the number of *Hulale* prayed per day in any given monastery was very often a matter of local custom more than official legislation.

The historical development of the different "hours" is a fascinating area of study that has been somewhat neglected in the past few decades.[13] This is not the place to go into great detail in this matter, but a few interesting traditional attributions may be edifying. The division of the prayer services into two "choirs" which recite or sing Psalms and Hymns in alternation, for example, is attributed to the famous Patriarch-Martyr Shim'un Bar Sabba'e.[14] Many of the poetic theological *Madrashe* (meditative doctrinal poems) are attributed to St. Ephrem, and apparently intended for women to sing.[15] The petitions (or at least a portion of them) at the end of the services were apparently added due to the advice of Mar Marutha at the above-mentioned Synod of Isaac in 410 AD, to whom also are attributed the beautiful Martyr Hymns of Evening and Morning Prayer.[16] The Trisagion ("Holy God, Holy Mighty One, Holy Immortal One...") was translated from Greek and inserted into the various liturgies by Mar Abba the Great in the 6th Century, who also composed the antiphons and prayers within the Psalter, and possibly created its division into *Marmyatha*.[17] The ornamented Our Father said at the beginning and end of many of the prayers was inserted by Timothy I in the 8th Century.[18] Above all, the most significant major reform of the liturgy of the Church of the East, including the liturgy of the hours and the liturgical year, was done during the time of Patriarch Isho'yahb III in the 600s. There he likely combined many monastic elements with the pre-existing cathedral offices, and collected, composed, or

---

[12] See Gregory Woolfenden, *Daily Liturgical Prayer*, 123; Mateos, *Lelya-Sapra*, III.2.
[13] See the Bibliography for some of the major works in this area.
[14] See Robert Taft, *The Liturgy of the Hours in East and West*, 226; Sarhad Jammo, *The Chaldean Liturgy*, 8; Varghese Pathikulangara, *Divine Praises and the Liturgical Year*, 24.
[15] Juan Mateos, *Lelya-Sapra*, IV.2. Excursus A.
[16] See Awa Royel, "Singing Hymns to the Martyrs," 8.
[17] See Gregory Woolfenden, *Daily Liturgical Prayer,* 135.
[18] See Gregory Woolfenden, *Daily Liturgical Prayer*, 121; Juan Mateos, *Lelya-Sapra*, I.1, Excursus A, notes that this practice had previously been forbidden by Isho'yahb III, and that Timothy prescribed it to be said *twice*, at the beginning and end of services, after a Jacobite monk asked why the Nestorians do not pray the Lord's Prayer at the end of their offices.

commissioned many of the beautiful *'onyatha* or Hymns contained in this volume.[19] Later, in the middle ages, other wonderful compositions were added to the existing sets of prayers, written by poets like George Warda,[20] and long (sometimes tedious) theological prayers intended to begin Sunday Morning Prayer were written by Patriarch Elias III, also known as Abu Ḥalim.[21]

I will now give a short description of the two most important Cathedral hours, Evening and Morning Prayer. Starting, as the liturgical day does, with *Ramsha*/Evening Prayer, we can look at a basic structural outline as it is found and practiced today, omitting the priest prayers which are interspersed between each element:

Ornamented Our Father
Marmytha Psalms
[Sundays/Feasts: Hymn of Incense]
Lakhu Mara with Lucernary Rite
Psalmody and Hymns "Before"
Central Evening Psalms 140, 141, 118:105–12, and 116
Psalmody and Hymns "After"
Petitions
Trisagion
Basilica/Seasonal Hymn
Seasonal Psalmody on Sundays or "Letter" Psalms on Weekdays
[Weekdays outside Lent: Martyr Hymns]
Ornamented Our Father

The basic primordial "core" of *Ramsha* or Evening Prayer is the set of Psalms 140, 141, 118:105–12, and 116, the most ancient parts being 140 and 118:105–12.[22] This is prayed daily, and is most likely the most ancient part of the prayer. "Before and after" these Psalms, other Psalms were selected to vary for each day of the week in a two-week cycle. Being part of the Cathedral office, the "before and after" Psalms were topical and selective, and not an attempt to divide the Psalter to be recited completely over some given period of time as in the monastic Psalm divisions. Petitions marked the end of the prayer, followed by a blessing and the sign of peace. Later, but still early enough to be

---

[19] See Baby Varghese, *The Early History of the Syriac Liturgy*, 116–17.
[20] See Anton Pritula, *The Warda: An East Syriac Hymnological Collection*.
[21] Robert Taft, *The Liturgy of the Hours in East and West*, 228.
[22] Gregory Woolfenden, *Daily Liturgical Prayer*, 126–27.

mentioned by all extant commentaries, the beautiful hymn *Lakhu Mara*[23] was placed as an opening hymn to the prayer accompanied by a "Lucernary" ritual, where the curtain of the sanctuary was opened, incense was burned, and the lamps were lit.[24] Probably at the time of Abba the Great, the Trisagion was placed at the end, as a final hymn to be sung after the Petitions.[25] Martyr Hymns were sung after the conclusion of Evening Prayer, during a procession to the reliquary of the parish.[26] Again, Isho'yahb added *'onyatha* or Hymns to the "before and after" Psalmodies, as well as seasonal hymns called, on Sundays, "Basilica Hymns," and attached the monastic *Marmytha* Psalms (which would have been prayed earlier in the afternoon) to the beginning, and the "Letter Psalms" (named after the lettered sections of Psalm 118, prayed later in the night by monastics) to the end of Evening Prayer. Finally, Timothy I added his ornate Our Father to each prayer's beginning and end.[27] *Ramsha* therefore developed from the inside-out, with various elements being added to the beginning and end over the centuries.

The structure and development of *Ṣapra* or Morning Prayer is much simpler, which alone is a sign of the prayer's antiquity:

>Psalm 100
>Psalm 91
>Psalm 104
>Psalm 113
>Psalm 93
>Psalm 148
>[On Weekdays: Psalm 149]
>Psalm 150

---

[23] Juan Mateos, "L'office divin," 277, is certain that this hymn is quite ancient.
[24] See Juan Mateos, "L'office du matin et du soir," 78–79; Gregory Woolfenden, *Daily Liturgical Prayer*, 123.
[25] Gregory Woolfenden, *Daily Liturgical Prayer*, 125; Sarhad Jammo, "L'office du soir chaldeean," 190–91;
[26] See Awa Royel, "Singing Hymns to the Martyrs," 7; Gregory Woolfenden, *Daily Liturgical Prayer*, 130.
[27] See Juan Mateos, "L'office divin," 253–75; Sarhad Jammo, "L'office du soir chaldeean," 187–208, recognizes the beginning of the Cathedral office is indicated by the opening of the outer curtain during *Lakhu Mara*; he also posits the possibility that the Basilica Hymns were settled at the time of Abba the Great, since they are mentioned by Gabriel Qatraya. See also Robert Taft, *The Liturgy of the Hours in East and West*, 235.

Psalm 116
[On Sundays: Seasonal Hymn with Lucernary Rite
Popular Hymn "At Dawn of Morning"
"Light" Hymns of Ephrem and Narsai
Canticle from Daniel 3:57–88
The Gloria in Excelsis Deo]
[On Weekdays:
Lakhu Mara with Lucernary Rite
Psalm 51
Hymn of Praise "Glory to you, our God"]
Trisagion
Ornamented Our Father
[On Weekdays outside Lent: Martyr Hymns
then the complete "At Dawn of Morning" set of hymns]

Again we find an ancient "core" of the prayer in the form of selected Psalms which are prayed every day. The majority of Morning Prayer being Psalms, and the fact that the prayer is almost entirely disconnected from the liturgical season, both attest to the antiquity of this liturgy.[28] Scholars speculate about which portions of this morning Psalmody are the oldest,[29] but the list above is the received ritual still in use today. The avoidance of Psalm 149 on Sundays and Feasts is likely due to the fact that those are the days when public officials would be most likely to attend services, and the Church preferred not to sing the verse about binding kings in chains in front of them.[30] The contrast between singing the Daniel canticle on Sundays versus Psalm 51 on weekdays illustrates the different spiritual aspects of glorification and penitence proper to each. It is likely that the two "Light" hymns of Ephrem and Narsai were intended to be alternated from Sunday to Sunday, and even that Narsai himself composed his hymn for this purpose, but the current practice is to sing both of them together.[31]

---

[28] See Gabriele Winkler, "Das Offizium," 303; Juan Mateos, "L'office divin," 270–71.

[29] Gregory Woolfenden, *Daily Liturgical Prayer,* 143, posits that "the most ancient part of sapra must be psalms 148–50 and 116"; Juan Mateos, "L'office divin," 271–72, posits Psalms 100, 91, and 112 as the oldest, noting 91 as possibly deriving from Jewish synagogue usage.

[30] See Juan Mateos, *Lelya-Sapra,* I.1.5; Robert Taft, *The Liturgy of the Hours in East and West,* 233.

[31] See Juan Mateos, *Lelya-Sapra,* I.1.5.c.

III.   THE LITURGICAL YEAR

Rather than discuss the possible historical development of the liturgical year, which is admittedly cloudier than that of the "hours," I will instead discuss the fully-developed year season-by-season, and make some final conclusions about the concept of the year as a whole, seen in terms of the Jubilee Year of Leviticus 25.[32]

The current liturgical year begins with *Subara*, literally translated as "Annunciation" but basically corresponding to Advent, the (more or less) four weeks preceding Christmas.[33] Along with it we can consider Christmas itself (celebrated on December 25th), and the (more or less) two Sundays between it and Epiphany, as making up one thematic season together, with Christmas as the centerpiece. The liturgical Mass readings focus on the preparation for the birth of Christ, the actual event of the Nativity, and the events following it such as the presentation in the temple. The prayers and hymns contained in the "Propers" for this season have the same focus as well. Though there are no indications in any of this that the season is one of fasting or penitence, there is a longstanding practice of considering Advent to be a season of preparation for Christmas analogous to Lent, the preparation for Easter, and therefore there is a practice of fasting as a spiritual preparation for receiving Christ into the world and into one's soul.[34] The year begins, therefore, with the beginning of the Gospel.

The second major season is *Dinḥa*, which literally means "the dawn," and which is rendered "Epiphany" in this volume. This season centers thematically around the feast day of Epiphany, which takes place on January 6th. In the Church of the East, Epiphany is the memorial of the baptism of Christ (not of the visit of the Magi as in some Western traditions), and the season celebrates the revelation of the Son of God to the world through this event at the beginning of his ministry as well as the revelation of the Holy Trinity. The Epiphany season is flexible in length, and can be as short as 5 weeks or as long

---

[32] In this I follow closely the arguments of Sarhad Jammo, *The Chaldean Liturgy*, 24–28.

[33] In translating these terms, I have generally opted to use the better-known equivalents rather than a literal rendering of the term, e.g. "Advent" rather than "Annunciation" for *Subara*, "Lent" rather than "the Great Fast" for *Ṣawma Rabba*, "Epiphany" rather than "the Dawning" for *Dinḥa*, etc., except where the literal meaning of the term might be relevant.

[34] Discussed by Juan Mateos, *Lelya-Sapra*, II.1.1.

as 8 weeks, due to the variable date of Easter and the rigidity of the length of Lent as 40 days exactly.

Within the season of Epiphany, after the fifth Sunday of this season and three weeks before the beginning of Lent, the Church of the East celebrates the *Ba'utha* or Supplication of the Ninevites. This three-day season of penitence commemorating the visit of Jonah to the city of Nineveh is one of the great treasures of the liturgy of the Church of the East, which was put together after a famine during the 6th Century.[35] The hymns and prayers arranged for this season are drawn from the works of Ephrem (for Monday and Tuesday) and Narsai (for the first section of Wednesday), and showcase the brilliance of the Church of the East's ability to take already-existing literary material and repurposing it for its different needs. In this case, the metrical homilies of Ephrem and Narsai were divided into sections, and given varying (and very beautiful) melodies to be sung during these three days of intense fasting and prayer. The selection from Jonah therein is taken from the RSV.

The season of *Ṣawma Rabba* (the "Great Fast") or Lent begins on a Sunday, though the fasting does not begin until that Monday (and indeed, the themes of the hymns of that Sunday are not clearly connected to Lent, to the point where there is debate whether the season did not originally begin later).[36] Counting forty days from that Monday, omitting Sundays as a day of rest and celebration of the Resurrection, we number the fast days until Wednesday of Holy Week, and begin the Triduum on Passover Thursday.[37] Thematically, Lent in the Church of the East is less about ashes and remembrance of death, and more about accompanying Christ in the wilderness as he wages battle, as the Head of the human race and the example for us all, against Satan .

Holy Week contains a number of liturgical masterpieces in its Propers, and from Palm Sunday the Church re-presents almost a day-to-day depiction of the events of Christ's life leading up to his crucifixion and resurrection. Easter itself begins a new season named after it, and extending for forty days until Ascension Thursday, and a bit longer still until Pentecost Sunday. Each day of the week following Easter is celebrated as if it were a Sunday, and the week is collectively called "the Week of Weeks." The second Sunday of the

---

[35] See Juan Mateos, *Lelya-Sapra*, II.1.3.
[36] This possibility is discussed by Juan Mateos, *Lelya-Sapra*, II.1.3.
[37] See Juan Mateos, *Lelya-Sapra*, II.1.3.2.

Easter Season is given the title "New Sunday," and it celebrates the renewal of the human race in the glorified risen body of Christ, as well as the ceremonial changing of the white garments worn by those who were baptized the previous week at the Easter Vigil. The Propers for this Sunday include the beautiful hymn *Apin Shalḥyton*, "Though you may take off," attributed to Shim'un Bar Sabba'e.

Pentecost begins the season of the Apostles, where the missionary commission of Christ is commemorated, showing that the life of the Church flows directly from the life of Christ. From this season forward, the Martyr Hymns are especially appropriate, since the witness of the martyrs is among the greatest glories of the Church. For seven weeks, the work and witness of the apostles is celebrated, and many of the liturgical hymns discuss the priesthood of the Church, and its power to bring light to the world and to forgive sins.

Naturally flowing from the season of the Apostles is the season usually called "Summer," but whose original name comes from the hymn of the first Friday of the season, *Ḥallelayn*, "Wash me…" In this volume, this original name is approximated by the name "Repentance," and it is always given along with the name "Summer" to avoid confusion. It is here that some ancient sources are in particular tension with the current practice of numbering, and it appears that what is now the *second* Sunday of "Summer" was at some point the *first* Sunday of *Ḥallelayn*.[38] This shift in numbering would affect the seasons before and after it as well (and would make sense of the Memorial of the Twelve Apostles, which currently falls on the First Sunday of Summer and not in the season of the Apostles at all). In any case, the traditional numbering is given in this volume. The season of Summer or Repentance is about the fruit of the preaching of the Church, which is the conversion of souls and their return to God. As such its theme is penitence, and the hymns assigned for this season are among the most passionate in asking God for forgiveness and help in fighting against temptation.

After the season of Summer/Repentance until the end of the liturgical year, every Sunday contains Propers (some of which are included in this volume) for a primordial season "of the Cross." The reforms of Isho'yahb III seem to have introduced two overlapping seasons on top of this original one,

---

[38] See Sarhad Jammo, *The Chaldean Liturgy*, 24–26; Juan Mateos, *Lelya-Sapra*, II.6.4; Varghese Pathikulangara, *Divine Praises and the Liturgical Year*, 193.

those of Elijah and of Moses.[39] Some commentaries, like the Introduction of the monk BrykhYsho' which follows this Preface, attempt to tie the season of Elijah and the Cross together thematically by asserting the Cross as the "sign of Elijah" to come at the end of days, but it is quite difficult to see what Moses has to do with any of this, or why his season (celebrated for four weeks at most) would come after that of Elijah, when the person of Moses came so much earlier than the person of Elijah. This season is also famous for the confusing naming of Sundays such as "the First Sunday of the Cross and Fourth of Elijah." The original season of the Cross, during which the Feast of the Finding of the Cross is celebrated (on September 13th), was another flexible season like that of Epiphany, to make up the weeks increasing or decreasing depending on the date of Easter. It commemorates not only the finding of the wood of the cross by Helena, but the victory of the cross of Christ in the world following the repentance of the nations after the preaching of the apostles. There is logic here, following the seasons commemorating the life of Christ up to the Ascension, then counting the nine days to Pentecost, then following the preaching of the Apostles, to the repentance of the world and of each of our souls, to the victory of Christ, again both in the world and in each of our souls. This logic is confused by the overlapping themes of Elijah and Moses, but the original Propers "of the Cross" are still retained as a foundation. Further evidence of the unity of this season under the theme of the Cross is the "continuation" of the Sunday Basilica Hymn, "Through the great power of the Cross..." (see p. 23). There is no distinct continuation hymn for Elijah or for Moses. All the Sundays of these seasons share the one hymn whose theme is the Cross.

    The final season of the liturgical year is that of the Sanctification or the Dedication of the Church. This season is truly exceptional because it is only four weeks long, whereas even the pseudo-season of Moses had at some point seven theoretical Sundays, despite the fact that they would never be celebrated. In the case of the season of the Church, we have a different kind of season. The theme is no longer one tied to the earthly history of salvation, whether pointed to the life of Christ, the preaching of the apostles, or the victory of the cross. Now, the Church celebrates its wedding in the eternity of heaven, its union with the heavenly Bridegroom. The hymns of this season

---

[39] See Sarhad Jammo, *The Chaldean Liturgy*, 24; Juan Mateos, *Lelya-Sapra*, II.7.3.

reflect this future glorification, but also relate a kind of piety toward the priesthood which constitutes an important serving class in the Church.

The word for "season" in Aramaic is *shawo'a*, which is related to the word for "seven." Theoretically, each of the major seasons of the liturgical calendar has seven weeks.[40] In some cases, such as Lent or Summer, the number of weeks is exactly seven. In other cases, such as Advent/Christmas, there are six Sundays and a major Feast which "counts" as the seventh week of the *shawo'a*, or in the case of Epiphany and the Cross season, there are "around" seven weeks, but there is flexibility in making the season longer or shorter in order to accommodate the varying dates of Easter. But the basic idea of a season is the number seven. Jammo notices a beautiful undercurrent unifying the entire liturgical year.[41] Multiply these seven weeks with the number of full seasons:

1. Advent/Christmas
2. Epiphany
3. Lent
4. Easter/Ascension
5. Pentecost/Apostles
6. Summer/Repentance
7. Cross

Seven sevens equal forty-nine, and the final capstone season reaching into eternity, that of the Sanctification of the Church, gives us a Jubilee like the one described in Leviticus 25:8–14:

> And you shall count seven weeks of years, seven times seven years, so that the time of the seven weeks of years shall be to you forty-nine years. Then you shall send abroad the loud trumpet on the tenth day of the seventh month; on the day of atonement you shall send abroad the trumpet throughout all your land. And you shall hallow the fiftieth year, and proclaim liberty throughout the land to all its inhabitants; it shall be a jubilee for you, when each of you shall return to his property and each of you shall return to his family. A jubilee shall that fiftieth year be to you; in it you shall neither sow, nor reap what grows of itself, nor gather the grapes from the undressed vines. For it is a jubilee; it shall be holy to you; you shall eat what it yields out of the field. In this year of jubilee each of you shall return to his property. And if you sell to your

---

[40] See Juan Mateos, *Lelya-Sapra*, I.1.
[41] Sarhad Jammo, *The Chaldean Liturgy*, 28.

neighbor or buy from your neighbor, you shall not wrong one another.

In this understanding of the liturgical year, we who live in the Christian dispensation are in a perpetual jubilee. In Christ, liberty is always given to slaves, debts are always erased, and rest is always found in our union with God, year after year.

IV. THE THEOLOGY OF THE CHURCH OF THE EAST

The proverbial elephant in the room is the supposed Nestorianism of the Church of the East, a heresy condemned in 431 AD at the Council of Ephesus under the most interesting conditions.[42] A great deal can be said about the teaching of Nestorius and the details surrounding the Council, much less the timeline whereby the Church of the East made any official pronouncement on Nestorius,[43] or ever began calling itself Nestorian, which was certainly later. However, this space is more reasonably spent discussing the Christology of the Church of the East as it is prayed in its liturgy, which is arguably its most important expression.[44] After this, I will make some comments on the Church of the East's ecclesiology in relation to the See of Rome and its relevance to the current volume.

While the debate between Nestorius and Cyril of Alexandria was originally about the term "mother of God" in reference to the Virgin Mary, the theological underpinning was quickly revealed as the identity of Jesus Christ. Is Jesus God, and not also man, or is he both, and if so, how? Cyril, stressing the Divinity of the Person of Christ, felt no compunction referring to his mother as "mother of God." Nestorius, stressing the distinction between Christ's Divinity and his humanity and limiting himself to terms found in the Scriptures, preferred the term "mother of Christ" or "mother of the Lord." Oversimplifying a very complicated history, Nestorius was eventually accused of dividing Christ into two separate persons: one God and one man. This teaching (whether or not it was truly the opinion of Nestorius) was condemned at the Council of Ephesus, and the Church of the East, who had

---

[42] See David Wilmshurst, *The Martyred Church*, 23–32; Christoph Baumer, *The Church of the East*, 42–50.

[43] Around 497. See David Wilmshurst, *The Martyred Church*, xiv, 68–70, 102–15.

[44] See Arthur John Maclean, *East Syrian Daily Offices*, vii, and his further comments on xxv.

already embraced the Scriptural interpretation of Theodore of Mopsuestia as its own, eventually aligned itself with Theodore's alleged student Nestorius.[45] Twenty years after the Council of Ephesus, another Council was held at Chalcedon. This Council condemned a thinker named Eutyches, who took Cyril's teaching and exaggerated it to the point of denying Christ's humanity after the Incarnation, saying he had only one Nature after the union. This Council clarified that Jesus Christ is:

> the same perfect in divinity and perfect in humanity, the same truly God and truly man, of a rational soul and a body; consubstantial with the Father as regards his divinity, and the same consubstantial with us as regards his humanity; like us in all respects except for sin; begotten before the ages from the Father as regards his divinity, and in the last days the same for us and for our salvation from Mary, the virgin God-bearer, as regards his humanity; one and the same Christ, Son, Lord, only-begotten, acknowledged in two natures which undergo no confusion, no change, no division, no separation; at no point was the difference between the natures taken away through the union, but rather the property of both natures is preserved and comes together into a single person and a single subsistent being; he is not parted or divided into two persons, but is one and the same only-begotten Son, God, Word, Lord Jesus Christ.[46]

The question here is whether the Church of the East's Christology, as expressed in its liturgy, is Chalcedonian. I cannot answer this question comprehensively here but will give representative examples of Christological texts found in this book that strongly suggest the answer is "yes."[47]

The first is the standard final blessing of Sunday Evening Prayer, which is found on p. 29 of this volume:

---

[45] Discussed by Bawai Soro, *The Church of the East*, 185–88.
[46] Norman Tanner, ed., *Decrees of the Ecumenical Councils*, vol. 1, 86
[47] See Juan Mateos, "L'office divin," 253; Arthur John Maclean, *East Syrian Daily Offices*, xxv: "The infrequent occurrence of Nestorian language will perhaps surprise the reader. If we put aside the mention of the names of Nestorius, Theodore the Interpreter, and Diodorus of Tarsus, and a very few passages (almost all of which are capable of an orthodox interpretation), we shall find no trace of heterodoxy in the following pages...we find much [in this book] that is quite inconsistent with true Nestorianism." See also the often-cited work by Sebastian Brock, "The Nestorian Church: A Lamentable Misnomer."

> Glory to you, O Jesus our victorious King, eternal Image of the Father, Begotten One without beginning, above the ages and creations, without whom we have neither hope nor expectation, O Creator! By the prayer of the just and chosen who have pleased you from the beginning, grant forgiveness for our sins, absolution for our faults, deliverance from our troubles and response to our requests. Bring us to your joyous Light and guard us, through your living cross, from all perils, hidden or manifest; now, at all times, and forever and ever.

This prayer, which is said at least once a week and is an option even daily, addresses Jesus from the start, which is the human name given to him by Mary and Joseph. Jesus is then given several titles that belong to God the Word, such as "eternal Image of the Father," and "Begotten One without beginning," and one title belonging to the Godhead as such, namely "Creator." To call Jesus Christ "the Creator" is nothing more or less than to use the "communication of idioms" which is the hallmark of the Christology of the Council of Ephesus, and the justification for Mary's title as "mother of God." There can be no doubt of the unity of Christ's Person in those reciting and receiving this blessing on a regular basis, nor any possibility of a separation of the Word of God from the man Jesus Christ.

A more particularly Christological text is found in the liturgy of Christmas Day, beginning on p. 398. This hymn, which is translated in selection in this volume, belongs to the later (possibly medieval) development of the Ḥudhra, and so is an expression of a Church in its full maturity. The hymn discusses the distinct natures of the Son of God and their proper operations:

> The Son of God showed the unveiled truth to his Church betrothed when he chose, in his love, to come to the world and proclaim and teach his Divinity and his humanity. * For he had been in the womb of his Father, before the ages, without beginning – truly, he is God indeed. * He came to us in the latter times, put on our body and saved us through it – truly, he is man indeed. * The prophets proclaimed him in their revelations, the just revealed him through their mysteries – truly, he is God indeed. * He was carried in the womb for nine months, and was also born as a man – truly, he is man indeed. * The angels glorified him – he is God indeed. He was placed in a manger – he is man indeed. The star proclaimed him – he is God indeed. He suckled milk – he is man indeed…

The distinct operations of Christ's two natures of Divinity and Humanity are described in a way identical to that of Pope Leo's letter to Flavian, canonized at the Council of Chalcedon: "The activity of each form is what is proper to it in communion with the other: that is, the Word performs what belongs to the Word, and the flesh accomplishes what belongs to the flesh. One of these performs brilliant miracles, the other sustains acts of violence."[48] Also perfectly in line with Chalcedon is the fact in the hymn that it is one and the same grammatical subject "he" who is "God indeed" and at the same time "man indeed." This again expresses perfect unity of Person along with distinctness of natures, each with its proper activity.

Another particularly Christological hymn is the famous *Brykh Ḥannana* of Babai the Great, sung during the Advent and Christmas seasons, and found on p. 159 in a singable (yet accurate) translation. In this hymn, among other things, Mary is said to "bear...the Son of God,"[49] practically giving her the title insisted on by Cyril and rejected by Nestorius.[50] It continues, speaking with precision: "For Christ is One, the Son of God, by all adored in two Natures." Yet again, the grammatical subject is singular, and is the Person of Jesus Christ. The hymn does introduce the technical term *qnoma* (plural *qnome*) which signifies that each of the two natures of Christ are individual natures rather than universal ones: Christ is the Son of God, not the Father or the Holy Spirit, and he is the Son of Mary named Jesus, not Socrates or Abraham or anyone else. There is no perfect equivalent to this term in English, and I have either transliterated it or rendered it "Individual" in this volume.

The two largest extant branches of the Church of the East named above, the Chaldean Catholic Church and the Malabar Church, are Eastern Churches *sui iuris* of the Catholic Church. The histories of the splitting of these branches, the various unions with Rome over the past five centuries, and the separation of the Malabar Church from the jurisdiction of the Chaldean Patriarchate, are extremely fascinating yet heated and complex issues.[51] Chaldean Patriarch

---

[48] Norman Tanner, ed., *Decrees of the Ecumenical Councils*, vol. 1, 79.

[49] *Dla zuwwagha yildath Maryam l'ammanuel bra d-Alaha*. Thomas Darmo, *Ḥudhra*, vol. 1, 118.

[50] The use of the title "Mother of God" in the Church of the East is discussed by Stefanos Alexopoulos and Maxwell E. Johnson, *Introduction to Eastern Christian Liturgies*, 160, and Sebastian Brock, "Mary in Syriac Tradition," 182–91.

[51] See David Wilmshurst, *The Martyred Church*, 316–51; Christoph Baumer, *The Church of the East*, 247–68. Especially fascinating is the Latin volume compiling evidence that the Church of

Putrus Eliya XII, introducing the printed *Ḥudhra* for the first time in 1887, rejoices in the fact of his Church's union with the Catholic Church and brags of the addition of new Roman feast days such as those of saints Barbara, Nicholas, and Joseph, while expressing relief at the cleansing of the "bitter poison of the heresy of Byzantium" (i.e. Nestorianism) from the pages of the liturgy.[52] Over seventy years later, Metropolitan Thomas Darmo and Patriarch Eshai Shim'un XXIII bemoan the corruption caused to the liturgy by the "upside-down Chaldeans," and boast of the publication of the true, pristine *Ḥudhra*, un-besmirched by outside interference.[53]

It is clear to me after spending decades translating and comparing the various editions of the *Ḥudhra* that both sides were exaggerating to the point of absurdity. On the one hand, the liturgies added from the Roman Calendar were either pieced together from already-extant hymns (such as that for the feast of *Corpus Christi*), or were newly composed with such mediocrity that they are barely celebrated (if noticed at all) today, and were not worth including in the present volume. On the other hand, the so-called "corruptions" inflicted upon the texts by the officers of the Catholic Church are universally both minor and unnecessary. I would venture a very liberal guess that no more than one hundred words were changed in the selection of the *Ḥudhra* presented here, and in not one case was there a theological necessity to do so.[54] The translations in this volume are therefore based on a comparative study of the 1886 Chaldean Hudhra and the Darmo *Ḥudhra* of 1960, but follow the latter where there are textual differences. A typical of example of this would be the use of the term "mother of Christ," which would in any case be ridiculous to call inaccurate. In other (again very rare) cases, the names of figures like Theodore and Nestorius are given in parentheses or in footnotes, in order to respect the Catholic sensibilities of the majority of the people who might make use of this book. In a similar vein, some hymns from the Catholic Feast of *Corpus Christi* were included since they are original to

---

the East had always embraced a Catholic ecclesiology written by Archbishop George 'Abdysho' Khayyat, *Romanorum Pontificum Primatus*.

[52] This volume, xliii. Robert Taft, *The Liturgy of the Hours in East and West*, 228, discusses the history of the publication of the *Ḥudhra*.

[53] This volume, lxi.

[54] See Awa Royel, "From Mosul to Turfan," 33, footnote 2: "Mar Thoma Darmo...undertook the task of printing the Assyrian edition of the hudra, though almost identically based on the Paul Bedjan edition, excluding all of the Latin feasts."

the Church of the East. Indeed, piety toward the Eucharist is, despite Patriarch Eshai Shim'un's complaint against the term transubstantiation,[55] as central to and compatible with the spirituality of the Church of the East as the veneration of Mary and the other saints.[56]

V. SELECTION AND TRANSLATION

The complete *Ḥudhra* is several thousand pages long, and any attempt to translate it, much less publish the translation, will take the better part of a lifetime and a committee of dedicated translators and editors. Having neither at my disposal, I decided to build upon the previous translated selections I have been working on for these many years and put together a single volume that will hopefully be of some use both to the devoted faithful of the Church of the East in all its branches, as well as to interested scholars.

The "Ordinaries," that is, the repeating portions of all the liturgical prayers, are translated here in full, in addition to the full Psalter (translated directly from the Aramaic, but admittedly with some mental reference to the Grail Psalter I prayed in the Roman Breviary as a seminarian), and the Martyr Hymns, all as contained in the *Kthawa da-Qdham wad-Bathar*, the "Book of Before and After." The Psalter is divided into the numbered *Hulale* and non-numbered *Marmyatha*, and includes the antiphons and priestly prayers attributed to Abba the Great. The hymns "before and after," the Martyr Hymns, and many other hymns and glorifications, are translated "singable" according to the traditional melodies (specifically those of Mosul, though adaptable to other variations). This was sometimes accomplished by taking a bit of liberty with English word order rather than sacrificing the literal meaning of the original text, and in a few cases, the melody was changed to one which is better known. In the cases of singable *'onyatha*/hymns, the melody name or *resh qala* is given in *red italics*. Rubrics, as the name implies, are printed in plain red, and the antiphons beginning or within hymns or Psalms are printed in **bold red**. Recordings of all singable portions of this book can be found at the website **beforeandafter.cc**. The ornate Our Father, the *Lakhu Mara*, and the

---

[55] This volume, lxii.
[56] Arthur John Maclean, *East Syrian Daily Offices,* xix: "Their addresses to St. Mary (in devotion to whom they yield to none) and their invocations of saints are remarkably staid."

Trisagion are always also given in transliteration, to facilitate praying them in the original language even when the rest of the service is in English.

The seasonal "Propers" given for each Sunday, Feast, and ferial day of the year are where the selection was most critical, since they make up the vast bulk of the *Ḥudhra*. For each week of the liturgical year, the Sunday's Evening Psalmody (*shuraya*), Basilica Hymn, Vigil Hymn (*'onytha d-qale d-shahra*), Madrasha (where there is one), Morning Hymn (*'onytha d-Ṣapra*), one Daniel Verse (*d-barekh*), and the Sanctuary Hymn (*'onytha d-Qanke*) are translated. The Morning Hymn, Daniel Verse, and Sanctuary Hymn are always singable. During the prayers of weekdays, I recommend praying the Evening Psalmody (which is marked with italics for singing according to the melody noted on p. xxxiv) and the Sanctuary Hymn of that Sunday, which is why I titled each set of Propers "First Week of Advent" rather than "First Sunday of Advent." All of the *Ba'utha* selections are singable aside from the reading from Jonah.

Between the traditional Ordinary and the Psalter, I provide the attempted Reform of the liturgy of the hours used in the Chaldean Catholic Diocese of St. Peter the Apostle in San Diego, California, originally published in a volume titled "Emmanuel." The principles of this Reform can be found in Jammo's *The Chaldean Liturgy: At the Gate of God*, and represent, in my view, a marvelous example of a liturgical reform that respects its traditional source material and adapts it for practical modern usage. This section of the present volume is, I think, particularly suited for community or personal daily prayer, but it can be safely ignored by anyone uninterested in it. In a similar vein, at the end of this book, I present a re-purposing of some of the traditional prayers and hymns for newer devotional practices such as Eucharistic Adoration, the Way of the Cross, and a Novena to Mar Abba the Great.

SOURCES FOR TRANSLATION
(Aramaic page numbers in italics)

	This volume	Bedjan *Ḥudhra*	Darmo *Ḥudhra*
Sunday Ordinaries	1–60	*1–18; 20–39*	*67–110*
Weekday Ordinaries	61–140	*40–42; 373–98*	*1–66*
Psalter	257–352	*216–337*	*241–392*
Martyr Hymns	353–88	*347–73*	*420–63*
Seasonal Propers (selected)	389–578	*53–end*	*113–end*

VI. Glossary

Abu Ḥalim: The Patriarch Eliah III of the 12th Century; also the name of a collection of prayers composed by him and others, specifically to introduce Morning Prayer for Sundays and Feasts.

Basilica Hymn: the Proper *'onytha* of each Sunday and Feast Day. Possibly named thus because of a connection to an ancient royal procession.[57]

Ba'utha: lit. "supplication." The *Ba'utha* of the Ninevites is a three-day period of fasting commemorating Jonah's visit to Nineveh. There were also a *Ba'utha* "of the Virgins," and one "of Mar Zayya," now obsolete.

Before and After: as a book title, it refers to a volume containing the Ordinaries of the liturgy of the hours, as well as the full Psalter and Martyr Hymns. The name comes particularly from the Psalmodies and Hymns ordered "before and after" the central Psalms of Evening Prayer.

Da-ḥraye: "latter"

Da-qdham: lit. "before"

Dinḥa: lit. "dawning"; the Feast of the Epiphany (the Baptism), and the corresponding season.

D-bathar: lit. "after"

D-qadhmaye: "former"

D-qanke: lit. "of the sanctuary."

Gazza: lit. "treasury." In manuscripts, the collection of Propers for Feast Days, in particular the Propers of the night services.

Giyyore: the antiphons within the Psalms attributed to Abba the Great

Hpakhta: lit. "a transition"; a portion of a prayer service between two sections.

Ḥudhra: lit. "cycle." As a book title, it can refer either to the complete published liturgy of the hours of the Church of the East, or, in manuscripts, to the collection of Propers for Sundays and Feast Days, as well as, at times, ordinary days.

Hulala, pl. ***Hulale:*** lit. "halleluiah-ing"; a larger division of the Psalms, usually made up of 3 *marmyatha*.

Kashkul: lit. "containing all." In manuscripts, the collection of the Propers for weekday prayer services.

---

[57] See Gregory Woolfenden, *Daily Liturgical Prayer*, 125; Varghese Pathikulangara, *Divine Praises and the Liturgical Year*, 52–53.

Khamis: An author from the 14th Century; also the name of a collection of hymns attributed to him.

Lilya: night prayer. Lit. "night."

Liturgical Season: a section of the liturgical year, thematically connected to some event or division of the life of Christ or salvation history.

Madrasha: a doctrinal hymn, often attributed to Ephrem.

Mar: lit. "lord"; a title used for either saints or bishops.

Marmytha, pl. *Marmyatha*: a collection of around 3 Psalms, prayed at the beginning of Evening Prayer.

Mawtwa: lit. "sitting"; a portion of a prayer service to be prayed while seated.

'Onytha: lit. "responsory," translated "hymn" in this volume due to the frequency of its use. Earlier English translations rendered this "anthem" due to its occasional use during processions.

Ordinary: the portions of a prayer service repeated on some regular prayers. Opposite: Propers.

Propers: the portions of a prayer service intended for ("proper to") a particular day. Opposite: Ordinary.

Qaltha: lit. "little song"; short hymns for night services, attributed to Narsai.

Qanona: lit. "canon," generally an antiphon related to a Psalm.

Qnoma (pl. *qnome*): "individual"; Three in the Trinity and Two in Christ.

Ramsha: evening prayer. Lit. "evening."

Resh Qala: the name of a melody.

Ṣapra: morning prayer. Lit. "morning."

Ṣawma: lit. "fasting"; the season of Lent.

Subara: lit. "annunciation"; the season of Advent.

Shahra: vigil prayer (particular to Sundays and Feasts). Lit. "vigil."

Shawo'a: a liturgical season.

Shuḥlape: a collection of hymns, organized according to melody. It is included in the printed editions of the *Ḥudhra*.

Shuraya: a Psalmody set for a prayer service.

Soghytha: a dialogue-poem between two or more characters.

Tishbuḥta: a glorification

Warda: An author from the 13th Century; also the name of a collection of poems including his works and those of others.

Yalda: the Nativity.

VII. Bibliography and Correspondence Charts

Printed Editions of the Ḥudhra

Bedjan, Paul. Editor. *Breviarium iuxta ritum Syrorum Orientalium id est Chaldaeorum*. 3 vols. Paris: Lutetiae Parisiorum, 1886. Reprinted in Rome in 1938 and 2002.

Darmo, Thomas. Editor. *Ḥudhra*. 3 vols. Thrishur, India: Mar Narsai Press, 1960.

Selected Manuscripts

Ḥudhra
- Vat. syr. 83 (1537): Assemani, *Catalogue* II, 456–57.
- Vat. syr. 86 (16th Century): Assemani, *Catalogue* II, 476–80.
- Vat. syr. 87 (third part of the Ḥudra, 15th Century): Assemani, *Catalogue* II, 269.
- Borgia syr. 85 (without date): Scher, *Notice*, 269.
- Borgia syr. 150 (15th Century): Scher, *Notice*, 281.
- Cambridge Add. 1981 (1607): Wright-Cook, *Catalogue*, 163–93.
- Mus. Brit. Add. 7177 (1484): Forshall, *Catalogue*, 55–56.

Gazza
- Cambridge Add. 1980 (1729): Wright-Cook, *Catalogue*, 147–63.
- Mus. Brit. Add. 7179 (15th Century): Forshall, *Catalogue*, 474–76.

Kashkul
- Vat. syr. 84 (1572): Assemani, *Catalogue*, 467–74.
- Vat. syr. 85 (1562): Assemani, *Catalogue*, 474–76.

Psalter
- Berlin orient. quart. 803 (18th Century): Sachau, *Catalogue*, 122–27.
- Mus. Brit. Add. 14,675 (13th Century): Wright, *Catalogue*, 129–31.
- Mus. Brit. Add. 17,219 (13th Century): Wright, *Catalogue*, 134–36.
- Cambridge Add. 1966 (1826): Wright-Cook, *Catalogue*, 25–38.

Book of Before and After
- Cambridge Add. 1979 (1707): Wright-Cook, *Catalogue*, 140–47.

Warda
- Cambridge Add. 1982 (1697): Wright-Cook, *Catalogue*, 193–265.

Khamis
- Cambridge Add. 1991 (1729): Wright-Cook, *Catalogue*, 365–86.

Abu-Ḥalim
- Cambridge Add. 1978 (1785): Wright-Cook, *Catalogue*, 121–40.

Secondary Sources

Alexopoulos, Stefanos, and Maxwell E. Johnson. *Introduction to Eastern Christian Liturgies.* Collegeville, Minnesota: Liturgical Press Academic, 2022.

Baumer, Christoph. *The Church of the East: An Illustrated History of Assyrian Christianity.* New York: I.B. Tauris, 2006.

Becker, Adam. *Fear of God and the Beginning of Wisdom: The School of Nisibis and the Development of Scholastic Culture in Late Antique Mesopotamia.* Philadelphia: University of Pennsylvania Press, 2006.

———. *Sources for the Study of the School of Nisibis.* Liverpool: Liverpool University Press, 2008.

Bradshaw, Paul. F. *Daily Prayer in the Early Church: A Study of the Origin and Early Development of the Divine Office.* Eugene, Oregon: Wipf and Stock, 1981.

Brock, Sebastian, Aaron M. Butts, George A. Kiraz, and Lucas Van Rompay. Editors. *Gorgias Encyclopedic Dictionary of the Syriac Heritage.* Piscataway, New Jersey: Gorgias Press, 2011.

Brock, Sebastian. "The Nestorian Church: A Lamentable Misnomer." *Bulletin of the John Rylands Library* 78, no. 3 (1996): 23–35.

———. "Mary in Syriac Tradition." In *Mary's Place in Christian Dialogue,* edited by A. Stacpoole, 182-91. Wilton: Morehouse-Barlow, 1982.

Chabot, Jean-Baptiste. Editor. *Syndicon Orientale.* Paris: Imprimerie Nationale, 1902.

Hunter, E. C. D., and J. F. Coakley. *A Syriac Service-Book [Hudra] from Turfan.* Turnhout: Berliner Turfantexte 39, 2017.

Jammo, Sarhad. "L'Office du soir chaldéen au temps de Gabriel Qatraya." *L'Orient Syrien* 12 (1967): 187–210.

———. *The Chaldean Liturgy: At the Gate of God.* El Cajon, California: Chaldean Media Center, 2014.

Khayyat, George 'Abdysho'. *Romanorum Pontificum Primatus.* Rome: Propaganda Fide, 1870.

King, Daniel, ed. *The Syriac World.* New York: Routledge, 2019.

Kuruthukulankara, P. *The Feast of the Nativity of our Lord in the Chaldean and Malabar Liturgical Year.* Kottayam: Oriental Institute of Religious Studies India 127, 1989.

Maclean, A. J. *East Syrian Daily Offices*. London: Rivington, Percival, & Co, 1894.

Macomber, William F. "A List of Known Manuscripts of the Chaldean Hudra." *Orientalia Christiana Periodica* 36 (1970): 120–34.

Mateos, Juan. "L'office du matin et du soir dans le rite chaldéen." *Le Maison-Dieu* 64 (1960): 65–89.

―――――. *Lelya-Sapra. Les offices chaldéens de la nuit et du matin*. Orientalia Christiana Analecta 156. Rome: Pontificale Institutum Studiorum Orientalium, second edition, 1992.

―――――. *Lelya-Sapra: Essai d'interpretation des matines chaldeennes*. Orientalia Christiana Analecta 156 (1959).

―――――. "Les différentes espèces de vigiles dans le rite chaldéen." *Orientalia Christiana Periodica* 27 (1961): 46–67.

―――――. "Les matines chaldéennes, maronites et syriennes." *Orientalia Christiana Periodica* 26 (1960): 51–73.

―――――. "Un office de minuit chez les chaldéens." *Orientalia Christiana Periodica* 25 (1959): 103–13.

―――――. "L'office divin chez les chaldéens." *Lex Orandi* 35: 253–81.

Moffett, Samuel Hugh. *A History of Christianity in Asia, vol. I*. San Francisco: Harper, 1992.

Moolan, John. "The History and Structure of the Syro-Malabar Liturgical Seasons." *Christian Orient* 25 (2004): 83–96.

―――――. *The Period of Annunciation-Nativity in the East Syrian Calendar*. Kottayam: Oriental Institute of Religious Studies India 90, 1985.

Pathikulangara, Varghese. *Divine Praises and the Liturgical Year*. Kottayam: Denha Services, 2000.

―――――. *Resurrection, Life and Renewal: A Theological Study of the Liturgical Celebrations of the Great Saturday and Sunday of the Resurrection in the Chaldeo-Indian Church*. Bangalore: Dharmaram Publications, 1982.

Pritula, Anton. *The Warda: An East Syriac Hymnological Collection; Study and Critical Edition*. Wiesbaden: Harrassowitz Verlag, 2015.

Pudicherry, Sylvester. *Ramsha: An Analysis and Interpretation of the Chaldean Vespers*. Bangalore: Dhamaram College Studies 9, 1972.

Royal, Mar Awa III. "Singing Hymns to the Martyrs: The 'Antiphons of the Sahde' in the Assyrian Church of the East." *Journal of the Canadian Society for Syriac Studies* 12 (2012): 3–11.

_____. "From Mosul to Turfan: The Hudra in the Liturgy of the Assyrian Church of the East: A Survey of its Historical Development and its Liturgical Anomalies at Turfan." *Ex Fonte - Journal of Ecumenical Studies in Liturgy* 1 (2022): 31–57.

Soro, Bawai. *The Church of the East: Apostolic and Orthodox.* San Jose, California: Adiabene Publications, 2007.

Taft, Robert, SJ. *The Liturgy of the Hours in East and West.* Collegeville, Minnesota, 1993.

_____. "On the Use of the Bema in the East-Syrian Liturgy." *Easter Churches Review* 3 (1970), pages 30–9.

_____. "Some Notes on the Bema in the East and West Syrian Traditions." *Orientalia Christiana Periodica* 34 (1968): 326–59.

Tanner, Norman P., SJ. *Decrees of the Ecumenical Councils.* 2 vols. Washington, D.C.: Georgetown University Press, 1990.

Tisserant, Eugene. "Nestorienne (l'Eglise)." *Dictionnaire de theologie catholique* 11.1. Paris, 1931.

Varghese, Baby. "East Syrian Liturgy During the Sassanid Period." *The Harp: A Review of Syriac and Oriental Ecumenical Studies* 15 (2002): 205–18.

_____. *The Early History of the Syriac Liturgy: Growth, Adaptation, and Inculturation.* Wiesbaden: Harrassowitz Verlag, 2021.

Vellian, Jacob. *East Syrian Evening Services.* Kottayam: Indian Institute for Eastern Churches, 1971.

Vööbus, Arthur. *History of the School of Nisibis.* Belgium: Peeters, 1965.

Wilmshurst, David. *The Martyred Church: A History of the Church of the East.* London: East and West Publishing, 2011.

Winkler, Gabriele. "Das Offizium am Ende des 4. Jahrhunderts und das heutige chaldäische Offizium, ihre strukturellen Zusammenhänge." *Ostkirchliche Studien* 19 (1970): 289–311.

_____. "Über die Kathedralvesper in der verschiedenen Riten des Ostens und Westens." *Archiv für Liturgiewissenschaft* 16 (1974): 53–102.

Woolfenden, Gregory W. *Daily Liturgical Prayer: Origins and Theology.* Burlington, Vermont: Ashgate, 2004.

Psalm Numberings

Hebrew	Greek	Aramaic
1–8	1–8	1–8
9–10	9	9–10
11–113	10–112	11–113
114–15	113	114
116:1–9	114	115:1–9
116:10–19	115	115:1–9
117–46	116–45	116–45
147:1–11	146	146
147:12–20	147	147
148–50	148–50	148–50

Hulala Numbering
(*Marmytha* divisions indicated by semicolons)

Hulala 1: Psalms 1–4; 5–7; 8–10.
Hulala 2: Psalms 11–14; 15–17; 18–21.
Hulala 3: Psalms 22–24; 25–27; 28–30.
Hulala 4: Psalms 31–32; 33–34; 35–36.
Hulala 5: Psalms 37; 38–40.
Hulala 6: Psalms 41–43; 44–46; 47–49.
Hulala 7: Psalms 50–52; 53–55; 56–58.
Hulala 8: Psalms 59–61; 62–64; 65–67.
Hulala 9: Psalms 68; 69–70.
Hulala 10: Psalms 71–72; 73–74; 75–77.
Hulala 11: Psalms 78; 79–81.
Hulala 12: Psalms 82–84; 85–86; 87–88.
Hulala 13: Psalms 89; 90–92.
Hulala 14: Psalms 93–95; 96–98; 99–101.
Hulala 15: Psalms 102–3; 104; 105.
Hulala 16: Psalms 106; 107–8; 109–11.
Hulala 17: Psalms 112–14; 115–17; 118: *alap–kap*.
Hulala 18: Psalms 118: *lamadh–taw*; 119–24; 125–30.
Hulala 19: Psalms 131–34; 135–37; 138–40.
Hulala 20: Psalms 141–43; 144–46; 147–50.
Hulala 21: Exodus 15:1–21, Isaiah 42:10–14; Deuteronomy 32:1–21; 32:21–43.

Table of Psalmody Melodies

Fixed Evening Psalms
Melody: Harmony beginning Ps 141:   Harmony beginning Ps 118:

Developed from the melody of the Sunday Ramsha Marmytha

Psalm Tones "Before & After"

Taken from a Psalm melody of the Pontifical Rites

Penitential Morning Psalm 51
Melody 1:   Melody 2:

Taken from a Lenten melody for Morning Prayer Psalms

Morning Meditation Psalms

Traditional

Seasonal Psalmodies

Taken from the melody of the traditional Mass Marmytha

Petitions

Taken from the melody of the weekday Ramsha Petitions

All recordings available at: beforeandafter.cc

Sunday and Feast Day Mass Readings

First Sunday of *Subara*/Advent: Genesis 17:1–27; Isaiah 42:18–43:13; Ephesians 5:21–6:9; Luke 1:1–25

Second Sunday of Advent: Numbers 22:20–23:2; Isaiah 43:14–44:5; Colossians 4:2–end; Luke 1:26–56

Third Sunday of Advent: Genesis 18:1–19; Judges 13:2–24; Ephesians 3:1–end; Luke 1:57–end

Fourth Sunday of Advent: Genesis 24:50–end; 1 Samuel 1:1–18; Ephesians 5:5–21; Matthew 1:18–end

Christmas: Isaiah 7:10–16, 9:1–8; Micah 4:1–5:10; Galatians 3:15–4:7; Luke 2:1–21

First Sunday after Christmas: Genesis 21:1–21; 1 Samuel 1:19–28; Galatians 4:18–5:1; Matthew 2:1–23

Second Sunday after Christmas: Exodus 2:1–10; Isaiah 49:1–6; 2 Timothy 2:16–end; Luke 2:21–end

Feast of *Dinḥa*/Epiphany: Numbers 24:2–end; Isaiah 4:2–6, 11:1–6, 9–11, 12:1–6; Titus 2:11–3:8; Matthew 3

First Sunday of Epiphany: Exodus 3:1–15; Isaiah 44:21–45:4; 2 Timothy 3:1–15; Luke 4:14–30

Second Sunday of Epiphany: Numbers 10:29–11:10; Isaiah 45:11–18; Hebrews 3:1–4:7; John 1:1–29

Third Sunday of Epiphany: Numbers 11:11–20; Isaiah 45:18–46:4; Hebrews 3:14–4:10; John 1:29–42

Fourth Sunday of Epiphany: Numbers 11:23–12:end; Isaiah 46:5–end; Hebrews 7:18–end; John 1:43–2:12

Fifth Sunday of Epiphany: Deuteronomy 18:9–22; Isaiah 48:12–20; Hebrews 6:9–7:3; John 3:1–21

Ba'utha Monday: 1 Timothy 2:1–3:11; Matthew 5:17–38

Ba'utha Tuesday: Romans 12; Luke 18:1–14

Ba'utha Wednesday: Colossians 3:1–4:2; Matthew 6:1–19

Sixth Sunday of Epiphany: Deuteronomy 24:9–end; Isaiah 43:7–17; Hebrews 8:1–9:11; John 3:22–4:4

Seventh Sunday of Epiphany: Deuteronomy 14:2–15:4; Isaiah 42:5–9, 14–17; 1 Timothy 6:9–21; Matthew 7:28–8:13

Eighth Sunday of Epiphany: Exodus 15:22–26, 16:4–11; Isaiah 44:23–45:8; Ephesians 1:15–2:8; John 5:19–30

Friday of the Deceased: 1 Corinthians 25:34–57; John 5:19–30

First Sunday of Ṣawma/Lent: Exodus 34:1–7, 27–35; Isaiah 58:1–12, 14–end; Ephesians 4:17–5:4, 5:15–21; Matthew 3:16–4:11
Second Sunday of Lent: Genesis 5:19–31; Joshua 4:15–24; Romans 6:1–23; Matthew 7:15–27
Third Sunday of Lent: Genesis 7:1–24; Joshua 5:13–6:5; Romans 7:14–25; Matthew 20:17–28
Fourth Sunday of Lent: Genesis 11:1–32; Joshua 6:27–7:15; Romans 8:12–27; Matthew 21:23–46
Fifth Sunday of Lent: Genesis 16:1–16; Joshua 9:15–27; Romans 12:1–21; John 7:37–52, 8:12–20
Sixth Sunday of Lent: Genesis 19:1–7, 9–26; Joshua 21:43–22:9; Romans 14:10–23; John 9:39–10:21
Hosanna Sunday: Genesis 49:1–12, 22–26; Zechariah 3:7–4:6, 11–end; 7:9–10; 8:4–5, 12–19; 9:9–12; Romans 11:13–24; Matthew 20:29–21:22
Passover Thursday: Exodus 12:1–21; Zechariah 9:9–13,11:4–6,12–14; 12:9–end, 13:7–end; 1 Corinthians 5:7–9, 10:15–18, 11:23–end; Matthew 26:17–25, John 13:22–28, Matthew 26:25, John 13:3–16, Matthew 26:26–31
Passion Friday: Isaiah 52:13–53:end; Daniel 9:21–end; Galatians 2:17–3:15; Matthew 27:1–33, Luke 23:27–31, Matthew 27:33–44, Luke 23:39–44, Matthew 27:45–55, John 19:31–38, Matthew 27:57–62.
Resurrection Sunday/Easter: (Evening): 1 Corinthians 15:20–29; Matthew 28:1–end; (Morning): Isaiah 60:1–8; 1 Samuel 2:1–11; Romans 5:20–6:end, Hebrews 13:20–end; John 20:1–18
New Sunday/Second Sunday of Easter: Isaiah 55:4–13; Acts 4:32–5:11; Colossians 1:1–20; John 20:19–31
Third Sunday of Easter: Isaiah 56:1–7; Acts 5:34–42; Ephesians 1:1–14; John 14:1–14
Fourth Sunday of Easter: Isaiah 49:13–23; Acts 8:14–25; Ephesians 1:15–2:7; John 16:16–33
Fifth Sunday of Easter: Isaiah 49:7–13; Acts 9:1–19; Hebrews 10:19–36; John 21:1–14
Sixth Sunday of Easter: Isaiah 51:9–11; 52:7–12; Acts 10:1–16; Ephesians 2:4–22; John 17:1–26
Ascension Thursday: 2 Kings 2:1–16; Acts 1:1–15; 1 Timothy 1:18–2:end, 3:14–end; Luke 24:36–end

Sunday after the Ascension: Isaiah 6:1–13; Acts 1:15–end; Philippians 1:27–2:11; Mark 16:2–end

Pentecost Sunday: Exodus 19:1–9; 20:18–21; Acts 2:1–21; 1 Corinthians 12:1–27; John 14:15–16, 25–26; 15:26–16:15

Second Sunday of the Apostles: Joel 2:15–26; Acts 4:5–22; 1 Corinthians 5:6–6:11; Luke 7:31–end

Third Sunday of the Apostles: Deuteronomy 1:3–17; Isaiah 1:1–9; 1 Corinthians 7:1–7; Luke 10:23–end

Fourth Sunday of the Apostles: Deuteronomy 1:16–33; Isaiah 1:10–20; 1 Corinthians 9:13–end; Luke 6:12–36

Fifth Sunday of the Apostles: Deuteronomy 1:33–2:1; Isaiah 1:21–end; 1 Corinthians 14:1–19; Luke 12:16–34

Sixth Sunday of the Apostles: Deuteronomy 4:1–10; Isaiah 2:1–19; 1 Corinthians 10:14–32; Luke 12:57–13:17

Seventh Sunday of the Apostles: Deuteronomy 4:10–24; Isaiah 5:8–25; 1 Corinthians 15:58–16:all; Luke 13:22–end

Feast of the Transfiguration: Isaiah 6; Acts 1:15–end; 1 Timothy 1:18–2:end, 3:14–end; Matthew 16:24–17:10

First Sunday of Summer/Nosard`el: 1 Kings 18:30–39; Acts 5:12–32; 1 Corinthians 4:9–16; Luke 14:1–14

Second Sunday of Summer: Deuteronomy 4:32–40; Isaiah 3:16–4:6; 2 Corinthians 3:4–18; Luke 15:4–end

Third Sunday of Summer: Deuteronomy 5:1–16; Isaiah 5:1–7; 2 Corinthians 7:1–11; John 9:1–38

Fourth Sunday of Summer: Deuteronomy 5:16–6:3; Isaiah 9:8–end; 2 Corinthians 10:1–18; Mark 7:1–23

Fifth Sunday of Summer: Leviticus 23:33–43; Isaiah 28:14–22; 2 Corinthians 12:14–21; Luke 16:19–17:10

Sixth Sunday of Summer: Leviticus 19:1–4; 9–14; Isaiah 29:13–end; 1 Thessalonians 2:1–12; Luke 17:5–19

Seventh Sunday of Summer: Leviticus 19:15–19; 20:9–14; Isaiah 30:1–15; 1 Thessalonians 2:14–3:13; Luke 18:1–14

Feast of the Holy Cross: Isaiah 52:13–53:end; Acts 2:14–37; 1 Corinthians 1:18–end; Luke 24:13–36

First Sunday of Elijah: Deuteronomy 6:20–7:7; Isaiah 31:1–9; 2 Thessalonians 1:1–12; Luke 18:35–19:10

Second Sunday of Elijah: Deuteronomy 7:7–12; Isaiah 30:15–26; 2 Thessalonians 2:15–3:18; Matthew 13:1–23

Third Sunday of Elijah: Deuteronomy 7:12–26; Isaiah 32:1–33:6; Philippians 1:12–25; Matthew 13:24–34

First Sunday of the Cross/Fourth of Elijah: Deuteronomy 8:11–20; Isaiah 33:13–24; Philippians 1:27–2:11; Matthew 4:12–5:16

Second Sunday of the Cross/Fifth of Elijah: Deuteronomy 9:1–8; Isaiah 25:1–8; Philippians 3:1–14; Matthew 17:14–end

Third Sunday of the Cross/Sixth of Elijah: Deuteronomy 9:13–22; Isaiah 26:1–19; Philippians 4:4–end; Matthew 15:21–38

Fourth Sunday of the Cross/Seventh of Elijah: Deuteronomy 10:12–22; Isaiah 13:1–14; 1 Corinthians 14:1–33; Matthew 18:1–18

First Sunday of Moses: Deuteronomy 11:1–12; Isaiah 40:1–17; 2 Corinthians 1:23–2:16; Matthew 20:1–16

Second Sunday of Moses: Deuteronomy 11:13–12:1; Isaiah 40:18–41:7; Galatians 5:1–end; Luke 8:41–end

Third Sunday of Moses: Deuteronomy 12:1–29; Isaiah 41:8–21; Galatians 6; John 5:1–19

Fourth Sunday of Moses: Deuteronomy 12:29–14:3; Isaiah 41:21–43:5; 1 Timothy 5:1–17; Matthew 8:23–9:10

First Sunday of the Sanctification of the Church: Exodus 40:17–end; Isaiah 6:1–13; 1 Corinthians 12:28–13:13; Matthew 16:13–19

Second Sunday of the Church: Exodus 39:32–40:16; 1 Kings 8:10–29; Hebrews 8:1–9:1; Matthew 12:1–21

Third Sunday of the Church: Numbers 7:1–10, 9:15–18; Isaiah 54:1–15; Hebrews 9:5–15; John 2:12–22

Fourth Sunday of the Church: 1 Kings 6:1–19; Hezekiah 43:1–7, 44:1–5; Hebrews 9:16–end; Matthew 22:41–23:22

Introduction
On the Ordering of the *Ḥudhra* and the Seasons, etc.
According to the Rite of the Upper Monastery

Monk BrykhYsho', abbot of Beth-Qoqa, known as Bar Ishkape (13th Century). May his prayer assist and aid our weakness, amen.

First of all, I make known to you with some sentences that I have written, O beloved reader, that you may understand that these seasons were not organized in a hasty or *ad hoc* way, but rather with perfect knowledge and precise and true inquiry, beginning with the blessed Isho'yahb of Adiabene, Catholicos (may his memorial be with the righteous and his prayers be on us).

He began with the beginning of the dispensation of Christ, that is, from when Gabriel announced to the Virgin Mary the glorious birth of Christ. For all this season, hymns, etc. were organized which remind us of all that happened at the time of his annunciation and his birth.

After Christmas there are two Sundays. The first reminds us of all that happened and took place after the death of the children. The second Sunday reminds us of his going up to the temple, the prophecies that were proclaimed about him, and his being carried by the old man Simeon, and speak to us of the whole stretch of the thirty years before the baptism of our Savior.

Next he organized the season of the Baptism: from the day of his baptism up to the moment of his struggle with Satan. For this season of Baptism he organized '*onyatha, qanone* and '*unnaye*, and all the events that correspond to the three years that followed the baptism of our Savior.

He next indicates the holy Lent, and the struggle and combat he had with Satan, the hater of justice, and for this season he organized '*onyatha* and every rubric to show the blessings prepared for those who fast.

After this he went on and indicated, in his heavenly organization, his Passover and his passion, death, burial, and resurrection, his Ascension, and the space of forty days after the resurrection and the ten days after the ascension of our Lord into the heavens. For each he organized '*onyatha* and '*unnaye*, appropriate and fitting for the time or the occasion.

He instructed us, in his organization of the season of the Apostles, about the Holy Spirit that came down upon them and about their preaching in every place; then, about the doctrine of the true faith that they taught in the Church; the persecutions, tortures, and death they underwent and endured from the persecutors, the conversion of the nations to the true faith and their repentance to God caused by them.

As for the season of Summer, he gave to it the name of *Ḥallellayn*; here is what it is about: when the holy apostles went out to the four corners of the creation, they preached, taught, made disciples, and baptized the whole world, tore down the altars in the temples of idols, and the places of the worship of demons; they broke up images and statues, purified and cleansed creation, washed away the filth of sin, abomination, and demonic decay. From then and up to the end of the year, the faithful, all the children of the church, call upon and cry out to God and ask of him for the forgiveness of their trespasses. This is why they say "Wash me (*ḥallelayn*) by the tears..." All the *'onyatha* and *qanone* of this season also refer to repentance and growing closer to God; and although, among the *'onyatha*, there are some that are composed in the singular, they refer primarily to the whole of the faithful, the children of the Church.

He then added, after this season, that of Mar Elijah, which is the last of the whole year; this is why he gave it the name of Mar Elijah. Its subject is the following: after the whole providence of our Savior and the conversion of the nations by the hands of the apostles, and the times and the years and the months, such as they are (that which, although it is hidden from us, is unveiled to the Knower of all) then, at the end of ages, Elijah the zealous prophet will be sent, and by his zeal and his wrath he will destroy every trick and snare of the one who will be named and called the son of perdition; he will confound him and cover him with shame, and he will consume and destroy him with the fire of his zeal.

He established for this season the commemoration of the Cross, because of the story of the saving Cross carried in the hands of Elijah; it is with this that he will fight and do battle, and by it that he will vanquish the son of perdition and convert the peoples to the worship of the Cross. This holy man gave and ordered as a title for this season the sign of the Cross; the reason that it was placed last is that Elijah will come at the end of the times, before the coming of Christ.

There are Sundays after this season of Mar Elijah; we celebrate sometimes one, sometimes two or three of them before the Sanctification of the Church. Here is their meaning: those on earth have no knowledge of the time when the coming of our Lord will take place, as he said: "the day and the hour no one knows, not even the angels in heaven, but only the Father," and all the rest of the passage, that we take from the mouth of the Holy One from whom we have learned it.

    Last of all this holy man established the Sundays of the Sanctification of the Church, as the end after the coming of Elijah, and after the destruction, the uprooting, and the condemnation of the son of perdition. Then from the heavens of his glorious holiness the heavenly Bridegroom will appear and bring back all men from the dust; he will show the righteous in the heights and the sinners he will send to Gehanna. The holy Church, the bride of Christ, which is the saints and the true faithful, will go out to meet him with joy, extolling him in all honor, the true Bridegroom, Jesus our Savior. He will take the Church as his bride and raise her up with him to heaven; he will bring her into his bridal chamber and seat her at his right hand, and he will gladden her with every good thing that does not pass away or perish. She will rejoice in him and exult and be glad; and with glorious voices and sweet songs will sing praises with the heavenly choirs. May our Lord make us also worthy of delighting with his saints, amen.

Introduction of Chaldean Patriarch Putrus Eliya XII, 1887

Putrus Eliya XII, by grace the Catholicos-Patriarch of Babylon, to our most-honored brethren, the venerable Metropolitans and Bishops, and our beloved sons, the splendid priests and monks, and the chosen deacons, and the other members of the Church, peace and blessings in our Lord.

After the light of the Gospel radiated the glory of the Lord upon this our eastern corner, especially through those three glorious lights, namely, Mar Thomas, Mar Addai, and Mar Mari, the blessed apostles, preachers of the truth, and messengers of righteousness, in a space of a short time, the mighty cloud of idolatry was stripped from its face, it was doubly brightened by the splendid rays of the truly glorious faith in the one living God of three adorable Individuals, the thicket of error which the evil one had sown in her from the ages was uprooted, it flourished and abounded in the seed of the good teaching of the truth, the thistles of all kinds of vices with which she was covered were taken up, she was adorned like a lovely meadow with the beautiful blossoms of the well-ordered habits of virtue, and her beauty gleamed before the eyes of all with the adorned lilies of noble works, for the precious blood of the victorious martyrs who were killed for the sake of Jesus watered her thirst and her tribulation. And it so happened that the number of Christians greatly increased like seed from within it, and then churches were established, and hermitages and monasteries were completed in many places, as the books remembering ecclesiastical stories witness, that these lands along with their ancient remnants remain until today. Because of this, our venerable fathers were consumed by the love of the Lord, and the holy fire of divine grace ignited in their heart and exhorted them, and they mused on arriving at the state of spiritual perfection. These chosen vessels of honor and revered dwellings of the Holy Spirit began, as if to refresh the thirst of their hearts, to sing the Psalms of David the king and prophet on Sundays and days set apart and specified, and became concerned to organize rites of various prayers filled with the spirit of divine work, which they celebrated together. Then the flower, this our glorious liturgy of canonical prayers, became a tradition, which was held, and is now held, completely without change, in all the dioceses and churches of our Chaldean nation. Thus every discerning person sees clearly how ancient these liturgical prayers are which are offered up every day in our churches, since they were arranged and passed down to us, hand to hand, from the apostles who made disciples in the East, from their holy disciples, from people who put on God, and from their composition, and they are kept at all times and celebrated vigilantly and diligently. Indeed, besides the Psalms which rise up in their multitude in all of their parts, and are as the foundation of the liturgy, there are among them compositions of Mar Marutha of Myparqat, and of Mar Shim'un Bar Sabba'e the Catholicos and victorious martyr, and of Mar Ephrem the great teacher, and others of the first teachers who shone in teaching and burned with the zeal of the house of the Lord. Because from the fifth century, when, for reasons unveiled to those who know, the bitter poison of the heresy of Byzantium seeped within these lands, and the beauty of that honored pearl, that is, the faith of true glory which our victorious fathers bought by the blood of their necks, was ruined, some things were added to the prayers composed by the intelligent teachers of that religion. A few services were arranged by Mar Yawsep II, which are those celebrated on the Memorial of St. Barbara, that of St. Nicholas, that of the Massacre of the Children, of the Feast of the Circumcision, the Bringing of Our Lord to the Temple, of St. Joseph the Betrothed of the Virgin Mary, the Annunciation of the Virgin, Corpus Christi (and the Heart of Jesus); and the rite of the Conception of the Holy Virgin without Stain was arranged by Fr. Damian.

It is clear to all those who are convinced by the ecclesiastical histories that in the fourth century after the birth of our Lord, this our honored liturgy was arranged in a splendid arrangement, and complete in all its essential parts, since it was fixed and finalized at the Synod of Mar Isaac and Mar Marutha, which was in the year 410 AD, that "the prayers of the liturgy are to be celebrated according to the manner of the church of Seleucia-Ctesiphon."

The parts of these liturgical prayers in the *Ḥudhra* of the whole year, aside from Lent, are three, namely, evening prayer, night prayer, and morning prayer. Evening prayer, in thanksgiving for the provision of the things of the daytime; morning prayer, in thanksgiving that we have been raised from the sleep which symbolizes death, and for our protection against dangers; and the service of night prayer, taken from the word of our Lord and of David. For David says: "In the middle of the night, I arose to give thanks to you for your just judgments." And our Lord admonishes us: "Stay awake, for you do not know at what hour your Lord comes," in the evening, or in the middle of the night, or when the rooster crows. But during the time of Lent, besides these prayers, our fathers of venerable memory set apart others, namely *Quta'a*, *'Iddana*, and *Suba'a*.

In the seventh century, [the liturgy's] parts were arranged in the Upper Monastery of Mar Gabriel and Mar Abraham, the disciples of Mar Eugene the blessed, which is near the city of Mosul, when with keen mind, sharp faculties, and great discernment, it was divided into the known seasons, namely, Advent, Christmas, Epiphany, Lent, Resurrection, Ascension, Pentecost or Apostles, Summer, Elijah, Cross, Moses, and the Sanctification of the Church. And for each of these seasons, and the feasts and memorials which occurred in them, they arranged proper services, prayers, and marvelous hymns, according to the subject of the particular feast or memorial, and the theme of the season. And so there is the glorious Conception of our Lord Jesus Christ, and his Birth, and his Circumcision, and his Baptism, and his holy Fasting, and his Preaching, and his Passion and his Death, and his Resurrection, and his Ascension, and the Descent of the Spirit Paraclete upon the Blessed Apostles, and their Tribulations and Preaching and Conversion of the Nations. And after the entire providence of our Savior and the conversion of the nations by the hands of the apostles and their true successors, and after the interval of years until the end of time, Elijah the Zealous is sent, and in his zeal he shames the one who is called and is the son of perdition, and thereafter the sign of the Son of God will be seen, namely the holy Cross, and then after the eradication, uprooting, and condemnation of the son of perdition, the heavenly Bridegroom will dawn from the holy and glorious heavens, and will raise all from the dust, and raise the good to the height above and dismiss the sinners to the fire of Gehenna. And the end, just as the same holy Church who is the betrothed of Christ, which is the saints and the true believers, will go out to meet him in joy as she extolls and glorifies him with all honors. Then the Bridegroom of Truth, Jesus our Savior, will receive his betrothed, the holy Church, and raise her with him to heaven, and bring her into the eternal bride chamber, and sit her at his right hand, and delight her with his visage, and make her young with the light of his face, and she will rejoice and extoll in him, and with glorious songs and sweet melodies sing glory to him in the Church of the first-born of heaven, forever and ever, with the assemblies of the heavenly, as she sang to him here in the Church on earth.

This splendid and marvelous arrangement of the yearly cycle of liturgical prayers, which was held from the first centuries, and is held now in perfect harmony in all our churches, and the divine care having established us, without worthiness, upon this Patriarchal Seat of Babylon, we were eagerly desirous and planning, against all difficulties which happened upon us, that editions of our glorious liturgy should be printed and distributed in order to fulfill the needs of the churches in all our Patriarchal territory. And thus when the holy Congregation of the Propaganda [Fide] had approved our wish, Mar John Simeon, Cardinal all-honorable, the head of said Congregation, wrote to us that we may examine and arrange a complete and corrected edition, scoured of all novelties, corruptions, and errors, so as to set them for printing. We then arose gladly and gathered the editions most ancient and accurate, and, comparing them with one another, we corrected, fashioned, and arranged a complete edition, free and separated, not only from everything fixed against the subjects of the Catholic Faith, but also against the luster of our Aramaic language. And in this whole work we followed the footsteps of those who preceded us, and guarded the true arrangement of the liturgy in all diligence. We only cast away and removed from its holy names that dark fog which was seen in it afterward because of the negligence of writers and the insolence of those with an unhealthy mind, and returned it to its original clarity, and its clear originality.

The hymns of evening and night prayer of ordinary days which were set apart on their own in the book of the *Kashkul* we arranged in their places following after their own Sunday in the *Ḥudhra*, and then attached the *Gazza* which gathered all the prayers of the feasts and memorials, and we divided all of these books of the liturgy into three volumes: the first volume, from Advent until the beginning of the great Lent; the second from the beginning of Lent until Pentecost; the third from Pentecost until the end of the season of the Sanctification of the Church. And we placed the general Introduction at the beginning of each volume as an additional commentary on the quality of the perfection of the service of the canonical prayers. And we arranged in it the prayers of priests and the glorifications in their places, and assembled the prayers for help and their *shuḥlape*, and the funeral hymns, with the Psalms of David, and the petitions, the martyr hymns, the "before and after," the common prayers of Wednesdays of the first and second cycles, and the "ordering of the month," and from them a common section was composed, which can be found at the end of each of the three volumes.

At the end, we appointed our brother, the all-honored Mar 'Abdysho' Khayyaṭ, Metropolitan of Amid, as manager, due to his education in the rites of the Church, and sent him to Rome, that he may lead this work before the holy Congregation as in our person, that which was requested humbly by our beloved son, Father Paul Bedjan, the Persian Lazirite (who took pains in praiseworthy zeal to gather the necessities required for this great work), in order to print the books mentioned above in complete keeping of our arrangement. This same holy Congregation of the Propaganda [Fide] increased its gracefulness with us and put up also half the cost of their publication.

Many benefits indeed are reaped from the printing of this liturgy: aside from the fact that there will no longer be a chance or opportunity to add or subtract anything from it, and there is one harmony and one equality and one goal of the liturgy, as there has been from the beginning in all our dioceses and churches; and aside from the fact that copies will be multiplied and increased in every place, that indeed there may not be a scarcity of these books, even for those who should and must pray this service alone, such as those who are on a journey, a new treasure of beautiful examples is opened also before lovers of learning, in which many of the foundational matters of the Catholic Faith are established, such as the original sin we inherited from our first father, and the freedom of the human will, and the necessity of the grace of Christ, and the Sacraments of the New Testament, and prayer for the dead, and the propriety of images of the providence of Christ, and the honor due to the dwellings of the saints, and the reliance on the intercession of the blessed who rule in heaven, and the fastings and services of the Church, and the superiority of the holy virgin Mary above all the saints, and the perpetual punishments of Gehanna, and the truth of the Sacrifice which is offered in the Divine Mysteries, and the transubstantiation of bread and wine into the Body and Blood of Christ, and the finding of the presence of Christ in the Sacrament of the Eucharist, and the authority of the priesthood in the Church to forgive sins, and the necessity of sacramental confession for the absolution of faults, and the headship of the Roman Pontiff, and many more which are found other than those listed by us now. Nevertheless, the benefits of this our liturgy are great not only at a glance at that which we have spoken, but also because of the lucidity of the paternal language which is in it, and the luster of its phrases, and the greatness of its thoughts, and the high quality of its understanding, such that it is seen to be and is in truth the very blossom of the Aramaic language.

Therefore, we willingly order that this edition be distributed in all our Patriarchal territory, and verify and ratify its acceptance, and we witness that the services and prayers contained in this edition complete perfectly the liturgy of the Patriarchal See of Babylon, and we decree and command, by our patriarchal authority, that it be kept in every diocese and church in all its requirements, without alteration and without subtraction, and in harmony, as the custom has been held among us Chaldeans until now.

In conclusion, if this liturgy is thus so ancient, and its compositions so beautiful, and its divisions so many, and its benefits so overflowing, how right it is for all of us to hold it in honor, and fulfill it in splendor and diligence, and keep it in faithfulness as an honored trust, and pass it on in its essence to the ages to come, as it has been passed on to us from our venerable fathers of blessed memory. Thus we trust, O venerable brothers and beloved sons, your praiseworthy zeal and the goodness of your wills, that you will keep all the canons, services, and prayers in this edition completely and earnestly. As we command all our people to be thankful for the gift of the holy Congregation of Propaganda [Fide], which is always careful to keep and promote in every place the honored things of our fathers, and to plead to God in your prayers for the victory of the Holy Catholic Church, and for all those who participated in this work, and especially for our Chaldean race, that its original beauty may be doubled, and it may be like a glorious olive tree in the house of God. We give you, as a pledge of love, the paternal blessing: may the grace of our Lord Jesus Christ, and the love of God the Father, and the communion of the Holy Spirit be with you all, amen.

At the Patriarchal residence in Mosul,
15 February, 1887 AD
+ Putrus Eliya XII
by grace the Catholicos-Patriarch of Babylon

INTRODUCTION OF EUGENE CARDINAL TISSERANT, 1938

To the Most-Blessed Mar Joseph Emmanuel II Thomas, Catholicos-Patriarch of Babylon, and the exalted Metropolitans and Bishops, and the revered Priests and Monks, and the entire blessed ecclesial assembly of the Rite of the East Syrians in Mesopotamia and in Malabar,

This canonical prayer of the Rite of the East Syrians has been in preparation for printing for fifty years' time. This has come about by the praiseworthy diligence of Patriarch Mar Eliya XII, who departed from this temporal world in the year 1894. Then a commemorated high priest was set apart and appointed to fulfill this great task: Mar 'Abdysho' Khayyaṭ, the renowned and eminent teacher, who was the Metropolitan of 'Ammid in that time, and became afterwards the Patriarch, and who passed on to the land of delights in the year 1899; [also] to the honored Father Paul Bedjan, the Persian Lazirite, who died in the year 1920. These two then, of blessed memory, diligently examined and arranged the bulk of prayers and services, according to the manuscripts that were most ancient and accurate. They corrected it and took out and rejected all corruptions and novelties from it. This work of theirs provided an honor and a boast for the rite of the East Syrians. On that account, it is right that it be guarded completely. Because of this, the Apostolic See, when it approved, with a rejoicing heart, their just request, which had been offered many times, it judged and decided that the prayers of their honored rite should be set down anew in print.

Let it be known to you, that the size of the first printing was made smaller, but its substance remained clear and easy to read. This was done, then, that one may find it ready to pray alone. Again, there was great diligence in the correction of the volumes, such that this new printing on high-quality paper may please and be enjoyed by everyone.

Furthermore, the antiquity and richness, and the marvelous elegance of the rite of the East Syrians, does not need explanation or verification, for they are obvious to everyone in marvelousness and great wonder. And all those who are educated in the rites of the Church witness with one accord, that this rite has been kept and passed down faithfully in the ancient tradition of the universal prayer of the Christian Church. This is the reason which moved and incited the Apostolic See to guard all the marvelous rites of the

Easterners completely, for they are like jewels fastened in the crown of Jesus the great King.

Indeed, without prayer, spiritual life cannot exist. It is obvious and clear also that without community prayer, there is no place for common Christian life for our Church or our people. Therefore it is expedient and appropriate for the whole rank of the Church, the lone vision and example before the eyes of all, to be in this spiritual and Christian life. A cleric therefore should be a man of prayer, insofar as he is a man of God. This suffices to convince us and show us the prime necessity and the just fittingness of daily prayer, in order to guard the spirit of our priesthood. Indeed, we are the salt of the earth and the light of the world, and this is according to the glorious will of Christ our Lord. Therefore, without prayer, there is no power in us to enlighten souls nor to keep them in divine life. We are certain, therefore, that this canonical prayer that was newly printed will be for you as a particular grace of God, adored be his Name, and like a gift of compassion of the Apostolic See, for the guarding and the perfect completion of your canonical prayer.

With these very desires and wishes, we extend to you the new printing of the canonical prayer, as we request you to pray for the upholding and health of the High Pontiff, Pope Pius XI, who rules blessedly, and for the good workers who labored and prepared this new printing, and thus also that you may pray for my weak self.

Rome, on the Feast of the Epiphany of Our Lord, 6 January 1938
Eugene Cardinal Tisserant
Prefect of the Eastern Congregation

INTRODUCTION OF METROPOLITAN THOMAS DARMO, 1960

After the coming of our Savior Jesus Christ to this world, twelve blessed apostles were chosen to announce the life-giving news, as he said to them: "Go and announce to the whole world and baptize them in the Name of the Father, and of the Son, and of the Holy Spirit." After this, the light of his announcement, that is, the holy Gospel, shone upon this eastern corner, especially through those three pillars of light, namely the glorious lamps Mar Toma, he who after his preaching and building churches in these our lands, then by the command of his Lord came to India, and Mar Addai and Mar Mari, the blessed apostles, and preachers of the truth, and announcers of justice. After a short time had passed, when they had gone out and preached and taught and made disciples and baptized many, and uprooted the high places and idol houses and houses of demon worship, and broke the images and carvings, and purified and scoured the creation, and washed it from the grime of sin and satanic abomination and filth, they were adorned, like precious and lovely meadows, with the beautiful blossoms of orderly, virtuous works.

Then churches were established, and hermitages and monasteries were crowned in many places, as the holy writings of the ecclesiastical histories witness of these eastern lands, and indeed an ancient remnant stands until today. Because of these things, our venerable and holy fathers were constantly consumed by the love of the Lord, and these pure and chosen vessels of honor and splendid dwellings of the Holy Spirit began, as if whetting their thirst, to sing the Psalms of David, he who is named prophet and king and the heart of the Lord, on Sundays and on days set apart and known. And they became concerned with arranging liturgies of various prayers filled with the spirit of divine labor, which they celebrated in assembly, and without variation, in all the dioceses and churches of our Assyrian nation in all lands. Since from the blessed and holy apostles, disciple-makers of the East, they passed down to their blessed disciples, and from the holy fathers and persons clothed with God, and from the compositions of these skillful saints, it was arranged and passed down to us, hand to hand, and kept at all times diligently, without change and without alteration, and it was celebrated excellently, in all diligence. Besides the Psalms which rise up as a majority in all its parts, and which are as a foundation of the liturgy, there are among them compositions by Mar Marutha of Mipraqat, and there are of Mar Shim'un Bar Sabba'e, the

Catholicos of the East and victorious martyr, and there are of Mar Ephrem the Syrian, the great and victorious teacher, and there are of the other early teachers, and teachers of the truth, who were shining with teaching and burning with zeal for the house of the Lord.

The blessed Mar 'Abdysho', Metropolitan of Soba and Armenia, in the abridged collection of the Synodical Canons which he collected, writes thus: "Regarding how many and what are the prayers appointed for each one of the ranks of Christians: the good and merciful one, our Lord Jesus Christ our God, and knower of the weakness of our nature and its frailties, through his prophets in his Divinity, and through his apostles in his humanity as well as his Divinity, according to our weakness, arranged for us seven times of prayer. The fathers of the world, then, since they also went according to this path, arranged these seven times for anchorite and sojourning hermits. Then those after them made the service of each time complete with three and three *Hulale*. The modest priests in the world, and the orderly faithful who possess love of prayer also are enjoined to keep this arrangement."

Therefore, the fathers after these, when they saw that the laypeople were not equal to this love of [liturgical] service, and there were among them those who were working in their labors, gave them a hand in fulfilling their service according to what was commanded: they measured also according to the tangle of weakness, and commanded that laypeople may not cease from four services. These are the four: evening prayer, the prayer before sleep, night prayer, and morning prayer. These limit the canon of the word of our Lord.

Evening prayer, then, for the thanksgiving for the things provided during the day. The prayer before sleep, that he may keep us from all foolish visions and dreams and anxieties, and to give us sleep and rest at night. Night prayer, taken from the word of our Lord and from David. For David says: "In the middle of the night I arose to give thanks to you for your just judgment," and our Lord also thus enlightens us and says: "Stay awake, for you do not know at what hour your Lord comes, in the evening, or in the middle of the night, or when the rooster crows." Morning prayer, in thanksgiving that we have been raised from sleep, which symbolizes death, and for our protection from temptations and dangers.

During the time of Lent, besides these, our holy fathers of venerable memory set apart other prayers, namely: *Quta'a*, *'Iddana*, and *Suba'a*.

In the seventh century, its sections were arranged in the Upper Monastery of Mar Gabriel and Mar Abraham, disciples of the blessed Mar Eugene, above the city of Mosul, when with keen mind, sharp faculties, and great and marvelous discernment, it was divided into the distinct and known seasons.

This adorned, lovely, and marvelous arrangement of the yearly cycle of liturgical prayers, which was held in the first centuries is now also held in full harmony in all our churches in all our lands.

The hymns of evening and night prayer of ordinary days which were set apart on their own in the book of the *Kashkul* we arranged in their places following after their own Sunday in the *Ḥudhra*, and also the prayers of Patriarch Mar Eliya III Abuḥalym, each one in its place. We then attached the *Gazza* in which were contained all the prayers of feasts and memorials, and divided all these liturgical books into three volumes, and the book of Before and After is fully found at the beginning of each of the three volumes, and the explanatory composition of the readings, the *Shuraye*, the Apostle, the *Zumara*, the Gospel, of each of the three volumes, each day in its place. Aside from those from the first Sunday of *Subara* until the great *Ṣawma*, and of *Ba'utha*, and of the Friday of the Deceased, which were separated from their places.

The first volume is from *Subara* until the beginning of the great *Ṣawma*; the second, from the beginning of the great *Ṣawma* until Pentecost; the third, from Pentecost until the end of the season of the Sanctification of the Church.

As an introduction and further commentary on the quality of the fulfillment of the celebration of the canonical prayers, we placed a general introduction at the beginning of each volume, and arranged in it the prayers of the priests and the glorifications, in their places.

And we gathered the Hymns for Assistance and their *shuḥlape*, and the Hymns of the Deceased, with the Psalms of David and the petitions, and the Martyr Hymns of ordinary days and Sundays, and the Common Hymns of Wednesday of the first and second [cycles], and the ordering of the month, and from them, a general section was fashioned, to be found at the end of each of the three volumes.

Let us now turn to the goal of the printing of this *Ḥudhra* for the first time in the history of the world and of our Church; this is not hidden, but rather known to all the sons of our Church and Assyrian nation. That the word may not be lengthened, we now show in summary to the educated readers how we began in this good and holy work.

So then, after I arrived at this blessed land of India, in the year 1952 AD, we began to build churches hand in hand, and our seminary, and other things. At this point I made it known to His Holiness the Patriarch that we wished to print the *Ḥudhra* of our Church, and I asked him for help, that is, for the costs. When he heard about the publication of the *Ḥudhra*, he rejoiced and was glad, and said in his letters dated 30 July 1956, 5 February 1958, and 14 March 1958, "if only this holy book could be printed, and we eagerly desire this good work. Nevertheless," he said, "this work requires great cost, and at this time we find it difficult to thus gather money. However, the sons of our Church in the United States of America receive many wages, and have much money. So because of this, we cannot help you in this work..."

I then asked his Blessedness Mar Yawsep to gather some money from the sons of our Church in Iraq, that is, Mesopotamia, for the costs of the printing of our *Ḥudhra*. In his letter dated 26 February 1958, he gave me the same answer as that of His Holiness the Patriarch. When I received these replies, I was greatly and exceedingly sad, but I trusted in the Lord.

Then immediately afterward, I wrote to His Holiness the Patriarch thus: "I, by the power of the great God, will begin this work. If the Lord helps me and I find and gather the costs, how good and lovely. Indeed, I have trust and faith and great hope that he will aid me." With that trust I began to write to the faithful of our beloved and praiseworthy Assyrian Church and Nation in personal letters. Thus, "through a scroll of a voice from the East," in the time of three years more or less, I received some amount of a little money from here or there, and this amount was not enough to begin the work. But even then, we had nothing but hope.

After we had finished building our seminary, according to the custom due to the great heat of Trishur, I went up to Kunoor, a village built on hills, for some rest and for a change of weather. The athlete Inassu knew we were seeking to print the book of the *Ḥudhra*, and were seeking costs, etc. He, from his love and zeal toward our Church, helped us with the cost of paper for two volumes. By the power of the great God and the help of this faithful man, we began the printing. If it were not for this man, we would not have been able to begin this work, for this we plead to the Lord to repay him with a reward of heavenly benefits in both worlds.

Then the sons of our Church and nation, after they heard and knew about the great sacrifice of this man, began also to give. They sent from the United States of America, and Iraq, that is Mesopotamia, and Syria and Lebanon, and Iran, but the most from the Press of Mar Narsai in Trishur.

Before we began, according to the general legal canons of publishing books, requesting and seeking ancient and accurate manuscripts which were placed as a foundation for the book which was being published, before we went to ask and see from people outside, by the compassion of our good God, we found the books (*Ḥudhre*) which we were in need of in our own archive, and they had been in the archives from the days of the deceased Mar Timothy, Metropolitan of our Church in this land. They were compared and examined and investigated in all diligence and great care. These editions of the *Ḥudhra* are as written below.

1. The first manuscript. This is noted in its colophon: "This book of the *Ḥudhra* was completed by the help of our Lord on the day of Friday, 28 April, the second Sunday of the Resurrection, whose 'onytha is 'Your resurrection, O Lord, has adorned...' in the year 1909 of the blessed Greeks. This book was written in the blessed and beatified village, priestly in its orthodox faith, of Alqaye, which is set and ordered under the shelter of St. George the victorious martyr, and the companionship of Mar Addai and Mar Mari, the blessed apostles, under the leadership of the Father of Fathers, Mar Eliya, Catholicos-Patriarch of the East, and in the days of the diligent leader and amazing pastor and marvelous guide Mar Yawsep bishop of Azerbaijan, that is, the blessed and beatified land of Armenia...this book was written by the hands of Deacon Ḥnanysho', lazy servant, in the year numbered 1909."

2. The second manuscript is of Alkosh, and this is written in its colophon: "This book of the *Ḥudhra* of the entire year was finished and completed in the blessed month of June, on its 11th day, on Saturday, the vigil of the fourth Sunday of the Apostles, whose 'onytha is 'O Lord, when the assembly,' of the year one-thousand nine-hundred and ninety-two of the blessed Greeks...this book of the *Ḥudhra* was written in the blessed and beatified village, noble in orthodox faith, Alkosh, the village of Nahum the Prophet, which is settled and ordered and built near the holy dwelling of Mar Rabban Hormizd the Persian...it was written in the days of the Father and Lord of the Fathers...Mar Eliya Catholicos Patriarch of the head of all corners, the East, and of all the ends of the world of righteous glory. The weak and repentant priest George,

son of priest Israel, son of the priest Hormizd, son of the deceased priest Israel Alkoshaya, wrote, or rather ruined and blotted [it]."

3. The third manuscript, in three volumes of the *Ḥudhra*, in which are contained the *Gazza*, the *Kashkul*, and the Before and After, printed the second time in the publishing house of William of Rogolen in the city of Leipzig, in the country of Germany, in the year 1938 AD. It was of the deceased Rubel, son of the faithful Muhatas, of the village of Mar Bhysho'. He compared the manuscripts which were very old and accurate of the *Ḥudhra* of our Church, and he examined and searched it with great diligence, lest some theological fault pass through into this our holy, lovely, and adorned liturgy. He prepared it for publication, but before he began this good work, he was summoned by our Lord. This manuscript remembered above was sent to us by Deacon George of the house of Benjamin, Ashithnaya.

Thus also his deceased teacher, priest Joseph Qilayta had this intention from the beginning, until the last hour of his life, to print the *Ḥudhra* of our Church. He prepared everything needed for its printing, but there were people who stood against him and hated him, and they took the printing from him, and did not allow him to print it, and they themselves did not print it. He also, while in this diocese, was summoned by his Lord, and they did not allow him to complete his virtuous work. The very same thing happened to us during our days. This parable of our Savior is true, where he says: "Woe to you who close the door of the kingdom of heaven before men, for you neither enter, nor do you allow them to enter." Matthew 13:14; Luke 11:52.

4. The book of Sukale, which shows the liturgy of the services of the Church and its tradition, which was made and composed in great examination by priest Abraham Shikwana, which is known as Beth Qasha, in the year 1898 AD.

5. The *Kashkul*: this is noted in its colophon: "This book of the *Kashkul* was completed and took final form and completion in the blessed month of September, on the 6th day, on a Friday, of the year one-thousand eight-hundred and ninety-five of Alexander, son of Phillip the Macedonian, and of the birth of Christ, one-thousand, five-hundred, and eight-five (four)…in the blessed and beatified city, priestly in its orthodox faith, dwelling-place for the sick, Kotamangalam, in the church of St Mary the Holy Virgin (which is in the land of India today), under the headship of the Father of Fathers and the Leader of Shepherds, the venerable and fount of veneration, pure and fountain

of purity, Mar Shim'un Catholicos-Patriarch of the East...and in the days of the wakeful leader and amazing and faithful guide, marvelous judge and attentive navigator, and true shepherd, Mar Abraham the bishop metropolitan of India...these pages were written, that is scratched and ruined, spoiled and tarnished, by a sinful man, more sinful than the sinners of sinners, the miserable one, he who is not worthy to be remembered by name in the holy books due to the greatness of his faults...Matthew son of Joseph the priest."

It should be known that this book was not printed by our hands casually or by happenstance, but rather care and great diligence were shown, that it might be complete in everything required of it. It was examined, compared, and printed with the manuscripts mentioned above, and after they were tested and searched with much care and great diligence, as the writers of the manuscripts confessed and said in the introductions they made to their books. These are the manuscripts printed, especially those two books of the *Ḥudhra* mentioned above. We set them as a foundation for this book, that we may lay out in print for the sons of the holy, apostolic, catholic Church of the East without alteration or change.

This also should be made known: I confess and make known that I am not very learned or educated, nor was I expert fully enough for this book of our beautiful and marvelous *Ḥudhra*, to enter this arena of printing it, in which is contained all the points of religion and theology of our holy Church, of true glory. Nevertheless, my love and zeal toward our Church enticed and beguiled me, and strengthened me and dragged me, to this work which is far above my strength. I thought, indeed, that the healthy and true teaching of our holy fathers should not perish. It was right for me to enter, and I entered this arena according to my bodily weakness and my lacking in teaching, by the power and aid of the Lord of all, he who gives sight to the blind, walking to the lame, speech to the stammering and dumb, health to the sick, wisdom and knowledge and teaching to the simple, and good hope to each one who believes in him. He helped me and strengthened me to finish this work.

Many obstacles came before us. Nevertheless, that which was worst of all was that the workers, that is, the printers, that is, those who arrange the letters in our press, were Hindus, and Indian Christians, who knew nothing, and were not experts or could learn the meaning of a single word or letter of our Aramaic language. Because of this, innumerable obstacles were before us, until indeed we verified and read and examined every single section six or seven times or more, before we could send it to the printer.

Therefore, let it be known to your love, O my brethren in our Lord, all who are familiar with this book, especially the educated clerics, that you may find some errors or blunders of grammar, etc. Correct them by the love of our Lord, and pray for my frailty.

This also, even more, should be remembered: that we have great gratitude for our sons in the Spirit, priest Francis son of the faithful David of the house of Ollukkaran, and deacon Joseph son of the faithful Thomas of the house of Arangyassery, head of the Press of Mar Narsai, for the love and zeal toward our Church they showed in the publication of this book. Though they are not well-studied in our Aramaic language, still according to their ability they aided me, and greatly labored and took care to correct errors, etc. and did not shrink from this work night and day and at all hours, according to the necessity of the time. Deacon George also, son of the faithful John of the house of Immaty, and deacon Raphael, son of the faithful Joseph of the house of Poovathingal, aided us greatly whenever they found opportunity or time.

Now then, we lift up glory, honor, exaltation and halleluiah to the blessed, glorious, and holy Name of our good God for the providence and help toward our weakness, he who by his eternal mercies gave us health of body and spirit, and strengthened and aided us to print this book of the *Ḥudhra*, which there is great need for. Indeed, after almost two thousand years more or less, this is the first time of its printing and its entering into print fully, without subtraction and without alteration, according to the true liturgy of the holy apostolic catholic Church of the East, besides the fact that copies can be produced and multiplied in every place, that there be no need for these books, as there has been, ever again.

At the end, we have great and constant gratefulness toward all the clerics and faithful men and women of our loved and beloved Church and nation who helped us, whether by donations or by prayers or by work or by showing their ecclesial love and zeal, for this book. And now by the Lord's aid, we have come to the end.

We pray, therefore, and plead from the Lord, that he may reward you and accept your sacrifice, as that of Abraham, Isaac, and Jacob, and as the widow's penny. We pray also, and plead from the Lord, for peace and serenity in the world, and for the upholding of our holy Church, and for all readers and hearers who make use of this book, that they may be enriched and pluck heavenly benefits from it for both worlds, amen.

Written down in the Metropolitan villa in Trishur of southern India,

> December 25, the day of the Birth of our Lord,
> in the year of our Lord 1960,
> + the weak Thomas Darmo
> by grace, the Metropolitan of the Church of the East in India.

Introduction of Assyrian Patriarch Eshai Shim'un XXIII, 1961

From the Patriarchal Palace of the Church of the East:
receive prayers and blessings.

To our brethren in spiritual shepherdhood, leaders and shepherds, the venerable metropolitans and bishops, and to our beloved sons the chosen priests and deacons, and the other splendid clerics, and to the whole group of the sons of the holy apostolic catholic Church of the East, and of all the ends of the world: may grace and blessings dwell among you.

When the blessed apostles preached the life-filled Gospel in our eastern corner, after a short time the shadow caused by idolatry was exterminated, and idols and images of the custom of paganism from the face of the earth, and the radiance of the rays of the light of the true and whole faith radiated, that of the one Divine Nature, impassible and immortal, living forever and ever.

And the thorns of error which the evil one had sown in the field of mankind were uprooted through the victorious blood of the blessed apostles and true preachers.

Then the Church was adorned, the splendid bride, with beautiful blossoms, and the adorned flowers of virtuous manners, and she became intoxicated by the pure and victorious blood of the martyrs and confessors, on behalf of him who saved the beloved and holy catholic Church from slavery to idols and adoration of images by his holy blood, in order to shepherd the rational flock. By the grace of our Lord and God, leaders and shepherds were set apart in an election of the Holy Spirit, that through them, the authority of the Spirit may be fulfilled, to bind and to loose on earth and heaven, namely, those first Fathers in whose heart a holy fire burned, and even more so were consumed by commenting on and interpreting the Scriptures of the Old and New, as witness the books of the histories of our eastern Church.

Even more so, this our marvelous and gorgeous liturgy of prayers, which was passed down to our first fathers from the tradition of the Apostles, when its foundation was first composed by the blessed Apostles, and then hand to hand was crowned and decorated with the beauty of its spiritual solemnity by men clothed with God, among whom were Mar Shim'un bar Sabba'e, Catholicos and victorious martyr, and Mar Ephrem the Great, and Mar

Marutha, Bishop of Maphraqat, and others among them, breathing the Holy Spirit.

It is clear to all who know and are educated, who are experts in the histories of the apostolic Church of the East, that in the Fourth Century AD, this our liturgy was arranged in a marvelous and gorgeous arrangement in all its essential parts, and was settled and sealed at the Synod of Mar Isaac the Catholicos-Patriarch, and Mar Marutha, and the Fathers, leaders of the Church of the East, that happened in 410 AD.

In the Fifth Century, the glorifications, petitions, 'onyatha, and madrashe were added to the seasons, composed by our illustrious teachers, zealous and victorious in spiritual love, and longing for divine things: Mar Babai the Great, and Mar Babai of Nisibis, and Mar Narsai the Harp of the Spirit, and Ḥnana the Solitary, and Mar Abraham of Seleucia, and the others.

In the Seventh Century, then, it was arranged and crowned in the Upper Monastery of Mar Gabriel and Mar Abraham, disciples of the blessed Mar Eugene, which is near the city of Mosul in the land of Assyria. Those pillars of fire and rays of light, in the discernment of their mind and the clarity of their powers, and in the sharpness of their intelligence, divided this liturgy into the known seasons, namely *Subara*, Nativity, Epiphany, *Ṣawma*, Resurrection, Ascension, Pentecost or Apostles, Summer, Elijah, Cross, Moses, and the Sanctification of the Church. All these are arranged cyclically in a year, and each one of these seasons, and the feasts and memorials they contain, arrange in an orderly way the services and prayers and marvelous hymns, according to the topic of the proper feast or the memorial, that the topic of the providence of God the Father through his only-begotten Son for the salvation of our Adamic race is shown as the topic of that season. Such as the glorious conception of our Lord Jesus Christ, and his birth, and his baptism, and his holy fasting, and his preaching, and his suffering, and the death of his humanity, and his resurrection, and his ascension, and the descent of the Spirit, the Paraclete, upon the blessed apostles, and their struggle and preaching and the discipling of the nations, and after a measure of some years, at the end of times, Elijah the zealous will be sent, and in his zealousness, he will shame the one who is called and is the son of perdition, and then the sign of the Son of God will be seen, namely, the holy Cross, and thus after the eradication and uprooting and condemnation of the son of perdition, the heavenly Bridegroom will dawn from his glorious holy heavens, and will raise all from the dust, and lift up the good to the heights above, and will dismiss sinners to the unending fire of Gehanna, and because the holy Church is the betrothed of Christ, she will come out to meet him in joy as she extolls him with all honors, and he the Bridegroom of Truth, Jesus Christ our Savior, will receive his betrothed, the holy Church, and bring her up with him to heaven, and bring her to the eternal bridechamber, and sit her at his right hand, and gladden her in his vision, and renew her by the light of his face, and she will rejoice and extoll in him, and with glorious songs and beautiful hymns, will sing to him in the Church a glorification forever and ever with the heavenly assemblies, as she sang to him here in the Church on earth.

The parts of the prayers of this our liturgy, according to the intention of the Fathers, outside of *Ṣawma*, are three: namely, Evening Prayer, Night Prayer, and Morning Prayer, and the others set apart of *Suba'a*, Midnight, and *Quta'a*, and *'Iddana*, according to the word of our Lord: "awake, for you do not know at what hour your Lord comes, in the evening, or in the middle of the night, or when the cock crows."

Thus when this our lovely and beautiful liturgy was arranged and settled from the first centuries in all its spiritual services, constant thanksgivings and adorations were offered to the Divinity, according to the word of the Apostle, in Colossians 2:18.

It is also right to make known that this our liturgy is divided into three volumes: first from *Subara* until the beginning of the great *Ṣawma*; second from the beginning of the great *Ṣawma* until Pentecost; third from Pentecost until the end of the season of the Sanctification of the Church.

And in each volume, the book of the *Gazza*, and the *Kashkul*, are fully arranged, and the Psalms of David, and the glorifications, the petitions, and the prayers of Mar Eliya III, Patriarch, Abuḥalym, and at the end of each volume, we attached the book of Before and After completely.

With this, then, our brethren and the sons of our Liturgy, the upside-down Chaldeans introduced Roman customs into this our liturgy of the Eastern Fathers. The first who added in the printing was Putrus Eliya XII, their Patriarch, by the order of his master, His Excellency the Cardinal John Simeone, and by an endowment of his supposed mother, the Congregation of the Propaganda, in the year 1887 AD.

Indeed, they ruined the beauty of its original composition, and its foundational essence. They added and planted in it the cursed customs and thoughts of the Romans, namely "God was born of Mary, and suffered, and died." Indeed they confess that he was immortal from the beginning, but became mortal in the latter times – see the *Qalta* of the Sixth Sunday of the Resurrection, or the Second Sunday of the Cross, in the printing of the Chaldeans.

The upside-down Chaldeans also confess in the transubstantiation of bread and wine in the holy Mysteries, to the flesh and blood of God the Word. Indeed they confess that the Nature of God the Word became flesh to a man hypostatically/substantially.

Not only do they deny the divine revelations that were shown to us through the prophets and sealed through the witness of the Evangelists, and explained and interpreted by the blessed apostles, but whether knowingly or unknowingly, they deny the faith of our Fathers of Nicaea, who confessed as lords: Mar Ephrem the Great and Athanasius the Renowned in true glory. Mar Athanasius, the Patriarch of Alexandria, confesses thus in a book *On the Incarnation*: "God the Word, when he saw that there is no other Mediator in whom to renew the ruined man, aside from that of death, and since it was impossible for God the Word to die, since he is immortal in his Nature, therefore took for himself a body of mortal nature, so that that mortal body, in its unity with God the Word, on behalf of all men may taste death, for since it is mortal and corruptible in its nature, because of this God the word dwelt in it, and made it one with him in a unity of dwelling, that he may therefore be incorruptible, and eradicate the corruptibility of all men through the grace of his resurrection." (Rowan Greer, *Theodore of Mopsuestia*, Pub Faith Press, London, p. 14–15). It is clear that the upside-down Chaldeans inserted foreign customs of the Latins into the eastern Liturgy in their edition, since prayers were added of Barbara, and Nicholas, and the Slaughter of the Children, and the Feasts of the Circumcision of our Lord, and the Presentation at the Temple, and St Joseph the betrothed of the Virgin Mary, and the Annunciation of the Virgin, the Body of Christ, the Heart of our Lord, and the Conception of the Virgin, and other Roman customs that were never known in our eastern liturgy.

Thus by the grace of God the Father, and the mercy of the Son, and the compassion of the Holy Spirit, we have printed it in its primordial essence and original substance, which was arranged by our Fathers of true glory, Mar Shim'un bar Sabba'e the Catholicos and victorious martyr, and Mar Ephrem the Great, namely upon the foundation of their faith, which is upon the temple of God the Word.

That is, God the Word took for himself a perfect man from the virgin Mary, and made him his Temple, and dwelt in him. The Evangelists witness: "'Tear down this temple and in three days I will raise it up;' but he spoke of the temple of his body." John 2:19–22. "That Temple in which dwells the complete fullness of Divinity in a fleshy way." Colossians 2:9.

For this, the Fathers of the East placed and founded their faith upon the Evangelical and Apostolic Faith. Mar Shim'un bar Sabba'e the Catholicos, in the Glorification "Glory to you, O Lord who created us": "Glory to you, holy Son, who wore our body and saved us" (see the *Shubaha* of ferial days during the Great *Ṣawma*).

Mar Ephrem the Great: "God the Word, Only-Begotten of the Father: may I please you alone, in the humanity which you wore" (see the Glorification of morning prayer of ferial Saturdays, "Blessed is the Being who made us").

Likewise: "the Word from the Father, did not take the likeness of a servant from the angels, but rather from the seed of Abraham, and in our humanity came in his grace to save our race from error" (see the first Sunday of *Subara*, the Responsory of the Basilica).

So we, by the aid of grace and the will of the Holy Spirit, have returned this our liturgy to its original clarity and its primordial and substantial arrangement, cleansed and purified from all alien unhealthy ideas.

We have corrected and set in order, and for this edition, our liturgy has wholly been examined, and searched by comparing the oldest manuscripts found in our time.

For this good work, and great labor, we established as manager our beloved brother Mar Thomas Darmo, Metropolitan of Malabar and all India, that he, as in our own person, may guide this work.

Thus it is also right to make known that the honored Inassu son of the faithful Thomas of the house of Olluqaran, victorious in all athleticism, faithful and God-fearing, who by a willing sacrifice took from his own the finances – not small – to begin this good and holy work of the printing of this book of the *Ḥudhra*. It is indeed obvious that without his donations, this work would not have succeeded. For this reason, we also grant him our Paternal blessings to dwell with him, and pray that he and the members of his family may be blessed with all heavenly and earthly blessings, in this world and that to come.

And we praise the diligent zeal and well-ordered care of our beloved sons, priest Francis son of the faithful David of the house of Ollukkaran, and deacon Joseph son of the faithful Thomas of the house of Arangyassery, and deacon George son of John of the house of Immathy, and all the faithful in the city of Trishur, and all the sons of the Church of the East in India, that they may be blessed by all blessings of the spirit in heaven through Jesus Christ our Lord.

On behalf of all the sons of our Church in the various lands who by their good will sent respectable donations, and made full sacrifices for the costs of printing, we pray that they be blessed with all blessings of the sprit in heaven and on earth, yes and amen.

Therefore we willingly permit, and approve, and ratify, that this edition of the *Ḥudhra* be distributed in all our Patriarchal territory, and we command and order by our Patriarchal authority, that this edition be kept in all the parishes of our holy apostolic catholic Church of the East and of all the ends of the earth, without alteration or subtraction, and that there should not be given place or chance to introduce additional corrupted heretical thoughts into it.

And let there be one communion and one harmony in all the Church together, and that editions may be increased and multiplied for the use of clerics, priests and deacons, and all those who love to pray in every place.

And as a gift of love, we give you our apostolic patriarchal blessings, and may the Grace of our Lord Jesus Christ, and the love of God the Father, and the communion of the Holy Spirit be with you all, amen.

Given at the Patriarchal palace
in the city of San Francisco, California
in the United States of America.
12 January 1961 AD

+ Mar Eshai Shim'un XXIII
by grace,
Catholicos-Patriarch of the East

The Service of Evening Prayer
for Feasts, Sundays, and Memorials

The Presider begins – the bishop, or, if there is not one present, the Archdeacon begins, or, if there is not one, the priest earliest ordained among the priests on his side. Know also, if the prayer of the day is of the "former," [the left side, facing the altar] they begin on the "former" side, and if the "latter," on the "latter" side. This is known from the *Ḥudhra*, outside of Lent: if the Vigil Hymns of the Sunday have "The Lord reigns," it is of the "former," and if they have "Thus Moses glorified," it is of the "latter." So if the Sunday is of the "former," so are Monday, Wednesday, and Friday; and Tuesday, Thursday, and Saturday are of the "latter." So also are Feasts and Memorials which fall on them. It is vice-versa, if the Sunday is of the "latter."

Presider: Glory to God in the highest 3x, peace on earth, and good hope to the sons of men, at all times, forever.

They say: *Barekh mar.*

And continue, singing:

Our Father who art in heaven,	Abbun dba-shmayya
hallowed be your name.	nithqaddash shmakh,
Your kingdom come.	tethe malkuthakh,
Holy, holy, you are holy.	**qaddysh, qaddysh, qaddysh-at,**
Our Father in heaven:	**Abbun dba-shmayya.**
heaven and earth are full	**Damlen shmayya w-ar'a**
of the greatness of your glory;	**rabbuth shuḥakh,**
angels & men cry out to you:	**'yre w-nasha qa'en lakh**
holy, holy, you are holy.	**qaddysh, qaddysh, qaddysh-at.**
Our Father who art in heaven,	Abbun dba-shmayya
hallowed be thy name.	nithqaddash shmakh,
Thy kingdom come,	tethe malkuthakh,
thy will be done on earth	nehwe ṣiw-yanakh
as it is in heaven.	aykanna dba-shmayya ap b-ar'a,
Give us this day our daily bread	haw lan laḥma d-sunqanan
and forgive us our trespasses,	yawmana wa-shwoq lan ḥawbayn
as we forgive those	wa-ḥtahayn aykanna d-ap ḥnan
who trespassed against us.	shwaqn l-ḥay-yawayn,
And lead us not into temptation,	w-la ta'lan l-nisyona
but deliver us from evil,	illa paṣan min bysha
for thine is the kingdom,	mittul d-dhylakh-y malkutha,

Sunday Evening Prayer

the power and the glory,
now and forever.
Presider: Glory to the Father, to the Son and to the Holy Spirit.
People: From age to age, amen, amen. Our Father who art in heaven, hallowed be your name. Your kingdom come.
Holy, holy, you are holy. Our Father in heaven: heaven and earth are full of the greatness of your glory; angels & men cry out to you: holy, holy, you are holy.

w-ḥayla w-tish-buḥta
l-'alam 'almyn, amen.
Presider: *Shuḥa l-Abba wla-Bra wal-Ruḥa d-Qudsha.*
People: *Min 'alam wa-'dham-ma l-'alam amen w-amen.*
Abbun dba-shmayya nithqaddash shmakh, tethe malkuthakh,
Qaddysh, qaddysh, qaddysh-at, Abbun dba-shmayya.
Damlen shmayya w-ar'a rabbuth shuḥakh,
'yre w-nasha qa'en lakh qaddysh, qaddysh, qaddysh-at.

Server: Let us pray. Peace be with us.
Priest: We confess your Divinity, O Lord, with spiritual praises, adore your Majesty with earthly adorations, and glorify your hidden Nature with pure intentions and holy, unstained thoughts, O Lord of all, Father, Son and Holy Spirit, forever.
On Memorials: We confess your Divinity, O Lord 2x, we adore your Majesty, and lift up unending praise to your glorious Trinity, at all times, Lord of all, Father, Son and Holy Spirit, forever.
People: Amen.

MARMYTHA
Psalm 65

To you is glory due in Zion, O God. **Halleluiah.**
    To you is glory due in Zion, O God.
And to you vows are fulfilled: hear my prayer!
    To you all flesh will come.
The words of the wicked are stronger than I,
    but you forgive my sins.
Blessed is he in whom you are pleased,
    and whom you bring near to dwell in your lodging.
Who is filled with the good things of your house,
    with the holiness of your temple,
    and with your awesome righteousness.

Sunday Evening Prayer

Answer, O God our Savior!
    The Hope of all the ends of the earth,
    and of the distant nations!
He establishes the mountains in his power;
    they are made strong by his might!
He stills the roarings of the sea
    and the sound of their waves.
The nations and the dwellers of earth are awestruck,
    by your signs and the procession of morning and evening.
You have surrounded the earth with glory.
    You have given it rest and greatly enriched it.
The vessels of God are filled with water:
    you prepared their food when you fashioned them.
You have drenched the furrows, that fruits may grow.
    Through dew the growth increases and is blessed.
Bless the crown of the year in your grace,
    and your calves will be fed with grass.
    They will be fed from the lodgings in the wilderness.
With glory the hills will be girt,
    and the choice lambs will be clothed.
The valleys will be filled with crops:
    they will shout with joy and praise!

Psalm 66

Glorify the Lord, all the earth!
    Sing to the honor of his name, sing to the honor of his glory!
Say to God: "How awesome are your works!"
    Because of your great strength, your enemies are convicted.
Through all the earth they shall adore and sing to you,
    and glorify your name forever,
and say "Come and see the works of God,
    whose marvels are many for the sons of men!
For he turned the sea to dry land,
    and they passed through the river on foot."
There, let us rejoice in him whose greatness rules forever.
    His eyes look upon the nations, so rebels will never be exalted.
O nations, bless God, and make his voice of his glory heard.

Sunday Evening Prayer

    For he placed our souls in life and did not let our foot stumble.
For you have tested us, O God, and tried us, like they test silver.
    You have brought us to the net, and laid a burden on our backs.
You let men ride upon our heads,
    brought us to fire and water, and brought us out to rest.
I will come to your house with respect and repay you my vows,
    that which my lips have spoken and my mouth in distress.
I will raise up burnt offerings with the smoke of rams,
    and make a sacrifice of bullocks and goats.
Come and hear, and I will make known to you,
    all you servants of God, what he has done for my soul.
I called to him with my mouth, and he answered me,
    and I exalted him with my tongue.
"O Lord, if you see malice in my heart, you will not save me."
    Then God heard the sound of my petition.
Blessed be the Lord,
    who did not let my prayer or his grace pass from me.

Psalm 67

O God, have mercy on us!
    Bless us, and let your face shed its light upon us.
That your ways be known upon earth
    and all nations learn your salvation.
Let the peoples confess you, O God;
    let all the peoples confess you.
Let the kingdoms be glad and exult
    for you judge the nations uprightly
    and guide the nations on earth.
Let the peoples confess you, O God;
    let all the peoples confess you.
The earth has yielded its fruit
    for God, our God, has blessed us.
May God still give us his blessing
    and all the ends of the earth will fear him.

Glory to the Father, to the Son and to the Holy Spirit.
    From age to age, amen, amen.
Halleluiah, halleluiah, halleluiah.

Sunday Evening Prayer

[During Advent and Christmas Seasons, they sing:
MARMYTHA
Psalm 87

Its foundations are on his holy mountain: **Halleluiah.**
    Its foundations are on his holy mountain:
the Lord loves the gates of Zion
    more than all of Jacob's dwellings.
Honorable things are said in you,
    O village of our God.
You will be remembered in Egypt and known in Babylon,
    Philistia, Tyre, and among the Cushites.
That man will be born there,
    and of Zion it shall be said:
the Great One shall be born there,
    and he has established her.
The Lord will count his people in his register:
    that man will be born there.
The leaders who dwell in you will rejoice,
    as well as all the lowly within you.

Psalm 88

O Lord God of my salvation,
    By day I cried out, and by night before you.
May my prayer enter before you;
    turn your ear to my pleading,
for my soul is filled with evils,
    and my life has reached Sheol.
I am considered among those who have descended to the cave,
    and have become like a man without help,
a freeborn man among the dead,
    like the murdered buried in tombs,
those whom you have not remembered,
    and those destroyed by your hands.
You have brought me down to the lowest cave,
    to the darkness and the shadow of death.
Your wrath has devoured me,
    and you have brought all your waves against me.

Sunday Evening Prayer

You have distanced those who know me,
> and made me impure to them.

I am prevented from leaving,
> and my eye pines due to my humiliation.

I have called you, O Lord, every day,
> and extended my hands toward you.

Lo, will you work miracles for the dead?
> Will warriors rise and give thanks to you?

Will those in the tomb discuss your grace,
> and those in destruction your faithfulness?

Will your marvel be made known in the darkness,
> and your righteousness in a land that was lost?

But I cry out to you, O Lord,
> and present my prayer to you in the morning.

Do not forget my soul, O Lord,
> nor turn your face from me.

I am miserable and weary from my youth:
> I have been raised up, and humbled, and broken,

and your wrath has passed over me,
> and your tempest has silenced me.

I am surrounded as with waters the whole day,
> and they come against me as one.

You have distanced my friends and companions from me,
> and removed those who know me.

Glory to the Father, to the Son and to the Holy Spirit.
> **From age to age, amen, amen.**

Halleluiah, halleluiah, halleluiah.]

People: Let us pray. Peace be with us.
The Prayer of "Like a Cloud" for Sundays and Feasts: It is right at all times for us to thank, adore and glorify the great and awesome, holy and blessed, lofty and incomprehensible name of your glorious Trinity, and your grace toward our race, O Lord of all, Father, Son and Holy Spirit, forever. [Thus all prayers end, aside from those signed in the name of our Lord alone, when they say "Lord of all, forever."]
They answer: Amen.

The priest on the "latter" side begins, if the beginning of Ramsha is at the "former" side, and vice-versa:

- How lovely are your tabernacles, Lord God almighty!
- My soul longs and yearns for the courts of the Lord!
Like a cloud of fine incense and the smell of a sweet thurible,
accept, O Christ our Savior, the pleading and the prayer of your servants!
They repeat it, and then "glory" it.
[On Feasts of the Lord, they say it five times, as in the *Ḥudhra* or *Gazza*.]

[Prayer of "Like a Cloud" for Memorials:
To you, O Good and Kind One, Merciful and Compassionate, O great King of Glory, O Being who exists from eternity, we give thanks, adore, and glorify you at all times, Lord of all, Father, Son, and Holy Spirit, forever.
- I will bless the Lord at all times.
- And at all times, his praises in my mouth.
Like a cloud…
They repeat it, and then "glory" it.]

Server: Peace be with us.
Prayer of *Lakhu Mara* for Sundays, Feasts, and Memorials: And for all your benefits and graces to us that cannot be repaid, we give you thanks and praise you unceasingly in your crowned Church, full of all benefits and blessings, for you are Lord and Creator of all, Father, Son, and Holy Spirit, forever.

And they say:

<small>LAKHU MARA</small>

We give you thanks,	*Lakhu Mara d-kulla*
O Lord of all,	*mawdenan,*
we glorify you,	*w-lakh Yshoʾ Mshyḥa*
Jesus Christ;	*mshabḥynan*
you raise our bodies	*d-attu Mnaḥmana*
into life,	*d-paghrayn,*
you are the Savior	*w-attu Paroqa*
of our souls.	*d-nawshathan.*

Sunday Evening Prayer

I rejoiced when I heard them say: we are going to the house of the Lord!	*Ḥdhyth kadh amryn waw ly: l-bayteh d-Marya azynan!*
We give you thanks...	*Lakhu Mara d-kulla...*
Glory to the Father, to the Son and to the Holy Spirit. From age to age, amen, amen.	*Shuḥa l-Aḇḇa w-laḆra wal-Ruḥa d-Qudsha min 'alam wa'dhamma l-'alam amen, w-amen.*
We give you thanks...	*Lakhu Mara d-kulla...*

On Feasts of the Lord, they say it five times, as written in the *Ḥudhra* or *Gazza*.

Prayer of the Psalmodies and Responsories "Before": Lord, you are indeed the One who raises our bodies, the true Savior of our souls, and the constant Guardian of our lives. It is thus our duty to thank, adore and glorify you who are Lord of all forever.

On Sundays, they say the Psalmody of "Before and After" as in the *Ḥudhra*.

PSALMODIES "BEFORE"
First Sunday (Psalm 47:1–5)

All peoples, *clap* your hands,
   Halleluiah, halleluiah, *h*alleluiah.
All peoples, *clap* your hands,
   cry to God *with* shouts of joy!
For the Lord, the Most High, *we* must fear,
   great king ov*er* all the earth.
He subdues peoples *un*der us
   and nations *un*der our feet.
Our inheritance, our glory, *is* from him,
   given to Ja*cob* out of love.

[And, from Ascension to Advent, Psalm 47:5–9]
God goes up with *shouts* of joy;
   the Lord goes up *with* trumpet blast.
Sing praise for *God*, sing praise,
   sing praise to *our* king, sing praise.
God is king of *all* the earth,
   sing praise *with* all your skill.

God is king *ov*er the nations;
    God reigns on *his* holy throne.
Glory to the Father, to the Son and to the *Ho*ly Spirit.
    From age to age, *a*men, amen.
Halleluiah, *ha*lleluiah, *ha*lleluiah.

Second Sunday (Psalm 65:1–5)

To you is glory due in Zi*on*, O God.
    Halleluiah, halleluiah, *ha*lleluiah.
To you is glory due in Zi*on*, O God.
    And to you vows are fulfilled: hear my prayer!
        To you *all* flesh will come.
The words of the wicked are stron*ger* than I,
    but you *for*give my sins.
Blessed is he in whom *you* are pleased,
    and whom you bring near to *dwell* in your lodging.
Who is filled with the good things *of* your house,
    with the holiness of your temple,
    and with your awe*some* righteousness.
Answer, O *God* our Savior!
    The Hope of all the *ends* of the earth.
Glory to the Father, to the Son and to the *Ho*ly Spirit.
    From age to age, *a*men, amen.
Halleluiah, *ha*lleluiah, *ha*lleluiah.

Third Sunday (Psalm 89:1–5)

I will sing the grace of the *Lord* forever,
    Halleluiah, halleluiah, *ha*lleluiah.
I will sing the grace of the *Lord* forever,
    and make known his faithfulness with my *mouth* for the ages.
For you said the world was *built* in grace,
    and your faithful*ness* fashioned heaven.
I established a covenant *with* my chosen,
    and vowed to Da*vid* my servant:
I will establish your *seed* forever,
    and build your *throne* for the ages.

Glory to the Father, to the Son and to the *Ho*ly Spirit.
  From age to age, *a*men, amen.
Halleluiah, *h*alleluiah, *h*alleluiah.

Fourth Sunday (Psalm 93)

The Lord is king, with majes*ty* enrobed;
  Halleluiah, halleluiah, *h*alleluiah.
The Lord is king, with majes*ty* enrobed;
  the Lord is clothed with might and power.
  he constructed the world *to* be unshaken.
Your throne is established from *the* beginning:
  and you exist, O Lord, from *e*ternity.
The rivers have lifted *up*, O Lord,
  the rivers have lifted up their voice,
  the rivers have lifted up *in* purity.
Even mightier than the roar of *ma*ny waters
  are the sur*gings* of the sea.
Glorious are you, O *Lord*, on high,
  and your testimonies *are* greatly faithful.
And holiness is fitting *to* your house,
  O Lord, until *the* end of days.
Glory to the Father, to the Son and to the *Ho*ly Spirit.
  From age to age, *a*men, amen.
Halleluiah, *h*alleluiah, *h*alleluiah.

Fifth Sunday (Psalm 125:1–7)

When the Lord delivered Zi*on* from bondage,
  Halleluiah, halleluiah, *h*alleluiah.
When the Lord delivered Zi*on* from bondage,
  it *seemed* like a dream.
Then was our mouth *filled* with laughter,
  on our *lips* there were songs.
The heathens themselves *said*: "What marvels
  the *Lord* worked for them!"
What marvels the Lord *worked* for us!
  In*deed* we were glad.

Deliver us, O Lord, *from* our bondage
    as *streams* in dry land.
Those who are sow*ing* in tears
    will *sing* when they reap.
They go out full of tears, carrying seed *for* the sowing:
    they come back full of song, car*ry*ing their sheaves.
Glory to the Father, to the Son and to the *Ho*ly Spirit.
    From age to age, *a*men, amen.
Halleluiah, *ha*lleluiah, *ha*lleluiah.

Sixth Sunday (Psalm 49:1–5)

Hear this, *all* you peoples,
    Halleluiah, halleluiah, *ha*lleluiah.
Hear this, *all* you peoples,
    give heed, all who dwell in the world,
    men both high and low, rich *and* poor alike!
My lips will speak *words* of wisdom.
    My heart *is* full of insight.
I will turn my mind *to* a parable,
    with the harp I *will* solve my problem.
Glory to the Father, to the Son and to the *Ho*ly Spirit.
    From age to age, *a*men, amen.
Halleluiah, *ha*lleluiah, *ha*lleluiah.

Seventh Sunday (Psalm 136:1–4)

By the rivers of *Ba*bylon
    Halleluiah, halleluiah, *ha*lleluiah.
By the rivers of *Ba*bylon
    there we sat and wept, *re*membering Zion;
on the poplars *that* grew there
    we *hung* up our harps.
For it was there *that* they asked us,
    our captors, for songs, our oppressors, for joy.
    "Sing to us," they said, "one *of* Zion's songs."
Glory to the Father, to the Son and to the *Ho*ly Spirit.
    From age to age, *a*men, amen.
Halleluiah, *ha*lleluiah, *ha*lleluiah.

Sunday Evening Prayer

HYMNS "BEFORE" – *'am kulhon qaddyshayk*

- Gladden your servant's soul.
Give rest, O Christ the King,
to all of your servants' souls,
with your saints in harmony,
where there is no suffering,
and no sickness or distress,
but only kingly eternal life.

- Our Lord is great and glorious!
Our support is in our God,
Fashioner of Adam's race,
Hope of both our death and life.
This world is not any thing,
as its comforts are as well,
and so, raise us, give us life in grace.

- Glory to the Father, to the Son and to the Holy Spirit.
Christ the King, our Savior:
raise us on the day you come,
and set us at your right hand,
with the just who did your will,
who believed, confessed your cross,
that, one with them,
we may live in you.

But on Feasts and Memorials, there is no Psalmody. They say only the Responsories of Before and After, as written in their places.

Server: Let us pray. Peace be with us.
The Prayer of Psalm 140: It is our duty, O Lord our God, to thank, adore and glorify you for your mercy and your providential will for us, at all times, O Lord of all, Father, Son and Holy Spirit, forever.
People: Amen.

Then a priest from the "latter" side begins, if the day's prayer is of the "former," and vice-versa, and says:

Sunday Evening Prayer

Psalm 140

I have called to you, Lord; hasten to *help* me!
> **Hearken to my words and *ac*cept my prayer.**

I have called to you, Lord; hasten to *help* me!
> Hearken to my words and *ac*cept my prayer.

Let my prayer arise before you like *in*cense,
> the offering of my hands like an eve*ning* oblation.

Set, O Lord, a guard over my *mouth*
> and a guard *o*ver my lips!

That my heart may not turn to an evil *deed*,
> or accompl*ish* works of wickedness.

May I not dine with evil *men*.
> Let a just man teach *me* and reprove me.

But let the oil of the wicked not anoint my *head*,
> for my prayer is *a*gainst their malice.

Their judges were thrown down by a rock-like *hand*,
> then they heard that *my* words were kind,

Like a plough that scatters the *ground*.
> Their bones were strewn at *the* mouth of Sheol.

To you, Lord God, I lift up my *eyes*:
> I trust you; do not cast *my* soul away!

Guard me from the hands of the *boastful*,
> who *set* traps for me.

Let the wicked fall together into their own *nets*
> while I pursue *my* way unharmed.

Psalm 141

With my voice I called to the *Lord*,
> with my voice *I* begged the Lord.

I lifted my pleading be*fore* him;
> I showed *him* my distress.

When my spirit trembled, you knew my *path*.
> On the way I walked they set *a* trap for me.

I looked to my right and *saw*:
> there was no *one* to advise me.

I had no means of es*cape*,
> not one who *cared* for my soul.

Sunday Evening Prayer

I cried to you, Lord; I said: you are my *hope*,
    all that I have in the *land* of the living.
Hearken then to my *plead*ing,
    for I am *brought* very low.
Rescue me from those who pur*sue* me,
    for they are *strong*er than I.
Bring my soul out of this *pris*on,
    that I may give *thanks* to your name.
Your just ones will a*wait* me
    as you *grant* me reward.

Psalm 118:105–12

Your word is a lamp for my *feet*
    and a *light* for my paths.
I have sworn and made up my *mind*
    to keep *your* just decrees.
Lord, I am deeply aff*lic*ted:
    give me *life* by your word.
Be pleased, Lord, with the words of my *mouth*
    and teach me *by* your decrees.
My soul is in your hands at all *times*;
    I will not *for*get your law.
Though sinners laid traps for *me*,
    I did not stray *from* your commands.
Your witness is my heritage for*ever*,
    for it is the *joy* of my heart.
I set my heart to carry out your *stat*utes
    in *truth*, for ever.

Psalm 116

O praise the Lord, all you *nat*ions,
    O praise *him*, all you peoples!
For mighty is his *love* for us;
    truly, he is the *Lord* forever.

Glory to the Father, to the Son and to the Holy *Spir*it.
    From age to age, *a*men, amen.

I have called to you, Lord; hasten to *help* me!
    Hearken to my words and *a*ccept my prayer.

Sunday Evening Prayer

Server: Let us pray. Peace be with us.
Prayer of the Shuraye and Responsories "After": Hear, O Lord our God, the prayer of your servants in your mercy; accept the supplication of your adorers in your compassion, and pity our sinfulness in your grace and mercies, O Healer of our bodies and Good Hope of our souls at all times O Lord of all, Father, Son and Holy Spirit, forever.
People: Amen.

Psalmodies "After"
First Sunday (Psalm 48:1–3)

Great is our Lord and highly *glo*rious,
    Halleluiah, halleluiah, *h*alleluiah.
Great is our Lord and highly *glo*rious,
    in the vill*age* of our God,
and on his holy and glo*ri*ous mountain.
    There is joy all *o*ver the earth.
The mountain of Zion which is on the outskirts *of* the north
    is the village *of* the great king.
God makes *known* his might
    in *her* palaces.
Glory to the Father, to the Son and to the *Ho*ly Spirit.
    From age to age, *a*men, amen.
Halleluiah, *h*alleluiah, *h*alleluiah.

Second Sunday (Psalm 66:1–4)

Cry out with joy to God *all* the earth,
    Halleluiah, halleluiah, *h*alleluiah.
Cry out with joy to God *all* the earth,
    O sing to the glo*ry* of his name.
O render him glo*ri*ous praise.
    Say to God: "How tremen*dous* are your deeds!
Because of the greatness *of* your strength
    your ene*mies* cringe before you.
Before you all the *earth* shall bow,
    shall sing to you, *sing* to your name!"

Sunday Evening Prayer

Glory to the Father, to the Son and to the *Ho*ly Spirit.
  From age to age, *a*men, amen.
Hallelu*i*ah, *ha*lleluiah, *ha*lleluiah.

Third Sunday (Psalm 89:5–9)

I will establish your *seed* forever,
  Halleluiah, halleluiah, *ha*lleluiah.
I will establish your *seed* forever,
    and build your *throne* for the ages.
The heavens confess your won*ders*, O Lord,
    and your faithfulness in the church of *your* holy ones.
Who compares to the Lord in the hea*vens* of heaven,
    and resembles the Lord among the *sons* of the angels?
God stands in the church of the *ho*ly ones,
    great and fearful for all who surround him.
    Lord God almighty, who is *mi*ghty like you?
Glory to the Father, to the Son and to the *Ho*ly Spirit.
  From age to age, *a*men, amen.
Hallelu*i*ah, *ha*lleluiah, *ha*lleluiah.

Fourth Sunday (Psalm 148:1–7)

Praise the Lord *from* the heavens,
    Halleluiah, halleluiah, *ha*lleluiah.
Praise the Lord *from* the heavens,
    praise *him* in the heights.
Praise him, *all* his angels,
    praise *him* all his hosts.
Praise him, *sun* and moon,
    praise him, *all* stars and lights.
Praise him hea*ven* of heavens.
  Waters above the heavens,
    praise the *name* of the Lord.
For he spoke, *and* they were;
  He commanded and *they* were created.
He fixed them fore*ver* and ever,
    gave a law which shall not pass away.
    Praise the *Lord* from the earth.

Glory to the Father, to the Son and to the *Ho*ly Spirit.
  From age to age, *a*men, amen.
Halleluiah, *ha*lleluiah, *ha*lleluiah.

Fifth Sunday (Psalm 126:1–5)

If the Lord does not *build* the house,
  Halleluiah, halleluiah, *ha*lleluiah.
If the Lord does not *build* the house,
  in vain do *its* builders labor;
if the Lord does not watch o*ver* the city,
  in vain does the *wat*chman keep vigil.
In vain is your ear*li*er rising,
  your going *la*ter to rest,
you who toil for the *bread* you eat,
  when he pours gifts *on* his beloved
while *they* slumber.
  Truly sons are the inheri*tance* of the Lord.
Glory to the Father, to the Son and to the *Ho*ly Spirit.
  From age to age, *a*men, amen.
Halleluiah, *ha*lleluiah, *ha*lleluiah.

Sixth Sunday (Psalm 129)

From the depths I have cried to *you*, O Lord,
  Halleluiah, halleluiah, *ha*lleluiah.
From the depths I have cried to *you*, O Lord,
  and *you* heard my voice.
Let your ears *be* attentive
  to the *sound* of my pleading.
If you keep *count* of sins,
    O Lord, who would be able to stand?
    For forgive*ness* is from you;
I have hoped *in* the Lord
  and my soul a*wait*ed his word.
It awaited the Lord from the *mor*ning watch
  until *the* morning watch.

Let Israel await *for* the Lord,
    for mer*cies* are from him,
and salvation e*ven* more so.
    He will save Israel *from* all its sin.
Glory to the Father, to the Son and to the *Ho*ly Spirit.
    From age to age, *a*men, amen.
Halleluiah, *ha*lleluiah, *ha*lleluiah.

Seventh Sunday (Psalm 137:1–4)

I thank you, Lord, with *all* my heart,
    Halleluiah, halleluiah, *ha*lleluiah.
I thank you, Lord, with *all* my heart,
    and sing to *you* before kings.
I will adore in your *ho*ly temple
    and thank your name,
    for your grace *and* for your truth.
For you exalted the name of your glory *o*ver all.
    On the day I called, *you* answered me.
You increased the strength *of* my soul.
    O Lord, let all the kings of the *earth* confess you,
Glory to the Father, to the Son and to the *Ho*ly Spirit.
    From age to age, *a*men, amen.
Halleluiah, *ha*lleluiah, *ha*lleluiah.

HYMNS "AFTER" FOR THE FORMER WEEK - *niṭṭayaw*

- Turn your ear, and answer me.
Messiah, who came to save
and renew Adam's face
which had rotted in disgrace,
who took on our flesh,
in it redeemed us,
giving us strength
to be raised from death:
forgive your servants in grace,
when you come again!

- Because of your grace, O God.
In grace, you created us
when the world first began,
vested us with radiance
in Paradise,
but in rebellion,
we sinned and fell.
Then you sent your Son,
and in his mercy we have
kingly, eternal life.

- Glory to the Father, to the Son and to the Holy Spirit.
We praise you, O Christ our King,
for you gained victory:
through your cross
you saved our race
from Satan's deceit.
May you renew us,
abolish death,
let your new life reign
and make us fit for mercy,
O Resurrecting King!

HYMNS "AFTER" FOR THE LATTER WEEK – *malka mnaḥmana*
- For he comes to judge the earth.
The King who raises:
he is dawning from above
in radiance, giving life to all,
and all together
will arise from every tomb,
and lift up praise
to their raising King!

- All you servants of God.
Let sadness pass by
from your hearts,
O mortal ones,
for his day dawns,

Sunday Evening Prayer

and will gladden us,
awaken us all,
when the watchers
will rejoice
before his throne,
on the day he comes.
- **Glory to the Father, to the Son and to the Holy Spirit.**
May our deceased live,
and their bodies all be raised
as prophesied
Isaiah, who said:
"The sleeping will rise,
and those buried in the earth."
For your renewal
is of Light and Truth.

PETITIONS

Server: Let us all stand composed.
In joy and gladness, let us implore *and* say: Lord, have mer*cy* on us.
People: Lord, have mer*cy* on us. | *Maran ith*raḥam *'layn.*
Server:
* O Father of mercies and God of every cons*o*lation, we *im*plore you...
* Our Savior, our Caretaker and Provider *for* all, we *im*plore you...
* For the peace, concord and well-being of the whole world and of *all* churches, we *im*plore you...
* For the well-being of our country and of all countries, and for the protection of all the faithful who inha*bit* them, we *im*plore you...
* For good weather, a fertile season, the abundance of fruits and all the poor *and* needy, we *im*plore you...
* For the health of our holy fathers: [Mar _____, High Pontiff, Pope of Rome,] Mar _____, Catholicos-Patriarch, Mar _____, Bishop/Metropolitan, and for all those in the same priest*ly* service, we *im*plore you...
* For the rulers of *this* world, we *im*plore you...
* O merciful God, who guides all in *his* mercy, we *im*plore you...
* For the priests and deacons of our Church, and for all of our Chris*tian* brethren, we *im*plore you...

Sunday Evening Prayer

* O Rich in his mercies and overflowing in his *com*passion, we *im*plore you...
* O One who is before the ages, and whose authority will remain *for*ever, we *im*plore you...
* O Kind One in his Nature, and Giver of all *good* things, we *im*plore you...
* O One who does not desire that a sinner should die, but rather that he should repent from evil *and* live, we *im*plore you...
* O One who is glorified in heaven and worshipped *on* earth, we *im*plore you...
* O One through whose holy <u>Birth</u> [or <u>Dawning</u>, or <u>Fasting</u>, or <u>Presentation</u>, or <u>Resurrection</u>, or <u>Ascension</u>, or <u>Descent</u>, or <u>Cross</u>] has gladdened earth and deligh*ted* heaven, we *im*plore you...
* O One whose Nature is Immortality, and who dwells in radi*ant* light, we *im*plore you...
* O Savior of all mankind, especially those who believe *in* him, we *im*plore you...
* Save us all, O Christ our Lord, in your grace, increase your peace and your tranquility within us and have mer*cy* on us...

Server: Let us entrust our souls mutually to the Father, and to the Son, and to *the* Holy Spirit.

People: To you, *O* Lord our God.

Priest: To you, Lord God almighty, do we entrust our bodies and souls, and from you, O Lord our God, do we ask for forgiveness of debts and sins. Grant this to us through your grace and mercies, as you always do, Lord of all, Father, Son, and Holy Spirit, forever.

The Server who said the Petitions says: Lift your voices, all you people, and glorify the living God.

People:

Holy God,	Qaddysha Alaha
Holy Mighty One,	Qaddysha Ḥayilthana,
Holy Immortal One:	Qaddysha La Mayotha
Have mercy on us.	Ithraḥam 'layn.
Glory to the Father, to the Son and to the Holy Spirit.	*Shuḥa l-Aḅḅa w-laḄra wal-Ruḥa d-Qudsha.*
Holy God...	Qaddysha Alaha...
From age to age, amen, amen.	*Min 'alam wa'dhamma l-'alam amen, w-amen.*
Holy God...	Qaddysha Alaha...

Sunday Evening Prayer

They say: Let us pray. Peace be with us.

The prayers after "Holy God" for Sundays and Feasts: To you, O Holy One who is holy in his Nature and glorious in his Existence, and high and exalted above all in his Divinity, the Nature that is holy and blessed from eternity, do we give thanks, adore and glorify at all times, O Lord of all, Father, Son and Holy Spirit, forever.

For Memorials: O Holy, Glorious, Mighty and Immortal One, who dwells in the saints and delights in them: we implore you: turn to us, O Lord, pardon us and have mercy on us as you always do, Lord of all: Father, Son, and Holy Spirit, forever.

People: Amen.

The Server who said the Petitions: Bless me, sir. Bow your heads for the laying-on of hands, and accept the blessing.

The Presider says: May Christ adorn your service in the Kingdom of heaven.

The Prayer of the Basilica: When our souls are completed for the one perfect faith of the glorious Trinity, may we all become worthy, in the one harmony of love, to lift up glory, honor, thanksgiving, and adoration, at all times, Lord of all, Father, Son, and Holy Spirit, forever.

Here they say the *Suyake*, if there is one written in the rite of the day, and they say the BASILICA HYMN of the day, and repeat, and "glory" it (see pp. 389–578).

Then, From Advent to Epiphany:

- **From age to age, amen, amen.**

God advised and promised Abraham from the beginning, "through your seed, all the sinful nations shall be blessed, who were dead in their sins and lost in error." For he gathered them and healed their wounds, as the prophet saw from ages ago, "he will take on their wounds and carry their sicknesses." For this we cry out as we say: glory to you, O Son of the Lord of All!

During Epiphany:

- **From age to age, amen, amen.**

The three Individuals of Existence have dawned and been revealed in the created world in the latter times upon the Jordan: the Father who cried out and made his voice heard from on high: "this is my Son and my Beloved," and the Spirit who makes the true faith known to us.

Note that there is no "continuation" from Lent to Pentecost, for either the Basilica Responsory or the Night Responsory.

During the Season of the Apostles:
- From age to age, amen, amen.
O Christ, who chose his apostles and clothed them with the power of the Spirit, that they may be preachers in the world and reveal his glory and Divinity in creation through the mighty works of their hands: gladden your churches with peace and harmony, and lift up the head of the preachers of your name and the keepers of your commandments. With your right hand, O Lord, may our salvation be guarded, and may they preach your righteousness in the peace that comes from you.

During the Season of Summer until the Feast of the Cross:
- From age to age, amen, amen.
Answer your adorers, O Christ, and send us from your treasury pity, mercies, salvation and the forgiveness of sins; and, as you answered Daniel from the den of lions and the house of Hananiah in the furnace of fire, deliver us also, O Lord, from kings and rulers, evil people and rebellious demons, who advance to destroy us like lions. With your mighty power, pacify their ferocity, deliver us from their wickedness, abolish their dominion, and gladden us with your salvation, O Christ the King!

During the Season of the Cross until the Sanctification of the Church:
- From age to age, amen, amen.
Through the great power of the cross, the Church has gained a boast over death and over Satan, rejoices in salvation, and extols it in glory before the eyes of the enemies of Truth, for it exalted her abasement with the power that it made to dwell in her. And lo, on the day of its finding, her children shout with hymns of praise: "O General who gave victory to her in battle, keep your promise." The glory of your revelation is the boast of her children!

During the Sundays of the Sanctification of the Church:
- From age to age, amen, amen.
You have made this holy house, O Lord, the pedestal of your dwelling. Order it, O Lord, with your hands. May the prayers and tears of the weary be accepted

Sunday Evening Prayer

in it, may all benefits and gifts flow from it to your people and the sheep of your flock, those saved by your cross and taking refuge in the name of your Majesty.

Then also, from Christmas to Lent, and after Pentecost:
- Let all the people say: "Amen, amen."
O holy virgin Mary, mother of Jesus our Savior: plead and implore for mercies from the Child who dawned from your womb, that in his grace he may make times of distress pass by us and establish peace and serenity for us; and through your prayers, may the Church and her children be guarded from the evil one. On the glorious day when his Greatness is revealed, may we be worthy to delight with you in the bridal chamber of Light.

According to the current practice, here the Gospel of the day is read, and they say the *Zumara* of Psalm 140, as written in the *Ḥudhra* or *Gazza*.

Prayer before the Psalmody after the Basilica, for Advent, Christmas, and the season of Epiphany, and the season of the Resurrection, and Ascension, and Pentecost, and all Feasts of the Lord: To your wondrous and indescribable providence, O Lord, which was accomplished, completed and perfected in mercies and pity for the renewal and the salvation of our weak race through the Principal that is from us, do we lift up glory, honor, thanksgiving and adoration at all times, O Lord of all, Father, Son and Holy Spirit, forever.
People: Amen.
For the great Lent, and the season of Summer, and the season of Elijah until the Feast of the Cross, and for all Ordinary Days: Pity us, O Pitying One, in your grace, turn to us, O Merciful One, and do not turn your gaze and your providence away from us, for our hope and support are in you, at all times and ages, Lord of all, Father, Son, and Holy Spirit, forever.
For the Season of the Apostles: May the prayers of the holy apostles, O Lord, the pleading of the true preachers, and the begging and supplication of the victorious athletes, preachers of the truth, the evangelists of righteousness, sowers of peace in creation, be among us always, at all times and ages, Lord of all, Father, Son, and Holy Spirit, forever.
For the Season of the Cross: Sow, O Lord, your peace in every corner, establish your Church through your cross, and protect her children by your grace, for in

Sunday Evening Prayer

her we lift up glory, honor, thanksgiving, and adoration to you, at all times, Lord of all, Father, Son, and Holy Spirit, forever.

For the season of the Sanctification of the Church: Establish, O Lord, the pillars of your Church through your mercy, strengthen her foundations in your grace, and let your glory dwell in the Temple set apart for the honor of your service, all the days of the age, Lord of all, Father, Son, and Holy Spirit, forever.

For Feasts and Memorials of St. Mary: May the prayer of the holy Virgin, O Lord, the pleading of the Blessed Mother, and the supplication and petition of the one who is Full of Grace, the blessed St. Mary, be among us always, at all times and ages, Lord of all, Father, Son, and Holy Spirit, forever.

For the Memorial of the Patron Saint: May the prayer, petition, supplication, and begging of our splendid and holy patron, the victorious St. ____ and all his companions, be among us always, at all times and ages, Lord of all, Father, Son, and Holy Spirit, forever.

For Memorials of Martyrs and Confessors: May the prayers of your martyrs, O Lord, the petition of your confessors, and the supplication and pleading of the athletes who fulfilled your will, plead to your Divinity on our behalf, that you may accomplish your peace and serenity among us, all the days of the age, Lord of all, Father, Son, and Holy Spirit, forever.

For Memorials of Teachers: May the prayers of the holy priests, O Lord, the petition of the victorious teachers, and the supplication and pleading of the athletes who perfected your will, be among us always, at all times and ages, Lord of all, Father, Son, and Holy Spirit, forever.

For the Memorial of St. John the Baptist: May the prayer of the well-proven Baptist, the petition of the good ambassador, and the supplication and pleading of the true preacher, the splendid and holy martyr St John the victorious, be among us always, at all times and ages, Lord of all, Father, Son, and Holy Spirit, forever.

For the Wednesdays of the Entire Year: Arm us, O Lord our God, with a mighty and invincible armor, by the prayers of your blessed mother, the blessed St. Mary, and grant us part and portion with her in the heavenly banquet, Lord of all, forever.

For the Fridays of the Entire Year: Raise, O Lord, our deceased in your mercy, raise them up at your right hand, clothe them with splendid glory in your Kingdom, and mingle them among the just who fulfilled your will, in the Jerusalem above, Lord of all, Father, Son, and Holy Spirit, forever.

Sunday Evening Prayer

They say the PSALMODY of the day, as written in the *Ḥudhra* or *Gazza* (see pp. 389–578), and at the end of the Psalmody, they say *Abbun d-bashmayya* in a simple tone (see above, p. 1).

The Presider prays: May your holy name, O Lord our God, be glorified, your Divinity adored, your Lordship honored, your Greatness made victorious, your Existence exalted, and may the eternal mercies of your glorious Trinity surround your people and the sheep of your flock, Lord of all, Father, Son, and Holy Spirit, forever.

Again: May your Divinity be blessed in heaven and on earth, O Lord, your Lordship adored, and the adorable and glorious name of your glorious Trinity hallowed, glorified, lifted up, and exalted at all times, Lord of all, Father, Son, and Holy Spirit, forever.

Here they pray the *Suba'a*, if there is one. Prayer before *Suba'a*: Make us worthy, O Lord our God, for an evening of peace, a night of restfulness, a morning of blessed hopes, and a daytime of good works, that in them we may please your Divinity, all the days of our lives, Lord of all, Father, Son, and Holy Spirit, forever.

Prayer after *Suba'a*: O Opener of the door to those who knock, and Answerer of the requests of those who ask: open, O Lord our God, the door of mercies to our prayer, accept our petition, and answer our requests in your mercies, from the your rich and overflowing treasury, O Kind One who does not withhold his mercies or his gifts from the needy and afflicted, his servants who call and plead to him at all times and ages, Lord of all, Father, Son, and Holy Spirit, forever.

Another: O Hearer of the voice of the righteous and just who please him at all times, who does the will of those who fear him: hear, O Lord, the prayer of your servants in your mercy, accept the supplication of your adorers in your compassion, and pity the afflicted and downtrodden, your servants who plead to you at all times and ages, Lord of all, Father, Son, and Holy Spirit, forever.

Here each of the priests says a prayer from among those written here, according to priority of ordination:

For Assistance: O Lord, may the assistance of your mercies, the aid of your grace, the hidden and glorious power of your glorious Trinity, and your merciful and compassionate right hand, dwell with and accompany your weak adorers from your holy house filled with all assistance and blessing, through the prayers of the blessed St. Mary, and the prayers of all your saints who pleased you, Lord of all, Father, Son, and Holy Spirit, forever.

Another: By your blessing, O Lord our God, may your servants be blessed, by the providence of your will, may your adorers be kept, and may the constant serenity of your Divinity, and the permanent peace of your Majesty, rule among your people and your Church all the days of the age, Lord of all, Father, Son, and Holy Spirit, forever.

Another: May the blessing of the Blesser of all, the peace of the Pacifier of all, the pity of the Pitier of all, and the protection of our adorable God, be among us, with us, and around us, and keep us from the evil one and his hosts, at all times and ages, Lord of all, Father, Son, and Holy Spirit, forever.

Another: By your blessing, O Lord our God, my we be blessed, by your providence may we be kept, may your power come to our aid, your assistance accompany us, your right hand dwell among us, your peace rule in us, your cross be our great fortress and refuge, and may we be guarded under its wings from the evil one and his hosts, at all times and ages, Lord of all, Father, Son, and Holy Spirit, forever.

Another: Blessed, O Lord, are the mercies of your grace, and adorable are the promises of your Majesty, which always teach us to look to you, exalt in you, and not lose hope in you, all the days of our lives, Lord of all, Father, Son, and Holy Spirit, forever.

Another: May your blessing, O Lord our God, descend upon your people, and may your mercy always be upon us weak sinners, O our Good Hope and Merciful Refuge, Forgiver of sins and faults, Lord of all, Father, Son, and Holy Spirit, forever.

Another: May the peace of the Father be with us, the love of the Son be among us, may the Holy Spirit guide us according to his will, and upon us be his mercies and compassion, at all times and ages, Lord of all, Father, Son, and Holy Spirit, forever.

Sunday Evening Prayer

Another: May your peace, O Lord, dwell in us, your serenity rule in us, and your love increase among us, all the days of our lives, Lord of all, Father, Son, and Holy Spirit, forever.

Another: Protect us, O Lord, by your right hand, keep us under your wings, and may your assistance accompany us, all the days of our lives, Lord of all, Father, Son, and Holy Spirit, forever.

Another: Grant us, O Lord, perpetual peace, charity, love of learning, life, blessings, and joys, and provision that does not fail, all the days of our lives, Lord of all, Father, Son, and Holy Spirit, forever.

Another: Be an unsleeping guardian for the sheepfold where your flock dwells, lest it be harmed by the wolves that thirst for the blood of your sheep, for you are the unfailing Sea, Lord of all, Father, Son, and Holy Spirit, forever.

Another: Bless us, O Lord, by your blessings, surround us by the wall of your providence; may we never lack in good things, and dine in your banquet of light, Lord of all, Father, Son, and Holy Spirit, forever.

Another: Come, O Lord, to our assistance in your mercy, be revealed to us in your compassion, and straighten our journeys by the paths of righteousness, all the days of our lives, Lord of all, Father, Son, and Holy Spirit, forever.

Another: May your grace dawn upon us, O Lord, when your justice judges us, and may your mercies come to our aid on the day your Majesty dawns, Lord of all, Father, Son, and Holy Spirit, forever.

Another: May your blessing, your grace, and your merciful and compassionate right hand dwell with and accompany the assembly of your adorers who call and plead to you at all times and ages, Lord of all, Father, Son, and Holy Spirit, forever.

Of Mary: May the prayer of the holy Virgin, O Lord, the pleading of the Blessed Mother, the supplication and petition of the one who is Full of Grace, the blessed St. Mary, the great power of the victorious Cross, the divine assistance, and the petition of St. John the Baptist, be among us always, at all times and ages, Lord of all, Father, Son, and Holy Spirit, forever.

Of the Apostles: May the prayers of the holy apostles, O Lord, the pleading of the true preachers, the begging and supplication of the victorious athletes, preachers of the truth, the evangelists of righteousness, sowers of peace in creation, be among us always, at all times and ages, Lord of all, Father, Son, and Holy Spirit, forever.

Of the Saints: May the prayer, the petition, the pleading, and the supplication of our splendid and holy patron St. Thomas the blessed apostle, St. Addai and St. Mari the evangelizers of the East, St. Stephen the first-born of the martyrs, St. Simon Bar Sabba'e, St. Jacob, St. Ephrem, the powerful warrior St. George the victorious martyr, St. Quryaqos, St. Pithyon, St. Hormizd, St. Eugene the blessed and all the spiritual ranks, St. Barbara, Shmoni and her sons, Miskenta and her two sons, and all the martyrs and saints of our Lord, always be for us a great fortress and mighty refuge which saves, delivers, redeems, and protects our bodies and souls from the evil one and his hosts, at all times and ages, Lord of all, Father, Son, and Holy Spirit, forever.

Here the Presider concludes, and if he is not present, a priest from the "latter" side concludes. If the prayer began on the "latter" side, the final blessing is on the "former" side.

Final blessing: Glory to you, O Jesus our victorious King, eternal Image of the Father, Begotten One without beginning, above the ages and creations, without whom we have neither hope nor expectation, O Creator! By the prayer of the just and chosen who have pleased you from the beginning, grant forgiveness for our sins, absolution for our faults, deliverance from our troubles and response to our requests. Bring us to your joyous Light and guard us, through your living cross, from all perils, hidden or manifest; now, at all times, and forever and ever. *He signs the cross upon the people.*

Another: May the prayer of your miserable servants be accepted, O Lord our God, before the judgment-seat of your Divinity, and may this, our assembly, be pleasing to your Majesty, that it may receive, from you through grace, the health of the body, the protection of the soul, an abundance of sustenance, the absolution of debts, the forgiveness of sins, constant peace, O Lord, and enduring tranquility, and the unity of love which will not pass away or dissolve from among us, for all the time the world remains, now, at all times, and forever and ever.

Another: Blessed be God forever, and glorified be his holy name unto the ages; from him do we beg, and to the overflowing sea of his compassion do we plead, that he make us worthy for radiant glory in his kingdom, for delight with his holy angels, for unveiled faces before him and for place at his right hand in the Jerusalem above, in his grace and mercies, now, at all times, and forever and ever.

Another: May God the Lord of all, in whose house we have assembled, and before whose greatness we have prayed for the great hope of his compassion, hear our prayer in his mercy, accept our pleading in his pity, cleanse and scour the filth of our debts and sins with the overflowing hyssop of his benevolence, give rest to the souls of our deceased in the glorious dwelling-places of his kingdom, and sprinkle the dew of his kindness upon us all. And upon us and all creatures, may the right hand of his providence rest, in his grace and mercies, now, at all times, and forever and ever.

Another: May God the Lord of all, who has placed his praises in our mouths, his songs upon our tongues, his hymns in our throats, his confession on our lips, and his faith in our hearts, hear our prayers, accept our supplication, be pleased with our pleadings, forgive our trespasses, and answer our appropriate and blameless requests. And from the great treasury of his compassion, may he make his mercies and pity overflow upon us and upon the whole world to its ends, now, at all times, and forever and ever.

Another: May the name of God the Lord of all, the Orderer of times and ages, be praised among us, and upon us weak sinners, the whole world to its ends, the holy Church and her children, our parents and brethren, our monks and teachers, our deceased and those who have passed away and departed from among us, and our entire Christian brethren, may the right hand of his providence and his compassion rest, now, at all times, and forever and ever.

Another: To God be glory; to the angels, honor; to Satan, shame; to the cross, adoration; to the Church, exaltation; to the deceased, resurrection; to the repentant, acceptance; to the captive, freedom; to the sick and infirm, health and healing; to the four corners of the world, great peace and serenity; and also upon us, who are weak and sinners: may pity and mercies come and rest, overflow and dwell, rule and settle upon you constantly, now, at all times, and forever and ever.

They recite the Nicean Creed: "Truly indeed, and without division, We believe in one God..."

The Service of Night Prayer
for Feasts, Sundays, and Memorials

The Presider begins: Glory to God in the highest 3x, peace on earth, and good hope to the sons of men, at all times, forever.
They say: *Barekh mar.*
And continue, singing:

Our Father who art in heaven,	*Aḇḇun dba-shmayya*
hallowed be your name.	*nithqaddash shmakh,*
Your kingdom come.	*tethe malkuthakh,*
Holy, holy, you are holy.	*qaddysh, qaddysh, qaddysh-at,*
Our Father in heaven:	*Aḇḇun dba-shmayya.*
heaven and earth are full	*Damlen shmayya w-ar'a*
of the greatness of your glory;	*rabbuth shuḥakh,*
angels & men cry out to you:	*'yre w-nasha qa'en lakh*
holy, holy, you are holy.	*qaddysh, qaddysh, qaddysh-at.*
Our Father who art in heaven,	*Aḇḇun dba-shmayya*
hallowed be thy name.	*nithqaddash shmakh,*
Thy kingdom come,	*tethe malkuthakh,*
thy will be done on earth	*nehwe ṣiw-yanakh*
as it is in heaven.	*aykanna dba-shmayya ap b-ar'a,*
Give us this day our daily bread	*haw lan laḥma d-sunqanan*
and forgive us our trespasses,	*yawmana wa-shwoq lan ḥawbayn*
as we forgive those	*wa-ḥṭahayn aykanna d-ap ḥnan*
who trespassed against us.	*shwaqn l-ḥay-yawayn,*
And lead us not into temptation,	*w-la ta'lan l-nisyona*
but deliver us from evil,	*illa paṣan min bysha*
for thine is the kingdom,	*miṭṭul d-dhylakh-y malkutha,*
the power and the glory,	*w-ḥayla w-tish-buḥta*
now and forever.	*l-'alam 'almyn, amen.*
Presider: Glory to the Father, to the Son and to the Holy Spirit.	**Presider:** *Shuḥa l-Aḇḇa wla-Ḇra wal-Ruḥa d-Qudsha.*
People: From age to age, amen, amen. Our Father who art in heaven, hallowed be your name. Your kingdom come.	**People:** *Min 'alam wa-'dham-ma l-'alam amen w-amen. Aḇḇun dba-shmayya nithqaddash shmakh, tethe malkuthakh,*

Sunday Night Prayer

Holy, holy, you are holy.	*Qaddysh, qaddysh, qaddysh-at,*
Our Father in heaven:	*Aḇḇun dba-shmayya.*
heaven and earth are full	*Damlen shmayya w-ar'a*
of the greatness of your glory;	*rabbuth shuḥakh,*
angels & men cry out to you:	*'yre w-nasha qa'en lakh*
holy, holy, you are holy.	*qaddysh, qaddysh, qaddysh-at.*

They continue: Arise for prayer. Let us pray. Peace be with us.

The Presider says the prayer of the first *Hulala*: Let us arise, O Lord, in the hidden power of your Divinity, be confirmed through the marvelous hope of your Majesty, lifted up and strengthened by the great arm of your Greatness, and made worthy by the help of your grace to lift up glory, honor, thanksgiving, and adoration to you, at all times, Lord of all, Father, Son, and Holy Spirit, forever.

They serve the *Hulale*, and at the end of each *Hulala*, they add "glory.." and "from age..." and continue, singing: Halleluiah, halleluiah, glory to you, O God, halleluiah, halleluiah, glory to you, O God, halleluiah, halleluiah, Lord, have mercy on us. Let us pray. Peace be with us.

Prayer of the second *Hulala*: Strengthen, O Lord our God, our weakness by your mercy, hearten and aid our meagre soul by your grace, wake the lethargy of our conscience, cut away the heaviness of our bodies, wash and scour the filth of our debts and sins, enlighten the darkness of our minds, and extend and grant us the power and hand of your assistance, that in it we may rise and thank you, and glorify you unceasingly all the days of our lives, Lord of all, Father, Son, and Holy Spirit, forever.

Prayer of the third *Hulala*: May the hidden power of your Divinity, O Lord, the marvelous aid of your Majesty, and the great assistance of your compassion, strengthen the weakness of our miserable nature to lift up glory, honor, thanksgiving, and adoration to you, at all times, Lord of all, Father, Son, and Holy Spirit, forever.

THE ORDERING OF THE *HULALE* FOR THE SERVICE OF NIGHT PRAYER OF SUNDAYS, FEASTS, AND MEMORIALS

1. The First Sunday of the "former" weeks: They serve from "Do not be jealous" 3 *Hulale*, with the Psalm "Glorify the Lord who strengthens us," according to its melody. [*Hulala* 5, Psalm 37 to *Hulala* 7, Psalm 58, with Psalm 81]

Sunday Night Prayer

The Second Sunday of the "former" weeks: They serve from "God stands," 3 *Hulale*, with the Psalm "Glorify the Lord who strengthens us," according to its melody. [*Hulala* 9, Psalm 68 to *Hulala* 11, Psalm 80, with Psalm 81]
2. The First Sunday of the "latter" weeks: They serve from "God stood" 3 *Hulale*, with the Psalm "Out of the depths," according to its melody. [*Hulala* 12, Psalm 82 to *Hulala* 14, Psalm 101, with Psalm 129]
The Second Sunday of the "latter" weeks: They serve from "Give thanks to the Lord" 3 *Hulale*, with the Psalm "Out of the depths," according to its melody. [*Hulala* 16, Psalm 106 to *Hulala* 18, Psalm 130, with Psalm 129]
3. On all Feasts and Memorials, they serve from "God stood," 3 Hulale with the Giyyore. [*Hulala* 12, Psalm 82 to *Hulala* 14, Psalm 101]
On the Feasts of Christmas and Epiphany, they serve from "God stood," 4 *Hulale*, with the Giyyore. [*Hulala* 12, Psalm 82 to *Hulala* 15, Psalm 105]

Note that the *Qalta*, if the prayer began on the "former" side, begins on the "latter," and vice-versa.
Prayer of the *Qalta*: Glory is due to your hidden Nature, O Lord, which is incomprehensible and uncontainable by the thought or idea of all creatures, and songs of thanksgiving are right, and adoration in heaven and earth is appropriate and owed, Lord of all, Father, Son, and Holy Spirit, forever.

They say the *Qalta* of the day, as in the *Ḥudhra*, in its melody.

The Psalmody of the *Qalta*, for the "former" Sundays of Advent:
Psalm 40: Hoping, I hoped in the Lord, * and he turned to me and heard my petition, * and brought me up from the cave of wretchedness and the filth of decay, * and established my feet upon the rock and ordered my journeys. * He gave my mouth a new praise, praise to God, * that many may see and rejoice, * and hope in the Lord. * Blessed is the man who relies on the name of the Lord, * and does not turn toward idolatry, * or to a deceitful word. * Lord our God, you have accomplished many things, * your marvels and your considerations toward us – and there is none like you! * I showed and said, that they are more than can be numbered. * You were not pleased by sacrifices and offerings, * so ears you opened up for me, * and did not ask for burned offerings on behalf of sinners. * Then I said, Lo, I come, * that, as is written of me in the titles of the Scriptures. * I wished to do your will, O God, * and your

Sunday Night Prayer

law within my recesses. * I announced your justice in the great church, * and did not stop my lips. * O Lord, you know, * that I did not hide your justice within my heart, * but rather spoke your salvation and your faithfulness. * I did not hide your grace or faithfulness from the great church. * And may you not, O Lord, withhold your mercies from me. * Rather, may your mercies and faithfulness guard me at all times.

Continue, Psalm 120: I lift my eyes to the mountain: * from where shall come my help? * My help comes from the Lord * who made heaven and earth. * May he never allow your foot to stumble, * nor let your guardian sleep. * No, he sleeps not nor slumbers, * Israel's guardian. * The Lord is your guardian, * he will place his right hand upon you. * By day the sun shall not smite you, * nor the moon in the night. * The Lord will guard you from all evils, * the Lord will guard your soul. * The Lord will guard your going and your coming * both now and forever.

Continue, Psalm 88:10–11: Lo, will you work miracles for the dead? * Will warriors rise and give thanks to you? * Will those in the tomb discuss your grace, * and those in destruction your faithfulness?

Continue, Psalm 137:7–8: Extend your hand and save me. * Let your right hand rest upon me, O Lord. * Lord, your mercies are forever, * do not leave the works of your hands.

* **Glory to the Father, to the Son, and to the Holy Spirit.** Halleluiah, halleluiah, halleluiah. * **From age to age, amen, amen.** Hoping, I hoped in the Lord, and he turned to me and heard my petition, halleluiah.

The Psalmody of the *Qalta*, for the "latter" Sundays of Advent:

Psalm 48:1–11: Great is our Lord and highly glorious, * in the village of our God, * and on his holy and glorious mountain. * There is joy all over the earth. * The mountain of Zion which is on the outskirts of the north * is the village of the great king. * God makes known his might in her palaces. * Lo, kings are present and pass away together; * they saw, marveled, shook, and were seized by tremors, * and pangs like a woman in labor. * Thousands from Tarshish were broken by a mighty wind. * As we heard, thus we have seen * in the village of the almighty Lord, * in the village of our God. * God will establish it forever. * Our hope, O God, is in your grace, within your temple. * As is your name, O God, so are your glories. * Your right hand is filled with justice until the ends

Sunday Night Prayer

of the earth. * Mount Zion rejoices and the daughters of Judah extoll, * because of your judgments, O Lord.

Continue, Psalm 122: To you I lift my eyes, Dweller of heaven, * like the eyes of servants toward their masters, * and like the eyes a handmaid toward her mistress. * Thus are our eyes are toward you, O Lord our God, * until you have mercy on us. * Have mercy on us, Lord, have mercy on us.

Continue, Psalm 102:26–27: They will pass, but you will remain, * and all of them will perish like clothing, * and will change like a cloak. * But you, O Lord, are as you are, and your years do not end.

Continue, Psalm 137:7–8: Extend your hand and save me. * Let your right hand rest upon me, O Lord. * Lord, your mercies are forever, * do not leave the works of your hands.

* **Glory to the Father, to the Son, and to the Holy Spirit.** Halleluiah, halleluiah, halleluiah. * **From age to age, amen, amen.** Great is our Lord and highly glorious, in the village of our God, halleluiah.

The Psalmody of the *Qalta*, for the "former" Sundays of the Whole Year:
Psalm 86: Turn your ear, O Lord, and answer me, * for I am poor and needy. * Protect my soul, for you are good. * Save your servant, O God in whom he hopes. * Have mercy on me, Lord, * for I call to you every day. * Gladden the soul of your servant, * for to you, O Lord, I lift up my soul, * because you are good, O Lord, * and your grace is great toward all who call to you. * Attend to my prayer, O Lord, * and hear the sound of my pleading. * On the day of my distress I called you and you answered me. * There is none like you, O Lord my God, and there is nothing like your works. * All the peoples you have made * come and adore you, O Lord, * and glorify your name, for you are great. * You perform marvels, you alone, O God. * Show me, O Lord, your path, and I will walk it in truth. * Gladden my heart in those who fear your name. * I will thank you, O Lord my God, with all my heart, * and I will glorify your name forever. * For your grace has increased for me, * and you saved my soul from the lower Sheol. * O God, the wicked have risen against me, * and the assembly of the mighty seek my soul, and do not consider you. * You, O Lord God, are merciful and compassionate, * patient and abounding in grace and truth. * Turn to me and have mercy on me; * give strength to your servant, and save the son of your handmaid. * Accomplish a good sign with me, * that my haters may see and be ashamed, * for you, O Lord, have helped me and comforted me.

Sunday Night Prayer

Continue, Psalm 120: I lift my eyes to the mountain: * from where shall come my help? * My help comes from the Lord * who made heaven and earth. * May he never allow your foot to stumble, * nor let your guardian sleep. * No, he sleeps not nor slumbers, * Israel's guardian. * The Lord is your guardian, * he will place his right hand upon you. * By day the sun shall not smite you, * nor the moon in the night. * The Lord will guard you from all evils, * the Lord will guard your soul. * The Lord will guard your going and your coming * both now and forever.

Continue, Psalm 88:10–11: Lo, will you work miracles for the dead? * Will warriors rise and give thanks to you? * Will those in the tomb discuss your grace, * and those in destruction your faithfulness?

Continue, Psalm 137:7–8: Extend your hand and save me. * Let your right hand rest upon me, O Lord. * Lord, your mercies are forever, * do not leave the works of your hands.

* **Glory to the Father, to the Son, and to the Holy Spirit.** Halleluiah, halleluiah, halleluiah. * **From age to age, amen, amen.** Turn your ear, O Lord, and answer me, for I am poor and needy, halleluiah.

The Psalmody of the *Qalta*, for the "latter" Sundays of the Whole Year: Psalm 91: He who dwells in the shelter of the Most High * and is adorned by the shadow of God * says to the Lord: "My refuge, * my stronghold, my God in whom I trust!" * For he will deliver you from the fowler's trap * and from the deceitful conversation. * He will conceal you with his pinions and under his wings you will find refuge. * His truth will surround you like an armor. * You will not fear the terror of the night * nor the arrow that flies by day, * nor the plague that prowls in the darkness * nor the scourge that lays waste at noon. * Thousands may fall at your side, a myriad at your right, * you, it will never approach. * You need only look with your eyes * to see how the wicked are repaid, * you who have said: "Lord, my refuge, * who has made his dwelling on high!" * Upon you no evil shall fall, * no plague approach where you dwell. * For you has he commanded his angels, * to keep you in all your ways. * They shall bear you upon their hands * lest you stumble with your feet. * On the viper and the serpent you will tread * and trample the lion and the dragon. * "Because he seeks me, I will save him and strengthen him. * Because he knows my name, he will call and I will answer him. * I am with him in distress. * I will strengthen him and honor him. * With length of life I will content him; I shall let him see my salvation."

Continue, Psalm 122: To you I lift my eyes, Dweller of heaven, * like the eyes of servants toward their masters, * and like the eyes a handmaid toward her mistress. * Thus are our eyes are toward you, O Lord our God, * until you have mercy on us. * Have mercy on us, Lord, have mercy on us.

Continue, Psalm 102:26–27: They will pass, but you will remain, * and all of them will perish like clothing, * and will change like a cloak. * But you, O Lord, are as you are, and your years do not end.

Continue, Psalm 137:7–8: Extend your hand and save me. * Let your right hand rest upon me, O Lord. * Lord, your mercies are forever, * do not leave the works of your hands.

* **Glory to the Father, to the Son, and to the Holy Spirit.** Halleluiah, halleluiah, halleluiah. * **From age to age, amen, amen.** He who dwells in the shelter of the Most High and is adorned by the shadow of God, halleluiah.

The Psalmody of the *Qalta*, for the "former" Sundays of the Sanctification of the Church:

Psalm 45: My heart overflows with noble words. * I will speak my works to the king. * My tongue is the pen of a skillful scribe. * He is more beautiful in his aspect than the sons of men. * Mercies are poured upon your lips, * and for this, God has blessed you forever. * O mighty one, gird your sword upon your back; * your splendor and glory; your glory victorious. * Ride upon a truthful word, and a just humility. * Your law is in the fear of your right hand. * Your arrows are sharp, and peoples fall beneath you, * into the heart of the enemies of the king. * Your throne, O God, is forever and ever. * The scepter of your kingdom is a simple scepter. * You loved justice and hated evil, * and for this, God your God has anointed you * with the oil of gladness more than your companions. * Myrrh, cassia, and aloes * perfume all your garments. * Your joy is from the noble temple and from myself. * The daughter of the king stands in glory, * and the queen at your right hand, * dressed in the gold of Ophir. * Listen, O daughter, and see, and incline your ear, * and forget your people and the house of your father, * for the king desires your beauty. * Because he is your Lord, adore him, * and the daughter of Tyre will adore him. * The wealthy among the people will seek your face with offerings. * All the beauty of the princess is from within, * and she adorns her clothing with fine gold. * She goes

Sunday Night Prayer

to the king with offerings, * and brings her virgin companions with her. * They go with gladness and joy, * and enter the temple of the king. * In place of your fathers, you will have sons. * Make them rulers over all the earth. * That your name be remembered from age to age. * For this, the peoples will thank you forever and ever.

Continue, Psalm 120: I lift my eyes to the mountain: * from where shall come my help? * My help comes from the Lord * who made heaven and earth. * May he never allow your foot to stumble, * nor let your guardian sleep. * No, he sleeps not nor slumbers, * Israel's guardian. * The Lord is your guardian, * he will place his right hand upon you. * By day the sun shall not smite you, * nor the moon in the night. * The Lord will guard you from all evils, * the Lord will guard your soul. * The Lord will guard your going and your coming * both now and forever.

Continue, Psalm 88:10–11: Lo, will you work miracles for the dead? * Will warriors rise and give thanks to you? * Will those in the tomb discuss your grace, * and those in destruction your faithfulness?

Continue, Psalm 137:7–8: Extend your hand and save me. * Let your right hand rest upon me, O Lord. * Lord, your mercies are forever, * do not leave the works of your hands.

* **Glory to the Father, to the Son, and to the Holy Spirit.** Halleluiah, halleluiah, halleluiah. * **From age to age, amen, amen.** My heart overflows with noble words. I will speak my works to the king, halleluiah.

The Psalmody of the *Qalta*, for the "latter" Sundays of the Sanctification of the Church:

Psalm 84: How lovely are your tabernacles, Lord almighty. * My soul yearns for the courts of the Lord. * My heart and my flesh glorify the living God. * Even the bird finds a home and the sparrow a nest. * Fledglings grow near your altar, O Lord almighty. * My King and my God, blessed are they who dwell in your house. * They will glorify you forever. * Blessed is the man who trusts in you, * and who has your paths in his heart. * They will pass through the depth of lamentation and make it a dwelling place. * Even the lawmaker will be clothed with a blessing. * They will go from strength to strength, * and be seen by the God of gods in Zion. * O Lord God almighty, hear my prayer, * and attend, O God of Jacob. * See, O God our help, * and look upon the face of your Anointed One. * For one day in your court is greater than a thousand. * I wished to dwell

Sunday Night Prayer

in the house of God, * more than to dwell in the dwelling of the wicked. * For the Lord God is our nourisher and our help. * The Lord will give mercies and honor, * and not hold back his blessings * from those who walk in innocence. * Lord God almighty, * blessed is the man who hopes in you.

Continue, Psalm 122: To you I lift my eyes, Dweller of heaven, * like the eyes of servants toward their masters, * and like the eyes a handmaid toward her mistress. * Thus are our eyes are toward you, O Lord our God, * until you have mercy on us. * Have mercy on us, Lord, have mercy on us.

Continue, Psalm 102:26–27: They will pass, but you will remain, * and all of them will perish like clothing, * and will change like a cloak. * But you, O Lord, are as you are, and your years do not end.

Continue, Psalm 137:7–8: Extend your hand and save me. * Let your right hand rest upon me, O Lord. * Lord, your mercies are forever, * do not leave the works of your hands.

* **Glory to the Father, to the Son, and to the Holy Spirit.** Halleluiah, halleluiah, halleluiah. * **From age to age, amen, amen.** How lovely are your tabernacles, Lord almighty. My soul yearns for the courts of the Lord, halleluiah.

On Feasts and Memorials, there is no *Qalta*.

They answer: Let us pray. Peace be with us.

MAWTWA

The Presider says the prayer before the Sunday *Mawtwa*: May our prayer please you, O Lord, our petition enter before you, and from the great treasury of your mercy, may the requests of our neediness be answered, at all times and ages, Lord of all, Father, Son, and Holy Spirit, forever.

They begin, on the "former" side, the Responsories for Assistance of the *Mawtwa* of the Sunday, and continue with the Prayer as in the *Ḥudhra*. If more than one Prayer is in the *Ḥudhra*, and there is not space for all of them to be said, they say first two verses of each one, and that of Mary, and of the Cross, and of the Saints, and the Patron, and the Deceased, and the entire final Prayer, and the "Glory."

Sunday Night Prayer

On Feasts and Memorials, the Presider prays: To you, O Treasury of assistance, Fount of all blessings, overflowing Sea of mercy and compassion, great Abyss of forgiveness and absolution, we plead: turn to us, O Lord, forgive us, and have mercy on us, as you always do, Lord of all, Father, Son, and Holy Spirit, forever.
They begin the *Mawtwa* as it is in the *Gazza*, and at the end they say: Let us pray. Peace be with us.

THE PRAYER OF THE CANON

On Sundays, they pray the Canon of the Season, and on Feasts and Memorials, that of the day. They begin the Canon on the "latter" side, and when it is finished, they begin the Glorification on the "former" side, according to the *Ḥudhra* or the *Gazza*. A server on the "former" side says the Petitions of the day, and they say: Let us pray. Peace be with us.

The Presider says the Prayers before the Madrasha: From you, Merciful and Compassionate One, from the great wealth of the kindness of your Love, and from the overflowing treasury of your compassion, we ask aid, redemption, protection, and healing for the wounds of our bodies and souls. Grant this in your grace and mercies, as you do at all times, Lord of all, Father, Son, and Holy Spirit, forever.

Another: Blessed and adorable, marvelous and glorious, high, exalted, and incomprehensible are the eternal mercies of your glorious Trinity, which freely pity sinners, O our Good and Merciful Hope, Forgiver of debts and sins, Lord of all, Father, Son, and Holy Spirit, forever.

> He begins the Madrasha of the day, as in the *Ḥudhra* or the *Gazza* (see pp. 389–578).

Suyake: as in the *Ḥudhra*. A priest says the Prayer before the first Psalm: Glory is due to your hidden Nature, O Lord, which is incomprehensible and uncontainable by the thought or idea of all creatures, and songs of thanksgiving are right, and adoration in heaven and earth is appropriate and owed, Lord of all, Father, Son, and Holy Spirit, forever.

They begin the Psalm on the "latter" side, then say: Let us pray. Peace be with us.

Sunday Night Prayer

A priest says the Prayer: To you, O Hidden in his Existence, Secret in his Divinity, Indescribable in his Glory, O great King of glory, Being who is from eternity, we give thanks, adore, and glorify you at all times, Lord of all, Father, Son, and Holy Spirit, forever.

They say the second Psalm, on the "former" side, and continue: Let us pray. Peace be with us.

THE VIGIL HYMNS

The Presider says the Prayer: May the hymns of our halleluiahs and the melodies of our songs please you, O Lord our God, and in your grace accept the rational fruits of our lips, which we offer in thanksgiving to your glorious Trinity, night and day, Lord of all, Father, Son, and Holy Spirit, forever.

They begin, on the "former" side, on the "former" Sundays, the *Hulala* "The Lord reigns" and they serve the entire *Marmytha* [Psalms 93–95] in its melody. On "latter" Sundays "Then they praised" [Exodus 15:1–22, Isaiah 42:10–14, 45:8]. At the end of each *Marmytha*, they "glory" and "from age," and add: Halleluiah, halleluiah, halleluiah.

They say: Let us pray. Peace be with us.

A priest says the prayer: Make us worthy, O Lord our God, to sing glory to your glorious Trinity night and day, with the watchers and the assemblies of angels, through songs filled with thanksgiving, Lord of all, Father, Son, and Holy Spirit, forever.

They begin, on the "latter" side, "Sing a new song to the Lord" and the entire *Marmytha* [Psalms 96–98] in its melody. On "latter" Sundays the *Marmytha* [Deuteronomy 32:1–21].

Then the next priest says the prayer: It is right for all the rational natures you created, O Lord, to lift up constant glory, unceasing halleluiahs, and glorifications without end, to your glorious Trinity, night and day, Lord of all, Father, Son, and Holy Spirit, forever.

They begin, on the "former" side, "The Lord reigns, let the nations tremble," and the whole *Marmytha* [Psalms 99–101] in its melody. On "latter" Sundays, the *Marmytha* [Deuteronomy 32:21–44].

Sunday Night Prayer

On Feasts and Memorials, they serve the Psalms of the Vigil Hymns in their melody, as in the *Gazza*.

The Presider says the prayer: By the rational mouths you created, O Lord, the glorifying tongues you fashioned, and the entire assembly of the lofty and the lowly, the name of your Divinity and Majesty is adored, glorified, honored, exalted, confessed, and blessed, in heaven and on earth, Lord of all, Father, Son, and Holy Spirit, forever.

They begin, on the "latter" side, the Night Responsory as in the *Ḥudhra* (see pp. 389–578). Then they "glory" it, and continue:

- **From age to age, amen, amen.** O Christ, do not neglect us, or abandon your adorers, for we take refuge in you, O Lord. Lead us in your path of life, that we may all sing glory to you, Lord God.
- **Let all the people say, amen, amen.** O holy virgin Mary, mother of Jesus our Savior, plead with us to Christ, that he may let his peace dwell among us, and protect us from all dangers, night and day.

Know that from Lent until Pentecost, there is no "From age," and during Advent, there is no "Let all the people."

On Feasts and Memorials, the say the Night Responsory, as in the *Ḥudhra* or *Gazza*, and when they finish, they say: Let us pray. Peace be with us.

On Sundays, a priest says the Prayer of the *Shubaḥa*: To you be glory from every mouth, thanksgiving from every tongue, and adoration, honor, and exaltation from every creature, O Secret and glorious Being who dwells in the highest heavens, Lord of all, Father, Son, and Holy Spirit, forever.

They begin, on the "former" side, the *Shubaḥa*, as in the *Ḥudhra*. On Feasts of the Lord, they say the Night Responsories, with the prayers of the priests, according to the rite of the Feasts. The priest says the prayer of the Canon, and on Memorials, the prayer of the Canon of the day: To your wondrous and indescribable providence, O Lord, which was accomplished, completed and perfected in mercies and pity for the renewal and the salvation of our weak race through the Principal that is from us, do we lift up glory, honor, thanksgiving and adoration at all times, O Lord of all, Father, Son and Holy Spirit, forever.

They begin the Canon, as in the Ḥudhra or Gazza. On Sundays, the begin the Hpakhta of Tawdy l-Ṭawa, as in the Ḥudhra, and they continue with this Glorification by Mar Narsai:

All thanks to him who saved our race
    from slavery to sin and death!
He reconciled us with the hosts
    above, who scorned us for our sin.
    Blessed is he who had mercy,
        who sought and found us, and rejoiced.
    He symbolized our straying and
        returning in his parable:
He named our race the heir and son,
    who strayed, returned, who died and rose.
He gladdened all the hosts above
    through our return and our rising.
The great love which the Lover of
        our race showed cannot be described:
    For from our race, he took on flesh,
        and reconciled us to himself.
It is a thing too great for us;
    it is a new thing he has done:
he has made his temple our flesh,
    in which he is worshipped by all.
    O Come, earthly and heavenly,
      and marvel at our lofty place:
    our race has reached the greatest height
    of infinite Divinity!
Heaven and earth and all therein
    give thanks to him who renewed us,
For he has wiped our sins away,
    named us his name, and has crowned us.
    Worthy is he of praise and thanks
        from every mouth, who raised us up.
    Let us proclaim our praise to him,
    forever and ever, amen.

Then on Feasts, after the *Hpakhta*, they begin the Glorification as in the *Ḥudhra* or the *Gazza*. On Memorials, they say this Glorification of Mar Abraham of Nithpar:

Glory to him who has made known
> his glory to mankind in love.

He created a mute thing of dust,
> and gave it a soul of treasures.

He placed his thanks in lowly flesh,
> that the whole world may sing him praise.

Come, rational, and sing his praise,
> before we doze the sleep of death.

During the night, remember death,
> which shuts and silences our mouths.

The just who praise him during night
> are alive even when they die,

but the evil who deny him
> are dead even during their lives.

Let us now wake our flesh in prayer
> and praise the Hidden Majesty,

that we may be like the virgins
> who were praised in the parable.

On that night when he shakes the world,
> may we meet the Son while awake.

Let us not drown in our desires,
> but see his glory when he dawns.

Let us be watchful servants when
> he leads forth those in his chamber.

The evil will be suffering;
> the door of mercies will be shut.

Thus, while we live, let us labor,
> for after death is our reward.

The flesh that is wearied in prayer
> will fly in air the day he comes,

will see the Lord while without shame,
> and will enter in the kingdom.

The angels and the just love him,
> who have kept vigil in their prayer.

Sunday Night Prayer

Blest is he who made us vessels
　　to praise him, though we are of dust.
Praise him who gave us earthly ones
　　a share with those who are above,
that we may sing, on every night,
　　and every time, "holy his name."
Let us together sing his praise
　　forever and ever, amen.

When it is finished, a server says the Petitions, as in the *Ḥudhra* or *Gazza* of the day. If there is not one there, he says these petitions:

Server: Let us all stand composed. In joy and gladness, let us implore *and* say: Lord, have mer*c*y on us.

People: Lord, have mer*c*y on us. | *Maran ithraḥam 'layn.*

* O One who taught us to pray with*out* weariness, we *im*plore you...
* O One who kept vigil in prayer to God for the salvation of *our* race, we *im*plore you...
* O One who gave us an example of his mercy in our earth*ly* fathers, we *im*plore you...
* O One who saved us from violent deaths, and in whom we hope for *sal*vation, we *im*plore you...
* O One who saved us from the dominion of darkness and brought us into the kingdom of his belo*ved* Son, we *im*plore you...
* O One who said: "ask and it shall be given to you, seek and you shall find, knock and the treasure of mercies will be opened *for* you," we *im*plore you...
* For the health of our holy fathers: [Mar _____, High Pontiff, Pope of Rome,] Mar _____, Catholicos-Patriarch, Mar _____, Bishop/Metropolitan, and for all those in the same priest*ly* service, we *im*plore you...
* For the priests and deacons of our Church, and for all of our Chris*tian* brethren, we *im*plore you...
* O Compassionate God, who guides all in *his* mercy, we *im*plore you...
* O One who is glorified in heaven and worshipped *on* earth, we *im*plore you...
* Give us victory, O Christ our Lord, in your coming, give peace to your Church saved by your precious Blood, and have mer*c*y on us...
* Let us entrust our souls mutually to the Father, and to the Son, and to *the* Holy Spirit.

People: To you, *O* Lord our God.

THE SERVICE OF MORNING PRAYER
OF FEASTS, SUNDAYS, AND MEMORIALS

The Presider begins the prayers before the Morning Psalms: Make us worthy, O Lord our God, that, according to the will of your Divinity and your glorious Majesty, we may serve before you purely and honorably, attentively and diligently, justly and uprightly, in holiness and without fault. May our Service be to your satisfaction, O Lord, our prayer to your appeasement, our imploring for your honor, and our supplication for your reconciliation. And may the mercies and the compassion of your Divinity be for the remission of the debts of your people, and the forgiveness of the sins of all the sheep of your flock, whom you have chosen for yourself in your grace and in your mercies, O Lord of all: Father, Son and Holy Spirit, forever.

People: Amen. *Barekh mar.*

Another: Enlighten us, O Lord, in your Light, gladden us by your coming, delight us in your salvation, and let us share in your Mysteries. Grant, and make us worthy, that with the heavenly assemblies clothed with light and the legions of angels, with hymns filled with thanksgiving, we may sing praise to your glorious Trinity. O Creator with dominion over all! O Creator who is not in need of the service of creatures! O Creator of light in his grace, and Orderer of darkness in his Wisdom, Knowledge and Divinity, incomprehensible to the spiritual and the physical, O Lord of all, Father, Son and Holy Spirit, forever.

People: Amen.

Or the two prayers as in the *Ḥudhra* or *Gazza*.

They begin on the "former" side, singing:

Psalm 100

Glorify the Lord, all the earth!

They say the *Brashyth* verse as in the *Ḥudhra*, or if there is not one, they say:

    O Giver of Light, O Lord: we lift up praise to you!
    Glorify the Lord, all the earth!
Serve the Lord in *gla*dness.
    O Giver of Light, O Lord: we lift up praise to you!
Enter before *him* with praise.
    Know he is the *Lord* our God:
he made us; it *was* not we.
    We are his people, the sheep *of* his flock.

Sunday Morning Prayer

Enter his gates with thanksgiving and his *courts* with praise.
>Give thanks to him *and* bless his name,
for the Lord is good and eter*nal* is his grace,
>and his faithfulness is *un*to the ages.
Glory to the Father, to the Son and to *the* Holy Spirit.
>**From age to age, *a*men, amen.**
Glorify the Lord, all the earth!
>**O Giver of Light, O Lord: we lift up praise to you!**
Or the *Brashyth* Verse, if there is one.

Server: Let us pray. Peace be with us.
Priest: To you, O Lord, all the creatures you have created lift up praise and thanksgiving; for to them, you alone are the true Light, and the Enlightener of ages and creatures in his grace and mercies, Lord of all, Father, Son and Holy Spirit, forever.
People: Amen.

Psalm 91

He who dwells in the shelter of the Most High
>**Glorious is your faithfulness, O Christ our Savior.**
[On days there is a *Brashyth* Verse, they say the first two lines of the Psalm and continue: When the Creator constructed the light, the angels marveled at it, and when it dawns every morning, they praise him, and we as well.]
He who dwells in the shelter of the Most High
>and is adorned by the shadow of God
says to the Lord: "My refuge, my stronghold,
>my God in whom I trust!"
For he will deliver you from the fowler's trap
>and from the deceitful conversation.
He will conceal you with his pinions
>and under his wings you will find refuge.
>His truth will surround you like an armor.
You will not fear the terror of the night
>nor the arrow that flies by day,
nor the plague that prowls in the darkness
>nor the scourge that lays waste at noon.
Thousands may fall at your side,

Sunday Morning Prayer

    a myriad at your right,
        you, it will never approach.
You need only look with your eyes
    to see how the wicked are repaid,
you who have said: "Lord, my refuge,
    who has made his dwelling on high!"
Upon you no evil shall fall,
    no plague approach where you dwell.
For you has he commanded his angels,
    to keep you in all your ways.
They shall bear you upon their hands
    lest you stumble with your feet.
On the viper and the serpent you will tread
    and trample the lion and the dragon.
"Because he seeks me,
    I will save him and strengthen him.
Because he knows my name,
    he will call and I will answer him.
I am with him in distress.
    I will strengthen him and honor him.
With length of life I will content him;
    I shall let him see my salvation."

Glory to the Father, to the Son and to the Holy Spirit.
    From age to age, amen, amen.
 He who dwells in the shelter of the Most High
    Glorious is your faithfulness, O Christ our Savior.
[Or: When the Creator constructed the light, the angels marveled at it, and when it dawns every morning, they praise him, and we as well. Glory to the Father, to the Son and to the Holy Spirit. From age to age, amen, amen. **When you created the abundant light, the spiritual beings praised you, and they understood that the One who created that light created them.** He who dwells in the shelter of the Most High, and is adorned by the shadow of God. **You are glorified by angels and praised by men, and all together they cry out and say blessed is your** (Advent, Birth, Baptism, Fasting, Resurrection, Ascension, Descent of your Holy Spirit) **O Christ our Savior!**]

Sunday Morning Prayer

Server: Let us pray. Peace be with us.
Priest: Glorious, O Lord, is the great faithfulness of your Divinity, and high and exalted is the awesome sanctuary of your authority. Nor are they put to shame who hope and trust in you, call upon your holy name, and entreat you at all times and ages, O Lord of all, Father, Son, and Holy Spirit, forever.
People: Amen.

Psalm 104

Bless the Lord, my soul!
    To you is glory due, O God!
Bless the Lord, my soul!
    Lord God, how great you are,
clothed in majesty and glory,
    wrapped in light as in a robe!
You stretch out heaven like a tent.
    He makes his dwelling above the rains.
He makes the clouds his chariot,
    he walks with wings of wind,
he makes the winds his messengers
    and burning fire his servants.
He founded the earth on its bases,
    to be unshaken from age to age.
You wrapped it with the firmament like a cloak:
    the waters stood above the mountains.
At your threat they took to flight;
    at the voice of your thunder they fled.
The mountains rose and the plains were lowered
    to the place which you had appointed.
You set limits for them
    lest they return to cover the earth.
You sent springs to the valleys:
    they flow in between the hills.
They give drink to all the beasts of the field;
    the wild animals quench their thirst.
Upon them dwell the birds of heaven;
    from the mountains they sing their song.

Sunday Morning Prayer

From his dwelling he waters the hills;
> earth drinks its fill of the fruit of your work.

You make the grass grow for cattle
> and the plants for man's labor,

That he may bring forth bread from the earth:
> wine gladdens the heart of man;

Oil makes his face rejoice;
> and bread sustains man's heart.

The trees of the Lord drink their fill.
> **To you is glory due, O God!**

Psalm 113

Praise, O servants of the Lord,
> praise the name of the Lord!
>
> **To you is glory due, for you are the Creator of light!**

May the name of the Lord be blessed,
> from age to age!

From the dawning of the sun to its setting,
> great is the name of the Lord!

High above all nations is the Lord,
> and above the heavens his honor.

Who is like the Lord, our God,
> who sits on high and sees below?

Who sits on high and sees below,
> in the heavens and on the earth?

From the dust he lifts up the poor man,
> and lets him sit with the rulers of the people.

He sets the barren woman in a home,
> and makes her the joyful mother of children.

Glory to the Father, to the Son and to the Holy Spirit.
> **From age to age, amen, amen.**

Praise, O servants of the Lord,
> praise the name of the Lord!
>
> **To you is glory due, for you are the Creator of light!**

Server: Let us pray. Peace be with us.

Sunday Morning Prayer

Priest: You, O Lord, are the Creator of light in your grace, and the Orderer of darkness in your wisdom, and the Enlightener of creation through your glorious Light. To you, O Lord, is constant unending glory due, and to your name is owed thanksgiving and adoration in heaven and on earth, O Lord of all, Father, Son and Holy Spirit, forever.
People: Amen.

Psalm 93

The Lord is King, with majesty enrobed.
    We adore you, O Being without beginning!
    The Lord is King, with majesty enrobed.
The Lord is clothed with might and power.
    He constructed the world to be unshaken.
Your throne is established from the beginning:
    and you exist, O Lord, from eternity.
The rivers have lifted up, O Lord,
    the rivers have lifted up their voice,
    the rivers have lifted up in purity.
Even mightier than the roar of many waters
    are the surgings of the sea.
Glorious are you, O Lord, on high,
    and your testimonies are greatly faithful.
And holiness is fitting to your house,
    O Lord, until the end of days.
    We adore you, O Being without beginning!

Psalm 148

Praise the Lord from the heavens,
    praise him in the heights.
Praise him, all his angels,
    praise him all his hosts.
Praise him, sun and moon,
    praise him, all stars and lights.
    Praise him heaven of heavens.
Waters above the heavens,
    praise the name of the Lord.
For he spoke, and they were;
    he commanded and they were created.

Sunday Morning Prayer

He fixed them forever and ever,
    gave a law which shall not pass away.
Praise the Lord from the earth,
    sea creatures and all oceans,
fire and hail, snow and mist,
    stormy winds that obey his word;
all mountains and hills, all fruit trees and cedars,
    beasts wild and tame, reptiles and birds on the wing;
all earth's kings and peoples,
    earth's princes and rulers;
young men and maidens,
    old men together with children.
Let them praise the name of the Lord,
    for his name alone is great,
    and his glory is through earth and heaven.
He exalts the horn of his people
    and the praise of all his just,
of the sons of Israel,
    of the people that is near to him.

Psalm 150

Praise God in his holy place,
    praise him in his mighty firmament.
Praise him for his power,
    praise his surpassing greatness.
O praise him with sound of trumpet,
    praise him with lute and harp.
Praise him with timbrel and tambourine,
    praise him with pleasant strings.
O praise him with resounding cymbals,
    praise him with hymns and cries!
Praise the Lord with every breath!

Psalm 116

O praise the Lord, all you nations,
    O praise him, all you peoples!
For mighty is his love for us;
    truly is he the Lord forever.

Sunday Morning Prayer

Glory to the Father, to the Son and to the Holy Spirit.
   From age to age, amen, amen.
Praise the Lord with every breath!
   O Christ the Light, we praise you!
Server: Let us pray. Peace be with us.
Priest: To you, O Christ the true Light, the glorious Image of the Father, who was revealed and dawned in the world for the renewal and the redemption of our nature through the Principal that is from us, do we lift up glory, honor, thanksgiving and adoration at all times, Lord of all, forever.
People: Amen.

> **MORNING HYMN (see pp. 389–578)**

- From age to age, amen, amen. – *b-madnaḥay ṣapra*
At dawn of morning, we lift glory to your name,
   for you have saved us and all the world.
      Grant us in your grace
      that our day be filled with peace,
      and we beg you to forgive our sins.
Deny not our hope, do not close your door to us,
   do not hold back of your saving grace,
      and do not treat us
      as our deeds deserve, O Lord,
      for you alone know how weak we are.
Sow, Lord, in the world, love and peace and harmony,
   uphold our priests, kings and governors,
      grant peace to countries,
      heal the sick, protect the poor,
      forgive the sins of the sons of men.
Server: Let us pray. Peace be with us.
Priest: Make us all worthy O Lord, in your grace and mercies, to rejoice and delight in the glorious light of your revelation and the joyful dawning of your coming, that which all the creatures you have created look to, hope for and await, with all the true sons of your Mysteries in the Jerusalem above, O Lord of all, Father, Son and Holy Spirit, forever.
People: Amen.

Sunday Morning Prayer

Morning Hymn of Mar Ephrem

Light has dawned upon the just, and joy to the upright of heart.
Nuhra dnaḥ l-zad-y-qi wla-try-ṣay libba ḥadhu-tha.

Jesus Christ, our sovereign Lord,
dawning from the Father's Womb,
came and brought us out of darkness,
bright'ning us with his radiant Light!

> Day has dawned upon mankind,
> and the power of darkness fled;
> brightness dawning from his radiant
> Light has brightened our darkened eyes.

His glory he dawned on earth,
brightening the lowest depths;
death was darkened, darkness banished,
and the gates of Sheol were destroyed.

> He enlightened all mankind,
> which had been in dark before,
> and the dead, who had been buried,
> rose and praised, for they had been saved.

He, the Savior, gave us life,
to the Father's Womb returned;
he will come again in glory,
bright'ning those who bide his return.

> Our King will come again!
> Let us light our lamps and go,
> ready to rejoice in him,
> as he rejoiced in us and gave us joy!

Let us lift up praise to him,
to the Father giving thanks,
who in mercy sent him to us,
our Salvation and all our Hope.

> From the silence his day dawns,
> and his saints are all awake,
> and all those who labored, wearied
> and prepared are lighting their lamps.

All the watchers in the heights
laud the glory of the just,
placing crowns upon their heads,
shouting together: "halleluiah!"
> Brethren, rise up and prepare,
> give thanks to our Savior King,
> who in glory will return and
> gladden us with his radiant Light!

Morning Hymn of Mar Narsai

The light of the dawning of Christ has gladdened earth and heaven.
Nuhra d-dhinḥeh da-Mshyḥa ḥad-dy l-ar'a wla-shmayya.
Error, like the darkest night,
had been spread across the world,
but the Light of the Messiah
dawned and gave the world clarity.
> History, from Adam on,
> had resembled darkest night,
> and the day of Christ's unveiling
> was the daylight hours' running-course.

Our Lord even compared
morning to his preaching's start,
and the evening to the ending,
when the world will rest from its work.
> Priests and kings and prophets had
> waited with this hope in mind,
> and the Maker gave them comfort
> in the day that he was revealed.

In his day all creatures rest,
who had once been crushed in sin,
and the world begins to ponder
the meaning of the world to come.
> The New Covenant he gave
> to all who accept his creed,
> and with his own Blood he sealed it,
> that his promise might never fail.

Sunday Morning Prayer

With his promised Paradise,
he made fast the course of man,
and behold, on earth and heaven
all await his coming again.
> The new coming of the King
> who rules from our race has neared:
> come, let us prepare to meet him
> with the hosts of heaven above!

Let us take the oil of love
for that day filled with despair,
lest we hear the voice then saying,
"begone, I know not of your works."
> While we live, then, let us work
> in the vineyard of the Word,
> that we may then hear the voice which says:
> "Come and receive what was vowed!"

Let us fix our mind's sojourn
with the hope of life to come,
and arrive, through love and faith, then,
at the harbor of all delights!

Light has dawned upon the just, and joy to the upright of heart.
Nuhra dnaḥ l-zad-y-qi wla-try-ṣay libba ḥadhu-tha.

DANIEL 3:57–88

Bless the Lord, you works of *the* Lord!
Bless the *Lord*, heavens of the Lord!

DANIEL VERSE (see pp. 389–578)

Bless the Lord, you works of *the* Lord!
Bless the *Lord*, heavens of the Lord!
> Bless the Lord, angels of *the* Lord!
> Bless the *Lord*, waters above!

Bless the Lord, hosts of *the* Lord!
Bless the *Lord*, O sun and moon!
> Bless the Lord, O stars of *heaven*!
> Bless the *Lord*, O rain and dew!

Bless the Lord, all *you* winds!
Bless the *Lord*, O fire and heat!

Sunday Morning Prayer

    Bless the Lord, O night *and* day!
    Bless the *Lord*, light and darkness!
Bless the Lord, O cold *and* heat!
Bless the *Lord*, O ice and snow!
    Bless the Lord, lightning *and* cloud!
    Bless the *Lord*, O all the earth!
Bless the Lord, mountains *and* hills!
Bless the *Lord*, all that grows on earth!
    Bless the Lord, O seas and *rivers*!
    Bless the *Lord*, springs of water!
Bless the Lord, fish and sea *creatures*!
Bless the *Lord*, all birds of the sky!
    Bless the Lord, beasts, wild *and* tame!
    Bless the *Lord*, O sons of men!
Bless the Lord, O sons *of* men!
Bless the *Lord*, house of Israel!
    Bless the Lord, O priests of *the* Lord!
    Bless the *Lord*, servants of the Lord!
Bless the Lord, O souls of *the* just!
Bless the *Lord*, humble of heart!

DANIEL VERSE (see pp. 389–578)

Glory to the Father, to the Son and to the Holy *Spi*rit.
From age to *age*, amen, amen.

DANIEL VERSE (see pp. 389–578)

Bless the Lord, you works of *the* Lord!
Bless the *Lord*, heavens of the Lord!

DANIEL VERSE (see pp. 389–578)

On Sundays and Feasts of the Lord

Server: Peace be with us.
Priest says the prayer of the Glorification: We glorify, exalt, sing halleluiah and praise the hidden and mysterious, blessed and incomprehensible Nature of your glorious Trinity at all times, O Lord of all, Father, Son and Holy Spirit, forever.
People: Amen.

Sunday Morning Prayer

They begin the Glorification from the "former" side:
Glory to *God* in the highest!
Peace on earth!
Good hope to *the* sons of men!
We adore, glorify, *and* exalt you!
Being *with*out beginning!
Secret, incompre*hen*sible Nature!
Father, Son *and* Holy Spirit!
King of Kings *and* Lord of Lords!
Who dwells *in* radiant Light!
Which none *on* earth can see!
Holy, Almighty, Im*mor*tal alone!
We *give* thanks to you!
Through our Media*tor* Jesus Christ!
The Sav*ior* of the world!
The Son *of* the Most High!
The liv*ing* Lamb of God!
Who takes away the *sin* of the world!
Have *mer*cy on us!
Who sits at the right *hand* of his Father!
Accept our *sup*plication!
For you are *our* God and Lord!
You are *our* King and Savior!
You are the Forgi*ver* of our sins!
The eyes of all look to *you*, Jesus Christ!
Glory *to* God your Father!
To you and to *the* Holy Spirit!
Forever and *ev*er, amen!

Prayer of the Glorification for Memorials: say the Prayer of the Shuraya *and Canon of that day; the Glorification of the day as in the* Gazza.

Prayer of Qaddysha Alaha *for Sundays and Feasts:* To you, O Lord, to your Christ, and to your living, holy, life-giving, and divine Spirit, we lift up glory, honor, thanksgiving, and adoration, at all times, Lord of all, Father, Son, and Holy Spirit, forever.

For Memorials: Glory to your name, adoration to your Majesty, and constant thanksgiving are due to your glorious Trinity, at all times, Lord of all, Father, Son, and Holy Spirit, forever.

Server: Lift your voices, all you people, and glorify the living God.
People, in the melody of Memorials: Holy God... and then *Aḥḥun d-bashmayya* (see above).

People: Let us pray. Peace be with us.
The Presider says the prayer of Sundays and Feasts: O Merciful One whose name is holy, whose temple is holy, whose dwelling-place is holy, whose heavenly powers are holy, who hallow him with their halleluiahs, who is hallowed by the spiritual and the physical with holy and unceasing hymns: hallow, O Lord our God, the temple of our souls, purify our intentions, forgive our faults, cleanse our impurities, and make us, O Lord, pure temples of your exalted Divinity, and adorned dwelling-places fit for the honor of the service of your love, O Hallower of all by the power of his Word and his Spirit, Lord of all, forever.
Another: Holy are you, O Lord, essentially; glorious are you eternally; high and exalted above all incomprehensibly; and adored by angels and men in Trinity and Unity; O great King of glory, Being who is from eternity: we thank, adore, and glorify you at all times, Lord of all, Father, Son, and Holy Spirit, forever.

On Memorials, they say: O Merciful One whose name is holy, Kind and Just One from eternity, whose grace and compassion overflow: may the sweet mercy of your love overflow, O Lord our God, upon the souls of your adorers who call and plead to you at all times and ages, Lord of all, Father, Son and Holy Spirit, forever.
Another: Bless, O Lord, your servants in your grace, guard your adorers from all dangers in the overflowing greatness of your compassion, shepherd, guide, aid and protect our lives under the wings of your providential love, and save, redeem, and deliver our bodies and souls from the evil one and his hosts, at all times and ages, Lord of all, Father, Son, and Holy Spirit, forever.

The priests on both sides pray, in order of their ordination, the prayers above as on page 26.

Final Blessing of Morning Prayer

Bestow, O Lord our God, in your grace, at this morning hour, redemption upon the oppressed, freedom upon the captive, refreshment upon the weary, healing upon the sick, closeness upon the distant, protection upon the near, forgiveness upon sinners, acceptance upon the repentant, exaltation upon the just, care upon the poor, finding upon the lost, return upon the exiled, a gracious and acceptable memory upon the deceased, and mercies and pity upon all things created and made. Accomplish, among us and among all men, those things which aid us who are weak and sinners and which please your Majesty, in your grace and mercies, now, at all times, and forever and ever.

They enter the altar and begin the great Sanctification, and they complete it as in the Ḥudhra or Gazza.

THE SERVICE OF EVENING PRAYER
FOR ORDINARY DAYS

Presider: Glory to God in the highest 3x, peace on earth, and good hope to the sons of men, at all times, forever. *They say: Barekh mar.*
And continue, singing in a simple tone:

Our Father who art in heaven,	*Aḅḅun dba-shmayya*
hallowed be your name.	*nithqaddash shmakh,*
Your kingdom come.	*tethe malkuthakh,*
Holy, holy, you are holy.	***qaddysh, qaddysh, qaddysh-at,***
Our Father in heaven:	***Aḅḅun dba-shmayya.***
heaven and earth are full	***Damlen shmayya w-ar'a***
of the greatness of your glory;	***rabbuth shuḥakh,***
angels & men cry out to you:	***'yre w-nasha qa'en lakh***
holy, holy, you are holy.	***qaddysh, qaddysh, qaddysh-at.***
Our Father who art in heaven,	*Aḅḅun dba-shmayya*
hallowed be thy name.	*nithqaddash shmakh,*
Thy kingdom come,	*tethe malkuthakh,*
thy will be done on earth	*nehwe ṣiw-yanakh*
as it is in heaven.	*aykanna dba-shmayya ap b-ar'a,*
Give us this day our daily bread	*haw lan laḥma d-sunqanan*
and forgive us our trespasses,	*yawmana wa-shwoq lan ḥawbayn*
as we forgive those	*wa-ḥtahayn aykanna d-ap ḥnan*
who trespassed against us.	*shwaqn l-ḥay-yawayn,*
And lead us not into temptation,	*w-la ta'lan l-nisyona*
but deliver us from evil,	*illa paṣan min bysha*
for thine is the kingdom,	*miṭṭul d-dhylakh-y malkutha,*
the power and the glory,	*w-ḥayla w-tish-buḥta*
now and forever.	*l-'alam 'almyn, amen.*
Presider: Glory to the Father, to the Son and to the Holy Spirit.	**Presider:** *Shuḥa l-Aḅḅa wla-Bra wal-Ruḥa d-Qudsha.*
People: *From age to age, amen, amen. Our Father who art in heaven, hallowed be your name. Your kingdom come.*	**People:** *Min 'alam wa-'dham-ma l-'alam amen w-amen. Aḅḅun dba-shmayya nithqaddash shmakh, tethe malkuthakh,*
Holy, holy, you are holy.	***Qaddysh, qaddysh, qaddysh-at,***
Our Father in heaven:	***Aḅḅun dba-shmayya.***

Weekday Evening Prayer

heaven and earth are full of the greatness of your glory; angels & men cry out to you: holy, holy, you are holy.	*Damlen shmayya w-ar'a rabbuth shuḥakh, 'yre w-nasha qa'en lakh qaddysh, qaddysh, qaddysh-at.*

Server: Let us pray. Peace be with us.
Priest: We confess your Divinity, O Lord 2x, we adore your Majesty, and lift up unceasing praise to your glorious Trinity, at all times, Lord of all, Father, Son and Holy Spirit, forever.
People: Amen.

> They serve the two *MARMYATHA* of the day as in the "Before and After"
> See pp. 69–115

Server: Let us pray. Peace be with us.
Prayer of *Lakhu Mara*: And for all your benefits and graces to us that cannot be repaid, we give you thanks and praise you unceasingly in your crowned Church, full of all benefits and blessings, for you are Lord and Creator of all, Father, Son, and Holy Spirit, forever.
People: Amen.
And they say:

We give you thanks, O Lord of all, we glorify you, Jesus Christ; you raise our bodies into life, you are the Savior of our souls.	*Lakhu Mara d-kulla mawdenan, w-lakh Ysho' Mshyḥa mshabḥynan d-attu Mnaḥmana d-paghrayn, w-attu Paroqa d-nawshathan.*
I rejoiced when I heard them say: we are going to the house of the Lord!	***Ḥdhyth kadh amryn waw ly: l-bayteh d-Marya azynan!***
We give you thanks…	*Lakhu Mara d-kulla…*
Glory to the Father, to the Son and to the Holy Spirit. From age to age, amen, amen.	***Shuḥa l-Abba w-laBra wal-Ruḥa d-Qudsha min 'alam wa'dhamma l-'alam amen, w-amen.***
We give you thanks…	*Lakhu Mara d-kulla…*

Weekday Evening Prayer

Server: Let us pray. Peace be with us.
Prayer of the Psalmodies and Responsories "Before": Lord, you are indeed the One who raises our bodies, the true Savior of our souls, and the constant Guardian of our lives. It is thus our duty to thank, adore and glorify you who are Lord of all forever.
People: Amen.

They say the PSALMODIES AND HYMNS "BEFORE" of the day.
See pp. 69–115.

Server: Let us pray. Peace be with us.
The Prayer of Psalm 140: It is our duty, O Lord our God, to thank, adore and glorify you for your mercy and your providential will for us, at all times, O Lord of all, Father, Son and Holy Spirit, forever.
People: Amen.

Psalm 140

I have called to you, Lord; hasten to *help* me!
    Hearken to my words and *a*ccept my prayer.
I have called to you, Lord; hasten to *help* me!
    Hearken to my words and *a*ccept my prayer.
Let my prayer arise before you like *in*cense,
    the offering of my hands like an eve*ning* oblation.
Set, O Lord, a guard over my *mouth*
    and a guard *o*ver my lips!
That my heart may not turn to an evil *deed*,
    or accompl*ish* works of wickedness.
May I not dine with evil *men*.
    Let a just man teach *me* and reprove me.
But let the oil of the wicked not anoint my *head*,
    for my prayer is *a*gainst their malice.
Their judges were thrown down by a rock-like *hand*,
    then they heard that *my* words were kind,
Like a plough that scatters the *ground*.
    Their bones were strewn at *the* mouth of Sheol.
To you, Lord God, I lift up my *eyes*:
    I trust you; do not cast *my* soul away!

Guard me from the hands of the *boastful*,
>   who *set* traps for me.
Let the wicked fall together into their own *nets*
>   while I pursue *my* way unharmed.

Psalm 141

With my voice I called to the *Lord*,
>   with my voice *I* begged the Lord.
I lifted my pleading be*fore* him;
>   I showed *him* my distress.
When my spirit trembled, you knew my *path*.
>   On the way I walked they set *a* trap for me.
I looked to my right and *saw*:
>   there was no *one* to advise me.
I had no means of es*cape*,
>   not one who *cared* for my soul.
I cried to you, Lord; I said: you are my *hope*,
>   all that I have in the *land* of the living.
Hearken then to my *plead*ing,
>   for I am *brought* very low.
Rescue me from those who pur*sue* me,
>   for they are *strong*er than I.
Bring my soul out of this *pri*son,
>   that I may give *thanks* to your name.
Your just ones will a*wait* me
>   as you *grant* me reward.

Psalm 118:105–12

Your word is a lamp for my *feet*
>   and a *light* for my paths.
I have sworn and made up my *mind*
>   to keep *your* just decrees.
Lord, I am deeply af*flic*ted:
>   give me *life* by your word.
Be pleased, Lord, with the words of my *mouth*
>   and teach me *by* your decrees.
My soul is in your hands at all *times*;
>   I will not *for*get your law.

Weekday Evening Prayer

Though sinners laid traps for *me*,
    I did not stray *from* your commands.
Your witness is my heritage for*ever*,
    for it is the *joy* of my heart.
I set my heart to carry out your *stat*utes
    in *truth*, for ever.

Psalm 116

O praise the Lord, all you *nat*ions,
    O praise *him*, all you peoples!
For mighty is his *love* for us;
    truly, he is the *Lord* forever.
Glory to the Father, to the Son and to the Holy *Spir*it.
    From age to age, *a*men, amen.
I have called to you, Lord; hasten to *help* me!
    Hearken to my words and *ac*cept my prayer.

Server: Let us pray. Peace be with us.
Prayer of the Shuraye and Responsories "After": Hear, O Lord our God, the prayer of your servants in your mercy; accept the supplication of your adorers in your compassion, and pity our sinfulness in your grace and mercies, O Healer of our bodies and Good Hope of our souls at all times O Lord of all, Father, Son and Holy Spirit, forever.
People: Amen.

They say the Psalmodies and Hymns "After" of the day.
See pp. 69–115.

Petitions

Server: Let us all stand composed.
In contrition and diligence, let us implore *and* say: Lord, have mer*cy* on us.
People: Lord, have mer*cy* on us. | Maran ithraḥam 'layn.
Server:
* O Father of mercies and God of every con*sol*ation, we *im*plore you...
* Our Savior, our Caretaker and Provider *for* all, we *im*plore you...
* For the peace, concord and well-being of the whole world and of *all* churches, we *im*plore you...

Weekday Evening Prayer

* For the well-being of our country and of all countries, and for the protection of all the faithful who inha*bit* them, we *im*plore you...

* For good weather, a fertile season, the abundance of fruits and all the poor *and* needy, we *im*plore you...

* For the health of our holy fathers: [Mar _____, High Pontiff, Pope of Rome,] Mar _____, Catholicos-Patriarch, Mar _____, Bishop/Metropolitan, and for all those in the same priest*ly* service, we *im*plore you...

* For the rulers of *this* world, we *im*plore you...

* O merciful God, who guides all in *his* mercy, we *im*plore you...

* For the priests and deacons of our Church, and for all of our Chris*tian* brethren, we *im*plore you...

* O Rich in his mercies and overflowing in his *com*passion, we *im*plore you...

* O One who is before the ages, and whose authority will remain *for*ever, we *im*plore you...

* O Kind One in his Nature, and Giver of all *good* things, we *im*plore you...

* O One who does not desire that a sinner should die, but rather that he should repent from evil *and* live, we *im*plore you...

* O One who is glorified in heaven and worshipped *on* earth, *we* implore you...

* O One through whose holy <u>Birth</u> [or <u>Dawning</u>, or <u>Fasting</u>, or <u>Presentation</u>, or <u>Resurrection</u>, or <u>Ascension</u>, or <u>Descent</u>, or <u>Cross</u>] has gladdened earth and deligh*ted* heaven, we *im*plore you...

* O One whose Nature is Immortality, and who dwells in radi*ant* light, we *im*plore you...

* O Savior of all mankind, especially those who believe *in* him, we *im*plore you...

* Save us all, O Christ our Lord, in your grace, increase your peace and your tranquility within us and have mer*cy* on us...

Server: Let us entrust our souls mutually to the Father, and to the Son, and to *the* Holy Spirit.

People: To you, *O* Lord our God.

Priest: To you, Lord God almighty, do we entrust our bodies and souls, and from you, O Lord our God, do we ask for forgiveness of debts and sins. Grant this to us through your grace and mercies, as you always do, Lord of all, Father, Son, and Holy Spirit, forever.

The Server who said the Petitions says: Lift your voices, all you people, and glorify the living God.

People:

Holy God,	Qaddysha Alaha
Holy Mighty One,	Qaddysha Ḥayilthana,
Holy Immortal One:	Qaddysha La Mayotha
Have mercy on us.	Ithraḥam 'layn.
Glory to the Father, to the Son	*Shuḥa l-Aḅḅa w-laḄra*
and to the Holy Spirit.	*wal-Ruḥa d-Qudsha.*
Holy God…	Qaddysha Alaha…
From age to age,	*Min 'alam wa'dhamma*
amen, amen.	*l-'alam amen, w-amen.*
Holy God…	Qaddysha Alaha…

They say: Let us pray. Peace be with us.
Priest: O Holy, Glorious, Mighty and Immortal One, who dwells in the saints and delights in them: we implore you: turn to us, O Lord, pardon us and have mercy on us as you always do, Lord of all: Father, Son, and Holy Spirit, forever.
People: Amen.

The Server who said the Petitions: Bless me, sir. Bow your heads for the laying-on of hands, and accept the blessing.
The Presider says: May Christ adorn your service in the Kingdom of heaven.
The Prayer of the Basilica: When our souls are completed for the one perfect faith of the glorious Trinity, may we all become worthy, in the one harmony of love, to lift up glory, honor, thanksgiving, and adoration, at all times, Lord of all, Father, Son, and Holy Spirit, forever.

*They say a S*EASONAL *H*YMN *OF THE* W*EEK (see pp. 389–578).*

Server: Let us pray. Peace be with us.
Priest: Pity us, O Pitying One, in your grace, turn to us, O Merciful One, and do not turn your gaze and your providence away from us, for our hope and support are in you, at all times and ages, Lord of all, Father, Son, and Holy Spirit, forever.
People: Amen.

*They say the and P*SALMODY *OF THE* W*EEK (see pp. 389–578).*

*They continue with A*ḅḅun *d-bashmayya (see above, p. 61).*

Weekday Evening Prayer

The Presider prays: May your holy name, O Lord our God, be glorified, your Divinity adored, your Lordship honored, your Greatness made victorious, your Existence exalted, and may the eternal mercies of your glorious Trinity surround your people and the sheep of your flock, Lord of all, Father, Son, and Holy Spirit, forever.

Again: May your Divinity be blessed in heaven and on earth, O Lord, your Lordship adored, and the adorable and glorious name of your glorious Trinity hallowed, glorified, lifted up, and exalted at all times, Lord of all, Father, Son, and Holy Spirit, forever.

People: Amen.

> They say the MARTYR HYMNS of the Day, pp. 353–88.

Then the Presider prays: To you who raise up your Church, crown your friends, uphold your saints, give victory to your athletes in their glorious and holy trials, we plead: turn to us, O Lord, forgive us and have mercy on us, as you always do, Lord of all, Father, Son, and Holy Spirit, forever.

Another: By the prayers of your saints, O Lord our God, guide us, and by the pleading of your true ones, let our sins pass, absolve our faults, raise our deceased, give success to our works, sanctify our souls and our bodies, make us worthy for beautiful glory of your kingdom, and mingle us with the just and righteous in the Jerusalem above who fulfilled your will, Lord of all, Father, Son, and Holy Spirit, forever.

The priests say the prayers of assistance in order, according to their number, and of Mary, and of the Apostles, and the Patron, and they conclude, as on p. 26 above.

CYCLE FOR WEEKDAY EVENING PRAYER

MONDAY EVENING PRAYER – WEEK I

MARMYTHA: Psalms 11–14; 15–17.

PSALMODY "BEFORE"
Psalm 12:1–6

Save me, Lord, for the good man has *dis*appeared,
    Halleluiah, halleluiah, *h*alleluiah.
Save me, Lord, for the good man has *dis*appeared,
    and faith has van*ished* from the earth.
Men speak vanity, a man to his friend with de*ceiv*ing lips.
    They speak *with* two faces.
May the Lord destroy all de*ceiv*ing lips,
    the tongues *that* speak proud things.
For they say: "our tongue will *make* us great;
    our lips are our own; *who* is our master?"
"Because of the oppression *of* the poor,
    and the groa*ning* of the needy,
I will arise now," *says* the Lord.
    "And I will grant salva*tion* openly."
Glory to the Father, to the Son and to the *Hol*y Spirit.
    From age to age, *a*men, amen.
Halleluiah, *h*alleluiah, *h*alleluiah.

HYMNS "BEFORE" – *ha shwan*

- Save me, Lord, the good man vanished.
Lo, the gracious one has vanished,
the just is gone,
none is honest among men!
Each one speaking with two faces,
and with his friend,
only words of deception!
From within, our race is filled with
envy, deceit and slander.
Love, the head of all commandments,
has been blotted from our minds and hearts.

The terror is great
that your wrath will destroy us,
but your justice has been silent,
leaving room for mercy.
O Lord, forgive us!
- In his words, the Lord is faithful.
Our Redeemer made a promise:
eternal life
to his friends, his beloved!
He enriched them with his knowledge,
and filled them with
wisdom to pray at all times:
Our Father
who art in heaven,
hallowed be thy name.
May thy kingdom come to us,
thy will be done on earth and heaven. Give
us the bread we need,
and lead us from temptation,
from the evil one deliver,
for thine is the kingdom,
the power and glory.
- Glory to the Father, to the Son, and to the Holy Spirit.
Virgin Mary, our great refuge,
who bore Life's Balm
for the wounded sons of Adam,
we take refuge in your pleading,
and by the prayers
of St. John,
defeat the devil.
By the prayer of
all the prophets,
apostles, martyrs, holy ones,
by the prayers of our patron,
confessors, St. George, the mighty strength
of the holy cross,

the crowning of the holy Church,
we entreat the Lord and Christ,
that he may grant his mercies
to all our souls.

Psalmody "After"
Psalm 15:1–5

Lord, who shall be admitted *to* your tent
Halleluiah, halleluiah, *ha*lleluiah.
Lord, who shall be admitted *to* your tent
    and dwell on *your* holy mountain?
He who walks *with*out fault;
    he *who* acts with justice
and speaks the truth *from* his heart;
    he who does not slan*der* with his tongue.
He who does no wrong *to* his brother,
    who casts no *slur* on his neighbor.
Who holds the godless *in* disdain,
    but honors those *who* fear the Lord.
Glory to the Father, to the Son and to the *Ho*ly Spirit.
    From age to age, *a*men, amen.
Halleluiah, *ha*lleluiah, *ha*lleluiah.

Hymns "After" – *abba ḥannana*

- He who was before all time.
O kind Father,
O Son of mercy,
O Spirit of love,
who makes holy the impure:
make holy our
flesh and soul,
and have mercy on us!
- Holy and awesome is his name.
May the hallowings
of the hosts above
plead to your Justice

on our souls' behalf,
by the request
of the Son,
and have mercy on us!
- **Glory to the Father, to the Son, and to the Holy Spirit.**
Mary, mother of
the great King of kings,
plead to Christ your Son,
who dawned from your womb,
to pity us
and let us
enter his kingdom.
- **From age to age, amen, amen.**
Through the prayers of
all your saints, O Christ,
prophets, apostles,
martyrs, all the just,
protect the Church
you have saved
from all evil things.
- **Let all the people say "amen, amen."**
Holy patron,
be a guide for us
in the ways of life
that appease your Lord,
that through your prayers
we find help
and delight with you.

"Letter" Psalm: Psalm 118, Alap-Beth.

Tuesday Evening Prayer – Week I

Marmytha: Psalms 25–27; 28–30.

Psalmody "Before"
Psalm 17:1–6

Hear, O *ho*ly Lord,
    Halleluiah, halleluiah, *h*alleluiah.
Hear, O *ho*ly Lord,
    and look *up*on my pleading.
Hearken *to* my prayer,
    for it is not said *with* lying lips.
From you my judg*ment* comes forth:
    may your eyes see *in*tegrity.
You search my heart, you visit *me* by night.
    You test me and you find *in* me no wrong.
The works of men have not *crossed* my mouth,
    even in the spea*king* of my lips.
Rather, you have kept me from *evil* ways;
    you placed my journeys firm*ly* on your paths.
There was no faltering *in* my steps.
    I called you for *you* answered me.
Glory to the Father, to the Son and to the *Ho*ly Spirit.
    From age to age, *a*men, amen.
Halleluiah, *h*alleluiah, *h*alleluiah.

Hymns "Before" – *nuhra w-bar nuhra*

- Hear, O God, and have mercy.
Hearer who does not turn,
Answerer, Savior, and Redeemer:
hear our pleading, Lord,
and respond to our requests.

- The Lord is faithful in his words.
Lord Jesus Christ, you said:
"to the one who knocks
upon the door, it will open;
his requests will find response."

Tuesday Evening Prayer – Week I

- Glory to the Father, to the Son, and to the Holy Spirit.
The holy Virgin's prayer,
Mary, mother of the Christ,
protect us from all harm
and the evil one, our foe.
- From age to age, amen, amen.
Prophets and apostles,
martyrs, priests and wise teachers:
your supplication be
our fortress both night and day.
- Let all the people say "amen, amen."
O holy patron, friend
of the heavenly Bridegroom:
entreat on our behalf
from the Lord whose love you know.

PSALMODY "AFTER"
Psalm 21:1–5

Lord, may your strength give joy *to* the king;
    Halleluiah, *h*alleluiah, *h*alleluiah.
Lord, may your strength give joy *to* the king;
    may your salva*tion* gladden him!
You granted him his *heart's* desire;
    you refused not the pra*yer* of his lips.
You met him with *a* good blessing;
    you set a glorious crown *up*on his head.
He asked you for life and this *you* have given,
    days that will last *from* age to age.
Glory to the Father, to the Son and to the *Ho*ly Spirit.
    From age to age, *a*men, amen.
Halleluiah, *h*alleluiah, *h*alleluiah.

Tuesday Evening Prayer – Week I
Hymns "After" – *lilya mikkel*

- O Lord, hear my prayer!
We beg you, O Lord our God,
and implore your Majesty:
as you made us in your grace,
give us life when you come!
For you pity sinful ones,
have mercy when we repent,
and you forgive all our sins
in the mercies of your grace.

- Hearken to my words and accept them.
O God, who accepted the
lamb of innocent Abel,
the off'ring of just Noah
and of faithful Abraham:
accept our petitions, Lord,
respond to all our requests,
and let your peace dwell in us
during all our days!

- Glory to the Father, to the Son, and to the Holy Spirit.
O Mary, holy virgin,
mother of our Savior, Christ:
may your prayer be a guard
for the Church upon earth.
Through you, may our pray'r be heard
as befits our humbleness,
and with you, may we see Christ
on the day when he comes.

- From age to age, amen, amen.
We commemorate the just
and take refuge in their prayers,
and to you we cry through them:
O Lord, pity us!
Establish their love in us,
make our mouth proclaim their truth,

confirm their true faith in us,
Hope of his true ones!
- Let all the people say "amen, amen."
Noble are you, blessed one;
full of sweetness is the crown
of your heav'nly victories
you won with nobility!
You beat down the enemy
who fought you in the battle,
and your victory is known
in heaven and on earth!

"Letter" Psalm: Psalm 118, Gamal–Dalath.

Wednesday Evening Prayer – Week I

Marmytha: Psalms 62–64; 65–67.

Psalmody "Before"
Psalm 23:1–4

The Lord *is* my Shepherd;
** Halleluiah, halleluiah, *h*alleluiah.**
The Lord *is* my Shepherd;
  there is no*thing* I shall want.
To green pas*tures* he brings me;
  to rest*ful* waters he leads me.
He turns my *soul* and guides me
  along *the* paths of truth.
Because of your name, even if *I* should walk
  in the valleys of *the* shadows of death,
no evil would I fear, for *you* are with me:
  your crook and your *staff* comfort me.
Glory to the Father, to the Son and to the *Ho*ly Spirit.
** From age to age, *a*men, amen.**
Halleluiah, *h*alleluiah, *h*alleluiah.

Hymns "Before" – ḥannana wamle raḥme

- During day and night.
- All times and all ages.
May the virgin Mary's prayer,
mother of our Savior Christ,
be our fortress at all times
of the night and of the day.
- Glory to the Father, to the Son, and to the Holy Spirit.
Prophets, may you pray for peace,
and apostles, for accord.
Martyrs, priests and wise teachers:
may your prayer be our guard.
- From age to age, amen, amen.
Plead and beg, O great patron,
from Christ whose Love you espoused,

that the Church who celebrates
you be aided by your prayers.
- Let all the people say "amen, amen."
Hearer of your servant's prayers,
Answerer of our requests:
Hear the sound of all our pray'rs,
and answer all our requests.

PSALMODY "AFTER"
Psalm 24:1–6

The Lord's is the earth *and* its fullness,
   Halleluiah, halleluiah, *h*alleluiah.
The Lord's is the earth *and* its fullness,
   the world *and* all its peoples.
For he set its foundations *on* the seas;
   on the rivers *he* made it firm.
Who shall climb the mountain *of* the Lord?
   Who shall stand on *his* holy mountain?
The man with clean hands *and* pure heart,
   who has not sworn de*ceit* in his soul.
He shall receive a blessing *from* the Lord
   and justice *from* God our Savior.
Glory to the Father, to the Son and to the *Ho*ly Spirit.
   From age to age, *a*men, amen.
Halleluiah, *h*alleluiah, *h*alleluiah.

HYMNS "AFTER" – *kul nishma*

- From her the earth is filled.
- The mountains are covered by her wings.
Mary, who bore
Life's Balm for the sons of Adam:
by your pray'r may we find mercy
when he comes.
- Glory to the Father, to the Son, and to the Holy Spirit.
A Spring of Life
you made for us, Lord, and all those

who receive your Mysteries
and love your name.
- From age to age, amen, amen.
Holy patron,
friend of Jesus Christ the Savior:
plead to him for pity,
mercies on our souls.
- Let all the people say "amen, amen."
Help us, O Lord,
send peace to us, banish Satan,
guard your Church and keep her children
from all harm.

WEDNESDAY MARIAN HYMNS – *la bahtynan*
- Holy is the dwelling-place of the Most High.
- I will glorify the Word of God.
The Virgin bore the Son-Word
with great glory in her womb,
and was mother and handmaid
to Jesus Christ, the Savior.
For this, all who dwell on earth
celebrate her holy day
and call us to the feast of Light,
to joy which is unending.
Thus every generation
gives her blessing constantly,
and glory to the One
who chose her as his dwelling.
- Glory to the Father, to the Son, and to the Holy Spirit.
Like incense Aaron offered,
let our pleading rise to you;
like the Ninevites' begging,
may you accept our prayer,
O Lord, and respond to us
from your treasure of mercy.
As you answered Daniel

within the den of lions,
respond, aid your worshippers,
in this time of trouble,
for our trust is in you,
Lord who loves his servants.
- From age to age, amen, amen.
The bones of the saints are like
fine pearls upon our King's crown:
their beauty shines forth on earth.
Come, let us celebrate them
in great love with spiritual hymns,
from morning till eventide,
remembering their noble deeds,
asking mercy of God,
that he may allow his peace
to dwell on the earth,
and that the Church and her children be
kept safe by their prayers.
- Let all the people say "amen, amen."
Blest are you, O great patron,
who was attacked for the truth,
and bore suffering and pain
that he may gain the kingdom.
What man can relate the tale
of the labors you performed
in vigil, penance and pray'r?
Your prayer be a fortress
for sinners who trust in you,
and may we be worthy to give praise to the Lord
who raised you to glory.

WEDNESDAY MARIAN PSALMODY

Psalm 45:14–17: All the beauty of the princess is from within, * and she adorns her clothing with fine gold. * She goes to the king with offerings, * and brings her virgin companions with her. * They go with gladness and joy, * and enter the temple of the king.

THURSDAY EVENING PRAYER – WEEK I
MARMYTHA: Psalms 96–98; 99–101.

PSALMODY "BEFORE"
Psalm 25:1–5

To you, O Lord, I lift *up* my soul.
Halleluiah, halleluiah, *h*alleluiah.
To you, O Lord, I lift *up* my soul.
    I trust you, my God, let me not *be* put to shame.
Do not let my enemies boast *o*ver me,
    for those who hope in you shall not *be* put to shame.
Let the wicked be *put* to shame
    in *their* vanity.
Lord, show *me* your ways;
    make your *paths* known to me.
Lead me in your *truth* and teach me,
    for you are God my Savior; in you I *hope* every day.
Glory to the Father, to the Son and to the *Ho*ly Spirit.
    From age to age, *a*men, amen.
Halleluiah, *h*alleluiah, halleluiah.

HYMNS "BEFORE" – *attu nuhra*

- O Lord, you know.
You know more, O Lord, than all
what aids us: order our life
in your grace, let your mercy
be moved by our sinfulness;
your Mercy be our Doctor
and your Love be our Teacher.
Praise to you, mercy to us!
- Lord, your mercies are eternal.
We call to your overflowing
mercies of grace, O Christ,
for our weakness and its aid.
Because of our troubled times,
and this world scorched by its sins,

grant us peace unshaking where
we may thank you at all times.
- Glory to the Father, to the Son, and to the Holy Spirit.
Holy blessed virgin Mary,
mother of Jesus Christ:
beg and plead mercies for us,
lest we sinners be destroyed,
for we take shelter in you.
May your prayer be our guard,
in this world and that to come.
- From age to age, amen, amen.
By the pray'rs of all of those
who pleased you, and all the just,
the prophets, apostles and
teachers, martyrs, priests and monks,
protect your Church on the earth,
that they lift up praise to you,
Father, Son and Holy Spirit!
- Let all the people say "amen, amen."
Let us keep with diligence the
glorious memorial
of our great, splendid patron,
a vessel most merciful,
worthy of his Lord's service,
who would daily light his lamp.
May his prayer be our guard.

PSALMODY "AFTER"
Psalm 28:1–6

To you, O *Lord*, I called,
    Halleluiah, halleluiah, *ha*lleluiah.
To you, O *Lord*, I called,
    my God, do not *be* silent with me.
If you are silent with me, I will be *ha*nded over
    with those who have gone down *in*to the cave.

Hear the sound of my pleading as I *call* to you,
    as I lift up my hands to *your* holy temple.
Do not count me a*mong* the wicked,
    or with those *who* do evil,
who speak words of peace *to* their neighbors
    but have e*vil* in their hearts.
Repay them according *to* their works,
    and accor*ding* to their malice.
For they ignore the deeds *of* the Lord
    and the *work* of his hands.
May he ruin them and ne*ver* rebuild them.
        Blessed be the Lord for he has heard
            the *sound* of my pleading.

Glory to the Father, to the Son and to the *Ho*ly Spirit.
    From age to age, *a*men, amen.
Halleluiah, *h*alleluiah, *h*alleluiah.

Hymns "After" – *la miṭṭalmyn*

- I have called to you, Lord, every day.
The weary call to you, Merciful One;
in you they take refuge, Friend of man!
In your mercy, be the guard of their lives;
save them from the evil one –
they hope in you.
- From the depths of his heart.
Jonah called to you, and you answered him;
Hananiah from the fire; you rescued him.
All creation calls in groaning to you:
pity it, be merciful,
as is your way!
- Glory to the Father, to the Son, and to the Holy Spirit.
Mary, blest mother of the King of kings:
offer prayer with us to Jesus your Son,
that he let his peace dwell in all the world,
and the Church and all her sons
be kept from harm.

- From age to age, amen, amen.
Blessed was your land, O you noble ones,
our Messiah's workers bearing life to men!
Bring your treasure of graces to the poor,
and protect the land from evil
and from harm.
- Let all the people say "amen, amen."
Plead for all of us from your Lord, the Christ,
O splendid, holy patron, friend of the Son,
so that, through your pray'rs, all who are distressed
may be guarded and be aided
and redeemed.

"Letter" Psalm: Psalm 118, Zayn–Ḥeth.

Friday Evening Prayer – Week I

Marmytha: Psalms 85–86; 87–88.

Psalmody "Before"
Psalm 75:1–4

We give thanks to *you*, O God,
    Halleluiah, halleluiah, *h*alleluiah.
We give thanks to *you*, O God,
    we give you thanks and call upon your name.
        We recount *your* marvelous deeds.
"When I reach the ap*poin*ted time,
    then I will judge with *in*tegrity.
The earth and its inhabitants *will* be humbled."
    You have ordered its *in*habitants.
Glory to the Father, to the Son and to the *Ho*ly Spirit.
    From age to age, *a*men, amen.
Halleluiah, *h*alleluiah, *h*alleluiah.

Hymns "Before" – *talmydhaw*

- Give thanks to him and bless his name.
Give thanks, O mortals, to the Son who saved
us from slavery to death,
which had strangled us in sin,
for he went down into Sheol
and raised the dead from the grave.
Who can repay the grace of God
granted to the race of all mortal men?
- My mouth will wisdom speak.
Take refuge in repentance, sinful ones,
for the time is so short:
this world blooms and dies away!
There will be, for the repentant, joy,
death for the unjustified.
For if you judged justly, O Lord,
who on earth would be without any fault?

Friday Evening Prayer – Week I

- Glory to the Father, to the Son, and to the Holy Spirit.
We implore you, O Christ the King of kings,
that you may forget the
faults of all who have received
your Flesh and your Blood, and may you stand
for them on the day they rise,
that they be saved from Gehenna
and meet you in praise, with the hosts above!

Psalmody "After"
Psalm 82:1–4

God stands in the assem*bly* of angels.
    Halleluiah, halleluiah, *h*alleluiah.
God stands in the assem*bly* of angels.
    In the midst of *the* angels he judges.
"How long will you *judge* unjustly
    and favor the *cause* of the wicked?
Do justice for orphans *and* the poor,
    vindicate the hum*ble* and the needy.
Rescue the weak *and* the poor
    from the *hand* of the wicked."
Glory to the Father, to the Son and to the *Ho*ly Spirit.
    From age to age, *a*men, amen.
Halleluiah, *h*alleluiah, *h*alleluiah.

Hymns "After" – *push bashlama*

- I will bless the Lord at all times.
Blest your day, Son of the Mighty,
which tears open the womb of Sheol!
Glorious is your day of raising,
which all ages await with longing.
- They will pass, but you will remain.
Lo, this world is passing quickly,
and its pleasures are all empty!
Blest is he who made provision
for the world that lasts forever.

- Glory to the Father, to the Son and to the Holy Spirit.
No hope do we have to boast in
save your cross, O our Absolver,
for it is our mighty fortress,
and it saves us from all peril.

Friday Psalmody

Psalm 115:11–13: What shall I repay the Lord, for all his rewards are upon me? * I will receive the cup of salvation * and call upon the name of the Lord. * I will fulfill my vows to the Lord, * before all the people.

Saturday Evening Prayer – Week I

MARMYTHA: **Psalms 144–46; 147–50.**

PSALMODY "BEFORE"
Psalm 30:1–5

I will exalt you, Lord, for you lif*ted* me up,
    Halleluiah, halleluiah, *h*alleluiah.
I will exalt you, Lord, for you lif*ted* me up,
    and did not let my enemies re*joice* over me.
O Lord my God, I *cried* to you
    and *you* have healed me.
You raised my *soul* from Sheol,
    given me life apart from those who sank *in*to the cave.
Sing to the Lord, *you* his chosen,
    confess the memory of *his* holiness.
Glory to the Father, to the Son and to the *Ho*ly Spirit.
    From age to age, *a*men, amen.
Halleluiah, *h*alleluiah, *h*alleluiah.

HYMNS "BEFORE" – *ḥannana dapthyḥ*

- In him our heart is glad.
- **We hope in his holy name.**
May the cross which caused
us such benefits,
and through which our whole
mortal race was freed,
may it be, O Lord,
a_mighty castle wall,
where we may defeat
the evil one and all his schemes.
- **Glory to the Father, to the Son, and to the Holy Spirit.**
Sanctify your Church,
Savior, in mercy,
and let your grace dwell
in your temple set apart.
Set your altar up

strong within its walls,
where we may receive
your Flesh and your Blood.
- From age to age, amen, amen.
Lord, who promised us
in his great mercy:
"He who asks, receives,
and who seeks will find":
from you we implore
strength and aid all times
to fulfill your will
in our works and deeds.

PSALMODY "AFTER"
Psalm 54:1–6

O God, save me *by* your name;
    Halleluiah, halleluiah, *h*alleluiah.
O God, save me *by* your name;
    give me jus*tice* by your strength.
O God, *hear* my prayer;
    hearken to the *words* of my mouth.
For strangers have ri*sen* against me,
    the wicked seek my life.
        They have no regard *for* you, O God.
But I have God *for* my help.
    The Lord *up*holds my soul.
Glory to the Father, to the Son and to the *Ho*ly Spirit.
    From age to age, *a*men, amen.
Halleluiah, *h*alleluiah, *h*alleluiah.

HYMNS "AFTER" – *shlama l-sahde*

- From the ends to the ends of the earth.
- From the rising of the sun to its setting.
Cross that prevailed in creation's four corners:
guard those who kneel to you,
through Divinity's mercy.

- Glory to the Father, to the Son and to the Holy Spirit.
On Golgotha, the Church saw Lord Jesus Christ,
knelt down and worshipped him,
lifting praise to his Sender.
- From age to age, amen, amen.
O Lord may the prayer of your servants not
be out of vanity,
but for forgiveness and grace.

"LETTER" PSALM: Psalm 118, Ṭeth–Kap.

Monday Evening Prayer – Week II

Marmytha: Psalms 11–14; 15–17.

Psalmody "Before"
Psalm 42:1–5

Like the deer that yearns for *ru*nning streams,
    Halleluiah, halleluiah, *h*alleluiah.
Like the deer that yearns for *ru*nning streams,
    so my soul yearns *for* you, Lord God.
My soul thirsts for you, O *li*ving God;
    when can I come *and* see your face?
My tears have become my food, O God, by *day* and night,
    as they say to me every day: "*Where* is your God?"
I recall these things with a *wea*ry soul,
    for I would go to your mighty fortress,
        even to *the* house of God.
Glory to the Father, to the Son and to the *Ho*ly Spirit.
    From age to age, *a*men, amen.
Halleluiah, *h*alleluiah, *h*alleluiah.

Hymns "Before" – *sahde brykhe*

- Like the deer that yearns for running streams.
Who will give to me
a wellspring of tears
and a contrite heart,
that I may cry,
weep and groan
in thund'ring lamentation
over all the years gone by
wasted on such worthless things?
Empty vanities, not good works!
- Woe is me, my journey is repeated.
What has come of me?
Evil set a trap
for me, and I fell.

Monday Evening Prayer – Week II

You, Lord, created me free,
but I broke all your commands;
and because the evil one
saw me weak, he captured me.
Lord, deliver me from his snares!
- **Glory to the Father, to the Son, and to the Holy Spirit.**
By the prayers of the Virgin Mary,
the blessed mother,
may your worshippers be kept
from all the deceiver's schemes.
Grant us to fulfill your will
in our words as in our deeds,
and to sing you praise at all times.
- **From age to age, amen, amen.**
By the prayers of your saints who have kept
all of your commands,
prophets and apostles
teachers, martyrs,
priests and monks,
guard the Church that worships you
from all the deceiver's schemes,
and give us the strength to do your will.
- **Let all the people say "amen, amen."**
O garment of grace by the Spirit weaved,
O holy patron,
by your faithfulness and deeds,
you made grace flow like a spring
and watered your flock with words
of the life of Spirit, and
so, the crown of victory is yours!

Monday Evening Prayer – Week II

Psalmody "After"
Psalm 122:1–4

To you have I lifted *up* my eyes,
    Halleluiah, halleluiah, *h*alleluiah.
To you have I lifted *up* my eyes,
    you *who* dwell in heaven:
like the eyes of slaves *to* their lords;
    like the eyes of a hand*maid* to her mistress.
So our eyes are to you, O *Lord* our God,
    till you have mercy on us.
        Have mercy on *us*, Lord, have mercy.
Glory to the Father, to the Son and to the *Ho*ly Spirit.
    From age to age, *a*men, amen.
Halleluiah, *h*alleluiah, *h*alleluiah.

Hymns "After" – *byadh shlama*

- To you I lifted up my eyes, Dweller of heaven.
To you I lift my eyes, you who dwell in heaven:
you brought me into being and your will made me.
Send me your strength and my sickness heal,
and treat my wounds with your mercy's balm,
for you are the true Doctor, who treats without charge.
In your mercies, heal all of my wounds!

- May your mercies quickly come to us.
May your mercies come quickly, Lord of compassion;
to you we stretch our hands and our hearts to heaven;
we beg and plead that you may forgive
our faults and a-bsolve all of our sins,
redeem us from the evil one who attacks us,
and strengthen us to do all you will.

- Glory to the Father, to the Son, and to the Holy Spirit.
The pray'r of Mary who bore you, John who baptized you,
Peter and Paul the preachers and the evangelists,
Stephen and the whole host of teachers,
our patron and all of our deceased,
the twelve confessors and holy George the martyr,
protect our land and all who dwell therein!

- From age to age, amen, amen.
By your ascension, Jesus, you raised our abasement;
in love you seated us at the right of the Father.
By the descent of the Holy Ghost,
you made us wise; through your cross of light
you gave us understanding, and by the holy Church,
you hallowed us: glory to your providence!

"Letter" Psalm: Psalm 118, Lamadh–Mym.

TUESDAY EVENING PRAYER – WEEK II

MARMYTHA: Psalms 25–27; 28–30.

PSALMODY "BEFORE"
Psalm 67:1–6

May God have mer*cy* on us,
    Halleluiah, halleluiah, *h*alleluiah.
May God have mer*cy* on us,
    bless us, and let his *face* shine on us.
That his ways be *known* on earth
    and his salvation *a*mong all peoples.
Let the peoples confess *you*, O God;
    let all *the* peoples confess you.
Let the kingdoms be *glad* and praise,
    for you judge the nations uprightly
        and guide *the* nations on earth.
Let the peoples confess *you*, O God;
    let all *the* peoples confess you.
Glory to the Father, to the Son and to the *Ho*ly Spirit.
    From age to age, *a*men, amen.
Halleluiah, *h*alleluiah, *h*alleluiah.

HYMNS "BEFORE" – ḥannana wamle raḥme

- Let your face shine on us and we shall be saved.
Pitying and Merciful,
do not turn your gaze from us:
send us pity, mercies, re-
demption from your treasury.
- Till you have mercy on us.
O Lord, we knock at your door,
and ask for mercies from you.
Open to us, and respond,
Kind One who does not withhold.
- Glory to the Father, to the Son, and to the Holy Spirit.
May the virgin Mary's prayer,
mother of our Savior Christ,

be our fortress at all times
of the night and of the day.
- **From age to age, amen, amen.**
Prophets, may you pray for peace,
and apostles, for accord.
Martyrs, priests and wise teachers:
may your prayer be our guard.
- **Let all the people say "amen, amen."**
Plead and beg, O great patron,
from Christ whose Love you espoused,
that the Church who celebrates
you be aided by your prayers.

Psalmody "After"
Psalm 40:14–17

Be pleased, O Lord, to de*li*ver me.
    Halleluiah, halleluiah, *h*alleluiah.
Be pleased, O Lord, to de*li*ver me.
    O Lord, has*ten* to my aid.
May those who seek to kill my *soul* be buried.
    May they be turned back and buried,
        those *who* wish me evil.
May they marvel at the repetition *of* their shame,
    those who say to me, *a*ha, aha.
May all who seek you re*joice* in you.
    May they always *say*, God is great.
Glory to the Father, to the Son and to the *Ho*ly Spirit.
    From age to age, *a*men, amen.
Halleluiah, *h*alleluiah, *h*alleluiah.

HYMNS "AFTER" – *ḥannana dapthyḥ*

- Redeem me and deliver me, in this age and forever.
O God, who redeemed Hezekiah's house,
saved Jerusalem from the Assyrian:
rest your hand on us,
save your worshippers,
keep us all, O Lord,
from the mighty sword.

-From the depths of his heart.
When King David called,
Lord, you answered him,
and you eased his pain
and cast down his foes.
And we also call:
persecution end,
and uphold the Church
who adores your cross.

- Glory to the Father, to the Son, and to the Holy Spirit.
The holy Virgin
is a great fortress
for the faithful who
always ask her prayers.
By her mighty pray'r,
may our Church be blessed,
and be given priests,
harmony and peace.

- From age to age, amen, amen.
Prophets, apostles,
teachers and martyrs,
beg mercy from God
for the world entire:
harmony for priests,
benevolence for kings,
forgiveness of sins
for the Church's sons.

- **Let all the people say "amen, amen."**
O holy patron,
the Messiah's friend,
who gained the kingdom
through labor and works:
plead mercies for us
from him who chose you,
that he may pity
us and save our souls.

"Letter" Psalm: Psalm 118, Simkath–'e.

Wednesday Evening Prayer – Week II

Marmytha: Psalms 62–64; 65–67.

Psalmody "Before"
Psalm 72:1–4

O God, give your judgment *to* the king;
    Halleluiah, halleluiah, *h*alleluiah.
O God, give your judgment *to* the king;
    to the *king's* son your justice,
that he may judge your peo*ple* in justice,
    and your *poor* in right judgment.
May the mountains bear peace *for* your people,
    and *the* hills, your justice,
That he may judge the poor *of* the people,
    save the children of the needy, *and* crush the tyrant.
Glory to the Father, to the Son and to the *Ho*ly Spirit.
    From age to age, *a*men, amen.
Halleluiah, *h*alleluiah, *h*alleluiah.

Hymns "Before" – *sahdaw dabra*

- There will I raise David to honor.
- He has chosen a dwelling-place for himself.
From Abraham and David's house,
the Creator chose a virgin,
and sent her his hidden pow'r.
By the Holy Spirit's pow'r,
she conceived and bore the Savior
who is Judge of height and depth.
- Glory to the Father, to the Son, and to the Holy Spirit.
How right it is to glorify
within this one, holy house,
where are prophets, apostles,
martyrs and priests and teachers,
where the sacred table is,
which forgives all Adam's sons.

- From age to age, amen, amen.
Blessed is one hired like you,
O patron, who spiritual wealth
gathered, filling his vessel
with all blessings, who made forth
and found his way to harbor,
to the place of all the just.
- Let all the people say "amen, amen."
O Lord, may your kingdom come,
your will be done here on earth,
as it is there in heaven.
Give to us the bread we need,
and lead us from temptation;
save us from the evil one.

Psalmody "After"
Psalm 101:1–6

Of grace and justice *I* will sing,
    Halleluiah, halleluiah, *h*alleluiah.
Of grace and justice *I* will sing,
    and I *will* praise you, Lord.
I will walk in your way *with*out blame;
    when, Lord, will *you* come to me?
I will walk with blameless heart with*in* my house;
    I will not set what is base *be*fore my eyes.
I have hated *e*vildoers;
    they shall not *come* near to me.
A wicked heart must de*part* from me;
    I *have* not known evil.
He who slanders his friend in secret I *have* destroyed;
    of proud eyes and haughty heart *I* have not dined with.
I look to the faithful in the land that they may *dwell* with me.
    He who walks faultless on *the* way shall serve me.
Glory to the Father, to the Son and to the *Ho*ly Spirit.
    From age to age, *a*men, amen.
Halleluiah, *h*alleluiah, *h*alleluiah.

Wednesday Evening Prayer – Week II

HYMNS "AFTER" – *la miṭṭalmyn*

- **For he is your Lord; adore him.**
- **Plead to him and petition him to forgive us.**

Mary, blest mother of the King of kings:
with us offer pray'r to Christ who is of you,
that he let his peace dwell in all the world,
and the Church and all her sons be kept from harm.

- **Glory to the Father, to the Son, and to the Holy Spirit.**

Blessed was your land, O you noble ones,
our Messiah's workers bearing life to men!
Bring your treasure of graces to the poor,
and protect the land from evil and from harm.

- **From age to age, amen, amen.**

Plead for all of us from your Lord, the Christ,
O splendid, holy patron, friend of the Son,
so that, through your pray'rs, all who are distressed
may be guarded and be aided and redeemed.

- **Let all the people say "amen, amen."**

O God who forgave Nin'veh, forgive us,
and turn not your gaze from our malicious age.
If you closed your door against sinful ones,
whose door could we knock upon, O Friend of man?

WEDNESDAY MARIAN HYMNS – *lakh dayyana*

- **Protect us from the malice of the evil one.**
- **Protect me, and guard me from my enemies.**

Under the wings of your prayers,
Virgin Mary, we take shelter.
May they guard us now and at all times;
in them may we find pity on
judgment day.

- **Glory to the Father, to the Son, and to the Holy Spirit.**

By the pray'rs of all the prophets,
who had proclaimed your great mysteries,
the apostles, who preached your holy gospel,

and the martyrs, priests and teachers,
Christ, protect us.
- **From age to age, amen, amen.**
Holy patron, pray for the sick,
that the Lord may heal in mercy.
Let your prayer be finest incense,
and a thurible pleasing unto
God for sinners.
- **Let all the people say "amen, amen."**
Hear our pleading, Hope of our lives,
respond to all our requests.
Grant us healing from our maladies,
that we may give thanks to you;
have mercy on us.

WEDNESDAY MARIAN PSALMODY

Exodus 15:20–21: Mary, the sister of Aaron, took a tambourine in her hand, * and all the women went after her with tambourines and timbrels. * Mary sang to them: * Glorify the splendid God.

THURSDAY EVENING PRAYER – WEEK II

MARMYTHA: Psalms 96–98; 99–101.

PSALMODY "BEFORE"
Psalm 118:41–48

Lord, let your mercies *come* upon me,
    Halleluiah, halleluiah, *h*alleluiah.
Lord, let your mercies *come* upon me,
    and the *sal*vation you promised.
I shall answer *those* who taunt me,
    for I *trust* in your words.
Let not the word of truth die *from* my mouth,
    for I trust *in* your decrees.
I shall keep your law for *e*ver and ever,
    and walk in freedom for I de*light* in your precepts.
I will speak of your justice *be*fore kings
    and *not* be ashamed.
I will consider your commands which *I* have loved;
    I will lift my hands to your commands *which* I have loved,
I will pon*der* your statutes.
    I will glory in *your* faithfulness.
Glory to the Father, to the Son and to the *Ho*ly Spirit.
    From age to age, *a*men, amen.
Halleluiah, *h*alleluiah, *h*alleluiah.

HYMNS "BEFORE" – *shlama nisge lakh*

- Lord, let your mercies come upon me, the salvation you promised.
May your mercies which made us aid us now;
may they heal our wounds with your mercy's balm.
- Turn to me and have mercy on me.
Come, Lord, to our aid, strengthen our frailty;
in you is our hope during night and day.
- Glory to the Father, to the Son, and to the Holy Spirit.
Let us all recall the virgin Mary,
the mother of Christ, upon the altar.

- From age to age, amen, amen.
Those sent by the Son, Sole-Begotten's friends:
pray that there be peace in all creation.
- Let all the people say "amen, amen."
O holy patron, may you be recalled
with the just victors, and the crowned martyrs.

PSALMODY "AFTER"
Psalm 118:121–28

O Just and *Right*eous One:
    Halleluiah, halleluiah, *h*alleluiah.
O Just and *Right*eous One:
    do not abandon me *to* my oppressors.
Comfort your servant *with* good things,
    and the braggarts *will* not oppress me.
My eyes yearn for *your* salvation
    and the pro*mise* of your justice.
Treat your servant according *to* your mercies,
    and *teach* me your law.
I am your servant; *give* me knowledge,
    and I *shall* know your testimony.
It is time to work *for* the Lord,
    for they have nul*li*fied your law.
That is why I loved *your* commands
    more than *gold* and fine gems:
I love all *your* commands
    and hate all *the* paths of the wicked.
Glory to the Father, to the Son and to the *Ho*ly Spirit.
    From age to age, *a*men, amen.
Halleluiah, *h*alleluiah, *h*alleluiah.

Thursday Evening Prayer – Week II
Hymns "After" – *lzaddyqe la qrayt*

- You are righteous, O Lord, and your judgments are just.
You have not called the
righteous to repent,
but rather have told
sinners to turn back.
Hear us in mercy,
O Christ our Savior,
and forgive our debts
and sins in your grace.

- Turn to me and have mercy on me.
Turn and hear the pray'r
of your servants, Lord,
receive our pleading,
respond to our needs,
take the binding of
the deceitful one,
that our Church be saved
from his envy's filth.

- Glory to the Father, to the Son, and to the Holy Spirit.
Mary, mother of
the great King of kings,
plead to Christ, that he
may pity our lot,
keep wars from the ends
of the earth, and bless
the crown of the year
in his guarding grace.

- From age to age, amen, amen.
By the prayers of
your saints, Christ our Lord,
prophets, apostles,
martyrs, all the just,
keep your worshippers
from all harmful things,

let them lift up praise
to you night and day.
- Let all the people say "amen, amen."
Holy patron, friend
of the Heavenly Groom,
may your prayer be
a refuge for us,
and, the day your Lord
dawns in his glory,
plead to him, that we
may see his kingdom.

"Letter" Psalm: Psalm 118, Qop–Resh.

Friday Evening Prayer – Week II

Marmytha: Psalms 85–86; 87–88.

Psalmody "Before"
Psalm 95

Come, let *us* praise the Lord,
> **Halleluiah, halleluiah, *hal*leluiah.**

Come, let us *praise* the Lord,
> and sing to *our* God, the Savior.

Let us come before him *gi*ving thanks,
> and glori*fy* him with songs.

For our God is *a* great Lord,
> the great King *o*ver all the gods,

in whose hands are the foundations *of* the earth
> and the *heights* of the mountains.

His is the sea, *for* he made it,
> and the dry *land* his hands made.

Come, let us bless and *wor*ship him,
> and kneel before *the* Lord who made us.

For he is our God, and we *are* his people,
> and the *sheep* of his flock.

Glory to the Father, to the Son and to the *Ho*ly Spirit.
> **From age to age, *a*men, amen.**

Halleluiah, *hal*leluiah, *hal*leluiah.

Hymns "Before" – *shlyḥe qaddyshe*

- Come, let us praise the Lord.
O mortals, come,
let us thank and praise
him who has destroyed
death and all its power,
and has given life to men
by his dying on the cross.

- Come, let us bless and adore.
We worship you,
O Redeeming Lord,

for you raise and save
all the baptized
who have passed on
and who have
confessed your name,
and your dying on the cross.
- **Glory to the Father, to the Son and to the Holy Spirit.**
Glory to you
who have promised life
to the mortal race
through your rising up
from the grave,
let us give you thanks
and praise, you alone
who raise the dead.

PSALMODY "AFTER"
Psalm 138:1–5

O Lord, you search me *and* you know me;
    Halleluiah, halleluiah, *h*alleluiah.
O Lord, you search me *and* you know me;
    you know my sit*ting* and my standing.
You discern my intentions *from* above;
    you know my paths and *trace* all my ways.
Before ever a word is *on* my tongue,
    you know it, *O* Lord my God.
In all things, from begin*ning* to end,
    you molded me and placed *your* hand on me.
Glory to the Father, to the Son and to the *Ho*ly Spirit.
    From age to age, *a*men, amen.
Halleluiah, *h*alleluiah, *h*alleluiah.

HYMNS "AFTER" – *ythya dabrimzeh*

- **You molded me and placed your hand on me.**
In Genesis, God
formed Adam from earth on Friday, and breathed

spirit into him,
giving speech to him, that he may sing him praise.
- **An ignorant and unwise people.**
On Friday, mankind
crucified our Lord upon Golgotha,
and that day the Lord
killed murderous Death, and raised up our race.
- **Glory to the Father, to the Son and to the Holy Spirit.**
Let us groan and beg
and through mercy plead grace and forgiveness from
the Merciful One
who opens his door to all who turn to him.

Friday Psalmody

Psalm 40:7–10: I showed and said, that they are more than can be numbered. * You were not pleased by sacrifices and offerings, * so ears you opened up for me, * and did not ask for burned offerings on behalf of sinners. * Then I said, Lo, I come, * that, as is written of me in the titles of the Scriptures.

Friday Evening Prayer – Week III

Marmytha: Psalms 85–86; 87–88.

Psalmody "Before"
Psalm 144:1–7

I will exalt you, O *Lord* my King;
  Halleluiah, halleluiah, *h*alleluiah.
I will exalt you, O *Lord* my King;
  I will bless your name *for*ever and ever.
I will bless you day *a*fter day
  and praise *your* name forever.
The Lord is great, highly *to* be praised,
  his greatness *can*not be measured.
Age to age shall pro*claim* your works,
  shall *de*clare your might,
shall speak of your *fear*ful strength,
  tell the tale of *your* wonderful works,
shall re*count* your greatness,
  and recall *your* many graces.
Glory to the Father, to the Son and to the *Ho*ly Spirit.
  From age to age, *a*men, amen.
Halleluiah, *h*alleluiah, *h*alleluiah.

Hymns "Before" – ḥadhu ḥayla

- I will exalt you, O Lord my King.
Christ the King, our Savior,
raise us on the day you come;
stand us up at your right hand
on the day your greatness dawns.
- I hope in you, my God; I shall not be put to shame.
We adore your cross, O Lord,
in which is resurrection,
and through which our dead are raised,
and their bodies glorified.
- Glory to the Father, to the Son and to the Holy Spirit.
God the Father: give me life;
Christ the Son: raise up my death;
Holy Spirit, Paraclete: lead me to the land of light!

Friday Evening Prayer – Week II-III

Psalmody "After"
Psalm 144:18–21

The Lord is close to all who call to *him* in truth,
   Halleluiah, halleluiah, *ha*lleluiah.
The Lord is close to all who call to *him* in truth,
      He does the will *of* those who fear him.
He hears their pleading *and* saves them.
      The Lord pro*tects* all who fear him;
the wicked he *will* destroy.
      Let me speak the praises of the *Lord* with my mouth.
Let all *the* sons of flesh
      bless his holy name *for*ever and ever.
Glory to the Father, to the Son and to the *Ho*ly Spirit.
      From age to age, *a*men, amen.
Halleluiah, *ha*lleluiah, *ha*lleluiah.

Hymns "After" – *nittayaw*

- His salvation is close to those who fear him.
The time comes when this world will
come to end, and its joys
will be made undone, destroyed!
Hear, mortal ones:
turn back from your sins, before the day
when death comes, and each one
is repaid for his works,
in the dread judgment!
- Like a lion which snarls and roars.
Death is planned for every one
and destroys me as well.
Thus I tremble and I quake,
due to my sins!
For they are greater than other men's,
and Death owns my soul.
You are my help, O Savior:
I wait upon you!

- Glory to the Father, to the Son and to the Holy Spirit.
We praise you, O Christ our King,
for you gained victory:
through your cross you saved our race
from Satan's deceit.
May you renew us, abolish death,
let your new life reign
and make us fit for mercy,
O Resurrecting King!

Friday Psalmody

Psalm 31:21–24: How great is the grace you save for those who fear you, * for those who hope in you before the sons of men. * You cover them with the shelter of your face * from the tumult of the sons of men. * You hide them from danger under your shadow. * Blessed is the Lord who chose his elect in the mighty village.

Saturday Evening Prayer – Week II
Marmytha: Psalms 144–46; 147–50.

Psalmody "Before"
Psalm 123:1–6

"If the Lord had not been *on* our side,"
    Halleluiah, halleluiah, *h*alleluiah.
"If the Lord had not been *on* our side,"
    let *I*srael say.
"If the Lord had not been *on* our side
    when *men* rose against us,
then would they have swallowed *us* alive
    when *their* anger was kindled.
Then would the waters *have* engulfed us,
    the torrent *gone* over us;
over our head *would* have swept
    all *the* raging waters.
Blessed be the Lord who *did* not give us
    a *prey* to their teeth!"
Glory to the Father, to the Son and to the *Ho*ly Spirit.
    From age to age, *a*men, amen.
Halleluiah, *h*alleluiah, *h*alleluiah.

Hymns "Before" – *m'yna dṭawatha*

- In him our heart rejoices.
- He abolishes wars from the ends of the earth.
Your cross, O Savior,
which united height and depth
by its great power,
and its glorious might,
unite the whole world
that is troubled by its sins,
and make your peace
dwell in all the earth.
- Glory to the Father, to the Son, and to the Holy Spirit.
Guard your holy Church

from all perils, Jesus, Lord,
who came to save
the whole human race:
make us all worthy,
in fear and in trembling,
to lift praise to your Divinity.
- From age to age, amen, amen.
Grant us what you know
will befit us, Life-Giver,
for we know not
what to ask of you.
For one thing only:
that your will
be done in us,
and your mercies
may defend us all.

Psalmody "After"
Psalm 124:1–2

Those who put their trust in the Lord *on* Mount Zion,
    Halleluiah, halleluiah, *h*alleluiah.
Those who put their trust in the Lord *on* Mount Zion,
    will not shake, but *will* stand forever.
Jerusalem! The moun*tains* surround her,
    so the Lord surrounds his people *both* now and forever.
Glory to the Father, to the Son and to the *Ho*ly Spirit.
    From age to age, *a*men, amen.
Halleluiah, *h*alleluiah, *h*alleluiah.

Hymns "After" – *kulnishma*

- That he may show forth his greatness.
- Show forth your greatness and come to save us.
O cross, which showed
marvelous wonders to the sons of men:
drive out dangers from the souls
marked by your sign.

- Glory to the Father, to the Son, and to the Holy Spirit.
Lord, be a guard
for the churches in all nations,
and let your truth rampart them
with armor strong.
- From age to age, amen, amen.
Help us, O Lord,
send peace to us, banish Satan,
guard your Church and keep her children
from all harm.

"Letter" Psalm: Psalm 118, Shyn–Taw.

THE SERVICE OF NIGHT PRAYER
FOR ORDINARY DAYS

Presider: Glory to God in the highest 3x, peace on earth, and good hope to the sons of men, at all times, forever.
They say: *Barekh mar.*
And continue, singing in a simple tone:

Our Father who art in heaven,	*Abbun dba-shmayya*
hallowed be your name.	*nithqaddash shmakh,*
Your kingdom come.	*tethe malkuthakh,*
Holy, holy, you are holy.	***qaddysh, qaddysh, qaddysh-at,***
Our Father in heaven:	***Abbun dba-shmayya.***
heaven and earth are full	***Damlen shmayya w-ar'a***
of the greatness of your glory;	***rabbuth shuhakh,***
angels & men cry out to you:	***'yre w-nasha qa'en lakh***
holy, holy, you are holy.	***qaddysh, qaddysh, qaddysh-at.***
Our Father who art in heaven,	*Abbun dba-shmayya*
hallowed be thy name.	*nithqaddash shmakh,*
Thy kingdom come,	*tethe malkuthakh,*
thy will be done on earth	*nehwe siw-yanakh*
as it is in heaven.	*aykanna dba-shmayya ap b-ar'a,*
Give us this day our daily bread	*haw lan lahma d-sunqanan*
and forgive us our trespasses,	*yawmana wa-shwoq lan hawbayn*
as we forgive those	*wa-htahayn aykanna d-ap hnan*
who trespassed against us.	*shwaqn l-hay-yawayn,*
And lead us not into temptation,	*w-la ta'lan l-nisyona*
but deliver us from evil,	*illa pasan min bysha*
for thine is the kingdom,	*mittul d-dhylakh-y malkutha,*
the power and the glory,	*w-hayla w-tish-buhta*
now and forever.	*l-'alam 'almyn, amen.*
Presider: Glory to the Father, to the Son and to the Holy Spirit.	Presider: *Shuha l-Abba wla-Bra wal-Ruha d-Qudsha.*
People: From age to age, amen, amen. Our Father who art in heaven, hallowed be your name. Your kingdom come.	People: *Min 'alam wa-'dham-ma l-'alam amen w-amen. Abbun dba-shmayya nithqaddash shmakh, tethe malkuthakh,*

116

Weekday Night Prayer

Holy, holy, you are holy.	*Qaddysh, qaddysh, qaddysh-at,*
Our Father in heaven:	*Aḅḅun dba-shmayya.*
heaven and earth are full	*Damlen shmayya w-ar'a*
of the greatness of your glory;	*rabbuth shuḥakh,*
angels & men cry out to you:	*'yre w-nasha qa'en lakh*
holy, holy, you are holy.	*qaddysh, qaddysh, qaddysh-at.*

They continue: Arise for prayer. Let us pray. Peace be with us.

Presider: May we arise, O Lord, by your power, be confirmed in your hope, raised and strengthened by the great arm of your might, and made worthy, by the help of your grace, to lift up glory, honor, thanksgiving, and adoration to you, at all times, Lord of all, Father, Son, and Holy Spirit, forever.

Each day, they serve 3 *Hulale,* **and at the end of each** *Hulala,* **they say, plainly:** Halleluiah, halleluiah, glory to you, O God; halleluiah, halleluiah, glory to you, O God; halleluiah, halleluiah, Lord, have mercy on us.

They continue: Let us pray. Peace be with us.

After the first *Hulala,* **the Presider says:** Strengthen, O Lord our God, our weakness by your mercy, hearten and aid our meagre soul by your grace, wake the lethargy of our conscience, cut away the heaviness of our bodies, wash and scour the filth of our debts and sins, enlighten the darkness of our minds, and extend and grant us the power and hand of your assistance, that in it we may rise and thank you, and glorify you unceasingly all the days of our lives, Lord of all, Father, Son, and Holy Spirit, forever.

They serve the second *Hulala,* **and a priest says the prayer:** May the hidden power of your Divinity, O Lord, the marvelous aid of your Majesty, and the great assistance of your compassion, strengthen the weakness of our miserable nature to lift up glory, honor, thanksgiving, and adoration to you, at all times, Lord of all, Father, Son, and Holy Spirit, forever.

They serve the third *Hulala,* **and when it is finished, they answer:** Halleluiah, halleluiah. Let us pray. Peace be with us.

Weekday Night Prayer

INSTRUCTION

On Monday, they serve *Hulale* 1–3 [Psalms 1–30].
On Tuesday, they serve *Hulale* 4–6 [Psalms 31–49].
On Wednesday, they serve *Hulale* 7–9 [Psalms 50–70].
On Thursday, they serve *Hulale* 10, 11, 15 [Psalms 51–58; 102–5].
On Friday, they serve *Hulale* 16–18 [Psalms 106–30].
On Saturday, they serve *Hulale* 19–21 [Psalms 131–50; Exodus 15:1–22; Isaiah 42:10–14; Deuteronomy 32:1–44].

PRAYER OF THE *MAWTWA*

May our miserable prayer arise before you like incense, O Lord our God, may our feeble supplication enter before you, may your mercies be advocates for our guiltiness, and may the requests of our neediness be answered from the great treasury of your compassion, at all times and ages, Lord of all, Father, Son and Holy Spirit, forever.

> The *Mawtwa* of the Day, as in the *Kashkul*,
> and they "glory" on the first verse.

- From age to age, amen, amen. – *talmydhaw*

O our merciful God, forgive us all;
    let not your inheritance fall to the nations' envy.
    Look down from your throne and see the fight
    imposed by our enemies.
    Dawn to us through your grace's help,
    lest the nations question "where is your God?"
O our merciful God, keep your servants,
    from those who despise us,
    who wish to reap what we sowed.
    May your mighty truth empower us,
    that our enemies be shamed,
    and let your grace surround us all,
    that we rest in it, and give thanks to you.
By the prayers of your mother, Jesus, Lord,
    pacify the whole world that is troubled by its sins;
    take away all conflicts from the earth;
    reconcile Church and state,
    that in love and in harmony,
    we may give her praise during all our days.

Weekday Night Prayer

May the just who have pleased you, Jesus, Lord,
    prophets and apostles, martyrs, teachers from all lands,
    plead to you on all our souls' behalf,
    that you have compassion,
    and with them, make us all worthy
    to give thanks to you on the day you come.
Blessed are you, O holy patron,
    who accomplished victory in the vineyard of the Lord
    and received reward for all your works,
    the reward of heaven's bliss:
    may your prayers be upon us all,
    and make us worthy to be heaven's heirs.

Prayer of the *Shubaḥa*: To you glory from the lofty, thanksgiving from the lowly, and adoration, honor and exaltation from all you have created and fashioned, in heaven and earth, Lord of all, Father, Son, and Holy Spirit, forever.

MONDAY
Psalm 13

How long, O Lord, *will* you forget me?
    Glory to you, O God.
How long, O Lord, *will* you forget me?
    How long *will* you hide your face?
How long will there be *grief* in my soul,
    this sorrow *in* my heart all day?
How long shall my e*ne*my prevail?
    Look at me, *an*swer me, Lord God!
Give light to my eyes lest I fall *a*sleep in death,
    lest my enemy say: "*I* have overcome him";
lest my foes rejoice *to* see my fall.
    As for me, *I* trust in your grace.
Let my heart rejoice in *your* saving help;
    let me *praise* the Lord who saved me.
Glory to the Father, to the Son and to *the* Holy Spirit.
    From age to *age*, amen, amen.
Glory to you, O God.

Weekday Night Prayer

GLORIFICATION OF MAR ABRAHAM

Savior, turn toward your *lo*wly servants' prayers,
> our pleading accept, re*spond* to our needs,

for you are the hope and *re*fuge of the weak.
> Through your help, let us de*feat* Satan's wiles.

Lo, he lays traps for our *souls* both night and day,
> and, in malice, he wants *to* strike us down.

Send your power, O Lord, and *cut* up his snares,
> lest he capture us in*to* sin's abyss.

May your grace's strength make *our* conscience strong,
> that we may please you, O *Mer*ciful One.

Make us all worthy to *sing*, when you come,
> an unceasing praise, for*ev*er, amen.

TUESDAY
Psalm 28

To you, *O* Lord, I called,
> ***Glo*ry to you, O God.**

To you, *O* Lord, I called,
> my God, do not *be* silent with me.

If you are silent with me, I will *be* handed over
> with those who have gone *down* into the cave.

Hear the sound of my pleading as *I* call to you,
> as I lift up my hands *to* your holy temple.

Do not count me *a*mong the wicked,
> or with *those* who do evil,

who speak words of *peace* to their neighbors
> but have *e*vil in their hearts.

Repay them accor*ding* to their works,
> and ac*cor*ding to their malice.

For they ignore the deeds of the Lord and the *work* of his hands.
> May he ruin them *and* never rebuild them.

Blessed be the Lord *for* he has heard
> all the *sound* of my pleading.

The Lord is my help and my shield; in *him* my heart trusts
> and my flesh rejoices; *I* thank him with praise.

Weekday Night Prayer

The Lord is the *strength* of his people,
   a fortress of the sal*vation* of his Christ.
Save your people and bless *your* heritage.
   Be their shepherd *and* guide them forever.
Glory to the Father, to the Son and to *the* Holy Spirit.
   From age to *age*, amen, amen.
***Glo*ry to you, O God.**

GLORIFICATION OF MAR ABBA

Earth and heaven and all *that* they contain
   cannot make you known, who *or*der all things!
Too small are they both to *tell* of your love,
   the heights of your grace, and *your* great mercies
that you sent to our most *un*worthy race.
   Kind and Gracious One, who *took* on our flesh,
who saved us from death and *has* ascended,
   who sits above all, as *Lord* and Ruler:
all the hosts of angels *be*fore you kneel,
   and together praise you *un*ceasingly:
O Father, and Son, and *their* Holy Spirit;
   all glory to you, from *age* unto age!

WEDNESDAY
Psalm 67

May God have *mer*cy on us,
   ***Glo*ry to you, O God.**
May God have *mer*cy on us,
   bless us, and let *his* face shine on us.
That his ways *be* known on earth
   and his sal*va*tion among all peoples.
Let the peoples con*fess* you, O God;
   let all the *peo*ples confess you.
Let the kingdoms *be* glad and praise,
   for you judge the nations uprightly
      and *guide* the nations on earth.
Let the peoples con*fess* you, O God;
   let all the *peo*ples confess you.

Weekday Night Prayer

The earth has *yiel*ded its fruit,
> for *God*, our God, has blessed us.

May God still *give* us his blessing,
> and all the ends *of* the earth will fear him.

Glory to the Father, to the Son and to *the* Holy Spirit.
> **From age to *age*, amen, amen.**

***Glo*ry to you, O God.**

GLORIFICATION OF MAR THOMAS OF URHAI

May your mercies be on our sins,
> O Christ, Friend of the penitent.

Give ear to us, our Kind Doctor;
> remove the sores of wickedness.

Because you know our suffering,
> heal our wounds with your medicine.

Apply your mercy to our scars,
> and heal us, Lord, as is your way.

With the dew that is of your grace,
> cleanse our defects, as is your will.

Let us together praise your name:
> Father, and Son, and Holy Spirit,
> forever and ever, amen.

THURSDAY
Psalm 54

O God, save *me* by your name,
> ***Glo*ry to you, O God.**

O God, save *me* by your name,
> and *judge* me by your might.

O *God*, hear my prayer;
> hearken to *the* words of my mouth.

For strangers have *ri*sen against me;
> the *wi*cked seek my soul.

They have no regard *for* you, O God:
> O God my help, up*hol*der of my soul.

Bring evil upon *my* enemies
> and si*lence* them by your truth;

and I will sacrifice to *you* in discernment,
    and confess that your *name*, O Lord, is good.
For you have delivered *me* from all troubles,
    and my eyes have seen *the* fall of my enemies.
Glory to the Father, to the Son and to *the* Holy Spirit.
    From age to *age*, amen, amen.
Glory to you, O God.

GLORIFICATION OF MAR EPHREM

Accept, Lord, the pleading of all,
    which we bring forth in petition.
Hear, God, the voice of your servants,
    the groaning of those who praise you.
You are our King; in your great name
    we have true hope and confidence.
Grant that we may all gain one mind,
    without division, in the faith,
as we confess that, by your will
    all things were made out of nothing.
Your Essence can never be searched
    by creatures, you who dwell in Light!
By your making, Lord, your richness
    was made known to your handiwork.
For you are Lord and Fashioner
    Almighty, who provides for all.
We deeply long for forgiveness:
    bestow it, as you always do.
And grant that we may spiritually
    apply your balm onto our wounds.
We ask for mercies, Lord of all:
    grant your wealth to our poverty.
Your mercy be a steady guide
    for those who waver and who stray
in the deceit of Satan's way,
    and tread their consciences a path,
that they may know it was your plan
    that our enslaved race was freed.

Thus, with perfect, innocent heart,
> may we serve you as is your will,
and always do, with diligence,
> all that pleases Divinity,
and lift up praise with one accord
> to Father, Son and Holy Spirit,
who saved us through our Principal;
> did not treat us as we deserve.
Glory to him from all on earth,
> forever and ever, amen.

FRIDAY
[Option: Psalm 95

Come, let *us* praise the Lord,
> ***Glo**ry to you, O God.*
Come, let *us* praise the Lord,
> and sing *to* our God, the Savior.
Let us come before *him* giving thanks,
> and glor*ify* him with songs.
For our God *is* a great Lord,
> the great King *o*ver all the gods,
in whose hands are the found*a*tions of the earth
> and the *heights* of the mountains.
His is the sea, *for* he made it,
> and the *dry* land his hands made.
Come, let us bless *and* worship him,
> and kneel be*fore* the Lord who made us.
For he is our God, and *we* are his people,
> and the *sheep* of his flock.
Glory to the Father, to the Son and to *the* Holy Spirit.
> **From age to *age*, amen, amen.**
***Glo*ry to you, O God.]**

GLORIFICATION OF MAR ABRAHAM OF NITHPAR

Glory to him who has made known
> his glory to mankind in love.
He created a mute thing of dust,
> and gave it a soul of treasures.

He placed his thanks in lowly flesh,
    that the whole world may sing him praise.
Come, rational, and sing his praise,
    before we doze the sleep of death.
During the night, remember death,
    which shuts and silences our mouths.
The just who praise him during night
    are alive even when they die,
but the evil who deny him
    are dead even during their lives.
Let us now wake our flesh in prayer
    and praise the Hidden Majesty,
that we may be like the virgins
    who were praised in the parable.
On that night when he shakes the world,
    may we meet the Son while awake.
Let us not drown in our desires,
    but see his glory when he dawns.
Let us be watchful servants when
    he leads forth those in his chamber.
The evil will be suffering;
    the door of mercies will be shut.
Thus, while we live, let us labor,
    for after death is our reward.
The flesh that is wearied in prayer
    will fly in air the day he comes,
will see the Lord while without shame,
    and will enter in the kingdom.
The angels and the just love him,
    who have kept vigil in their prayer.
Blest is he who made us vessels
    to praise him, though we are of dust.
Praise him who gave us earthly ones
    a share with those who are above,
that we may sing, on every night,
    and every time, "holy his name."
Let us together sing his praise
    forever and ever, amen.

Weekday Night Prayer

SATURDAY
Psalm 150

Praise God in *his* holy place.
> *Glo*ry to you, O God.

Praise God in *his* holy place,
> praise him *in* his mighty firmament.

Praise him *for* his power,
> praise *his* surpassing greatness.

O praise him *with* sound of trumpet,
> praise *him* with lute and harp.

Praise him with timbrel *and* tambourine,
> praise him with pleasant strings.
> Praise him *with* resounding cymbals,

Praise him *with* hymns and cries!
> Praise the *Lord* with every breath!

Glory to the Father, to the Son and to *the* Holy Spirit.
> **From age to *age*, amen, amen.**

*Glo*ry to you, O God.

GLORIFICATION OF MAR EPHREM

Blest be him who made us, *sav*ed us in his Christ,
> who called us to know the *ho*ly Trinity.

God the Word, Only-Be*got*ten of the Father:
> may I please you in our *man*hood you wore,

and may I never be *sil*ent, Christ, my Lord,
> to give thanks to *your* name at all times.

PETITIONS

Server: Let us all stand composed. In contrition and diligence, let us implore *and* say: Lord, have mer*cy* on us.

Response: Lord, have mer*cy* on us. | *Maran ith*raḥ*am 'layn.*

* Almighty Lord, Eternal Being who dwells in the high*est* heavens, we *im*plore you...

* O One in the abounding love with which he loved us has fashioned our race in his Ho*nor's* image, we *im*plore you...

Weekday Night Prayer

* O One who promised benefits to his friends through Abraham the faithful, and through the revelation of Christ was made known to *his* Church, we *im*plore you...

* O One who does not wish the destruction of our race, but rather its repentance from the error of darkness to the knowledge of *the* truth, we *im*plore you...

* O One who is alone the Maker and Fashioner of creatures, and who dwells in radi*ant* light, we *im*plore you...

* For the health of our holy fathers: [Mar _____, High Pontiff, Pope of Rome,] Mar _____, Catholicos-Patriarch, Mar _____, Bishop/Metropolitan, and for all those in the same priest*ly* service, we *im*plore you...

* O Compassionate God, who guides all in *his* mercy, we *im*plore you...

* O One who is glorified in heaven and worshipped *on* earth, we *im*plore you...

* Give us victory, O Christ our Lord, in your coming, give peace to your Church saved by your precious Blood, and have mer*cy* on us...

Server: Let us entrust our souls mutually to the Father, and to the Son, and to *the* Holy Spirit.

Response: To you, *O* Lord our God.

The Service of Morning Prayer
For Ordinary Days

The Presider says the prayer before the ferial morning Psalms: O Tender, Merciful and Compassionate One, whose door is open to the repentant, and who calls unceasingly to sinners, that they may approach him in repentance: open, O Lord our God, the door of mercies to our prayer, accept our supplication, and grant our requests in your mercies from your rich and overflowing treasury, O Gracious One who does not withhold his mercies or his gifts from the needy and afflicted, his servants who call and plead to him at all times and ages, Lord of all, Father, Son and Holy Spirit, forever.

Another: All the creatures you have created enter before you O Lord; they kneel and adore you, praise and hallow you, ask and entreat you, implore and beseech you, confess and glorify you; for by your command they were constructed, and through your will they came to be; you are the Cause of their existence, and the Breath and Spiration of our lives, O Lord of all, Father, Son and Holy Spirit, forever.

People: Amen.

Weekday Morning Prayer

Psalm 100

Glorify the Lord, all the earth!
> **O Giver of Light, O Lord: we lift up praise to you!**
> Glorify the Lord, all the earth!

Serve the Lord in *gla*dness.
> **O Giver of Light, O Lord: we lift up praise to you!**
> Enter before *him* with praise.

Know he is the *Lord* our God:
> he made us; it *was* not we.

We are his people, the sheep *of* his flock.
> Enter his gates with thanksgiving
>> and his *courts* with praise.

Give thanks to him *and* bless his name,
> for the Lord is good and eter*nal* is his grace,
> and his faithfulness is *un*to the ages.

Glory to the Father, to the Son and to *the* Holy Spirit.
> **From age to age, *a*men, amen.**

Glorify the Lord, all the earth!
> **O Giver of Light, O Lord: we lift up praise to you!**

Server: Let us pray. Peace be with us.

Priest: To you, O Lord, do we lift up praise and confession, and to your living and holy name do we offer adoration and thanksgiving at all times, O Lord of all, Father, Son and Holy Spirit, forever.

People: Amen.

Psalm 91

He who dwells in the shelter of the Most High
> **Glorious is your faithfulness, O Christ our Savior.**

He who dwells in the shelter of the Most High
> and is adorned by the shadow of God

says to the Lord: "My refuge, my stronghold,
> my God in whom I trust!"

For he will deliver you from the fowler's trap
> and from the deceitful conversation.

He will conceal you with his pinions
> and under his wings you will find refuge.
>> His truth will surround you like an armor.

You will not fear the terror of the night
    nor the arrow that flies by day,
nor the plague that prowls in the darkness
    nor the scourge that lays waste at noon.
Thousands may fall at your side,
    a myriad at your right,
    you, it will never approach.
You need only look with your eyes
    to see how the wicked are repaid,
you who have said: "Lord, my refuge,
    who has made his dwelling on high!"
Upon you no evil shall fall,
    no plague approach where you dwell.
For you has he commanded his angels,
    to keep you in all your ways.
They shall bear you upon their hands
    lest you stumble with your feet.
On the viper and the serpent you will tread
    and trample the lion and the dragon.
"Because he seeks me,
    I will save him and strengthen him.
Because he knows my name,
    he will call and I will answer him.
I am with him in distress.
    I will strengthen him and honor him.
With length of life I will content him;
    I shall let him see my salvation."

Glory to the Father, to the Son and to the Holy Spirit.
   From age to age, amen, amen.
He who dwells in the shelter of the Most High
   Glorious is your faithfulness, O Christ our Savior.

Server: Let us pray. Peace be with us.
Priest: Glorious, O Lord, is the great faithfulness of your Divinity, and high and exalted is the awesome sanctuary of your authority. Nor are they put to shame who hope and trust in you, call upon your holy name, and entreat you at all times and ages, O Lord of all, Father, Son, and Holy Spirit, forever.

Psalm 104

Bless the Lord, my soul!
May the glory of the Lord be forever!
Bless the Lord, my soul!
    Lord God, how great you are,
clothed in majesty and glory,
    wrapped in light as in a robe!
You stretch out heaven like a tent.
    He makes his dwelling above the rains.
He makes the clouds his chariot,
    he walks with wings of wind,
he makes the winds his messengers
    and burning fire his servants.
He founded the earth on its bases,
    to be unshaken from age to age.
You wrapped it with the firmament like a cloak:
    the waters stood above the mountains.
At your threat they took to flight;
    at the voice of your thunder they fled.
The mountains rose and the plains were lowered
    to the place which you had appointed.
You set limits for them
    lest they return to cover the earth.
You sent springs to the valleys:
    they flow in between the hills.
They give drink to all the beasts of the field;
    the wild animals quench their thirst.
Upon them dwell the birds of heaven;
    from the mountains they sing their song.
From his dwelling he waters the hills;
    earth drinks its fill of the fruit of your work.
You make the grass grow for cattle
    and the plants for man's labor,
That he may bring forth bread from the earth:
    wine gladdens the heart of man;
Oil makes his face rejoice;

and bread sustains man's heart.
The trees of the Lord drink their fill. **May the glory of the Lord be forever!**

Psalm 113

Praise, O servants of the Lord,
    Glory to the One who created light!
Praise, O servants of the Lord,
    praise the name of the Lord!
May the name of the Lord be blessed,
    from age to age!
From the dawning of the sun to its setting,
    great is the name of the Lord!
High above all nations is the Lord,
    and above the heavens his honor.
Who is like the Lord, our God,
    who sits on high and sees below?
Who sits on high and sees below,
    in the heavens and on the earth?
From the dust he lifts up the poor man,
    and lets him sit with the rulers of the people.
He sets the barren woman in a home,
    and makes her the joyful mother of children.

Psalm 93

The Lord is King, with majesty enrobed.
    The Lord is clothed with might and power.
    He constructed the world to be unshaken.
Your throne is established from the beginning:
    and you exist, O Lord, from eternity.
The rivers have lifted up, O Lord,
    the rivers have lifted up their voice,
    the rivers have lifted up in purity.
Even mightier than the roar of many waters
    are the surgings of the sea.
Glorious are you, O Lord, on high,
    and your testimonies are greatly faithful.
And holiness is fitting to your house,
    O Lord, until the end of days.

Weekday Morning Prayer

Psalm 148

Praise the Lord from the heavens,
    praise him in the heights.
Praise him, all his angels,
    praise him all his hosts.
Praise him, sun and moon,
    praise him, all stars and lights.
    Praise him heaven of heavens.
Waters above the heavens,
    praise the name of the Lord.
For he spoke, and they were;
    he commanded and they were created.
He fixed them forever and ever,
    gave a law which shall not pass away.
Praise the Lord from the earth,
    sea creatures and all oceans,
fire and hail, snow and mist,
    stormy winds that obey his word;
all mountains and hills, all fruit trees and cedars,
    beasts wild and tame, reptiles and birds on the wing;
all earth's kings and peoples,
    earth's princes and rulers;
young men and maidens,
    old men together with children.
Let them praise the name of the Lord,
    for his name alone is great,
    and his glory is through earth and heaven.
He exalts the horn of his people
    and the praise of all his just,
of the sons of Israel,
    of the people that is near to him.

Psalm 149

Sing a new song to the Lord,
    his glory in the church of his just.
Let Israel rejoice in its Maker,
    and the sons of Zion exalt in their King.

May they glorify his name with timbrel and tambourine,
> and sing to him with harps.
For the Lord has delighted in his people,
> and given the poor salvation.
The just will be strengthened in honor,
> and glorify him on their beds,
> and exalt God in their throats.
A two-edged sword is in their hands,
> to make vengeance upon the nations,
and chastisement upon the peoples,
> to bind their kings in chains,
and their honored ones in fetters of iron,
> to carry out the sentence that was written.
> Glory to all his just.

Psalm 150

Praise God in his holy place,
> praise him in his mighty firmament.
Praise him for his power,
> praise his surpassing greatness.
O praise him with sound of trumpet,
> praise him with lute and harp.
Praise him with timbrel and tambourine,
> praise him with pleasant strings.
O praise him with resounding cymbals,
> praise him with hymns and cries!
Praise the Lord with every breath!

Psalm 116

O praise the Lord, all you nations,
> O praise him, all you peoples!
For mighty is his love for us;
> truly is he the Lord forever.

Glory to the Father, to the Son and to the Holy Spirit.
> **From age to age, amen, amen.**

Glorify the Lord, all the earth!
> **O Giver of Light, O Lord: we lift up praise to you!**

Server: Let us pray. Peace be with us.

Weekday Morning Prayer

Prayer of *Lakhu Mara*: It is the duty, O Lord, of heaven, earth and all therein to thank, adore and glorify you for all of your benefits and graces whose greatness cannot be repaid, O Lord of all, Father, Son and Holy Spirit, forever.
People:

LAKHU MARA

We give you thanks,	Lakhu Mara d-kulla
O Lord of all,	mawdenan,
we glorify you,	w-lakh Ysho' Mshyḥa
Jesus Christ;	mshabḥynan
you raise our bodies	d-attu Mnaḥmana
into life,	d-paghrayn,
you are the Savior	w-attu Paroqa
of our souls.	d-nawshathan.
In the morning, O Lord,	***Marya, b-ṣapra***
you hear my voice,	***tishma' qal,***
and in the morning	***wab-ṣapra***
I prepare and present	***ittayaw***
myself to you.	***w-ithḥze lakh.***
We give you thanks…	Lakhu Mara d-kulla…
Glory to the Father, to the Son	***Shuḥa l-Abba w-laBra***
and to the Holy Spirit.	***wal-Ruḥa d-Qudsha***
From age to age,	***min 'alam wa'dhamma***
amen, amen.	***l-'alam amen, w-amen.***
We give you thanks…	Lakhu Mara d-kulla…

Server: Let us pray. Peace be with us.
Prayer of Psalm 51: To you who resurrects our bodies in his mercies, and who answers and saves our souls by the silent command of his will, O great King of glory, Being who exists from eternity: we thank, adore, and glorify you, at all times, Lord of all, Father, Son, and Holy Spirit, forever.

Psalm 51

Have mercy on me, God, in *your* grace,
    and in your great mercies, *blot* out my sins.
Have mercy on me, O Lord.
Have mercy on me, God, in *your* grace,
    and in your great mercies, *blot* out my sins.

Wash me thoroughly from *my* guilt
    and purify *me* of my sins.
    For I know my *tres*passes,
        my sins are al*ways* before me.
    Against you alone *have* I sinned,
        and have evil *done* before you.
That you may be just in *your* word,
    and grant justice *when* you judge:
in *my* guilt was I conceived,
    and with sin my *moth*er bore me.
    But you delighted *in* the truth;
        and showed me the se*crets* of your wisdom.
    Sprinkle me with hyssop, and I *shall* be clean;
        wash me with it, I shall be *whi*ter than snow.
May your delight and gladness sus*tain* me,
    and my humble *bones* will rejoice.
Turn your face from *my* sins,
    and blot out all *of* my misdeeds.
    A pure heart create in *me*, O God,
        renew your creating *Spi*rit in me.
    Cast me not from *your* presence,
        nor deprive me of *your* Holy Spirit.
Rather, return your joy and salvation *to* me,
    may your glorious *Spi*rit sustain me,
that I may teach the wicked *your* ways,
    and sinners may *turn* back to you.
    Rescue me from bloodshed, *my* just God,
        and my tongue shall praise *your* righteousness.
    O Lord, open *my* lips;
        my mouth shall *speak* forth your praise.
You were not pleased in sac*ri*fice,
    nor considered *burnt* offerings.
The sacrifice of God is a hum*ble* spirit.
    God will not spurn *a* heart contrite.

Glory to the Father, to the Son and to the Ho*ly* Spirit.
    From age to age, *a*men, amen.
    Have mercy on me, O Lord.

Weekday Morning Prayer

Have mercy on me, God, in *your* grace,
  and in your great mercies, *blot* out my sins.
  Christ the King, have *mer*cy on me!

Morning Glorification

Glory to you, our God!
Thanksgiving to you,
  our Maker!
We bless you,
  our Fashioner!
O Tender Lord!
O Merciful God!
O Compassionate Creator!
O Savior, our Guardian!
Our Helper and Upholder!
We adore you, O Lord,
for patient is your Spirit
and great is your grace!
O Merciful One, forgive us
and have pity on us!
Turn to us in the greatness
of your mercies!
Our Support
and mighty Stronghold!
O Lord our God,
show us your face,
and we shall be saved!
O Accepter of the repentant
in his mercies:
accept our prayer
and our service!
O Hearer of the voice
of his adorers:
let our imploring
come before you,
and have mercy on us!

O Forgiver of the debts
of mortals in his pity,
forgive us our debts
and sins in your pity!
O Absolver of the sins
of mankind in his grace:
absolve our many sins,
and have mercy on us!
O Good Hope of mankind,
grant us peace and serenity,
that we may confess your Trinity,
O Lord of all, forever, amen.
Repeat 3x from "O Good Hope…"

They say: Let us pray. Peace be with us.
Prayer of Holy God: O Christ, O Good Hope of mankind and peaceful harbor granting peace to creatures: may you, O Lord, accomplish your peace and tranquility among us, that in it we may give thanks to you and praise you unceasingly all the days of our lives, O Lord of all, forever.

Server:

Lift your voices, all you people, and glorify the living God.	*Arym qalkhon, w-shabbaḥ kulleh ʿamma, l-Alaha ḥayya.*

People (in the melody of ordinary days):

Holy God,	Qaddysha Alaha
Holy Mighty One,	Qaddysha Ḥayilthana,
Holy Immortal One:	Qaddysha La Mayotha
Have mercy on us.	Ithraḥam ʿlayn.
Glory to the Father, to the Son and to the Holy Spirit.	*Shuḥa l-Aḅba w-laḄra wal-Ruḥa d-Qudsha.*
Holy God…	Qaddysha Alaha…
From age to age, amen, amen.	*Min ʿalam waʾdhamma l-ʿalam amen, w-amen.*
Holy God…	Qaddysha Alaha…

And they say *Aḅḅun d-bashmayya* in a simple tone (see above).

Weekday Morning Prayer

The Presider says the prayer before the Martyr Hymns: O Merciful One whose name is holy, Kind and Just One from eternity, whose grace and compassion overflow: may the sweet mercy of your love overflow, O Lord our God, upon the souls of your adorers who call and plead to you at all times and ages, Lord of all, Father, Son and Holy Spirit, forever.

Another: Bless, O Lord, your servants in your grace, guard your adorers from all dangers in the overflowing greatness of your compassion, shepherd, guide, aid and protect our lives under the wings of your providential love, and save, redeem, and deliver our bodies and souls from the evil one and his hosts, at all times and ages, Lord of all, Father, Son, and Holy Spirit, forever.

They say the morning MARTYR HYMNS of the day (pp. 353–88)

Every day, after the Martyr Hymns, they continue: – *m'yna d-ṭawatha*
At dawn of morning, we lift glory to your name,
>> for you have saved us and all the world.
>> Grant us in your grace
>> that our day be filled with peace,
>> and we beg you to forgive our sins.
Deny not our hope, do not close your door to us,
>> do not hold back of your saving grace,
>> and do not treat us
>> as our deeds deserve, O Lord,
>> for you alone know how weak we are.
Sow, Lord, in the world, love and peace and harmony,
>> uphold our priests, kings and governors,
>> grant peace to countries,
>> heal the sick, protect the poor,
>> forgive the sins of the sons of men.
Your grace protect us on the path we walk, O Lord,
>> as to David, the young man, from Saul.
>> Grant us in mercy
>> what we need for our sojourn,
>> that as you will, we may walk in peace.

The grace that guarded Moses the prophet at sea,
> and Daniel in the lion's den,
> and Hananiah's
> family in the furnace,
> protect us, Lord, from the evil one.

Continue:
We awake in the morning and adore the Father,
lift up praise to the Son and confess the Holy Spirit.
> May the grace of the Father, the mercy of the Son
> and the compassion of the Spirit – the Trinity's Mystery –
> be for our benefit all of our days.

Our help is in you, O true Doctor, Supporter:
apply the medicine of your mercies
and heal our wounds, lest we perish completely.
> Without your aid, we become even weaker,
> O Christ, who supports those who do his will:
> protect your adorers, that they keep your commands.

Let us plead in groaning and beg for mercies,
asking forgiveness from the Merciful One
who opens his door to all who turn to him.
> Day after day I promise you that tomorrow I will repent,
> but my days pass away and are gone, and my sins remain.
> O Christ, forgive me, and have mercy on me.

The Presider prays the prayer of the Martyrs: May the martyrs, O Lord our God, who defeated, humbled and eradicated the error of idolatry by the power and aid that is from you, and who lifted up and raised the true faith of your name, beg and plead on our behalf to your Majesty on the great and glorious day your Justice dawns from heaven, O Just and Merciful Judge and Forgiver of sins and faults, Lord of all, Father, Son and Holy Spirit, forever.

Another: To you, O Great, Beautiful and True Hope, whom the just and the prophets awaited in their age, the righteous pleased with their works, and the martyrs appeased by the precious blood that flowed from their necks, we beg and plead: grant us, O Lord our God, that we may take refuge in the power that is hidden in their bones and be aided by their prayers, and that with them, among them, within their ranks, around their dwellings, and in the glorious temples that were set apart for the honor of their service, we may be worthy to lift up glory, honor, thanksgiving and adoration to you, Lord of all, Father, Son and Holy Spirit, forever.

The priests pray and conclude as above on p. 26.

[During Lent, they replace the following antiphons:
Psalm 91: **You are my security, O Christ; I will never be put to shame.**
Psalm 104: **May the glory of the Lord be forever.**
Prayer after Psalm 104: To you, O Creator of all natures, Maker of all that exists, and Fashioner of height and depth in his grace and mercies, we lift up glory, honor, thanksgiving, and adoration, at all times, Lord of all, Father, Son, and Holy Spirit, forever.
Psalm 113: **Glory to him who created light.**
Psalm 93: **We adore your Divinity, O Lord.**
Psalm 148: Praise the Lord from the heavens, **Let them glorify God**...
   Praise the Lord from the earth, **Give Glory to God.**
Psalm 149: **To him is glory due.** Ending: **O Son of God, forgive us.**
Psalm 150: **To the Father, Son, and Holy Spirit.**
Psalm 116: **O Christ the Light, we praise you.**
Lakhu Mara: **To show your grace in the morning, and your faithfulness during times of night.**

During Lent they also pray:

MIDDAY PRAYER

They pray one *Hulala*, then continue with the Lenten Glorification and priestly prayer on p. 176.
Then they pray a seasonal glorification, and the Petitions on p. 240.
They pray *Qaddysha Alaha* and *Aḇḇun dba-shmayya*, and conclude as above on p. 26.]

Emmanuel Sunday Evening Prayer

Presider: Glory to God in the highest, peace on earth, and good hope to men, at all times and forever.
People:
Our Father who art in heaven,
hallowed be your name.
Your kingdom come.
Holy, holy, you are holy.
Our Father in heaven:
heaven and earth are full
of the greatness of your glory;
angels & men cry out to you:
holy, holy, you are holy.
Our Father who art in heaven,
hallowed be thy name.
Thy kingdom come,
thy will be done on earth
as it is in heaven.
Give us this day our daily bread
and forgive us our trespasses,
as we forgive those
who trespassed against us.
And lead us not into temptation,
but deliver us from evil,
for thine is the kingdom,
the power and the glory,
now and forever.
Presider: Glory to the Father, to the Son and to the Holy Spirit.
People: From age to age, amen, amen. Our Father who art in heaven, hallowed be your name. Your kingdom come.
Holy, holy, you are holy.
Our Father in heaven:

Aḅḅun dba-shmayya
nithqaddash shmakh,
tethe malkuthakh,
qaddysh, qaddysh, qaddysh-at,
Aḅḅun dba-shmayya.
Damlen shmayya w-ar'a
rabbuth shuḥakh,
'yre w-nasha qa'en lakh
qaddysh, qaddysh, qaddysh-at.
Aḅḅun dba-shmayya
nithqaddash shmakh,
tethe malkuthakh,
nehwe ṣiw-yanakh
aykanna dba-shmayya ap b-ar'a,
haw lan laḥma d-sunqanan
yawmana wa-shwoq lan ḥawbayn
wa-ḥtahayn aykanna d-ap ḥnan
shwaqn l-ḥay-yawayn,
w-la ta'lan l-nisyona
illa paṣan min bysha
miṭṭul d-dhylakh-y malkutha,
w-ḥayla w-tish-buḥta
l-'alam 'almyn, amen.
Presider: Shuḥa l-Aḅḅa wla-Bra wal-Ruḥa d-Qudsha.
People: Min 'alam wa-'dham-ma l-'alam amen w-amen.
Aḅḅun dba-shmayya nithqaddash shmakh, tethe malkuthakh,
Qaddysh, qaddysh, qaddysh-at,
Aḅḅun dba-shmayya.

heaven and earth are full of the greatness of your glory; angels & men cry out to you: holy, holy, you are holy.	*Damlen shmayya w-ar'a rabbuth shuḥakh, 'yre w-nasha qa'en lakh qaddysh, qaddysh, qaddysh-at.*

Server: Let us pray. Peace be with us.

Presider: We confess your Divinity, O Lord, with spiritual praises, adore your Majesty with earthly adorations, and glorify your hidden Nature with pure intentions and holy, unstained thoughts, O Lord of all, Father, Son and Holy Spirit, forever.

People: Amen.

Marmytha
Psalm 65

To you is glory due in Zion, O God. **Halleluiah.**
 To you is glory due in Zion, O God.
And to you vows are fulfilled: hear my prayer!
 To you all flesh will come.
The words of the wicked are stronger than I,
 but you forgive my sins.
Blessed is he in whom you are pleased,
 and whom you bring near to dwell in your lodging.
Who is filled with the good things of your house,
 with the holiness of your temple,
 and with your awesome righteousness.
Answer, O God our Savior!
 The Hope of all the ends of the earth,
 and of the distant nations!
He establishes the mountains in his power;
 they are made strong by his might!
He stills the roarings of the sea
 and the sound of their waves.
The nations and the dwellers of earth are awestruck,
 by your signs and the procession of morning and evening.
You have surrounded the earth with glory.
 You have given it rest and greatly enriched it.
The vessels of God are filled with water:

you prepared their food when you fashioned them.
You have drenched the furrows, that fruits may grow.
    Through dew the growth increases and is blessed.
Bless the crown of the year in your grace,
    and your calves will be fed with grass.
    They will be fed from the lodgings in the wilderness.
With glory the hills will be girt,
    and the choice lambs will be clothed.
The valleys will be filled with crops:
    they will shout with joy and praise!

Glory to the Father, to the Son and to the Holy Spirit.
    From age to age, amen, amen.
Halleluiah, halleluiah, halleluiah.

[During Advent and Christmas Seasons, they sing:

MARMYTHA

Psalm 87

Its foundations are on his holy mountain: **Halleluiah.**
    Its foundations are on his holy mountain:
the Lord loves the gates of Zion
    more than all of Jacob's dwellings.
Honorable things are said in you,
    O village of our God.
You will be remembered in Egypt and known in Babylon,
    Philistia, Tyre, and among the Cushites.
That man will be born there,
    and of Zion it shall be said:
the Great One shall be born there,
    and he has established her.
The Lord will count his people in his register:
    that man will be born there.
The leaders who dwell in you will rejoice,
    as well as all the lowly within you.

Glory to the Father, to the Son and to the Holy Spirit.
    From age to age, amen, amen.
Halleluiah, halleluiah, halleluiah.]

Emmanuel Sunday Evening Prayer

INCENSE AND LUCERNARY RITE

Server: Let us pray. Peace be with us.

Priest: To you, O Gracious and Kind One, Compassionate and Merciful, the great King of Glory, the Being who is from eternity: we give thanks, adore and glorify you at all times, Lord of all, Father, Son and Holy Spirit, forever.

People: Amen.

HYMN OF INCENSE – *akh 'iṭra*

- **How lovely are your tabernacles, Lord God almighty!**
- **My soul longs and yearns for the courts of the Lord!**

Like a cloud of fine incense and the smell of a sweet thurible,
accept, O Christ our Savior, the pleading and the prayer of your servants!

They bring the thurible before the sanctuary.

Server: Peace be with us.

Presider: To you, O great Sun of Righteousness who dawned in the latter days for the salvation of mankind and who enlightens the darkness of our minds at all times of night and day: we ask you, O Lord our God, to enlighten the paths of our lives by your life-giving teaching and to strengthen our hearts by your faithful promise, as we light our lamps with the oil that is from your grace, and come out to meet you with hosannas.

And for all your benefits and graces toward us that cannot be repaid, we give you thanks and praise you unceasingly in your crowned Church, full of all benefits and blessings, for you are the Lord and Creator of all, forever.

People: Amen.

LAKHU MARA

We give you thanks,	*Lakhu Mara d-kulla*
O Lord of all,	*mawdenan,*
we glorify you,	*w-lakh Ysho' Mshyḥa*
Jesus Christ;	*mshabḥynan*
you raise our bodies	*d-attu Mnaḥmana*
into life,	*d-paghrayn,*
you are the Savior	*w-attu Paroqa*
of our souls.	*d-nawshathan.*

Emmanuel Sunday Evening Prayer

I rejoiced when I heard them say: we are going to the house of the Lord!	*Ḥdhyth kadh amryn waw ly: l-bayteh d-Marya azynan!*
We give you thanks...	*Lakhu Mara d-kulla...*
Glory to the Father, to the Son and to the Holy Spirit.	*Shuḥa l-Aḅḅa w-laḄra wal-Ruḥa d-Qudsha*
From age to age, amen, amen.	*min ʿalam waʾdhamma l-ʿalam amen, w-amen.*
We give you thanks...	*Lakhu Mara d-kulla...*

They open the curtain, incense the sanctuary and light the lucernary.
Server: Let us pray. Peace be with us.
Priest: Lord, you are indeed the One who raises our bodies, the true Savior of our souls, and the constant Guardian of our lives. It is thus our duty to thank, adore and glorify you who are Lord of all forever.
People: Amen.

PSALMODIES & HYMNS "BEFORE"
Former Sunday (Ps. 49:1–5)

Hear this, *all* you peoples,
   Halleluiah, halleluiah, *h*alleluiah.
Hear this, *all* you peoples,
   give heed, all who dwell in the world,
   men both high and low, rich *and* poor alike!
My lips will speak *words* of wisdom.
   My heart *is* full of insight.
I will turn my mind *to* a parable,
   with the harp I *will* solve my problem.
Glory to the Father, to the Son and to the *H*o*l*y Spirit.
   From age to age, *a*men, amen.
Halleluiah, *h*alleluiah, *h*alleluiah.

Hymns – *shlyḥe qaddyshe*

- Come, let us praise the Lord.
O mortals, come,
let us thank and praise
him who has destroyed
death and all its power,

and has given life to men
by his dying on the cross.
- **Come, let us bless and adore.**
We worship you,
O Redeeming Lord,
for you raise and save
all the baptized
who have passed on
and who have
confessed your name,
and your dying on the cross.
- **Glory to the Father, to the Son and to the Holy Spirit.**
Glory to you
who have promised life
to the mortal race
through your rising up
from the grave,
let us give you thanks
and praise, you alone
who raise the dead.

Latter Sunday (Ps. 136:1–4)

By the rivers of *Ba*bylon
    Halleluiah, halleluiah, *h*alleluiah.
By the rivers of *Ba*bylon
    there we sat and wept, *r*emembering Zion;
on the poplars *that* grew there
    we *hung* up our harps.
For it was there *that* they asked us,
    our captors, for songs, our oppressors, for joy.
    "Sing to us," they said, "one *of* Zion's songs."
Glory to the Father, to the Son and to the *Ho*ly Spirit.
    From age to age, *a*men, amen.
Halleluiah, *h*alleluiah, *h*alleluiah.

Hymns - *'am kulhon qaddyshayk*

- Gladden your servant's soul.
Give rest, O Christ the King,
to all of your servants' souls,
with your saints in harmony,
where there is no suffering,
and no sickness or distress,
but only kingly eternal life.

- Our Lord is great and glorious!
Our support is in our God,
Fashioner of Adam's race,
Hope of both our death and life.
This world is not any thing,
as its comforts are as well,
and so, raise us, give us life in grace.

- Glory to the Father, to the Son and to the Holy Spirit.
Christ the King, our Savior:
raise us on the day you come,
and set us at your right hand,
with the just who did your will,
who believed, confessed your cross,
that, one with them,
we may live in you.

FIXED EVENING PSALMODY

Server: Let us pray. Peace be with us.
Presider: It is our duty, O Lord our God, to thank, adore and glorify you for your mercy and your providential will for us, at all times, O Lord of all, Father, Son and Holy Spirit, forever.
People: Amen.

Emmanuel Sunday Evening Prayer

Psalm 140

I have called to you, Lord; hasten to *help* me!
    Hearken to my words and *a*ccept my prayer.
I have called to you, Lord; hasten to *help* me!
    Hearken to my words and *a*ccept my prayer.
Let my prayer arise before you like *in*cense,
    the offering of my hands like an eve*ning* oblation.
Set, O Lord, a guard over my *mouth*
    and a guard *o*ver my lips!
That my heart may not turn to an evil *deed*,
    or accompl*ish* works of wickedness.
May I not dine with evil *men*.
    Let a just man teach *me* and reprove me.
But let the oil of the wicked not anoint my *head*,
    for my prayer is *a*gainst their malice.
Their judges were thrown down by a rock-like *hand*,
    then they heard that *my* words were kind,
Like a plough that scatters the *ground*.
    Their bones were strewn at *the* mouth of Sheol.
To you, Lord God, I lift up my *eyes*:
    I trust you; do not cast *my* soul away!
Guard me from the hands of the *boastful*,
    who *set* traps for me.
Let the wicked fall together into their own *nets*
    while I pursue *my* way unharmed.

Psalm 141

With my voice I called to the *Lord*,
    with my voice *I* begged the Lord.
I lifted my pleading be*fore* him;
    I showed *him* my distress.
When my spirit trembled, you knew my *path*.
    On the way I walked they set *a* trap for me.
I looked to my right and *saw*:
    there was no *one* to advise me.
I had no means of es*cape*,
    not one who *cared* for my soul.

Emmanuel Sunday Evening Prayer

I cried to you, Lord; I said: you are my *hope*,
    all that I have in the *land* of the living.
Hearken then to my *plead*ing,
    for I am *brought* very low.
Rescue me from those who pur*sue* me,
    for they are *strong*er than I.
Bring my soul out of this *pri*son,
    that I may give *thanks* to your name.
Your just ones will a*wait* me
    as you *grant* me reward.

Psalm 118:105–12

Your word is a lamp for my *feet*
    and a *light* for my paths.
I have sworn and made up my *mind*
    to keep *your* just decrees.
Lord, I am deeply affl*ic*ted:
    give me *life* by your word.
Be pleased, Lord, with the words of my *mouth*
    and teach me *by* your decrees.
My soul is in your hands at all *times*;
    I will not *for*get your law.
Though sinners laid traps for *me*,
    I did not stray *from* your commands.
Your witness is my heritage for*ever*,
    for it is the *joy* of my heart.
I set my heart to carry out your *stat*utes
    in *truth*, for ever.

Glory to the Father, to the Son and to the Holy *Spir*it.
    From age to age, *a*men, amen.
I have called to you, Lord; hasten to *help* me!
    Hearken to my words and *accept* my prayer.

Server: Let us pray. Peace be with us.

Priest: Hear, O Lord our God, the prayer of your servants in your mercy; accept the supplication of your adorers in your compassion, and pity our sinfulness in your grace and mercies, O Healer of our bodies and Good Hope of our souls at all times O Lord of all, Father, Son and Holy Spirit, forever.

Emmanuel Sunday Evening Prayer

PSALMODIES & HYMNS "AFTER"
Former Sunday (Ps. 89:5–9)

The heavens proclaim your won*ders*, O Lord;
Halleluiah, halleluiah, *h*alleluiah.
The heavens proclaim your won*ders*, O Lord;
    and your faithfulness in the *church* of your saints.
Who is like the Lord in the hea*ven* of heavens,
    or compares to him among *the* sons of God?
God stands in the church *of* the saints,
    great and fearful *to* all around him.
O Lord *God* almighty,
    who is po*wer*ful like you?
Glory to the Father, to the Son and to the *Ho*ly Spirit.
    From age to age, *a*men, amen.
Halleluiah, *h*alleluiah, *h*alleluiah.

Hymns – *niṭṭayaw*

- Turn your ear, and answer me.
Messiah, who came to save
and renew Adam's face
which had rotted in disgrace,
who took on our flesh,
in it redeemed us,
giving us strength
to be raised from death:
forgive your servants in grace,
when you come again!
- Because of your grace, O God.
In grace, you created us
when the world first began,
vested us with radiance
in Paradise,
but in rebellion,
we sinned and fell.
Then you sent your Son,
and in his mercy we have
kingly, eternal life.

Emmanuel Sunday Evening Prayer

- Glory to the Father, to the Son and to the Holy Spirit.
We praise you, O Christ our King,
for you gained victory:
through your cross
you saved our race
from Satan's deceit.
May you renew us,
abolish death,
let your new life reign
and make us fit for mercy,
O Resurrecting King!

Latter Sunday (Ps. 126:1–5)

If the Lord does not *build* the house,
    Halleluiah, halleluiah, *h*alleluiah.
If the Lord does not *build* the house,
    in vain do *its* builders labor;
if the Lord does not *guard* the village,
    in vain do *its* watchmen keep vigil.
In vain is their ear*lier* rising,
    their going later to rest and eating *their* bread in toil.
Thus he grants his be*loved* slumber,
    for sons are *the* Lord's inheritance.
Glory to the Father, to the Son and to the *Ho*ly Spirit.
    From age to age, *a*men, amen.
Halleluiah, *h*alleluiah, *h*alleluiah.

Hymns– *malka mnaḥmana*

- For he comes to judge the earth.
The King who raises:
he is dawning from above
in radiance, giving life to all,
and all together
will arise from every tomb,
and lift up praise
to their raising King!

Emmanuel Sunday Evening Prayer

- All you servants of God.
Let sadness pass by
from your hearts,
O mortal ones,
for his day dawns,
and will gladden us,
awaken us all,
when the watchers
will rejoice
before his throne,
on the day he comes.
- Glory to the Father, to the Son and to the Holy Spirit.
May our deceased live,
and their bodies all be raised
as prophesied
Isaiah, who said:
"The sleeping will rise,
and those buried in the earth."
For your renewal
is of Light and Truth.

LITURGICAL SEASON

Server: Lift your voices, all you people, and glorify the living God.
People:

Holy God,	*Qaddysha Alaha*
Holy Mighty One,	*Qaddysha Ḥayilthana,*
Holy Immortal One:	*Qaddysha La Mayotha*
Have mercy on us.	*Ithraḥam 'layn.*
Glory to the Father, to the Son	***Shuḥa l-Aḅḅa w-laḄra***
and to the Holy Spirit.	***wal-Ruḥa d-Qudsha.***
Holy God...	*Qaddysha Alaha...*
From age to age,	***Min 'alam wa'dhamma***
amen, amen.	***l-'alam amen, w-amen.***
Holy God...	*Qaddysha Alaha...*

They say: Let us pray. Peace be with us.

Priest: To you, O Holy One who is holy in his Nature and glorious in his Existence, and high and exalted above all in his Divinity, the Nature that is holy and blessed from eternity, do we give thanks, adore and glorify at all times, O Lord of all, Father, Son and Holy Spirit, forever.
People: Amen.

EVENING PSALMODY OF THE WEEK (see pp. 389–578)

Server: Let us pray. Peace be with us.
Priest: To your wondrous and indescribable providence, O Lord, which was accomplished, completed and perfected in mercies and pity for the renewal and the salvation of our weak race through the Principal that is from us, do we lift up glory, honor, thanksgiving and adoration at all times, O Lord of all, Father, Son and Holy Spirit, forever.
People: Amen.

BASILICA HYMN OF THE WEEK (see pp. 389–578)

Then, From Advent to Epiphany:

- Glory to the Father, to the Son, and to the Holy Spirit.
God advised and promised Abraham from the beginning, "through your seed, all the sinful nations shall be blessed, who were dead in their sins and lost in error." For he gathered them and healed their wounds, as the prophet saw from ages ago, "he will take on their wounds and carry their sicknesses." For this we cry out as we say: glory to you, O Son of the Lord of All!

During Epiphany:

- Glory to the Father, to the Son, and to the Holy Spirit.
The three Individuals of Existence have dawned and been revealed in the created world in the latter times upon the Jordan: the Father who cried out and made his voice heard from on high: "this is my Son and my Beloved," and the Spirit who makes the true faith known to us.

Note that there is no "continuation" from Lent to Pentecost.

During the Season of the Apostles:
- Glory to the Father, to the Son, and to the Holy Spirit.
O Christ, who chose his apostles and clothed them with the power of the Spirit, that they may be preachers in the world and reveal his glory and Divinity in creation through the mighty works of their hands: gladden your churches with peace and harmony, and lift up the head of the preachers of your name and the keepers of your commandments. With your right hand, O Lord, may our salvation be guarded, and may they preach your righteousness in the peace that comes from you.

During the Season of Repentance:
- Glory to the Father, to the Son, and to the Holy Spirit.
Answer your adorers, O Christ, and send us from your treasury pity, mercies, salvation and the forgiveness of sins; and, as you answered Daniel from the den of lions and the house of Hananiah in the furnace of fire, deliver us also, O Lord, from kings and rulers, evil people and rebellious demons, who advance to destroy us like lions. With your mighty power, pacify their ferocity, deliver us from their wickedness, abolish their dominion, and gladden us with your salvation, O Christ the King!

During the Season of the Cross:
- Glory to the Father, to the Son, and to the Holy Spirit.
Through the great power of the cross, the Church has gained a boast over death and over Satan, rejoices in salvation, and extols it in glory before the eyes of the enemies of Truth, for it exalted her abasement with the power that it made to dwell in her. And lo, on the day of its finding, her children shout with hymns of praise: "O General who gave victory to her in battle, keep your promise." The glory of your revelation is the boast of her children!

During the Crowning of the Church:
- Glory to the Father, to the Son, and to the Holy Spirit.
You have made this holy house, O Lord, the pedestal of your dwelling. Order it, O Lord, with your hands. May the prayers and tears of the weary be accepted in it, may all benefits and gifts flow from it to your people and the sheep of your flock, those saved by your cross and taking refuge in the name of your Majesty.

Then also, from Christmas to Lent, and after Pentecost:

- From age to age, amen, amen.

O holy virgin Mary, mother of Jesus our Savior: plead and implore for mercies from the Child who dawned from your womb, that in his grace he may make times of distress pass by us and establish peace and serenity for us; and through your prayers, may the Church and her children be guarded from the evil one. On the glorious day when his Greatness is revealed, may we be worthy to delight with you in the bridal chamber of Light.

PETITIONS

Server: Let us all stand composed.

In faith and hope, let us implore and say: Lord, have mercy on us.

People: Lord, have mer*cy* on us. | *Maran ithraḥam 'layn.*

Server:

* O Father of mercies and God of every con*so*lation, we *im*plore you…

* Our Savior, our Caretaker and Provider *for* all, we *im*plore you…

* For the peace, concord and well-being of the whole world and of *all* churches, we *im*plore you…

* For the well-being of our country and of all countries, and for the protection of all the faithful who inha*bit* them, we *im*plore you…

* For good weather, a fertile season, the abundance of fruits and all the poor *and* needy, we *im*plore you…

* For the health of our holy fathers: [Mar _____, High Pontiff, Pope of Rome,] Mar _____, Catholicos-Patriarch, Mar _____, Bishop/Metropolitan, and for all those in the same pries*tly* service, we *im*plore you…

* For the priests and deacons of our Church, and for all of our Chris*tian* brethren, we *im*plore you…

* O One who does not desire that a sinner should die, but rather that he should repent from evil *and* live, we *im*plore you…

* O One through whose holy <u>Birth</u> [or <u>Dawning</u>, or <u>Fasting</u>, or <u>Resurrection</u>, or <u>Ascension</u>, or <u>Spirit</u>, or <u>Cross</u>] has gladdened earth and deligh*ted* heaven, we *im*plore you…

* Save us all, O Christ our Lord, in your grace, increase your peace and your tranquility within us and have mer*cy* on us…

Server: Let us entrust our souls mutually to the Father, and to the Son, and to *the* Holy Spirit.

People: To you, O Lord our God.

During Lent, the say the LENTEN PETITIONS on p. 180.

Presider: To you, Lord God almighty do we entrust our bodies and our souls, and from you, O Lord our God, do we receive all benefits and blessings; and so, as the crown of our prayer, in that confidence that is from you, we call together upon you and say thus:
People: *Aḥḥun dba-shmayya...*(as above, p. 141)

Server: *Barekh mar.*
Server says to the people: Bow your heads for the prayer and accept the blessing.

FINAL BLESSING

Presider: Glory to you, O Jesus our victorious King, eternal Image of the Father, Begotten One without beginning, above the ages and creations, without whom we have neither hope nor expectation, O Creator! By the prayer of the just and chosen who have pleased you from the beginning, grant forgiveness for our sins, absolution for our faults, deliverance from our troubles and response to our requests. Bring us to your joyous Light and guard us, through your living cross, from all perils, hidden or manifest; now, at all times, and forever and ever.

Emmanuel Sunday Vigil

Server: Peace be with us.

Presider: May our prayer rise before you like incense, O Lord, may our supplication enter your presence, and may the requests of our neediness be answered from the great treasury of your mercy, at all times and ages, O Lord of all, Father, Son and Holy Spirit, forever.

People: Amen.

A Seasonal Hymn of the Week (see pp. 389–578)

Server: Let us pray. Peace be with us.

Priest: To your wondrous and indescribable providence, O Lord, which was accomplished, completed and perfected in mercies and pity for the renewal and the salvation of our weak race through the Principal that is from us, do we lift up glory, honor, thanksgiving and adoration at all times, O Lord of all, Father, Son and Holy Spirit, forever.

People: Amen.

Weekly Psalmody (see pp. 389–578)

Seasonal Glorification (see pp. 159–66)

Server: Let us pray. Peace be with us.

Priest: To you, O Hidden one in his Being, mysterious in his Divinity and incomprehensible in his glory, the great King of glory, the Being who exists from eternity: we give thanks, adore and glorify you at all times, Lord of all, Father, Son and Holy Spirit, forever.

People: Amen.

Basilica Hymn of the Week (see pp. 389–578)

Emmanuel Sunday Vigil

PETITIONS

Server: Let us all stand composed. In faith and hope, let us implore *and* say: Lord, have mer*cy* on us.

People: Lord, have mer*cy* on us. | *Maran ithraḥam ʿlayn.*

Server:

* O One who taught us to pray with*out* weariness, we *im*plore you...

* O One who kept vigil in prayer to God for the salvation of *our* race, we *im*plore you...

* O One who gave us an example of his mercy in our earth*ly* fathers, we *im*plore you...

* O One who saved us from violent deaths, and in whom we hope for *sal*vation, we *im*plore you...

* O One who saved us from the dominion of darkness and brought us into the kingdom of his belo*ved* Son, we *im*plore you...

* O One who said: "ask and it shall be given to you, seek and you shall find, knock and the treasure of mercies will be opened *for* you," we *im*plore you...

* For the health of our holy fathers: [Mar _____, High Pontiff, Pope of Rome,] Mar _____, Catholicos-Patriarch, Mar _____, Bishop/Metropolitan, and for all those in the same priest*ly* service, we *im*plore you...

* For the priests and deacons of our Church, and for all of our Chris*tian* brethren, we *im*plore you...

* O Compassionate God, who guides all in *his* mercy, we *im*plore you...

* O One who is glorified in heaven and worshipped *on* earth, we implore you...

* Give us victory, O Christ our Lord, in your coming, give peace to your Church saved by your precious Blood, and have mer*cy* on us...

Server: Let us entrust our souls mutually to the Father, and to the Son, and to *the* Holy Spirit.

People: To you, *O* Lord our God.

FINAL BLESSING

Presider: Be a guardian that never sleeps and a surrounding wall in which your flock may dwell, that they may not be harmed by the wolves that thirst for the blood of your sheep, for you are the Sea that never fails, O Lord of all, Father, Son and Holy Spirit, forever.

Seasonal Glorifications

Subara and Nativity
Attributed to Babai the Great

O blessed Mercy, Gracefulness,
    who led our life through the prophets:
Isaiah saw, with Spirit's eye,
    the marvel Child of Divinity.
    For Mary bore, in virgin womb,
        'Ammanuel, the Son of God.
    For from her womb, the Spirit formed
        the Flesh made One, as is written,
to be the Dwelling-Place adored
    of the Radiance from the Father,
and, from his first conception made
    in honor One, in a wonder,
    that all in him may be fulfilled
        for salvation of all people.
    The angels cried, when he was born,
        "halleluiah," in heaven above,
and those on earth in love adored,
    through their offerings, in one honor.
For Christ is One, the Son of God,
    by all adored in two Natures:
    as God Divine, of Father born,
        eternally, from all ages;
    humanity, of Mary born,
        as is written, in his body.
As God, without a mother born,
    without father in his manhood.
Two Qnome, Natures unconfused,
    one Person, single Sonship.
    And, where the Godhead deigns to dwell,
        three Qnome, one Divinity.
    Therefore, the Sonship of the Son:
        in two Natures, single Person.

For thus the holy Church has learned:
    confess the Son who is the Christ.
Adore we your Divinity
    and your Manhood undivided.
One Power and One Majesty,
    One Will, One Mind and One Glory,
to Father, Son and Holy Ghost,
    from age to age, amen, amen.

Epiphany
Attributed to Babai of Nisibis

Praise the mercies that sent you to us,
    O Christ the Sun of Righteousness,
O Light that shone from David's house,
    and called the nations to repent!
Come, penitent, plead for mercies
    while there is time for penitence.
Each one forgive all in his heart,
    ask for mercies with unveiled face.
Hear our pleading, grant our requests,
    O Christ, who loves the penitent.
Do not turn from our pleading, Lord,
    for we approach with groaning souls!
You know our wickedness is great,
    extend your Mercy's hand to us.
You likened us to the younger son,
    who wasted his inheritance.
We have sinned and have enraged you:
    forgive us, O merciful Lord!
May your mercies be moved by our sins,
    for we were bought by your own Blood.
With the widow we plead, O Judge:
    forgive our faults, erase our sins,
O Gracious One who takes himself
    the full weight of our sinfulness!
May your cross be our great fortress,
    that drives away the devil's power.

On the day when all Adam's sons
    shake off all the dust of the ground,
and everyone wakes from the sleep
    of unescaped mortality,
in that judgment when good and bad
    are given pay for all they did,
your Pity be our advocate,
    and judge us not to be condemned.
On that day when your mercies dawn,
    let us meet you as is your will,
and sing praise to Divinity
    with all the saints who have loved you,
and let us all lift up glory
    to Father, Son and Holy Spirit.
To him be praise from all the Church,
    forever and ever, amen.

BA'UTHA AND LENT

In pain and tears and fervent prayer,
    we cry to you, good Lord above!
Be our healer and our wise guide:
    deep are our wounds; bitter our pain.
We have no right to plead to you:
    our faults abound, our malice soars.
The sea and land, and all therein,
    have quaked and raged due to our sin.
In our own time, as Scripture says,
    the end of days has come upon us.
In mercy, save us from distress,
    for height and depth have been confused.
O Good Shepherd, come tend your flock,
    for whose sake you endured the cross.
Make peace for us in Church and world,
    that we may live a tranquil life.
May we be yours, as is your will:
    Father, and Son, and Holy Spirit.
    From age to age, amen, amen.

Emmanuel Sunday Vigil

HOLY WEEK
Attributed to Theodore the Interpreter

Glory to *God* in the highest!
Peace on earth!
Good hope to *the* sons of men!
We adore, glorify, *and* exalt you!
Being *wi*thout beginning!
Secret, incompre*hen*sible Nature!
Father, Son *and* Holy Spirit!
King of Kings *and* Lord of Lords!
Who dwells *in* radiant Light!
Which none *on* earth can see!
Holy, Almighty, Im*mor*tal alone!
We *give* thanks to you!
Through our Media*tor* Jesus Christ!
The Sav*ior* of the world!
The Son *of* the Most High!
The liv*ing* Lamb of God!
Who takes away the *sin* of the world!
Have *mer*cy on us!
Who sits at the right *hand* of his Father!
Accept our *sup*plication!
For you are *our* God and Lord!
You are *our* King and Savior!
You are the Forgi*ver* of our sins!
The eyes of all look to *you*, Jesus Christ!
Glory *to* God your Father!
To you and to *the* Holy Spirit!
Forever and *ever*, amen!

Easter, Ascension, Apostles and Cross
Attributed to Narsai

All thanks to him who saved our race
    from slavery to sin and death!
He reconciled us with the hosts
    above, who scorned us for our sin.
    Blessed is he who had mercy,
        who sought and found us, and rejoiced.
    He symbolized our straying and
        returning in his parable:
He named our race the heir and son,
    who strayed, returned, who died and rose.
He gladdened all the hosts above
    through our return and our rising.
    The great love which the Lover of
        our race showed cannot be described:
    For from our race, he took on flesh,
        and reconciled us to himself.
It is a thing too great for us;
    it is a new thing he has done:
he has made his temple our flesh,
    in which he is worshipped by all.
    O Come, earthly and heavenly,
      and marvel at our lofty place:
    our race has reached the greatest height
      of infinite Divinity!
Heaven and earth and all therein
    give thanks to him who renewed us,
For he has wiped our sins away,
    named us his name, and has crowned us.
    Worthy is he of praise and thanks
        from every mouth, who raised us up.
    Let us proclaim our praise to him,
        forever and ever, amen.

Emmanuel Sunday Vigil
REPENTANCE

O soul that aged in wickedness,
    awake, be new through penitence!
With pain and tears, take medicine
    and bandage up your fallen face.
Cry out and lay out all your sins,
    that the Kind One may pity you.
Because you loved passing beauty,
    yours is destroyed, daughter of Light.
You ruined your body's temple,
    through weakness, you made it a slave.
O wretched one, till when will you
    take comfort in such passing things?
Quake and be frightened of that fire
    that you enkindle with your deeds.
So many sins have drowned your head
    like water, from the time of youth.
You drown in the sea of despair,
    because you dismissed penitence.
O you who are slave to desire,
    remember those who came before.
How long will your Judge be patient,
    while you keep drowning in your sins?
Do not forget that awful day
    when your secrets will be revealed.
Who will make an excuse for you?
    There, each one will defend himself.
Sufferings will pour out like soldiers,
    will ruin you, and will move on.
Good Hope who dawned upon our lives,
    pity the soul that forgets you!
I am your sheep, but I was trapped
    by the devil in wickedness.
Come, Lord, find me – seek what is yours,
    for I wasted your inheritance.

You bore the cross for all sinners:
    I am of them – remember me!
The devil has robbed me from you,
    strike him and take me from his hands.
O Lover of Mankind, love me,
    for I have no hope beside you.
Glory to you, O Son of God,
    who is so patient with sinners.
Thanksgiving to you from the lost,
    whom you have found and saved from death.
All glory to your Father, ours,
    and to the Spirit, Paraclete.
Let us all lift up praise to you,
    forever and ever, amen.

Church
Attributed to George of Nisibis

Glory to you, O Christ our King,
    O Son of God, adored by all.
You are our Lord, you are our God,
    the Head of life, our blessed Hope.
All those above and those below,
    praise you in song, with one accord.
As they confess you, Hidden One
    who was revealed in our flesh and blood.
When you unveiled your love and wished
    to come in flesh and free our race,
you healed our wounds, forgave our sins,
    and raised our death in your mercies.
You founded the one Church on earth,
    after the model of heaven.
In types, you signed; in love, betrothed;
    in mercy, took; in pain, made whole.
The hater of mankind shakes her,
    in impudence, through his servants.

Do not forget the holy Church,
    and make true your promise to her.
Let her beauty not be besmirched,
    nor her richness be bankrupted.
Remember your words to Peter:
    complete in deed the promise made.
Strengthen her doors, make strong her bars,
    raise up her horn, exalt her floors.
Bless her sons and guard her children,
    raise up her priests and shame her foes.
Let your peace dwell within her gates,
    eradicate all that divides.
Grant us to dwell in peace and love,
    in the true confession of faith,
as we keep true to our household,
    in good hope and in perfect love.
May our deeds be pleasing to you;
    may we find mercy when you judge.
And may we lift up perfect praise,
    to Father, Son, and Holy Spirit.
To him glory in every age,
    and every time, amen, amen.

Emmanuel Sunday Morning Prayer

Same as the Traditional Morning Prayer, ending after Daniel 3:57–88, or after "Glory to God in the Highest" if Mass does not follow. See p. 46.

Emmanuel Weekday Evening Prayer

Server: Peace be with us.

Presider: It is right at all times for us to thank, adore and glorify the great and awesome, holy and blessed, lofty and incomprehensible name of your glorious Trinity, and your grace toward our race, O Lord of all, Father, Son and Holy Spirit, forever.

People: Amen.

Lucernary

We give you thanks,	Lakhu Mara d-kulla
O Lord of all,	mawdenan,
we glorify you,	w-lakh Ysho' Mshyḥa
Jesus Christ;	mshabḥynan
you raise our bodies	d-attu Mnaḥmana
into life,	d-paghrayn,
you are the Savior	w-attu Paroqa
of our souls.	d-nawshathan.
I rejoiced when I heard	**Ḥdhyth kadh amryn waw ly:**
them say: we are going	**l-bayteh d-Marya**
to the house of the Lord!	**azynan!**
We give you thanks…	Lakhu Mara d-kulla…
Glory to the Father, to the Son	**Shuḥa l-Aḫḫa w-laḆra**
and to the Holy Spirit.	**wal-Ruḥa d-Qudsha**
From age to age,	**min 'alam wa'dhamma**
amen, amen.	**l-'alam amen, w-amen.**
We give you thanks…	Lakhu Mara d-kulla…

They open the curtain, incense the sanctuary, and light the lucernary.

Server: Let us pray. Peace be with us.

Priest: Lord, you alone are the Lamp of Truth who puts away the cloud of ignorance from our minds in his guiding light, and the one in whose loving scent our souls find delight and are renewed. Accept the rational oblations of our hearts, O Lord our God, at this eventide, for to you do we lift up glory, honor, thanksgiving and adoration, Lord of all forever.

People: Amen.

Psalmody & Hymns "Before" (see pp. 185–224)

Emmanuel Weekday Evening Prayer

Fixed Evening Psalmody

Server: Let us pray. Peace be with us.

Priest: It is our duty, O Lord our God, to thank, adore and glorify you for your mercy and your providential will for us, at all times, O Lord of all, Father, Son and Holy Spirit, forever.

People: Amen.

Psalm 140

I have called to you, Lord; hasten to *help* me!
  Hearken to my words and *ac*cept my prayer.
I have called to you, Lord; hasten to *help* me!
  Hearken to my words and *ac*cept my prayer.
Let my prayer arise before you like *in*cense,
  the offering of my hands like an eve*ning* oblation.
Set, O Lord, a guard over my *mouth*
  and a guard *o*ver my lips!
That my heart may not turn to an evil *deed*,
  or accompl*ish* works of wickedness.
May I not dine with evil *men*.
  Let a just man teach *me* and reprove me.
But let the oil of the wicked not anoint my *head*,
  for my prayer is *a*gainst their malice.
Their judges were thrown down by a rock-like *hand*,
  then they heard that *my* words were kind,
Like a plough that scatters the *ground*.
  Their bones were strewn at *the* mouth of Sheol.
To you, Lord God, I lift up my *eyes*:
  I trust you; do not cast *my* soul away!
Guard me from the hands of the *boastful*,
  who *set* traps for me.
Let the wicked fall together into their own *nets*
  while I pursue *my* way unharmed.

Psalm 141

With my voice I called to the *Lord*,
  with my voice *I* begged the Lord.
I lifted my pleading be*fore* him;
  I showed *him* my distress.

When my spirit trembled, you knew my *path*.
    On the way I walked they set *a* trap for me.
I looked to my right and *saw*:
    there was no *one* to advise me.
I had no means of es*cape*,
    not one who *cared* for my soul.
I cried to you, Lord; I said: you are my *hope*,
    all that I have in the *land* of the living.
Hearken then to my *plead*ing,
    for I am *brought* very low.
Rescue me from those who pur*sue* me,
    for they are *strong*er than I.
Bring my soul out of this *pris*on,
    that I may give *thanks* to your name.
Your just ones will a*wait* me
    as you *grant* me reward.

Psalm 118:105–12

Your word is a lamp for my *feet*
    and a *light* for my paths.
I have sworn and made up my *mind*
    to keep *your* just decrees.
Lord, I am deeply aff*lic*ted:
    give me *life* by your word.
Be pleased, Lord, with the words of my *mouth*
    and teach me *by* your decrees.
My soul is in your hands at all *times*;
    I will not *for*get your law.
Though sinners laid traps for *me*,
    I did not stray *from* your commands.
Your witness is my heritage for*ever*,
    for it is the *joy* of my heart.
I set my heart to carry out your sta*tutes*
    in *truth*, for ever.

*Glory to the Father, to the Son and to the Holy Spir*it.
    From age to age, amen, amen.
I have called to you, Lord; hasten to *help* me!
    Hearken to my words and accept my prayer.

Emmanuel Weekday Evening Prayer

Server: Let us pray. Peace be with us.
Priest: Hear, O Lord our God, the prayer of your servants in your mercy; accept the supplication of your adorers in your compassion, and pity our sinfulness in your grace and mercies, O Healer of our bodies and Good Hope of our souls at all times, Lord of all, Father, Son and Holy Spirit, forever.
People: Amen.

> PSALMODY & HYMNS "AFTER" (see pp. 185–224)

LITURGICAL SEASON

Server: Lift your voices, all you people, and glorify the living God.
People:

Holy God,	*Qaddysha Alaha*
Holy Mighty One,	*Qaddysha Ḥayilthana,*
Holy Immortal One:	*Qaddysha La Mayotha*
Have mercy on us.	*Ithraḥam 'layn.*
Glory to the Father, to the Son and to the Holy Spirit.	***Shuḥa l-Aḇḇa w-laḂra wal-Ruḥa d-Qudsha.***
Holy God...	*Qaddysha Alaha...*
From age to age, amen, amen.	***Min 'alam wa'dhamma l-'alam amen, w-amen.***
Holy God...	*Qaddysha Alaha...*

They say: Let us pray. Peace be with us.
Priest: O Holy, Glorious, Mighty and Immortal One, who dwells in the saints and delights in them: we implore you: turn to us, O Lord, pardon us and have mercy on us as you always do, Lord of all: Father, Son, and Holy Spirit, forever.
People: Amen.

> EVENING PSALMODY OF THE WEEK (see pp. 389–578)

Server: Let us pray. Peace be with us.
Priest: To your wondrous and indescribable providence, O Lord, which was accomplished, completed and perfected in mercies and pity for the renewal and the salvation of our weak race through the Principal that is from us, do we lift up glory, honor, thanksgiving and adoration at all times, O Lord of all, Father, Son and Holy Spirit, forever.
People: Amen.

> A SEASONAL HYMN OF THE WEEK (see pp. 389–578), and then,
> from Seasons of the Apostles to the Church, the MARTYR HYMNS (pp. 353–88)

PETITIONS

Server: Let us all stand composed. In faith and hope, let us implore *and* say: Lord, have mer*cy* on us.

People: Lord, have mer*cy* on us. | *Maran ithraḥam 'layn.*

Server:

* O Father of mercies and God of every consolation, we *im*plore you...

* Our Savior, our Caretaker and Provider *for* all, we *im*plore you...

* For the peace, concord and well-being of the whole world and of *all* churches, we *im*plore you...

* For the well-being of our country and of all countries, and for the protection of all the faithful who inha*bit* them, we *im*plore you...

* For good weather, a fertile season, the abundance of fruits and all the poor *and* needy, we *im*plore you...

* For the health of our holy fathers: [Mar _____, High Pontiff, Pope of Rome,] Mar _____, Catholicos-Patriarch, Mar _____, Bishop/Metropolitan, and for all those in the same priest*ly* service, we *im*plore you...

* For the priests and deacons of our Church, and for all of our Chris*tian* brethren, we *im*plore you...

* O Rich in his mercies and Overflowing in his com*passion*, we *im*plore you...

* O Kind One in his Nature who is the Giver of all *good* things, we *im*plore you...

* O One who is glorified in heaven and worshipped *on* earth, we *im*plore you...

* O One through whose holy <u>Birth</u> [or <u>Dawning</u>, or <u>Fasting</u>, or <u>Resurrection</u>, or <u>Ascension</u>, or <u>Spirit</u>, or <u>Cross</u>] has gladdened earth and deligh*ted* heaven, we *im*plore you...

* Save us all, O Christ our Lord, in your grace, increase your peace and your tranquility within us and have mer*cy* on us...

Server: Let us entrust our souls mutually to the Father, and to the Son, and to *the* Holy Spirit.

People: To you, *O* Lord our God.

Presider: To you, Lord God almighty, do we entrust our bodies and our souls, and from you, O Lord our God, do we receive all benefits and blessings; and so, as the crown of our prayer, in that confidence that is from you, we call together upon you and say thus:

Emmanuel Weekday Evening Prayer

People:
Our Father who art in heaven,
hallowed be your name.
Your kingdom come.
Holy, holy, you are holy.
Our Father in heaven:
heaven and earth are full
of the greatness of your glory;
angels & men cry out to you:
holy, holy, you are holy.
Our Father who art in heaven,
hallowed be thy name.
Thy kingdom come,
thy will be done on earth
as it is in heaven.
Give us this day our daily bread
and forgive us our trespasses,
as we forgive those
who trespassed against us.
And lead us not into temptation,
but deliver us from evil,
for thine is the kingdom,
the power and the glory,
now and forever.
Presider: Glory to the Father, to the Son and to the Holy Spirit.
People: From age to age, amen, amen. Our Father who art in heaven, hallowed be your name. Your kingdom come.
Holy, holy, you are holy.
Our Father in heaven:
heaven and earth are full
of the greatness of your glory;
angels & men cry out to you:
holy, holy, you are holy.

Aḅḅun dba-shmayya
nithqaddash shmakh,
tethe malkuthakh,
qaddysh, qaddysh, qaddysh-at,
Aḅḅun dba-shmayya.
Damlen shmayya w-ar'a
rabbuth shuḥakh,
'yre w-nasha qa'en lakh
qaddysh, qaddysh, qaddysh-at.
Aḅḅun dba-shmayya
nithqaddash shmakh,
tethe malkuthakh,
nehwe ṣiw-yanakh
aykanna dba-shmayya ap b-ar'a,
haw lan laḥma d-sunqanan
yawmana wa-shwoq lan ḥawbayn
wa-ḥtahayn aykanna d-ap ḥnan
shwaqn l-ḥay-yawayn,
w-la ta'lan l-nisyona
illa paṣan min bysha
mittul d-dhylakh-y malkutha,
w-ḥayla w-tish-buḥta
l-'alam 'almyn, amen.
Presider: *Shuḥa l-Aḅḅa wla-Bra wal-Ruḥa d-Qudsha.*
People: *Min 'alam wa-'dham-ma l-'alam amen w-amen.*
Aḅḅun dba-shmayya nithqaddash shmakh, tethe malkuthakh,
Qaddysh, qaddysh, qaddysh-at,
Aḅḅun dba-shmayya.
Damlen shmayya w-ar'a
rabbuth shuḥakh,
'yre w-nasha qa'en lakh
qaddysh, qaddysh, qaddysh-at.

172

Server: *Barekh mar.*

Server says to the people: Bow your heads for the prayer and accept the blessing.

Final Blessings

Monday

May the prayer of your miserable servants be accepted, O Lord our God, before the judgment-seat of your Divinity, and may this, our assembly, be pleasing to your Majesty, that it may receive, from you through grace, the health of the body, the protection of the soul, an abundance of sustenance, the absolution of debts, the forgiveness of sins, constant peace, O Lord, and enduring tranquility, and the unity of love which will not pass away or dissolve from among us, for all the time the world remains, now, at all times, and forever and ever.

Tuesday

Blessed be God forever, and glorified be his holy name unto the ages; from him do we beg, and to the overflowing sea of his compassion do we plead, that he make us worthy for radiant glory in his kingdom, for delight with his holy angels, for unveiled faces before him and for place at his right hand in the Jerusalem above, in his grace and mercies, now, at all times, and forever and ever.

Wednesday

May God the Lord of all, in whose house we have assembled, and before whose greatness we have prayed for the great hope of his compassion, hear our prayer in his mercy, accept our pleading in his pity, cleanse and scour the filth of our debts and sins with the overflowing hyssop of his benevolence, give rest to the souls of our deceased in the glorious dwelling-places of his kingdom, and sprinkle the dew of his kindness upon us all. And upon us and all creatures, may the right hand of his providence rest, in his grace and mercies, now, at all times, and forever and ever.

Thursday

May God the Lord of all, who has placed his praises in our mouths, his songs upon our tongues, his hymns in our throats, his confession on our lips, and his faith in our hearts, hear our prayers, accept our supplication, be pleased with our pleadings, forgive our trespasses, and answer our appropriate and blameless requests. And from the great treasury of his compassion, may he make his mercies and pity overflow upon us and upon the whole world to its ends, now, at all times, and forever and ever.

Friday

May the name of God the Lord of all, the Orderer of times and ages, be praised among us, and upon us weak sinners, the whole world to its ends, the holy Church and her children, our parents and brethren, our monks and teachers, our deceased and those who have passed away and departed from among us, and our entire Christian brethren, may the right hand of his providence and his compassion rest, now, at all times, and forever and ever.

Saturday

To God be glory; to the angels, honor; to Satan, shame; to the cross, adoration; to the Church, exaltation; to the deceased, resurrection; to the repentant, acceptance; to the captive, freedom; to the sick and infirm, health and healing; to the four corners of the world, great peace and serenity; and also upon us, who are weak and sinners: may pity and mercies come and rest, overflow and dwell, rule and settle upon you constantly, now, at all times, and forever and ever.

Emmanuel Weekday Evening Prayer for Lent

Server: Peace be with us.

Presider: It is right at all times for us to thank, adore and glorify the great and awesome, holy and blessed, lofty and incomprehensible name of your glorious Trinity, and your grace toward our race, O Lord of all, Father, Son and Holy Spirit, forever.

People: Amen.

Lucernary

We give you thanks,	Lakhu Mara d-kulla
O Lord of all,	mawdenan,
we glorify you,	w-lakh Ysho' Mshyḥa
Jesus Christ;	mshabḥynan
you raise our bodies	d-attu Mnaḥmana
into life,	d-paghrayn,
you are the Savior	w-attu Paroqa
of our souls.	d-nawshathan.
I rejoiced when I heard	**Ḥdhyth kadh amryn waw ly:**
them say: we are going	**l-bayteh d-Marya**
to the house of the Lord!	**azynan!**
We give you thanks...	Lakhu Mara d-kulla...
Glory to the Father, to the Son	**Shuḥa l-Aḇḇa w-laḆra**
and to the Holy Spirit.	**wal-Ruḥa d-Qudsha**
From age to age,	**min 'alam wa'dhamma**
amen, amen.	**l-'alam amen, w-amen.**
We give you thanks...	Lakhu Mara d-kulla...

They open the curtain, incense the sanctuary, and light the lucernary.

Server: Let us pray. Peace be with us.

Priest: Lord, you alone are the Lamp of Truth who puts away the cloud of ignorance from our minds in his guiding light, and the one in whose loving scent our souls find delight and are renewed. Accept the rational oblations of our hearts, O Lord our God, at this eventide, for to you do we lift up glory, honor, thanksgiving and adoration, Lord of all forever.

People: Amen.

Lenten Glorification

Halleluiah, halleluiah, halleluiah.
Glory to you, O God, halleluiah, halleluiah. 2x
Lord, have mercy on us.
You are glorious, O Lord,
and to you praise is always due
forever, amen.
Glory to Christ the Lord,
and thanks to him who gave our mouths
the grace to hallow with his praise.
Glory to Christ the Lord,
and thanks to him who gave our mouths
the grace to sing hymns of his praise.
Glory to Christ the Lord,
and thanks to him who gave our mouths
the grace to glory in his praise.
Father, Son and Holy Spirit: praise to you forever, amen. 3x
Our mouth is too small to thank you, O Lord,
all the days of life we have by your grace.
Our mouth is too small to praise you, O Lord,
all the days of life we have by your grace.
Our mouth is too small to glorify you, Lord,
all the days of life we have by your grace
to the mortal race, O Merciful One;
pity us in grace, have mercy on us.
For no living thing is just before you:
turn us, Lord, from error and sin:
for you are God and glory is due to you forever, amen.

Server: Let us pray. Peace be with us.

Priest: May your grace, O Lord, descend for the aid of your adorers, your mercies overflow for the support of those who call your name, and may you be revealed to us for the salvation of your people and the redemption of all the sheep of your flock from all dangers, hidden or manifest, Lord of all: Father, Son and Holy Spirit, forever.

People: Amen.

Psalmody & Hymns "Before" (see pp. 185–224)

Fixed Evening Psalmody

Server: Let us pray. Peace be with us.
Priest: It is our duty, O Lord our God, to thank, adore and glorify you for your mercy and your providential will for us, at all times, O Lord of all, Father, Son and Holy Spirit, forever.
People: Amen.

Psalm 140

I have called to you, Lord; hasten to *help* me!
    Hearken to my words and *ac*cept my prayer.
I have called to you, Lord; hasten to *help* me!
    Hearken to my words and *ac*cept my prayer.
Let my prayer arise before you like *in*cense,
    the offering of my hands like an eve*ning* oblation.
Set, O Lord, a guard over my *mouth*
    and a guard *o*ver my lips!
That my heart may not turn to an evil *deed*,
    or accomp*lish* works of wickedness.
May I not dine with evil *men*.
    Let a just man teach *me* and reprove me.
But let the oil of the wicked not anoint my *head*,
    for my prayer is *a*gainst their malice.
Their judges were thrown down by a rock-like *hand*,
    then they heard that *my* words were kind,
Like a plough that scatters the *ground*.
    Their bones were strewn at *the* mouth of Sheol.
To you, Lord God, I lift up my *eyes*:
    I trust you; do not cast *my* soul away!
Guard me from the hands of the *boastful*,
    who *set* traps for me.
Let the wicked fall together into their own *nets*
    while I pursue *my* way unharmed.

Psalm 141

With my voice I called to the *Lord*,
    with my voice *I* begged the Lord.
I lifted my pleading be*fore* him;
    I showed *him* my distress.

Emmanuel Weekday Evening Prayer for Lent

When my spirit trembled, you knew my *path*.
    On the way I walked they set *a* trap for me.
I looked to my right and *saw*:
    there was no *one* to advise me.
I had no means of es*cape*,
    not one who *cared* for my soul.
I cried to you, Lord; I said: you are my *hope*,
    all that I have in the *land* of the living.
Hearken then to my *plead*ing,
    for I am *brought* very low.
Rescue me from those who pur*sue* me,
    for they are *strong*er than I.
Bring my soul out of this *pris*on,
    that I may give *thanks* to your name.
Your just ones will a*wait* me
    as you *grant* me reward.

Psalm 118:105–12

Your word is a lamp for my *feet*
    and a *light* for my paths.
I have sworn and made up my *mind*
    to keep *your* just decrees.
Lord, I am deeply affl*ic*ted:
    give me *life* by your word.
Be pleased, Lord, with the words of my *mouth*
    and teach me *by* your decrees.
My soul is in your hands at all *times*;
    I will not *for*get your law.
Though sinners laid traps for *me*,
    I did not stray *from* your commands.
Your witness is my heritage for*ever*,
    for it is the *joy* of my heart.
I set my heart to carry out your *stat*utes
    in *truth*, for ever.
Glory to the Father, to the Son and to the Holy *Spir*it.
    From age to age, *a*men, amen.
I have called to you, Lord; hasten to *help* me!
    Hearken to my words and *ac*cept my prayer.

Emmanuel Weekday Evening Prayer for Lent

Server: Let us pray. Peace be with us.
Priest: Hear, O Lord our God, the prayer of your servants in your mercy; accept the supplication of your adorers in your compassion, and pity our sinfulness in your grace and mercies, O Healer of our bodies and Good Hope of our souls at all times, Lord of all, Father, Son and Holy Spirit, forever.
People: Amen.

PSALMODY & HYMNS "AFTER" (see pp. 185–224)

LITURGICAL SEASON

Server: Lift your voices, all you people, and glorify the living God.
People:

Holy God,	Qaddysha Alaha
Holy Mighty One,	Qaddysha Ḥayilthana,
Holy Immortal One:	Qaddysha La Mayotha
Have mercy on us.	Ithraḥam 'layn.
Glory to the Father, to the Son and to the Holy Spirit.	***Shuḥa l-Abba w-laBra wal-Ruḥa d-Qudsha.***
Holy God…	Qaddysha Alaha…
From age to age, amen, amen.	***Min 'alam wa'dhamma l-'alam amen, w-amen.***
Holy God…	Qaddysha Alaha…

They say: Let us pray. Peace be with us.
Priest: O Holy, Glorious, Mighty and Immortal One, who dwells in the saints and delights in them: we implore you: turn to us, O Lord, pardon us and have mercy on us as you always do, Lord of all: Father, Son, and Holy Spirit, forever.
People: Amen.

EVENING PSALMODY OF THE WEEK (see pp. 475–500)

Server: Let us pray. Peace be with us.
Priest: To your wondrous and indescribable providence, O Lord, which was accomplished, completed and perfected in mercies and pity for the renewal and the salvation of our weak race through the Principal that is from us, do we lift up glory, honor, thanksgiving and adoration at all times, O Lord of all, Father, Son and Holy Spirit, forever.
People: Amen.

A SEASONAL HYMN OF THE WEEK (see pp. 475–500)

Lenten Evening Petitions

Server: Let us pray. Peace be with us. Bend *your* knees. Let us pray and plead from *God* the Lord of all...

People: Amen.

Server: ...that he may hear the sound of our prayer, accept our pleading and have mer*cy* on us.

Server: For the Holy Catholic Church, here and in eve*ry* land, we pray and plead from God the Lord of all...

People: Amen.

Server: ...that his peace and serenity may dwell in her until the *end* of time.

Server: For our fathers *the* bishops, we pray and plead from God the Lord of all...

People: Amen.

Server: ...that they may stand at the head of their churches without guilt or fault all the days *of* their lives.

* For the health of our holy fathers: [Mar _____, High Pontiff, Pope of Rome,] Mar _____, Catholicos-Patriarch, Mar _____, Bishop/Metropolitan, and for all those in the same pries*tly* service, we *im*plore you...

People: Amen.

Server: ...that he may protect and uphold them at the head of their churches, and that they may shepherd and serve them, and prepare a perfect people that is zealous in good and *no*ble works.

Server: For priests and deacons, servants of *the* truth, we pray and plead from God the Lord of all...

People: Amen.

Server: ...that they may serve before him with a good heart and *pure* intention.

Server: For the pure and holy rank of monks and sisters in our holy Catho*lic* Church, we pray and plead from God the Lord of all...

People: Amen.

Server: ...that they may complete the good race of their sanctification, and accept the hope and promise of the land of the living *from* the Lord.

Server: For this land and its inhabitants, for this city and those who dwell in it, and especially for our *ass*embly, we pray and plead from God the Lord of all...

People: Amen.

Server: ...that he may spare us in his grace of war and captivity, earthquake and famine, plague and all evil afflictions hostile *to* the body.

Server: For those who have strayed from this true faith, and are captive to the snares *of* satan, we pray and plead from God the Lord of all...
People: Amen.
Server: ...that he may convert their hardness of heart, and that they may confess the one God, the Father of Truth and his Son, our Lord *Jesus* Christ.
Server: For those sick with serious diseases and tempted by e*vil* spirits, we pray and plead from God the Lord of all...
People: Amen.
Server: ...that he may send them an angel of mercy and healing to heal, aid and comfort them in his great grace *and* his mercies.
Server: For the poor and the oppressed, for orphans and widows, for the downtrodden and weak, for the distressed in spirit throughout *this* world, we pray and plead from God the Lord of all...
People: Amen.
Server: ... that the Lord may guide them in his grace, grant them comfort by his mercy, and save them from *the* unjust.
Server: Pray and plead from God the Lord of all, that you may become for him a kingdom - priests, a holy people. Cry out to the Lord God almighty with your all your heart and all your soul, for he is God, the merciful, compassionate and benevolent Father, who does not wish the destruction of his creature, but rather its repentance toward him, and its life *in* his presence. * It is especially fit that we pray, thank, adore, glorify, honor, and exalt the one God, the adorable Father, the Lord of all, who has accomplished the great hope and the salvation of our souls through his Christ, that he may complete his grace, his mercy and his compassion in us un*til* the end.
People: Amen.
Server: Stand in the strength of God.
People: Glory to the strength of God.
Server: In pleading and supplication, we ask for an angel of *peace* and mercies...
People: ...from you, O Lord.
Server: Day and night, all the days of our lives, for constant peace in your Church, and life without *sin*, we ask...
People: ...from you, O Lord.
Server: For the harmony of love and perfect unity in the accord of the Holy Sp*irit*, we ask...

Emmanuel Weekday Evening Prayer for Lent

People: ...from you, O Lord.

Server: For the forgiveness of sins that cleanses our hearts and pleases your Divini*ty*, we ask...

People: ...from you, O Lord.

Server: For the mercies of the Lord and his pity, constantly and at all *times*, we ask...

People: ...from you, O Lord.

Server: Let us entrust our souls mutually to the Father, and to the Son, and to *the* Holy Spirit.

People: To you, *O* Lord our God.

Presider: To you, Lord God almighty, do we entrust our bodies and our souls, and from you, O Lord our God, do we receive all benefits and blessings; and so, as the crown of our prayer, in that confidence that is from you, we call together upon you and say thus:

People:

Our Father who art in heaven,	*Abbun dba-shmayya*
hallowed be your name.	*nithqaddash shmakh,*
Your kingdom come.	*tethe malkuthakh,*
Holy, holy, you are holy.	***qaddysh, qaddysh, qaddysh-at,***
Our Father in heaven:	***Abbun dba-shmayya.***
heaven and earth are full	***Damlen shmayya w-ar'a***
of the greatness of your glory;	***rabbuth shuhakh,***
angels & men cry out to you:	***'yre w-nasha qa'en lakh***
holy, holy, you are holy.	***qaddysh, qaddysh, qaddysh-at.***
Our Father who art in heaven,	*Abbun dba-shmayya*
hallowed be thy name.	*nithqaddash shmakh,*
Thy kingdom come,	*tethe malkuthakh,*
thy will be done on earth	*nehwe siw-yanakh*
as it is in heaven.	*aykanna dba-shmayya ap b-ar'a,*
Give us this day our daily bread	*haw lan lahma d-sunqanan*
and forgive us our trespasses,	*yawmana wa-shwoq lan hawbayn*
as we forgive those	*wa-htahayn aykanna d-ap hnan*
who trespassed against us.	*shwaqn l-hay-yawayn,*
And lead us not into temptation,	*w-la ta'lan l-nisyona*
but deliver us from evil,	*illa pasan min bysha*
for thine is the kingdom,	*mittul d-dhylakh-y malkutha,*

the power and the glory, | w-ḥayla w-tish-buḥta
now and forever. | l-'alam 'almyn, amen.
Presider: Glory to the Father, to the Son and to the Holy Spirit. | **Presider:** Shuḥa l-Abba wla-Bra wal-Ruḥa d-Qudsha.
People: From age to age, amen, amen. Our Father who art in heaven, hallowed be your name. Your kingdom come. | **People:** Min 'alam wa-'dham-ma l-'alam amen w-amen. Abbun dba-shmayya nithqaddash shmakh, tethe malkuthakh,
Holy, holy, you are holy. Our Father in heaven: heaven and earth are full of the greatness of your glory; angels & men cry out to you: holy, holy, you are holy. | **Qaddysh, qaddysh, qaddysh-at, Abbun dba-shmayya. Damlen shmayya w-ar'a rabbuth shuḥakh, 'yre w-nasha qa'en lakh qaddysh, qaddysh, qaddysh-at.**

Server: *Barekh mar.*

Server says to the people: Bow your heads for the prayer and accept the blessing.

FINAL BLESSINGS

Monday

May the prayer of your miserable servants be accepted, O Lord our God, before the judgment-seat of your Divinity, and may this, our assembly, be pleasing to your Majesty, that it may receive, from you through grace, the health of the body, the protection of the soul, an abundance of sustenance, the absolution of debts, the forgiveness of sins, constant peace, O Lord, and enduring tranquility, and the unity of love which will not pass away or dissolve from among us, for all the time the world remains, now, at all times, and forever and ever.

Tuesday

Blessed be God forever, and glorified be his holy name unto the ages; from him do we beg, and to the overflowing sea of his compassion do we plead, that he make us worthy for radiant glory in his kingdom, for delight with his holy angels, for unveiled faces before him and for place at his right hand in the Jerusalem above, in his grace and mercies, now, at all times, and forever and ever.

Wednesday

May God the Lord of all, in whose house we have assembled, and before whose greatness we have prayed for the great hope of his compassion, hear our prayer in his mercy, accept our pleading in his pity, cleanse and scour the filth of our debts and sins with the overflowing hyssop of his benevolence, give rest to the souls of our deceased in the glorious dwelling-places of his kingdom, and sprinkle the dew of his kindness upon us all. And upon us and all creatures, may the right hand of his providence rest, in his grace and mercies, now, at all times, and forever and ever.

Thursday

May God the Lord of all, who has placed his praises in our mouths, his songs upon our tongues, his hymns in our throats, his confession on our lips, and his faith in our hearts, hear our prayers, accept our supplication, be pleased with our pleadings, forgive our trespasses, and answer our appropriate and blameless requests. And from the great treasury of his compassion, may he make his mercies and pity overflow upon us and upon the whole world to its ends, now, at all times, and forever and ever.

Friday

May the name of God the Lord of all, the Orderer of times and ages, be praised among us, and upon us weak sinners, the whole world to its ends, the holy Church and her children, our parents and brethren, our monks and teachers, our deceased and those who have passed away and departed from among us, and our entire Christian brethren, may the right hand of his providence and his compassion rest, now, at all times, and forever and ever.

Saturday

To God be glory; to the angels, honor; to Satan, shame; to the cross, adoration; to the Church, exaltation; to the deceased, resurrection; to the repentant, acceptance; to the captive, freedom; to the sick and infirm, health and healing; to the four corners of the world, great peace and serenity; and also upon us, who are weak and sinners: may pity and mercies come and rest, overflow and dwell, rule and settle upon you constantly, now, at all times, and forever and ever.

EMMANUEL CYCLE FOR WEEKDAY EVENING PRAYER

MONDAY EVENING PRAYER – WEEK I

PSALMODY "BEFORE"
Psalm 12:1–6

Save me, Lord, for the good man has *dis*appeared,
    Halleluiah, halleluiah, *h*alleluiah.
Save me, Lord, for the good man has *dis*appeared,
    and faith has van*ished* from the earth.
Men speak vanity, a man to his friend with de*cei*ving lips.
    They speak *with* two faces.
May the Lord destroy all de*cei*ving lips,
    the tongues *that* speak proud things.
For they say: "our tongue will *make* us great;
    our lips are our own; *who* is our master?"
"Because of the oppression *of* the poor,
    and the groa*ning* of the needy,
I will arise now," *says* the Lord.
    "And I will grant salva*tion* openly."
Glory to the Father, to the Son and to the *Ho*ly Spirit.
    From age to age, *a*men, amen.
Halleluiah, *h*alleluiah, *h*alleluiah.

HYMNS "BEFORE" – *ha shwan*

- Save me, Lord, the good man vanished.
Lo, the gracious one has vanished,
the just is gone,
none is honest among men!
Each one speaking with two faces,
and with his friend,
only words of deception!
From within, our race is filled with
envy, deceit and slander.
Love, the head of all commandments,
has been blotted from our minds and hearts.

The terror is great
that your wrath will destroy us,
but your justice has been silent,
leaving room for mercy.
O Lord, forgive us!
- **In his words, the Lord is faithful.**
Our Redeemer made a promise:
eternal life
to his friends, his beloved!
He enriched them with his knowledge,
and filled them with
wisdom to pray at all times:
Our Father
who art in heaven,
hallowed be thy name.
May thy kingdom come to us,
thy will be done on earth and heaven. Give
us the bread we need,
and lead us from temptation,
from the evil one deliver,
for thine is the kingdom,
the power and glory.
- **They kept his witness, and the covenant he gave them.**
Virgin Mary, our great refuge,
who bore Life's Balm
for the wounded sons of Adam,
we take refuge in your pleading,
and by the prayers
of St. John,
defeat the devil.
By the prayer of
all the prophets,
apostles, martyrs, holy ones,
by the prayers of our patron,
confessors, St. George, the mighty strength
of the holy cross,

the crowning of the holy Church,
we entreat the Lord and Christ,
that he may grant his mercies
to all our souls.

Psalmody "After"
Psalm 15:1–5

Lord, who shall be admitted *to* your tent
    Halleluiah, halleluiah, *ha*lleluiah.
Lord, who shall be admitted *to* your tent
    and dwell on *your* holy mountain?
He who walks *with*out fault;
    he *who* acts with justice
and speaks the truth *from* his heart;
    he who does not slan*der* with his tongue.
He who does no wrong *to* his brother,
    who casts no *slur* on his neighbor.
Who holds the godless *in* disdain,
    but honors those *who* fear the Lord.
Glory to the Father, to the Son and to the *Ho*ly Spirit.
    From age to age, *a*men, amen.
Halleluiah, *ha*lleluiah, *ha*lleluiah.

Hymns "After" – *abba ḥannana*

- He who was before all time.
O kind Father,
O Son of mercy,
O Spirit of love,
who makes holy the impure:
make holy our
flesh and soul,
and have mercy on us!
- Holy and awesome is his name.
May the hallowings
of the hosts above
plead to your Justice

on our souls' behalf,
by the request
of the Son,
and have mercy on us!
- **Holy is the dwelling-place of the Most High.**
Mary, mother of
the great King of kings,
plead to Christ your Son,
who dawned from your womb,
to pity us
and let us
enter his kingdom.
- **They kept his witness, and the covenant he gave them.**
Through the prayers of
all your saints, O Christ,
prophets, apostles,
martyrs, all the just,
protect the Church
you have saved
from all evil things.
- **May the memorial of the just be forever.**
Holy patron,
be a guide for us
in the ways of life
that appease your Lord,
that through your prayers
we find help
and delight with you.

Tuesday Evening Prayer – Week I

Psalmody "Before"
Psalm 17:1–6

Hear, O *ho*ly Lord,
    Halleluiah, halleluiah, *h*alleluiah.
Hear, O *ho*ly Lord,
    and look *up*on my pleading.
Hearken *to* my prayer,
    for it is not said *with* lying lips.
From you my judg*ment* comes forth:
    may your eyes see *in*tegrity.
You search my heart, you visit *me* by night.
    You test me and you find *in* me no wrong.
The works of men have not *crossed* my mouth,
    even in the spea*king* of my lips.
Rather, you have kept me from *e*vil ways;
    you placed my journeys firm*ly* on your paths.
There was no faltering *in* my steps.
    I called you for *you* answered me.
Glory to the Father, to the Son and to the *Ho*ly Spirit.
    From age to age, *a*men, amen.
Halleluiah, *h*alleluiah, *h*alleluiah.

Hymns "Before" – *nuhra w-bar nuhra*

- Hear, O God, and have mercy.
Hearer who does not turn,
Answerer, Savior, and Redeemer:
hear our pleading, Lord,
and respond to our requests.
- The Lord is faithful in his words.
Lord Jesus Christ, you said:
"to the one who knocks
upon the door, it will open;
his requests will find response."

- Holy is the dwelling-place of the Most High.
The holy Virgin's prayer,
Mary, mother of the Christ,
protect us from all harm
and the evil one, our foe.
- They kept his witness, and the covenant he gave them.
Prophets and apostles,
martyrs, priests and wise teachers:
your supplication be
our fortress both night and day.
- May the memorial of the just be forever.
O holy patron, friend
of the heavenly Bridegroom:
entreat on our behalf
from the Lord whose love you know.

Psalmody "After"
Psalm 21:1–5

Lord, may your strength give joy *to* the king;
    Halleluiah, halleluiah, *h*alleluiah.
Lord, may your strength give joy *to* the king;
    may your salva*tion* gladden him!
You granted him his *heart's* desire;
    you refused not the pra*yer* of his lips.
You met him with *a* good blessing;
    you set a glorious crown *up*on his head.
He asked you for life and this *you* have given,
    days that will last *from* age to age.
Glory to the Father, to the Son and to the *Ho*ly Spirit.
    From age to age, *a*men, amen.
Halleluiah, *h*alleluiah, *h*alleluiah.

HYMNS "AFTER" – *lilya mikkel*

- O Lord, hear my prayer!
We beg you, O Lord our God,
and implore your Majesty:
as you made us in your grace,
give us life when you come!
For you pity sinful ones,
have mercy when we repent,
and you forgive all our sins
in the mercies of your grace.

- Hearken to my words and accept them.
O God, who accepted the
lamb of innocent Abel,
the off'ring of just Noah
and of faithful Abraham:
accept our petitions, Lord,
respond to all our requests,
and let your peace dwell in us
during all our days!

- Holy is the dwelling-place of the Most High.
O Mary, holy virgin,
mother of our Savior, Christ:
may your prayer be a guard
for the Church upon earth.
Through you, may our pray'r be heard
as befits our humbleness,
and with you, may we see Christ
on the day when he comes.

- They kept his witness, and the covenant he gave them.
We commemorate the just
and take refuge in their prayers,
and to you we cry through them:
O Lord, pity us!
Establish their love in us,
make our mouth proclaim their truth,
confirm their true faith in us,
Hope of his true ones!

- May the memorial of the just be forever.
Noble are you, blessed one;
full of sweetness is the crown
of your heav'nly victories
you won with nobility!
You beat down the enemy
who fought you in the battle,
and your victory is known
in heaven and on earth!

Wednesday Evening Prayer – Week I

Psalmody "Before"
Psalm 23:1–4

The Lord *is* my Shepherd;
    Halleluiah, halleluiah, *h*alleluiah.
The Lord *is* my Shepherd;
    there is no*thing* I shall want.
To green pas*tures* he brings me;
    to rest*ful* waters he leads me.
He turns my *soul* and guides me
    along *the* paths of truth.
Because of your name, even if *I* should walk
    in the valleys of *the* shadows of death,
no evil would I fear, for *you* are with me:
    your crook and your *staff* comfort me.
Glory to the Father, to the Son and to the *Ho*ly Spirit.
    From age to age, *a*men, amen.
Halleluiah, *h*alleluiah, *h*alleluiah.

Hymns "Before" – *la bahtynan*
- Holy is the dwelling-place of the Most High.
- I will glorify the Word of God.
The Virgin bore the Son-Word
with great glory in her womb,
and was mother and handmaid
to Jesus Christ, the Savior.
For this, all who dwell on earth
celebrate her holy day
and call us to the feast of Light,
to joy which is unending.
Thus every generation
gives her blessing constantly,
and glory to the One
who chose her as his dwelling.

Emmanuel Wednesday Evening Prayer – Week I

- We your people and the sheep of your flock.
Like incense Aaron offered,
let our pleading rise to you;
like the Ninevites' begging,
may you accept our prayer,
O Lord, and respond to us
from your treasure of mercy.
As you answered Daniel
within the den of lions,
respond, aid your worshippers,
in this time of trouble,
for our trust is in you,
Lord who loves his servants.

- They kept his witness, and the covenant he gave them.
The bones of the saints are like
fine pearls upon our King's crown:
their beauty shines forth on earth.
Come, let us celebrate them
in great love with spiritual hymns,
from morning till eventide,
remembering their noble deeds,
asking mercy of God,
that he may allow his peace
to dwell on the earth,
and that the Church and her children be
kept safe by their prayers.

- May the memorial of the just be forever.
Blest are you, O great patron,
who was attacked for the truth,
and bore suffering and pain
that he may gain the kingdom.
What man can relate the tale
of the labors you performed
in vigil, penance and pray'r?

Your prayer be a fortress
for sinners who trust in you,
and may we be worthy to give praise to the Lord
who raised you to glory.

Priest: Arm us, O Lord our God, with a mighty and invincible armor, by the prayers of your blessed mother, the blessed St. Mary, and grant us part and portion with her in the heavenly banquet, Lord of all, forever.

PSALMODY "AFTER"
Psalm 24:1–6

The Lord's is the earth *and* its fullness,
    Halleluiah, halleluiah, *h*alleluiah.
The Lord's is the earth *and* its fullness,
    the world *and* all its peoples.
For he set its foundations *on* the seas;
    on the rivers *he* made it firm.
Who shall climb the mountain *of* the Lord?
    Who shall stand on *his* holy mountain?
The man with clean hands *and* pure heart,
    who has not sworn de*ceit* in his soul.
He shall receive a blessing *from* the Lord
    and justice *from* God our Savior.
Glory to the Father, to the Son and to the *Ho*ly Spirit.
    From age to age, *a*men, amen.
Halleluiah, *h*alleluiah, *h*alleluiah.

HYMNS "AFTER" – *kul nishma*

- **From her the earth is filled.**
- **The mountains are covered by her wings.**

Mary, who bore
Life's Balm for the sons of Adam:
by your pray'r may we find mercy
when he comes.

- We your people and the sheep of your flock.
Help us, O Lord,
send peace to us, banish Satan,
guard your Church and keep her children
from all harm.

- They kept his witness, and the covenant he gave them.
A Spring of Life
you made for us, Lord, and all those
who receive your Mysteries
and love your name.

- May the memorial of the just be forever.
Holy patron,
friend of Jesus Christ the Savior:
plead to him for pity,
mercies on our souls.

Thursday Evening Prayer – Week I

Psalmody "Before"
Psalm 25:1–5

To you, O Lord, I lift *up* my soul.
    Halleluiah, halleluiah, *h*alleluiah.
To you, O Lord, I lift *up* my soul.
    I trust you, my God, let me not *be* put to shame.
Do not let my enemies boast *over* me,
    for those who hope in you shall not *be* put to shame.
Let the wicked be *put* to shame
    in *their* vanity.
Lord, show *me* your ways;
    make your *paths* known to me.
Lead me in your *truth* and teach me,
    for you are God my Savior; in you I *hope* every day.
Glory to the Father, to the Son and to the *Ho*ly Spirit.
    From age to age, *a*men, amen.
Halleluiah, *h*alleluiah, *h*alleluiah.

Hymns "Before" – *attu nuhra*

- O Lord, you know.
You know more, O Lord, than all
what aids us: order our life
in your grace, let your mercy
be moved by our sinfulness;
your Mercy be our Doctor
and your Love be our Teacher.
Praise to you, mercy to us!

- Lord, your mercies are eternal.
We call to your overflowing
mercies of grace, O Christ,
for our weakness and its aid.
Because of our troubled times,
and this world scorched by its sins,
grant us peace unshaking where
we may thank you at all times.

- Holy is the dwelling-place of the Most High.
Holy blessed virgin Mary,
mother of Jesus Christ:
beg and plead mercies for us,
lest we sinners be destroyed,
for we take shelter in you.
May your prayer be our guard,
in this world and that to come.
- They kept his witness, and the covenant he gave them.
By the pray'rs of all of those
who pleased you, and all the just,
the prophets, apostles and
teachers, martyrs, priests and monks,
protect your Church on the earth,
that they lift up praise to you,
Father, Son and Holy Spirit!
- May the memorial of the just be forever.
Let us keep with diligence the
glorious memorial
of our great, splendid patron,
a vessel most merciful,
worthy of his Lord's service,
who would daily light his lamp.
May his prayer be our guard.

Psalmody "After"
Psalm 28:1–6

To you, O *Lord*, I called,
    Halleluiah, halleluiah, *h*alleluiah.
To you, O *Lord*, I called,
    my God, do not *be* silent with me.
If you are silent with me, I will be *ha*nded over
    with those who have gone down *in*to the cave.
Hear the sound of my pleading as I *call* to you,
    as I lift up my hands to *your* holy temple.

Do not count me a*mong* the wicked,
>   or with those *who* do evil,
who speak words of peace *to* their neighbors
>   but have e*vil* in their hearts.
Repay them according *to* their works,
>   and accor*ding* to their malice.
For they ignore the deeds *of* the Lord
>   and the *work* of his hands.
May he ruin them and ne*ver* rebuild them.
>   Blessed be the Lord for he has heard
>   >   the *sound* of my pleading.

Glory to the Father, to the Son and to the *Ho*ly Spirit.
>   **From age to age, *a*men, amen.**
Halleluiah, *h*alleluiah, *h*alleluiah.

Hymns "After" – *la miṭṭalmyn*

- I have called to you, Lord, every day.
The weary call to you, Merciful One;
in you they take refuge, Friend of man!
In your mercy, be the guard of their lives;
save them from the evil one –
they hope in you.

- From the depths of his heart.
Jonah called to you, and you answered him;
Hananiah from the fire; you rescued him.
All creation calls in groaning to you:
pity it, be merciful,
as is your way!

- Holy is the dwelling-place of the Most High.
Mary, blest mother of the King of kings:
offer prayer with us to Jesus your Son,
that he let his peace dwell in all the world,
and the Church and all her sons
be kept from harm.

- They kept his witness, and the covenant he gave them.
Blessed was your land, O you noble ones,
our Messiah's workers bearing life to men!
Bring your treasure of graces to the poor,
and protect the land from evil
and from harm.
- May the memorial of the just be forever.
Plead for all of us from your Lord, the Christ,
O splendid, holy patron, friend of the Son,
so that, through your pray'rs, all who are distressed
may be guarded and be aided
and redeemed.

Friday Evening Prayer – Week I

Psalmody "Before"
Psalm 75:1–4

We give thanks to *you*, O God,
>   **Halleluiah, halleluiah, *h*alleluiah.**

We give thanks to *you*, O God,
>   we give you thanks and call upon your name.
>>   We recount *your* marvelous deeds.

"When I reach the ap*poin*ted time,
>   then I will judge with *in*tegrity.

The earth and its inhabitants *will* be humbled."
>   You have ordered its *in*habitants.

Glory to the Father, to the Son and to the *Ho*ly Spirit.
>   **From age to age, *a*men, amen.**

Halleluiah, *h*alleluiah, *h*alleluiah.

Hymns "Before" – *talmydhaw*

- Give thanks to him and bless his name.
Give thanks, O mortals, to the Son who saved
us from slavery to death,
which had strangled us in sin,
for he went down into Sheol
and raised the dead from the grave.
Who can repay the grace of God
granted to the race of all mortal men?

- My mouth will wisdom speak.
Take refuge in repentance, sinful ones,
for the time is so short:
this world blooms and dies away!
There will be, for the repentant, joy,
death for the unjustified.
For if you judged justly, O Lord,
who on earth would be without any fault?

- Save your people, and the sheep of your flock.
We implore you, O Christ the King of kings,
that you may forget the
faults of all who have received
your Flesh and your Blood, and may you stand
for them on the day they rise,
that they be saved from Gehanna
and meet you in praise, with the hosts above!

Priest: Raise, O Lord, our deceased in your mercy, raise them up at your right hand, clothe them with splendid glory in your Kingdom, and mingle them among the just who fulfilled your will, in the Jerusalem above, Lord of all, Father, Son, and Holy Spirit, forever.

Psalmody "After"
Psalm 82:1–4

God stands in the assem*bly* of angels.
    Halleluiah, halleluiah, *h*alleluiah.
God stands in the assem*bly* of angels.
    In the midst of *the* angels he judges.
"How long will you *judge* unjustly
    and favor the *cause* of the wicked?
Do justice for orphans *and* the poor,
    vindicate the hum*ble* and the needy.
Rescue the weak *and* the poor
    from the *hand* of the wicked."
Glory to the Father, to the Son and to the *Ho*ly Spirit.
    From age to age, *a*men, amen.
Halleluiah, *h*alleluiah, *h*alleluiah.

HYMNS "AFTER" – *push bashlama*

- I will bless the Lord at all times.
Blest your day, Son of the Mighty,
which tears open the womb of Sheol!
Glorious is your day of raising,
which all ages await with longing.

- They will pass, but you will remain.
Lo, this world is passing quickly,
and its pleasures are all empty!
Blest is he who made provision
for the world that lasts forever.

- Glory to the Father, to the Son and to the Holy Spirit.
No hope do we have to boast in
save your cross, O our Absolver,
for it is our mighty fortress,
and it saves us from all peril.

Saturday Evening Prayer – Week I

Psalmody "Before"
Psalm 30:1–5

I will exalt you, Lord, for you lif*ted* me up,
  Halleluiah, halleluiah, *h*alleluiah.
I will exalt you, Lord, for you lif*ted* me up,
  and did not let my enemies re*joice* over me.
O Lord my God, I *cried* to you
  and *you* have healed me.
You raised my *soul* from Sheol,
  given me life apart from those who sank *in*to the cave.
Sing to the Lord, *you* his chosen,
  confess the memory of *his* holiness.
Glory to the Father, to the Son and to the *Ho*ly Spirit.
  From age to age, *a*men, amen.
Halleluiah, *h*alleluiah, *h*alleluiah.

Hymns "Before" – *ḥannana dapthyḥ*

- **In him our heart is glad.**
- **We hope in his holy name.**
May the cross which caused
us such benefits,
and through which our whole
mortal race was freed,
may it be, O Lord,
a mighty castle wall,
where we may defeat
the evil one and all his schemes.
- **Save your people, and the sheep of your flock.**
Sanctify your Church,
Savior, in mercy,
and let your grace dwell
in your temple set apart.

Set your altar up
strong within its walls,
where we may receive
your Flesh and your Blood.
- We your people and the sheep of your flock.
Lord, who promised us
in his great mercy:
"He who asks, receives,
and who seeks will find":
from you we implore
strength and aid all times
to fulfill your will
in our works and deeds.

Psalmody "After"
Psalm 54:1–6

O God, save me *by* your name;
    Halleluiah, halleluiah, *h*alleluiah.
O God, save me *by* your name;
    give me jus*tice* by your strength.
O God, *hear* my prayer;
    hearken to the *words* of my mouth.
For strangers have ri*sen* against me,
    the wicked seek my life.
        They have no regard *for* you, O God.
But I have God *for* my help.
    The Lord *up*holds my soul.
Glory to the Father, to the Son and to the *Ho*ly Spirit.
    From age to age, *a*men, amen.
Halleluiah, *h*alleluiah, *h*alleluiah.

Hymns "After" – *shlama l-sahde*

- From the ends to the ends of the earth.
- From the rising of the sun to its setting.
Cross that prevailed in creation's four corners:
guard those who kneel to you,
through Divinity's mercy.
- Glory to the Father, to the Son and to the Holy Spirit.
On Golgotha, the Church saw Lord Jesus Christ,
knelt down and worshipped him,
lifting praise to his Sender.
- From age to age, amen, amen.
O Lord may the prayer of your servants not
be out of vanity,
but for forgiveness and grace.

Monday Evening Prayer – Week II

Psalmody "Before"
Psalm 42:1–5

Like the deer that yearns for *ru*nning streams,
    Halleluiah, halleluiah, *h*alleluiah.
Like the deer that yearns for *ru*nning streams,
    so my soul yearns *for* you, Lord God.
My soul thirsts for you, O *li*ving God;
    when can I come *and* see your face?
My tears have become my food, O God, by *day* and night,
    as they say to me every day: "*Where* is your God?"
I recall these things with a *wea*ry soul,
    for I would go to your mighty fortress,
        even to *the* house of God.
Glory to the Father, to the Son and to the *Ho*ly Spirit.
    From age to age, *a*men, amen.
Halleluiah, *h*alleluiah, *h*alleluiah.

Hymns "Before" – *sahde brykhe*

- Like the deer that yearns for running streams.
Who will give to me
a wellspring of tears
and a contrite heart,
that I may cry,
weep and groan
in thund'ring lamentation
over all the years gone by
wasted on such worthless things?
Empty vanities, not good works!
- Woe is me, my journey is repeated.
What has come of me?
Evil set a trap
for me, and I fell.
You, Lord, created me free,
but I broke all your commands;
and because the evil one

saw me weak, he captured me.
Lord, deliver me from his snares!
- Holy is the dwelling-place of the Most High.
By the prayers of the Virgin Mary,
the blessed mother,
may your worshippers be kept
from all the deceiver's schemes.
Grant us to fulfill your will
in our words as in our deeds,
and to sing you praise at all times.
- They kept his witness, and the covenant he gave them.
By the prayers of your saints who have kept
all of your commands,
prophets and apostles
teachers, martyrs,
priests and monks,
guard the Church that worships you
from all the deceiver's schemes,
and give us the strength to do your will.
- May the memorial of the just be forever.
O garment of grace by the Spirit weaved,
O holy patron,
by your faithfulness and deeds,
you made grace flow like a spring
and watered your flock with words
of the life of Spirit, and
so, the crown of victory is yours!

Psalmody "After"
Psalm 122:1–4

To you have I lifted *up* my eyes,
    Halleluiah, halleluiah, *ha*lleluiah.
To you have I lifted *up* my eyes,
    you *who* dwell in heaven:
like the eyes of slaves *to* their lords;
    like the eyes of a hand*maid* to her mistress.

So our eyes are to you, O *Lord* our God,
    till you have mercy on us.
        Have mercy on *us*, Lord, have mercy.
Glory to the Father, to the Son and to the *Ho*ly Spirit.
    From age to age, *a*men, amen.
Halleluiah, *h*alleluiah, *h*alleluiah.

Hymns "After" – *byadh shlama*

- To you I lifted up my eyes, Dweller of heaven.
To you I lift my eyes, you who dwell in heaven:
you brought me into being and your will made me.
Send me your strength and my sickness heal,
and treat my wounds with your mercy's balm,
for you are the true Doctor, who treats without charge.
In your mercies, heal all of my wounds!

- May your mercies quickly come to us.
May your mercies come quickly, Lord of compassion;
to you we stretch our hands and our hearts to heaven;
we beg and plead that you may forgive
our faults and a-bsolve all of our sins,
redeem us from the evil one who attacks us,
and strengthen us to do all you will.

- Holy is the dwelling-place of the Most High.
The pray'r of Mary who bore you, John who baptized you,
Peter and Paul the preachers and the evangelists,
Stephen and the whole host of teachers,
our patron and all of our deceased,
the twelve confessors and holy George the martyr,
protect our land and all who dwell therein!

- The Lord is my shepherd, there is nothing I shall want.
By your ascension, Jesus, you raised our abasement;
in love you seated us at the right of the Father.
By the descent of the Holy Ghost,
you made us wise; through your cross of light
you gave us understanding, and by the holy Church,
you hallowed us: glory to your providence!

Tuesday Evening Prayer – Week II

Psalmody "Before"
Psalm 67:1–6

May God have mer*cy* on us,
  Halleluiah, halleluiah, *h*alleluiah.
May God have mer*cy* on us,
  bless us, and let his *face* shine on us.
That his ways be *known* on earth
  and his salvation *a*mong all peoples.
Let the peoples confess *you*, O God;
  let all *the* peoples confess you.
Let the kingdoms be *glad* and praise,
   for you judge the nations uprightly
     and guide *the* nations on earth.
Let the peoples confess *you*, O God;
  let all *the* peoples confess you.
Glory to the Father, to the Son and to the *Ho*ly Spirit.
  From age to age, *a*men, amen.
Halleluiah, *h*alleluiah, *h*alleluiah.

Hymns "Before" – ḥannana wamle raḥme
- Let your face shine on us and we shall be saved.
Pitying and Merciful,
do not turn your gaze from us:
send us pity, mercies, re-
demption from your treasury.
- Till you have mercy on us.
O Lord, we knock at your door,
and ask for mercies from you.
Open to us, and respond,
Kind One who does not withhold.
- Holy is the dwelling-place of the Most High.
May the virgin Mary's pray'r,
mother of our Savior Christ,
be our fortress at all times
of the night and of the day.

- They kept his witness, and the covenant he gave them.
Prophets, may you pray for peace,
and apostles, for accord.
Martyrs, priests and wise teachers:
may your prayer be our guard.
- May the memorial of the just be forever.
Plead and beg, O great patron,
from Christ whose Love you espoused,
that the Church who celebrates
you be aided by your pray'rs.

Psalmody "After"
Psalm 40:14–17

Be pleased, O Lord, de*liv*er me.
    Halleluiah, halleluiah, *h*alleluiah.
Be pleased, O Lord, to de*liv*er me.
    O Lord, has*ten* to my aid.
May those who seek to kill my *soul* be buried.
    May they be turned back and buried,
        those *who* wish me evil.
May they marvel at the repetition *of* their shame,
    those who say to me, *a*ha, aha.
May all who seek you re*joice* in you.
    May they always *say*, God is great.
Glory to the Father, to the Son and to the *Ho*ly Spirit.
    From age to age, *a*men, amen.
Halleluiah, *h*alleluiah, *h*alleluiah.

Hymns "After" – *ḥannana dapthyḥ*

- Redeem me and deliver me, in this age and forever.
O God, who redeemed Hezekiah's house,
saved Jerusalem from the Assyrian:
rest your hand on us,
save your worshippers,
keep us all, O Lord,
from the mighty sword.

-From the depths of his heart.
When King David called,
Lord, you answered him,
and you eased his pain
and cast down his foes.
And we also call:
persecution end,
and uphold the Church
who adores your cross.

- Holy is the dwelling-place of the Most High.
The holy Virgin
is a great fortress
for the faithful who
always ask her prayers.
By her mighty pray'r,
may our Church be blessed,
and be given priests,
harmony and peace.

- They kept his witness, and the covenant he gave them.
Prophets, apostles,
teachers and martyrs,
beg mercy from God
for the world entire:
harmony for priests,
benevolence for kings,
forgiveness of sins
for the Church's sons.

- May the memorial of the just be forever.
O holy patron,
the Messiah's friend,
who gained the kingdom
through labor and works:
plead mercies for us
from him who chose you,
that he may pity
us and save our souls.

Wednesday Evening Prayer – Week II

Psalmody "Before"
Psalm 72:1–4

O God, give your judgment *to* the king;
  Halleluiah, halleluiah, *h*alleluiah.
O God, give your judgment *to* the king;
  to the *king's* son your justice,
that he may judge your peo*ple* in justice,
  and your *poor* in right judgment.
May the mountains bear peace *for* your people,
  and *the* hills, your justice,
That he may judge the poor *of* the people,
  save the children of the needy, *and* crush the tyrant.
Glory to the Father, to the Son and to the *Ho*ly Spirit.
  From age to age, *a*men, amen.
Halleluiah, *h*alleluiah, *h*alleluiah.

Hymns "Before" – *sahdaw dabra*

- There will I raise David to honor.
- He has chosen a dwelling-place for himself.
From Abraham and David's house,
the Creator chose a virgin,
and sent her his hidden pow'r.
By the Holy Spirit's pow'r,
she conceived and bore the Savior
who is Judge of height and depth.
- We your people and the sheep of your flock.
How right it is to glorify
within this one, holy house,
where are prophets, apostles,
martyrs and priests and teachers,
where the sacred table is,
which forgives all Adam's sons.

Emmanuel Wednesday Evening Prayer – Week II

- May the memorial of the just be forever.
Blessed is one hired like you,
O patron, who spiritual wealth
gathered, filling his vessel
with all blessings, who made forth
and found his way to harbor,
to the place of all the just.
- Keep your mercies for your friends.
O Lord, may your kingdom come,
your will be done here on earth,
as it is there in heaven.
Give to us the bread we need,
and lead us from temptation;
save us from the evil one.

Priest: Arm us, O Lord our God, with a mighty and invincible armor, by the prayers of your blessed mother, the blessed St. Mary, and grant us part and portion with her in the heavenly banquet, Lord of all, forever.

Psalmody "After"
Psalm 101:1–6

Of grace and justice *I* will sing,
 Halleluiah, halleluiah, *h*alleluiah.
Of grace and justice *I* will sing,
 and I *will* praise you, Lord.
I will walk in your way *with*out blame;
 when, Lord, will *you* come to me?
I will walk with blameless heart with*in* my house;
 I will not set what is base *be*fore my eyes.
I have hated *e*vildoers;
 they shall not *come* near to me.
A wicked heart must de*part* from me;
 I *have* not known evil.
He who slanders his friend in secret I *have* destroyed;
 of proud eyes and haughty heart *I* have not dined with.

I look to the faithful in the land that they may *dwell* with me.
    He who walks faultless on *the* way shall serve me.
Glory to the Father, to the Son and to the *Ho*ly Spirit.
    From age to age, *a*men, amen.
Halleluiah, *h*alleluiah, *h*alleluiah.

HYMNS "AFTER" – *lakh dayyana*

- Protect us from the malice of the evil one.
- Protect me, and guard me from my enemies.
Under the wings of your prayers,
Virgin Mary, we take shelter.
May they guard us now and at all times;
in them may we find pity on
judgment day.
- They kept his witness, and the covenant he gave them.
By the pray'rs of all the prophets,
who had proclaimed your great mysteries,
the apostles, who preached your holy gospel,
and the martyrs, priests and teachers,
Christ, protect us.
- May the memorial of the just be forever.
Holy patron, pray for the sick,
that the Lord may heal in mercy.
Let your prayer be finest incense,
and a thurible pleasing unto
God for sinners.
- Save your people and the sheep of your flock.
Hear our pleading, Hope of our lives,
respond to all our requests.
Grant us healing from our maladies,
that we may give thanks to you;
have mercy on us.

Thursday Evening Prayer – Week II

Psalmody "Before"
Psalm 118:41–48

Lord, let your mercies *come* upon me,
    Halleluiah, halleluiah, *h*alleluiah.
Lord, let your mercies *come* upon me,
    and the *sal*vation you promised.
I shall answer *those* who taunt me,
    for I *trust* in your words.
Let not the word of truth die *from* my mouth,
    for I trust *in* your decrees.
I shall keep your law for e*ver* and ever,
    and walk in freedom for I de*light* in your precepts.
I will speak of your justice *be*fore kings
    and *not* be ashamed.
I will consider your commands which *I* have loved;
    I will lift my hands to your commands *which* I have loved,
I will pon*der* your statutes.
    I will glory in *your* faithfulness.
Glory to the Father, to the Son and to the *Ho*ly Spirit.
    From age to age, *a*men, amen.
Halleluiah, *h*alleluiah, *h*alleluiah.

Hymns "Before" – *shlama nisge lakh*

- Lord, let your mercies come upon me, the salvation you promised.
May your mercies which made us aid us now;
may they heal our wounds with your mercy's balm.
- Turn to me and have mercy on me.
Come, Lord, to our aid, strengthen our frailty;
in you is our hope during night and day.
- Holy is the dwelling-place of the Most High.
Let us all recall the virgin Mary,
the mother of Christ, upon the altar.

- They kept his witness, and the covenant he gave them.
Those sent by the Son, Sole-Begotten's friends:
pray that there be peace in all creation.
- May the memorial of the just be forever.
O holy patron, may you be recalled
with the just victors, and the crowned martyrs.

Psalmody "After"
Psalm 118:121–28

O Just and *Right*eous One:
    Halleluiah, halleluiah, *h*alleluiah.
O Just and *Right*eous One:
    do not abandon me *to* my oppressors.
Comfort your servant *with* good things,
    and the braggarts *will* not oppress me.
My eyes yearn for *your* salvation
    and the pro*mise* of your justice.
Treat your servant according *to* your mercies,
    and *teach* me your law.
I am your servant; *give* me knowledge,
    and I *shall* know your testimony.
It is time to work *for* the Lord,
    for they have nul*li*fied your law.
That is why I loved *your* commands
    more than *gold* and fine gems:
I love all *your* commands
    and hate all *the* paths of the wicked.
Glory to the Father, to the Son and to the *Ho*ly Spirit.
    From age to age, *a*men, amen.
Halleluiah, *h*alleluiah, *h*alleluiah.

Hymns "After" – *lzaddyqe la qrayt*

- You are righteous, O Lord, and your judgments are just.
You have not called the
righteous to repent,
but rather have told
sinners to turn back.
Hear us in mercy,
O Christ our Savior,
and forgive our debts
and sins in your grace.

- Turn to me and have mercy on me.
Turn and hear the pray'r
of your servants, Lord,
receive our pleading,
respond to our needs,
take the binding of
the deceitful one,
that our Church be saved
from his envy's filth.

- Holy is the dwelling-place of the Most High.
Mary, mother of
the great King of kings,
plead to Christ, that he
may pity our lot,
keep wars from the ends
of the earth, and bless
the crown of the year
in his guarding grace.

- They kept his witness, and the covenant he gave them.
By the prayers of
your saints, Christ our Lord,
prophets, apostles,
martyrs, all the just,
keep your worshippers
from all harmful things;

let them lift up praise
to you night and day.
- May the memorial of the just be forever.
Holy patron, friend
of the Heavenly Groom,
may your prayer be
a refuge for us,
and, the day your Lord
dawns in his glory,
plead to him, that we
may see his kingdom.

Friday Evening Prayer – Week II

Psalmody "Before"
Psalm 144:1–7

I will exalt you, O *Lord* my King;
> **Halleluiah, halleluiah, *h*alleluiah.**

I will exalt you, O *Lord* my King;
> I will bless your name *for*ever and ever.

I will bless you day *a*fter day
> and praise *your* name forever.

The Lord is great, highly *to* be praised,
> his greatness *can*not be measured.

Age to age shall pro*claim* your works,
> shall *de*clare your might,

shall speak of your *fear*ful strength,
> tell the tale of *your* wonderful works,

shall re*count* your greatness,
> and recall *your* many graces.

Glory to the Father, to the Son and to the *Ho*ly Spirit.
> **From age to age, *a*men, amen.**

Halleluiah, *h*alleluiah, *h*alleluiah.

Hymns "Before" – *ḥadhu ḥayla*

- I will exalt you, O Lord my King.
Christ the King, our Savior,
raise us on the day you come;
stand us up at your right hand
on the day your greatness dawns.

- I hope in you, my God; I shall not be put to shame.
We adore your cross, O Lord,
in which is resurrection,
and through which our dead are raised,
and their bodies glorified.

- Glory to the Father, to the Son and to the Holy Spirit.
God the Father: give me life;
Christ the Son: raise up my death;
Holy Spirit, Paraclete: lead me to the land of light!

Priest: Raise, O Lord, our deceased in your mercy, raise them up at your right hand, clothe them with splendid glory in your Kingdom, and mingle them among the just who fulfilled your will, in the Jerusalem above, Lord of all, Father, Son, and Holy Spirit, forever.

PSALMODY "AFTER"
Psalm 138:1–5

O Lord, you search me *and* you know me;
    Halleluiah, halleluiah, *h*alleluiah.
O Lord, you search me *and* you know me;
    you know my sit*ting* and my standing.
You discern my intentions *from* above;
    you know my paths and *trace* all my ways.
Before ever a word is *on* my tongue,
    you know it, *O* Lord my God.
In all things, from begin*ning* to end,
    you molded me and placed *your* hand on me.
Glory to the Father, to the Son and to the *Ho*ly Spirit.
    From age to age, *a*men, amen.
Halleluiah, *h*alleluiah, *h*alleluiah.

HYMNS "AFTER" – *ythya dabrimzeh*

- You molded me and placed your hand on me.
In Genesis, God
formed Adam from earth on Friday, and breathed
spirit into him,
giving speech to him, that he may sing him praise.
- An ignorant and unwise people.
On Friday, mankind
crucified our Lord upon Golgotha,
and that day the Lord
killed murderous Death, and raised up our race.
- Glory to the Father, to the Son and to the Holy Spirit.
Let us groan and beg
and through mercy plead grace and forgiveness from
the Merciful One
who opens his door to all who turn to him.

Saturday Evening Prayer – Week II

Psalmody "Before"
Psalm 123:1–6

"If the Lord had not been *on* our side,"
   Halleluiah, halleluiah, *h*alleluiah.
"If the Lord had not been *on* our side,"
   let *I*srael say.
"If the Lord had not been *on* our side
   when *men* rose against us,
then would they have swallowed *us* alive
   when *their* anger was kindled.
Then would the waters *have* engulfed us,
   the torrent *gone* over us;
over our head *would* have swept
   all *the* raging waters.
Blessed be the Lord who *did* not give us
   a *prey* to their teeth!"
Glory to the Father, to the Son and to the *Ho*ly Spirit.
   From age to age, *a*men, amen.
Halleluiah, *h*alleluiah, *h*alleluiah.

Hymns "Before" – *m'yna dṭawatha*

- In him our heart rejoices.
- He abolishes wars from the ends of the earth.
Your cross, O Savior,
which united height and depth
by its great power,
and its glorious might,
unite the whole world
that is troubled by its sins,
and make your peace
dwell in all the earth.
- We your people and the sheep of your flock.
Guard your holy Church
from all perils, Jesus, Lord,

who came to save
the whole human race:
make us all worthy,
in fear and in trembling,
to lift praise to your Divinity.
- **Protect your people and the sheep of your flock.**
Grant us what you know
will befit us, Life-Giver,
for we know not
what to ask of you.
For one thing only:
that your will
be done in us,
and your mercies
may defend us all.

Psalmody "After"
Psalm 124:1–2

Those who put their trust in the Lord *on* Mount Zion,
    Halleluiah, halleluiah, *h*alleluiah.
Those who put their trust in the Lord *on* Mount Zion,
    will not shake, but *will* stand forever.
Jerusalem! The moun*tains* surround her,
    so the Lord surrounds his people *both* now and forever.
Glory to the Father, to the Son and to the *Ho*ly Spirit.
    From age to age, *a*men, amen.
Halleluiah, *h*alleluiah, *h*alleluiah.

Hymns "After" – *kulnishma*

- **That he may show forth his greatness.**
- **Show forth your greatness and come to save us.**
O cross, which showed
marvelous wonders to the sons of men:
drive out dangers from the souls
marked by your sign.

- We your people and the sheep of your flock.
Lord, be a guard
for the churches in all nations,
and let your truth rampart them
with armor strong.
- Protect your people and the sheep of your flock.
Help us, O Lord,
send peace to us, banish Satan,
guard your Church and keep her children
from all harm.

Emmanuel Weekday Morning Prayer

Presider: All the creatures you have created enter before you O Lord; they kneel and adore you, praise and hallow you, ask and entreat you, implore and beseech you, confess and glorify you; for by your command they were constructed, and through your will they came to be; you are the Cause of their existence, and the Breath and Spiration of our lives, O Lord of all, Father, Son and Holy Spirit, forever.
People: Amen.

Psalm 100

Glorify the Lord, all the earth!
>**O Giver of Light, O Lord: we lift up praise to you!**
>Glorify the Lord, all the earth!

Serve the Lord in *gla*dness.
>**O Giver of Light, O Lord: we lift up praise to you!**
>Enter before *him* with praise.

Know he is the *Lord* our God:
>he made us; it *was* not we.

We are his people, the sheep *of* his flock.
>Enter his gates with thanksgiving
>>and his *courts* with praise.

Give thanks to him *and* bless his name,
>for the Lord is good and eter*nal* is his grace,
>and his faithfulness is *un*to the ages.

Glory to the Father, to the Son and to *the* Holy Spirit.
>**From age to age, *a*men, amen.**

Glorify the Lord, all the earth!
>**O Giver of Light, O Lord: we lift up praise to you!**

Server: Let us pray. Peace be with us.
Priest: To you, O Lord, do we lift up praise and confession, and to your living and holy name do we offer adoration and thanksgiving at all times, O Lord of all, Father, Son and Holy Spirit, forever.
People: Amen.

Emmanuel Weekday Morning Prayer

We give you thanks,
O Lord of all,
we glorify you,
Jesus Christ;
you raise our bodies
into life,
you are the Savior
of our souls.
**In the morning, O Lord,
you hear my voice,
and in the morning
I prepare and present
myself to you.**
We give you thanks…
**Glory to the Father, to the Son
and to the Holy Spirit.
From age to age,
amen, amen.**
We give you thanks…

Lakhu Mara d-kulla
mawdenan,
w-lakh Ysho' Mshyḥa
mshabḥynan
d-attu Mnaḥmana
d-paghrayn,
w-attu Paroqa
d-nawshathan.
*Marya, b-ṣapra
tishma' qal,
wab-ṣapra
itṭayaw
w-ithḥze lakh.*
Lakhu Mara d-kulla…
*Shuḥa l-Abba w-laBra
wal-Ruḥa d-Qudsha
min 'alam wa'dhamma
l-'alam amen, w-amen.*
Lakhu Mara d-kulla…

Server: Let us pray. Peace be with us.
Priest: It is the duty, O Lord, of heaven, earth and all therein to thank, adore and glorify you for all of your benefits and graces whose greatness cannot be repaid, O Lord of all, Father, Son and Holy Spirit, forever.
People: Amen.
Server: Lift your voices, all you people, and glorify the living God.
People:

Holy God,
Holy Mighty One,
Holy Immortal One:
Have mercy on us.
**Glory to the Father, to the Son
and to the Holy Spirit.**
Holy God…
**From age to age,
amen, amen.**
Holy God…

Qaddysha Alaha
Qaddysha Ḥayilthana,
Qaddysha La Mayotha
Ithraḥam 'layn.
*Shuḥa l-Abba w-laBra
wal-Ruḥa d-Qudsha.*
Qaddysha Alaha…
*Min 'alam wa'dhamma
l-'alam amen, w-amen.*
Qaddysha Alaha…

Emmanuel Weekday Morning Prayer

Server: Let us pray. Peace be with us.
Priest: O Merciful One whose name is holy, Kind and Just One from eternity, whose grace and compassion overflow: may the sweet mercy of your love overflow, O Lord our God, upon the souls of your adorers who call and plead to you at all times and ages, Lord of all, Father, Son and Holy Spirit, forever.
People: Amen.

PENITENTIAL PSALM
Psalm 51

Have mercy on me, God, in *your* grace,
    and in your great mercies, *blot* out my sins.
    Have mercy on me, O Lord.
Have mercy on me, God, in *your* grace,
    and in your great mercies, *blot* out my sins.
Wash me thoroughly from *my* guilt
    and purify *me* of my sins.
    For I know my *tres*passes,
        my sins are al*ways* before me.
    Against you alone *have* I sinned,
        and have evil *done* before you.
That you may be just in *your* word,
    and grant justice *when* you judge:
in *my* guilt was I conceived,
    and with sin my *mot*her bore me.
    But you delighted *in* the truth;
        and showed me the se*crets* of your wisdom.
    Sprinkle me with hyssop, and I *shall* be clean;
        wash me with it, I shall be *whi*ter than snow.
May your delight and gladness sus*tain* me,
    and my humble *bones* will rejoice.
Turn your face from *my* sins,
    and blot out all *of* my misdeeds.
    A pure heart create in *me*, O God,
        renew your creating *Spi*rit in me.
    Cast me not from *your* presence,
        nor deprive me of *your* Holy Spirit.

Rather, return your joy and salvation *to* me,
> may your glorious *Spi*rit sustain me,
that I may teach the wicked *your* ways,
> and sinners may *turn* back to you.
>> Rescue me from bloodshed, *my* just God,
>> and my tongue shall praise *your* righteousness.
> O Lord, open *my* lips;
>> my mouth shall *speak* forth your praise.
You were not pleased in sac*ri*fice,
> nor considered *burnt* offerings.
The sacrifice of God is a hum*ble* spirit.
> God will not spurn *a* heart contrite.

Glory to the Father, to the Son and to the Ho*ly* Spirit.
> **From age to age, *a*men, amen.**
> **Have mercy on me, O Lord.**

Have mercy on me, God, in *your* grace,
> and in your great mercies, *blot* out my sins.
> **Christ the King, have *mer*cy on me!**

Server: Let us pray. Peace be with us.

Priest: O Tender, Merciful and Compassionate One, whose door is open to the repentant, and who calls unceasingly to sinners, that they may approach him in repentance: open, O Lord our God, the door of mercies to our prayer, accept our supplication, and grant our requests in your mercies from your rich and overflowing treasury, O Gracious One who does not withhold his mercies or his gifts from the needy and afflicted, his servants who call and plead to him at all times and ages, Lord of all, Father, Son and Holy Spirit, forever.

People: Amen.

Morning Glorification

Glory to you, our God!
Thanksgiving to you,
> our Maker!
We bless you,
> our Fashioner!
O Tender Lord!
O Merciful God!

Emmanuel Weekday Morning Prayer

O Compassionate Creator!
O Savior, our Guardian!
Our Helper and Upholder!
We adore you, O Lord,
for patient is your Spirit
and great is your grace!
O Merciful One, forgive us
and have pity on us!
Turn to us in the greatness
of your mercies!
Our Support
and mighty Stronghold!
O Lord our God,
show us your face,
and we shall be saved!
O Accepter of the repentant
in his mercies:
accept our prayer
and our service!
O Hearer of the voice
of his adorers:
let our imploring
come before you,
and have mercy on us!
O Forgiver of the debts
of mortals in his pity,
forgive us our debts
and sins in your pity!
O Absolver of the sins
of mankind in his grace:
absolve our many sins,
and have mercy on us!
O Good Hope of mankind,
grant us peace and serenity,
that we may confess your Trinity,
O Lord of all, forever, amen.

Emmanuel Weekday Morning Prayer

Server: Let us pray. Peace be with us.
Priest: O Christ, O Good Hope of mankind and peaceful harbor granting peace to creatures: may you, O Lord, accomplish your peace and tranquility among us, that in it we may give thanks to you and praise you unceasingly all the days of our lives, O Lord of all, forever.
People: Amen.

Morning Meditation

Server: Peace be with us.
Priest: To your wondrous and indescribable providence, O Lord, which was accomplished, completed and perfected in mercies and pity for the renewal and the salvation of our weak race through the Principal that is from us, do we lift up glory, honor, thanksgiving and adoration at all times, O Lord of all, Father, Son and Holy Spirit, forever.
People: Amen.

A Seasonal Hymn of the Week (see pp. 389–578), and then, from Seasons of the Apostles to the Church, the Martyr Hymns (pp. 353–88)

- **Holy is the dwelling-place of the Most High.** - *talmydhaw*
By the prayers of your mother, Jesus, Lord,
pacify the whole world that is troubled by its sins;
take away all conflicts from the earth;
reconcile Church and state, that in love and in harmony,
we may give her praise during all our days.
- **They kept his witness, and the covenant he gave them.**
May the just who have pleased you, Jesus, Lord,
prophets and apostles, martyrs, teachers from all lands,
plead to you on all our souls' behalf,
that you have compassion, and with them, make us all worthy
to give thanks to you on the day you come.
- **May the memorial of the just be forever.**
Blessed are you, O holy patron,
who accomplished victory in the vineyard of the Lord
and received reward for all your works,
the reward of heaven's bliss: may your prayers be upon us all,
and make us worthy to be heaven's heirs.

Server: Let us pray. Peace be with us.
Priest: May our miserable prayer arise before you like incense, O Lord our God, may our feeble supplication enter before you, may your mercies be advocates for our guiltiness, and may the requests of our neediness be answered from the great treasury of your compassion, at all times and ages, Lord of all, Father, Son and Holy Spirit, forever.
People: Amen.

MONDAY
Psalm 13

How long, O Lord, *will* you forget me?
    Glory **to you, O God.**
How long, O Lord, *will* you forget me?
    How long *will* you hide your face?
How long will there be *grief* in my soul,
    this sorrow *in* my heart all day?
How long shall my e*ne*my prevail?
    Look at me, an*s*wer me, Lord God!
Give light to my eyes lest I fall *a*sleep in death,
    lest my enemy say: "*I* have overcome him";
lest my foes rejoice *to* see my fall.
    As for me, *I* trust in your grace.
Let my heart rejoice in *your* saving help;
    let me *praise* the Lord who saved me.
Glory to the Father, to the Son and to *the* Holy Spirit.
    From age to *age*, amen, amen.
Glory **to you, O God.**

Glorification of Mar Abraham

Savior, turn toward your *lo*wly servants' prayers,
    our pleading accept, re*spond* to our needs,
for you are the hope and *re*fuge of the weak.
    Through your help, let us de*feat* Satan's wiles.
Lo, he lays traps for our *souls* both night and day,
    and, in malice, he wants *to* strike us down.
Send your power, O Lord, and *cut* up his snares,
    lest he capture us in*to* sin's abyss.

May your grace's strength make *our* conscience strong,
> that we may please you, O *Mer*ciful One.

Make us all worthy to *sing*, when you come,
> an unceasing praise, for*ev*er, amen.

TUESDAY
Psalm 28

To you, *O* Lord, I called,
> **Glo*ry* to you, O God.**

To you, *O* Lord, I called,
> my God, do not *be* silent with me.

If you are silent with me, I will *be* handed over
> with those who have gone *down* into the cave.

Hear the sound of my pleading as *I* call to you,
> as I lift up my hands *to* your holy temple.

Do not count me *a*mong the wicked,
> or with *those* who do evil,

who speak words of *peace* to their neighbors
> but have *e*vil in their hearts.

Repay them accor*ding* to their works,
> and ac*cor*ding to their malice.

For they ignore the deeds of the Lord and the *work* of his hands.
> May he ruin them *and* never rebuild them.

Blessed be the Lord *for* he has heard
> all the *sound* of my pleading.

The Lord is my help and my shield; in *him* my heart trusts
> and my flesh rejoices; *I* thank him with praise.

The Lord is the *strength* of his people,
> a fortress of the sal*va*tion of his Christ.

Save your people and bless *your* heritage.
> Be their shepherd *and* guide them forever.

Glory to the Father, to the Son and to *the* Holy Spirit.
> **From age to *age*, amen, amen.**

Glo*ry* to you, O God.

Glorification of Mar Abba

Earth and heaven and all *that* they contain
    cannot make you known, who *or*der all things!
Too small are they both to *tell* of your love,
    the heights of your grace, and *your* great mercies
that you sent to our most *un*worthy race.
    Kind and Gracious One, who *took* on our flesh,
who saved us from death and *has* ascended,
    who sits above all, as *Lord* and Ruler:
all the hosts of angels *be*fore you kneel,
    and together praise you *un*ceasingly:
O Father, and Son, and *their* Holy Spirit;
    all glory to you, from *age* unto age!

WEDNESDAY
Psalm 67

May God have *mer*cy on us,
    *Glo*ry to you, O God.
May God have *mer*cy on us,
    bless us, and let *his* face shine on us.
That his ways *be* known on earth
    and his salva*tion* among all peoples.
Let the peoples con*fess* you, O God;
    let all the *peo*ples confess you.
Let the kingdoms *be* glad and praise,
    for you judge the nations uprightly
        and *guide* the nations on earth.
Let the peoples con*fess* you, O God;
    let all the *peo*ples confess you.
The earth has *yiel*ded its fruit,
    for *God*, our God, has blessed us.
May God still *give* us his blessing,
    and all the ends *of* the earth will fear him.
Glory to the Father, to the Son and to *the* Holy Spirit.
    From age to *age*, amen, amen.
***Glo*ry to you, O God.**

Glorification of Mar Thomas of Urhai

May your mercies be on our sins,
> O Christ, Friend of the penitent.

Give ear to us, our Kind Doctor;
> remove the sores of wickedness.

Because you know our suffering,
> heal our wounds with your medicine.

Apply your mercy to our scars,
> and heal us, Lord, as is your way.

With the dew that is of your grace,
> cleanse our defects, as is your will.

Let us together praise your name:
> Father, and Son, and Holy Spirit,
> forever and ever, amen.

THURSDAY
Psalm 54

O God, save *me* by your name,
> **Glo*ry* to you, O God.**

O God, save *me* by your name,
> and *judge* me by your might.

O *God*, hear my prayer;
> hearken to *the* words of my mouth.

For strangers have *ri*sen against me;
> the *wic*ked seek my soul.

They have no regard *for* you, O God:
> O God my help, up*hol*der of my soul.

Bring evil upon *my* enemies
> and si*lence* them by your truth;

and I will sacrifice to *you* in discernment,
> and confess that your *name*, O Lord, is good.

For you have delivered *me* from all troubles,
> and my eyes have seen *the* fall of my enemies.

Glory to the Father, to the Son and to *the* Holy Spirit.
> **From age to *age*, amen, amen.**

Glo*ry* to you, O God.

Glorification of Mar Ephrem

Accept, Lord, the pleading of all,
    which we bring forth in petition.
Hear, God, the voice of your servants,
    the groaning of those who praise you.
You are our King; in your great name
    we have true hope and confidence.
Grant that we may all gain one mind,
    without division, in the faith,
as we confess that, by your will
    all things were made out of nothing.
Your Essence can never be searched
    by creatures, you who dwell in Light!
By your making, Lord, your richness
    was made known to your handiwork.
For you are Lord and Fashioner
    Almighty, who provides for all.
We deeply long for forgiveness:
    bestow it, as you always do.
And grant that we may spiritually
    apply your balm onto our wounds.
We ask for mercies, Lord of all:
    grant your wealth to our poverty.
Your mercy be a steady guide
    for those who waver and who stray
in the deceit of Satan's way,
    and tread their consciences a path,
that they may know it was your plan
    that our enslaved race was freed.
Thus, with perfect, innocent heart,
    may we serve you as is your will,
and always do, with diligence,
    all that pleases Divinity,
and lift up praise with one accord
    to Father, Son and Holy Spirit,

who saved us through our Principal;
>   did not treat us as we deserve.
Glory to him from all on earth,
>   forever and ever, amen.

FRIDAY
Psalm 95

Come, let *us* praise the Lord,
>   ***Glo**ry to you, O God.*
Come, let *us* praise the Lord,
>   and sing *to* our God, the Savior.
Let us come before *him* giving thanks,
>   and glo*ri*fy him with songs.
For our God *is* a great Lord,
>   the great King *over* all the gods,
in whose hands are the founda*tions* of the earth
>   and the *heights* of the mountains.
His is the sea, *for* he made it,
>   and the *dry* land his hands made.
Come, let us bless *and* worship him,
>   and kneel be*fore* the Lord who made us.
For he is our God, and *we* are his people,
>   and the *sheep* of his flock.
Glory to the Father, to the Son and to *the* Holy Spirit.
>   **From age to *age*, amen, amen.**
***Glo**ry to you, O God.*

Glorification of Mar Abraham of Nithpar

Glory to him who has made known
>   his glory to mankind in love.
He created a mute thing of dust,
>   and gave it a soul of treasures.
He placed his thanks in lowly flesh,
>   that the whole world may sing him praise.
Come, rational, and sing his praise,
>   before we doze the sleep of death.

During the night, remember death,
  which shuts and silences our mouths.
The just who praise him during night
  are alive even when they die,
but the evil who deny him
  are dead even during their lives.
Let us now wake our flesh in prayer
  and praise the Hidden Majesty,
that we may be like the virgins
  who were praised in the parable.
On that night when he shakes the world,
  may we meet the Son while awake.
Let us not drown in our desires,
  but see his glory when he dawns.
Let us be watchful servants when
  he leads forth those in his chamber.
The evil will be suffering;
  the door of mercies will be shut.
Thus, while we live, let us labor,
  for after death is our reward.
The flesh that is wearied in prayer
  will fly in air the day he comes,
will see the Lord while without shame,
  and will enter in the kingdom.
The angels and the just love him,
  who have kept vigil in their prayer.
Blest is he who made us vessels
  to praise him, though we are of dust.
Praise him who gave us earthly ones
  a share with those who are above,
that we may sing, on every night,
  and every time, "holy his name."
Let us together sing his praise
  forever and ever, amen.

Saturday
Psalm 150

Praise God in *his* holy place.
   ***Glo*ry to you, O God.**
Praise God in *his* holy place,
   praise him *in* his mighty firmament.
Praise him *for* his power,
   praise *his* surpassing greatness.
O praise him *with* sound of trumpet,
   praise *him* with lute and harp.
Praise him with timbrel *and* tambourine,
   praise him with pleasant strings.
   Praise him *with* resounding cymbals,
Praise him *with* hymns and cries!
   Praise the *Lord* with every breath!
Glory to the Father, to the Son and to *the* Holy Spirit.
   From age to *age*, amen, amen.
***Glo*ry to you, O God.**

Glorification of Mar Ephrem

Blest be him who made us, *sav*ed us in his Christ,
   who called us to know the *ho*ly Trinity.
God the Word, Only-Be*got*ten of the Father:
   may I please you in our *man*hood you wore,
and may I never be *sil*ent, Christ, my Lord,
   to give thanks to *your* name at all times.

Morning Petitions

Server: Let us all stand composed. In faith and hope, let us implore *and* say: Lord, have mer*c*y on us.

People: Lord, have mer*c*y on us. | *Maran ithraḥam 'layn.*

* Almighty Lord, Eternal Being who dwells in the high*est* heavens, we *im*plore you...

* O One who is alone the Maker and Fashioner of creatures, and who dwells in radi*ant* light, we *im*plore you...

* O One in the abounding love with which he loved us has fashioned our race in his Ho*nor's* image, we *im*plore you...

* O One who promised benefits to his friends through Abraham the faithful, and through the revelation of Christ was made known to *his* Church, we *im*plore you...

* O One who does not wish the destruction of our race, but rather its repentance from the error of darkness to the knowledge of *the* truth, we *im*plore you...

* For the health of our holy fathers: [Mar _____, High Pont*iff*, Pope of Rome,] Mar _____, Catholicos-Patriarch, Mar _____, Bishop/Metropolitan, and for all those in the same priest*ly* service, we *im*plore you...

* O Compassionate God, who guides all in *his* mercy, we *im*plore you...

* O One who is glorified in heaven and worshipped *on* earth, we *im*plore you...

* Give us victory, O Christ our Lord, in your coming, give peace to your Church saved by your precious Blood, and have mer*c*y on us...

Server: Let us entrust our souls mutually to the Father, and to the Son, and to *the* Holy Spirit.

People: To you, *O* Lord our God.

Emmanuel Weekday Morning Prayer

[Lenten Morning Petitions]

Server: Let us all stand composed. In faith and hope, let us implore *and* say: Lord, have mer*cy* on us.

People: Lord, have mer*cy* on us. | *Maran ithraḥam ʻlayn.*

* Our all-merciful God, who freely justi*fies* sinners, we *im*plore you...

* O Good Shepherd who came searching for us and gave himself up on our *be*half, we *im*plore you...

* O Just Judge, who is patient in hope of our *re*pentance, we *im*plore you...

* O Doctor of mankind who came and was revealed in the flesh, who forgave our faults and healed *our* wounds, we *im*plore you...

* O Lord, who granted good hope through the tax collectors and sinners he accepted and *for*gave, we *im*plore you...

* For the health of our holy fathers: [Mar _____, High Pontiff, Pope of Rome,] Mar _____, Catholicos-Patriarch, Mar _____, Bishop/Metropolitan, and for all those in the same priest*ly* service, we *im*plore you...

* O Compassionate God, who guides all in *his* mercy, we *im*plore you...

* O One who is glorified in heaven and worshipped *on* earth, we *im*plore you...

* For sinners to repent, for the repentant to be justified, and for the justified to be *per*fected, we *im*plore you...

* Pity and forgive us, O Christ our Lord, in your grace, and let your mercies overflow upon us all in your pity , and have mer*cy* on us...

Server: Let us entrust our souls mutually to the Father, and to the Son, and to *the* Holy Spirit.

People: To you, *O* Lord our God.]

Presider: To you, Lord God almighty, do we entrust our bodies and our souls, and from you, O Lord our God, do we receive all benefits and blessings; and so, as the crown of our prayer, in that confidence that is from you, we call together upon you and say thus:

People:

Our Father who art in heaven,	Aḅḅun dba-shmayya
hallowed be your name.	nithqaddash shmakh,
Your kingdom come.	tethe malkuthakh,
Holy, holy, you are holy.	**qaddysh, qaddysh, qaddysh-at,**
Our Father in heaven:	**Aḅḅun dba-shmayya.**
heaven and earth are full	**Damlen shmayya w-ar'a**
of the greatness of your glory;	**rabbuth shuḥakh,**
angels & men cry out to you:	**'yre w-nasha qa'en lakh**
holy, holy, you are holy.	**qaddysh, qaddysh, qaddysh-at.**
Our Father who art in heaven,	Aḅḅun dba-shmayya
hallowed be thy name.	nithqaddash shmakh,
Thy kingdom come,	tethe malkuthakh,
thy will be done on earth	nehwe ṣiw-yanakh
as it is in heaven.	aykanna dba-shmayya ap b-ar'a,
Give us this day our daily bread	haw lan laḥma d-sunqanan
and forgive us our trespasses,	yawmana wa-shwoq lan ḥawbayn
as we forgive those	wa-ḥtahayn aykanna d-ap ḥnan
who trespassed against us.	shwaqn l-ḥay-yawayn,
And lead us not into temptation,	w-la ta'lan l-nisyona
but deliver us from evil,	illa paṣan min bysha
for thine is the kingdom,	miṭṭul d-dhylakh-y malkutha,
the power and the glory,	w-ḥayla w-tish-buḥta
now and forever.	l-'alam 'almyn, amen.

Presider: Glory to the Father, to the Son and to the Holy Spirit.
People: From age to age, amen, amen. Our Father who art in heaven, hallowed be your name. Your kingdom come.
Holy, holy, you are holy.
Our Father in heaven:

Presider: *Shuḥa l-Aḅḅa wla-Bra wal-Ruḥa d-Qudsha.*
People: *Min 'alam wa-'dham-ma l-'alam amen w-amen. Aḅḅun dba-shmayya nithqaddash shmakh, tethe malkuthakh,* **Qaddysh, qaddysh, qaddysh-at, Aḅḅun dba-shmayya.**

heaven and earth are full of the greatness of your glory; angels & men cry out to you: holy, holy, you are holy.	*Damlen shmayya w-ar'a rabbuth shuḥakh, 'yre w-nasha qa'en lakh qaddysh, qaddysh, qaddysh-at.*

Server: *Barekh mar.*

Server says to the people: Bow your heads for the prayer and accept the blessing.

Final Blessing

Presider: Bestow, O Lord our God, in your grace, at this morning hour, redemption upon the oppressed, freedom upon the captive, refreshment upon the weary, healing upon the sick, closeness upon the distant, protection upon the near, forgiveness upon sinners, acceptance upon the repentant, exaltation upon the just, care upon the poor, finding upon the lost, return upon the exiled, a gracious and acceptable memory upon the deceased, and mercies and pity upon all things created and made. Accomplish, among us and among all men, those things which aid us who are weak and sinners and which please your Majesty, in your grace and mercies, now, at all times, and forever and ever.

Shorter Prayers

Daily Personal Prayer

In the morning, when you wake from sleep: - *m'yna d-ṭawatha*
At dawn of morning, we lift glory to your name,
    for you have saved us and all the world.
        Grant us in your grace that our day be filled with peace,
        and we beg you to forgive our sins.
Deny not our hope, do not close your door to us,
    do not hold back of your saving grace,
    and do not treat us as our deeds deserve, O Lord,
        for you alone know how weak we are.
Sow, Lord, in the world, love and peace and harmony,
    uphold our priests, kings and governors,
        grant peace to countries, heal the sick, protect the poor,
        forgive the sins of the sons of men.
Your grace protect us on the path we walk, O Lord,
    as to David, the young man, from Saul.
        Grant us in mercy what we need for our sojourn,
        that as you will, we may walk in peace.
The grace that guarded Moses the prophet at sea,
     and Daniel in the lion's den,
     and Hananiah's family in the furnace,
     protect us, Lord, from the evil one.

Continue:
We awake in the morning and adore the Father,
lift up praise to the Son and confess the Holy Spirit.
    May the grace of the Father, the mercy of the Son
    and the compassion of the Spirit – the Trinity's Mystery –
    be for our benefit all of our days.
Our help is in you, O true Doctor, Supporter:
apply the medicine of your mercies
and heal our wounds, lest we perish completely.
    Without your aid, we become even weaker,
    O Christ, who supports those who do his will:
    protect your adorers, that they keep your commands.

Shorter Prayers

Let us plead in groaning and beg for mercies,
asking forgiveness from the Merciful One
who opens his door to all who turn to him.
> Day after day I promise you that tomorrow I will repent,
> but my days pass away and are gone, and my sins remain.
> O Christ, forgive me, and have mercy on me.

At night, before you sleep:
Psalm 120: I lift my eyes to the mountain: * from where shall come my help? * My help comes from the Lord * who made heaven and earth. * May he never allow your foot to stumble, nor let your guardian sleep. * No, he sleeps not nor slumbers, Israel's guardian. * The Lord is your guardian, * he will place his right hand upon you. * By day the sun shall not smite you, * nor the moon in the night. * The Lord will guard you from all evils, * the Lord will guard your soul. * The Lord will guard your going and your coming * both now and forever. * Glory to the Father, to the Son and to the Holy Spirit. * From age to age, amen, amen. *Halleluiah, halleluiah, halleluiah.

Nighttime Hymn of Mar Ephrem – *maran ithraḥam 'layn*

* O Lord, have mercy on us; Lord, accept our services.
Lord, turn not your face away; from sinners who call to you.
> * Send to me a guardian, to protect me as I sleep,
> and, by your own living Flesh, save me from all evil things.

* Guide my sleep throughout this night, that it be filled with your peace;
lest the evil one harm me, or thoughts filled with wickedness.
> * Through the holy cross, O Lord, on which you humbled yourself,
> grant me restful sleep tonight, and deliver me from harm.

* May your Body I received, guard me from evil desires;
may the Blood you shed for me, grant me rest within your peace.
> * May the fortress of your mercy guard my soul, which is your image,
> may your right hand guard my flesh, which your hand has fashioned.

* May the stronghold of your mercy shelter me, a mighty shield,
and when I am fast asleep, may your power be my guard.
> * Let my slumber come ascend, incense to your holy throne.
> By your mother's intercession, keep the devil from my bed.

* By your sacrifice for all, chase the evil one away;
your promise fulfill in me; by your cross protect my life.
> * That I rise and serve you well, thanking you for all your love;
> Glory to you, and your Father, and your hallowing Spirit.

SHORTER EVENING PRAYER

Opening Prayer: It is right at all times for us to thank, adore and glorify the great and awesome, holy and blessed, lofty and incomprehensible name of your glorious Trinity, and your grace toward our race, O Lord of all, Father, Son and Holy Spirit, forever.

We give you thanks, O Lord of all, we glorify you, Jesus Christ;
you raise our bodies into life, you are the Savior of our souls.
**I rejoiced when I heard them say:
we are going to the house of the Lord!**
We give you thanks...
**Glory to the Father, to the Son and to the Holy Spirit.
From age to age, amen, amen.**
We give you thanks...

Prayer: It is our duty, O Lord our God, to thank, adore and glorify you for your mercy and your providential will for us, at all times, O Lord of all, Father, Son and Holy Spirit, forever.

Psalm 140

I have called to you, Lord; hasten to *help* me!
   Hearken to my words and *a*ccept my prayer.
I have called to you, Lord; hasten to *help* me!
   Hearken to my words and *a*ccept my prayer.
Let my prayer arise before you like *in*cense;
   the offering of my hands like an eve*ning* oblation.
Set, O Lord, a guard over my *mouth*
   and a guard *o*ver my lips!
That my heart may not turn to an evil *deed*,
   or accompl*ish* works of wickedness.
May I not dine with evil *men*.
   Let a just man teach *me* and reprove me.
But let the oil of the wicked not anoint my *head*,
   for my prayer is *a*gainst their malice.
Their judges were thrown down by a rock-like *hand*,
   then they heard that *my* words were kind,
Like a plough that scatters the *ground*.
   Their bones were strewn at *the* mouth of Sheol.

Shorter Prayers

To you, Lord God, I lift up my *eyes*:
> I trust you; do not cast *my* soul away!

Guard me from the hands of the *boastful*,
> who *set* traps for me.

Let the wicked fall together into their own *nets*
> while I pursue *my* way unharmed.

Psalm 118:105–12

Your word is a lamp for my *feet*
> and a *light* for my paths.

I have sworn and made up my *mind*
> to keep *your* just decrees.

Lord, I am deeply aff*lic*ted:
> give me *life* by your word.

Be pleased, Lord, with the words of my *mouth*
> and teach me *by* your decrees.

My soul is in your hands at all *times*;
> I will not *for*get your law.

Though sinners laid traps for *me*,
> I did not stray *from* your commands.

Your witness is my heritage for*ever*,
> for it is the *joy* of my heart.

I set my heart to carry out your *stat*utes
> in *truth*, for ever.

Glory to the Father, to the Son and to the Holy *Spir*it.
> **From age to age, *a*men, amen.**

I have called to you, Lord; hasten to *help* me!
> **Hearken to my words and *accept* my prayer.**

Prayer: Hear, O Lord our God, the prayer of your servants in your mercy; accept the supplication of your adorers in your compassion, and pity our sinfulness in your grace and mercies, O Healer of our bodies and Good Hope of our souls at all times, Lord of all, Father, Son and Holy Spirit, forever.

Holy God, Holy Mighty One, Holy Immortal One: Have mercy on us.
> **Glory to the Father, to the Son and to the Holy Spirit.**

Holy God...
> **From age to age, amen, amen.**

Holy God...

Shorter Prayers

Let us all stand composed. In faith and hope, let us implore *and* say: Lord, have mer*cy* on us.

Response: Lord, have mer*cy* on us.

* O Father of mercies and God of every con*so*lation, we *im*plore you...

* Our Savior, our Caretaker and Provider *for* all, we *im*plore you...

* For the peace, concord and well-being of the whole world and of *all* churches, we *im*plore you...

* O Kind One in his Nature who is the Giver of *good* things, we *im*plore you...

* O One who is glorified in heaven and worshipped *on* earth, we *im*plore you...

* Save us all, O Christ our Lord, in your grace, increase your peace and your tranquility within us and have mer*cy* on us...

* Let us entrust our souls mutually to the Father, and to the Son, and to *the* Holy Spirit.

Response: To you, *O* Lord our God.

Prayer: To you, Lord God almighty, do we entrust our bodies and our souls, and from you, O Lord our God, do we receive all benefits and blessings; and so, as the crown of our prayer, in that confidence that is from you, we call together upon you and say thus:

Our Father who art in heaven, hallowed be your name. Your kingdom come. **Holy, holy, you are holy. Our Father in heaven: heaven and earth are full of the greatness of your glory; angels & men cry out to you: holy, holy, you are holy.** Our Father who art in heaven, hallowed be thy name. Thy kingdom come, thy will be done on earth as it is in heaven. Give us this day our daily bread and forgive us our trespasses, as we forgive those who trespassed against us. And lead us not into temptation, but deliver us from evil, for thine is the kingdom, the power and the glory, now and forever.

(Presider): Glory to the Father, to the Son and to the Holy Spirit.

People: From age to age, amen, amen. Our Father who art in heaven, hallowed be your name. Your kingdom come. **Holy, holy, you are holy. Our Father in heaven: heaven and earth are full of the greatness of your glory; angels & men cry out to you: holy, holy, you are holy.**

FINAL BLESSING

May the peace of the Father be with us, the love of the Son be among us, and may the Holy Spirit guide us according to his will. Upon us be his mercies and compassion at all times and ages, Lord of all, Father, Son and Holy Spirit, forever.

Shorter Prayers

SHORTER MORNING PRAYER

Opening Prayer: All the creatures you have created, O Lord, enter before you; they kneel and adore you, sing and hallow you, ask and entreat you, implore and beseech you, confess and glorify you, for by your command were they constructed, and through your will came they to be; for you are the Cause of their existence, and the Breath and Spiration of our lives, O Lord of all, Father, Son and Holy Spirit, forever.

Psalm 100

Glorify the Lord, all the earth!
> **O Giver of Light, O Lord: we lift up praise to you!**
> Glorify the Lord, all the earth!

Serve the Lord in *gla*dness.
> **O Giver of Light, O Lord: we lift up praise to you!**
> Enter before *him* with praise.

Know he is the *Lord* our God:
> he made us; it *was* not we.

We are his people, the sheep *of* his flock.
> Enter his gates with thanksgiving
>> and his *courts* with praise.

Give thanks to him *and* bless his name,
> for the Lord is good and eter*nal* is his grace,
> and his faithfulness is *un*to the ages.

Glory to the Father, to the Son and to *the* Holy Spirit.
> **From age to age, *a*men, amen.**

Glorify the Lord, all the earth!
> **O Giver of Light, O Lord: we lift up praise to you!**

Prayer: To you, O Lord, do we lift up praise and confession, and to your living and holy name do we offer adoration and thanksgiving at all times, O Lord of all, Father, Son and Holy Spirit, forever.

> We give you thanks, O Lord of all, we glorify you, Jesus Christ;
> you raise our bodies into life, you are the Savior of our souls.
> **In the morning, O Lord, you hear my voice,**
> **and in the morning I prepare and present myself to you.**
> We give you thanks…
> **Glory to the Father, to the Son and to the Holy Spirit.**
> **From age to age, amen, amen.**
> We give you thanks…

Shorter Prayers

Prayer: It is the duty, O Lord, of heaven, earth and all therein to thank, adore and glorify you for all of your benefits and graces whose greatness cannot be repaid, O Lord of all, Father, Son and Holy Spirit, forever.

Morning Hymn of Praise

Glory to you, our God!
Thanksgiving to you, our Maker!
We bless you, our Fashioner!
O Tender Lord! O Merciful God! O Compassionate Creator!
O Savior, our Guardian! Our Helper and Upholder!
We adore you, O Lord,
for patient is your Spirit and great is your grace!
O Merciful One, forgive us and have pity on us!
Turn to us in the greatness of your mercies!
Our Support and mighty Stronghold!
O Lord our God, show us your face, and we shall be saved!
O Accepter of the repentant in his mercies:
accept our prayer and our service!
O Hearer of the voice of his adorers:
let our imploring come before you, and have mercy on us!
O Forgiver of the debts of mortals in his pity,
forgive us our debts and sins in your pity!
O Absolver of the sins of mankind in his grace:
absolve our many sins, and have mercy on us!
O Good Hope of mankind,
grant us peace and serenity,
that we may confess your Trinity,
O Lord of all, forever, amen.

Petitions

Let us all stand composed. In faith and hope, let us implore *and* say: Lord, have mer*cy* on us.

Response: Lord, have mer*cy* on us.

* Almighty Lord, Eternal Being who dwells in the high*est* heavens, we *im*plore you...

* O One who is alone the Maker and Fashioner of creatures, and who dwells in radi*ant* light, we *im*plore you...

Shorter Prayers

* O One in the abounding love with which he loved us has fashioned our race in his Ho*nor's* image, we *im*plore you...
* O One who promised benefits to his friends through Abraham the faithful, and through the revelation of Christ was made known to *his* Church, we *im*plore you...
* O One who does not wish the destruction of our race, but rather its repentance from the error of darkness to the knowledge of *the* truth, we *im*plore you...
* O One who is glorified in heaven and worshipped *on* earth, we *im*plore you...
* Give us victory, O Christ our Lord, in your coming, give peace to your Church saved by your precious Blood, and have mer*cy* on us...
* Let us entrust our souls mutually to the Father, and to the Son, and to *the* Holy Spirit.

Response: To you, *O* Lord our God.
Prayer: To you, Lord God almighty, do we entrust our bodies and our souls, and from you, O Lord our God, do we receive all benefits and blessings; and so, as the crown of our prayer, in that confidence that is from you, we call together upon you and say thus:

Our Father who art in heaven, hallowed be your name. Your kingdom come. **Holy, holy, you are holy. Our Father in heaven: heaven and earth are full of the greatness of your glory; angels & men cry out to you: holy, holy, you are holy.** Our Father who art in heaven, hallowed be thy name. Thy kingdom come, thy will be done on earth as it is in heaven. Give us this day our daily bread and forgive us our trespasses, as we forgive those who trespassed against us. And lead us not into temptation, but deliver us from evil, for thine is the kingdom, the power and the glory, now and forever.
(Presider): Glory to the Father, to the Son and to the Holy Spirit.
People: From age to age, amen, amen. Our Father who art in heaven, hallowed be your name. Your kingdom come. **Holy, holy, you are holy. Our Father in heaven: heaven and earth are full of the greatness of your glory; angels & men cry out to you: holy, holy, you are holy.**

FINAL BLESSING

May your grace dawn upon us, O Lord, when your Justice judges us, and may your mercies come to our aid on the day that your greatness dawns, O Lord of all, Father, Son and Holy Spirit, forever.

Shorter Prayers

SHORTER SUNDAY MORNING PRAYER

Priest: Enlighten us, O Lord, in your Light, gladden us by your coming, delight us in your salvation, and let us share in your Mysteries. Grant, and make us worthy, that with the heavenly assemblies clothed with light and the legions of angels, with hymns filled with thanksgiving, we may sing praise to your glorious Trinity. O Creator with dominion over all! O Creator who is not in need of the service of creatures! O Creator of light in his grace, and Orderer of darkness in his Wisdom, Knowledge and Divinity, incomprehensible to the spiritual and the physical, O Lord of all, Father, Son and Holy Spirit, forever.
People: Amen.

Psalm 100

Glorify the Lord, all the earth!
    O Giver of Light, O Lord: we lift up praise to you!
    Glorify the Lord, all the earth!
Serve the Lord in *gla*dness.
    O Giver of Light, O Lord: we lift up praise to you!
Enter before *him* with praise.
    Know he is the *Lord* our God:
he made us; it *was* not we.
    We are his people, the sheep *of* his flock.
Enter his gates with thanksgiving and his *courts* with praise.
    Give thanks to him *and* bless his name,
for the Lord is good and eter*nal* is his grace,
    and his faithfulness is *un*to the ages.
Glory to the Father, to the Son and to *the* Holy Spirit.
    From age to age, *a*men, amen.
Glorify the Lord, all the earth!
    O Giver of Light, O Lord: we lift up praise to you!

Server: Let us pray. Peace be with us.
Priest: To you, O Christ the true Light, the glorious Image of the Father, who was revealed and dawned in the world for the renewal and the redemption of our nature through the Principal that is from us, do we lift up glory, honor, thanksgiving and adoration at all times, Lord of all, forever.
People: Amen.

MORNING HYMN (see pp. 389–578)

Shorter Prayers

- From age to age, amen, amen. – *b-madnaḥay ṣapra*
At dawn of morning, we lift glory to your name,
    for you have saved us and all the world.
        Grant us in your grace, that our day be filled with peace,
        and we beg you to forgive our sins.
Deny not our hope, do not close your door to us,
    do not hold back of your saving grace,
        and do not treat us, as our deeds deserve, O Lord,
        for you alone know how weak we are.
Sow, Lord, in the world, love and peace and harmony,
    uphold our priests, kings and governors,
        grant peace to countries, heal the sick, protect the poor,
        forgive the sins of the sons of men.

Server: Let us pray. Peace be with us.
Priest: Make us all worthy O Lord, in your grace and mercies, to rejoice and delight in the glorious light of your revelation and the joyful dawning of your coming, that which all the creatures you have created look to, hope for and await, with all the true sons of your Mysteries in the Jerusalem above, O Lord of all, Father, Son and Holy Spirit, forever.
People: Amen.

MORNING HYMN OF MAR EPHREM

Light has dawned upon the just, and joy to the upright of heart.
Nuhra dnaḥ l-zad-y-qi wla-try-ṣay libba ḥadhu-tha.
Jesus Christ, our sovereign Lord,
dawning from the Father's Womb,
came and brought us out of darkness,
bright'ning us with his radiant Light!
    Day has dawned upon mankind,
    and the power of darkness fled;
    brightness dawning from his radiant
    Light has brightened our darkened eyes.
His glory he dawned on earth,
brightening the lowest depths;
death was darkened, darkness banished,
and the gates of Sheol were destroyed.
    He enlightened all mankind,
    which had been in dark before,
    and the dead, who had been buried,
    rose and praised, for they had been saved.

Shorter Prayers

He, the Savior, gave us life,
to the Father's Womb returned;
he will come again in glory,
bright'ning those who bide his return.
> Our King will come again!
> Let us light our lamps and go,
> ready to rejoice in him,
> as he rejoiced in us and gave us joy!

Let us lift up praise to him,
to the Father giving thanks,
who in mercy sent him to us,
our Salvation and all our Hope.
> From the silence his day dawns,
> and his saints are all awake,
> and all those who labored, wearied
> and prepared are lighting their lamps.

All the watchers in the heights
laud the glory of the just,
placing crowns upon their heads,
shouting together: "halleluiah!"
> Brethren, rise up and prepare,
> give thanks to our Savior King,
> who in glory will return and
> gladden us with his radiant Light!

Morning Hymn of Mar Narsai

The light of the dawning of Christ has gladdened earth and heaven.
Nuhra d-dhinḥeh da-Mshyḥa ḥad-dy l-ar'a wla-shmayya.

Error, like the darkest night,
had been spread across the world,
but the Light of the Messiah
dawned and gave the world clarity.
> History, from Adam on,
> had resembled darkest night,
> and the day of Christ's unveiling
> was the daylight hours' running-course.

Our Lord even compared
morning to his preaching's start,
and the evening to the ending,
when the world will rest from its work.

Shorter Prayers

    Priests and kings and prophets had
    waited with this hope in mind,
    and the Maker gave them comfort
    in the day that he was revealed.
In his day all creatures rest,
who had once been crushed in sin,
and the world begins to ponder
the meaning of the world to come.
    The New Covenant he gave
    to all who accept his creed,
    and with his own Blood he sealed it,
    that his promise might never fail.
With his promised Paradise,
he made fast the course of man,
and behold, on earth and heaven
all await his coming again.
    The new coming of the King
    who rules from our race has neared:
    come, let us prepare to meet him
    with the hosts of heaven above!
Let us take the oil of love
for that day filled with despair,
lest we hear the voice then saying,
"begone, I know not of your works."
    While we live, then, let us work
    in the vineyard of the Word,
    that we may then hear the voice which says:
    "Come and receive what was vowed!"
Let us fix our mind's sojourn
with the hope of life to come,
and arrive, through love and faith, then,
at the harbor of all delights!
Light has dawned upon the just, and joy to the upright of heart.
Nuhra dnaḥ l-zad-y-qi wla-try-ṣay libba ḥadhu-tha.

Shorter Prayers

Daniel 3:57–88

Bless the Lord, you works of *the* Lord!
Bless the *Lord*, heavens of the Lord!

Daniel Verse (see pp. 389–578)

Bless the Lord, you works of *the* Lord!
Bless the *Lord*, heavens of the Lord!
    Bless the Lord, angels of *the* Lord!
    Bless the *Lord*, waters above!
Bless the Lord, hosts of *the* Lord!
Bless the *Lord*, O sun and moon!
    Bless the Lord, O stars of *heaven*!
    Bless the *Lord*, O rain and dew!
Bless the Lord, all *you* winds!
Bless the *Lord*, O fire and heat!
    Bless the Lord, O night *and* day!
    Bless the *Lord*, light and darkness!
Bless the Lord, O cold *and* heat!
Bless the *Lord*, O ice and snow!
    Bless the Lord, lightning *and* cloud!
    Bless the *Lord*, O all the earth!
Bless the Lord, mountains *and* hills!
Bless the *Lord*, all that grows on earth!
    Bless the Lord, O seas and *rivers*!
    Bless the *Lord*, springs of water!
Bless the Lord, fish and sea *creatures*!
Bless the *Lord*, all birds of the sky!
    Bless the Lord, beasts, wild *and* tame!
    Bless the *Lord*, O sons of men!
Bless the Lord, O sons *of* men!
Bless the *Lord*, house of Israel!
    Bless the Lord, O priests of *the* Lord!
    Bless the *Lord*, servants of the Lord!
Bless the Lord, O souls of *the* just!
Bless the *Lord*, humble of heart!

Daniel Verse (see pp. 389–578)

Glory to the Father, to the Son and to the Holy *Spir*it.
From age to *age*, amen, amen.

Daniel Verse (see pp. 389–578)

Shorter Prayers

Server: Peace be with us.
Priest: We glorify, exalt, sing halleluiah and praise the hidden and mysterious, blessed and incomprehensible Nature of your glorious Trinity at all times, O Lord of all, Father, Son and Holy Spirit, forever.
People: Amen.

Glory to <i>God</i> in the highest!
Peace on earth!
Good hope to <i>the</i> sons of men!
We adore, glorify, <i>and</i> exalt you!
Being <i>wit</i>hout beginning!
Secret, incompre<i>hen</i>sible Nature!
Father, Son <i>and</i> Holy Spirit!
King of Kings <i>and</i> Lord of Lords!
Who dwells <i>in</i> radiant Light!
Which none <i>on</i> earth can see!
Holy, Almighty, Im<i>mor</i>tal alone!
We <i>give</i> thanks to you!
Through our Media<i>tor</i> Jesus Christ!
The Sav<i>ior</i> of the world!
The Son <i>of</i> the Most High!
The liv<i>ing</i> Lamb of God!
Who takes away the <i>sin</i> of the world!
Have <i>mer</i>cy on us!
Who sits at the right <i>hand</i> of his Father!
Accept our <i>sup</i>plication!
For you are <i>our</i> God and Lord!
You are <i>our</i> King and Savior!
You are the Forg<i>iver</i> of our sins!
The eyes of all look to <i>you</i>, Jesus Christ!
Glory <i>to</i> God your Father!
To you and to <i>the</i> Holy Spirit!
Forever and <i>ever</i>, amen!

The Book of Psalms

Hulala I

Prayer: Make us worthy, O Lord our God, to be guided by the virtuous habits that please your Majesty, let our will be in your law, and may we meditate upon it night and day, Lord of all, Father, Son, and Holy Spirit, forever.

Psalm 1: Blessed is the man who walks not on the path of the wicked, * and stands not with the conscience of sinners. * Blessed is one who has carried your yoke and meditated upon your law, O Lord, night and day. And sits not in the company of scoffers, * but whose will is in the law of the Lord, * and who meditates upon his law day and night. * He will be as a tree planted by a stream of water, * who gives his fruits in season and whose leaves do not fall. * He completes all he does. * Not so are the wicked, * but rather like chaff the wind scatters. * For this, the wicked will not stand up to judgment, * nor sinners in the assembly of the just. * For the Lord knows the path of the just, * and the path of the wicked is destroyed.

Psalm 2: Why do the nations rage, * and the peoples go after vanity? * Like a horse without discernment, the insolent were emboldened and crucified Christ. The kings of the earth and rulers arose, * and took counsel together, * regarding the Lord and regarding his anointed, * that he may cut their punishment short, * and cast their yoke away from us. * He who sits in heaven laughs, * and the Lord scoffs at them. * Thus he will speak of them in his wrath, * and in his wrath he will set fire to them: * I have established my king upon Zion, my holy mountain, * that my covenant may be spoken. * The Lord said to me, You are my son, * and today I have begotten you. * Ask me and I will give you * the nations for your inheritance, * and your borders will cover the earth. * You will shepherd them with an iron staff, * and you will shake them like a potter's vessels. * Thus will kings be taught, * and the judges of the earth be instructed. * They work for the Lord in fear, * and cling to him in trembling. * They kiss the son lest he be angered, * and are scattered from his path. * For a little while, his wrath will burn, * and blessed are all who trust in him.

Psalm 3: O Lord, how many are my distresses, * how many have risen against me? * Because I spoke your truth, O Lord, evil men have risen against me; save me from their violence. How many say to my soul: * You have no salvation in your God. * You, O Lord, are my help and my honor, * and the one who lifts up my head. * With my voice I called to the Lord, * and he answered me from his holy mountain. * I laid down, and slept, and was awakened, * for the Lord sustained me. * I will not fear the armies of the nation, * who surround me and come against me. * Arise, O Lord my God, and save me, * for you strike all my enemies upon their faces, * and break the teeth of the wicked. * Salvation is the Lord's, * and upon your people, your blessing forever.

Psalm 4: When I called you, you answered me, * my God, and the Savior of my justice. * There is none like the Lord, in whom I hope, for he redeemed me from the deceptions and wiles of the wicked. You comforted me in my distresses. * Have mercy on me and hear my prayer. * Sons of men, how long * will you obscure my honor, * and love vanity, * and seek after deception forever? * Know that the Lord has set apart his chosen in a marvel. * The Lord will hear when I call to him. * Be angry, but do not sin. * Speak in your hearts, and consider upon your beds. * Offer sacrifices of justice and hope in the Lord. * There are many who say, Who will show us the good man, * and extend the light of his countenance upon us? * O Lord, you granted your joy to my heart, * more than their times of journeying, and wine, and oil. * Increase in peace together, * and I will lay down and sleep. * For you, O Lord, have let me dwell alone in peace.

Marmytha

Prayer: Attend, O Lord, to the words of our prayers, and turn your ear to the sound of our groaning, and do not turn your face from the sound of our supplication, O Kind One in whom we place our trust at all times and ages, Lord of all, Father, Son, and Holy Spirit, forever.

Psalm 5: Attend to my words, O Lord, and understand my plan. * Attend to the sound of my groaning, my King and my God. * You have led me, O Lord, to instruct me; do not disregard my petition. For to you do I pray. * O Lord, in the morning, you hear my voice, * and in the morning, I prepare and present myself to you. * For you are God, who does not desire wickedness: * the evil man does not dwell with you, * and the boastful do not stand before your eyes. * You have hated all who do evil, * and destroyed those who speak lies. * The Lord rejects the man who sheds blood and the deceiver. * I will enter your house through your great grace, * and will worship in your holy temple. * Guide me, O Lord, in your fear and in your justice. * Because of my enemies, straighten your path before me, * for there is no righteousness in their mouth, * but rather wickedness within them. * Their throats are open graves, * and their tongues turn about. * Condemn them, O God, * and they will fall from their foundations. * Drive them out in their great malice, * for they have embittered you. * All who hope in you will rejoice; * forever they will praise you, and you will dwell within them. * All who love your name will be strengthened in you, * for you bless the just. * O Lord, you will clothe me as if holding a shield.

Psalm 6: O Lord, do not reprove me in your wrath, * nor send me away in your anger. * Pity my weakness, my Fashioner, and guide me in your love. Have mercy on me, O Lord, for I am sick. * Heal me, O Lord, for my bones tremble, * and my soul is greatly shaken. * Until when, O Lord? * Turn to me, Lord, and deliver my soul. * Save me because of your grace. * For your remembrance is not in death, * and who thanks you in Sheol? * I am wearied by my sighs, I soak my bed every night, * and dampen my mattress with tears. * My eye is pained by your wrath, * and I am disturbed by all my enemies. * May all evildoers be taken away from me, * because the Lord heard the sound of my cry. * Hear my petition, O Lord; accept my prayer, O Lord. * May all my enemies be shamed and destroyed, * overturned and suddenly scattered.

Psalm 7: O Lord my God, I hoped in you; save me, * and deliver me from those who pursue me. * Blessed be God who directs and comforts his servants. Lest he break my soul like a lion, * and there be no one to save and deliver. * O Lord my God, if I have done this, * and if there is evil by my hands, * and if I have repaid one who has done me evil, * and if I have harmed my enemy needlessly, * let the enemy pursue my soul and overcome it, * and press my life into the ground, * and throw my glory into the dust. * Arise, O Lord, in your wrath, * and prevail over the neck of my enemies. * Awake for me in the judgment you commanded, * and the church of the peoples will surround you. * For its sake, return to the heights. * O Lord, judge the nations. * Judge me, O Lord, according to my justice and according to my innocence. * Bring complete evil upon the wicked, * and establish the just. * O Searcher of heart and recesses, * O just God, my help! * O God who saves the upright of heart, * O God, judge of truth, who is not wrathful every day! * If he does not return, he sharpens his sword, and aims his bow. * He prepared and prepares him vessels of wrath. * He makes arrows for those who burn, * for the wicked man ruins, and conceives malice, and begets depravity. * He digs a well and delves it, * and falls in the pit he made. * Return his evil upon his head, * and bring down his

The Psalter

malice upon his assault. * I will thank the Lord according to my justice, * and sing to the name of the exalted Lord.

Marmytha

Prayer: It is our duty, O Lord, to thank, adore, and glorify you, O Hidden One in his Existence who has fashioned your praise from the mouth of children and infants, Lord of all, Father, Son, and Holy Spirit, forever.

Psalm 8: O Lord, my Lord, how glorious is your name through all the earth, * for you have granted your glory to heaven. * O Son whom children praised in Jerusalem with their hosannas, save your adorers who plead to you. From the mouth of children and infants, * you have fashioned your praise * because of your enemies – * that the enemy taking vengeance may be silenced. * For they have seen the heavens, the work of your fingers, * the moon and the stars which you fashioned. * Who is man, that you remember him, * and the son of man, that you command him? * You have made him little less than the angels, * and clothed him with honor and glory, * and given him authority over the work of your hands, * and placed everything under his feet: * all sheep and cattle, * and even the beast of the wilderness and the birds of heaven, * and the fish of the sea who pass through the roads of the seas. * O Lord our Lord, how glorious is your name in all the earth!

Psalm 9: I will thank the Lord with all my heart, * and make known all his wonders. * We thank you who turned us toward knowledge of you, through your mercies, and shamed our enviers. I will rejoice and be glad in you, * and sing to your exalted name. * When my enemies are turned back, * they will be measured and scattered before you. * For you have accomplished my repayment and my judgment, * and sat upon the just judgment seat. * You rebuked the nations and scattered the wicked, * and erased their names forever and ever. * My enemies were finished by the sword forever. * You uprooted villages and destroyed their remembrance. * But the Lord stands forever, * and fashions his throne for judgment, * that he may judge the world in truth, * and the nations in uprightness. * May the Lord be a house of refuge for the poor, * and their help in a time of distress. * May all who know your name hope in you, * for you do not abandon those who seek you, O Lord. * Sing to the Lord who dwells in Zion, * and show the nations his deeds, * for he seeks to remember their bloodshed, * and will not forget the cry of the poor. * Have mercy on me, Lord, * and see my subjection from those who hate me. *

The Psalter

Bring me up from the gates of death, * for I have made known all your wonders. * In the gates of the daughter of Zion, * I will rejoice in your salvation. * The nations will drown in the well they made, * and their feet will be caught in the trap they set. * The Lord will make known the judgment he makes, * and will shut down the wicked by the work of his hands. * The wicked will be returned to Sheol, and all the nations who forget God. * For the poor man will not be forgotten forever, * and the hope of the poor will not be lost forever. * Arise, O Lord, and let not the son of man be strengthened. * Let the nations be judged before your face. * Establish a lawmaker for them, * that the nations may know that they are sons of men.

Psalm 10: Why, O Lord, do you stand far off, * and turn away your gaze in a time of distress? * Because the wicked lay in wait for the just in their ambush, and anger your name, destroy their intention, O Lord. The poor man burns through the arrogance of the wicked; * let them be caught by the plan that they devised. * Because the wicked man is boastful in the desires of his soul, * the evil man is blessed, but angers the Lord, * and the wicked man is not held back in his arrogance. * There is no God in any of his intentions. * His paths are loose at all times, * and your judgment is too lofty for him. * He despises all his enemies. * He says in his heart, I will not be moved for ages. * He considers evil, and his mouth is full of cursing. * Fraud and deceit under his tongue – malice and depravity. * He sits in the dwelling in ambush, * and in hiding he kills the just man. * His eyes strike the poor, * and he schemes to rob the poor man in the net of his trap. * He himself will be humbled and fall, * and upon his bones will be sickness and wounds. * He says in his heart that God has forgotten, * he has turned his face and never sees. * Arise, O Lord my God, and raise your hand, * and do not forget the poor man. * Why does the sinner anger God, * and say in his heart that he does not avenge? * You see that there is evil and wrath, * and you look, that it may be completed by your hands. * The poor man is forgiven by you, * and you are the help of the orphan. * Break the arm of the sinner and the evil man. * Avenge his sin, and let him never be found. * The Lord is King forever and ever. * The nations are scattered from his earth. * You hear the hope of the poor, O Lord, * and your ears hear the readiness of their heart, * to judge orphans and the poor, * that the sons of man may no longer increase destruction on the earth.

The Psalter
Hulala II

Prayer: O Lord, establish your hope in us, fill our soul with your assistance, may your grace forgive our sins, and the eternal mercies of your glorious Trinity come to the aid of your adorers, who call and plead to you at all times and ages, Lord of all, Father, Son, and Holy Spirit, forever.

Psalm 11: I hoped in the Lord; how can you say to my soul, * fly and dwell in the mountains like a bird? * Sinners plot against me; I hoped in you, O Lord. For lo, sinners have drawn their bow, * and fixed their arrows on the string, to shoot at the upright of heart in the gloom. * Because they destroyed what you have prepared, * what can the just man do? * The Lord is in his holy temple. * The Lord is in heaven, his throne. * His eyes see and his vision examines the sons of men. * The Lord examines the just and the wicked, * and his soul hates those who love evil. * Nets will fall upon the wicked like rain, * fire and brimstone, * and a striking wind as their dinner plate. * For the Lord is just and loves justice, * and his face sees uprightness.

Psalm 12: Save me, Lord, for the good man has disappeared, * and faith has vanished from the earth. * Deceit has increased and love has grown cold; Christ, do not turn away. Men speak vanity, * a man to his friend with deceiving lips. * They speak with two faces. * May the Lord destroy all deceiving lips, * the tongues that speak proud things. * For they say: Our tongue will make us great; * our lips are our own; who is our master? * Because of the oppression of the poor and the groaning of the needy, * I will arise now, says the Lord. * And I will grant salvation openly. * The speech of the Lord is a pure speech, * choice silver found in the earth, * cleansed as one out of seven. * May you, O Lord, protect them. * Redeem me and deliver me from this age forever, * for the wicked surround and march * like the corrupted hill of the sons of Edom.

Psalm 13: How long, O Lord, will you forget me? * How long will you hide your face? * Shepherd me and save me, O Lord, that I may give you thanks. How long will there be grief in my soul, * this sorrow in my heart all day? * How long shall my enemy prevail? * Look at me, answer me, Lord God! * Give light to my eyes lest I fall asleep in death, * lest my enemy say: I have overcome him; * lest my foes rejoice to see my fall. * As for me, I trust in your grace. * Let my heart rejoice in your saving help; * let me praise the Lord who saved me.

Psalm 14: The wicked man says in his heart, There is no God. * They are corrupted and polluted in their schemes. * Redeem your Church from evil men, O Lord of creatures. There is no one who does good. * The Lord gazes down from heaven upon the sons of men, * to see if anyone is intelligent and seeks God. * They all turned away together and were rejected. * There is none who does good, not even one. * And those who do evil do not know, * those who devour my people like eating bread. * They did not call to the Lord. * There, they feared greatly, * for the Lord is in the court of the just. * They were shamed by the mind of the poor man, * for the Lord is his support. * Who will bring salvation to Israel from Zion? * When will the Lord return the resting place to his people? * Jacob shall rejoice, and Israel shall be glad.

Marmytha

Prayer: Make us worthy, O Lord our God, that with our intentions purified and sanctified in the truth, we may dwell in your holy dwelling, and walk on your path without fault, all the days of our lives, Lord of all, Father, Son, and Holy Spirit, forever.

Psalm 15: Lord, who shall be admitted to your tent * and dwell on your holy mountain? * Let me stand before your holy altar with pure intentions, O Lord. He who walks without fault; he who acts with justice * and speaks the truth from his heart; he who does not slander with his tongue. * He who does no wrong to his brother, * who casts no slur on his neighbor. * Who holds the godless in disdain, * but honors those who fear the Lord. * He vows to his friend and does not lie, * and gives his money without interest, * and takes no bribe against an innocent man. * Whoever does this is righteous, * and will not be shaken forever.

Psalm 16: Protect me, O God, for I trust in you. * I said to the Lord, You are my Lord. * Glorious is your trust, our Fashioner, in which my misery rejoices. And my good is from you, * so also to the holy and glorious ones on earth, * in whom is all my pleasure. * Let their latest wounds increase quickly, * lest I pour out their libations of blood, * or remember their names with my lips. * O Lord, the portion of my inheritance and my sustenance, * you return my inheritance to me. * Cords fell upon me among the best, * and my inheritance has pleased me. * I will bless the Lord who advised me, * and who has guided my recesses during nights. * I placed the Lord before me at all times, * and he was at my right, lest I tremble. * Because of this, my heart rejoiced and my honor extolled, * and my flesh will dwell in serenity. * For you did not leave my soul in Sheol, * or allow your venerable one to see corruption. * May you show me your path of life, * and I will be satisfied by the joy of your person, * and by the sweetness of the victory of your right hand.

Psalm 17: Hear, O holy Lord, and look upon my pleading. * Hearken to my prayer, for it is not said with lying lips. * O Lord my God, have mercy on me, for I am persecuted unjustly. From you my judgment comes forth: * may your eyes see integrity. * You search my heart, you visit me by night. * You test me and you find in me no wrong. * The works of men have not crossed my mouth, * even in the speaking of my lips. * Rather, you have kept me from evil ways; you placed my journeys firmly on your paths. * There was no faltering in my steps. * I called you for you answered me. * O God, turn your ear to me and hear my words. * Accomplish a marvel for your venerable one, * O Savior of those who hope, * from those who stand against your right hand. * Protect me as the pupil of the eye, * and keep me in the shadow of your wings, * from the sinners who mock me, * and the enemies of my soul who stand against me. * Shut the mouths who speak arrogance. * They praised me and now they surround me. * They set their eyes to lift me upon the earth. * They are like a lion who seeks to destroy, * and like a lion's cub sitting in secret. * Arise, O Lord, before their face, and make them kneel. * Deliver my soul from the wicked and from destruction, * and from the dead who die by your hand, O Lord, * and from the dead in the ditch. * Divide them in life, * and fill their stomachs with your treasures. * Let the sons be filled and the rest of their sons be forgiven. * But let me see your face in justice, * and be filled when your faithfulness is awakened.

Marmytha

Prayer: O glorious Power of his servants, mighty trust of his adorers, and fortified house of refuge for those who fear him, who aids and exalts the horn of their salvation: it is our duty to thank, adore, and glorify you, Lord of all, Father, Son, and Holy Spirit, forever.

Psalm 18: I love you, O Lord, my strength and my trust, * my refuge and my deliverer. * Heaven and earth and all they contain, the lofty and the lowly, bless and adore God their Creator. O mighty God, in whom I trust, * my help and the Horn of my salvation, * and my glorious house of refuge. * I will call to the Lord, and be saved from my enemies, * for the cords of death have surrounded me, * and the feet of the wicked disturb me. * The cords of Sheol encircle me, * and the traps of death are set for me. * In my distress, I called to the Lord and I called to God, * and he heard my voice from his temple, * and my cry before him entered his ears. * The earth was troubled and shook, * and the foundations of the mountains shook and were troubled. * For they were scorched. * Smoke rose in his wrath, * and fire from his face kindled, * and coals burned from him. * Heaven came down and descended, * and the cloud under his feet. * He rode upon the cherubim and flew, * and soared upon wings of spirit. * He placed darkness as his hiding place and surrounded his roof. * The darkness of water in the clouds of the air * from the brightness of his roof. * His clouds made hail and coals of fire, * and the Lord thundered in heaven. * The Exalted One gave his voice: * hail and coals of fire. * He sent his arrows and scattered them. * He increased his lightnings and set them on fire. * Springs of water were seen, * and the foundations of the world were revealed, * by your rebuke, O Lord, * and from the breath of spirit of your wrath. * Send from the heights and silence me, * and receive me from the many waters, * and deliver me from my mighty enemies, * and from my haters, who are stronger than I am. * They set out against me on the day of my travails, * and the Lord became a savior to me, * and brought me out to relief, * and delivered me, for he rejoiced in me. * The Lord repaid me according to my justice, * and fulfilled me according to the purity of my hands. * For I have kept the ways of the Lord, * and have not rebelled against my God. * For all your judgments against me, * I did not cross his laws, * and have been faultless with him. * I have been careful not to sin: * the Lord rewarded me according to my justice, * and according to the purity of my hands before his eyes.

Division: You are loyal to the loyal, * and innocent with the innocent, * and elected with the elect, * and crafty with the crafty. * For you save a humble people, * and humble arrogant eyes. * You light my lamp, * O Lord my God, who brightens my darkness. * For in you, I chase off marauders, * and in my God, I leap over a fortress. * O God, faultless in his path. * The word of the Lord searches, * and helps all who trust in him. * For there is no God other than the Lord, * and there is none mighty like our God. * O God who girds me with strength, * and provides my path without fault. * He makes my feet as a deer and upholds me upon a hill. * He trains my hands for battle, * and sets my arms like a bow of brass. * You gave me the shield of salvation. * Your right hand helped me, and your discipline raised me. * You widened my steps under me, lest my ankles slip. * I will pursue my enemies and overcome them, * and not return until I have finished them. * I will strike them, and they will not be

The Psalter

able to stand, * and they will fall beneath my feet. * You will gird me with strength for battle, * and make those who stand against me kneel before me, * and break my enemies before me, * and silence those who hate me. * They will cry out and not have a savior. * They will implore the Lord, and he will not answer them. * I will crush them like dirt upon the wind, * and will stomp them like slime in the marketplace. * You will deliver me from the judgments of the people, * and make me the head of the nations. * The people I did not know will work for me, * and ears will truly hear me. * Strange sons will be subjected to me. * Strange sons will be stopped, and be crippled by their chains. * The Lord is alive, and my Strengthener is blessed. * My God and my Savior is exalted. * God who gave me vengeance, * and subjected the nations under me, * and delivered me from my enemies, * and exalted me over those who stand against me, * and delivered me from wicked men. * For this, I will thank you among the nations, O Lord, * and sing to your name, which raises the salvation of his king, * and accomplishes the grace of his anointed, * to David and his seed, forever.

Marmytha

Prayer: To you, O Hidden from all in his Existence, and revealed and dawned in the marvelous works of his providence, whose enormous power is shown by heaven and earth, it is our duty to thank, adore, and glorify you, Lord of all, Father, Son, and Holy Spirit, forever.

Psalm 19: The heavens proclaim the glory of God, * and the firmament shows the work of his hands. * God who exists eternally is adorable; he created the rational to contemplate his other works, and to know his glory. Day to day, the word pours forth, * and night to night, the mind shows forth. * There is no word or words, * that are not heard by their sound. * Their gospel goes through all the earth, * and their words to the ends of the earth. * Through them, he set a tent for the sun, * and he comes out like a bridegroom from his chamber. * He rejoices like a warrior in his course, * and his route is from the ends of heaven, * and his dining upon the ends of the heaven. * Nothing can hide from its heat. * The law of the Lord is faultless, and returns the soul. * The witness of the Lord is faithful and instructs children. * The commands of the Lord are upright and gladden the heart. * The command of the Lord is well-chosen, and enlightens the eyes. * The fear of the Lord is pure, and stands forever. * The judgments of the Lord are in truth, and fair in everything. * They are more desirable than gold and fine gems, * and sweeter than honey and a honeycomb. * Even your servant is careful with them. * If he keeps them, he will be rewarded greatly. * Who is taught by mistakes? * Give me victory over hidden things, * and keep your servant away from the evil man, * lest the wicked reign over me. * Let me be cleansed from my sins. * May the words of my mouth be according to your will. * The thought of my heart is before you, O Lord, my help and my savior.

Psalm 20: May the Lord answer you on the day of distress, * and may the name of the God of Jacob help you. * Our trust is in God, who can save the humble. May he send you help from his holy place, * and aid you from Zion. * May the Lord remember all your offerings, * and anoint your burned offerings. * May the Lord give you according to your heart, * and fulfill all your thoughts. * Let us glory in your salvation, * and be lifted up in the name of our God. * May the Lord accomplish all you will. * Henceforth may it be known that God has saved his anointed, * and answered him from his holy heaven * by the power of the salvation of his right hand. * These with chariots and these with horses, * and we are strengthened by the name of the Lord our God. * They will kneel and fall, * and we will stand and be ready. * May the Lord our King save us, * and answer us on the day we call him.

Psalm 21: Lord, may your strength give joy to the king; * may your salvation gladden him! O Lord, who lets the distress of his servants pass, and gladdens them by his power. You granted him his heart's desire; * you refused not the prayer of his lips. * You met him with a good blessing; * you set a glorious crown upon his head. * He asked you for life and this you have given, * days that will last from age to age. * His glory grows in your salvation. * You placed glory and splendor upon him. * For you have granted him blessing forever and ever, * and gladdened him with the gladness of your Person. * For the king hopes in the Lord, * and is not shaken in the grace of the Most High. * Your hand will find all your enemies, * and your right hand will find your haters. * Make them like an oven of fire on the day of wrath. * May the Lord burn them in his wrath, * and fire consume them, * and their fruits be destroyed from the earth, * and their seed from among the sons of men. * Because they set evil before you, * they will be overcome and unable to prevail. * May you place a mark upon them, * and your aim fasten upon their faces. * The Lord is exalted in your might. * Let us sing and glorify your greatness.

Hulala III

Prayer: O glorious Divinity, filled with mercies and pity, hope, life, and salvation for all creatures, it is our duty to thank, adore, and glorify you at all times, O Lord of all, Father, Son, and Holy Spirit, forever.

Psalm 22: My God, my God, why have you abandoned me? * And have taken away my salvation by my own ignorant words. * *My God, my God, do not desert me due to men who do not consider you.* My God, I called to you by day and you did not answer me, * and at night, and you did not remain with me. * You are holy, and Israel sits in your glory. * In you my fathers hoped. * They hoped in you, and you delivered them. * They cried to you, and were delivered. * They hoped in you and were not shamed. * I am a worm, and not a son of man; * a reproach of the sons of men and an abomination of the people. * All who see me mock me. * They shoot out their lips and shake their heads. * He trusts that the Lord will deliver him, * and take him out, if he is pleased by him. * For you are my trust from the womb, * and my hope from my mother's breasts. * I was cast upon you from the womb, * and from my mother's belly, my God, you did not leave me. * For distress approached me, and there is none to help. * Many bulls surrounded me, * and the bullocks of Bashan encircle me, * and open their mouths at me, * like a lion that roars and snatches. * I am thrown as into water, * and all my bones are scattered, * and my heart is like wax, * and my recesses melt within me. * My strength dries up like a potsherd, * and my tongue cleaves to my jaw. * You have cast me upon the dust of death. * For dogs have encircled me, * and the assembly of the wicked have surrounded me. * They have pierced my hands and feet, * and weakened all my bones. * They look upon me and see, * and divide my garments among them. * They cast lots for my clothing. * But you, O Lord, will not leave me.

Division: God, God, come to my aid, * and deliver my soul from the blade, * and my loneliness from the hand of dogs. * Save me from the mouth of the lion, * and my humility from the great horn, * that I may preach your name to my brethren, * and glorify you in the assembly. * Those who fear the Lord will praise him, * and all the seed of Jacob will honor him, * and all the seed of Israel will fear him. * For he did not despise or look down on the cry of the poor man, * or turn his face away from him. * When he cried to him, he heard him. * My glory in the great church is from you. * I will fulfill my vows before those who fear him. * The poor will eat and be filled, * and those who seek the Lord will glorify him, * and their heart will live forever. * All the ends of the

The Psalter

earth will remember and turn toward the Lord, * and all the families of the nations will worship before him. * For the kingdom is the Lord's, * and he has authority over the nations. * All the hungry of the earth will eat and worship before the Lord, * and all clothed in dirt will bless before him. * My soul lives for him. * The seed that he worked will preach its generation for the Lord. * They will come and show his justice * to the people who are born, what the Lord has done.

Psalm 23: The Lord is my Shepherd; there is nothing I shall want. * To green pastures he brings me, * *We cast our care upon you, O Provider for his family.* To restful waters he leads me. * He turns my soul and guides me along the paths of truth. * Because of your name, even if I should walk * in the valleys of the shadows of death, * no evil would I fear, for you are with me: * your crook and your staff comfort me. * You have prepared a banquet for me in the sight of my foes. * My head you have anointed with oil; my cup is overflowing. * Surely goodness and kindness shall follow me * all the days of my life. * In the Lord's own house shall I dwell for ever and ever.

Psalm 24: The Lord's is the earth and its fullness, * the world and all its peoples. * *Let us take pains to do what is right, that the Almighty may save us.* For he set its foundations on the seas; * on the rivers he made it firm. * Who shall climb the mountain of the Lord? * Who shall stand on his holy mountain? * The man with clean hands and pure heart, * who has not sworn deceit in his soul. * He shall receive a blessing from the Lord * and justice from God our Savior. * This is the age which seeks and hopes, * for the countenance of your face, O God of Jacob. * Lift up your heads, O doors, * be opened, doors from of old, * that the King of honors may enter. * Who is this King of honors? * The mighty and powerful Lord. * The Lord is a mighty warrior. * Lift up your heads, O doors, * be opened, doors from of old, * that the King of honors may enter. * Who is this King of honors? * The almighty Lord. * He is the honored King forever.

Marmytha

Prayer: Upon you, O Lord our God, hangs the gaze of our souls, for our hope and trust is in you, and from you we ask forgiveness for our faults. Grant this in your grace and mercies, as you always do, Lord of all, Father, Son, and Holy Spirit, forever.

Psalm 25: To you, O Lord, I lift up my soul. * I trust you, my God, let me not be put to shame. * I lift my eyes to you, O Lord, for you are my true hope. Do not let my enemies boast over me, * for those who hope in you shall not be put to shame. * Let the wicked be put to shame in their vanity. * Lord, show me your ways; * make your paths known to me. * Lead me in your truth and teach me, * for you are God my Savior; * in you I hope every day. * Remember your mercies, O Lord, which are eternal, and your graces. * Remember not the sins of my youth, * but remember me in your many mercies, * because of your grace, O God. * God is good and righteous. * Because of this, he corrects sinners on the path, * and leads the humble in judgment, * and teaches the poor his way. * All the ways of the Lord are grace and truth * for those who keep his covenant and his witness. * For your name, O Lord, forgive my sin, which is great. * Who is the man who fears the Lord, * and who teaches his chosen path, * and whose soul returns in grace, * and whose seed inherits the earth? * The mind of the Lord is upon those who fear him, * and he makes his covenant known to them. * My eyes are always toward the Lord, * for he brought my feet out of the trap. * Turn to me and have mercy on me, * for I am alone and poor. * The tribulations of my heart increased, and you brought me out. * See my subjugation and my labor, and forgive me all my sin. * See that my enemies have multiplied, * and they hate me with an evil hatred. * Protect my soul, and deliver me, for I hope in you. * Let the innocent and upright come to me, for I wait upon you. * God will save Israel from all its tribulations.

Psalm 26: Judge me, O Lord, for I have walked in innocence. * I trust in the Lord, I shall not tremble. * O Judge and head of judges, let my head not be lowered in your judgment. Try me, O Lord, and test me, * and search out my inner life and my heart. * Because your mercies are before my eyes, * I have walked in faith, * and not sat among the evil, * or entered among the impertinent. * I have hated the assembly of the wicked, * and not sat among the malicious. * I have washed my hands in purity, * and encircled your altar, O Lord, * that I may make the sound of your glory heard, * and make known all of your wonders. * O Lord, I have loved the service of your house, * and the place of the dwelling of your glory. * Do not destroy me with sinners, * or my life with men of bloodshed, * in whose hand is deceit, and whose right hand is filled with bribery. * I have walked in innocence. * Save me and have mercy on me. * My leg stands in uprightness, * and in the church I will bless the Lord.

The Psalter

Psalm 27: The Lord is my light and my salvation; whom shall I fear? * The Lord is the strength of my life; who will shake me? * Do not cast me from before your face, O Searcher of hidden things. When the evil approached me to devour my flesh, * my enemies and those who hate me, * they were crushed together and fell. * If a host encamps against me, my heart would not fear, * and if an army stands against me, in this would my heart trust: * that I have asked the Lord for one thing, and I have sought it: * to dwell in the house of the Lord all the days of my life, * and see the sweetness of the Lord, and seek out his temple. * For he will hide me in his shelter on the evil day, * and hide me in the shadow of his dwelling, and lift me upon a rock. * Henceforth, my head will be exalted over my enemies who surround me. * I will make sacrifices of praise in his dwelling. * I will glorify and sing to the Lord. * Hear my voice, O Lord, when I call to you. * Have mercy on me, and answer me. * My heart speaks of you, and my face seeks your face. * Lord, do not turn your face from me, * and do not afflict your servant in wrath. * You have been my help, O Lord. * Do not cast me away, and do not abandon me, my God and my Savior. * For my father and mother have abandoned me, but the Lord took me in. * Teach me your path, O Lord, * and lead me in your upright ways. * Do not hand me over to my enemies. * For false witnesses stand against me and speak evil. * But I have believed that I will see the blessings of the Lord in the land of the living. * Hope in the Lord and let your heart be strengthened. * Hope in the Lord.

Marmytha

Prayer: We call to you, O Lord, take refuge in you, and ask for forgiveness of debts and sins. Grant this in your grace and mercies, as you always do, Lord of all, Father, Son, and Holy Spirit, forever.

Psalm 28: To you, O Lord, I called, my God, do not be silent with me. * If you are silent with me, I will be handed over with those who have gone down into the cave. * To you our souls cry out: come to our aid and save us. Hear the sound of my pleading as I call to you, * as I lift up my hands to your holy temple. * Do not count me among the wicked, or with those who do evil, * who speak words of peace to their neighbors but have evil in their hearts. * Repay them according to their works, and according to their malice. * For they ignore the deeds of the Lord and the work of his hands. * May he ruin them and never rebuild them. * Blessed be the Lord for he has heard all the sound of my pleading. * The Lord is my help and my shield; * in him my heart trusts and my flesh rejoices; * I thank him with praise. * The Lord is the strength of his people, * a fortress of the salvation of his anointed. * Save your people and bless your heritage. * Be their shepherd and guide them forever.

Psalm 29: Bring forth to the Lord, O sons of men, * bring forth to the Lord glory and honor. * O Kind One whose mercies overflow, to whom glory is due. Bring forth to the Lord honor to his name. * Adore the Lord in his holy courtyard. * The voice of the Lord is upon the waters. * The glorious God thunders. * The Lord is upon the many waters. * The voice of the Lord in power, the voice of the Lord in glory. * The voice of the Lord which shatters cedars, * and the Lord breaks the cedars of Lebanon. * He makes them dance like calves, * Lebanon and Sirion, like the sons of bulls. * The voice of the Lord splitting the furnace of fire. * The voice of the Lord which shakes the wilderness, * and the Lord shakes the wilderness of Kadesh. * The voice of the Lord which shakes the trees and uproots the forests. * In his temple, everyone speaks praise. * The Lord overturns the flood. * The Lord sits as King forever. * The Lord gives power to his people, * and the Lord blesses his people with peace.

Psalm 30: I will exalt you, Lord, for you lifted me up, * and did not let my enemies rejoice over me. * We thank your name, you who have saved us, and broken our enemies by your power. O Lord my God, I cried to you and you have healed me. * You raised my soul from Sheol, * given me life apart from those who sank into the cave. * Sing to the Lord, you his chosen, * confess the memory of his holiness. * For there is rebuke in his wrath, and life in his will. * Weeping remains in the evening, but joy is in the morning. * I said in my serenity, I will never tremble. * O God, by your will, you established power upon my praise, * but you turned your face and I trembled. * I cried to you, Lord, and begged you. * What benefit is there in my blood, if I descend into corruption? * Dust does not thank you, or show your faithfulness. * Hear, O God, and have mercy. * O Lord, be a help to me. * For you turned my mourning into joy. * You loosened my sackcloth and girded me with joy. * For this, I will sing praise to you and not be silent. * O Lord my God, I will thank you forever.

Hulala IV

Prayer: To you our Hope and Trust, our Help and Provider, and the great Refuge of our weakness, we plead: turn to us, O Lord, forgive us, and have mercy on us, as you always do, Lord of all, Father, Son, and Holy Spirit, forever.

The Psalter

Psalm 31: I hope in you, O Lord, and will never be put to shame. * You bring me out in your justice. * Like a dead man, they have forgotten me in my distress; comfort me, O Lord. Turn your ear to me and answer me quickly. * O God, be a help for me, a refuge, and save me. * For you are my strength and my refuge. * Comfort me, O Lord, because of your name, * and take me out of this trap they set for me. * For you are my help, and my spirit waits for you. * You have saved me, Lord God of truth. * You hated those who kept vain religions. * But I have hoped in you, O Lord. * I will rejoice and be glad in your grace. * For you saw my humiliation and knew the distress of my soul. * You did not hand me over to my enemies. * You upheld my feet in an open space. * Have mercy on me, O Lord, for I am in distress. * My eye is disturbed in wrath, my soul and my stomach. * For my life passes in misery, * and my years in groanings. * My strength is sickened in poverty, * and my bones disturbed by all my enemies. * I have become a mockery to my neighbors, * and a fright to those who know me. * Those who see me in the market deride me. * I am lost from the heart like a dead man, * and have become like a broken vessel. * For I have heard the mocking of many, * when they all advise me together, * and think they will take my soul. * But I trust in you, O Lord, * and said, you are my God, O Lord, and the times are in your hands. * Save me from my enemies and from those who pursue me. * Brighten your face upon your servant, and save me in your grace. * O Lord, I will not be shamed, for I have called to you. * The wicked will be shamed, and be brought down to Sheol, * and the lips of the evil will be shut. * For they speak wickedness and folly about the just man. * How great is your grace which you keep for those who fear you, * for those who hope in you before the sons of men. * You cover them in the shelter of your person * from the abuse of the sons of men. * You cover them in your shadow from strife. * Blessed is the Lord who chose his elect in the mighty village. * I said in my haste that I was lost from your eyes. * But you heard the sound of my pleading when I called to you. * Love the Lord, you his just. * The Lord protects the faithful, * and repays the evil their works. * Let your hearts be strengthened and fortified, * all who hope in the Lord.

Psalm 32: Blessed is the man whose evil is forgiven, * and whose sin is covered. * Our Upholder, the Friend of Man: let us please him, that he may have pity on us. Blessed is the son of man whose sin the Lord does not consider. * There is no deceit in his heart. * Because I was silent, my bones were worn out, * as I moaned the whole day. * For night and day, your hand weighed heavy upon me, * and the wound returned in my chest to kill me. * I confessed my sins to you, and did not hide my faults from you. * I said that I will confess my faults to the Lord. * And you forgave all my sins. * For this, I will pray to you whenever you choose, in the appointed time. * The turbulence of many waters * will not approach him. * You guard me and protect me from my enemies. * Glory and salvation surround me, for I have been understood by you, * and confessed the road to you, that you may go and I may set my eye upon you. * Do not be like horse or mare, who are not wise, * whom they subdue with a harness from their youth, * and do not approach. * Many are the wounds of the wicked man, * but whoever hopes in the Lord, grace surrounds him. * Rejoice, O just, and be delighted in the Lord. * Glorify him, all you upright of heart.

Marmytha

Prayer: O glorified by the just, adored by the upright of heart, and confessed and blessed in heaven and on earth: it is our duty to thank, adore, and glorify you, at all times, Lord of all, Father, Son, and Holy Spirit, forever.

Psalm 33: Glorify the Lord, you just, * and glory is due for the upright. * *Glory is just for the righteous, and thanksgiving is right for them.* Thank him with the harp, * and with ten-stringed lyre sing to him. * Praise him with a new praise, * and speak in a lovely voice. * For the word of the Lord is upright, * and all his works are faithful. * He loves justice and right judgment. * The earth is filled with the grace of the Lord. * Heaven was made by the word of the Lord, * and all its hosts by the spirit of his mouth. * The waters of the sea assembled as in a wineskin, * and he placed the chasms in reservoirs. * Let all the earth fear the Lord, * and all who dwell in the world tremble before him. * For he spoke and they were, he commanded and they were established. * The Lord eradicates the counsel of the nations, * and the Lord eradicates the thoughts of the nations. * The mind of the Lord stands forever, * and the thought of his heart for the ages. * Blessed is the people whose God is the Lord, * the people he has chosen for his inheritance. * The Lord looks down from heaven, * and sees all the sons of men. * He sees all the dwellers of earth from his throne, * whose hearts he fashioned together. * They are instructed in all their works. * The King is not saved through great power, * nor the warrior delivered in his great power. * The salvation of the horse is a lie, * for in his great power he cannot deliver his rider. * The eyes of the Lord are upon the just, * who await his grace. * For he delivers their souls from death, * and gives them life during famine. * Our soul waits for the Lord, * for he is our aid and our help, * and in him our heart rejoices, * for in his holy name is our hope. * May your grace be upon us, O Lord, * since we wait for you.

Psalm 34: I will bless the Lord at all times, * and at all times his praises in my mouth. * Blessed is the King who gave victory to his athletes in their trials. My soul exults in the Lord. * Hear, O poor, and rejoice. * Exalt the Lord with me, * and lift his name together. * I pleaded to the Lord and he answered me, * and delivered me from all my distresses. * Look to him and hope in him, * and let your faces not be impudent. * This is the poor man who calls him and he answers, * and redeems from all his tribulations. * The dwelling of the angels of the Lord * surrounds those who fear him and delivers them. * Taste and see that the Lord is good. * Blessed are all who trust in him. * The rich are impoverished and hunger, * and those who plead to the Lord lack no good thing. * Come, sons, and hear me, * and I will teach you the fear of God. * Who is the man who desires life, * and loves to see good days? * Keep your tongue from evil, * and your lips from speaking deceit. * Depart from evil and do good. * Seek peace and pursue it. * The eyes of the Lord are upon the just, * and his ears hear them. * The face of the Lord is against the wicked, * to erase their memory from the earth. * The just cry out and the Lord hears them and delivers them. * The Lord is close to the broken hearted, * and saves the humble in spirit. * Many are the troubles of the just man, * and the Lord delivers him from all of them. * He protects all his bones, * that not one of them will be broken. * Evil kills the wicked, * and the haters of the just will perish. * The Lord saves the souls of his servants, * and all who hope in him will not be condemned.

Marmytha

Prayer: We plead to you, O Judge whose judgment is upright, whose testing is filled with righteousness, and whose trial is filled with mercies and forgiveness: turn to us, forgive us, and have mercy on us, Lord of all, Father, Son, and Holy Spirit, forever.

Psalm 35: Judge in my favor, O Lord, and fight those who would fight me. * Take up weapon and shield, and arise to help me. * Those with fervor for your zeal are persecuted; Christ, do not turn away. Take out the blade and thunder against my pursuers. * Say to my soul, I am your savior. * May those who seek

The Psalter

my soul be shamed and buried. * May they be turned back and ashamed, * those who devise evil for me. * May they be as dust before a wind. * May the angels of the Lord pursue them. * May their path be darkened, and may there be pitfalls upon it. * May the angels of God pursue them. * For they have set traps for me, * and spread out a net for my soul. * May evil suddenly come upon them, * and the net they set for me catch them, * and may they fall into the pit that they dug. * Then let my soul rejoice in God, * and be pleased in his salvation. * Let all my bones say, * O Lord, who is like you? * For you deliver the poor man from his enemy, * and the humble and poor man from the one who robs him in violence. * False witnesses arose, * and asked me a thing they did not know. * They repaid me evil for good, * and destroyed my soul from among the sons of men. * Because of their sickness, I put on sackcloth, * and humbled my soul in fasting, * and returned my prayer to my recesses. * I walked like a friend and a brother, * and was laid low like one who sits in lamentation. * They gathered and rejoiced in my suffering, * and gathered against me for a long time, and I did not know. * They gnashed their teeth against me in their pride and their mockery.

Division. O Lord, I have seen enough. * Return my soul from their tumult, * and my loneliness from the lionesses. * I will thank you in the great church, * and sing to you among the many nations. * Let my enemies not rejoice over me, * and the liars who hate me for no reason, * who signal with their eyes but do not speak peace, * and think of deceit for the humble man on earth. * They open their mouth against me and say: * aha, aha, we have seen him with our eyes. * You have seen, O God: do not abandon me, Lord, and do not leave me. * Awake for judgment, my God and my Lord, and see my injustice. * Judge me according to your justice O Lord, * lest they rejoice over me and say in their heart: * Our soul has rested, and our condemnation. * May they be shamed and buried together, those who wish me evil, * and may those who exalt over me be clothed with shame. * May those who wish for my vindication glorify and rejoice, * and always say the Lord is great, * for he willed peace for his servant. * My tongue will thank your justice, * and praise you all the day.

Psalm 36: The evil man considers wickedness in his heart, * for there is no fear of God before his eyes. * You are good, just, and wise, O mighty Lord. It is hateful in his eyes to leave his sins behind and hate them. * The word of his mouth is harm and deceit, * and he does not wish to do good. * He considers harm on his couch, * and he walks on the ugly path, that he may do evil. * O

The Psalter

Lord, your mercies are in heaven, * and your faithfulness unto the heaven of heavens. * Your justice is like the mountain of God, * and your judgments like the great firmament. * You save the sons of men and beasts, O Lord. * How many are your mercies, O God. * The sons of men are covered in the shadow of your wings. * They drink from the best things of your house, * and you give them drink from your pleasant valley. * For the fount of life is with you, * and in your light we see light. * Keep your mercies for your friends, * and your justice for the upright of heart. * Let the mighty foot not come against us, * and the hands of the wicked not shake us. * For all evildoers will fall there, * and they will be crushed and be unable to stand.

HULALA V

Prayer: O Good and Kind One, Pitying and Merciful, O Great King of glory, Being who exists from eternity: we thank, adore, and glorify you at all times, Lord of all, Father, Son, and Holy Spirit, forever.

Psalm 37: Do not be jealous of the wicked, * or envy evildoers. * **Your righteousness dawns suddenly, and scatters the wicked.** For they dry up quickly like grass, * and shrivel like the green of the field. * Hope in God and do good. * Dwell on the earth and seek faithfulness. * Hope in the Lord and give him the request of your heart. * Straighten your path before the Lord, and hope in him. * He will accomplish and bring about your justice like light, * and your judgments like noontime. * Plead to the Lord and pray before him, * and do not envy the man who does evil, and whose path is prosperous. * Rest from the anger and rest from wrath. * Do not envy evildoing. * For the evil perish, * and those who hope in the Lord inherit the earth. * In a short time, you will seek the wicked man and he is naught. * You will look for him in his place, and not find him. * But the poor will inherit the earth, * and delight in great peace. * The wicked man plots against the just man, * and gnashes his teeth against him. * But the Lord will laugh at him, * for he knows that his day has come. * The wicked draw a sword and bend a bow, * to kill the humble and the poor, and those whose path is straight. * Their sword will enter their own heart, * and their bows will be broken. * The little bit of the just man is more * than the many possessions of the wicked. * For the arms of the wicked will be broken. * The Lord will feed the just, * and the Lord knows the days of the innocent, * and their inheritance will be forever. * They will not be shamed by an evil hour, * and they will be full during days of hunger. * For the wicked will be destroyed, * and the fattened enemies of the Lord will be finished, and vanish like smoke. * The wicked man borrows and does not repay, * and the just man gives in mercy.

Division. For the blessed of the Lord inherit the earth, * and the cursed will vanish. * The steps of a man are fashioned before the Lord, * and he fashions his path. * If he falls he will not be injured, * for the Lord holds his hand. * I was young and grew old, and have not seen a just man abandoned, * nor his seed seeking bread. * Rather, all the day he has mercy and lends, * and his seed is blessed. * Depart from evil and do good. * Rest forever, for the Lord loves just judgment, * and does not abandon his just ones, * but guards them forever. * He destroys the seed of the wicked, * and the just inherit the earth, * and dwell upon it forever. * The mouth of the just man speaks wisdom, * and his tongue speaks just judgment. * The law of God in his heart, and his steps do not shake. * The wicked man awaits the just, and seeks to kill him, * but the Lord will not abandon him into his hands. * Rather, he will condemn him in judgment. * Hope in the Lord and keep his path, * and he will lift you up to inherit the earth. * You will see, when the wicked vanish, * for I have seen the wicked bragging, * and lifted up like the trees of the field. * But when I passed by, he was naught. * I sought him and did not find him. * Keep innocence and choose uprightness, * for the man of peace has a good end, * and sinners will vanish together. * The end of the wicked is destruction. * The Lord is the savior of the just, * and helps them in times of trouble. * The Lord helps them and delivers them, * and delivers them from the wicked. * He saves them, for they hoped in him.

Marmytha

Prayer: O Lord, do not rebuke us in your anger or your wrath, nor repay us as our ignorance deserves, but rather, in your mercies and forgiveness, turn to us, forgive us, and have mercy on us.

Psalm 38: O Lord, do not rebuke me in your anger, * or chasten me in your wrath. * May our discipline be seasoned by your mercies, O Pitying One. For your arrows have fastened upon me, * and your hand has rested upon me. * There is no peace for my flesh before your wrath, * nor peace for my bones before my sins. * For my faults have passed over my head, * and have become too heavy for me like a heavy burden. * My wounds have rotted and festered, * because of my faults I tremble greatly. * All the day I walk in sadness, * for my ankles are filled with trembling, * and there is no peace for my flesh. * I tremble and shake greatly, * and I groan from the murmuring of my heart. * O Lord, all my desire is before you, * and my groanings are not hidden from you. * My heart is overturned and my strength leaves me, * and the light of my eyes is not with me. * My friends and companions stand against my wound, * and my neighbors stand far away from me. * Those who seek my soul seize me and wish evil upon me. * They speak evil and deceit. * They rebuke me all the day. * But I am like a deaf man and do not hear, * like a mute man and do not open my mouth. * I have become like a man who does not hear, * and has no rebuke in his mouth. * For I awaited you, O Lord, * and you answered me, O Lord my God. * For I have said, they will not rejoice over me, * and will not boast over me when my feet slip. * For I am prepared for suffering, * and my wound is before me at all times. * For I have shown you my faults, * and been cleansed of my sins. * My enemies are strengthened and see, * and those who hate me wrongly are many. * They repay me evil for good, * and malign me because I pursued good. * Do not abandon me, O Lord my God, or be far from me, * but rather hasten to my aid and save me.

Psalm 39: I said I will keep my path and not sin with my tongue. * I will guard my mouth from evil because the wicked are before me. * **The evil distress me, O Lord; my true hope is in you.** I was silent and gloomy, I mourned the good, and my wound was renewed. * My heart burned within me, and fire seized my flesh. * I spoke with my tongue, and the Lord showed me my end, * and how long was the measure of my days, * that I may know why I remain. * For lo, you grant me days in measure, * and my lifetime is as nothing before you. * For all the sons of men stand as a vapor, * and a man walks in an image, and fades like a vapor. * He sets down treasures and does not know who will take them up. * Now, then, who will be my hope besides you, O Lord? * Deliver me from all my faults. * May the envy of the wicked not subject me. * I was mute and did not open my mouth, for you have accomplished it. * Let your punishment pass me by, and the blow of your hand. * I am finished by the rebuke on behalf of my sins. * You lead a man and let his desires pass by like rubbish. * All the sons of men are like vapor. * Hear, O Lord, my prayer and my petition, and attend to my tears. * Do not be silent with me, for I journey with you, * and am a sojourner like all my forefathers. * Save me, and I will rest, * until I move on, and am no longer.

The Psalter

Psalm 40: Hoping, I hoped in the Lord, * and he turned to me and heard my petition. * There is no numbering your blessings to us, O Pitying One. And brought me up from the cave of wretchedness and the filth of decay, * and established my feet upon the rock and ordered my journeys. * He gave my mouth a new praise, praise to God, * that many may see and rejoice, * and hope in the Lord. * Blessed is the man who relies on the name of the Lord, * and does not turn toward idolatry, * or to a deceitful word. * Lord our God, you have accomplished many things, * your marvels and your considerations toward us – and there is none like you! * I showed and said, that they are more than can be numbered. * You were not pleased by sacrifices and offerings, * so ears you opened up for me, * and did not ask for burned offerings on behalf of sinners. * Then I said, Lo, I come, * that, as is written of me in the titles of the Scriptures, * I wished to do your will, O God, * and your law within my recesses. * I announced your justice in the great church, * and did not stop my lips. * O Lord, you know, * that I did not hide your justice within my heart, * but rather spoke your salvation and your faithfulness. * I did not hide your grace or faithfulness from the great church, * and may you not, O Lord, withhold your mercies from me. * Rather, may your mercies and faithfulness guard me at all times. * For innumerable evils surround me, * and my sins overcome me, and I am unable to see. * They are more than the hairs of my head, and my heart abandons me. * Be pleased, O Lord, to deliver me. * O Lord, hasten to my aid. * May those who seek to kill my soul be buried. * May they be turned back and buried, * those who wish me evil. * May they marvel at the repetition of their shame, * those who say to me, aha, aha. * May all who seek you rejoice in you. * May they always say, God is great, * those who love your salvation, * and I who am poor and needy. * O Lord, they think of me; * you are my help and my deliverer; O God, do not delay.

Hulala VI

Prayer: O Rich in his love, Overflowing in his mercy, Kind in his goodness, Incomprehensible in his glory, great King of glory, Being who exists from eternity: we thank, adore, and glorify you at all times, Lord of all, Father, Son, and Holy Spirit, forever.

Psalm 41: Blessed is the man who looks upon the poor; * on the day of evil, the Lord will deliver him. * Blessed is the one who finds mercies in your just judgment. The Lord will protect him, give him life and blessings on the earth,

The Psalter

* and will not hand him over to his enemies. * The Lord will sustain him on his sickbed, * and turn over his couch in his sickness. * I said, You are my Lord, have mercy on me. * Heal my soul, for I have sinned against you. * My enemies speak evil of me. * When will he die and his name be lost? * When they came to see me, * they spoke deception, * and forged evil in their heart. * They went out to the market and spoke. * All those who hate me murmured against me together, * and thought evil of me. * They thought with an evil mind: * Henceforth he will be buried and not be able to rise. * Even the man who greeted me, in whom I trusted. * He who ate my bread, in whom I trusted, greatly deceived me. * But you, O Lord, have mercy on me, * and raise me, and repay them. * In this I knew that you delight in me: * that my enemy did not do evil to me. * But you sustained me in my innocence, * and raised me before you forever. * Blessed is the Lord, God of Israel, * from age to age, amen, amen.

END OF BOOK ONE.

BOOK TWO

Psalm 42: Like the deer that yearns for running streams, * so my soul yearns for you, Lord God. * *I beseech you, my God: in your mercies, turn to me.* My soul thirsts for you, O living God; * when can I come and see your face? * My tears have become my food, O God, * by day and night, * as they say to me every day: "Where is your God?" * I recall these things with a weary soul, * for I would go to your mighty fortress, * even to the house of God. * Many rejoiced with a song of praise and thanksgiving. * Why are you cast down, my soul, and why do you groan? * Await God, for again I will thank him, * the Savior of my countenance and my God. * My soul is cast down within me, * for I recall you from the land of Jordan. * From Hermon and from the small mountain. * Abyss calls to abyss, * sound to sound of the waters of your fountains. * All your waves and billows passed over me. * In daytime, the Lord commands his mercies, * and at night his praises: * pray with me to the living God. * I said to God, why have you forgotten me, * and why do I walk sadly, * in the distress of my enemies? * My enemies envy me enough to break my bones, * and they said to me every day, Where is your God? * Why are you cast down, my soul, and why do you groan? * Await for God, for again I will thank him, * the Savior of my countenance and my God.

Psalm 43: Judge for me, O God, and defend my cause, * from a people without compassion. * *Judge for me, O Lord, against those who malign me, and extend your aid to me.* Deliver me from evil and deceitful men. * For you are the God of my strength; why have you forgotten me? * And why do I walk sadly, * in the distress of my enemies? * Send your light and your faith, and comfort me. * Bring me to your holy mountain and to your dwelling. * I will come to the altar of God, * and to the God who gladdens my youth. * I will thank you with harp, O God my God. * Why are you cast down, my soul, and why are you saddened? * Await for God, for I will thank him again, * the Savior of my countenance and my God.

Marmytha

Prayer: O our Creator and maker of our blessings, who holds and leads our souls through the gentle signal of his will, great King of glory, Being who exists from eternity: we thank, adore, and glorify you, at all times, Lord of all, Father, Son, and Holy Spirit, forever.

Psalm 44: O God, we have heard with our ears, * and our fathers have declared to us. * O Creator who redeemed our forefathers by his might, save your adorers through our pleading. What you did in their days, * in the days of long ago. * Your hand scattered the people and planted them, * you brought evil upon the kingdoms and established them. * For they did not inherit the earth in their battle, * nor did their arm save them, * but rather your right hand and your arm, * the light of your face, which delighted in them. * You are God my King, * who commanded the salvation of Jacob. * In you we pierce through our enemies, * and for your name we tread upon those who hate us. * For we do not trust in bows, * nor that our arms will save us. * You have saved us from those who hate us, * and shamed our enemies. * We praise you, O God, all the day, * and thank your name forever. * But now you have forgotten us and shamed us, * and do not go out with our army. * Rather you turned us back, and our enemies plunder. * You gave us over like sheep to be devoured, * and scattered us among the nations. * You sold your people without a price, * and did not reject their offer. * You have made us a taunt to our neighbors, * and a byword and mockery to those around us. * You have made us an example among the peoples, * and a taunt among the nations. * My shame is before me all the day, * and my shamefacedness covers me. * From the voice that reviles and scorns, * and before the enemy who takes revenge. * All these things happened to us and we did not forget you, * or deny your covenant, * or turn our backs, * or turn our steps away from your path. * For you have humbled us in the land yet again, * and covered us in the shadows of death. * But we did not forget the name of our God, * or extended our hands to strange gods. * It is God who searches these things, * for he knows the thoughts of the heart. * For your sake, we are killed daily, * and are considered as sheep for the slaughter. * Awake, and do not sleep, O Lord, * remember us and do not forget us, * and do not turn your face from us, * or forget our humiliation and our troubles. * For our soul is reduced to the dust, * and our stomach cleaves to the earth. * Arise, help us, and save us, because of your mercies.

Psalm 45: My heart overflows with noble words. * I will speak my works to the king. * *Glory to you, our Savior, who has honored the Church you chose, and adorned her with all beautiful things.* My tongue is the pen of a skillful scribe. * He is more beautiful in his aspect than the sons of men. * Mercies are poured upon your lips, * and for this, God has blessed you forever. * O mighty one, gird your sword upon your back; * your splendor and glory; your glory victorious. * Ride upon a truthful word, and a just humility. * Your law is in the fear of your right hand. * Your arrows are sharp, and peoples fall beneath you, * into the heart of the enemies of the king. * Your throne, O God, is forever and ever. * The scepter of your kingdom is a simple scepter. * You loved justice and hated evil, * and for this, God your God has anointed you * with the oil of gladness more than your companions. * Myrrh, cassia, and aloes * perfume all your garments. * Your joy is from the noble temple and from myself. * The daughter of the king stands in glory, * and the queen at your right hand, * dressed in the gold of Ophir. * Listen, O daughter, and see, and incline your ear, * and forget your people and the house of your father, * for the king desires your beauty. * Because he is your Lord, adore him, * and the daughter of Tyre will adore him. * The wealthy among the people will seek your face with offerings. * All the beauty of the princess is from within, * and she adorns her clothing with fine gold. * She goes to the king with offerings, * and brings her virgin companions with her. * They go with gladness and joy, * and enter the temple of the king. * In place of your fathers, you will have sons. * Make them rulers over all the earth. * That your name be remembered from age to age. * For this, the peoples will thank you forever and ever.

Psalm 46: Our God, our mighty refuge, * and our help in times of trouble. * *God our help lest we be defeated by the ruin of captors: gladden us in your salvation.* You are found by us at every time. * For this, we do not fear, * when the earth shakes and the mountains shake in the heart of the seas. * The waters will be troubled and return, * and the mountains will shake by his might. * The streams of the rivers will rejoice in the city of our God. * Holy is the dwelling-place of the Most High. * God is not shaken within her. * God helps her during morningtide. * The nations shook and the kingdoms trembled. * He raised his voice and the earth shook. * The almighty Lord is with us, * and our help is the God of Jacob. * Come and see the works of God, * who works marvels on the earth, * and eradicates wars from the ends of the earth. * He breaks bows and he breaks spears, * and he burns chariots with fire. * Turn back and know that I am God. * I am exalted among the peoples, and I am exalted on the earth. * The almighty God is with us, * and our help is the God of Jacob.

Marmytha

Prayer: O illustrious and honored King, whom the peoples and nations revere, and whose Majesty they adore: it is our duty to thank, adore, and glorify you, Lord of all, Father, Son, and Holy Spirit, forever.

Psalm 47: All you peoples, clap your hands, * and glorify God with a song of praise. * Blessed is he who came down and gave us his Body for food, and erased the debts of his flock by his Blood. For the Lord is exalted and awesome. * He is the great King over all the earth, * who subjugates the peoples under us, * and the nations under our feet. * He chose us for his inheritance, and the honor of Jacob whom he loved. * God ascends in glory, the Lord with the sound of trumpet. * Sing to God in glory, sing to our King. * For the King of all the earth is God; sing him praise. * God rules over the nations. * God sits on his holy throne. * The leaders of the peoples were turned toward the God of Abraham. * For the ends of the earth are God's, and he is greatly exalted.

Psalm 48: Great is our Lord and highly glorious, * in the village of our God, * Rejoice and be glad, race of Adam which was exalted through Christ who rose and defeated death through his death. And on his holy and glorious mountain. * There is joy all over the earth. * The mountain of Zion which is on the outskirts of the north * is the village of the great king. * God makes known his might in her palaces. * Lo, kings are present and pass away together; * they saw, marveled, shook, and were seized by tremors, * and pangs like a woman in labor. * Thousands from Tarshish were broken by a mighty wind. * As we heard, thus we have seen * in the village of the almighty Lord, * in the village of our God. * God will establish it forever. * Our hope, O God, is in your grace, within your temple. * As is your name, O God, so are your glories. * Your right hand is filled with justice until the ends of the earth. * Mount Zion rejoices and the daughters of Judah extoll, * because of your judgments, O Lord. * Walk around Zion and encircle it, and count her towers. * Set your hearts upon her strength, and uproot her palaces, * that you may declare to the next generation * that this is God our God, * forever and forever and ever, * for he guides us beyond death.

Psalm 49: Hear this, all you peoples, * give heed, all who dwell in the world. * Henceforth hear, O rulers of the people: work for God, the Lord of all. Men both high and low, * rich and poor alike! My lips will speak words of wisdom. * My heart is full of insight. * I will turn my mind to a parable, * with the harp I will solve my problem. * I will not fear in evil days, * the malice of my enemies surrounding me, * all who trust in their own strength, * and pride in the greatness of their wealth. * The brother does not save, * and man does not give God his salvation. * The salvation of their soul is precious. * Labor for an age, and live from age to age, * and you will never see corruption. * Then you see the wise dying, * and the ignorant and mindless perishing. * They leave their possessions to others, * their tombs their houses forever, * and their dwellings for the ages, * but they had reputations on the earth. * The son of man is not understood in his honor, * but is handed over to the beast, and resembles it. * This is their path, the stumbling block to their soul, * and the end of those pleased with their mouth. * They will be handed over to Sheol like sheep, and death will shepherd them. * The upright will rule over them in the morning, * and Sheol will wear out their image. * They will reject their glories. * God will save my soul, * and will raise me up from the hand of Sheol. * Do not fear when a man gains wealth, * and the honor of his house increases. * For he does not bring anything to his death, * nor does his glory go down with him. * For himself, he blesses his own life, * and thanks you when you speak well of him, * but he will reach the age of his fathers. * He will never see the light. * The son of man is not understood in his honor, * but rather is handed over to the animal, and resembles it.

HULALA VII

Prayer: O God of gods, and Lord of lords, great King of glory, Being who exists from eternity: we thank, adore, and glorify you, at all times, Lord of all, Father, Son, and Holy Spirit, forever.

Psalm 50: The God of gods, the Lord, speaks, * and calls the earth from the dawning of the sun to its setting. * Blessed is he who undid and ended all sacrifices through the sacrifice of his Beloved. From Zion, God shows a glorious crown. * God will come and not be silent, * and fire will devour before him, * and will burn well around him. * He will call to heaven from above, * and the earth to judge his people. * His chosen will be gathered to him, * who make his covenant with sacrifice. * The heavens will show his justice, * for God is the judge. * Hear, my people, and I will tell you, * Israel, and I will witness. * I am God, your God. * I do not reprove you over your sacrifices, * and your offerings are before me always. * I do not receive bulls from your house, * nor goats from your folds, * for all the animals of the wilderness are mine, * and the beasts and bulls of the mountains. * I know all the birds of heaven, * and the animals of the wilderness are mine. * If I hunger, I would not tell you, * for mine is the world in its fullness. * I do not eat the flesh of calves, * nor drink the blood of goats. * Sacrifice thanksgiving to God, * and fulfill your vows to the Most High. * Call me on the day of distress. * I will strengthen you, and you will praise me. * God says to the sinner: * What have you to do with the Scriptures of my commandments, * that you take my covenant into your mouth? * You have hated my instruction, * and thrown my words behind you. * If you had seen a thief, you would have run with him, * and would set your portion with the adulterer. * Your mouth has spoken evils, * and your tongue has spoken deceit. * You sat and spoke against your brother, * and have slandered your mother's son. * All these you have done, and I was silent with you. * You thought I am an evil man, like you. * So I reprove you, and set these things before your eyes. * Let those who forget God learn these things, * lest they are made to kneel and there is no one to deliver. * Whoever sacrifices thanksgiving, he will praise me. * There I will show him the path of the salvation of our God.

Psalm 51: Have mercy on me, God, in your grace, * and in your great mercies, blot out my sins. * Through the hyssop of your mercies, let my stains be cleansed, O Pitying One. Wash me thoroughly from my guilt, * and purify me of my sins. * For I know my trespasses, * my sins are always before me. * Against you alone have I sinned, * and have evil done before you. * That you may be just in your word, * and grant justice when you judge: * in my guilt was I conceived, * and with sin my mother bore me. * But you delighted in the truth; * and showed me the secrets of your wisdom. * Sprinkle me with hyssop, and I shall be clean; * wash me with it, I shall be whiter than snow. * May your delight and gladness sustain me, * and my humble bones will rejoice. * Turn your face from my sins, * and blot out all of my misdeeds. * A pure heart create in me, O God, * renew your creating Spirit in me. * Cast me not from your presence, * nor deprive me of your Holy Spirit. * Rather, return your joy and salvation to me, * may your glorious Spirit sustain me, * that I may teach the wicked your ways, * and sinners may turn back to you. * Rescue me from bloodshed, my just God, * and my tongue shall praise your righteousness. * O Lord, open my lips; * my mouth shall speak forth your praise. * You were not pleased in sacrifice, * nor considered burnt offerings. * The sacrifice of God is a humble spirit. * God will not spurn a heart contrite. * Bring good to Zion by your will, * and build the walls of Jerusalem. * Then you will be pleased with sacrifices of truth and burnt offerings, * and then they will offer bulls upon your altar.

Psalm 52: Why do you boast of evil, warrior, * and why does your tongue plot evil every day against the venerable one? * Blessed is he who exalts the humble and makes the illustrious fall. You accomplish deceit like a sharp blade. * You loved evil things more than good things, * and deception more than speaking justice. * You loved all who spoke evil, * and deceptive tongues. * For this, God will uproot you, * and forever overthrow you from your dwelling, * and your roots from the land of life, * so that many may see and rejoice, * and hope in the Lord. * They will say, This is the man who did not make the Lord his trust, * but rather trusted in his great wealth and was exalted in his possessions. * I am like a glorious olive tree in the house of God. * I hoped in the grace of God, * forever, and from age to age. * I will thank you forever for what you have done, * and proclaim your name for the ages before your just ones.

Marmytha

Prayer: We plead to you who destroys the evil, scatters the proud, casts down the mighty, and keeps his covenant and his grace to those who fear his holy name: turn to us, forgive us, and have mercy on us, as you always do, Lord of all, Father, Son, and Holy Spirit, forever.

Psalm 53: The evil man says in his heart, There is no God. * They are destroyed and defiled in their evil. * Save your Church, O Knower of all. There is none who does good. * God looks down from heaven upon the sons of men, * to see if any are intelligent and seek God. * They have all turned away together and become defiled, * and there is none who does good, not even one, * and evildoers do not know. * Those who devoured my people like eating bread, * did not call to God. * There, they will fear greatly, * in a land where there was no fear. * For God will scatter the bones * of those who please the sons of men. * They were ashamed, for God rejected them. * Who will bring salvation to Israel from Zion? * When will the Lord return the dwelling to his people? * Rejoice, Jacob, and be glad, Israel.

Psalm 54: O God, save me by your name; * give me justice by your strength. * You are my true hope. O God, hear my prayer; * hearken to the words of my mouth. * For strangers have risen against me, * the wicked seek my life. * They have no regard for you, O God. * But I have God for my help. * The Lord upholds my soul. * Bring evil upon my enemies, * and silence them by your truth; * and I will sacrifice to you in discernment, * and confess that your name, O Lord, is good. * For you have delivered me from all troubles, * and my eyes have seen the fall of my enemies.

Psalm 55: Attend, O God, to my prayer, and do not turn away from my petition. * Hear me and answer me, answer my cry, and hear me. * To you, O God, I entrust my judgment. Because of my enemies and because of the distress of the evil man, * and because the wicked have looked down on me and envied me. * Fear has fallen upon me, * and the shadows of death have covered me. * I said, Who will give me wings like a dove, * to fly and dwell far away, * to fly and dwell in the wilderness, * to await him who will deliver me from the wind of the tempest? * O Lord, drown the devising of their tongues, * for I have seen conflict and judgment in the village. * Day and night, they surround its walls. * Evil and wickedness within her, and depravity. * Fraud and deceit do not end in her markets. * It is not that I endure my enemy envying me, * nor one who hates me exalting over me, that I may hide from him. * You, a man like me, * my companion and friend, * who ate dinner with me in the house of God, * as we were walking in harmony. * Bring death upon them, * and they will descend into Sheol while alive. * For there is evil within them. * But I will call to God, and God will save me. * In the evening, in the morning, and at noon, * I considered and spoke, and he heard my voice. * He delivered my soul from those who would rule over me, * for they would have conflict with me. * God will hear and humble them, * he who was before all time. * They have no substitute, and do not fear God. * They extended their hand upon his friend and violated his covenant. * They were troubled by the wrath of his face, and from the anger of his heart. * His words were softer than oil, but they were spears. * Cast your burden on the Lord, and he will sustain you. * He will never allow his just to tremble. * May you, O God, bring them down to the pit of destruction, * the men who shed blood and speak deceit. * May they not complete their days, and let me hope in you.

Marmytha

Prayer: Have mercy on us, O Lord our God, forgive, erase, and let pass our faults in the overflowing mercies of your grace, O Merciful One, and Forgiver of debts and sins, Lord of all, Father, Son, and Holy Spirit, forever.

Psalm 56: Have mercy on me, God, for man has tread upon me, * and all the day, the warrior has distressed me. * *Do not leave me with the deceit of liars, O Lord.* My enemies treaded on me all the day, * for many warriors have risen against me. * I will not fear during the day, for I trust in you. * In God is my pride; in God I hoped; I will not fear. * What will man do to me? * All the day they subject me, * and think evil of me. * They hide, and wait, and they keep watch over my steps. * As they waited for my soul, and they said: * He has no redeemer. * Judge them with the wrath of the nations. * O God, I will show you thanksgiving. * Set my tears before you, and in your book. * Then my enemies will be turned back, * and I will know that I have a God. * I will praise the word of God. * I trust in God; I will not fear. * What will man do to me? * I will fulfill my vows to you, O God, * and sacrifice to you in thanksgiving. * For you delivered my soul from death, * and my feet from stumbling, * that I may please you, O God, in the land of the living.

Psalm 57: Have mercy on me, O God, for my soul hopes in you, * and I take refuge in the shadow of your wings. * *Protect me from the trouble of man, my Lord and my God.* While they cause trouble, * I will call to the exalted God, to God my Savior, * that he may send from heaven and save me, * and rebuke my enemies. * God sent his grace and his truth, * and saved my soul from the dogs, * so I slept untroubled. * The sons of men: their teeth are spears and arrows, * and their tongue like a sharp sword. * Rise up to heaven, O God, * and your honor over all the earth. * They set traps for my feet, * and dug a pit for my soul, and fell in it. * My heart is ready, O God, my heart is ready. * I will praise and I will sing. * Awake, my harp; awake, lyre and harp. * I will awake in the morning. * I will thank you among the peoples, O God, and sing to your name among the nations. * For your grace is lifted up to heaven, * and your faithfulness to the heaven of heavens. * Rise up to heaven, O God, * and your honor over all the earth.

The Psalter

Psalm 58: Indeed, you truly speak justice, * and judge uprightly, you sons of men. * Protect the righteous, O God, and cast out the vicious. Lo, you all speak evil on the earth, * and your hands are tangled in evil. * The wicked are set apart from the belly, * and those who speak deception forgotten from the womb. * Their wrath like a poisonous snake, * and like a deaf serpent, * who stops its ears, that it may not hear * the sound of the charmer, or the conjurer, or the wise man. * May God break the teeth in their mouth, * and the Lord pull out the fangs of the lions. * May they vanish like spilled water, * and may he cast his arrows until they vanish. * May they be destroyed like wax which melts and falls before the fire. * May their thorns become brambles, * and may wrath disturb them. * May the just man who sees the repayment rejoice, * and wash his hands in the blood of the wicked. * Let the son of man say, There are fruits for the just man, * and there is a God who judges those on earth.

Hulala VIII

Prayer: Deliver us, O Lord our God, from the deceits and tricks of the enemy, the rebel, through your great and mighty power and your exalted and invincible arm, O Kind One in whom we place our trust at all times and ages, Lord of all, Father, Son, and Holy Spirit, forever.

Psalm 59: Deliver me from my enemies, O God, * and lift me away from those who stand against me. * The wicked have robbed and disturbed me; deliver me, O Lord my God. Deliver me from evildoers, * and save me from men of bloodshed. * For they lay in wait for my soul, * and their malice overpowers me. * Not because of my faults, O Lord, nor through my sins, * for they did not pursue me and lay traps for me in ignorance. * Awake and see, O Lord, almighty God. * O God of Israel, awake, * and command all the peoples. * Do not spare any of the wicked. * They return in the evening, howling like dogs, * and they surround the city. * The word of their mouth is a dispute on their lips; * and they say, Who will hear? * But you, laugh at them, O Lord, * and deride all the peoples. * I will praise you, O God, * for you are my refuge. * O God, may your grace come before me. * O God, show me my enemies. * Do not slay them, lest they forget my people, * but rather shake them by your power and bring them down, O Lord my trust. * The sin of their mouth they speak on their lips; * may they be trapped in their arrogance. * May they be mocked because of cursing and lying. * Scatter them in your wrath; scatter them, and let them not be found. * That they may know that God has authority over Jacob and over the ends of the earth. * They return in the evening, howling like dogs, * and they surround the city. * They seek to devour; let them not be fed or remain. * I will praise your power, * and praise your grace in the morning. * For you have become my refuge, * and my redeemer on the day of distress. * O God, I will sing to you, * for you are the God of my refuge and the God of my grace.

Psalm 60: O God, you have forgotten us, cast us out, and been angry with us. * You have shaken the earth and opened it up. * Save your adorers, O Christ, as you promised. Repair its brokenness, for it is sick. * You have shown harsh things to your people, * and given them foul wine to drink. * You gave those who fear you a sign, * lest they flee before the bow, * for your beloved will be armed. * Save me by your right hand and answer me. * God speaks in his holy place. * I am strengthened and I will divide Shechem. * I will measure out the depth of Succoth. * Mine is Gilead, and mine is Manasseh. * Ephraim is my helmet, * Judah my scepter, Moab my washbasin. * I will loosen my sandals upon Edom, and cry out in Philistia. * Who will lead me to Edom, * and who will bring me to the mighty city? * For lo, you have forgotten us, O God, and do not go out with our army. * Give us help against our enemies, * for the salvation of man is a lie.

Psalm 61: Hear my prayer, O God, and attend to my petition. * From the ends of the earth, I call to you, in the trepidation of my heart. * You are in every place, O God; accept our supplication. Upon the rock, you lifted me and comforted me. * For you have become my refuge, * and my high tower before my enemies, * that I may live in your dwelling forever, * and be covered in the shadow of your wings. * For you, O God, have heard my vows, * and given inheritance to those who fear your name. * You increased days upon days for the king, * and his years unto the ages. * May he be upheld forever before God. * Whom will grace and truth protect? * Thus I will sing to your name forever and ever, * as I fulfill my vows day after day.

Marmytha

Prayer: Our souls await you, O Lord, the eyes of our hearts look to your pity, and we ask forgiveness of our faults from you. Grant this in your grace and mercies, as you always do, Lord of all, Father, Son, and Holy Spirit, forever.

Psalm 62: My soul waits for the Lord, for my salvation is from him, * and he is my God and my Savior. * I am subjected to God, for he is my hope. And my great refuge, that I may not shake. * Until when will you provoke a man, that you may kill him, * like a leaning wall and like a broken fence? * Indeed, they consider how to cast him down from his honor, * and they run in deception. They bless with their mouths but curse in their hearts. * Await for God, my soul, for my salvation is from him, * and he is my God and my Savior, * and my refuge, lest I shake. * In God is my salvation and my honor; * my strength, my help, and my hope is God. * O people, hope in him at every hour, * and cast your hearts before him. * For God is our protection, * and all lying men are like vapor, * who are raised up for a time but perish together. * Do not rely on fraud, * and do not love violence. * When possessions increase, do not let your heart rejoice in them. * One thing has God said, * and two I have heard: * for might is of God, * and grace, O Lord, is yours, * for you repay a man according to his works.

Psalm 63: My God, my God, I await you. * My soul thirsts for you and my flesh waits for you. * In your mercies which are greater than life, forgive me, Pitying One. Like a thirsty and smitten land seeking water, * thus she looks to you in truth, * that I may see your might and your honor. * For your mercies are greater than life, * and my lips will praise you. * Thus will I bless you in my life, * and lift my hands in your name. * My soul is anointed as with cream and fat, * and my mouth praises you with lips of praise. * I remembered you upon my bed, * and considered you during the night. * For you have become my help, * and in the shadow of your wings I am glorified. * My soul goes out after you, * and your right hand sustains me. * They seek to destroy my soul, * and enter the depths of the earth. * They will be handed over to destruction, and become food for foxes. * But the king will rejoice in God, * and all who swear by him will take pride, * for the mouth of liars will be stopped.

Psalm 64: Hear my voice, O God, when I plead to you, * and protect me from the fear of my enemies. * From the evil of deceivers, protect me, my Lord and my God. Protect me from the malice of the evil one, * and from the returning of those who do evil, * who sharpen their tongues like a sword, * and their words like an arrow, * to cast down the innocent man in secret. * They will suddenly cast him down, and not be seen, * and their evil word will be strengthened. * They considered how to set traps, * and said, Who will see us? * The wicked were understood, and burned, * in order to decrease malice among the son of man, * and from the depth of his heart. * God will rise up and suddenly cast down arrows upon them, * and their tongues will become diseased, * and all who look upon them will fear, * and all the sons of men will

The Psalter

fear, * and the works of God will be shown. * They will look upon the works of his hands, * and the just will rejoice in the Lord and trust in him, * and all the upright of heart will praise him.

Marmytha

Prayer: To you is glory due in your chosen Church, to you is owed thanksgiving in glorious Zion, and adoration is right in your exalted dwelling, Lord of all, Father, Son, and Holy Spirit, forever.

Psalm 65: To you is glory due in Zion, O God. * And to you vows are fulfilled: hear my prayer! * Our paths do not prosper by our own hands, O Christ our Savior, for you are the fashioner of our deeds by your power and wisdom. To you all flesh will come. * The words of the wicked are stronger than I, * but you forgive my sins. * Blessed is he in whom you are pleased, * and whom you bring near to dwell in your lodging. * Who is filled with the good things of your house, * with the holiness of your temple, * and with your awesome righteousness. * Answer, O God our Savior! * The Hope of all the ends of the earth, * and of the distant nations! * He establishes the mountains in his power; * they are made strong by his might! * He stills the roarings of the sea * and the sound of their waves. * The nations and the dwellers of earth are awestruck, * by your signs and the procession of morning and evening. * You have surrounded the earth with glory. * You have given it rest and greatly enriched it. * The vessels of God are filled with water: * you prepared their food when you fashioned them. * You have drenched the furrows, that fruits may grow. * Through dew the growth increases and is blessed. * Bless the crown of the year in your grace, * and your calves will be fed with grass. * They will be fed from the lodgings in the wilderness. * With glory the hills will be girt, * and the choice lambs will be clothed. * The valleys will be filled with crops: * they will shout with joy and praise!

Psalm 66: Glorify the Lord, all the earth! * Sing to the honor of his name, sing to the honor of his glory! * Glory to you, our Creator, for you gave us rest at night and protected us, and woke us in the morning, that we may see your wonders by light. Say to God: How awesome are your works! * Because of your great strength, your enemies are convicted. * Through all the earth they shall adore and sing to you, * and glorify your name forever, * and say, Come and see the works of God, * whose marvels are many for the sons of men! * For he turned the sea to dry land, * and they passed through the river on foot. * There, let us rejoice in him whose greatness rules forever. * His eyes look upon the nations, that the insolent may never be exalted. * O nations, bless God, and make his voice of his glory heard. * For he placed our souls in life and did not let our foot stumble. * For you have tested us, O God, and tried us, like they test silver. * You have brought us to the net, and laid a burden on our backs. * You let men ride upon our heads, * brought us to fire and water, and brought us out to rest. * I will come to your house with respect and repay you my vows, * that which my lips have spoken and my mouth in distress. * I will raise up burnt offerings with the smoke of rams, * and make a sacrifice of bullocks and goats. * Come and hear, and I will make known to you, * all you servants of God, what he has done for my soul. * I called to him with my mouth, and he answered me, * and I exalted him with my tongue. * O Lord, if you see malice in my heart, you will not save me. * Then God heard the sound of my petition. * Blessed be the Lord, * who did not let my prayer or his grace pass from me.

Psalm 67: O God, have mercy on us! * Bless us, and let your face shed its light upon us. * O Christ, who gave the talents of spiritual silver to his servants: grant your help to your adorers who have accepted your Gift. That your ways be known upon earth * and all nations learn your salvation. * Let the peoples confess you, O God; * let all the peoples confess you. * Let the kingdoms be glad and exult * for you judge the nations uprightly * and guide the nations on earth. * Let the peoples confess you, O God; * let all the peoples confess you. * The earth has yielded its fruit * for God, our God, has blessed us. * May God still give us his blessing * and all the ends of the earth will fear him.

Hulala IX

Prayer: May the eternal mercies of your glorious Trinity be stirred up for the sake of weak sinners, your servants who call and plead to you at all times and ages, Lord of all, Father, Son, and Holy Spirit, forever.

Psalm 68: May God arise and may all his enemies be scattered, * and all those who hate him flee before him. * The time has come for idols to be uprooted, and only God, the Lord of all to be worshipped. Let them vanish like smoke vanishes, * and melt like wax before fire. * Let the wicked be scattered from before God, * and the just rejoice and be strengthened before God. * May they rejoice in his delight. * Sing to God and glorify his name. * Glorify, for the Lord's name rides on the west wind. * Be strengthened before the Father of orphans, * and the judge of widows. * God is in his holy dwelling. * God sets the lonely one in a home, * and sets captives free in prosperity, * and lets rebels go among the tombs. * God, when you went out before your people, * and passed over the desert, the earth quaked, * and the heavens poured down. * Before God, this mountain of Sinai; * before God, the God of Israel. * O God, you gave the rain of your will to your inheritance. * It was sick, and you restored it. * Your beasts dwelt in it. * You provided for the poor in your grace, O God. * The Lord will give the word of the good news in great power. * The kings of the armies will be gathered, * and the beauty of your house will be divided by robbery, * if you sleep among thorns. * The wings of the dove are covered in silver, * and its pinions in pure gold. * When God divided the king, it froze * in Zalmon, the mountain of God, * the mountains of Bashan, the mountains of Gibinyam. * O mountains of Bashan, why do you desire the mountains of Gibinyam? * The mountain that God chose to sit upon; * the Lord will dwell upon it forever. * God rides upon legions and thousands of powers. * The Lord is within them, his holy Sinai.

Division. You went up to the height, and dwelt in a dwelling, * and received gifts for the sons of men, * though rebels will not dwell before God. * Blessed be the Lord every day, for he chose us as his inheritance. * God is our Savior, God is our Deliverer. * The Lord God is the Lord of death and escape. * Therefore the Lord will cut off the head of his enemies, * the pupils of the heads of those who walk in their sins. * The Lord said, I will return you from among the fangs, * and return you from the depths of the sea. * For you have soaked your feet in blood, * and the tongue of your dogs in your enemies. * They see your footsteps, O God; * the footsteps of my God and my holy King. * The exalted are presented after those who glorify, * among the maidens who play upon timbrels in their assemblies. * Bless the Lord God from the fountains of Israel. * There Benjamin the least will be in silence. * The princes of Judah and their leaders; * the princes of Zebulun, and the princes of Naphthali. * God, command your might, * and strengthen, O God, this thing you have prepared for us * from your temple to Jerusalem. * To you will kings give offerings. * Rebuke the beasts of the reed, the assembly of calves. * The calves of the people who are covered with silver. * Scatter the people who desire war. * Ambassadors will come from Egypt, * and Ethiopia will extend a hand to God. * Kingdoms of the earth, praise God. * Sing to the Lord who rides on the heaven of heavens. * From the east he gives his voice, a mighty voice. * Give glory to God, * and to Israel, more than what is due. * For his might is in the heaven of heavens. * Fearful are you, O God, from your sanctuary. * The God of Israel, * he will give strength and might to his people; blessed be God.

Marmytha

Prayer: O Lord, save your people from the destruction of perdition, bring our souls away from the fraud of sinfulness, and let your truth set our steps upon the paths of justice, all the days of our lives, Lord of all, Father, Son, and Holy Spirit, forever.

Psalm 69: Save me, O God, for the waters have reached my soul. * I have drowned in the deep abyss, and there is nowhere to stand. * O Christ, forgive me. I have entered the deep waters, and the whirlpool has drowned me. * I am weary in my crying, and my throat is parched. * My eyes are dim as I await for my God. * Those who are my enemies without cause are more than the hair of my head, * and my wicked enemies are stronger than my bones. * The thing I did not steal, I had to return. * O God, you know my faults, * and my sins are not hidden from you. * Let those who hope in you not be ashamed by me. * O Lord God almighty, * may those who seek you not be put to shame, O God of Israel. * For your sake, I have accepted reproach, * and shame has covered my face. * I have become a stranger to my brothers, * and an alien to the sons of my mother. * For zeal of your house has consumed me, * and the reproach of your reproachers has fallen upon me. * I have humbled my soul in fasting, and become a reproach to them. * I have made my garment sackcloth, and become an example to them. * Those who sit at the gate discuss me, * and those who drink strong drink discuss me. * O Lord, I pray to you at the accepted time. * O God, in the greatness of your grace, answer me. * And in the greatness of your salvation, deliver me * from the grime, lest I drown, * and that I may be delivered from those who hate me and from the depth of the waters; * that the whirlpool of water may not drown me, * or the abyss swallow me, * or the mouth of the pit swallow me. * Answer me, O Lord, for your grace is good, * and turn to me in your great mercies. * Do not turn your face from your servant, * for I am greatly troubled; answer me. * Bring my soul to your salvation; * because of my enemies, save me. * You know my reproach, * and my shame is before all my enemies.

Division. Heal and bandage my broken heart. * I awaited for one to pity me, and there was none, * and for one to comfort, and I did not find. * They gave me gall for food, * and vinegar to quench my thirst. * May their table become a trap before them, * and their reward a stumbling-block. * May their eyes be darkened, that they may not see, * and their back always be bent. * Cast your wrath upon them, * and let the anger of your wrath overcome them. * May their dwelling place be destroyed, * and their inhabitances become uninhabitable. * For they pursue the one you have struck, * and added to the wounds of the murdered man. * Grant evil upon their evil, * that they may not enter in justice, * and they be erased from your book of life, * and not be written among your just. * I am poor and wounded. * May your salvation help me. * I will praise the name of God with glory, * and exalt him in thanksgiving. * I will please the Lord with fattened bulls, * horns and hooves. * The poor will see and rejoice, and their heart will live. * For the Lord hears the poor, * and does not despise the imprisoned. * Heaven and earth will praise him, * the seas and all that moves within them. * For God saves Zion, * and builds the villages of Judah, * that his servants may dwell in her and inherit her, * and those who love his name may live within her.

Psalm 70: Deliver me, O God, O Lord, come to my aid. * May those who seek my soul be put to shame and humiliation. * Help me, O Lord my God. May they be turned back and ashamed, * those who wish evil for me. * May they be amazed at the recounting of their shame, * those who say to me, Aha, aha. * May all who seek you rejoice, * and may they say at all times, God is great, * those who love your salvation. * But I am poor and needy; * O God, hasten to me. * O my help and my deliverer, O Lord, do not delay.

HULALA X

Prayer: In you, O Lord, we hope, in your mercies we trust, and from your grace we plead: be an aid to our weakness, O Lord, a refuge for our fallenness, a provider to our neediness, an assembler to our scatteredness, a savior to our affliction, a forgiver to our sinfulness, and do not turn your face from the sound of our pleading, O Kind One in whom our trust is place, at all times and ages, Lord of all, Father, Son, and Holy Spirit, forever.

Psalm 71: In you I have hoped, O Lord, let me never be put to shame, * and in your justice, deliver me. * Come, brethren, let us take refuge in prayer, for it is the mighty armor by which we can defeat Satan our enemy, the hater of our race. Turn your ear to me and save me. * Be a dwelling place where I may enter at all times, * and command my salvation. * For you are my refuge and my citadel. * O God, deliver me from the hand of the wicked, * and from the hand

The Psalter

of the malicious, evil man. * For you are my hope, O Lord. * O God, my trust from my youth; * I have been nourished by you from the womb, * and from my mother's belly, you are my trust. * I glorified you at all times. * I have been a marvel to many, * for you are my mighty trust. * May my mouth be filled with your praise, * and all the day your greatness. * Do not cast me away at a time of old age, * and do not abandon me when my strength is finished. * For my enemies said to me, * those who kept watch over my soul, * they took counsel together and said: * God has abandoned him; pursue him and take him, * for he has no deliverer. * O God, do not be distant from me. * O God, hasten to my aid. * May those who envy my soul be ashamed and humiliated. * Let shame accompany those who wish evil for me. * Then I will always pray and increase your praises, * and my mouth will announce your justice, * and all the day your praises. * For I have not known learning, * that I may enter into the might of the Lord, * and recall his justice on my own. * O God, be my teaching from my youth until now, * that I may show your wonders. * Do not abandon me during old age or elder years, * until I show your arm and your might to the generation to come. * Your justice, O God, is unto the height, * and the great deeds you have worked, O God; who is like you? * For you have shown me distress and great evil, * and returned and given me life. * You even returned and lifted me from the abysses of the earth. * You increased my greatness, and returned and comforted me. * I will thank you with the harp and sing to your truth. * O God, I will sing to you with the holy harp of Israel, * and my lips will praise as they sing to you, and my soul which you saved. * My tongue will thank your justice all the day, * for they have been shamed and humiliated, * those who wished me evil.

Psalm 72: O God, give your judgment to the king; * to the king's son your justice. * *The grace of God overflowed upon all from on high at the coming of Christ, the Savior of all creatures.* That he may judge your people in justice, * and your poor in right judgment. * May the mountains bear peace for your people, * and the hills, your justice, * that he may judge the poor of the people, * save the children of the needy, * and crush the tyrant. * May they fear you with the sun, * and before the moon unto the ages. * May he fall like rain upon the grass, * and like droplets that fall upon the earth. * May justice flourish in his days, * and great peace until the moon passes away. * May he seize all from sea to sea, * and from the rivers until the ends of the earth. * Before him may the islands kneel, * and may his enemies lick the dust. * The kings of Tarshish and the islands * will bring him offerings. * The kings of Sheba and Seba * will offer oblations. * All kings will worship him, * and all the peoples will serve him. * For he will deliver the poor man from the mighty one, * and the humble man who has no one to help. * He pities the humble and the poor, * and saves the souls of the humble. * He saves their souls from fraud and evil. * Their blood is precious in his eyes. * May he live and be given of the gold of Sheba, * and may they pray for him at all times, * and bless him all the day. * May he be like abundant grain in the land, * and may his fruits flourish on the mountaintops as in Lebanon. * May he blossom from his city like the grass of the earth. * May his name be forever; * and before the sun is his name. * May all the nations be blessed in him, * and all of them glorify him. * Blessed is the Lord, the God of Israel, * who has worked great wonders alone. * And blessed be his honored name forever. * May all the earth be filled with his honor, amen, amen.

END OF BOOK TWO.

BOOK THREE

Marmytha

Prayer: O patient in his grace, sharp avenger in his righteousness, great King of glory, Being who exists from eternity: we thank, adore, and glorify you at all times, Lord of all, Father, Son, and Holy Spirit, forever.

Psalm 73: God is good to Israel, and to the simple of heart. * But my feet stumble a bit. * *You are patient, O Lord, but your vengeance is sharp.* My steps fell as into nothing. * For I had envied the evil, * when I saw the peace of the wicked. * For they have no expectation of death, * and their folly is great. * They do not labor like others, * nor are stricken with the sons of men. * Because of this, contempt has taken them. * Their evil and their wickedness is hidden, * and their evil runs out like oil. * They act as if with thoughtful hearts. * They consider and speak evil, * and speak violence against the Most High. * They set their mouths in heaven, * and their lips walk on earth. * Because of this, my people return here, * and find them full. * They say, How will God know? * And, Is there knowledge in the Most High? * For lo, the wicked prosper in the world, * and are mighty in strength. * But I alone purify my heart, * and wash my hands in purity. * I have been struck all the day, * and rebuked in the morning. * Were I to say I will act like them, there would be envy in my eyes. * But then I enter the holy place of God, * and understand their end. * What is prepared for them is like their deceit, * and it will fall upon them as they fall. * Just as they were suddenly a marvel, * they will vanish and be finished in confusion. * Like the one who awakes when he sees a dream, * the Lord will treat their image with contempt in the village. * My heart was troubled and my belly shook, * but I was ignorant and did not know, * and was a beast with you. * Comfort me with your understanding, and guide me after your honor. * What do I have in heaven with you? * And what have I desired on earth? * You have held my right hand, * my heart is fulfilled, my flesh, and the strength of my heart. * My portion is in God forever, * for lo, those far from you will be scattered, * and you will destroy all who are lost to you forever. * But I wished to grow near to God. * Your name is best for me, O Lord my trust, * and I will make your wonders known.

Psalm 74: O God, why have you forgotten us forever, * and increased your anger with the sheep of your flock? * **O Lord of all, to whom all is revealed: do not leave your adorers.** Remember your church which you established from the beginning, * and save the tribe of your inheritance. * This is mount Zion, where you dwell. * Raise your servants over those who would take by force. * All who destroy are enemies to your sanctuary. * Your enemies boast during your feast. * They have made their signs into signs, * and you have known as an exalted one above. * They have rent the doors like forests with axes, * together with hatchets and pickaxes. * They have razed and burned your sanctuary with fire, * and smeared the dwelling of your name with dirt. * They said in their heart, We will destroy them together, * and destroy all the feasts of God from the earth. * They did not see their signs. * There is neither prophet nor wise man among us. * Until when, O God? * The enemy taunts, and angers your name constantly. * Why do you not return your hand, and your right hand from your feast? * Our God is the King, * who commanded from the beginning regarding the salvation of Jacob. * You divided the sea by your might, * and crushed the heads of the dragons in the sea. * You bruised the head of Leviathan, * and gave it as food to a mighty people. * You shook the fountains in the valleys. * You dried the mighty rivers. * Yours is the day and yours is the night. * You fashioned light and the sun. * You established all the limits of the earth. * You created summer and winter. * Remember, O Lord, the mockery of the enemy, * an ignorant people angering your name. * Do not give the soul who thanks you over to ruin, * or forget the souls of your humble ones forever. * Look, O Lord, upon your covenant, * for the dwellings of the

The Psalter

earth are filled with darkness and evil. * Let the poor man not sit shamefully. * Let the poor and humble praise your name. * Arise, O God, and make your judgments. * Remember your daily mockery from the ignorant, * and do not forget the voice of your enemies, * and the troubling of those who rise against us, * which increases at all times.

Marmytha

Prayer: We thank your compassion toward us, O Lord our God, adore the providence of your will for us, and we lift up praise at all times, Lord of all, Father, Son, and Holy Spirit, forever.

Psalm 75: We give thanks to you, O God, * we give you thanks and call upon your name. * **We honor the feast of your baptism, O Christ our Savior.** We recount your marvelous deeds. * When I reach the appointed time, * then I will judge with integrity. * The earth and its inhabitants will be humbled. * You have ordered its inhabitants. * You told fools not to be fools, * and to the wicked not to raise the horn, * or raise their horn to the heights, * or speak with a proud neck. * For exodus is not from the west, * nor from the wilderness of mountains, * for God is the judge; * he lowers one and exalts another. * For the cup is in the hand of the Lord, * and its mixture is of cloudy wine. * He looks down from one to the other. * His dregs drain and give drink to all the wicked of the earth. * But I will live forever, * and sing to the God of Jacob. * I will smite all the horns of the wicked, * and the horns of the just will be exalted.

Psalm 76: God is known in Judah, * and his great name in Israel. * **You are exalted forever, King of all creatures.** His abode is in Salem, * and his dwelling in Zion. * There he broke the arms of the archers, * the shield and sword of war. * You are shining and glorious from your mighty mountain. * All the ignorant of heart were troubled, * and warrior men slept their slumber. * Because of your rebuke, they could not use their hands, O God of Jacob. * Those who ride chariots slept, and you are fearful. * Who can stand before you in this wrath? * You hear judgment from heaven; * earth sees and fears, * when you arise to judge, O God, * and to save all the humble of the earth. * For the thought of man confesses you, * and you end the rest of his anger in wrath. * Vow and fulfill to the Lord your God, * all who surround him, bring offerings to the Fearful One, * who humbles the spirit of princes, * and is fearful over the kings of the earth.

Psalm 77: With my voice, I called to God and he heard, * and lifted my voice toward him, and he answered. * O Lord of all, revealed to all: may you protect your adorers. On the day of my distress, I cried out to the Lord, * and his hand pulled me at night and I was not silent. * There was no one to comfort my soul. * I remembered God and I trembled. * I considered, and my spirit shook, * and dizziness seized my eyes. * I was mute and did not speak. * I considered my days of old, * and remembered the years from ages ago. * I considered at night, and considered in my heart, * and examined my spirit and said, * The Lord has forgotten me forever, * and no longer favors me. * O, will he let his grace pass me by forever, * and make an end to his word unto the ages? * O, has God forgotten to have mercy, * or stopped his mercies in his wrath? * I said that it is my sickness, * and the right hand of the Most High is doubled. * For I remembered your marvels from of old, * and considered all your works, * and considered your deeds. * O God, your path is holy, * and there is no one as great as our God. * You are the God who has worked wonders, * and showed your might among the nations, * and saved your people by your arm, * the sons of Jacob and Joseph. * The waters saw you, O God, the waters saw you and feared. * Even the abysses shook, and the clouds rained water. * The heavens of heaven made a sound, * and even your arrows fly, * and the sound of your thunders in the spheres. * Your lightnings shine for the world. * The earth trembled and shook. * Your path is in the sea, and your ways through many waters. * Your footsteps are not known. * You led your people like sheep, * by the hand of Moses and Aaron.

Hulala XI

Prayer: To you O wise provider, O wondrous caretaker of his household, O great treasure bringing forth all benefits and blessings in his compassion: we implore you to turn to us, forgive us, and have mercy on us, as you always do, Lord of all, Father, Son, and Holy Spirit, forever.

Psalm 78: My people, attend to my law and take refuge, * incline your ears to the words of my mouth. * The sons of Israel, an unjust people. Lo, I will open my mouth in proverbs, * and speak parables from of old. * We knew the things we have heard, * and those things which our fathers made known to us, * which they did not hide from their sons, * but made them known to the next generation. * The glories of the Lord and his power, * and the wonders he worked. * For he established a witness in Jacob, * and placed his law in Israel, as he commanded our fathers, * to confess them to their sons, * that the next generation might know, * the sons that are born and stand. * That they may make them known to their sons, * that their hope may be in God, * lest they forget the works of God, * but rather keep his commands. * Let them not be as their fathers, * an evil and murmuring generation, * a generation which did not fasten its heart, * whose spirit did not believe in God. * The sons of Ephraim, who stretched a bow and cast an arrow, * and turned back on the day of battle. * For they did not keep the covenant of God, * and did not wish to walk in his law, * and forgot his works and his wonders, * which he showed before their fathers. * For he worked wonders in the land of Egypt, * and in the fields of Zoan. * He divided the sea, and let them pass; * he held up the waters as with a wineskin. * He led them by day with a cloud, * and the whole night with the brightness of fire. * He divided the rock in the wilderness, * and let them drink as from a great abyss. * He brought streams out of a rock, * and the waters streamed like rivers. * But the people increased in sinning, * and in murmuring against the Most High in their thirst. * They tested God in their heart, * to ask for food for their soul. * They spoke against God and said, * Can God prepare us tables in the wilderness? * If he struck the rock and waters streamed, and made the torrents stream? * Is he also able to give us bread? * Or prepare food for his people? * Because of this, the Lord heard and was angered, * and fire seized Jacob. * Wrath arose in Israel, * because they did not believe in God, * and did not hope in his salvation.

Division. He commanded the clouds from above, * and the doors of heaven were opened. * He brought down manna for them to eat, * and gave them the bread of heaven. * The son of man ate the bread of angels, * and he sent them game to eat. * He made the winds blow in the sky, * and led it to the south by his power. * He brought down meat for them like dust, * and winged birds like the sand of the seas. * They fell in their habitats around their camps; * they ate and were well filled, and he gave them their desires. * But they were not saved from their desires, * and while their food was in their mouth, * the wrath of God came upon them, * and he slew their wealthy ones, * and made the chosen of Israel kneel. * In all these things they sinned, * and again did not believe in his wonders. * They wasted their days in vanities, * and their years too quickly. * When he slew them, they sought him; * they returned and progressed toward him. * They remembered that God is their help, * and the exalted God their Savior. * They loved him with their mouth, but lied of him

with their tongue. * Their heart was not fastened upon him, and they did not believe in his covenant. * But he is merciful, forgives sins, and does not destroy. * He increasingly turned back his wrath, and did not awake his full anger. * He remembered that they are flesh, * a wind that goes and does not return. * They murmured in the wilderness, * and angered him in the desert. * They turned and tested God, * and provoked the Holy One of Israel. * They did not remember his hand on the day he saved them from distress, * he who accomplished his signs in Egypt, * and his marvels in the fields of Zoan. * For he turned their rivers to blood, * and their streams, lest they drink water. * He sent swarms upon them, and they devoured them, * and frogs, which destroyed them. * He gave their fields to the locust, * and the fruit of their labor to the young locust. * He destroyed their vines with hail, * and their figs with snow. * He gave their cattle over to hail, * and their possessions to fires. * He sent them the anger of his wrath; * anger, wrath, and distress. * He sent them through an evil angel, * and tread evil paths, * and did not spare their souls from death. * He gave their animals over to death, * and slew all the first born of Egypt, * the head of all the children in the dwelling of Ham.
Division. He led forth his people like sheep, * and led them like a flock in the wilderness. * He let them dwell in hope, and they did not fear. * The sea covered their enemies. * He brought them to his holy border, * this mountain that his right hand had gained. * He scattered the people before them, * and cast them down with the cord of his inheritance. * The tribes of Israel dwelt in their tents. * They tested and murmured to the exalted God, * and did not keep his testimonies. * They turned and lied like their fathers, * and were turned like a deceitful bow. * They angered him with their high places and moved him to zeal with their idols. * God heard and was angered, * and was greatly wrathful toward Israel. * He forgot the dwelling in Shiloh, * the dwelling where he dwelt among the sons of men. * He gave his people to captivity, and his glory into the hand of the foe. * He handed his people over to battle, and turned away from his inheritance. * Fire devoured their youths, * and their virgins were smitten. * Their priests fell in battle, * and their widows did not lament. * The Lord awoke as from sleep, * and like a man shaking off wine. * He struck his enemies behind him, * and made them the taunt of the nations. * He rejected the dwelling of Joseph, * and was not pleased with the tribe of Ephraim. * He chose the family of Judah * for mount Zion which he loved. * He built his sanctuary on the hill, * and established it on earth forever. * He

chose David his servant, * and led him from the sheepfolds, * and from following suckling sheep, * to shepherding Jacob his people, and Israel his inheritance. * He shepherded them in the innocence of his heart, * and by the skill of his hands, he led them.

Marmytha

Prayer: Save your people, O Lord, bless your inheritance, and let your glory dwell in the temple set apart for your honor, all the days of the age, Lord of all, Father, Son, and Holy Spirit, forever.

Psalm 79: O God, the peoples have entered before your inheritance, * and have defiled your holy temple. * Because we sinned, our oppressors subjugate us, and profane your holy place; O Merciful One, forgive us. They have made Jerusalem a ruin. * They gave the corpses of your servants as food for the birds of the sky, * and the flesh of your just to the beasts of the earth. * They spilled their blood like water around Jerusalem, and there is no one to bury them. * We have become the taunt of our neighbors, * and the mockery and derision of those around us. * How long will you be angry, O Lord, * and how long will your wrath burn like fire? * Cast your wrath upon the nations, those who do not know you, * and upon those kingdoms who do not call upon your name. * For they have devoured Jacob and destroyed his dwelling. * Let our early sins not be remembered against us; * let your mercies quickly come to us, * for we have been greatly humiliated. * Help us, O God our Savior, * for the sake of the honor of your name. * Forgive and deliver us from our sins, for your name, * lest the nations say, Where is their God? * Let it be known to the nations before our eyes, * the vengeance of the blood of your servants which was shed. * May the groaning of the prisoner come before you. * By your mighty arm, unbind the sons from death, * and repay our neighbors sevenfold in their bosom, * the taunt by which they taunted you, O Lord. * We are your people, and the sheep of your flock. * Let us thank you forever, * and make your wonders known unto the ages.

Psalm 80: Hear, O Shepherd of Israel, * and lead Joseph like a flock. * You protected our fathers in their age, those who pleased you. O Seer of all, save your church. You who sit upon the cherubim, be revealed, * to Ephraim, Benjamin, and Manasseh. * Show your might and come to save us. * Almighty God, turn to us, * brighten your face, and we will be saved. * Lord God almighty, * how long will you be angry over the prayer of your servant? * You fed them bread in tears, * and gave them tears to drink. * You have made us the scorn of our neighbors, * and our enemies mock us. * Turn to us, almighty God; * brighten your face, and we will be saved. * You brought a vine out of Egypt, * and you scattered the nations and planted her. * You looked upon her, and planted her roots. * With her, the earth is filled, * and the mountains are covered by her shade, * and her branches are over the cedars of God. * She cast out her branches to the sea, * and her shoots to the rivers. * Why have you opened up her wall? * All who pass by trample her. * The boar of the forest consumes her, * and the beasts of the field feed on her. * Turn to us, almighty God; * look from heaven and see. * Regard this vine, * and the stock your right hand has planted. * A son of man strengthened by you * has burned her branches with fire. * Let them be scattered by the rebuke of your face. * Let your right hand be upon the man, * and upon the son of man strengthened by you. * Let us not turn away from you, * but rather give us life and we will call upon your name. * Lord God almighty, turn to us; * brighten your face, and we will be saved.

Psalm 81: Glorify God who strengthens us, * and cry out to the God of Jacob. Blessed is the Lord who aids his holy ones to keep his words, and quickly destroys those who hate him. Take up timbrel and harp, * sweet ones, with the lyre. * Blow trumpets at the new moon, * and at the full moon, on feast days. * For it is a law for Israel, * and a judgment of the God of Jacob. * He placed it as a witness in Joseph, * when he left the land of Egypt. * He heard a language he did not know: * I let the yoke pass from his shoulder, * and unbound his hand from the basket. * He called me in distress and I delivered him, * and covered him in my glorious shelter. * I tested him in the waters of conflict. * Hear, my people, and I will speak; * Israel, and I will witness in you. * If you hear me, you will not have an alien God, * and you will not worship in a different religion. * I am the Lord your God, * who brought you up from the land of Egypt. * Open your mouth and I will fill it. * But my people did not hear my voice, * and Israel did not accept me. * They walked in the will of their heart, * and in the thought of their soul. * If only my people heard me, and Israel walked on my paths. * After a while, I would destroy their enemies, * and turn my hand against those who hate them. * Those who hate the Lord mocked him, * and their trembling is forever. * I would feed him with the finest wheat, * and satisfy him with honey from a rock.

The Psalter
Hulala XII

Prayer: O King whom kings adore, and the adorable honor of whose Majesty assemblies and legions of angels and archangels stand, serve, and extol in great fear and trembling: it is our duty to thank, adore, and glorify you, at all times, Lord of all, Father, Son, and Holy Spirit, forever.

Psalm 82: God stands in the assembly of angels. * In the midst of the angels he judges. * O judges, judge justly and keep away from evil. How long will you judge unjustly * and favor the cause of the wicked? * Do justice for orphans and the poor, * vindicate the humble and the needy. * Rescue the weak and the poor * from the hand of the wicked. * They neither know nor understand, * that they walk in darkness. * All the foundations of the earth shook. * I said, You are gods, * and sons of the Most High, all of you. * Henceforth, you will die like sons of men, * and will fall like one of the exalted. * Arise, O God, and judge the earth, * for you own all the nations.

Psalm 83: O God, who is like you? * Do not be silent or still, O God. * You have no equal among things made, O God almighty. Lo, your enemies are aware, * and those who hate you raise their head over your people. * In their cunning, they devise secrets, * and they consult themselves regarding the holy ones, saying: * Come, let us scatter them from the people, * and the name of Israel will not be remembered. * For they consider together in their hearts, * and set up a covenant against you. * The tent of Edom and the Arabs, * of Moab and Hagrites, * the border of Ammon and of Amalek, * of Philistia with those dwelling in Tyre, * and even the Assyrian has joined them, * and has become a help to the sons of Lot. * Do to them as you did to Midian and Sisera, * to Nabin at the river Kishon, * who were destroyed at Endor and became refuse for the earth. * Destroy them and scatter them, * like at Oreb and like Zeeb, like Zebah and Salmunna, * all of whose leaders said, * We will inherit the village of God. * O God, make them like a potter's wheel and like grass before the wind, * like fire passing over the forest, * like a furnace burning the mountains. * Thus pursue them with your windstorms, * and shake them with your tempests. * Fill their faces with shame, * and let them seek your name, O Lord. * Let them be shamed and shaken forever and ever; * let them be humiliated and scattered, * and let them know that your name alone, O Lord, * is exalted over all the earth.

Psalm 84: How lovely are your tabernacles, Lord almighty. * My soul yearns for the courts of the Lord. * How glorious and lovely is your sanctuary, O God who

sanctifies all. My heart and my flesh glorify the living God. * Even the bird finds a home and the sparrow a nest. * Fledglings grow near your altar, O Lord almighty. * My King and my God, blessed are they who dwell in your house. * They will glorify you forever. * Blessed is the man who trusts in you, * and who has your paths in his heart. * They will pass through the depth of lamentation and make it a dwelling place. * Even the lawmaker will be clothed with a blessing. * They will go from strength to strength, * and be seen by the God of gods in Zion. * O Lord God almighty, hear my prayer, * and attend, O God of Jacob. * See, O God our help, * and look upon the face of your Anointed One. * For one day in your court is greater than a thousand. * I wished to dwell in the house of God, * more than to dwell in the dwelling of the wicked. * For the Lord God is our nourisher and our help. * The Lord will give mercies and honor, * and not hold back his blessings * from those who walk in innocence. * Lord God almighty, * blessed is the man who hopes in you.

Marmytha

Prayer: O Lord, be pleased with the prayer of your servants, receive the service of your adorers, forgive the faults of those who praise you, and let the anger of your wrath pass over your family, O Kind One who cares for our lives at all times and ages, Lord of all, Father, Son, and Holy Spirit, forever.

Psalm 85: O Lord, you were pleased with your land, * and returned the dwelling to Jacob. * O Lord, send help and salvation to your adorers, by the great power of the cross. You forgave the sin of your people, * and covered all their sins. * You let all your anger pass, * and overturned the anger of your wrath. * Turn to us, O God our Savior, * and remove your wrath from us. * Do not be angry with us forever, * and do not keep your wrath for the ages. * Rather, turn to us and give us life, and your people will rejoice in you. * O Lord, show us your grace and grant us your salvation. * That we may hear what the Lord our God has spoken, * who spoke peace for his people with the just, * lest they be turned back. * His salvation is close to those who fear him. * Let his honor dwell in our land. * Grace and truth will meet; * justice and peace will kiss; * faithfulness will grow from the earth, * and justice will look down from heaven. * The Lord will even give his blessings, * and the earth will bear its harvest. * The just man will walk before him, * and place his footsteps on the earth.

The Psalter

Psalm 86: Turn your ear, O Lord, and answer me, * for I am poor and needy. * O Christ who loves the repentant: open the door to our prayer, and accept our petition. Protect my soul, for you are good. * Save your servant, O God in whom he hopes. * Have mercy on me, Lord, * for I call to you every day. * Gladden the soul of your servant, * for to you, O Lord, I lift up my soul, * because you are good, O Lord, * and your grace is great toward all who call to you. * Attend to my prayer, O Lord, * and hear the sound of my pleading. * On the day of my distress I called you and you answered me. * There is none like you, O Lord my God, and there is nothing like your works. * All the peoples you have made * come and adore you, O Lord, * and glorify your name, for you are great. * You perform marvels, you alone, O God. * Show me, O Lord, your path, and I will walk it in truth. * Gladden my heart in those who fear your name. * I will thank you, O Lord my God, with all my heart, * and I will glorify your name forever. * For your grace has increased for me, * and you saved my soul from the lower Sheol. * O God, the wicked have risen against me, * and the assembly of the mighty seek my soul, and do not consider you. * You, O Lord God, are merciful and compassionate, * patient and abounding in grace and truth. * Turn to me and have mercy on me; * give strength to your servant, and save the son of your handmaid. * Accomplish a good sign with me, * that my haters may see and be ashamed, * for you, O Lord, have helped me and comforted me.

Marmytha

Prayer: Establish, O Lord, the pillars of your Church through your mercy, strengthen her foundations in your grace, and let your glory dwell in the Temple set apart for the honor of your service, all the days of the age, Lord of all, Father, Son, and Holy Spirit, forever.

Psalm 87: Its foundations are on his holy mountain: * the Lord loves the gates of Zion, * God the Creator is adored, he who cares for all ages. More than all of Jacob's dwellings. * Honorable things are said in you, * O village of our God. * You will be remembered in Egypt and known in Babylon, * Philistia, Tyre, and among the Cushites. * That man will be born there, * and of Zion it shall be said: * the Great One shall be born there, * and he has established her. * The Lord will count his people in his register: * that man will be born there. * The leaders who dwell in you will rejoice, * as well as all the lowly within you.

Psalm 88: O Lord God of my salvation, * By day I cried out, and by night before you. * You are compassionate, O Fashioner; in your grace, forgive us. May my prayer enter before you; * turn your ear to my pleading, * for my soul is filled with evils, * and my life has reached Sheol. * I am considered among those who have descended to the cave, * and have become like a man without help, * a freeborn man among the dead, * like the murdered buried in tombs, * those whom you have not remembered, * and those destroyed by your hands. * You have brought me down to the lowest cave, * to the darkness and the shadow of death. * Your wrath has devoured me, * and you have brought all your waves against me. * You have distanced those who know me, * and made me impure to them. * I am prevented from leaving, * and my eye pines due to my humiliation. * I have called you, O Lord, every day, * and extended my hands toward you. * Lo, will you work miracles for the dead? * Will warriors rise and give thanks to you? * Will those in the tomb discuss your grace, * and those in destruction your faithfulness? * Will your marvel be made known in the darkness, * and your righteousness in a land that was lost? * But I cry out to you, O Lord, * and present my prayer to you in the morning. * Do not forget my soul, O Lord, * nor turn your face from me. * I am miserable and weary from my youth: * I have been raised up, and humbled, and broken, * and your wrath has passed over me, * and your tempest has silenced me. * I am surrounded as with waters the whole day, * and they come against me as one. * You have distanced my friends and companions from me, * and removed those who know me.

Hulala XIII

Prayer: Pour out your graces upon us, O Lord, increase your help toward us, and strengthen us as you always do, that we may be noble before you as you will, be guided according to your commands, and please your Divinity, all the days of our lives, Lord of all, Father, Son, and Holy Spirit, forever.

Psalm 89: I will sing the grace of the Lord forever, * and make known his faithfulness with my mouth for the ages. * The blessings God promised to Abram and David were fulfilled in deed during our days through Christ; glory to him. For you said the world was built in grace, * and your faithfulness fashioned heaven. * I established a covenant with my chosen, * and vowed to David my servant: * I will establish your seed forever, * and build your throne for the ages. * The heavens confess your wonders, O Lord, * and your faithfulness in the church of your holy ones. * Who compares to the Lord in the heavens of heaven, * and resembles the Lord among the sons of the angels?

The Psalter

* God stands in the church of the holy ones, * great and fearful for all who surround him. * Lord God almighty, * who is mighty like you, * and whose faithfulness surrounds you? * You are powerful in the splendor of the sea, * and you silence the shaking of its waves. * You humble the proud like the dead. * By your mighty arm you scatter your enemies. * Yours are the heavens and yours is earth; * you fashioned the world in its fullness. * You created the north and the south, * Tabor and Hermon glorify your name. * Yours is the arm and yours is the might. * Your hand is mighty and your right hand is exalted. * In justice and judgment, your throne is established. * In grace and truth your countenance is presented. * Blessed is the people who knows your glories. * O Lord, let them walk in the light of your countenance, * and rejoice in your name every day, * and be exalted in your justice. * For you are the glory of our might, * and by your will our horn is exalted. * For the Lord is our trust, * and the Holy One of Israel our King. * Of old he spoke in a vision, * when he spoke to his righteous ones: * I have set the crown upon one who is mighty, * I have exalted one chosen from the people. * I have found David, my servant; * with my holy oil I have anointed him; * so that my hand shall ever abide with him, * my mighty arm shall strengthen him. * His enemy will profit nothing, * and the son of the wicked will not humble him. * He will scatter his enemies before him, * and crush those who hate him. * My faithfulness and grace are with him, * and in my name his horn will be exalted.

Division. I will set his hand upon the sea, * and his right hand on the rivers. * He will call to me, You are my Father, * my God and my mighty Savior. * And I will make him a firstborn, * and lift him over the kings of the earth. * My grace will protect him forever, * and my covenant will be faithful in him. * I will set his seed forever, * and his throne like the days of heaven. * If his sons abandon my law, * and do not walk in my commands, * I will command their evil with a rod, * and their sins with a beating. * My grace will not pass from him, * and I will not be false in my faithfulness or despise my covenant. * That which came forth from my lips, I will not change. * I vowed one thing in my truth to David, and will not lie: * that his seed will be forever, * and his throne like the sun before me, * and will be established forever like the moon. * The witness in the sky is faithful, * but you have forgotten me and rejected me, * and turned the face of your anointed. * You rejected the covenant of your servant, * and thrown his crown to the ground. * You wrecked his fences and crushed his fortresses, * and all who pass on the road step on him. * He has

The Psalter

become a mockery to his neighbors, * and you have raised the right hand of his enemies. * You made all who hate him rejoice, * and overturned the help of his sword. * You have not helped him in battle. * You have removed his justifier, * and crushed his throne to the ground. * You reduced the days of his youth, * and clothed him with shame. * How long, O Lord, will you be angry forever, * will your wrath burn like fire? * Recall us from the ditch, * for it was not in vain that you created all the sons of men. * Who is the man who will live and not see death? * Who delivers his life from the hand of Sheol? * Where are your original graces, O Lord, * which you promised to David in faithfulness? * Remember, O Lord, the scorn of your servant, * that I bore the insults of the nations in my life. * Your enemies mocked me, O Lord, * and they mocked the footsteps of your anointed. * Blessed is the Lord forever, amen, amen.

END OF BOOK THREE.

BOOK FOUR
Marmytha

Prayer: To you who holds all by the power of his Word, who guides the ages and creatures by the silent signal of his will, O great King of glory, Being who exists from eternity: we thank, adore, and glorify you at all times, Lord of all, Father, Son, and Holy Spirit, forever.

Psalm 90: O Lord, you were a dwelling place for us for the ages, * since the mountains were brought forth. * O almighty Caretaker: pity our sinfulness. Until the earth perishes, * and until the world is destroyed, * and since the world was established, * forever and unto forever, you are God. * You returned the son of man to humility, * and said, Return, sons of men. * For a thousand years in your eyes * are like yesterday that has passed, * and like a watch of the night. * Their armies will become like sleep, * and they will change in the morning like grass, * which grows in the morning and then changes, * and in the evening withers and dries. * For we are finished by your wrath, * and tremble by your anger. * You placed our sins before you; * make us young by the light of your face. * For all our days are finished by your wrath, * and our years finish like a whisper. * The days of our years are seventy years, * and for the strong one, eighty years, * and most of these are labor and pains. * For humiliation has come upon us and struck us down. * Who knows the might of your wrath, and the fearfulness of your wrath? * Make us know the number of our days, * that we may enter the heart of your wisdom. * Turn to us, O Lord –

how long * will you not comfort your servants? * Feed us your grace in the morning. * Let us praise and rejoice all our days. * Gladden us, for our sin is dead, * and because of the years of evil we have seen. * May your works be seen by your servants, * and your splendor by their sons. * May the sweetness of the Lord our God be upon us, * whose handiwork established us, * and whose handiwork formed us.

Psalm 91: He who dwells in the shelter of the Most High * and is adorned by the shadow of God * You are my trust, O Christ; I will never be put to shame. Says to the Lord: My refuge, * my stronghold, my God in whom I trust! * For he will deliver you from the fowler's trap * and from the deceitful conversation. * He will conceal you with his pinions and under his wings you will find refuge. * His truth will surround you like an armor. * You will not fear the terror of the night * nor the arrow that flies by day, * nor the plague that prowls in the darkness * nor the scourge that lays waste at noon. * Thousands may fall at your side, a myriad at your right, * you, it will never approach. * You need only look with your eyes * to see how the wicked are repaid, * you who have said: "Lord, my refuge, * who has made his dwelling on high!" * Upon you no evil shall fall, * no plague approach where you dwell. * For you has he commanded his angels, * to keep you in all your ways. * They shall bear you upon their hands * lest you stumble with your feet. * On the viper and the serpent you will tread * and trample the lion and the dragon. * Because he seeks me, I will save him and strengthen him. * Because he knows my name, he will call and I will answer him. * I am with him in distress. * I will strengthen him and honor him. * With length of life I will content him; I shall let him see my salvation.

Psalm 92: It is good to give thanks to the Lord, * and sing praise to your name, O Most High. * O Mighty One who can do all things: protect those who worship you. To show your grace in the morning, * and your faithfulness at night. * I will play upon the ten-stringed harp, * and play upon the lyre. * For you gladdened me, O Lord, by your works, * and I praise with the works of your hands. * How great are your works, O Lord, * and how very deep are your thoughts! * Miserable man does not know, * and the ignorant man does not understand this. * Though the wicked are rewarded like grass, * and all evildoers flourish, * they will be destroyed forever and ever. * You, O Lord, are exalted forever. * Lo, your enemies, O Lord, * lo, your enemies will be destroyed, * and all evildoers will be scattered. * You raised up my horns like an ox, * and poured scented oil over me. * My eyes have seen my enemies, * and my ears will hear of the evil men who stood against me. * The just man will be rewarded like the palm tree, * and will flourish like the cedars of Lebanon, * which are planted in the house of the Lord, * and in the courts of our God. * They will be repaid and will grow into old age. * They will be rich and sweet, * and will show that the Lord is upright. * The Mighty One has no wrong.

Hulala XIV

Prayer: O Adorable and Glorious One, Splendid and Beautiful, Exalted above all in his Existence, Great King of glory, Being who exists from eternity: we thank, adore, and glorify you at all times and ages, Lord of all, Father, Son, and Holy Spirit, forever.

Psalm 93: The Lord is King, with majesty enrobed. * The Lord is clothed with might and power. * *We adore your Existence without beginning, glorious in the heights; protect your Church and deliver her.* He constructed the world to be unshaken. * Your throne is established from the beginning: * and you exist, O Lord, from eternity. * The rivers have lifted up, O Lord, * the rivers have lifted up their voice, * the rivers have lifted up in purity. * Even mightier than the roar of many waters * are the surgings of the sea. * Glorious are you, O Lord, on high, * and your testimonies are greatly faithful. * And holiness is fitting to your house, * O Lord, until the end of days.

Psalm 94: The Lord is a God of vengeance; * O God of vengeance, be revealed. * *O All-Knowing, All-Powerful, and All-Judging One, you are our Lord; save the servants who call to you.* Arise, O Judge of the earth. * Repay the proud their reward. * How long, O Lord, shall the wicked, * how long will the wicked brag? * They spew forth and speak evil, * and all evildoers say * that they humiliated your people, O Lord, * and subjugated your inheritance, * and killed orphans and inhabitants, * and destroyed orphans. * They say that the Lord does not see, * and the God of Jacob does not understand. * Understand, you miserable among the people. * How long will you not understand, you fools? * He who planted ears, does he not hear? * He who created eyes, does he not understand? * He who rebukes the peoples, does he not rebuke? * He who teaches the son of man knowledge, * the Lord knows the thoughts of the sons of men. * For they are a vapor. * Blessed is the man whom you rebuke, O Lord, * and whom you teach by your law, * and whom you give rest from evil days, * until a pit is dug for the wicked. * For the Lord does not forsake his people, * and does not abandon his inheritance. * For he will return judgment after the just man, * and after him all the upright of heart. * Who will stand for me against the evil, * and who will prepare for me against evildoers? * If the Lord was not my help, * my soul would soon have dwelt in misery. * I said that my foot slips, * but your grace supported me. * In the great pains of my heart, * your comforts saved my soul. * Let the throne of the evil not ruin your people, * who fashion evil against your law, * and set traps for the soul of the just man, * and are guilty of the blood of the innocent one. * But the Lord became my might, * the mighty God my help. * He overturned their evil upon them, * and silenced them by their own malice. * The Lord my God silenced them.

Psalm 95: Come, let us praise the Lord, * and sing to our God, the Savior. * Our Lord saved us from error, from faults, and from death in his pity; let us adore and glorify him. Let us come before him giving thanks, * and glorify him with songs. * For our God is a great Lord, * the great King over all the gods, * in whose hands are the foundations of the earth * and the heights of the mountains. * His is the sea, for he made it, * and the dry land his hands made. * Come, let us bless and worship him, * and kneel before the Lord who made us. * For he is our God, and we are his people, * and the sheep of his flock. * If you hear his voice today, * do not harden your hearts and anger him, * like those who murmured and like the day of the trial in the wilderness. * For your fathers tested me, * and they searched and saw my works for forty years. * I loathed that generation, * and said it is a people whose heart goes astray. * They did not know my paths, and so I vowed in my anger, they will not enter into my rest.

Marmytha

Prayer: O Lord, it is our duty to lift up new praise, exalted thanksgiving, humble adoration, and constant thanksgiving, to your glorious Trinity, at all times, Lord of all, Father, Son, and Holy Spirit, forever.

Psalm 96: Sing a new song to the Lord, * sing to the Lord, all the earth. * Blessed is your coming, O Christ the Savior of all, for you made us worthy to praise you with the spiritual beings. Praise the Lord and bless his name. * Proclaim his salvation from day to day. * Make his honor known among the nations, * and his works among all the nations. * For the Lord is great and highly glorious, * fearful over all the gods. * For all the gods of the nations are naught. * The Lord made heaven. * Splendor and glory are before him. * Might and glory in his holy place. * Give to the Lord, tribes of the nations, * give to the Lord glory and honor; * give to the Lord the honor due to his name. * Take offerings and enter his courts. * Adore the Lord in his holy courtyard. * Let the whole earth tremble before him. * Say among the nations that the Lord reigns. * He constructed the world to be unshaken. * He judges the nations in uprightness. * The heavens rejoice and the earth is glad. * The sea is joyful in its fullness. * The fields are strengthened, and all that is in them. * Therefore all the trees of the forest glorify, * before the Lord who comes to judge the earth. * He judges the world in justice, * and the nations in faithfulness.

Psalm 97: The Lord reigns, let the earth rejoice, * and let the many islands be glad. * O Church, sing praise to the Lord who renewed you, who exalted your lowliness by his ascension, and gladdened all. Clouds and darkness surround him. * He established his throne in justice and judgment. * Fire consumes before him, * and burns up his enemies. * His lightnings brighten the world. * The earth sees and trembles, * and the mountains are melted like wax * before the Lord, the Lord of all the earth. * The heavens show his justice, * and all the nations see his honor. * All who make idols are shamed, * those who pride in carvings. * All his angels adore him. * Zion hears and is glad, * and the daughters of Judah rejoice. * Because of your judgments, O Lord, * because you are the exalted Lord over all the earth. * You are greatly exalted over all gods. * The friends of the Lord hate evil, * and he protects the souls of his just. * He delivers them from the hand of the wicked. * Light dawns upon the just, * and joy to the upright of heart. * Rejoice, O just, in the Lord, * and confess the memory of his holiness.

Psalm 98: Sing a new song to the Lord, * for he has worked wonders. * Blessed is he who bowed down and was baptized by John in the Jordan, and forgave all by his baptism. His right hand has saved, and his holy arm. * The Lord has shown his salvation, * and unveiled his justice before the eyes of the nations. * He has remembered his grace and his faithfulness toward the house of Israel, * and all the shores of the earth have seen the salvation of our God. * Glorify the Lord, all the earth. * Be gladdened, sing, and glorify. * Sing to the Lord with harps and with the sound of singing, * and glorify before the King, the Lord, with lyre. * The sea trembles in its fullness, * the world and all who dwell in it. * The rivers clap their hands together, * and the mountains glorify before the Lord. * For he comes to judge the earth. * He judges the world in truth, * and the nations in uprightness.

The Psalter

Marmytha

Prayer: It is our duty to thank, adore, and glorify you who sit upon the chariot of the cherubim, are extolled by the legions of angels, whose signal shakes the earth and whose command terrifies the world, Lord of all, Father, Son, and Holy Spirit, forever.

Psalm 99: The Lord reigns; let the nations tremble. * He sits upon the cherubim, let earth shake. * There is nothing like your power, O Savior, for you filled your holy apostles with the Holy Spirit. The Lord is great in Zion, * and exalted over all the nations. * They confess your great and fearful name which is holy. * The might of the king loves judgment. * You established uprightness and judgment, * and you accomplished justice in Jacob. * Exalt the Lord our God, * and bow down before his footstool. * Holy among his priests were Moses and Aaron, * and Samuel among those who called his name. * They called the Lord and he answered them; * he spoke to them in the pillar of cloud. * They kept his witness, and the covenant he gave them; * O Lord, our God, you answered them. * O God, you were an avenger for them. * Repay them according to their deeds. * Exalt the Lord our God, * and adore at his holy mountain, * for the Lord our God is holy.

Psalm 100: Glorify the Lord, all the earth! * Serve the Lord in gladness. * The just are clothed with glory, and fly above the clouds to meet our Lord when he comes. Enter before him with praise. * Know he is the Lord our God: * he made us; it was not we. * We are his people, the sheep of his flock. * Enter his gates with thanksgiving and his courts with praise. * Give thanks to him and bless his name, * for the Lord is good and eternal is his grace, * and his faithfulness is unto the ages.

Psalm 101: Of grace and justice I will sing, * and I will praise you, Lord. * The Lord in whom I trust redeems me in his mercies from the haters who envy me. I will walk in your way without blame; * when, Lord, will you come to me? * I will walk with blameless heart within my house; * I will not set what is base before my eyes. * I have hated evildoers; * they shall not come near to me. * A wicked heart must depart from me; * I have not known evil. * He who slanders his friend in secret I have destroyed; * of proud eyes and haughty heart I have not dined with. * I look to the faithful in the land that they may dwell with me. * He who walks faultless on the way shall serve me. * One who works deceit will not sit in my house, * and deceptive speech will not remain before my

The Psalter

eyes. * In the morning I will silence all the wicked of the land, * and scatter from the city of the Lord * all who do evil.

Hulala XV

Prayer: O Pitier of the debts of sinners in his great patience: pity, O Lord our God, the misery, the lostness, and the lowliness of our weak nature, O Merciful One and Forgiver of debts and sins, Lord of all, Father, Son, and Holy Spirit, forever.

Psalm 102: O Lord, hear my prayer, * and let my cry come before you. * *Pity my lowliness, O Being who does not change.* Do not turn your face from me on the day of my distress, * but rather turn your ear to me on the day I call and quickly answer me. * For my days pass in smoke, * my bones flame white like furnaces, * and my heart burns like grass and dries up. * For I have forgotten the eating of bread; * my flesh clings to my bones because of the sound of my groaning, * I resemble the vulture of the wilderness, * and I have become like an owl in the wasteland. * I tremble and remain alone, * like a bird flying upon the rooftops. * All the day, my enemies taunt me, * and those who praise me swear by me. * For I have chewed ash like bread, * and have mixed my drink with tears. * Before your wrath and anger, * since you lifted me up and cast me away, * my days are brought down like a shadow, * and I dry up like grass. * But you, O Lord, stand forever, * and your memory unto the ages. * May you arise and have mercy on Zion, * for the time has come to have mercy on her. * For your servants have been pleased with her stones, and loved her soil. * May the nations fear your name, O Lord, * and all the kings of the earth your honor. * For the Lord will build Zion, * and will be seen in his glory; * he will return to the prayer of the poor, * and not despise their prayer. * This will be written for the next generation, * and the people that is created will praise the Lord, * for he will look down from his holy height. * The Lord looked down from heaven to earth, * to hear the groan of the prisoner, * and to free the sons from death, * that the name of the Lord may be made known in Zion, * and his glories in Jerusalem. * When the nations were gathered together, * and the kingdoms to serve the Lord, * they humbled my power upon the earth, * and the shortness of my days spoke to me. * Do not lift me up in the middle of my days; * your years are unto the ages. * You established the earth before us, * and the heavens are the work of your hands. * They will pass, but you will remain, * and they will all wear out like a garment, * and will be changed like a cloak. * But you are as you are, and your years do not end, * and the sons of your servants will dwell upon the earth, * and their seed will be established before you.

Psalm 103: Bless the Lord, my soul, * and all my bones, his holy name. * Blessed is the merciful Lord, whose grace is overflowing. Bless the Lord, my soul, * and do not forget all his rewards, * for he forgives all your sin, * and heals all your wounds. * He saves you from corruption, * and sustains you with grace and mercies. * He feeds your flesh with good things, * and renews your youth like an eagle. * The Lord accomplishes justice, * and judgment to all the unjust. * He shows his paths to Moses, * and his works to the sons of Israel. * The Lord is merciful and compassionate, * patient and great in his grace. * For he does not keep anger forever, * nor guard his wrath forever. * For he did not treat us according to our sins, * nor repay us according to our malice. * For as the heavens are exalted above the earth, * thus is the grace of the Lord over those who fear him. * And as far as the east is from the west, * thus far does he remove our sin from us. * As a father has compassion upon sons, * the Lord has compassion on those who fear him. * For he knows our fashioning, * and remembers that we are dust. * The son of man's days are like grass, * and he sprouts like the flower of the field. * But when the wind blows upon it, it is no more, * nor is its place even known. * The grace of the Lord is eternal, * and is unto the ages over those who fear him. * His justice is for the sons of their sons, * for those who keep his covenant, * and remember his commandments and act on them. * The Lord establishes his throne in heaven, * and his kingdom has authority over all. * His angels bless the Lord, * who have power and accomplish his commands. * All his hosts bless the Lord, * his servants who do his will. * All his works bless the Lord, * for his authority is over all the earth. * Bless the Lord, my soul.

Marmytha

Prayer: It is our duty to thank, adore, and glorify you who are clothed in splendor and beauty, and covered in indescribable light, by whose signal the worlds were created and creatures were fashioned, Lord of all, Father, Son, and Holy Spirit, forever.

Psalm 104: Bless the Lord, my soul! * Lord God, how great you are. * Adorable is the Creator, forever and ever. Clothed in majesty and glory, * wrapped in light as in a robe! * You stretch out heaven like a tent. * He makes his dwelling above the rains. * He makes the clouds his chariot, * he walks with wings of wind, * he makes the winds his messengers * and burning fire his servants. * He founded the earth on its bases, * to be unshaken from age to age. * You wrapped it with the firmament like a cloak: * the waters stood above the mountains. * At your threat they took to flight; * at the voice of your thunder they fled. * The mountains rose and the plains were lowered * to the place which you had appointed. * You set limits for them * lest they return to cover the earth. * You sent springs to the valleys: * they flow in between the hills. * They give drink to all the beasts of the field; * the wild animals quench their thirst. * Upon them dwell the birds of heaven; * from the mountains they sing their song. * From his dwelling he waters the hills; * earth drinks its fill of the fruit of your work. * You make the grass grow for cattle * and the plants for man's labor, * that he may bring forth bread from the earth: * wine gladdens the heart of man; * oil makes his face rejoice; * and bread sustains man's heart. * The trees of the Lord drink their fill, * the cedars of Lebanon which you planted. * There the birds settle, * and the stork has her nest in the fir trees. * The tall mountains are for the wild goats, * and the rocks a refuge for badgers.

Division. He made the moon for time, * and knew the time of the sun's courses. * He made darkness, and there was night, * and all the beasts of the field pass by during it. * The lions roar to destroy, * and seek their food from God. * When the sun dawns, they are gathered in, * and lie down in their dens. * Man goes out to his work, * and for his labor until evening. * How many are your works, O Lord, * all of them you created in wisdom. * The earth is filled with your possessions: * this is the great sea, an open space of hands, * in which are innumerable creeping things, * animals large and small, * and on it boats go by. * This is Leviathan, which you created to laugh at. * All of them wait for you, * to give them food in their time. * You give to them and they are satisfied. * You open your hand and they feed, * and you turn your face away and they tremble. * You take away their spirit and they die, * and return to their dust. * You send forth your Spirit, and they are created, * and you renew the face of the earth. * May the glory of the Lord be forever. * May the Lord rejoice in his works, * for he looks upon the earth and it shakes, * and rebukes the mountains, and they double over. * I will glorify the Lord in my life, * and sing to my God while I stand. * May my praise please him, * and I will rejoice in the Lord. * May sinners vanish from the earth, * and the evil not ravish it. * Bless the Lord, my soul.

The Psalter
Marmytha

Prayer: We thank you, our good God, we call your name to help us, and our lips speak your praise, for you are the Lord who does good for his adorers and has mercy upon all, Lord of all, Father, Son, and Holy Spirit, forever.

Psalm 105: Give thanks to the Lord and call upon his name, * and show his works among the nations. * **We thank the Lord, for he has been good to us, and we ask him to fill our needs, for his love overflows forever.** Praise and sing to him, * and make all his wonders known. * Praise his holy name. * May the heart of those who seek the Lord rejoice. * Seek the Lord and be strengthened, * and seek his face at all times. * Remember the wonders he worked, * his wonders and the judgment of his mouth. * Seed of Abraham his servant, * and sons of Jacob his chosen. * He is the Lord our God, * upon all the earth are his judgments. * Remember his covenant forever, * the word that he commanded for a thousand generations. * For he established his covenant with Abraham, * and his vows with Isaac, * and his witness with Jacob, * a covenant for Israel forever. * He said, I will give you the land of Canaan, * the borders of your inheritance, * though you were small in number, * you were small, and were sojourners in it. * They walked from people to people, * and from a kingdom to another people. * But he did not allow a man to oppress them; * he rebuked kings for their sake: * Do not approach my anointed, * or do harm to my prophets. * He called forth a famine upon the earth, * and broke every staff of their journey. * He sent a man before them. * Joseph was sold into slavery. * His feet were tied with chains, * and his soul was put into irons, * until his word unbound him, * the word of the Lord tested him. * The king sent and unbound him, * and made him a ruler over his people, * a lord over his house and a ruler over all his possessions, * to guide the rulers as he wished, * and instruct the elders.

Division. Israel entered Egypt, * and Jacob dwelt in the dwelling of Ham. * He greatly increased his people, * and made it stronger than its enemies. * He turned their heart to hate his people, * and to deceive his servants. * He sent Moses his servant and Aaron whom he chose. * He accomplished his signs and wonders through them in the land of Ham. * He sent darkness and caused it to be dark, and they murmured at his word. * He turned their water to blood, and caused their fish to die. * He made the frogs creep over their land, and in the courts of their kings. * He said that swarms would come, * and parasites in all their land. * He made their rain into hail, * and fire burned in their land. *

He struck their vines and figs, * and broke the trees of their borders. * He spoke, and locusts came, * and innumerable young locusts in all their land. * They devoured all the plants and fruits of their land. * He smote all the firstborn of Egypt, * the head of all their children. * He brought them out with silver and gold, * and none in their tribes became sick. * Egypt rejoiced in their exodus, * for fear had fallen upon them. * He spread a cloud over them and covered them, * and fire to light in the night. * They asked, and he gave them food, * and satisfied them with the bread of heaven. * He opened the rock, and water poured forth, * and water walked through a thirsty land. * For he remembered the word of his truth to Abraham his servant. * He brought out his people in rejoicing, * and its young men in glory. * He gave them the lands of the nations, * and they inherited the labors of the peoples, * that they may hold to his commands, * and keep his laws.

Hulala XVI

Prayer: Grant us, O Lord, to give thanks for your grace, make us worthy to make your wonders known, and strengthen us to confess, adore and praise the hidden and glorious power of your majestic Trinity, at all times, Lord of all, Father, Son, and Holy Spirit, forever.

Psalm 106: Give thanks to the Lord, for he is good, and his grace is forever. * Who will make known the wonders of the Lord? * Lord, forgive the sins of your servants who sinned and failed, who angered your name with their deeds; in your grace, pity them. And will make his glories heard? * Blessed are those who keep his judgments, * and do justice at all times. * Remember us, O Lord, in the will of your people, * and save us by your salvation, * that we may see the good things of your chosen, * rejoice in your joy, and glory in your inheritance. * We sinned, along with our fathers; we have been foolish and wicked. * Our fathers in Egypt did not understand your wonders, * and did not remember the greatness of your graces. * They contended upon the waters at the Red Sea, * and he saved them for the sake of his name, * that he may show forth his greatness. * He rebuked the Red Sea and it dried up, * and they walked upon the abyss as in the desert. * He saved them from the hand of the enemy, * and delivered them from the hand of the foe. * The waters covered up their foes, * and not one of them was soiled. * They believed his words and praised his glories. * But they quickly forgot God, * and did not consider his mind. * They desired deeply in the wilderness, * and they tested God in the desert. * He gave them their requests, * and sent plenty for their soul. * They became jealous of Moses in the tent, * and of Aaron, the holy one of God. * The earth opened up and swallowed Dathan, * and it covered the entire assembly of Abiram. * Fire broke out in their assemblies, * and a furnace burned the wicked. * They made a calf in Horeb and adored a molten image; * they changed their honor like a bull that eats grass. * They forgot the God who saved them, * who accomplished great things in Egypt, * and wonders in the land of Ham, * and fearful things in the Red Sea. * So he said he would destroy them.

Division. Were it not for Moses his chosen, * who stood in the breach before him, * and turned back his wrath, lest it destroy them. * But they despised the land of desire, * and did not believe in his word. * They complained in their tents, and did not hear the voice of the Lord. * He raised his hand against them that he would destroy them among the nations, * and scatter their seed among the nations, * and destroy them among the lands, * because they followed the idols of Peor, * and ate the sacrifices of the deceased, * and angered him by their works, and provoked him by their idols. * A plague overcame them suddenly, * and Phineas arose, prayed, and the plague was stopped. * This was reckoned a victory for him unto the ages and forever. * They angered him at the waters of strife, * and it went badly for Moses because of them. * For they embittered his spirit and he spoke with his lips. * They did not destroy the peoples of which the Lord had spoken, * but rather mingled among the peoples and learned their works. * They feared their idols and these became a stumbling block for them. * They sacrificed their sons and daughters to demons, * and they shed innocent blood. * The blood of their sons and daughters * they sacrificed to the idols of Canaan. * The land was polluted with blood, * and they were polluted in their deeds; they fornicated in their schemes. * The anger of the Lord was enflamed against his people, * and he rejected his inheritance. * He handed them over into the hands of the nations, * and those who hated them ruled over them. * Their enemies subjugated them, * and they were subjugated under their hands. * Many times he delivered them, * and they murmured in their thoughts. * They were humiliated in their evil; * he saw their turmoil and heard their pleading. * He remembered his covenant, and had mercy on them, * and he led them according to his great grace, * and gave to them in mercies before each of their captivities. * Save us, Lord our God, and gather us from among the nations, *

The Psalter

that we may thank your holy name, and glory in your inheritance. * Blessed is the Lord God of Israel, * forever and ever; * let all the people say, amen, amen.

END OF BOOK FOUR.

BOOK FIVE
Marmytha

Prayer: May your eternal grace, O Lord, in which the lofty and the lowly take refuge, stand for the guiltiness of our race, and protect us from the evil one and his hosts, at all times and ages, Lord of all, Father, Son, and Holy Spirit, forever.

Psalm 107: Give thanks to the Lord, for he is good, and his grace is forever. * Let those saved by the Lord say it. * **Blessed is our Savior.** Whom he saved from the hand of the foe, * and gathered them from all lands, * from the east and from the west, * and from the north and from the sea. * They were lost in the wilderness of the desert, and the path of the village of settlement they did not find. * They hungered and thirsted, and their soul was vexed. * They begged the Lord in their tribulations, * and he brought them away from their afflictions. * He made them walk in the path of truth, * going to the villages of settlement. * May his just ones give thanks to the Lord, * for his mercies are upon the sons of men. * He feeds vexed souls, * and fills hungry souls. * They sit in darkness and the shadows of death, * and are bound by poverty and in irons, * for they murmured against the word of God, * and rejected the mind of the Most High. * Their heart broke in laboring; * they were sick and there was none to help them. * They prayed to the Lord in their distress, * and he saved them from their troubles. * He brought them out from darkness and the shadows of death, * and he cut off their bonds. * May his just ones give thanks to the Lord, * for his mercies are upon the sons of men. * For he has broken doors of bronze, * and shattered bars of iron. * He helped them from the path of their sins, * and they were humbled by their evil. * Their soul hated all food, * and they reached the doors of death. * They begged the Lord in their tribulations, * and he brought them away from their afflictions. * He sent his word and healed them, * and delivered them from corruption. * May his just ones give thanks to the Lord, * for his mercies are upon the sons of men.

Division. They offered him sacrifices of praise, * and his servants praised his wonders. * Those who go down to the sea in boats, * and those who do their work upon many waters, * they saw the works of the Lord, * and his wonders in the depths of the sea. * For he established the wind of the storm, * and raised the waves of the sea. * They go up to heaven and they go down to the abyss, * and their soul is worn out within them. * They shook and trembled like drunken men, * and all their wisdom was lost. * They cried out to the Lord in their distress, * and he brought them away from their afflictions. * He calmed the storm and it was silenced, * and he gave rest to the waves of the sea. * They rejoiced when they had been silenced, * and he guided them to the port they sought. * May his just ones give thanks to the Lord, * for his mercies are upon the sons of men. * Praise him in the church of the nations, * and exalt him in the gathering of the elders. * For he made rivers like a desert, * and springs of water like thirsty ground, * fruitful earth into a salty waste, * due to the evil works of those who inhabit it. * He made a desert into pools of water, * and thirsty land into springs of water, * and let the hungry dwell there; * they built villages and dwelt in them. * They sowed fields and planted vineyards, * and they ate from the fruit of their harvests. * He blessed them and they greatly increased, * and did not decrease their cattle. * They decreased and were humbled in their great evil and trouble. * He poured evil upon the rulers, * and made them lost in the wilderness without paths. * He strengthened the poor and made their tribes like flocks, * that the just may see and rejoice. * But all the wicked shut their mouth. * Whoever is wise should keep these things, * and know the kindness of the Lord.

Psalm 108: My heart is ready, O God, my heart is ready. * I will glorify and sing in my honor. * O God, I thank you. Awake, my harp, awake lyre and harp, * and I will awake in the morning. * I will thank you among the nations, O God, * and sing to your name among the peoples. * For your grace is great unto heaven, * and your faithfulness unto the heavens of heaven. * Arise over heaven, O God, * and your honor over all the earth. * Because your beloved are saved, * save me by your right hand and answer me. * God speaks in his holy place. * I will praise and I will divide Shechem. * I will measure out the depth of Succoth. * Gilead is mine, and mine is Manasseh. * Ephraim is my helmet, * Judah my scepter, Moab my washbasin. * I will take off my sandals over Edom, and cry out over Philistia. * Who will bring me to the mighty village, * and who will lead me to Edom? * Lo, you have forgotten us, O God, and do not go out with our army. * Grant us strength over our enemies, * for the salvation of man is naught. * God will give us strength. * He will tread upon our enemies.

The Psalter
Marmytha

Prayer: O Lord, save your people from the wicked, deliver your flock from deceivers, and redeem your Church from those who hate and envy your name, for you are the glory of our strength and the crown of our pride, Lord of all, Father, Son, and Holy Spirit, forever.

Psalm 109: O God of my glory, do not be silent, * for the mouth of the wicked and the mouth of the deceiver is opened against me. * Save me, O Lord, from the wicked among the people and the peoples, who are gathered together against me to destroy me unjustly. They speak to me with a lying tongue and a voice of hatred. * They fight against me pointlessly. * In place of my love, they begrudge me, * but I had prayed for them. * They repay me evil in place of good, * and hatred in place of love. * Command evil upon them, * and let Satan stand at their right hand. * When they are judged, may they leave guilty, * and may their prayer be a sin. * May their days be few, * and may the things they keep be taken by another. * May their sons become orphans, * and their wives widows. * May the creditor come for all they have, * and strangers reduce their power. * Let there be no one to have mercy on them, * nor anyone to have compassion on their orphans. * Let their end be destruction, * and their name be erased in the age to come. * Let the evil of their fathers be remembered, * and the sins of their mothers not be erased. * Rather, let them be before the Lord at all times, * and their memory be destroyed from the earth, * because they did not remember to do good, * and persecuted the humble and the poor, * and the brokenhearted to his death. * They loved curses and did not wish for blessings, * and they wore curses like an armor. * They entered their bones like water and like oil. * May this be like a garment that covers, * and like a belt at all times. * This is the work of those who begrudge the Lord, * and those who speak evil of my soul. * But you, O Lord, act toward me according to your name; * because your grace is good, deliver me. * For I am poor and needy, * and my heart trembles within me, * and my steps go down like shadows. * I am shaken off like a locust, * and my knees are sick from fasting. * My flesh burns with oil, * and I have become a mockery to them. * They see me and wag their heads. * Help me, O Lord my God, and save me according to your grace, * that they may know that this is your hand, and that you have done this. * May they be cursed, * and may you be blessed and your servant rejoice. * May those who begrudged me be clothed with shame, * and may they wear it like a mantle. * I will give thanks to the Lord with my mouth, * and glorify him among many, * for he stood at the right hand of the poor man, * to save his soul from judgment.

Psalm 110: The Lord said to my Lord, sit at my right hand, * until I place your enemies as your footstool. * We give thanks to you, Lord Jesus, for in your humanity you are from David and from Abraham, and in your Existence from your Father. The Lord will send the staff of might from Zion, * and they will rule over your enemies, * your glorious people on the day of power. * In holy splendor from the womb, * I have begotten you from of old, O child. * The Lord has sworn and will not lie, * that you are a priest forever, * like Melchizedek. * The Lord is on your right. * On the day of wrath, he broke kings. * He will judge the peoples and fill them with corpses, * and cut off the heads of many in the land. * He will drink from the creek by the path. * Because of this, his head will be exalted.

Psalm 111: I will thank the Lord with all my heart * in company of the upright in the church. * All the upright give thanks with us to the Being who created us. Exalted are the works of the Lord, * sought by all who desire them. * His works are glorious and great, * and his justice stands forever. * He gives remembrance to his wonders. * The Lord is merciful and compassionate. * He gives food to those who fear him, * and his covenant is remembered forever. * He shows power to his people by his works, * that he may give inheritance to the nations. * The work of his hands is truth and judgment. * They stand forever and ever, * and they confirm all his commands. * They are made in justice and truth. * He sends salvation to his people, * and his covenant is remembered forever. * He is holy and fearful is his name. * The beginning of wisdom is the fear of the Lord, * and good understanding is for those who act on it. * His glory stands forever.

HULALA XVII

Prayer: Let us be yours, O Lord, and be in awe of you. Let us tremble at your word, shake at your judgment, be vigilant in your commands, and please your Divinity in good works of justice all the days of our lives, Lord of all, Father, Son, and Holy Spirit, forever.

Psalm 112: Blessed is the man who fears the Lord, * and is vigilant in his commands. * Blessed are those who walk without blame on the path of Christ, walk in his holy laws, and keep his commands. His seed will be powerful on the earth, * and he will be blessed in the age of the just. * possessions and wealth will increase in his house, * and his justice will stand forever. * Light has dawned in the darkness for the upright, * and he has mercy on the just. * The man who has mercy and lends is good, * and who considers his words in judgment. * He will never tremble. * May the memorial of the just be forever. * Let him not fear bad news, * he who settles his heart to trust in God. * He whose heart is firm will not fear, * even when he sees his enemies. * He scatters and gives to the poor, * and his justice stands forever and ever, * and his horn is exalted in glory. * The evil man sees and is enraged, * and he grinds his teeth and trembles, * and the desire of the wicked is destroyed.

Psalm 113: Praise, O servants of the Lord, * praise the name of the Lord! * Glorious is the Being who called the nations through his servants to know the things he set apart, and by whose power they were victorious on earth and in heaven, by the glory he shone for them. May the name of the Lord be blessed, * from age to age! * From the dawning of the sun to its setting, * great is the name of the Lord! * High above all nations is the Lord, * and above the heavens his honor. * Who is like the Lord, our God, * who sits on high and sees below? * Who sits on high and sees below, * in the heavens and on the earth? * From the dust he lifts up the poor man, * and lets him sit with the rulers of the people. * He sets the barren woman in a home, * and makes her the joyful mother of children.

Psalm 114: When Israel came out from Egypt, * and the sons of Jacob from an unknown people, * In the middle of the night, I arise to thank you, O Lord, for your judgments, and am amazed at the deeds of wisdom as I confess your name. Judah was his holy place, and Israel his glory. * The sea saw and fled, * and the Jordan turned back on itself. * The mountains danced like rams, * and the hills like lambs of the flock. * Why did you flee, O sea, * and Jordan, why did you turn back on yourself? * Mountains, why did you dance like rams, * and hills, like lambs of the flock? * The earth trembles before the Lord, * before the God of Jacob, * who turned a stone into pools of water, * and a rock truly into springs of water. * **Not to us,** Lord, not to us, * but to your name give honor, * because of your grace and your truth, * lest the nations say, Where is their God? * Our God is in heaven and does all he wills. * The idols of the nations are silver and gold, * the work of the hands of men. * They have a mouth but do not speak, * they have eyes but do not see, * they have ears but do not hear, * they have noses but do not smell. * They do not touch with their hands, * and they do not walk with their feet. * They do not speak with their throats. * May their makers become like them, * and all those who trust in them. * The house of Israel trusts in the Lord; * he is their help and their aid. * The house of Aaron trusts in the Lord; * he is their help and their aid. * Those who fear the Lord trust in the Lord; * he is their help and their aid. * The Lord remembers and blesses us; * he blesses the house of Israel; * he blesses the house of Aaron; * the Lord blesses those who fear him. * Small and great, * may the Lord add to you, * to you and to your sons. * You are the blessed of the Lord, * who made heaven and earth. * The heavens of heaven are the Lord's, * and the earth he has given to the sons of men. * The dead will not praise the Lord, * nor those who go down into the darkness. * But let us bless the Lord, * now and forever and ever.

Marmytha

Prayer: It is our duty to thank, adore, and glorify the overflowing, blessed, and incomprehensible mercies of your glorious Trinity, at all times, Lord of all, Father, Son, and Holy Spirit, forever.

Psalm 115: I love the Lord who heard the sound of my pleading, * and turned his ear to me on the day I call him. * *God alone is the Lord of our death and our lives.* For the cords of death surrounded me, * and the afflictions of Sheol reached me. * I have found distress and misery, * and called upon the name of the Lord. * O Lord, deliver my soul. * You are merciful and just, O Lord, * and you are a compassionate God. * The Lord protects the simple. * He humbles me and saves me. * Turn, O my soul, to your rest, * for the Lord repays you. * For he delivered my soul from death, * and my feet from stumbling, * that I may please you, O Lord, in the land of the living. * I have believed, and have spoken, and have been greatly humbled. * I said in my frustration that every man lies. * What will I repay the Lord for all his rewards toward me? * I will take the cup of salvation, * and call upon the name of the Lord. * I will repay my vows to the Lord, * before all the people. * Precious in the eyes of the Lord is the death of his just. * O Lord, I am your servant. * I am your servant and the son of your handmaid. * You undid my bonds. * I will sacrifice sacrifices of praise to you, * and call upon the name of the Lord. * I will repay my vows to the Lord, * before all the people, * and in the courts of the house of the Lord, * and within you, Jerusalem.

Psalm 116: O praise the Lord, all you nations, * O praise him, all you peoples! * *The people and the peoples, one Church, praise the Christ.* For mighty is his love for us; * truly, he is the Lord forever.

Psalm 117: Give thanks to the Lord, for he is good, and his mercies are forever. * Let Israel say that his mercies are forever. * There is no one mighty and merciful as the Lord our refuge. Let the house of Aaron say that his mercies are forever. * Let those who fear the Lord say that his mercies are forever. * I called to the Lord in my distress, * and the Lord heard me in deliverance. * The Lord is my help, I shall not fear. * What can man do for me? * The Lord is my help, and I will see those who hate me. * It is better to trust in the Lord, * than to trust in man. * It is better to trust in the Lord, * than to trust in the ruler. * All the nations surrounded me, * and I destroyed them in the name of the Lord. * They surrounded me and encircled me, * and I destroyed them in the name of the Lord. * They surrounded me like hornets, and went out like fire in the grass. * In the name of the Lord I destroyed them. * I was struck down and overthrown and fell, * and the Lord helped me. * My power and my glory is the Lord, and he has become my Savior. * The voice of praise and salvation in the assembly of the just. * The right hand of the Lord has accomplished power; * the right hand of the Lord has lifted me up; * the right hand of the Lord has accomplished power and I will not die. * Rather I will live and make known the works of the Lord. * Leading, the Lord has led me, and has not handed me over to death. * Open the doors of justice to me, * that I may enter them and give thanks to the Lord. * This is the door of the Lord, in which the just enter. * I will thank you for you have answered me, and have become my Savior. * The stone that the builders rejected * has become the head of the building. * This has happened before the Lord, and is a wonder in our eyes. * This is the day the Lord has made; * come, let us rejoice and be glad in it. * O Lord, save me; O Lord, deliver me. * Blessed is he who comes in the name of the Lord. * I bless you from the house of the Lord. * The Lord our God enlightens us. * Bind our feasts in fetters, * until the horns of the altar. * My God, I will thank you; my God, I will glorify you. * Give thanks to the Lord, for he is good, and his grace is forever.

Marmytha

Prayer: O Good One who does good for the good, Just One who loves the just, Holy One who dwells in the saints in whom his will rests: we plead to you; turn to us, O Lord, forgive us, and have mercy on us, as you do at all times, Lord of all, Father, Son, and Holy Spirit, forever.

Psalm 118, Alap: Blessed are those who are on the path without fault, * May you help my weakness, O Christ, that I may fulfill your will. And walk in the law of the Lord. * Blessed are those who keep his witness, * and seek him with all their heart, * and do not do evil, and walk on his paths. * You have commanded that your commands be kept well, * so I will apply the fashioning of my steps to keep your commands. * I will not be put to shame when I have kept all your commands. * I will thank you in the uprightness of my heart. * When I learned the judgments of your justice, * I kept your commands; may you not ever leave me.

Beth: In what can the young man purify his path, to keep your commands? * Establish me in your love, O Lord, and instruct my innocence by your Gospel. I have searched for you with all my heart; do not let me stray from your commands. * You have hidden your words in my heart, that I may not sin against you. * Blessed are you, O Lord; teach me your commands. * By my lips I have repeated all the judgments of your justice. * I have loved the path of your witness more than all wealth. * I have considered your commands, and known your ways. * I have considered your law, that I may not forget your words.

Gamal: Answer your servant, that I may live and keep your words. * Your teaching is choice, more precious than anything, and good, O Savior. Unveil my eyes, that I may see the wonders in your law. * I am a sojourner with you; do not hide your commands from me. * My soul wished and desired your judgments at all times. * Rebuke the nations, and those who stray from your commands be cursed. * Let scorn pass by me, for I have kept your witness. * The wicked have sat and considered me, * but I have considered your law. * I have considered your witness, and your good thoughtfulness.

Dalath: My soul clings to the dirt; give me life according to your word. * Those who hate the truth have stomped upon me; O Lord of all, may you help me. I have shown you my paths, and you answered me; teach me your law. * Show me the path of your commands, and I will consider your wonders. * My soul is smitten with thinking; give me life according to your word. * Let the path of the wicked pass by me, and teach me your law. * I have chosen the path of your faithfulness, and desired your judgments. * I have clung to your witness, O Lord, let me not be put to shame. * I have walked in your commands, for you have gladdened me.

Heh: Teach me, O Lord, the path of your commands, and I will keep them. * All error is vanity; O Christ, lead me by your truth. Teach me to keep your law, and I will keep it with all my heart. * Let me walk in the path of your commands, for I have wished for it. * Turn my heart to your witness, and not to parables. * Let my eyes pass, lest they see deception, and give me life on your paths. * Set your word firmly for your servant who fears you. * Let scorn pass by me, for your judgments are beautiful. * I have enjoyed your commands; give me life by your justice.

Waw: Lord, let your mercies come upon me, and the salvation you promised. * It is right that you are made victorious before all kings through your servants, O Lord. I shall answer those who taunt me, * for I trust in your words. * Let not the word of truth die from my mouth, * for I trust in your decrees. * I shall keep your law for ever and ever, * and walk in freedom for I delight in your precepts. * I will speak of your justice before kings * and not be ashamed. * I will consider your commands which I have loved; * I will lift my hands to your commands which I have loved, * I will ponder your statutes. * I will glory in your faithfulness.

Zayn: Remember your word to your servant, that in which I trust. * This time is like a dream; comfort me in your hope, O Lord. I am comforted by it in my humiliation. * Give me life because of your word. * The wicked trouble me, but I do not stray from your law. * I have remembered your judgments, O Lord, which are eternal, and have been comforted. * They have become an education for me. * Sadness has taken me, due to the sinners who have abandoned your law. * Your commands were like a song to me during my sojourn. * I have remembered your name at night, O Lord, and kept your law. * I have been comforted, for I have kept your commands.

Ḥeth: I have considered the portion of the Lord, that I may keep your commands. * I look toward your love at every hour; O Christ, save my oppression. I have awaited your face with all my heart; give me life according to your word. * I have considered my ways, and turned my feet to your paths. * I have prepared, and did not delay in keeping your commands. * The cords of the wicked have woven around me, and I have not strayed from your law. * In the middle of the night, I have arisen to thank you for your judgments, O Just One. * I am a friend to all who fear you, and of those who keep your commands. * The earth is filled with your mercies, O Lord; teach me your commands.

Ṭeth: Do good to your servant, O Lord, as you have spoken. * I love your Word more than all honor; O Lord, comfort me. Teach me good taste, gracefulness, and knowledge, * for I have believed in your commands. * Before I was humbled, I believed, and kept your word. * You are good, O Lord, and make me good; teach me your commands. * The malice of the proud has increased, but I have kept your commands with all my heart. * Their heart has curdled like milk, but I have kept your law. * It is better for me to be humbled, that I may learn your commands. * The law of your mouth is better for me than thousands of gold and silver pieces.

Yodh: Your hands have made and fashioned me; teach me your law. * You know more than all, O Lord, what aids us. That those who fear you may see and rejoice that I have hoped in your word. * I knew that your judgments are just, O Lord, and that your faithfulness humbled me. * Let your mercies comfort me, as you said to your servant. * Let your mercies come upon me, and I will live, for I have been instructed in your law. * Let the wicked who humiliated me in wickedness be ashamed, and I have considered your commands. * Let those who fear you turn to me, and those who know your witness. * My heart will consider your commands, and not be put to shame.

Kap: My soul has desired your salvation, and has hoped in your word. * O Righteous One and Lord to whom all is unveiled: save the troubled who call to you. My eyes await your word, for when will it comfort me? * For I have become like a wineskin in the hail, and have not forgotten your commands. * How many are the days of your servant, and when will you grant me judgment against those who pursue me? * The wicked have dug a pit for me, for they are not of your law. * All your commands are faithful, but the wicked pursue me. * For a while, they scattered me over the earth, but I did not abandon your commands. * According to your mercies, give me life, that I may keep the witness of your mouth.

Hulala XVIII

Prayer: O Being without beginning or end, hidden and incomprehensible Nature, Eternal and Infinite One, Creator, Maker, and Provider for all: it is our duty to thank, adore, and glorify you, at all times, Lord of all, Father, Son, and Holy Spirit, forever.

Lamadh: You are Lord forever, and your word stands in heaven. * There is no fear of mortals for those who fear the Lord which does not pass. And your faithfulness is unto the ages. * You fashioned the earth and established it. * If your law had not been a consideration for me, I would have perished in my poverty. * I will never forget your commands, for in them is my life. * I am yours; deliver me for I have kept your commands. * The wicked lie in wait for me to destroy me, but I have understood your witness. * I have seen a limit to all ends, but your command is so broad.

Mym: How much do I love your law, and consider it all the day. * O Lord who exalts the poor, and strikes down the exalted: glory to you. Make me wiser than my enemies, for I have kept your commands. * Make me understand more than all my teachers, for I have considered your witness. * I have understood more than the elders, for I have kept your commands. * I have stopped my feet from all evil paths, that I may keep your commands. * I have not turned away from your judgments, for you have instructed me. * Your words are sweet to my palate more than honey to the mouth. * I have considered your commands, and because of this I have hated the path of all the wicked.

Nun: Your word is a lamp for my feet and a light for my paths. * Your Word is light, life, and truth, O Savior. I have sworn and made up my mind to keep your just decrees. * Lord, I am deeply afflicted: give me life by your word. * Be pleased, Lord, with the words of my mouth, and teach me by your decrees. * My soul is in your hands at all times; I will not forget your law. * Though sinners laid traps for me, I did not stray from your commands. * Your witness is my heritage forever, for it is the joy of my heart. * I set my heart to carry out your statutes in truth, for ever.

Simkath: I have hated the wicked, and loved your law. * O Lord, establish your hope in us, that we may persist in your teaching. You are my shade and my refuge, and I hope in your word. * The wicked pass over me, for I keep the commands of my God. * Uphold me in your word, and I will live; do not shame me in my hope. * Help me and I will be saved, and learn your commands. * At all times, you reject those who forget you, for they are evil in their consideration. * Feed me and I will be saved, and will consider your commands at all times. * Touch my flesh with your fear, and I will fear your judgments.

'e: O Just and Righteous One: do not abandon me to my oppressors. * Help your Church, O Savior, for she loves you; do not turn away from her. Comfort your servant with good things, and the braggarts will not oppress me. * My eyes yearn for your salvation and the promise of your justice. * Treat your

The Psalter

servant according to your mercies, and teach me your law. * I am your servant; give me knowledge, and I shall know your testimony. * It is time to work for the Lord, for they have nullified your law. * That is why I loved your commands more than gold and fine gems: * I love all your commands and hate all the paths of the wicked.

Pe: Great are your testimonies; for this, my soul has kept them. * Save, O Lord, those who call your name, that those who oppress the truth may groan. Open up your word, and enlighten and instruct the youth. * I have opened my mouth, taken a breath, and awaited your salvation. * Turn to me and have mercy on me, for I have loved your name. * Fashion my steps on your paths, and let the wicked not rule over me. * Save me from those who oppress the son of man, that I may keep your commands. * Brighten your face upon your servant, and teach me your law. * Streams of tears come from my eyes because they have not kept your law.

Ṣade: You are just, O Lord, and your judgments are upright. * Be pleased with me, O Lord, and save me, that the lost may know your glory. I have commanded your witness in justice and faithfulness. * Zeal inflicts me at all times, because your enemies have forgotten your word. * Your word is precious, and your servant loves it. * I am small and miserable, but have not forgotten your commands. * Your justice stands forever and your law in truth. * Distress and anguish have reached me, but I have considered your commands. * Your witness is just forever; instruct me and I will live.

Qop: I have called you with all my heart; O Lord, answer me and I will keep your commands. * The sound of your glory, O God, never leaves the mouth of your servants. I have called you; save me and I will keep your witness. * I arose in the morning, cried out, and awaited your word. * My eyes arose to keep watch, that I may consider your word. * Hear my voice, O Lord, according to your mercies, and give me life by your judgments. * My evil pursuers have approached, and have gone far from your law. * You are near, O Lord, and all your commands are in the truth. * My eyes arose to keep watch, that I may consider your word. * I have known your witness from the beginning, for you have fashioned it from eternity.

Resh: See my humiliation and deliver me, for I have not forgotten your law. * First of all things is fear of you, O Lord; judge on my behalf. Make your judgment for me and deliver me, and give me life by your word. * Salvation is far from the wicked, for they do not seek your commands. * Many are your mercies, O Lord; give me life by your judgments. * My pursuers are many, and my enemies, but I have not turned away from your witness. * I have seen the wicked and known that they do not keep your word. * See that I have loved your commands, O Lord, and give me life by your grace. * The head of your word is truth, and all the judgments of your justice are eternal.

Shyn: The lofty pursue me vainly, but my heart fears your word. * Your glory, O Lord, is greater than all, and comforts me in my persecution at every hour. I have rejoiced in your word, like the one who has found great spoil. * I have hated evil, and despised it, and loved your law. * Seven times a day I have praised you for your judgments, O Just One. * Peace has increased for those who love your law, and they have no sickness. * I have hoped in your salvation, O Lord, and acted on your commands. * My soul has kept your witness, and loved it greatly. * I have kept your commands and your witness, and all my paths are before you.

Taw: Let my praise enter before you, O Lord, and give me life by your word. * Accept our supplication, O Lord, and fill our mouth with thanksgiving. Let my pleading come before you, and deliver me by your word. * Let my tongue overflow with your word, * for all your commands are in justice. * Let my lips speak your glories as you teach me your commands. * Let your hand help me, for I have desired your commands. * My soul has awaited for your salvation, and considered your law. * My soul lives and praises you, and your judgment helps me. * I was lost like a lost sheep; seek your servant, * for I have not forgotten your commands.

Marmytha

Prayer: We call to you in our troubles, take refuge in you in our oppressions, and ask forgiveness of our faults from you; grant this in your grace and mercies as you always do, Lord of all, Father, Son, and Holy Spirit, forever.

Psalm 119: I called to the Lord in my distress, * and the Lord answered me and delivered my soul. * The wicked send me far away; O Unlimited One, comfort me. From the lips of the wicked, * and from deceptive tongues; * what do they give you, and what do they add to you, * deceptive tongues? * The arrows of a man are sharp, * like the coals of an oak. * Woe is me, for my journey is extended, * and I have dwelt in the dwelling of Kedar. * My soul has dwelt for so long among those who hate peace, * but I have spoken of peace, * and they have fought against me.

Psalm 120: I lift my eyes to the mountain: * from where shall come my help? * I await you, More Awake than all; protect my weakness at every hour. My help comes from the Lord * who made heaven and earth. * May he never allow your foot to stumble, * nor let your guardian sleep. * No, he sleeps not nor slumbers, * Israel's guardian. * The Lord is your guardian, * he will place his right hand upon you. * By day the sun shall not smite you, * nor the moon in the night. * The Lord will guard you from all evils, * the Lord will guard your soul. * The Lord will guard your going and your coming * both now and forever.

Psalm 121: I rejoiced when I heard them say, * We are going to the house of the Lord. * Gladden us with your salvation, O Lord, and with the rejoicing of your churches. My feet were standing at your gates, Jerusalem. * Jerusalem, well-built, * like a city surrounded by a wall. * The tribes, the tribes of the Lord, go up to it, * a witness to Israel to make known the name of the Lord. * For there the thrones of judgment were lifted, * the thrones of the house of David. * Ask for the peace of Jerusalem; * may your friends prosper. * Let there be peace in your army, * and prosperity in your towers. * Because of my brethren and friends, * I will speak peace upon you. * Because of the house of the Lord our God, * I will seek your blessings.

Psalm 122: To you I lift my eyes, Dweller of heaven, * like the eyes of servants toward their masters, * O Merciful One, accept our pleading, and let those who despise me be overturned. And like the eyes of a handmaid toward her mistress. * Thus are our eyes are toward you, O Lord our God, * until you have mercy on us. * Have mercy on us, Lord, have mercy on us. * For we have heard enough of contempt, * and our soul is filled with plenty, * of the scorn of the mockers, * and the contempt of the arrogant.

Psalm 123: If the Lord had not been on our side, * let Israel say, If the Lord had not been on our side, * Blessed is our Maker, who redeems his adorers from evil men. When men rose against us, * then would they have swallowed us alive * when their anger was kindled. * Then would the waters have engulfed us, * the torrent gone over us; * over our head would have swept * all the raging waters. * Blessed be the Lord who did not give us * a prey to their teeth! * Our soul was rescued from the trap of the hunter like a bird. * The trap was broken, and we were delivered. * Our help is in the name of the Lord, * who made heaven and earth.

Psalm 124: Those who put their trust in the Lord on Mount Zion, * will not shake, but will stand forever. * The well-established never tremble, for their trust is in the Lord. Jerusalem! The mountains surround her, * so the Lord surrounds his people both now and forever. * For the tribe of the evil will never rest in the portion of the just, * and the just will never extend their hands in evil. * The Lord does good to the good, * and to the upright of heart. * But to those whose paths turn astray, * the Lord will lead them with evildoers. * Peace be upon Israel!

Marmytha

Prayer: Turn to us in your mercies, and accept us into your family, O Good Shepherd who came out to find us, found us who were lost, and rejoices in our return, in his grace and mercies, Lord of all, Father, Son, and Holy Spirit, forever.

Psalm 125: When the Lord returned the captive to Zion, * we were like those who rejoice. * I journey in your hope, O Lord, and in you I take shelter; help me. Then our mouth was filled with laughter and our tongue with glory. * Then they said among the nations, * The Lord has increased in doing these things; * the Lord has increased in doing this for us, and we are rejoicing. * The Lord has returned our captivity like channels in the south. * Those who sow in tears will reap in joy. * Walking, he walks and weeps, * he who carries the seed; * coming, he comes in joy, * he who carries the bundle.

Psalm 126: If the Lord does not build the house, * in vain do its builders labor. * Protect me under the wings of your sweetness, O Lord my God. If the Lord does not watch over the city, * in vain does the watchman keep vigil. * In vain is your earlier rising, * your going later to rest, * you who toil for the bread you eat, * when he pours gifts on his beloved while they slumber. * Truly sons are the inheritance of the Lord, * the reward of the fruits of the womb. * Like an arrow in the hand of a warrior, * thus are the sons of youth. * Blessed is the man whose quiver is filled with them; * he is not shamed when he speaks with his enemies at the gate.

Psalm 127: Blessed are all who fear the Lord, * and walk in his ways. * Overflow your gift, O Lord, upon your servants in your grace. The labor of your hands when you eat, O son of man; * blessed are you, and a blessing for your soul. * Your wife will be like a glorious vine in the yard of your house; * your sons like an olive shoot surrounding your table. * Thus will the man who fears the Lord be blessed. * The Lord will bless you from Zion, * and you will see the blessings

The Psalter

of Jerusalem all the days of your life. * You will see sons for your sons. * Peace upon Israel.

Psalm 128: Those who trouble me have increased from my youth; * let Israel say, Those who trouble me have increased from my youth. * O Lord, hear the sound of our pleading, and protect us from the evil one. But they have not overcome my power. * They struck me with stripes on my back, and they lengthened their humiliation. * The Lord is just, and cuts off the branches of the wicked. * Each one who hates Zion will be turned back, * and will be like grass on the rooftops. * For when the wind blows upon him, he withers and dries up, * and the reaper will not fill his bundle with him, * nor the carrier his shoulder. * Those who pass by will not say, * The blessing of the Lord upon you, * we bless you in the name of the Lord.

Psalm 129: From the depths I have cried to you, O Lord, and you heard my voice. * Let your ears be attentive to the sound of my pleading. * O Good, Just, and Pitying One: have mercy on me in your grace. If you keep count of sins, O Lord, who would be able to stand? * For forgiveness is from you; * I have hoped in the Lord and my soul awaited his word. * It awaited the Lord from the morning watch until the morning watch. * Let Israel await for the Lord, * for mercies are from him, * and salvation even more so. * He will save Israel from all its sin.

Psalm 130: O Lord, my heart is not exalted, and my eyes are not exalted, * and I have not walked with those too great for me. * Raise me from the dust, O Lord, that I may glorify and thank your name. Rather, I have humbled my soul like a weaning child with its mother. * It is like a weaning child with my soul. * Let Israel wait for the Lord, * both now and forever.

Hulala XIX

Prayer: O Hope of the just, Trust of the righteous, Comfort of the weary, and great refuge of those who call upon his holy name, we implore you: turn to us, O Lord, forgive us, and have mercy on us, as you always do, Lord of all, Father, Son, and Holy Spirit, forever.

Psalm 131: Lord, remember David and all his humiliation, * who swore to the Lord, and vowed to the God of Jacob. * O Christ, protect the priesthood, and let your peace dwell in churches. I will not enter under the roof of my house, * nor go into my bedroom, * nor give sleep to my eyes, * or slumber to my eyelids, * until I find a place for the Lord, * and a dwelling for the God of Jacob.

* Lo, we heard it in Ephrathah and found it in the fields. * Let us enter his dwelling and worship at his footstool. * Arise, O Lord, for your resting place, * you and the ark of your might. * Your priests will be clothed with justice, and your just ones with glory. * Because of David your servant, do not turn away the face of your anointed. * The Lord vowed to David in truth, and will not turn away from it, * that from the fruits of your loin I will make one sit upon your throne, * if your sons keep my covenant. * This is the witness I teach them, * and their sons also will sit forever and ever upon your throne. * For the Lord has been pleased with Zion, * and chosen her for himself for a dwelling place. * This is my resting place forever and ever. * Here I will sit, for I have desired her, * and I will bless her fishermen, * and feed her poor with bread. * I will clothe her high priests with salvation and her just ones with glory. * There I will make the horn of David dawn, * and light the lamp of his anointed. * I will clothe her enemies with shame, * and my holy place will flourish in it.

Psalm 132: How good and how beautiful it is, * when brothers dwell in peace together. * *Our Lord has promised an unending banquet and beatitude for his holy ones*. Like oil descending upon the head and upon the beard, * the beard of Aaron, descending on the collar of his robes, * and like the dew of Hermon descending upon mount Zion. * For there the Lord commanded blessing and life forever.

Psalm 133: Bless the Lord, all the servants of the Lord, * those who stand in the house of the Lord at night. * *It is always right for the holy ones to glorify you, our Savior*. Lift your hands to the holy place and bless the Lord. * We bless you, O Lord, from Zion, * you who made heaven and earth.

Psalm 134: Praise the name of the Lord, * praise, O servants of the Lord. * *The people praise you in its exodus, for you gave victory to their hands*. Those who stand in the house of the Lord, * and in the courts of the house of our God. * Praise the Lord for he is good. * Sing to his name for he is sweet. * For the Lord chose Jacob for himself, * and Israel for his assembly. * For I know that the Lord our Lord is greater than all gods. * The Lord does all he wills, * in heaven and earth, * in the sea and all the abysses. * He brings up clouds from the ends of the earth, * and makes lightning for rain. * He brought out winds from the storehouses * to strike down the firstborn of Egypt, * the sons of men and the beasts. * He sent signs and wonders into Egypt, * upon Pharaoh and upon all his servants. * For he struck down many nations, * and slew mighty kings. * Sihon, king of the Amorites, * and Og, king of Bashan, * and all the kingdoms of Canaan. * He gave their land an inheritance to Israel his people. * O Lord, your name is forever; O Lord, your memory is unto the ages. * For the Lord judges his people, * and is comforted by his servants. * The idols of the nations are silver and gold, * the work of human hands. * They have a mouth but do not speak; * they have eyes but do not see; * they have ears but do not hear. * There is no breath in their mouth. * May their makers become like them, * and all who trust in them. * Bless the Lord, those of the house of Israel. * Bless the Lord, those of the house of Aaron. * Bless the Lord, those of the house of Levi. * Bless the Lord, those who fear the Lord. * The Lord is blessed from Zion, * he who dwells in Jerusalem.

Marmytha

Prayer: O Good God and merciful King, who ordered the lights for the pleasure of our service, and in whose light we rejoice and delight, it is our duty to thank, adore, and glorify you, Lord of all, Father, Son, and Holy Spirit, forever.

Psalm 135: Give thanks to the Lord, for he is good, and his mercies are forever. * Give thanks to the God of gods, for his mercies are forever. * Let us thank our God, who saved his servants from evil and oppressive men who hate us for no reason, and from the hand of the wicked, in his great graces. Give thanks to the Lord of lords, for his mercies are forever. * To him who has alone worked great wonders, for his mercies are forever. * To him who made heaven in his wisdom, for his mercies are forever. * To him who made the earth firm on the waters, for his mercies are forever. * To him who made the great rivers, for his mercies are forever. * The sun to rule the day, for his mercies are forever. * The moon and stars to rule the night, for his mercies are forever. * Who struck down the firstborn of Egypt, for his mercies are forever. * Who brought out Israel from among them, for his mercies are forever. * By a mighty hand and an exalted arm, for his mercies are forever. * Who divided the Red Sea, for his mercies are forever. * Who let Israel pass within it, for his mercies are forever. * Who drowned Pharaoh and his army in the Red Sea, for his mercies are forever. * Who led his people through the wilderness, for his mercies are forever. * Who struck down great kings, for his mercies are forever. * Who smote mighty kings, for his mercies are forever. * Sihon, king of the Amorites, for his mercies are forever. * Og, the king of Bashan, for his mercies are forever. * He gave their land as an inheritance, for his mercies are forever. * An inheritance to Israel his servant, for his mercies are forever. * Who

The Psalter

remembered us in our humiliation, for his mercies are forever. * Who saved us from our enemies, for his mercies are forever. * Who gives food to all flesh, for his mercies are forever. * Give thanks to God in heaven, for his mercies are forever.

Psalm 136: By the rivers of Babylon, * there we sat and wept. * Because Jerusalem sinned, and did not accept the prophets and apostles who came to her, there was mercy for the nations. Remembering Zion; * on the poplars that grew there we hung up our harps. * For it was there that they asked us, * our captors, for songs, our oppressors, for joy. * Sing to us, they said, one of Zion's songs. * How can we sing the glories of the Lord in a strange land? * If I forget you Jerusalem, let my right hand be lost. * Let my tongue cleave to my palate if I do not remember you. * Rather, lift up Jerusalem to the head of my joys. * Remember the sons of Edom, O Lord, on the day of Jerusalem, * who said, Destroy it, destroy it down to its foundations. * O daughter of Babylon the despoiler: * blessed is he who repays you the payment you paid us. * Blessed is he who takes your children and dashes them on a rock.

Psalm 137: I thank you, Lord, with all my heart, * and sing to you before kings. * We adore your precious cross, O Lord Jesus, by which you saved our race. I will adore in your holy temple and thank your name, * for your grace and for your truth. * For you exalted the name of your glory over all. * On the day I called, you answered me. * You increased the strength of my soul. * O Lord, let all the kings of the earth confess you, * for they have heard the word of your mouth, * and let them glorify the ways of the Lord, * for the honor of the Lord is great. * The Lord is exalted and sees into the depths. * He knows from afar anyone who exalts himself. * If I walk in distress you will give me life. * In the anger of my enemies, * you extend your hand and save me. * Lord, let your right hand rest upon me. * Lord, your mercies are forever. * Do not turn away from the work of your hands.

Marmytha

Prayer: O Searcher of our thoughts, Examiner of our hearts, Knower of our secrets, Provider of our blessings, and Fashioner of height and depth in his grace and mercies: we lift up glory, honor, thanksgiving and adoration to you, at all times, Lord of all, Father, Son, and Holy Spirit, forever.

Psalm 138: O Lord, you search me and you know me, * you know my sitting and my standing. * O Knower of all before he created all: save me, Almighty

One. You discern my intentions from above; * you know my paths and trace all my ways. * Before ever a word is on my tongue, * you know it, O Lord my God. * In all things, from beginning to end, * you molded me and placed your hand on me. * This knowledge and wonder is too much for me. * I was strengthened, but my strength was not enough. * Where can I go from your spirit, * and where can I hide from before you? * If I ascend to heaven, you are there, * and if I go down to Sheol, you are there as well. * If I lift my wings like an eagle, * and dwell at the end of the sea, * your hand is there, and your right hand holds me and leads me. * I said that darkness enlightens me, * and night brightens my face, * but darkness is not too dark for you, * and night is bright like daytime, * and darkness like a light. * For you fashioned my recesses, * and accepted me from the womb of my mother. * I thank you for the wonder you worked. * For your works are exalted, and my soul truly knows. * My bones are not hidden from you, for you made them in secret. * I went down to the lowest parts of the earth, and my eyes saw my reward, * and all of them will be written in your scriptures. * Lo, the days were shortened and had no one in them. * But your mercies greatly honored me, O God, and greatly strengthened me. * I will count their princes, * and they will increase more than the dust. * I was awakened, and again I was with you. * If only God would smite sinners, * and let men of bloodshed pass by me, * for they speak of you and take the city vainly. * O Lord, I have hated those who hate you, * and have been angry at those who stand against you. * I hate them with a complete hatred, * and they are enemies to me. * Search me, O God, and know my heart, * and examine and know my steps. * See if there is a path of wickedness in me; * guide me in your way forever.

Psalm 139: Deliver me, Lord, from the evil man, * and protect me from wicked men. * **Protect me, O Lord my God, from the inclination and violence of evil men.** Who consider evil in their hearts, * and stir up disputes all the day. * They sharpen their tongue like a serpent, * and the wrath of the viper is under their lips. * Protect me, O Lord, from the hand of the wicked, * and protect me from violent men. * For they consider how to trip my steps, * and the proud set traps for me. * They lay out the cords of their nets upon my paths, * and throw nets upon me. * I said to the Lord, You are my God. * Hearken to the sound of my pleading, O Lord my mighty Savior. * My helmet on the day of battle, * do not grant the desire of the wicked, O Lord. * Let his intention not move ahead. * Let the evil of their lips cover them, * and let coals fall upon them. * Let them

The Psalter

fall into fire and be able to stand. * Let the talkative man not be upheld on the earth, * and let evil capture the wicked man into destruction. * I knew that the Lord grants judgment to the poor and to the humble. * Therefore the just will thank your name, * and the upright will sit before your face.

Psalm 140: I have called to you, Lord; hasten to help me! * Hearken to my words and accept my prayer. * Blessed are you, O Lord, who does not despise the pleading of your adorers. Let my prayer arise before you like incense, * the offering of my hands like an evening oblation. * Set, O Lord, a guard over my mouth * and a guard over my lips! * That my heart may not turn to an evil deed, * or accomplish works of wickedness. * May I not dine with evil men. * Let a just man teach me and reprove me. * But let the oil of the wicked not anoint my head, * for my prayer is against their malice. * Their judges were thrown down by a rock-like hand, * then they heard that my words were kind, * like a plough that scatters the ground. * Their bones were strewn at the mouth of Sheol. * To you, Lord God, I lift up my eyes: * I trust you; do not cast my soul away! * Guard me from the hands of the boastful, * who set traps for me. * Let the wicked fall together into their own nets * while I pursue my way unharmed.

Hulala XX

Prayer: We call to you, O Lord, to come to our aid, we take refuge in you, to come to help us, and we plead that you may assist our weakness to keep your life-giving and divine commands. Grant this in your grace and mercies, as you always do, Lord of all, Father, Son, and Holy Spirit, forever.

Psalm 141: With my voice I called to the Lord, with my voice I begged the Lord. * I lifted my pleading before him. * O Comfort of the lonely, you are almighty. I showed him my distress. * When my spirit trembled, you knew my path. * On the way I walked they set a trap for me. * I looked to my right and saw: there was no one to advise me. * I had no means of escape, * not one who cared for my soul. * I cried to you, Lord; I said: you are my hope, * all that I have in the land of the living. * Hearken then to my pleading, * for I am brought very low. * Rescue me from those who pursue me, * for they are stronger than I. * Bring my soul out of this prison, * that I may give thanks to your name. * Your just ones will await me * as you grant me reward.

Psalm 142: Hear my prayer, O Lord, and attend to my pleading. * Answer me by your word and by your justice. * I am reproached by those who hate the truth; save your servant, O God. Do not enter into judgment with your servant, * for no living thing is innocent before you. * For the enemy pursues my soul, * and he has humbled my life to the ground. * He has made me sit in the dark like the dead forever. * My spirit smites me and my heart shakes within me. * I remember you, O Lord, from of old, * and I consider all your works. * I consider the work of your hands, and extend my hands to you. * My soul thirsts for you like earth. * Answer me quickly, O Lord, for my spirit is finished. * Do not turn your face from me, lest I be finished with those who go down into the pit. * In the morning, let me hear your grace, * for I trust in you. * Show me your path, that I may go upon it, * for I lift my soul to you, O Lord. * Deliver me from my enemies, and teach me to do your will, * for you are my God. * Let your sweet Spirit lead me on the path of life. * For the sake of your name, O Lord, comfort me, * and for the sake of your justice, bring my soul out of distress. * By your grace, silence those who hate me, * and destroy the enemies of my soul, * for I am your servant.

Psalm 143: Blessed is the Lord, who has trained my hands for battle, * and my fingers for battle. * Blessed is the Lord who condemns the evil and gives victory to his family. My refuge and my deliverer; * my help in whom I trust, * who subjugates the nations beneath me. * O Lord, what is the son of man that you know him, * and the son of man, that you consider him? * The son of man is like a breath, * and his days pass like a shadow. * Bend heaven down, O Lord, and descend; * rebuke the mountains and they will smoke. * Flash your lightnings and set fire to them. * Send your arrows and scatter them. * Extend your hand from above, * and grant me silence from the many waters, * and from the hand of the wicked, * whose mouth speaks vanity, * and whose right hand is the right hand of evil. * O God, I will praise you with a new praise, * and sing to you with a ten-stringed harp. * For you gave salvation to the king, * and delivered David his servant from an evil sword. * Deliver me from the hand of the wicked, * whose mouth speaks vanity, * and whose right hand is the right hand of evil. * Their sons are raised like a vine from their youth, * and their daughters like brides adorned like temples. * Their chambers are filled and overflow, one by one. * Their sheep give birth and grow in their markets. * Their cattle grow strong and have none who are sterile. * There is neither ruin nor lamentation in their markets. * Blessed is the people who have this. * Blessed is the people whose God is the Lord.

The Psalter

Marmytha

Prayer: O King of kings and Lord of Lords, whose authority upholds and guides heaven and earth and all within them: it is our duty to thank, adore, and glorify you at all times, Lord of all, Father, Son, and Holy Spirit, forever.

Psalm 144: I will exalt you, O Lord my King; * I will bless your name forever and ever. * We thank you, our Maker who leads us by the light of day, brings us by evening to rest in the night, and who protects us. I will bless you day after day and praise your name forever. * The Lord is great, highly to be praised, * his greatness cannot be measured. * Age to age shall proclaim your works, * shall declare your might, * shall speak of your fearful strength, * tell the tale of your wonderful works, * shall recount your greatness, * and recall your many graces. * Your just will seek and will find. * The Lord is merciful and compassionate, * patient and abounding in grace. * The Lord is good, and his mercies are upon his servants. * Your servants will thank you, O Lord, * and your righteous will praise you, * and tell of the glory of your kingdom, * and speak of your might; * to show mankind your power * and the glory of your kingdom. * Your kingdom is a kingdom forever, * and your authority in every age. * The Lord is faithful in his words, * and just in all his deeds. * The Lord supports all who fall, * and upholds all who are bowed down. * The eyes of all hang upon you, * for you give them their food in their time. * You open your hand and satisfy the will of all who live. * The Lord is just in all his paths, * and compassionate in all his deeds. * The Lord is close to all who call to him in truth, * he does the will of those who fear him. * He hears their pleading and saves them. * The Lord protects all who fear him; * the wicked he will destroy. * Let me speak the praises of the Lord with my mouth. * Let all the sons of flesh bless his holy name forever and ever.

Psalm 145: Bless the Lord, my soul; * I will glorify the Lord in my life. * The heavenly and the earthly thank you, O Eternal Being, for in your great mercies you came down and took on our humanity. I will sing to my God as long as I stand. * Do not trust in the prince or in man, * who does not have salvation in his hand, * whose spirit departs and who returns to his dirt, * and on that day all his thoughts are lost. * Blessed is the one whose help is the God of Jacob, * and whose hope is in the Lord God, * who made heaven and earth, * the seas and all that is in them. * He keeps truth forever. * He makes judgment for the oppressed. * The Lord gives bread to the hungry. * The Lord unbinds the shackled. * The Lord opens the eyes of the blind. * The Lord upholds all who are bowed down. * The Lord loves the just, * and protects the poor. * He upholds orphans and widows. * He drowns the path of the wicked. * The Lord reigns forever, * and your God, O Zion, for the ages.

Psalm 146: It is good to sing to our God, and sweet, * and glory is due to him. * When you created this light, O God, the angels marveled at it, and when it dawns every morning, they glorify you, and we as well. The Lord builds Jerusalem, * and gathers the scattered of Israel. * He heals the broken hearted, and binds up their wounds. * He counts the number of the stars, * and calls each one by name. * The Lord is great and mighty is his power, * and there is no limit to his understanding. * The Lord exalts the poor, * and humbles the evil to the dirt. * Glorify the Lord in glory; * sing to the Lord with harps, * for he covers the heaven with clouds, * and gives rain upon the earth. * He makes grass grow upon the mountains. * He gives to beasts their food, * and to the sons of the ravens who call. * The Lord is not pleased by the power of the horse, * nor is he pleased by the legs of the warrior. * Rather the Lord is pleased with those who fear him, * and those who await his grace.

Marmytha

Prayer: Answer your Church who calls to you in groaning, O Lord, accept the supplication of your flock who knocks upon the door of your Majesty, and fulfill your promise to her, that the doors of Sheol and its rulers will not overcome it unto the ages, Lord of all, Father, Son, and holy Spirit, forever.

Psalm 147: Praise the Lord, Jerusalem; * praise your God, O Zion. * Blessed is he who established the Jerusalem above in place of Mount Zion. For he has strengthened the bars of your gates, * has blessed your sons within you, * has established your borders in peace, * and has fed you with finest wheat. * He sends his word upon the earth, * and his phrase runs quickly. * He gives snow like wool, * and scatters frost like ash. * He throws ice like morsels, * and who can stand before his cold? * He sends his word and he melts them. * He makes the winds blow and the waters flow. * He shows his word through Jacob, * and his laws and commands through Israel. * He has not done this for all nations. * He has not showed them his judgments.

Psalm 148: Praise the Lord from the heavens, * praise him in the heights. * The heavens of heaven glorify you, for you brought them into being. Praise him, all his angels, * praise him all his hosts. * Praise him, sun and moon, * praise him, all stars and lights. * Praise him heaven of heavens. * Waters above the heavens, * praise the name of the Lord. * For he spoke, and they were; * he commanded and they were created. * He fixed them forever and ever, * gave a law which shall not pass away. * Praise the Lord from the earth, * sea creatures and all oceans, * fire and hail, snow and mist, * stormy winds that obey his word; * all mountains and hills, all fruit trees and cedars, * beasts wild and tame, reptiles and birds on the wing; * all earth's kings and peoples, * earth's princes and rulers; * young men and maidens, * old men together with children. * Let them praise the name of the Lord, * for his name alone is great, * and his glory is through earth and heaven. * He exalts the horn of his people * and the praise of all his just, * of the sons of Israel, * of the people that is near to him.

Psalm 149: Sing a new song to the Lord, * his glory in the church of his just. * The nations sing glory to the God who saved them. Let Israel rejoice in its Maker, * and the sons of Zion exalt in their King. * May they glorify his name with timbrel and tambourine, * and sing to him with harps. * For the Lord has delighted in his people, * and given the poor salvation. * The just will be strengthened in honor, * and glorify him on their beds, * and exalt God in their throats. * A two-edged sword is in their hands, * to make vengeance upon the nations, * and rebuke upon the peoples, * to bind their kings in chains, * and their honored ones in fetters of iron, * to carry out the sentence that was written. * Glory to all his just.

Psalm 150: Praise God in his holy place, * praise him in his mighty firmament. * The Son of God has sanctified you, and invited you to his kingdom. Praise him for his power, * praise his surpassing greatness. * O praise him with sound of trumpet, * praise him with lute and harp. * Praise him with timbrel and tambourine, * praise him with pleasant strings. * O praise him with resounding cymbals, * praise him with hymns and cries! * Praise the Lord with every breath!

THE PSALMS OF THE BLESSED DAVID, WITH THEIR CANONS, ARE ENDED.

The number of the Psalms is 150, with 20 *Hulalas*, in 29 sections, 57 *Marmythas*, 4,833 verses, and 5 books, 19,934 nouns, 90,852 letters, 732 Lords, 400 Gods, 285 Becauses, 6 Moseses, 6 Aarons, 24 Jacobs, 1 Samuel, 2 Benjamins, 44 Israels, 5 Indeeds, 5 Buts. (Know also that in David there is no "underneath," as in Paul there is no "under"). 13 Unders, and 4 Now and forevers.

The Psalter

THE GLORIFICATIONS OF BLESSED MOSES

HULALA XXI

Prayer: To you, O Splendid and Excellent One, Powerful and Glorious One, Mighty Warrior, strong but merciful, great King of glory, Being who exists from eternity: we thank, adore, and glorify you at all times, Lord of all, Father, Son, and Holy Spirit, forever.

First Glorification (Exodus 15:1–21): Then Moses and the sons of Israel sang * this praise to the Lord, and said: * Blessed is the Being, the Creator, who delivered his people by every sign, and saved his Church through his Anointed. Let us glorify the splendid Lord, * who was victorious over the horses and their riders whom he cast into the sea. * He is mighty and glorious. * Yah is the Lord, and has become a Savior for us. * He is my God; I will glorify him. The God of my father; I will exalt him. * The Lord is a mighty warrior, the Lord is his name. * He cast the chariots of Pharaoh and his army into the sea, * and drowned the chosen warriors in the Red Sea. * The abysses covered them. * They descended to the depths and they drowned like rocks. * Your right hand, O Lord, is glorious in power. * Your right hand, O Lord, has destroyed your enemies. * In your great might, you have crushed those who hate you. * You sent your wrath, and devoured them like stubble. * At the breath of your face, the waters piled up. * The floods stood up like heaps. * The abysses congealed in the heart of the sea. * + The enemy said, I will pursue and overcome and divide the spoil. * My soul will swallow them. * I will draw my sword and my hand will destroy them. * Your wind blew and the sea covered them. * They drowned like lead in the mighty waters. * Who is like you, O Lord? * Who is like you, glorious in his holiness? * Powerful and glorious, a worker of wonders? * You lifted your right hand and the earth swallowed them. * By grace, you led this people whom you saved. * You led them by your strength to your holy dwelling. * The nations heard and trembled, * and fear seized those who sit in Philistia. * Then the great ones of Edom feared, * and trembling seized the men of Moab. * All the dwellers of Canaan were broken. * Fear and trembling fell upon them. * By your great arm, they sank like rocks, * until your people crossed, O Lord; * until this people you saved crossed. * You will bring them and plant them on the mountain of your inheritance. * O Lord, you made your holy place an establishment for your dwelling. * O Lord, establish it by your hands. * The Lord reigns forever and ever, * for the horses of Pharaoh and his chariots and horsemen entered the sea, * and the Lord overturned the water of the sea upon them. * The sons of Israel walked on dry land within the sea. * Then Miriam the prophetess, sister of Aaron, took a timbrel in her hand, * and all the women went out after her with timbrel and tambourine. * Miriam sang to them, * Glorify the glorious Lord, * who was victorious over the horses and their riders whom he cast into the sea.

The Glorification of Isaiah the Prophet (Isaiah 42:10–14): Sing a new song to the Lord, * his glory from the ends of the earth. * *Glory to the Lord, by whose might has destroyed the oppressor and saved his servants.* The cloaks of the sea in its fullness, * the coastlands and those who dwell in them. * Let the desert and its villages rejoice, * and let Kedar become meadows. * Let the inhabitants of Sela glorify, * and cry out from the mountaintops. * Let them give glory to the Lord, * and let them show his glories on the coastlands. * The Lord will come out like a warrior, * and like a man of war, he stirs up his zeal. * He will cry out, shout, and slay his enemies. * Heaven above will be pleased, * and the clouds will rain justice. * The earth will open and salvation will increase, * and justice will bloom together. * I am the Lord, who has created these things.

Marmytha

Prayer: Sow, O Lord, the good seed of your teaching within our heart, and let drops of your grace rain upon us, that we may grow as you will, and bear fruits pleasing to your Majesty all the days of our lives, Lord of all, Father, Son, and Holy Spirit, forever.

The Second Glorification of Moses (Deuteronomy 32:1–21): Attend, O heaven, and I will speak, * hear, O earth, the word of my mouth. * *Attend to my prayer, O Lord, and do not turn away from my pleading.* My teaching will drop like rain, * and my word will come down like dew, * and like wind upon the grass, * and like drops upon the crop. * For I will call upon the name of the Lord. * Grant greatness to our mighty God, * whose works are without blame, * and all his ways are well-judged. * God is faithful and not wicked; * he is just and upright. * The sons of fault have corrupted and are not his, * a crooked and perverted generation. * Do you repay these things to the Lord, * ignorant and unwise nation? * As if he were not your Father who has gained you, * the one who made you and fashioned you? * Remember the days from ages past, * and understand the years of generations ago. * Ask your father and he will show you, * and your grandfathers, and they will tell you, * of when the Most High divided the nations, * and when he distinguished the sons of men. * + He established borders for the nations according to the number of the sons of Israel, * for the portion of the Lord is his people, * and Jacob the cord of his inheritance. * He found him in a desert land and in the wilderness of the desert. * He cleaved to him, loved him, and kept him like the pupil of the eye, * and like an eagle who soars to its nest, * and has compassion over its brood. * He spreads his wings and embraces them, * and he takes them upon the might of his feathers. * The Lord alone led him, * and there was no strange god with him. * He sat him upon the might of the land, * and fed him the produce of the field. * He suckled him with honey from a rock, * and oil from the flinty rock. * Curds of cows and milk from sheep, * with the fat of lambs, * young males and goats, * with the finest of the wheat, * and he let him drink wine, the blood of grapes. * Israel became fat and kicked; * he got fat and thick, and gained wealth, * and forgot the God who made him, * and scoffed at the Mighty One who saved him. * They made him jealous with strangers, * and angered him with false religions. * They sacrificed to demons who were not gods, * gods they did not know. * The things that were done were new things, * and your fathers did not worship in these ways. * You strayed from the Mighty One who had begotten you, * and forgot the God who had glorified you. * The Lord saw and was angered, * for his sons and daughters had angered him. * He said, I will turn my face from them, * and will see what their end will be. * For they are an upside-down generation, * sons who have no faith. * They have made me jealous with their non-gods, * and angered me with their false worship.

Marmytha

Prayer: O Zealous and Just One, in whose zeal scatters the evil, and in whose wrath destroys the wicked, and who keeps his covenant and grace for those who fear his holy name: we implore you: turn to us, forgive us, and have mercy on us, as you always do, Lord of all, Father, Son, and Holy Spirit, forever.

Third Glorification of Moses (Deuteronomy 32:21–43): So I will make them jealous with those who are not my people, * and will anger them with an ignorant people. * Blessed is he who brought up an ignorant nation, and revealed future things to it. For a fire is kindled by my anger, * and it burns to the depths of Sheol. * It devours the earth and its fields, * and burns the

The Psalter

foundations of the mountains. * I will gather evil things against them, * and my arrows will devour them. * They will be destroyed by hunger, and evil spirits will end them. * I will abandon them to the bird, * and will drag them away with the tooth of the beast, * with the wrath of snakes who crawl on the ground. * The sword will lay waste from without, and fear from within, * even for the young men and the maidens, * the children with the old men.
* I said, Where are they? I will erase their memory from among men. * If the wrath of the enemy had not increased, * and their tormentors been exalted, * and they had said, Our hand will be raised up, * it was not the Lord who did this. * For it is a people whose mind is lost, * and they have no understanding. * If they were wise and understood this, * and considered their end, * one would pursue a thousand, and two would put ten thousand to flight. * But their might has handed them over, * and the Lord has imprisoned them. * For their might is not like our might, * and our enemies are not our judges. * For their vine is from the vine of Sodom, * and from the field of Gomorrah. * Their grapes are sour grapes, * and their clusters are bitter. * Their wrath is the wrath of the dragon, * and the head of an evil asp. * Lo, my people is hidden, and completely in the storehouse. * The vengeance which I avenge is mine, * in the time when their foot will slip. * For the day of their destruction is near, * and the thing to come is coming quickly. * For the Lord judges his people, * and is comforted by his servant. * For he has seen that the hand has reigned, * and there is none who helps or sustains. * He will say, Where are their mighty gods, * in whom they trusted? * They ate the fat of their sacrifices, * and drank the wine of their libations. * Let them stand now and help them, * and be protectors for them. * See now, that I am, * and there is no god other than me. * I bring death and I bring life. * I strike down and I heal. * None can escape my hand. * For I have lifted my hand to heaven, * and said that I live forever. * I will sharpen the tooth of my sword like lightning, * and my hand will seize the judgment. * I will return vengeance to those who hate me, * and finish my enemies. * I will make my arrows drunk with blood, * and my sword will eat flesh, * the blood of the killed and the captives, * and from the head of the scepter of the enemy. * Then the nations will glorify with him, * for the blood of his people will be avenged, * and he will take vengeance on those who hate him. * He will forgive the earth and his people.

THE MARTYR HYMNS
Attributed to Mar Marutha of Mephraqat

Prayer: May the martyrs, O Lord our God, who defeated, humbled and eradicated the error of idolatry by the power and aid that is from you, and who lifted up and raised the true faith of your name, beg and plead on our behalf to your Majesty on the great and glorious day your Justice dawns from heaven, O Just and Merciful Judge and Forgiver of sins and faults, Lord of all, Father, Son and Holy Spirit, forever.

Another: To you, O Great, Beautiful and True Hope, whom the just and the prophets awaited in their age, the righteous pleased with their works, and the martyrs appeased by the precious blood that flowed from their necks, we beg and plead: grant us, O Lord our God, that we may take refuge in the power that is hidden in their bones and be aided by their prayers, and that with them, among them, within their ranks, around their dwellings, and in the glorious temples that were set apart for the honor of their service, we may be worthy to lift up glory, honor, thanksgiving and adoration to you, Lord of all, Father, Son and Holy Spirit, forever.

MONDAY EVENING PRAYER – *abbun d-bashmayya*

- Praise the Lord, you righteous ones.
Holy martyrs, pray that there may be peace
and we may, with joy, celebrate your deeds.

- And glory is right for the innocent.
Martyrs, who desired to see Jesus Christ,
gained wings by the sword, and flew to heaven.

- And say in a lovely voice.
All the martyrs say, in their love for Christ:
"for your sake we will give our lives each day."

- Beg the Lord and be strengthened.
Martyrs, beg for mer-cy for all the world,
by the power hi-dden within your bones.

- They called the Lord, he answered them.
We call to the martyrs, our true refuge,
that they be inter-cessors for us all.

Martyr Hymns

- Like a city surrounded by a wall.
You are a great wall in our daily fight
that protects us all from our enemies.

- Both now and forever.
All the martyrs' prayers are our mighty wall,
that will chase away the deceiver's wars.

- They offered a sacrifice of praise.
O martyrs, who were sacrificed by priests,
may your prayer be a wall for our souls.

- I will bless the Lord at all times.
Blest your agony, O holy martyrs,
for you gained the king-dom by your necks' blood.

- And at all times his praises in my mouth.
How blessed is Christ, who raised his martyrs,
here upon the earth, and in heaven above.

- The friends of the Lord hate wickedness.
Martyrs of the Son, friends of the Only-Begotten,
pray that there be peace in cre-ation.

- Look to him and hope in him.
Martyrs saw the Son, crucified on wood,
and they bent their necks to the crowning sword.

- Turn your ear, O Lord, and answer me.
The cross of our Lord was dripping with blood;
the martyrs looked on, and they bent their necks.

- He opened the sea and let them pass.
The cross of the Christ was the martyrs' bridge;
the just walked across, to the land of life.

- Better than gold and precious jewels.
The martyrs are like precious pearls and jewels,
for their images are on the King's crown.

- The princess stands in beauty.
The most faithful Church is like a fine pearl,
and the martyrs are her obla-tions.

- At the gate of daughter Zion.
The great martyrs saw a pearl on Zion;
they ran and they bought it with their own blood.

Martyr Hymns

- More beautiful than the sons of men.
Flowers in gardens are so beautiful,
but even more so, martyrs in their deaths.
- How good and beautiful.
The most precious jewels and the finest pearls:
martyrs in the crown of the King of kings.
- Sing to the Lord with harp and song.
I heard the martyrs singing praise to God,
with King David's harp, around Paradise.
- His glory on earth and in heaven.
Glory to the voice who told the martyrs:
mix your blood with mine, and my life with yours.
- Hear this, all you nations.
Martyrs were wheat har-vested by the King,
and the Lord put them in the Kingdom's barn.
- Coming, he came in great joy.
The martyrs and priests, and all holy ones,
come with joy to meet Christ the day he comes.
- He rebukes kings to their face.
How right when Qurya-qos the little child,
faced the wicked king, and admonished him.
- A mother rejoicing in her sons.
Shmoni the faithful gave heart to her sons:
"my beloved sons, you may go in peace."
- Plead to the Lord and pray to him.
Ask your Lord for us, O martyr St. George,
pity, mercies, forgiveness of sins.
- Kings of earth and all nations.
Every age and time calls our Lady blest,
the virgin Mary, the mother of Christ.
- Glory to the Father, to the Son and to the Holy Spirit.
How blessed are you, O holy martyrs,
sowing seeds of peace throughout all the world.
- From age to age, amen, amen.
O holy patron, may you be recalled
with the victorious just, and the martyrs crowned.

Martyr Hymns

- Let all the people say: Amen, amen.
In your hands, O God, where mercies abound,
be our discipline, not the hands of men.
* Come, Lord, to our aid, strengthen our frailty;
in you is our hope during night and day.
* Christ, who does not turn from those who call him,
in mercy, let our prayer come to you.
* Our eyes look to you, that you may forgive
all our faults and blot out all of our sins.
* Lord, by your right hand, overthrow Satan;
he intoxicates our souls without wine.
* With the tax collector, we plead to you:
pity us, O God, have mercy on us.
* Your cross has saved us, and your cross saves us;
so may your cross be a wall for our souls.
* Let wars be erased, let conflicts subside,
and let your peace reign throughout all the earth.
* O Lord protect us, for we are like sheep,
among violent men who are worse than wolves.
* Sow your peace, O Lord, throughout all the world,
and let pass from it the correcting rod.
* Bless us and protect our assembly, Lord,
and let your great peace dwell within our lives.
* Lord, let your peace dwell in the four corners,
and destroy all those who would oppress us.
* O Lord, shut the mouth of all wicked men,
lest they speak evil of the Church's sons.

Martyr Hymns

MONDAY MORNING PRAYER – *sahdaw dabra*

- In the morning, O Lord, you hear my voice.
Morning, the time when the doors above are opened to us,
Lord, look kindly on our prayer, and answer all our requests,
granting hope and salvation to the souls who wait for you.

- And in the morning, I prepare and present myself to you.
The morning of the Lord has come, and from the silence, he dawns,
giving all the just their wage. Blessed is he who has worked
and labored in his vineyard, and received his wage from him.

- In the morning, make your grace heard to me.
Make us worthy, that morning when heaven and earth rejoice,
to rejoice with all the just, with the righteous in their deeds,
with the martyrs in their crowns, and the nations in mercy.

- In the morning, let my prayer come before you.
In the morning, Moses prayed, chosen one on the mountain;
there it was God answered him, and gave him a staff of help,
to descend, save Israel, from slavery to Egypt.

- To show your grace in the morning.
In the morning, Moses saw fearful visions on the mount:
God extolled by cherubim, carrying his chariot,
seraphim crying "holy," angels serving at his throne.

- Sing to the Lord with harp and song.
In the morning, David sang, the young man with voice and harp,
the songs of the Holy Ghost, and even the animals
came to hear his sweet verses, as he sang "halleluiah."

- We glorify him with song.
In the morning, martyrs sang a new song as they were judged:
"We will not deny our Christ, for he suffered, for our sake,
pain and death upon the cross, and saved our race from darkness."

- God sends his grace and his truth.
In the morning, innocent Noah sent a dove above,
due to water from the flood, and it came back to the ark,
carrying an olive leaf, sign of peace, serenity.

Martyr Hymns

- You gave a sign to those who fear you.
In the morning it was seen: sign of peace, serenity,
the bow of our Lord in clouds, and then the Creator vowed:
"I will not again make a flood to come, forever more."

- Before all the people.
In the morning, martyrs came, raised their voice as they were judged:
"We will not worship idols, for we worship one true God,
and confess his only Son, who delivers us from fire."

- Let your heart be given strength.
In the morning, the martyrs, took heart and said, one to one:
"The Lord will help us, fear not. What can mankind do to us?"
For its power will be naught; the Lord's Kingdom will endure.

- Hear this, all you peoples.
In the morning, it was heard: the voice speaking to athletes,
"Take your cross and follow me, for I am your Lord and Master,
and your God who gives you strength, and you are my disciples."

- He vindicates the oppressed.
In the morning, faithful one, Shmoni offered pray'r to God:
"O God, vindicate me from Antiochus, wicked one,
for he kills my sons like lambs, and growls at me like a lion."

- And your prayers be with us all.
Gaddai, Maccbai, and Tarsai, Hebron, Hebson, and Bakos,
seventh brother Yonadab, their teacher Eliazar,
mother Shmoni, faithful one: may their prayer be our wall.

- The dwelling of the angels of God.
In the morning, martyrs went, row by row of holy ones,
from the prison, as they said: "Hurry, king, and cut our heads,
for we will go to heaven, to our Lord who waits for us."

- For he has done a wonder.
What a wonder that was done, from end to end of the earth,
through the child Quryaqos, who was only three years old:
grace came down and dwelt in him, and he was strengthened in faith.

- Just and upright one.
May the martyr's prayer be our great refuge and our wall,
that the devil's arrows miss, and his spear not pierce our skin,
enemy who hates our race, who wishes to destroy us.

Martyr Hymns

- Come and hear, and I will make known to you.
Hear and marvel, O mankind: Virgin bore in Bethlehem,
the light of the world entire; we make her memorial
in the four corners of earth, and with angels in heaven.
- Glory to the Father, to the Son and to the Holy Spirit.
At morningtide, praise to you from those above and below,
Son who sits at God's right hand; the trumpet sounds, and they rise,
both old and young, whom you have created for your glory.
- From age to age, amen, amen.
Blessed is one hired like you, O patron, who spiritual wealth
gathered, filling his vessel with all blessings, who made forth
and found his way to harbor, to the place of all the just.
- Let all the people say: Amen, amen.
O Lord, may your kingdom come, your will be done here on earth,
as it is there in heaven. Give to us the bread we need,
and lead us from temptation; save us from the evil one.
* May the help which came to aid Moses, firstborn of prophets,
opened up the sea before all the people, may it come
and aid us who worship you, and sweetly forgive our sins.

Martyr Hymns

TUESDAY EVENING PRAYER – *istepanos urḥa drash*

- May the memorial of the just be forever.
The path treaded by Stephen was followed by the martyrs
who rejoice with the Bridegroom in the unceasing wedding feast.

- He feared not evil tidings.
When St. Stephen was being stoned he saw his Lord in heaven,
as the Spirit was weaving the crowns of all the faithful.

- He asked for life and this you gave.
St. Stephen asked for mercies for those who came to stone him:
"Lord, forgive and absolve them, they do not know what they do."

- From a people without mercy.
When St. Stephen was being killed, he asked mercy for killers,
like his Lord while on the cross, who asked forgiveness for us.

- And say in a lovely voice.
The martyrs cried out loudly, before the judges, and said:
"We will never deny Christ, who tasted death for our sake."

- Help us, O God our Savior.
O Christ, who with the martyrs, came down and helped them suffer:
our invincible armor, and our unbreakable wall.

- There is none like you, O God, and none like your works.
There is not one affliction that can make us deny you,
for all idols will perish, and you alone will not cease.

- Planted in the house of the Lord.
The martyrs in the temple are like trees in a garden,
and above them the altar; the Holy Spirit serves them.

- Servants who do his will.
The watchers come from their place, and sing glory with their songs,
to the bones of the faithful who obeyed their Creator.

- Offer him sacrifices of praise.
The martyrs burned were incense which fell into the fire,
and the smell of their burning, perfume within the temple.

- The cedars of Lebanon you planted.
Martyrs, cedars unbroken, unbent before their judges;
now kings worship at their graves, and ask for help from their bones.

Martyr Hymns

- Like a city surrounded by a wall.
O martyrs, walls unfalling, and blessed founts unfailing:
plead for mercy by your pray'rs, from God the Merciful One.

- Turn your ear, O Lord, and answer me.
Moses prayed, sea divided; Simon prayed, Satan vanquished;
Jesus prayed and tasted death, and gave life to lost Adam.

- Who is like the Lord in the heaven of heavens?
Time's sufferings compare not to the kingdom prepared for
the faithful from the beginning, those who are led by your name.

- How good and how lovely.
Sweet the scent of the garden within the holy temple:
martyrs enter and delight under the shadow of its leaves.

- Blessed are they who go on the path without fault.
Martyrs rejoice when they hear the Father's voice as he says:
"Come inherit the Kingdom which you have all awaited."

- They walk in the law of the Lord.
A great, unceasing blessing, was promised by Lord Jesus,
to those who loved and believed him, and kept all his commandments.

- Come, let us bless and adore him.
Come and be blessed by martyrs, come and be blessed by the priests;
may the prayers of them both be a great wall for our souls.

- O God, who is like you?
The death of the great athletes is like the death of our Lord;
his, the death on the cross, and theirs the sword and stoning.

- To the upright of heart.
The martyrs were invited to sweet, unceasing blessings,
and in place of their sufferings, they became heirs of heaven.

- Both small and great.
We take refuge in St. George, that by his pow'r and prayers,
the Lord will clear our pathways, and lift our body's burdens.

- I will speak peace unto you.
"O full of grace, blessed are you," the angel said to Mary,
"the Lord is with you, O maiden, from whom will dawn the Savior."

- Glory to the Father, to the Son and to the Holy Spirit.
Blessed are you, O builders who built a tower that fell not,
in the name of Lord Jesus, a dwelling-place in heaven.

Martyr Hymns

- From age to age, amen, amen.
Your crown of victory is for you above, O Patron;
at the end you will receive it, from the right hand of your Lord.
- Let all the people say: Amen, amen.
You who complete the day's course, and give the night for resting:
may your grace now complete us, O Lord, at night and daytime.
* O Christ, who kept us daytime, and led us to the evening:
may we rest in the night time, and thank you for your graces.
* O Lord, grant peace to our land, and bless us in our labors;
make us worthy for mercy, and unveiled face before you.
* Grant, in your grace and mercies, a restful slumber this night
to all the sick and weary, who call to you in distress.

Martyr Hymns

TUESDAY MORNING PRAYER – *sahde hwayton taggare*

- Let the righteous praise the Lord.
Martyrs, you were wise merchants, and your wage is in heaven.
You bought the Pearl of great price with the blood of your own necks.

- To the innocent, glory.
Martyrs entered happily the Jerusalem above,
and they bought with their own blood that land they had waited for.

- They walked from land unto land.
You may move from land to land, but you will not leave your Lord:
you bring the Treasure of Life to each land which you enter.

- The Lord dwells there forever.
In the place that has your bones, dwell peace and serenity.
The armies of the angels keep it and its people safe.

- Blessed is the people who have this.
Blessed is the place where the bones of martyrs are reserved,
When the light of the sun goes, light from their bones dawns on us.

- Light dawns in the darkness on the just.
Light dawns from your holy bones, and my mind is held captive:
I consider how you died, and I marvel at your crowns.

- More precious than gold and fine gems.
Your bones, martyrs, are fine pearls, and your bodies are incense;
the blood that poured from your necks, brought compassion to the world.

- Your grace is preached among the tombs.
Lo, your bodies in the church, and the keys of heaven yours.
Blessed ones, open your stores, and give help to those in need.

- Like a city surrounded by a wall.
Like the framework of a house, martyrs uphold all the world;
When the earth is in danger, they support it by their bones.

- I was strengthened but still had no strength.
The entire sea cannot pierce a wall your love surrounds,
nor can Satan overcome in the place your bones are kept.

- For your sake we are killed daily.
The Lord whose martyrs were killed for the sake of his glory,
on the day his cross will dawn, will stand them at his right side.

Martyr Hymns

- For there the Lord will grant life and blessing forever.
The place where martyrs were killed and their bodies torn apart,
there the Holy Spirit comes, and turns wilderness to peace.

- Come let us bless and worship him.
Come worship before their bones, the Strength hidden in their bones,
and because we saw their deaths, may we also see their crowns.

- They go to the sea in ships.
Martyrs, you were wise merchants, and went over sea and land;
by your tears, the sea was calmed, and by your prayers, the land.

- From the depths I cried to you, Lord, and you heard my voice.
The martyrs cried from the depths, and your grace replied to them.
From the depths, we cry to you: grant us help and salvation.

- I will bless the Lord at all times.
Blest, the Lord whose servants sleep, and who lifts their memory;
they are sleeping restfully, and yet, graces flow from them.

- How good and beautiful.
How your crowns are beautiful, which the faith has woven you,
and the Spirit has adorned with the most beautiful gems.

- Like a thirsty and parched land needing water.
Like a thirsty and parched land, needing water every day,
thus the martyrs were thirsting for the sweet love of their Lord.

- These are new things that were done.
Come in peace, O new bridegrooms, sons of holy baptism,
who were raised up by God's grace, in the holy Trinity.

- I have spoken of peace.
Peace be always on your bones, and rest unto your bodies,
for you imitated Christ, by whose death sinners may live.

- Give thanks to him and bless his name.
They always confessed the truth; they saw swords and did not shake;
they put on hidden armor, fashioned by the Holy Ghost.

- Both small and great ones.
One martyr said to his friend, and pitied his companion:
"Come, let us die for Jesus, and inherit life with him."

- The Lord is faithful in his words.
The word which our Lord had spoke, the martyrs heard and were strong:
"Whoever will die for me, he will have eternal life."

Martyr Hymns

- **More precious than gold and fine jewels.**
Similar to precious jewels, and like gold and finest pearls,
thus the martyrs longed to die for the sake of Christ their Lord.
- **How good and beautiful.**
How beautiful is the boat which carried Mar Quryaqos;
cherubim stood in array, and seraphim cried "holy."
- **From the dawning of the sun to its setting.**
Celebrated everywhere, is the great memorial
of victorious monk Hormizd: blest is he who has crowned him.
- **He will heal the broken hearted and bind up all their wounds.**
St. George, you were a doctor, without balms or medicines,
and to all who come for help, you grant aid by your prayers.
- **I rejoice in your blessings.**
Plead, O filled with gracefulness, to the Son who dawned from you:
that he may let his peace dwell in the Church bought by his Blood.
- **Glory to the Father, to the Son and to the Holy Spirit.**
Peace to you, who have conquered; peace to you, who defeated.
Peace to you, who have become sharers in Christ's suffering.
- **From age to age, amen, amen.**
Great is your truth, O patron, and exalted is your joy.
Plead to Christ for all of us, that we may share in your joy.
- **Let all the people say: Amen, amen.**
Hearer of your servants' prayer, Answerer of our requests:
hear our prayer and our voice, and answer us in mercy.
* You whose right hand is stretched out, and whose door is opened up:
open it to our pleading, and let our voice come to you.
* You whose chariot is fire, and whose court is of watchers:
let the liar be destroyed, and the evil one silenced.
* O True One who does not lie, who said "knock, it will open,"
look with favor on our pray'r, and answer our souls' request.

Martyr Hymns

WEDNESDAY EVENING PRAYER – *sahde qaddyshe d-ithqaṭṭal*

- For your sake we are killed daily.
O holy martyrs who suffered for the love of Christ the Lord,
plead on our behalf: beg for mercies from our God.

- In heaven and earth.
Great are your labors, and joyful is the memory of your fight,
you who were killed for Christ's sake, and who reign with him above.

- Plead to the Lord and be strengthened.
O martyrs, plead for the whole world which takes refuge in your bones,
that, by your holy prayers Christ may have mercy on us.

- How good and beautiful.
Serenity, peace, and union, fill the places where you dwelt,
and they are kept from dangers by your prayers, blessed ones.

- I will bless the Lord at all times.
Blessed is he who has made you blessed healers, true in faith,
and made your bones a refuge to all who approach in need.

- The dwelling of the angels of the Lord.
Rank after rank of the martyrs came before their pursuers
as they cried out to their Lord: "help your servants in their pain."

- Look to him and hope in him.
They looked to Christ, and they loved him, who gave his life for the Church;
they ran and they gave their lives, to be with him when he dawns.

- Offer him a sacrifice of praise.
O blessed ones, you were incense, oblations to the Father,
whom the Son has accepted, and whom the Spirit has crowned.

- Praise the Lord in the heights.
Up in the heights is the glory which martyrs wear in death,
in the land full of glory, whose life is greater than fear.

- More precious than gold and fine gems.
Crowns that are greater than jewels, and find gold and precious pearls,
Christ has placed upon your heads, and has gladdened you with him.

- Be strengthened and let your heart be strong.
O martyrs, you did not fear fire, or the sword of the judges,
for you were clothed with Christ's love, and endured all suffering.

Martyr Hymns

- Sing a new song to him.
Jesus has clothed with new glory those whom he chose for himself;
in place of pains and hardships, he has made them heirs above.

- Open the gates of justice to me.
Open your treasures, O blessed, and give help to those in need,
who look and wait for your pray'rs, that they may be kept from harm.

- Blessed are those on the path without blame.
Blessed are you, holy martyrs, friends of the Bridegroom above,
for you were all invited to the blessed life above.

- They walk in the law of the Lord.
Unceasing joys, and the kingdom that will never pass away
our Savior promised to those who have kept their love for him.

- Joseph was sold to slavery.
The bones of victorious Joseph brought ruin unto Egypt;
but the bones of the martyrs bring mercy to the whole world.

- You placed a glorious crown upon his head.
A glori-ous crown, most precious, granted the Lord of glory
to Quryaqos victorious, who had suffered for the truth.

- O just and upright one.
Martyr St. Sargis whose power shamed both Satan and his hosts:
may his prayer be our guard from the evil one, our foe.

- The Lord gives strength to his people.
May the great power that came down, to give strength to martyr George,
be with us: may it guard us from Satan and all his hosts.

- A choice treasure found on earth.
Your holy body, O Mary, is our store of benefits,
and, through its many graces, you enrich our poverty.

- Glory to the Father, to the Son and to the Holy Spirit.
Glory to Jesus, who raised you, and who made you stores of life
where all those who are weary may take refuge and be saved.

- From age to age, amen, amen.
O brave and victorious martyr, patron who gained the kingdom:
plead to Christ for his mercies, that peace may dwell in the world.

- Let all the people say: Amen, amen.
We lift up praise in the evening to you Lord, our mighty God,
and ask for your forgiveness, and that you may accept us.

Martyr Hymns

* Grant us a life without sin, Lord, love and peace and harmony,
and answer all that we ask, as befits your Majesty.
* Sow in us a love for prayer; let our pleading rise to you,
and grant us health of body, and great virtue of our soul.

WEDNESDAY MORNING PRAYER – *m'yna d-ṭawatha*

- Your servants will thank you, Lord.
O holy martyrs, teachers of the one true faith,
pray that there be peace in all the world,
that wars and battles may be taken from the earth,
and the Church sing glory through her sons.

- And your righteous will praise you.
The holy martyrs, who confessed you in their fight,
and satisfied you with their necks' blood,
may they be for us pleaders for our sinfulness,
that when you judge us, you have mercy.

- They speak praise of your kingdom.
The kingdom's glory was seen by the martyrs' minds
when they were tortured and killed,
and they accepted pain and grief in their bodies
as they rejoiced, when they were received.

- Their blood is precious in his eyes.
Let us all honor, with the Holy Spirit's songs,
the martyr's bones, for the pain they faced,
and find our help there on the day that we are judged
from the mercy and goodness of God.

- The Lord is glorified in the heights.
Your crowns in heaven, and on earth your gatherings,
O martyrs who preached of Christ the King;
in heaven and earth, your feast days we celebrate,
sowers of peace over all the world.

- Plead to the Lord and be strengthened.
Martyrs, beg mercies from the God of compassion,
that his peace may dwell in all the earth,
and when our Lord comes, and the clouds bear your bodies,
pray that, with you, we may see heaven.

Martyr Hymns

- **O Lord, in the morning, you hear my voice.**
At dawn, the martyrs, cried before their murderers:
"The Bridegroom we will never deny,
for he will save us from the hands of evil men,
and will clothe us in glory above."

- **In the morning, I prepare and present myself to you.**
On that great morning, when the King comes who crowned you,
prophets, apostles, martyrs and priests,
and places on you glory which will never end:
pray that, with you, we may see heaven.

- **Light has dawned in the darkness for the upright.**
Martyrs, sons of light, who hated this passing world,
and loved the Bridegroom who reigns above,
may you plead from him that he may grant us mercy
and save our souls on the day he comes.

- **Blessed are those on the path without fault.**
O blessed martyrs, victors over Satan's wiles,
who stomped on death, and defeated sin,
your prayers guard us like a strong surrounding wall,
from all the wiles of our enemy.

- **They walk in the law of the Lord.**
Gladness unfailing, the Kingdom that never ends,
our Savior promised to those he chose;
in place of torment, and the tortures they endured,
they will inherit eternal life.

- **O just and upright one.**
Small in his body, splendid martyr Quryaqos,
who made the king marvel at his words,
and then accepted the sword of the wicked king,
he was then crowned for our Savior's sake.

- **More beautiful than the sons of men.**
A lovely offshoot, and a splendid olive tree,
O great St. George, friend of Christ the Son,
by whose humbleness, and the love you have for him,
you bowed your head, and carried your cross.

- **She brings her virgin companions with her.**
O holy Virgin, Mary, mother, blessed one,
all generations will call you blest,
for you were worthy to carry Emmanuel,
whom the prophets preached in mystery.
- **Glory to the Father, to the Son and to the Holy Spirit.**
Praise to the Power that dwells in the martyrs' bones,
and whose voice thunders in all the world,
for from all churches, blessings flow from them to us,
and the truth shines from their words and deeds.
- **From age to age, amen, amen.**
You loved innocence, all the days you lived on earth,
O chosen one, you were unblemished
for the sake of Christ, and by your virtuous life,
you found a place among all the saints.
- **Let all the people say: Amen, amen.**
Grant us what you know will befit us, Life-Giver,
for we know not what to ask of you.
For one thing only: that your will be done in us,
and your mercies may defend us all.
* O Christ, who promised: "When you call, I will answer;
whoever knocks, it will be opened,"
let not your mercies or your grace be far from us;
in you we trust, to receive good things.

Martyr Hymns

THURSDAY EVENING PRAYER – *sahde brykhe*

- You, the blessed of the Lord.
The blessed martyrs considered pain and death a great benefit,
and accepted torturing as an honor and a gift,
and so, now, after their deaths, they distribute benefits
to the world from their treasury.

- They despised the world of desire.
The martyrs who saw this world passes on and the Truth remains,
left their houses and their plans, and possessions – vanities;
they befriended Fear of God, their necks leaving to the sword,
and inherited heaven's bliss.

- And say in a lovely voice.
All the martyrs say: "Our crown is intact, our reward is kept,
and the Kingdom we have gained, that of Christ whom we have loved.
Though passing through fire and sword, Christ our anguish comforted
in the joys of his Paradise."

- Your Kingdom is a kingdom forever.
Martyrs were invited to heaven above and eternal life;
that which ear has never heard, and which eye has never seen;
and into the heart of man, joys which never have entered,
for the victors who loved Jesus Christ.

- Take up armor and shield and come to my aid.
The martyrs of truth wore the Spirit's armor, and went down to fight.
Children and youth gathering to see the sight yet unseen:
men contending against death, and defeating it while killed.
Wonder marvelous too great for words!

- Look to him and hope in him.
O holy martyrs, you saw Jesus Christ reigning in heaven;
from life in this passing world, you arrived at perfection,
and were worthy to give praise, with the spirits gathering,
to our God, the Lord of creation.

- The eyes of the Lord are upon the just.
The holy martyrs looked at Jesus Christ with the Spirit's eye;
they mirrored him in their pains, for they heard his voice which said:
"he who bears his pains for me, here on earth from sons of men,
will delight in my paradise."

Martyr Hymns

- He spread a cloud and hid them.
A great cloud of light will carry the saints on the day they rise,
when the majesty is shown of the heav'nly King of kings.
There above, they will delight sitting placed at Christ's right hand,
for they loved and kept all his commands.

- They did not know or understand.
Though the king commanded the three children go into the furnace,
the fourth one who was with them sprinkled dew upon their face;
as hot as the fire burned, their faces were glorious.
Blessed is God who lifts up his saints.

- Before all the people.
All the martyrs say: "We will never de-ny the Son of God,
for we are Abraham's seed, and the heirs of Jacob's line.
For the God of our fathers, we have died a death in time,
and inherited eternal life.

- May his evil return to him.
Such a wicked king, who enraged with wrath and with jealousy,
brought sharp nails and fastened them into an innocent child.
But Christ came to help and aid the victor Mar Quryaqos;
may his prayers be a wall for us.

- He strengthened his heart and did not fear.
Martyr Mar Pithyon stood up valiantly before the magi,
and chastised their insolence in their great idolatry.
Rather, they must worship God, who made both heaven and earth,
and whose kingdom will last forever.

- From a merciless people.
Bitter sufferings and ugly torments, and various deaths,
were endured by the martyr, holy George victorious,
for the love of Christ the Lord, whom he loved more than his life:
blessed is he who crowns his martyrs.

- The Lord keeps his faithful ones.
By Mary's pray'rs, the virgin and the mother all-blessed,
may your worshippers be kept from all the deceiver's schemes;
Grant us to fulfill your will in our words as in our deeds,
and to sing you praise at all times.

Martyr Hymns

- Glory to the Father, to the Son and to the Holy Spirit.
Holy martyrs, hail! O friends of Christ, who won victory
and who gained the glorious crown, shaming Satan in the fight.
Blessed are you on that day when the light of Christ will dawn,
and you share the banquet with him.

- From age to age, amen, amen.
O garment of grace by the Spirit weaved, O holy patron,
by your faithfulness and deeds, you made grace flow like a spring
and watered your flock with words of the life of Spirit, and
so, the crown of victory is yours!

- Let all the people say: Amen, amen.
On sea and land, we call to you: come, Lord to our aid.
Answer him who calls on sea; turn to him who calls on land.
We call to you, Lord, as well: come and save us by your grace,
and protect us from the evil one.
* Christ, who pacified heaven and earth by his precious Blood:
reconcile priests and kings, and uphold your holy Church.
Let one goal of faithfulness reign in all who dwell on earth,
by your grace, compassionate God.
* By your great grace, bless and protect, O merciful Lord,
this land and those who live here from demons and evil men.
Grant increase in all good things, love, and peace, and harmony,
and good health of body and soul.
* Cast Satan out, the enemy of all righteousness,
from the houses where we live; let him never enter them.
Firmly place their foundation on the rock of faithfulness,
and grant life eternal to us.

Martyr Hymns

THURSDAY MORNING PRAYER – *shlama l-sahde*

- For he speaks peace to your people and to your just ones.
To martyrs, peace, to their bones greatest honor,
to their Lord glory, and to us, aid by their prayers.

- And in your light we see light.
Martyrs in light, and apostles with the Groom,
and lo, they sing praise, to the One who dwells in light.

- And say in a lovely voice.
The martyrs say, when they enter the kingdom:
"Glory to you, Lord; all who hope in you are saved."

- None who hope in you will be shamed.
The martyrs say: "We take refuge in your cross,
compassionate Lord. Let no violence come to us."

- He divided the sea and let them pass.
Martyrs, who passed over fire to Eden,
pray we never drown in the surging sea of sin.

- Their blood is precious in his eyes.
Christ, who received martyrs' blood when they were killed,
receive our pleading; open your door to our pray'r.

- The Lord is glorified above.
Heaven above, and a treasury unbound,
contain the good works of the martyrs, friends of Christ.

- Your throne is established from the beginning.
O Son who has set his Kingdom's throne above:
let your holy ones keep the earth which our sins shake.

- Sing to the Lord with harp and song.
With hallowings, and the songs of the Spirit,
the holy ones sing, and the armies quake in fear.

- O Lord, in the morning you hear my voice.
Every morning, the martyrs arise to pray,
and ask for your help for the souls of us sinners.

- In the morning, I prepare and present myself to you.
On the morning when the martyrs gain their prize,
have pity on us, at the hour when you come.

Martyr Hymns

- **Offer him a sacrifice of praise.**
Martyrs, who were pure oblations to their Lord:
may your prayer be our fortress both night and day.
- **Blessed are those on the path without fault.**
Martyrs rejoice when they hear the voice which says:
"Inherit new life, blessed ones of my Father."
- **They walk in the law of the Lord.**
Blessed are you whose Lord made you treasuries,
and who are recalled on the altar forever.
- **The Lord does good to the good.**
O athletes blest, who depicted their image
in heaven above, not on earth where all decays.
- **To the upright of heart.**
Martyrs are blest at the time when good and bad
are each set apart; they become the Kingdom's heirs.
- **The dwelling of the angels of the Lord.**
O Gregory, Basil, and John Chrysostom:
pray that we be kept from the dark of heresies.[58]
- **And your prayers for us all.**
O Mar Ephrem, and all teachers of the truth:[59]
may your prayer be our fortress both night and day.
- **A land where there is no fear.**
In the chamber full of light, at Christ's right hand,
there all the martyrs dwell in his unceasing delight.
- **How good and beautiful.**
How beautiful is the glory that the just
will wear on the day that the faithful are raised up.
- **In heaven and earth.**
Your flesh on earth, and your soul is in heaven,
O martyr St. George: plead for mercies from your Lord.
- **Light has dawned in the darkness for the upright.**
O Christ who dawned from the Virgin mother's womb,
by your mother's pray'r, keep your Church from every harm.

---

[58] Originally: "O Diodore, Theodore, Nestorius, pray lest the darkness of the Egyptians enter the Church."

[59] Originally: "O Mar Ephrem, Mar Narsai, Mar Abraham…"

Martyr Hymns

- Glory to the Father, to the Son and to the Holy Spirit.
Peace to the Church, and to all who dwell in her;
praise to the great Power who empowered the martyrs.
- From age to age, amen, amen.
Patron, who was pure oblation to his Lord,
may your petition be our fortress both night and day.
- Let all the people say: Amen, amen.
O Lord, may the prayer of your servants be
appea-sing to you, and grant forgiveness to us.
* Into your house I come and I worship at
your throne, Merciful One: forgive all my sins and faults.
* This holy house is a symbol of heaven;
let us all enter it in love and without deceit.

Martyr Hymns

Friday Evening Prayer – *mara d-kulla*

- All this happened, and we did not stray.
O Jesus Christ, the Savior, the Lord and King of glory,
the martyrs who have loved you have put the devil to shame.
With the angels rejoicing, they stand before God's throne now,
indeed, they have subjected the enemy beneath their feet.

- We have not denied your covenant.
O Jesus Christ, the Savior who died for our salvation,
and treads the path to heaven: the martyrs walked your footsteps!
They gave their bodies to torture, to fire and to torment,
and gained, by their own necks' blood, kingly, eternal life above!

- The sound of praise and salvation in the dwelling of the just.
At the voice of the martyrs, who sowed peace in creation,
the angels fly, descending, down to the sanctuary.
The ranks of angels cry out along with all the martyrs:
"Holy are you, O Lord of all, who raised the race of mortals!"

- For he has worked a marvel.
The splendid martyrs, athletes, set up a marvel for us:
they saw swords flash like lightning, and their murderers growling;
they did not shake or weaken in their great love of their Lord;
death they received like a gift, and did not cease confessing.

- They did not hold themselves back from death.
O killed who loved their Maker, and willingly received death,
became rational sacrifice for Christ the King who crowned them:
offer with us petition, on that great day of testing,
that we be saved from torture, and become heirs of heaven.

- Offer him a sacrifice of praise.
O martyrs, willing sacrifice, who pleased their Lord in their lives,
and by the blood of their necks gained the unending Kingdom:
plead and supplicate the Lord that we sinners may be saved,
for we take refuge in you; may peace increase among us.

- He sent his word and he healed them.
The martyrs became doctors throughout the whole creation;
they healed and made souls healthy who had been sickened with sin.
Thanks to the Lord who chose you, and placed his pow'r in your bones,
that you may be a harbor for all the race of mortals.

Martyr Hymns

- He brought them to the port they desired.
The place of holy relics is a port of serenity,
a fount of healing mercy which you have made, O Savior.
May the power that comes down and works always in their bones,
protect all your adorers from tricks of the deceiver.

- I will exalt you, O Lord my King.
The King above and his saints visit the ranks of faithful;
the order came they be killed, the just martyrs by the sword.
The Chaldeans then marveled; they raised their fingers and said:
"The God of the faithful is great; invisible, he saves them."

- The great King over all the gods.
The King of lofty places built his castle in heaven
and then named it Jerusalem of the firstborn, as written.
The ladder he established, in the Church, where he raises
his family to dwell in the Kingdom they inherit.

- Take up armor and shield and come to my aid.
The armor of the Spirit was worn by all the martyrs
when they extended their necks before the swords of their foes.
They disregarded tortures out of their love for Jesus,
and gained, by the blood of their necks, the Kingdom that does not end.

- The princess stands in beauty.
The Church resembles the ark; the altar is like the throne;
the martyrs, ranks of angels who all serve the Messiah.
It is built with jasper, with sapphires and crystals;
its builders Peter and Paul, as well as John and Andrew.[60]

- I will speak peace unto you.
Peace unto you, Quryaqos, athlete of Jesus the King;
peace to the place where you dwell, which gives health to the sickly.
Peace be unto your body, which is a fount of blessings,
peace to you and your mother; and thanks to God who triumphed.

- Plead to the Lord and pray to him.
O worker of the Spirit, splendid martyr Mar Sargys:
the great Pearl without blemish, brought shining light to your soul.
With your own blood you bought it, and gained unending fortune.
Pray for the Church and her sons, for love and peace and harmony.

---

[60] Originally: "as well as Theodore and Nestorius."

Martyr Hymns

- Lift the sword on your back, O warrior.
O general St. George who, looked down on death and the sword,
and bitter amputations, and every kind of torture,
you accomplished great wonders, and brought all men to the truth:
blest is he who gave victory, where error is defeated.

- They say this among the nations.
Blest are you, holy virgin, blest are you, Christ's own mother,
blest are you, whom all ages and generations call blest!
blest, you who pleased the Father, blest, you who housed the Savior,
blest, you whose name the Spirit made conquer in creation.

- Glory to the Father, to the Son and to the Holy Spirit.
Praise the Father who chose you, O splendid, holy martyrs;
glory to Christ, whose power upheld you in the battle;
glory now to the Spirit, who weaved your crowns in heaven.
Your prayer be our fortress, until the end of ages!

- From age to age, amen, amen.
O patron, splendid victor: your reward is in heaven.
Christ who formed you in virtue remembers you in the Church.
Your love was like incense; you pleased your Lord by your works.
Plead for us, that when he comes, he may have mercy on us.

- Let all the people say: Amen, amen.
O King of kings, our comfort, you are the Christ, our Savior:
forgive us who call to you in this time of great trouble.
Miseries now surround us, and every side has dangers.
May your mercies come quickly; brighten your face and save us.
* O Merciful forever, Compassionate for ages,
what is sin in creation, to mercies overflowing?
Sprinkle the dew of forgiveness upon the face of our race;
redeem us from the evil one, and from the sons of error.
* Adam and all the righteous, Moses and all the prophets,
Peter and all apostles, Stephen and all the martyrs,
Ephrem and all the teachers, Anthony and all hermits,
plead unto you, Lord Jesus, to have mercy on the world.
* May the deceased who wore you in the waters of baptism
be purified in body from all the stains of their sins.
May those who ate your Body and drank of your living Blood
be remembered by you, Lord, in the land of the righteous.

Martyr Hymns

Friday Morning Prayer – *brykh ḥayla*

- I will bless the Lord at all times.
Blest is the Power that is hidden and that dwells in martyrs' bones,
for though they are in their tombs, they chase out *de*mons from the world;
through their teaching they confronted
sinful nations, teaching them to a*dore* you,
who alone are Lord and God.

- And at all times, his praises in my mouth.
Blessed is Christ, who gave his apostles twelve a mighty arm,
and they went out to the world preaching his *Go*spel and his peace;
with the sword of God's own Spirit,
they beat darkness and turned us all *from* error
to the knowledge of the Truth.

- Great is the Lord and highly glorious.
Great is the truth of the holy martyrs who preached in the world.
With no fire and no sword they stood up *to* the pagan kings.
Nothing in the world could shake them,
for they trusted and confessed in *God* alone,
and saw persecution small.

- The Lord is faithful in his words.
In faithfulness, the just martyrs were tested and made victors.
For they knew the word was truthful which our *Lord* had said to them:
"He who confesses me in this world,
he will inherit the kingdom in hea*ven* above,
and my Father will know him."

- Look to him and hope in him.
With Spirit's eye, the true sons at God's right hand beheld the truth.
For there is a world above behind the *veil*, the holy place,
On the road of persecution,
they ran to find what they longed for and *crossed* the bridge,
of the cross to gain Eden.

- Let your right hand rest on us, O Lord.
Our Lord's right hand, which calls all to the Kingdom, blesses our Church,
which keeps vigil on the feast day which re*mem*bers the martyrs,
that by their prayers we are blessed,

Martyr Hymns

and that they may be our mighty fortress on *the* last day,
when height and depth are fulfilled.
- **The dwelling of the angels of the Lord.**
The blessed rank of the martyrs, splendid athletes, amazing ones:
how could they look down on this world and all *of* the joys it has?
By the glorious Pearl on the cross,
they looked and saw the truth with the *bri*ghtest eyes,
and desired to take it.
- **And your prayers for us all.**
Splendid martyrs, by your prayers give assistance to the poor,
for you have filled up the whole world by the *good* seed of your works,
and you pulled up all the weeds which
the evil one had planted, and put in their place the *Word* of God,
O athletes, workers of truth.
- **How good and beautiful.**
A spotless Pearl the athletes saw with their eyes on Golgotha,
and the wished to go and find it and buy *it* with their own blood.
They endured all kinds of torture,
for its sake and the reward of their work *now* is kept:
great delights which have no end.
- **Great over all the earth.**
Great and raised high is the glorious, honored place prepared for you.
Christ the King accomplished this for those who *strive* to be with him,
those who love him and confess him.
So now their feast day is known all o*ver* the earth;
blest is he who lifts his saints.[61]
- **Blessed are those on the path without fault.**
Victorious ones built on the foundation of the seventy-two,
Mar Eugene, Mar Shaleta, and Mar Me*lis* with Mar Babai,

---

[61] Two verses removed from the Catholic books:
 - **I stand my feet upon the rock.** The true ones built their foundation upon Simon Kepa's truth: Diodore, Theodore, with Nestorius, great Ephrem, Mar Narsai and Mar Barṣawma, the blessed pair, with Abraham and Job and John and Michael, the heirs of the Church.
 - **That will not shake forever and ever.** The saints built upon the foundation of the truth of St. Anthony, Mar Sabrisho', Mar Ḥnanysho', Mar John son of the seers, Maran'ammeh Zyzana, Mar Shuḥa Lmaran, peace upon him, the monk Pransi, Mar Yawsip, Mar Qnowaya, and Ysho'Sawran, Rabban Hormizd: their prayer be our fortress.

Martyr Hymns

ven'rable Jacob of Soba,
Mar Aḥḥa and Mar Yoḥannan:
may their prayers be our wall.[62]
- I will bless the Lord at all times.
Blessed is Christ, who strengthened Mar Quryaqos in his trial,
to stand before his pursuers and made *him* stronger than kings.
By the Spirit's pow'r he triumphed
and endured tortures as a sacrifice *for* his Lord,
and received a glorious crown.
- Be glad, sing and glorify.
In great gladness, splendid martyr George endured all afflictions.
Knowing that those who labor here will be *made* victorious.
For he heard St. Paul who had said:
"The sufferings of this present time can*not* compare
to the glories that will come."
- She brings her virgin companions with her.
Eternal Virgin, Mary, blessed mother, plead to Christ for us,
that his peace may dwell in us, in the tem*ple* reserved for him,
that, the day you are remembered,
he may help, as he did Abram, all *those* in need,
that they may receive his aid.
- Glory to the Father, to the Son and to the Holy Spirit.
To you be praise, gracious Lord, whose kindness has upheld the saints,
whose grace has given them aid to conquer *those* who hated them,
and who ruined satan's power
when he saw the martyrs stood, and were *not* made weak
due to their trust in the Lord.
- From age to age, amen, amen.
Splendid patron, who pleased God from his own youth like Samuel,
and in his humility resembled *the* prophet Moses,
in his zeal was like Elijah,

---

[62] The original has "Mar Kodahway" in place of Melis, and a "Mar Abraham" after Jacob of Soba. It also has the following verse, not present in the Catholic books:
- They walk in the law of the Lord. They walked in the steps, and mirrored the works of these skillful ones: Mar Andrew, Mar Olog, Mar John the Arab, monk Salara and his mother, with Mar Mikha, Abbot Yazdad, Mar Hareth: may their prayer protect our assembly.

Martyr Hymns

in love of his Lord was like *Abraham*:
may his prayer protect us.
- **Let all the people say: Amen, amen.**
We offer thanks to your great Divinity, O our Good Lord,
for by your grace you protected all those *who* adore your name,
Your door is opened to penance,
and you do not withhold *your* great Gift,
from your flock, O God adored.

SATURDAY EVENING PRAYER – *sahde qaddyshe lwyshay nuhra*

- **Their gospel goes through all the earth.**
The holy martyrs were clothed with light,
when they went out to preach to all the earth,
the majestic Trinity: Father, Son and Holy Spirit.
- **And their words to the world's ends.**
The martyrs were like the angels,
for on earth they walked, like the common man,
but in spirit, up above, with the angels they would stride.
- **Bless the Lord, all his angels.**
The holy martyrs could be compared
to the angels' ranks, while on earth below:
they would suffer as they preached of the glorious Trinity.
- **They go to the sea in ships.**
O laborers, by your blood you gained
treasure that will not decay for all time:
plead for us and beg from Christ that his peace may dwell on earth.
- **His servants who do his will.**
Angels descend from the land of light,
and sing glory upon bones of the saints,
to him who made earthly ones worthy of joy with angels.
- **More precious than gold and fine gems.**
Like finest gold and most precious gems,
the bones of the saints are placed in the churches of Christ;
they distribute help and aid to those who shelter in them.

Martyr Hymns

- Light has dawned in the darkness for the upright.
Just as the sun dawns upon the world,
so the works of the saints dawn in the churches of God,
and whoever trusts in them will not be harmed by the dark.

- Splendor and glory before him.
The blessed martyrs saw your glory,
when they suffered on the cross for the sake of your name,
and they cried out as they said: "For your sake we give our lives."

- He spread a cloud and covered them.
Hananaiah's house in the furnace:
the three children overcame the great flames.
May their prayer protect us from all the deceiver's schemes.

- Blessed are those on the path without fault.
Blest are the martyrs who loved the Christ,
and looked down on this world in the fire of his love;
now they have found the reward for their labors on the earth.

- They walk in the law of the Lord.
Blessed are you, holy martyrs,
athletes who became victors in the fight.
Your bodies are in the church, and your souls with the angels.

- The Lord gives power to his people.
Christ, who empowered Mar Quryaqos,
who did not become weak in the power of the truth:
guard our gathering through him, from the evil one always.

- The Lord is the strength of his people.
Christ, who empowered martyr Pithyon,
to stand before the evil of the faithless magi:
strengthen us to overcome persecution and passions.

- Blessings to you and your soul.
Blessed your spirit, martyr St. George,
for as your Lord willed, you labored in this passing world,
and have now received reward with the saints in the Kingdom.

- They cry out from the mountain tops.
Blessed are you, Virgin-Mother:
what the prophets spoke of, apostles knew:
you, a virgin, bore the Christ, by the Holy Spirit's powe'r.

Martyr Hymns

- **Glory to the Father, to the Son and to the Holy Spirit.**
O holy martyrs, peace unto you,
peace to you who have conquered in the fight,
peace to you who loved the Lord, in all purity of heart.
- **From age to age, amen, amen.**
To the perfection of all the saints,
our splendid patron arrived by the help of God's grace.
Christ who lifts his holy ones: guard our churches by his pray'r.
- **Let all the people say: Amen, amen.**
Answer, O Lord, answer, our great Hope;
answer, God our Savior, and hear the sound of our voice.
Answer us in your mercies, Kind One who does not withhold.
* Your cross, O Lord, be the guardian
of the gathering you chose to be your catholic Church;
help us to fulfill your will, as in heaven, so on earth.
* The prayer that we offer to you,
come before your Majesty, O Jesus our Savior:
may your grace give us the strength to tread on the enemy.
* Your teaching is like a lamp of light;
David the prophet witnesses, like apostle Paul.
Come let us enjoy its streams, and walk in obedience.
* Open, O Lord, your mercy's treasure,
that we may receive salvation for our sinful souls,
like the thief who stole your grace, who was promised paradise.

Martyr Hymns

SATURDAY MORNING PRAYER – *bṣapra sahde*

- In the morning, O Lord, you hear my voice.
In the morning, the martyrs were called
to death while the Spirit wove their crowns.

- And in the morning, I prepare and present myself to you.
In the morning, the martyrs ran hard
to take their prize, their undying crown.

- In the morning, make your grace heard to me.
In the morning, our Lord called to them:
"Receive your prize, faithful laborers."

- Look to him and hope in him.
In the morning, martyrs saw the Spirit
weave the crown placed upon their heads.

- Light dawns in the darkness for the upright.
In the morning, the martyrs dawn like the sun,
and go out to meet Christ the Bridegroom.

- He is holy and fearful is his name.
In the morning, the martyrs cried out
with the angels: "Holy, holy God."

- They will bring him offerings.
In the morning, martyrs offer offerings,
their mouths' prayer, and their neck's own blood.

- The offering of my hands like an evening oblation.
In the morning, martyrs offer incense
to the King, with their offerings.

- Like a cloud of fine incense and a scent acceptable to God.
In the morning, martyrs placed incense
for him whose throne is ring-ed with fire.

- Be strengthened and strong of heart.
In the morning, martyrs encouraged,
each, one to one: "mock the wicked king."

- Before all the people.
In the morning, martyrs cried in court:
"We will not de-ny the Bridegroom Christ."

Martyr Hymns

- He rebukes kings to their faces.
In the morning, martyrs stood and faced
the wicked kings, and rebuked them all.

- For your sake we are killed daily.
O killed like me, and persecuted
for me: you are with me in heaven.

- We are considered like sheep for the slaughter.
Martyrs to death, their Lord to the cross,
and the Spirit weaving all their crowns.

- Your throne is established from the beginning.
Throne established, and the Prince enthroned;
the martyrs come and receive their crowns.

- Small and lofty ones.
In the morning, martyrs run to drink
the Wine which was prepared with a spear.

- The Lord will give power to his people.
O Power which helped the martyrs in their fight,
be with us, Lord, who worship you now.

- Open the doors of justice for me.
In the morning, the King opens up
his treasure and martyrs take their crowns.

- That I may enter them and give thanks to the Lord.
In the morning, Christ opened up Paradise,
the thief entered, and gained the Kingdom.

- When God stands to judge.
In the morning, our Lord will stand up
to judge the world, and crown the martyrs.

- How good and beautiful.
How good it is that young Quryaqos
rebuked the king, in defense of Christ.

- A mother rejoicing with her sons.
In the morning, Shmony encouraged
her sons to be unshaken in faith.

- Blessings to you and your soul.
Blessed are you, O great martyr
George, who is singing with angels above.

Martyr Hymns

- The daughters of Judah rejoice.
The faithful Church sings, rejoicing, the
day she recalls the blessed Virgin.
- Glory to the Father, to the Son and to the Holy Spirit.
O martyrs, hail! Glory to your Lord!
And through your pray'rs mercies and pity!
- From age to age, amen, amen.
Splendid patron, friend of Christ, plead for us
from your Lord, that he has mercy.
- Let all the people say: Amen, amen.
At dawn we thank, and at dawn we praise
the Lord who is our unfailing Light.
* In the morning, let our prayer rise
before your throne, O Merciful God.
* In the morning, we give thanks to you
who have ordered light to please creatures.

Selections from the *Ḥudhra*
i.e., Seasonal Propers

Subara/Advent & Christmas

First Week of Advent

Evening Psalmody (from Psalm 89)
Of old he spoke in a *vi*sion,
    Halleluiah, halleluiah, hal*le*luiah.
Of old he spoke in a *vi*sion,
    when he spoke to his *right*eous ones:
"I have set the crown upon one who is *mi*ghty,
    I have exalted one chosen *from* the people.
I have found David, my *ser*vant;
    with my holy oil I have a*noin*ted him;
so that my hand shall ever abide with *him*,
    my mighty arm shall *streng*then him.
Glory to the Father, to the Son and to the Holy *Spi*rit.
    From age to age, a*men*, amen.
Halleluiah, halle*lu*iah, hal*le*luiah.

Basilica Hymn
- Hear, O Shepherd of Israel.
- He who was before the ages.
- Indeed, he did not take it from the angels, but from the seed of Abraham.
God the Word, who is from the Father, did not assume the form of a servant from the angels, but rather from the seed of Abraham, and came in our humanity, by his grace, to save our race from error.

Vigil Hymn
- O God, give your judgment to the king.
- This is the great wide sea, and your judgments are like a great abyss.
- O the depth of the riches and wisdom and knowledge of God! Man cannot search his judgments or seek out his ways.

What mind can comprehend the sea of your Compassion, O God, the Depth of riches and Mind of eternal thought, who was with God from the beginning? By his love he chose to send us his Word, and he was clothed with a garment of flesh from the holy Virgin, and went out into the world. She learned thus from the angel: "Peace to you, full of grace, for from you the Great One and the Savior of the ages will be born." O Incomprehensible One, Lord of all: glory to you!

Madrasha

- Watchers and children, sing glory before the Child of the Virgin by whom our race was saved.

* The Being above all bowed down in his love to exalt the humble to the name of his Greatness. He raised the lowly to a divine station, and opened the treasure of his wisdom to them, that they may be enriched by his portions and distribute his wealth, rejoice without suffering, and reign without fear.

* By his signal, he descended to earth to lift up the sons of earth. He sent, before his Love, a watcher to the sleeping, to preach to them in his name the gospel of reconciliation. He gave them peace stamped in his name, that by his name they may return from the wandering path the evil one had tread for them by the breaking of the command.

* He gave the name of his greatness to one of the heavenly, and he carried it without senses and flew, arriving to earth. He sowed it in the hearing of a rib from Adam: "Peace to you, daughter of weak Eve, for in you the door of life will be opened for mortals, that those subjugated to death may receive their freedom."

Morning Hymn– *nawde w-nisgodh leh*

Lift up thanks and praise
to the eternal King
in whose Light created light.

Daniel Verse

The watcher sent from heaven,
came in fear unto Mary.
He hailed her with a greeting of peace,
hope and life for us mortals.

Advent & Christmas

Sanctuary Hymn – *ḥannana dapthyḥ*
- **Come hear this, all you nations.**
- **A just and righteous one.**
Gabriel said un-to Zechariah:
You will have a son, and shall name him John.
He will tread the path for the King of Kings
who comes in glory to save all the world.

SECOND WEEK OF ADVENT

Evening Psalmody (from Psalm 103)
The grace of the Lord is e*ter*nal,
  Halleluiah, halleluiah, hal*le*luiah.
The grace of the Lord is e*ter*nal,
   and is unto the ages over *those* who fear him.
His justice is for the sons of their *sons*,
   for those who *keep* his covenant.
Glory to the Father, to the Son and to the Holy *Spi***rit.**
   From age to age, a***men*, amen.**
Halleluiah, halle*lu*iah, hal*le*luiah.

Basilica Hymn
- **He who was before the ages.**
- **His name was before the sun.**
- **This is the mystery hidden from the ages in God who created all.**
The great Mystery that had been hidden for centuries and for generations has been revealed to us in the final age: the Only-Begotten One, who was in the Womb of his Begetter, came and assumed the form of a servant in his grace; and he related and revealed to us the perfect faith of the Trinity.

Vigil Hymn
- **O God, have mercy on us.**
- **For you, O Lord, are good.**
- **You are merciful, O Lord, and just.**
O Lord, in your mercies, you bowed down toward the earthly, as the Friend of man. You know requests before they are made, and you know all actions

before they are done; you cause the change of ages and times, and never take away the blessings of your gift from the earthly. You look and see sinners, O Lord, and disregard our faults, for you are God, and in your mercies you bowed down toward the earthly, as the Friend of man. O Lord of all, glory to you!

Madrasha
- To you glory, radiant Son of virginity.
* This, the month that is forever filled with blessings: slaves have freedom, free men glory, doors have crownings, bodies feastings, violet garments thrown with love as unto princes.
* This, the month that will forever carry victory: freed is spirit, flesh is tempered, mortal woman bears the Living: Godhead now is reconciled with human nature.
* This, the month when slaves recline upon fine beddings, and the free recline on carpets, kings themselves asleep on matting: in a manger sleeps the Lord of all, for all's sake.

Morning Hymn – *nawde w-nisgodh leh*
In love, we present
our bodies and souls
to him who is Light from Light.

Daniel Verse
Gabriel the archangel
came to Mary from heaven.
He announced of the birth of the Christ,
who dawned for our salvation.

Sanctuary Hymn – *byadh shlama*
- **He makes the winds blow and the waters flow.**
In deepest winter, when all the earth is barren,
Lord Jesus was revealed in the womb of the Virgin.
He is the Cause of all benefits -
the greatest Hope of creation.
He is indeed the true Light, Lord and Messiah,
adorable with his Father and Spirit.

Advent & Christmas
Third Week of Advent

Evening Psalmody (from Psalm 8)
Who is man, that you remember *him*,
    Halleluiah, halleluiah, hal*le*luiah.
Who is man, that you remember *him*,
    and the son of man, that *you* command him?
You have made him little less than the *a*ngels,
    and clothed him with ho*nor* and glory,
and given him authority over the work of your *hands*,
    and placed everything un*der* his feet:
Glory to the Father, to the Son and to the Holy *Spi*rit.
    From age to age, *a*men, amen.
Halleluiah, halle*lu*iah, hal*le*luiah.

Basilica Hymn
- My heart overflows with noble words.
- He who was before the ages, and before the sun is his name.
- He is the living God, who stands forever.

He who is neither understood nor limited by creatures has accomplished his plan in our humanity: indeed, the divine Nature has joined to the human nature he has assumed, while not changing. The Virgin gave birth in holiness to Christ, the Power of God and his Wisdom. While adoring, we confess Him to be the one Son who is the Savior of the world.

Vigil Hymn
- I will exalt you, Lord, for you lifted me up.
- It was sick but you strengthened it.
- You pacified it and greatly enriched it.

You have visited creation, O Lord, through the true Son. The Child that is from you has been seen, he who, on the day of his annunciation, undid and erased the sound that decreed judgment upon our race: "You will return to dust, Adam, because you sinned." And the spiritual assemblies who had been distanced from our service because we sinned, he made preachers who cried out renewal to us as they said: "Good news upon you, O mortals who had corrupted, for lo, the Savior who will free you has arrived. Henceforth glorify Christ without ceasing, the Savior of the world."

Advent & Christmas

Madrasha

- Glory to the One who sent the watcher to Mary, and announced to her the conception of Jesus our Savior.

* Men heard a new thing in the conception of the daughter of man, for the daughter of man sprouted a Wheat Stalk without a seed, and buried in her mortality the Leaven of life. "Lo, you will conceive and bear a son," he said. When has this happened, or ever been heard, that virgins give birth to children without seed?

* "The power of the Most High will overshadow you," he said," to engrave the Image of man in the tablet of your body, and the Shoot of wonder will sprout from your womb. This is easy for his wisdom, for as he fashioned Adam, and made his rib into Eve, he can compose a Child within you without seed."

* The girl saw a man who was true in his promises, and she began to reveal to him the truth of her own mind, if she accepted the Seed which fell in her hearing: "Lo, I am the handmaid of the Lord; may the good news of your words be fulfilled in deed, and may the Image of the house of Adam rest in my body."

Morning Hymn – *nawde w-nisgodh leh*

In awe, let us all
sanctify our lips
praising him who gives us light.

Daniel Verse

Glorious is your unveiling,
which the prophets preached in symbols:
by your dawning from Mary,
you fulfilled their words in deed.

Sanctuary Hymn – *byadh shlama*

- **Proclaim his salvation from day to day.**

The greeting heard by Mary flowed with all graces:
she would conceive the Christ with no seed or joining:
on her alone would the Spirit come;
in her would dwell the Almighty's Power.
She is most-blessed of women, in her is our Hope:
Adored be God, who pitied our race!

Advent & Christmas
Fourth Week of Advent

Evening Psalmody (from Psalm 36)
How many are your mercies, O *God*.
    Halleluiah, halleluiah, hal*le*luiah.
How many are your mercies, O *God*.
    The sons of men are covered in the shadow *of* your wings.
They drink from the best things of your *house*,
    and you give them drink from your *plea*sant valley.
For the fount of life is with *you*,
    and in your light *we* see light.
Keep your mercies for your *friends*,
    and your justice for the up*right* of heart.
Glory to the Father, to the Son and to the Holy Sp*ir*it.
    From age to age, a*men*, amen.
Hal*le*luiah, halle*lu*iah, hal*le*luiah.

Basilica Hymn
- I will exalt you, O Lord my King.
- His lightning lights up the world. At the edge of the sky is his departure.
- The Ray of justice has shone from the house of David.

The Splendor of the Father who was revealed from the house of David in our humanity has been seen: he reigns over the house of Jacob, and there is no end to his authority. An angel announced to Mary; he gave a greeting full of mercies to the Virgin, and announced a hope full of blessings to the holy woman: "Peace be with you, blessed among women, full of hope! Peace be with you, and blessed are you, giver of birth without joining! For from you will dawn the Lord of height and depth and all within them! To him be glory from every mouth!" O Lord, glorious is the day of your annunciation!

Vigil Hymn
- Proclaim his salvation from day to day.
- The hope of all the ends of the earth.
- The world and all who dwell in it.

The whole creation to its ends is filled with good hope through your revelation in the flesh, Only-Begotten Word, who took on the vestment for his own Existence which the Signal had woven in the womb of flesh of the daughter of David, as it had been promised from of old: "I will sit one from among your seed forever and ever in heaven."

Madrasha

- Glorious is your annunciation, O Gladdener of all, Christ who came for our salvation.

* Who indeed, while mortal, can make known the One who gives life to all? For he left the height of his greatness, and was lowered to smallness. O One who lifted up all in his birth, lift up my miserable mind that I may make your birth known, not to reduce your greatness, but rather to preach your grace. Blessed is the One who was hidden and revealed in his histories.

* It is a great marvel that the Son dwelt entirely in the body. He dwelt in it entirely and it was enough for him; he lodged in it while not being limited. His will was entirely in it; his limit was not entirely in it. Who is sufficient to speak of this? While he was entirely dwelling in the body, he also was entirely dwelling everywhere. Blessed is he who is never limited.

* Your greatness is hidden from us, and your grace is unveiled to us. I will be silent, O Lord, about your greatness, and make known your grace. Your grace drew you back, and bowed you down to our humanity. Your grace made you a Child; your grace made you a Man. Your grace contracted and expanded. Blessed is your Power, which became small and increased.

Morning Hymn – *shlama l-sahde*

Good News of peace
the head of the angels preached,
when you were conceived,
Christ the Great Light of the world.

Daniel Verse

Blest, the Light from the Father,
whose rays shone in our nature,
who was born of Mary, David's child,
for all creatures' salvation.

Sanctuary Hymn – *byadh shlama*

- **These are new things he has done.**

Our Lady marveled at what the angel told her:
she who did not know man would conceive a child;
He who had made Adam from the dust,
and fashioned Eve without need for man,
who blest Sarah and Rachel and Eliza-beth,
would bring a child from the Virgin's womb.

Advent & Christmas
THE HOLY FEAST OF THE BIRTH OF OUR LORD

Evening Psalmody (from Psalm 87)
Its foundations are on his holy *moun*tain:
    Halle*luiah, halleluiah, hall*eluiah.
Its foundations are on his holy *moun*tain:
    the Lord loves the gates of Zion
        more than all *Ja*cob's dwellings.
Honorable things are said in *you*,
    O village *of* our God...
"It was there that he was *born*";
    and of Zion it *shall* be said:
"The Great Man was *born* there,
    and he *has* established her."
The Lord will count his people in his *reg*ister:
    "It was there that *he* was born."
Glory to the Father, to the Son and to the Holy *Spir*it.
    From age to age, a*men*, amen.
Halleluiah, halle*lu*iah, hall*e*luiah.

Basilica Hymn (selection) – *ḥannana da-pthyḥ*
- There I will make a horn to sprout for David.
In the flesh was born, from the house of David,
Christ our Life-Giver, whose birth gladdened all.
The Lord of glory is from the Father
and in human flesh: Christ, the seed of Abraham.
- From those who walk in innocence.
Christ the Lord was born of the Virgin Mary,
and is of the seed of David and Abraham.
His Majesty's power is placed in his hand;
his authority rules heaven and earth.
- Praise him and sing to him.
Angels glorified, and their ranks cried out:
"Glory in heaven, and peace upon earth!"
The whole mortal race sang and glorified,
on the birth of Christ, who has saved our race.

Advent & Christmas

- From then the nations will praise with him.
Nations and gentiles, come and glorify
Jesus Christ the Lord who has saved our race,
turned our ignorance to the light of truth,
and gave us, in grace, his eternal life.
- He will be like a tree planted near a stream of water.
The Fruit of Gladness dawned from Mary's womb;
he forgave our sins and erased our debts.
He came, searched for us, raised our death to life,
and renewed our race that had drowned in sin.
- Gladness over all the earth.
At the birth of Christ, the angels proclaimed:
"Glory in heaven and peace upon earth."
O mortals, come now, take the bond of sin,
the Fruit of Mary's womb has redeemed our race.

Vigil Hymn
- The Lord is King, enrobed with majesty.
- Who will make known the wonders of the Lord; Who is like you, Lord?
- For even if all creatures were one mouth and tongue, they would not suffice to make known your greatness, O Lord.
Who is able to relate your grace, O Maker? For you saved Adam from death through the Principal from our race. Thus all the nations who were sitting in darkness offer you praise without ceasing, and exult with their voices, glorifying in holiness, confessing with the holy cherubim and seraphim, saying: "Holy, holy, holy is the great day of your birth, for on it great hope and salvation came to us." O Christ who came for our salvation, forgive us and have mercy on us!
- From age to age, amen, amen. (selection) – *ayna d-athe l-ba'utha*
The Son of God showed the truth to his Church betrothed when he
chose, in love, to come reveal he is God and he is man.
>For he had been in the womb of his Father, for all time,
>without beginning or end: truly, he is God indeed.

He came to us in our days, was clothed in humanity,
and saved us as Son of Man, truly, he is man indeed.
>The prophets proclaimed him in their teachings and made him known
>through their inspired writings, truly, he is God indeed.

He was carried for nine months in the Virgin Mary's womb
and was born in a manger, truly, he is man indeed.
> Angels came and worshipped him, truly, he is God indeed.
> He was placed in a manger, truly, he is man indeed.

The star preached him in the East, truly, he is God indeed.
Mary fed him with her milk, truly, he is man indeed.
> The magi of Persia came and brought him glorious gifts
> and made offerings to him, truly, he is God indeed.

He was circumcised and made offerings in the temple
according to the old law, truly, he is man indeed.
> Simeon called him a light to the nations and the glory
> of the people Israel, truly, he is God indeed.

With Joseph and Mary he fled to Egypt from Herod,
the wicked, tyrannic king truly, he is man indeed.
> The shepherds ran in great joy to honor his holy birth,
> and they knelt and worshiped him, truly, he is God indeed.

He grew up before the Lord, and advanced in his stature,
in his wisdom and in grace, truly, he is man indeed.
> Blessed be God who provides the salvation of mankind!
> To him glory, and on us his great mercies, at all times.

Madrasha

- Glory to him who saved us by his birth from Mary, and granted us to share with him in the Kingdom.

* The height of the Lord of all is incomprehensible to all, and his limit cannot be imagined by the mind. It is the height of understanding by which he reigns: he becomes small and then great, while remaining the same; and while he has no limit, he becomes like one with a limit. Blessed is he who contracted his size to bring us near to him.

* His visage cannot be searched or imagined by the mind; he hears without ears; he speaks without mouth; he makes without hands; he sees without eyes. And the soul can neither persist nor cease considering what this means: he put on, in his grace, the vestment of our humanity, and named us in his likeness.

* There is no space that can surround or contain him, nor a depth that can search or suffice for him. His Existence is great, and so also his Fatherhood. He condemns and overwhelms space and mind. And if there is no space sufficient for his Existence, whose mind can suffice to examine his Fatherhood?

Madrasha 2

- Glory to the Child whose Father is of heaven, whose mother is of earth, and who is incomprehensible.

* I saw a great wonder in Bethlehem ministered to before the eyes of all creatures, for the star ministered before the Divine Prince. The star runs, the star leads, the star directs, the star announces; the star an ambassador, the star a preacher, the star arrives at the door of the house of the King.

* Peace to Mary who bore, and raised, and suckled, and carried, and rejoiced. Peace to the small manger that depicted a symbol of the holy altar. Peace to the cave, peace to the swaddling-cloths, peace to the Bridegroom, peace to Gabriel. Peace in heaven, peace on earth, peace to our entire assembly.

* There the books are fulfilled in the birth of the Son, the Lord of Mysteries. There the crowns of kings, the sons of warriors, are thrown before his feet. There is the gold, there is the myrrh, there is the frankincense, there is Joseph. There are the angels, there are the hallowings, there are the halleluiahs without end.

Morning Hymn – *abbun d-bashmayya*

Peace be unto you, O people of God:
Jesus Christ is born, the Light of the world.

Daniel Verse

Blest, the Child, who called Magi,
through a star, to adore him.
When they came, they brought gifts unto him:
gold and frankincense and myrrh.

Sanctuary Hymn – *byadh shlama*

- And before the sun is his Name.
The Child who had been hidden from all the angels,
has filled the earth with grace as the Savior of all:
he has come and was revealed through Flesh.
Thus we sing: Glo-ry to God on high!
And with the shepherds, preach him,
for peace upon earth.
May his good hope rest within our souls!

Advent & Christmas

The Solemnity of the Blessed Virgin Mary

Evening Psalmody (from Exodus 15)
Then Miriam the prophetess, sister of Aaron, took a timbrel in her *hand*,
    Halleluiah, halleluiah, hal*le*luiah.
Then Miriam the prophetess, sister of Aaron, took a timbrel in her *hand*,
    and all the women went out after her with timbrel and *tam*bourine.
Miriam sang to *them*,
    Glorify the *glo*rious Lord
Glory to the Father, to the Son and to the Holy *Spi*rit.
    From age to age, a*men*, amen.
Halleluiah, halle*lu*iah, hal*le*luiah.

Basilica Hymn
- Our God, our mighty stronghold.
- He has chosen a dwelling for himself.
The daughter of man became the Tree of Life for the whole mortal race, for the Glorious Fruit which dawned from her pours forth and grants all benefits. Come, O mortals, let us be brought near to the sweetness of his words, and sing praise to him!
- Glory to the Father and to the Son and to the Holy Spirit.
Through your pleading, O revered Mary, may peace reign in creation, and by your supplication, O full of hope, may the children of the Church be guarded. Come, O mortals, let us take refuge in the wings of the Blessed Mother, that we may be made worthy of forgiveness.

Vigil Hymn
- For he is your Lord, adore him.
- Plead to him and beg him, that he may forgive us.
The Church says to Mary: "Come, let us go together and plead to the Son of the Lord of all, on behalf of the wickedness of the world. You plead because you fed him with milk, and I will plead because he prepared his Blood for my wedding feast. You plead as a mother, and I as a bride, for he listens to his mother and answers his betrothed."

Advent & Christmas

Madrasha
- Blessed is the Fruit that dawned from you, O blessed woman.

* No one knows, O Lord, what to call your mother: if we call her a virgin, her Child arises; a married woman, no one has known her; and if your mother is incomprehensible, who could suffice for you!

* She alone is your mother, but your sister with all; she is your mother, she is your sister. She is also your betrothed, with all the chaste women. Lo, you have decorated the beauty of your mother with all things.

* Indeed, she was your betrothed, as was custom, before you came; but she conceived against custom after you came, O Holy One; and she was a virgin as she gave birth to you in holiness.

Morning Hymn – *abbun d-bashmayya*
Every age and time calls our Lady blest,
the virgin Mary, the mother of Christ.

Daniel Verse
On the feast day of Mary,
angels and men sing glory
for the Savior has dawned from her womb,
the Light come from the Father.

Sanctuary Hymn – *mara dkulla*
- **From the beginning to the end.**
O blessed virgin Mary, plead unto Christ for our sake,
that he may sow his mercies in us who shelter in you.
Let us rejoice on your feast day, and our sons be protected,
from all the false deceptions of the backbiter Satan.

The Commemoration of the Blessed Magi

Basilica Hymn
- **He speaks peace to his people and to his righteous ones.**
"Send our greeting to Jerusalem, and show this to the high priests," says Persia to the Magi. "With gold, go and honor the King who is born in Judah; with myrrh, proclaim his passion for our sake; with frankincense, show forth his Essence, for he shares with his Father in authority, and is the Lord God.

Indeed, the kingdom of Nimrod, who raised us, has approached, for lo, all nations are subjected under his rule. The star is before you: go, fall and adore him, and say to him, 'You are our King, and to you is thanksgiving due; O Lord of all, glory to you!'"

First Week after Christmas

Evening Psalmody (from Psalm 89)
Who is like the Lord in the heaven of *hea*vens,
   Hal*l*eluiah, halleluiah, hal*l*eluiah.
Who is like the Lord in the heaven of *hea*vens,
   or compares to him among the *sons* of God?
God stands in the church of the *saints*,
   great and fearful to *all* around him.
O Lord God al*migh*ty,
   who is power*ful* like you?
Glory to the Father, to the Son and to the Holy *Spi*rit.
   From age to age, a*men,* amen.
Hal*l*eluiah, halle*lu*iah, hal*l*eluiah.

Basilica Hymn
- I will exalt you, O Lord my King.
- As is your name, O Lord, so be your glories; O God, who is like you?
- He who is the invisible Image of God.
O Lord of all, while you are in the likeness of God, you assumed the likeness of a servant in your love, and you neither robbed your Divinity nor defrauded your humanity. Rather, in both natures you are truly one Son, undivided. Indeed, above you are without a mother, from the Father; and below, without a father, from a mother. Thus have the prophets anticipated and predicted; thus also have the apostles preached; and thus have the Fathers taught in the Church: so that, by their pleading and in their faith, you may protect us, O God, and have mercy on us.

Vigil Hymn
- Lord our Lord, how glorious is your name in all the earth.
- How lofty are your works, O Lord; I thank you for the wonder you worked.
- For this, the many nations praise you.

Because of the glorious greatness of the wonder of the day of your birth, the care that our Savior provided to all the heavenly and the race of the earthly, the angels looked from the heights to the depths in amazement, and they saw you, O Star of Light who dawned from Jacob. The magi's countenances looked from above without confusion, and saw there the Star of Bethlehem. They all gathered together in fear to the cave, and with fiery mouths and earthly lips, they hallowed and lifted praise to you. With them we glorify, that you may have mercy on us in the greatness of your mercies and your grace.

Madrasha

- Blessed is he who gladdened all by his birth, and accomplished the renewal of the race of mortals.

* On the day of your birth, Jesus our Savior, the magi rejoiced. They offered gifts on it; they kindled fire on it; they burned incense on it; the scribes were saddened on it; children were killed on it.

* Glory to the Hidden One whose birth was unveiled. Glory to the King whose bed was a manger. Glory to the child whose lamp was a star. Glory to the Bridegroom whose chamber was a cave. Glory to the Father, Son, and Holy Spirit.

* The mother who gave birth to him is worthy of blessings. The shoulder that carried him is worthy of memorial. The knees that lifted him are worthy of praise. The manger that sufficed for him is worthy of visitation. The cave where he slept is worthy of perfumes. The village where he was born is worthy of commemoration.

Morning Hymn – ḥannana dapthyḥ

In the flesh was born,
one from David's house,
Christ our Life-Giver,
whose birth gladdened all.
The Lord of glory
is from the Father,
and in human flesh:
Christ, the seed of Abraham.

Advent & Christmas

Daniel Verse
At your birth, Savior of all,
angels and men together
raised up praise and thanksgiving
to the Father who sent you.

Sanctuary Hymn – ḥannana dapthyḥ
- He who humbles the spirit of the powerful.
Because of the Child who came from Mary,
King Herod trembled, and Jerusalem.
Rachel wept and wailed;
children's blood was spilled.
But despite our sins,
all creatures were saved.

SECOND WEEK AFTER CHRISTMAS

Evening Psalmody (from Psalm 92)
How great are your works, O *Lord*,
    Halleluiah, halleluiah, hal*l*eluiah.
How great are your works, O *Lord*,
    and how very deep *are* your thoughts!
Miserable man does not *know*,
    and the ignorant man does not *un*derstand this.
Glory to the Father, to the Son and to the Holy *Spi*rit.
    From age to age, a*men*, amen.
Halleluiah, halle*lu*iah, hal*l*eluiah.

Basilica Hymn
- My heart overflows with noble words.
- He will sprout from his city like the grass of the earth.
- A comely and lovely plant; it produces leaves and forms almonds.
As is the staff of Aaron, which blossomed, so is the Virgin who conceived, O unbelieving ones! That which was neither planted nor watered, sprouted; the Virgin, then, without husband and seed conceived by the command of God. The staff showed a wonderful Fruit; and the Power of the Most High came and rested upon her who is full of grace, and made her worthy to give birth to Jesus

Christ, the Savior of the world, whom we adore and to whom we say: Great, O Lord, is the mystery of your gracious providence; glory to you!

Vigil Hymn
- **Praise the Lord from the heavens.**
- **More lovely in his looks than the sons of men.**
- **And lo, the star which they had seen in the east went before them.**

The course of the star above was to enlighten from east to west, and it was our preacher for your incomprehensible birth, not in words, but in radiance, and not in sound, but in its course. Indeed, it showed us and all creation the wonder of the revelation of your birth. O Savior of all, glory to you!

Madrasha
- Blessed is Christ, by whose birth gladdened earth and heaven.

* On this day, the Lord gladdened priests, kings, and prophets, and on it their words were fulfilled, and all were accomplished in deed. For on this day the virgin gave birth to Emmanuel in Bethlehem. The sound that Isaiah spoke today has become a reality.

* "This one will be born there," which is in the book which counts its people, the song that David sang, today is fulfilled. The word that Micah spoke, today is accomplished in deed, a Shepherd went out from Ephraim, and tended souls by his staff.

* Lo, the Star has dawned from Jacob, the Head has arisen from Israel. The prophecy that Balaam spoke today has an explanation. Indeed, the lofty Light has descended, and his beauty has dawned from a Body. The Dawn spoken of by Zechariah, today has shone in Bethlehem.

Morning Hymn – ḥannana dapthyḥ
Christ the Lord was born
of the Virgin Mary,
and is of the seed
of David and Abraham.
His Majesty's pow'r
is placed in his hand;
his authority
rules heaven and earth.

Daniel Verse
Blest, the Child dawned from Mary,
who, unveiled, brightened the world.
Through the star, messenger to your flock,
you revealed to us your power.

Sanctuary Hymn – *ḥannana dapthyḥ*
- **Hear this, all you nations.**
- **Henceforth praise him, all nations.**

Peoples and nations,
come and sing glory
to the Christ who saved
the whole human race.
He turned us from dark
to his radiant Light,
and gave us, in grace,
new, eternal life.

The Holy Feast of the Dawning of Our Lord
(*Dinḥa*/Epiphany)

Evening Psalmody (Psalm 29)
Bring forth to the Lord, O sons of men, * **Halleluiah, halleluiah, halleluiah.** Bring forth to the Lord glory and honor. * Bring forth to the Lord honor to his name. * Adore the Lord in his holy courtyard. * The voice of the Lord is upon the waters. * The glorious God thunders. * The Lord is upon the many waters. * The voice of the Lord in power, the voice of the Lord in glory. * The voice of the Lord which shatters cedars, * and the Lord breaks the cedars of Lebanon. * He makes them dance like calves, * Lebanon and Sirion, like the sons of bulls. * The voice of the Lord splitting the furnace of fire. * The voice of the Lord which shakes the wilderness, * and the Lord shakes the wilderness of Kadesh. * The voice of the Lord which shakes the trees and uproots the forests. * In his temple, everyone speaks praise. * The Lord overturns the flood. * The Lord sits as King forever. * The Lord gives power to his people, * and the Lord blesses his people with peace. * **Glory to the Father, to the Son and to the Holy Spirit. * From age to age, amen, amen. * Halleluiah, halleluiah, halleluiah.**

Basilica Hymn (selection)
- **Come, let us bless and adore him.**
- **We your people and the sheep of your flock.**

We adore your holy dawning, O Lord, which has gladdened us, for in it, by a wonder, you enlightened all the nations who sat in darkness and in the shadow of death. O Friend of mankind, glory to you!

- **Come, let us praise the Lord.**

Come, let us give thanks to Christ in whose revelation has freed us from error, has reconciled us with the Father by the oblation of his Body, and has pacified the exalted ones with us, who were enraged because of our wickedness. To him be glory, with his Sender!

Vigil Hymn
- **I will exalt you, O Lord my King.**
- **The great King over all the gods.**
- **He who loved us and gave himself for us has given us life by the washing of new birth.**

Epiphany

Christ the King freed creation and saved it from error by his revelation. He eradicated the authority of Satan, who had condemned our race in his envy. He became the glorious and perfecting Head of our faith by his baptism, in whose type we are baptized in the confession of the three Individuals of the Father, Son and Spirit, one Nature, one unlimited Power, he who is from eternity, and adored by all creatures.

Madrasha

\- Blessed is he who bowed down and was baptized in the Jordan river, and opened up heaven to mortals by his baptism.

* The image of the house of Adam, which was named the hidden image, rusted through sin, and became hateful through enticements. It overturned the decree of its miserable clay, and the hater mocked and derided it. The rational and the mute were saddened at its corruption, for the dwelling of their love had been wrecked by death.

* The Good One saw his image made hateful through sin, and he recast it in the crucible of water. He scoured its hatefulness, and plated its construction with the gold of the Holy Spirit. The heavenly marveled at the image, and those who were saddened at its decay rejoiced in its renewal. They returned to the order of the love required of them.

* The Signal joined them in one harmony to rejoice in the renewal of the image of the earthly one. They wove a crown of glory for the Hidden One with their songs, for he had renewed the image of man in his love, and revealed the love of his will to his creatures, for he wished that the image of his Hiddenness not be destroyed.

Morning Hymn – *abbun d-bashmayya*

The Light of the world has dawned from above:
Only-Begotten, Lord of creation.

Daniel Verse

Blest, he who opened heaven
by means of his baptism.
Fire and Spirit with water,
showed power to his people.

Epiphany

Sanctuary Hymn – *l-ḥayye w-ṭuwwe*
- **Your throne, O God, is forever.**
Cherubim stand in fear and awe
before your throne, O Mighty One;
they hide their faces with their wings,
lest they behold that fearful sight:
lest their eyes see your Divinity,
the Fire that burns bright unceasingly!
And yet you, so glorious,
choose to dwell among mankind,
not that you may burn,
but that you may shine.
Great, O Lord, is your compassion,
and your grace,
for you have visited our race!

MEMORIAL OF JOHN THE BAPTIST

Basilica Hymn
- **Chosen silver that is tried in the earth.**
- **Blessed is the people that has this.**
A portion of the heavenly treasure, which is desired by the angels, and by the prophets and apostles, and by the honored martyrs, Christ gave, in his grace, to the faithful Church: John the Baptist, he whose neck was sliced for the sake of the law of the love of God. Come, all you peoples, in awe and love, and in songs of the Holy Spirit, let us honor the day of his commemoration. He is indeed an unassailable rampart for our people.

FIRST WEEK OF EPIPHANY

Evening Psalmody (from Psalm 74)
Remember your *church*,
    Halleluiah, halleluiah, hal*le*luiah.
Remember your *church*
    which you established from *the* beginning,
and save the tribe of your in*her*itance.
    This is mount Zion, *where* you dwelt.

Epiphany

Glory to the Father, to the Son and to the Holy *Spi*rit.
    From age to age, a*men*, amen.
Halleluiah, halle*lu*iah, hall*e*luiah.

Basilica Hymn
- **Remember your Church, whom you chose from the beginning.**
- **You destroyed the nations and established her.**
- **That through the Church, the manifold Wisdom of God be made known.**

To your Church, O Savior, who has followed you perfectly by love and the faith which comes from baptism, you first showed the Individuals of glorious Divinity; and by her, the perfect teaching of the mystery of the Trinity was revealed to the spiritual assemblies. By your grace, O Lord, may the creed that has been delivered to her by you in your Gospel be preserved without stain.

Vigil Hymn
- **May God arise and scatter all his enemies.**
- **In vain do its builders labor.**
- **The Lord will scatter them from there to the face of the earth.**

The men who built the tower of Babylon wished to rise to the great difficulty of arriving at the height of heaven. By the act of beginning this insolence, the Holy Spirit showed them vain and impotent weakness, and the earthly nature was scattered. Not only did what they dared to do not finish, but ordinary speech became babbling. But in the river Jordan, glorious stairs were built through you, who are named the Mighty Rock, and all those who are baptized ascend to the height of heaven and are brought in. Thus you wished, for your grace is never ending. O Lord of all, glory to you!

Madrasha
- **Blessed is he who paid the debt of our fault, and gave us victory through the Son of our race.**
* The Hidden Will wished to renew all things by water and the Spirit. Like a disfigured image, he recast his fashioning in the furnace of the water of baptism, and scoured the filth of mortality from the mortals who were disfigured in sin. The rational image of the house of Adam was wrecked in sin, and its Craftsman recast it with fire and water.

* The Fashioner of all things renewed the work of his hands skillfully, for while he is who he is, he returned and cast a chosen vessel from it. He made Adam an image of dirt which became old and ruined, and returned to his dirt. Like a potter, he shattered his mortality, and anointed him with the Holy Spirit instead of gold.

* His Love bowed down and took on one member of mortals, and in him his wisdom was proclaimed, how he is a renewing Craftsman. In him the power of his Greatness was victorious, which is able to create and renew his works again. For he cast him first in the furnace of the Holy Spirit, and set the crown of glory upon him: the name of the Son.

Morning Hymn – *lakh mawdenan*
Give thanksgiving,
to the Christ who saved us from our error,
and who reconciled us to his Father through his Body,
and the angels who had turned away because of our sins:
praise unto him, with his Sender.

Daniel Verse
Christ, who freed us through his birth,
and who clothed us in baptism
with the Spirit, and sat us
in great glory in heaven.

Sanctuary Hymn – *mara d-kulla*
- I exalt you, Lord, for you lifted me up.
By your Dawning, you raised us
from our subjection to sin.
The world rose up to praise you,
for the salvation given.
Let us cry out together,
in one great sound of glory:
Blessed is Christ who saved us,
by his baptism, from the curse.

Epiphany

The Memorial of Sts. Peter and Paul, Apostles

Basilica Hymn
- In you, O Lord, I put my hope; I will never be put to shame.
- Nor will those who hope in you be put to shame.

"We are not ashamed, O Jesus, of your Gospel," cry out the true preachers, Peter, head of the apostles, and Paul, the teacher of the gentiles. For in the great city of Rome, the course of their work was completed: Peter, in the suffering of a cross, and Paul crowned with the sword. By the hand of the wicked Nero the blood of the saints was spilled. And lo, an imperishable crown is kept for them!

Daily Hymn - Let those saved by the Lord say.
Blessed are you, O famous Rome, city of kings, handmaid of the heavenly Bridegroom! For two true preachers were placed in you as in a harbor: Peter, he who is head of the apostles, upon whose truth our Savior built his faithful Church, and Paul the chosen and the apostle, and the builder of the churches of Christ; for we take refuge in their prayers, that mercies and pity may be upon our souls.

Second Week of Epiphany

Evening Psalmody (from Psalm 89)
Of old he spoke in a *vi*sion,
> Halleluiah, halleluiah, hal*le*luiah.

Of old he spoke in a *vi*sion,
> when he spoke to his *righ*teous ones:

"I have set the crown upon one who is *mi*ghty,
> I have exalted one chosen *from* the people.

I have found David, my *ser*vant;
> with my holy oil I have a*noin*ted him;

so that my hand shall ever abide with *him*,
> my mighty arm shall *streng*then him.

Glory to the Father, to the Son and to the Holy *Spi*rit.
> From age to age, a*men*, amen.

Halleluiah, halle*lu*iah, hal*le*luiah.

Basilica Hymn
- Of old he spoke in a vision to his righteous ones.
- In the days of long ago; Age unto age tells of your works.

Epiphany

O Lord, from the beginning, you spoke with our fathers in every manner and every type, and you taught them to worship your hidden and secret Nature. In the Last Days, however, you spoke to our race through your true Son, and in him you made known to us that your glorious Divinity is announced in three Individuals. To you do all the ranks of angels and men, who have been renewed in Christ, lift up glory.

Vigil Hymn
- O Lord, the God of my salvation.
- We your people, and the sheep of your flock.
- For your grace and for your truth.

O Lord, your flock gives thanks to you, for you descended to her in your compassion, and took from our race a Pledge of peace for the sake of your love, and made him a chosen Dwelling for your providential Will, a glorious Image of your invisible Nature, a splendid Icon of your Divinity, and the Mediator of your mercies toward its sons, the great High Priest in whom our debts are forgiven through his grace.

Madrasha
- Blessed is he who bowed down and was baptized in the Jordan river, and opened up heaven to mortals by his baptism.

* The image of the house of Adam, which was named the hidden image, rusted through sin, and became vicious from temptations. It overturned the decree of its miserable clay, and the hater mocked and derided it. The rational and the mute were saddened at its corruption, for the dwelling of their love had been wrecked by death.

* The Good One saw his image made hateful through sin, and he recast it in the crucible of water. He scoured its hatefulness, and plated its construction with the gold of the Holy Spirit. The heavenly marveled at the image, and those who were saddened at its decay rejoiced in its renewal. They returned to the order of the love required of them.

* The Signal joined them in one harmony to rejoice in the renewal of the image of the earthly one. They wove a crown of glory for the Hidden One with their songs, for he had renewed the image of man in his love, and revealed the love of his will to his creatures, for he wished that the image of his Hiddenness not be destroyed.

Morning Hymn – *abbun d-bashmayya*

Blessed is Christ, who made us holy
by his baptism, type of life above.

Daniel Verse

By your baptism, Savior,
you cleansed the filth of our race.
You forgave us and hallowed us,
and named us heirs of heaven.

Sanctuary Hymn – *sahde brykhe*

- **The Lord is great and highly to be praised.**
- **Great and awesome to all around him.**

"Great the Mystery
that has dawned on earth!"
the Apostle cries.
A heavenly Mystery,
that our God has taken flesh,
and has made it one with him,
working through it by his pow'r,
that in him we may gain paradise.

MEMORIAL OF THE FOUR EVANGELISTS
MATTHEW, MARK, LUKE AND JOHN

Basilica Hymn

- **Their gospel went out to all the earth.**
- **And their words to the ends of the world.**
- **For lo, their whisper goes out to all the earth.**

O holy apostles, who preached and taught the new Gospel in the four corners, uprooted the thorns that the evil one planted through his weeds, planted good seed by means of their teaching, fulfilled and completed the charge they received, and transmitted this to the teachers and priests: O victorious athletes, O true pillars: supplicate and plead to Christ for peace!

The Third Week of Epiphany

Evening Psalmody (from Psalm 66)
Through all the earth they shall adore and sing to *you*,
    Halleluiah, halleluiah, hal*le*luiah.
Through all the earth they shall adore and sing to *you*,
    and glorify your *name* forever,
and say "Come and see the works of *God*,
    whose marvels are many for the *sons* of men!
Glory to the Father, to the Son and to the Holy Sp*i*rit.
    From age to age, a*men*, amen.
Halleluiah, halle*lu*iah, hal*le*luiah.

Basilica Hymn
- **Come and praise the Lord.**
- **Come and see the works of God.**
- **For as is his greatness, so are his works.**
Come and be amazed, my beloved, at that wise Creator who, when he saw that his work was being mocked by the insolent, sent his beloved and assumed our image, and revealed and made known, in him, the mystery that had been hidden from ages and generations. By his hand he was expounded, like the voice of the prosperous worker. Therefore, O Lord, we cry out and say: O you who made peace with the ages by his epiphany: Glory to you!

Vigil Hymn
- **I will exalt you, O Lord my King.**
- **He forgives his land and his people.**
- **This is truly the Christ, the Life-giver of the world.**
Our Life-giver, the Lord of glory, was baptized in the river Jordan by his servant in order to forgive us, and with the Father who sent him and the Holy Spirit of truth, he purified and sanctified all springs, and gave life to the entire race of mortals. Great, O Lord, is your compassion to us; O Friend of man, glory to you!

Madrasha
- **Blessed is he by whose baptism sanctified the forgiving womb for our salvation through his glorious mystery.**

Epiphany

* The Radiance of the eternal Light without beginning symbolized himself by the sun, and dawned upon the world. He was hidden in his Begetter before the ages and generations, and he spread his glory upon all. For the Image of his Hiddenness to give life to our mortality, he engraved him in the daughter of man, and dawned to the mortal race with the name of the Son.

* The Sun, by a just act, justified sinners by the medicine of his words. He dawned with the name of the Sun, as prophecy had called him, and he confirmed the prophecy. The dawning of his revelation enlightened all the ends of the earth. By the force of his rays, he pursued darkness away, which had given birth to sadness for the race of the sons of Adam.

* The brightness of his rays he hid within his body, which his glory had engraved in the womb of the Virgin, that his visage might be plain before the eyes of humanity which longed for its salvation by the fulfillment of its needs. What love, which the world is not enough to thank, and what a wonder, which our race is insufficient to praise!

Morning Hymn – *abbun d-bashmayya*
Your dawning, O Christ, gladdened all creatures,
and promised blessings, and eternal life.

Daniel Verse
Glorious is your dawning,
Christ our King and Life-Giver,
which brought joy to the world to its ends,
and destroyed dark and error.

Sanctuary Hymn – *sahde brykhe*
- **That which was before all time.**
- **The Lord has shown forth his salvation.**

The great Secret hidden
from ages past
by the Maker's will,
earth and heaven later learned
in the Dawning of the Christ.
Men and angels then began
to relate the honored truth:
Trinity in one Divinity.

Epiphany

Memorial of St. Stephen, Martyr

Basilica Hymn
- Lord, who may dwell in your tabernacle?
- And I also will make him a firstborn
- A witness of the sufferings of Christ, and a sharer in the glory which is to be revealed.
You became the head of the martyrs of Christ, like Abel the first just man, O holy Stephen; indeed, when you were debating in the assembly of the wicked, you were seen to have the face of the angels. For this reason, they were enraged with envy, and with heavy stones killed you first, reflective of the victory of him who crowned you!

The Fourth Week of Epiphany

Evening Psalmody (from Psalm 110)
I have begotten you from of old, O *child*.
    Halleluiah, halleluiah, hal*le*luiah.
I have begotten you from of old, O *child*.
    The Lord has sworn and *will* not lie,
that you are a priest forever, like Mel*chi*zedek.
    The Lord is *on* your right.
Glory to the Father, to the Son and to the Holy *Spi*rit.
    From age to age, a*men*, amen.
Halleluiah, halle*lu*iah, hal*le*luiah.

Basilica Hymn
- How good and how pleasant.
- Radiance and glory are before him. His works are glorious and great.
- The earth is filled with his glory.
Glorious and beautiful was the day of your birth, O Savior, and pleasant and excellent also the feast of your dawning, O Christ our Life-Giver. At your birth, O Lord, the sheepfold and the cave, the crib and the swaddling clothes, the star and the magi, the shepherds and the angels, all served in reverence. At your great and honorable dawning, John served in fear, and the river Jordan announced your baptism; the Father with his voice, and the Holy Spirit by his hovering, witnessed, O Lord, to your Divinity. And we also glorify you: have mercy on us, O God!

Epiphany

Vigil Hymn
- **Praise the Lord from heaven.**
- **The Lord looks down from heaven; the Most High gives his voice.**
- **There was a voice from heaven, which spoke.**

The great mystery of the providence of God was revealed to us from heaven, when John, at the command of our Lord Jesus, baptized him, and saw the Holy Spirit of truth descend and dwell upon his head. He heard the voice of the Father from above crying out and saying: "This is my beloved Son, in whom I am well-pleased."

Madrasha
- Heaven and earth sing praise on the day of the baptism of the King of kings; he is worthy to be honored by all, who gladdened all by his dawning.

* I will relate the greatness of the revelation of the baptism of the Lord who mingled with his servants, God with the sons of men. Divinity today came to humanity to sanctify it. New life has dawned today, in which the dead are victorious over death.

* The Wealth above came down to earth, and scattered its treasure upon mankind. "Holy, holy," sing glory to the Father who gave us life in his Son. The Spirit's song is in the prophets, and his words again in the apostles, that the word of the prophet might be fulfilled: Day to day, he awaited.

* The heavens proclaimed a man whose splendor was exceeding through the clouds, as a Son, and the Scriptures were opened before him. His hidden splendor moved and came down; Mary stirred and received him; the waters of baptism stirred; the Spirit stirred and flew to him.

Morning Hymn - *sahde brykhe*
The Light dawned for us: the Radiant Day, through your words, O Christ.
We have all gathered in awe, and have taken refuge here,
in the house in which you dwell, to adore and praise your Name,
for all of your blessings to us.

Daniel Verse
Angels served your announcement;
Magi processed to your birth;
at your dawning, the Father spoke:
"this is my beloved Son."

Epiphany

Sanctuary Hymn – *lakhu qarenan*
- I will bless the Lord at all times.
- And at all times, his praise in my mouth.

Let us all bless God,
who sent his Belo-
ved to save our race.

MEMORIAL OF THE GREEK TEACHERS
Basil, Gregory and John, and their Companions
[Diodore, Theodore and Nestorious]

Basilica Hymn
- Your priests will wear justice, and your just ones glory.
- Holy are Moses and Aaron among his priests.

O holy priests, who worked and labored, in hunger and thirst, for the sake of the truth: who left books behind like treasures for the children of the Church, who enlightened them by the glorious light of their words, who demolished and uprooted the buildings of deception, and who established the faith of the apostles. O evangelists of the kingdom! O extollers of the priesthood! Plead to your Lord, that he may forgive us in his mercies!

- Glory to the Father and to the Son and to the Holy Spirit.

O holy priest, the Spring of Life, the Teaching of the Spirit made your mouth fruitful, and you interpreted the Scriptures of the Spirit in the power of grace, and enlightened the world by the radiance of your works, and gladdened angels and men through your word. O sea of wisdom, O spring of understanding: may your prayer be a refuge for our souls!

[- They are not in the work of man.
- They hungered and thirsted, and their soul was ill-treated.
- And they were poor and weak and ill-treated.

To laborious works of teaching our fathers were hired: Diodore, who was celebrated in learning, and Nestorious, who handed himself over for the sake of the truth, and Theodore the teacher, who made angels and men stand in great awe and wonder with the light of his teaching. And lo, the works and deeds of these athletes who loved Christ are announced throughout creation.]

The Fifth Week of Epiphany

Evening Psalmody (from Psalm 144)
The Lord is *good*,
>Halleluiah, halleluiah, hal*le*luiah.

The Lord is *good*,
>and his mercies are up*on* his servants.

Your servants will thank you, O *Lord*,
>and your righ*teous* will praise you,

and tell of the glory of your *king*dom,
>and speak *of* your might;

to show mankind your *pow*er
>and the glory *of* your kingdom.

Your kingdom is a kingdom for*ever*,
>and your authority *in* every age.

Glory to the Father, to the Son and to the Holy *Spi*rit.
>**From age to age, a*men*, amen.**

Halleluiah, halle*lu*iah, hal*le*luiah.

Basilica Hymn
- **The earth was defiled with blood.**
- **Their blood spilled like water in Jerusalem, and there was none to bury.**
- **He sent and killed all the children in Bethlehem and the area.**

The earth of Judah was defiled with the blood of children; but it was absolved by springs of water made holy. While Herod made the earth unclean by the murdering of children, you, O Lord, in your mercies, as a Kind One, absolved the whole creation by your holy Epiphany. Great is your gift and your compassion, O Lord; glory to you!

Vigil Hymn
- **Hear this, all you peoples.**
- **That he may show forth his greatness.**
- **Then when he came up from the water, heaven was opened to him.**

When our Savior went up from the waters of baptism, the evil one, the enemy, was troubled, and begin to say: "In my deceit, I subjugated Adam, the head of creatures, into sin, and by my flattery, I showed weak Eve the tree. I taught Cain how to murder a brother with a beating, and I advised Herod to slaughter the children. Who is this, who has such mighty power? John trembles at his word, and the Jordan flees from before him. He even commands the winds, and they are subjugated. Indeed, could his kingdom be mightier than ours?" Cast down the enemy, O Lord, for he has laid so many temptations upon us. O Lord, save us in your mercies; O Lord of all, glory to you!

Madrasha
- The children Herod killed in Bethlehem enjoy heaven, and extoll in Paradise.
* Who has ever seen children who have conquered kings, thrown down the mighty, overthrown warriors, humbled judges by heavenly judgment, all clothed with truth, and have stepped on the evil one, who troubles all, with their sandals? Glory to the Power who was an armor for his servants.
* The evil one said: "Woe is me, woe is me" as he wept, "for though I have conquered kings, I have fallen by their deaths. They conquered me and I did not know, and while they died they lived. They shine, and their crowns are woven by the blood of their necks. Woe is me; what has happened to me? For children have taken my crowns."
* "The sword which I sharpened has killed me, and I did not know. The secret I devised has ensnared me, and I was not aware. The stalks which I harvested have burned me by their power. The grapes that I picked have condemned me. For their death has lifted them up, and they have punished and bound me. Where can I run from Jesus, who has slain me?"

Morning Hymn – *abbun d-bashmayya*
Christ, who was baptized, and dawned on the world:
send your peace to dwell in all your elect.

Daniel Verse
Blest, the King who enlightened
creatures who were in darkness,
and who showed, in baptism,
the three Qnome of Godhead.

Sanctuary Hymn – *lakhu qarenan*
- I will bless the Lord at all times.
- And at all times, his praise in my mouth.
Blest is he who came
down and saved our race
when he dawned on earth.

The Supplication of the Ninevites (Ba'utha)

Monday of Ba'utha

Opening Hymn
In pain and tears and fervent prayer,
we cry to you, good Lord above!

> Be our healer and our wise guide:
> deep are our wounds; bitter our pain.

We have no right to plead to you:
our faults abound, our malice soars.

> The sea and land, and all therein
> have quaked and raged due to our sin.

In our own time, as Scripture says,
the end of days has come upon us.

> In mercy, save us from distress,
> for height and depth have been confused.

O Good Shepherd, come tend your flock,
for whose sake you endured the cross.

> Make peace for us in Church and world,
> that we may live a tranquil life.

May we be yours, as is your will:
Father, and Son, and Holy Ghost.
From age to age, amen, amen.

Response:	'unaya:
Lord, have mercy on us,	Maran, ithraḥam 'layn,
Lord, accept our supplication,	Maran, qabbil ba'uthan.
Lord, be pleased with your servants.	Maran, ith-ra'a l-'awdayk.

Monday of *Ba'utha*

From the Book of the Prophet Jonah

Now the word of the Lord came to Jonah the son of Amittai, saying, "Arise, go to Nineveh, that great city, and cry against it; for their wickedness has come up before me." But Jonah rose to flee to Tarshish from the presence of the Lord. He went down to Joppa and found a ship going to Tarshish; so he paid the fare, and went on board, to go with them to Tarshish, away from the presence of the Lord. But the Lord hurled a great wind upon the sea, and there was a mighty tempest on the sea, so that the ship threatened to break up. Then the mariners were afraid, and each cried to his god; and they threw the wares that were in the ship into the sea, to lighten it for them. But Jonah had gone down into the inner part of the ship and had lain down, and was fast asleep. So the captain came and said to him, "What do you mean, you sleeper? Arise, call upon your god! Perhaps the god will give a thought to us, that we do not perish." And they said to one another, "Come, let us cast lots, that we may know on whose account this evil has come upon us." So they cast lots, and the lot fell upon Jonah. Then they said to him, "Tell us, on whose account this evil has come upon us? What is your occupation? And whence do you come? What is your country? And of what people are you?" And he said to them, "I am a Hebrew; and I fear the Lord, the God of heaven, who made the sea and the dry land." Then the men were exceedingly afraid, and said to him, "What is this that you have done!" For the men knew that he was fleeing from the presence of the Lord, because he had told them. Then they said to him, "What shall we do to you, that the sea may quiet down for us?" For the sea grew more and more tempestuous. He said to them, "Take me up and throw me into the sea; then the sea will quiet down for you; for I know it is because of me that this great tempest has come upon you." Nevertheless the men rowed hard to bring the ship back to land, but they could not, for the sea grew more and more tempestuous against them. Therefore they cried to the Lord, "We beseech you, O Lord, let us not perish for this man's life, and lay not on us innocent blood; for you, O Lord, hast done as it pleased you." So they took up Jonah and threw him into the sea; and the sea ceased from its raging. Then the men feared the Lord exceedingly, and they offered a sacrifice to the Lord and made vows. And the Lord appointed a great fish to swallow up Jonah; and Jonah was in the belly of the fish three days and three nights. And the Lord spoke to the fish, and it vomited out Jonah upon the dry land. Then the word of the Lord came to Jonah the second time, saying, "Arise, go to Nineveh, that great city, and

Monday of *Ba'utha*

proclaim to it the message that I tell you." So Jonah arose and went to Nineveh, according to the word of the Lord. Now Nineveh was an exceedingly great city, three days' journey in breadth. Jonah began to go into the city, going a day's journey. And he cried, "Yet forty days, and Nineveh shall be overthrown!" And the people of Nineveh believed God; they proclaimed a fast, and put on sackcloth, from the greatest of them to the least of them. Then tidings reached the king of Nineveh, and he arose from his throne, removed his robe, and covered himself with sackcloth, and sat in ashes. And he made proclamation and published through Nineveh, "By the decree of the king and his nobles: Let neither man nor beast, herd nor flock, taste anything; let them not feed, or drink water, but let man and beast be covered with sackcloth, and let them cry mightily to God; yea, let every one turn from his evil way and from the violence which is in his hands. Who knows, God may yet repent and turn from his fierce anger, so that we perish not?" When God saw what they did, how they turned from their evil way, God repented of the evil which he had said he would do to them; and he did not do it. But it displeased Jonah exceedingly, and he was angry. And he prayed to the Lord and said, "I pray you, Lord, is not this what I said when I was yet in my country? That is why I made haste to flee to Tarshish; for I knew that you are a gracious God and merciful, slow to anger, and abounding in steadfast love, and repenting of evil. Therefore now, O Lord, take my life from me, I beseech you, for it is better for me to die than to live." And the Lord said, "Do you do well to be angry?" Then Jonah went out of the city and sat to the east of the city, and made a booth for himself there. He sat under it in the shade, till he should see what would become of the city. And the Lord God appointed a plant, and made it come up over Jonah, that it might be a shade over his head, to save him from his discomfort. So Jonah was exceedingly glad because of the plant. But when dawn came up the next day, God appointed a worm which attacked the plant, so that it withered. When the sun rose, God appointed a sultry east wind, and the sun beat upon the head of Jonah so that he was faint; and he asked that he might die, and said, "It is better for me to die than to live." But God said to Jonah, "Do you do well to be angry for the plant?" And he said, "I do well to be angry, angry enough to die." And the Lord said, "You pity the plant, for which you did not labor, nor did you make it grow, which came into being in a night, and perished in a night. And should not I pity Nineveh, that great city, in which there are more than a hundred and twenty thousand persons who do not know their right hand from their left, and also much cattle?"

Monday of *Ba'utha*

Petitions

* Let us all stand composed, in contrition and diligence, let us implore and say: Lord, have mercy on us.

Lord, have mercy on us.

* Eternal God, who from the beginning is good, and whose goodness never changes, we implore you: **Lord, have mercy on us.**

* He who has shown the wisdom of his power and revealed his blessedness in the creatures which he mysteriously fashioned, we implore you: **Lord, have mercy on us.**

* He who made known his great love, separated our nature from other creatures and made us in his own image, we implore you: **Lord, have mercy on us.**

* He who has shown the greatness of his overflowing, unending mercy for our progress and help, we implore you: **Lord, have mercy on us.**

* He who overflowed his great kindness in the latter days through the glorious appearance of his Son, to redeem our nature and to renew all creation, we implore you: **Lord, have mercy on us.**

* He who sanctified our nature by the holy body which he took from us and which he united to himself through his Son, our Lord, we implore you: **Lord, have mercy on us.**

* He who painted the image of our going astray and returning in the parable of the prodigal son who was given life, we implore you: **Lord, have mercy on us.**

* He who illumined the lamp of his humanity in the glorious rays of his Divinity, searched for our lost image in the mud of creation like the lost coin, and gladdened all the angels when he found us, we implore you: **Lord, have mercy on us.**

* He who calls us in his goodness and gave us the courage to offer him our needs at any time with hope in his reply, according to his incomparable goodness, we implore you: **Lord, have mercy on us.**

* He who lets us call him without end, and continually responds, most especially in the time of our needs, we implore you: **Lord, have mercy on us.**

* Hear our pleading; have mercy on us. **(kneel)**

Hear our pleading; have mercy on us.

Monday of *Ba'utha*

* Eternally Good, have mercy on us:
> (stand) **Hear our pleading; have mercy on us.**

* Forever Glorious, have mercy on us:
> (kneel) **Hear our pleading; have mercy on us.**

* Maker of Creation, have mercy on us:
> (stand) **Hear our pleading; have mercy on us.**

* Holy in his Nature, have mercy on us:
> (kneel) **Hear our pleading; have mercy on us.**

* He who orders all, have mercy on us:
> (stand) **Hear our pleading; have mercy on us.**

* He who honors us, have mercy on us:
> (kneel) **Hear our pleading; have mercy on us.**

* He who wants us to be saved, have mercy on us:
> (stand) **Hear our pleading; have mercy on us.**

* O our Helper, have mercy on us:
> (kneel) **Hear our pleading; have mercy on us.**

* Provider for all, have mercy on us:
> (stand) **Hear our pleading; have mercy on us.**

* O Merciful One, have mercy on us:
> (kneel) **Hear our pleading; have mercy on us.**

* Turn toward us, have mercy on us:
> (stand) **Hear our pleading; have mercy on us.**

* O great Support, have mercy on us:
> (kneel) **Hear our pleading; have mercy on us.**

* Come to our aid, have mercy on us:
> (stand) **Hear our pleading; have mercy on us.**

* Hear our cry and have mercy on us. **Lord, have mercy on us.**
* For the peace and harmony of the whole world and all churches, we implore you: **Lord, have mercy on us.**
* For our country and for all countries, and all the faithful who inhabit them, we implore you: **Lord, have mercy on us.**
* For the health of our holy fathers… and for all our priests, deacons and all those who serve with them, we implore you: **Lord, have mercy on us.**
* O Merciful God, who guides all in his mercy, we implore you: **Lord, have mercy on us.**

Monday of *Ba'utha*

* He who is glorified in heaven and worshiped on earth, we implore you: **Lord, have mercy on us.**
* Save us all, O Christ our Lord, in your grace, increase your peace and tranquility within us and have mercy on us: **Lord, have mercy on us.**
* Let us pray, peace be with us, and let us bend our knee.
(kneel)
* Arise in the power of God
    (stand) **Glory to the power of God.**

Mawtwa

Response:	*'unaya:*
Lord, have mercy on us,	Maran, ithraḥam 'layn,
Lord, accept our supplication,	Maran, qabbil ba'uthan.
Lord, be pleased with your servants.	Maran, ith-ra'a l-'awdayk.

Hpakhatha

It is time for penitence; let us labor in our prayer.
Leave off the labor of earth; for it makes us earthly ones.
Lift up your eyes to heaven; plead for pity and mercy.

Arise, O you sinful ones; let us become penitent.
Each one confess all his sins; and be absolved of his faults.
As God's mercies overflow; we must pour out our own souls.

Let us suffer in penance; that creatures may then rejoice.
As earthly beings are glad; in blessings that come from above,
Just so the angels await; the good fruits of the penitent.

Let our voices be one voice; and let us all share one will.
Let us bind up, with one love; our souls as well as our hymns.
Love, like a treasure's steward; opens the door to our prayer.

Let our mouths be, unto God; like incense filled with sweetness.
Let our fasting be to Christ; hyssop that whitens our hearts.
Let all of us plead to him: O Lord, have mercy on us!

Monday of *Ba'utha*
First Qiryana

You who come to *Ba'utha*, cleanse your soul from empty thoughts,
And prepare your ears to hear, like the earth prepared for sowing:
For the Seed of life will come, if your soul awakes for him.

Let each of us cleanse his ears, and his eyes before the Light.
For there may be a weak eye, that cannot behold his rays,
Or perhaps a sickly ear, that does not retain his words.

There may be a twisted will, one who needs Life's medicine.
There may be a body here, but its thoughts are gone astray.
We only his shadow see, while his mind cannot be seen.

It may be he thinks of food; lo, he eats and is not filled!
It may be a time to fast; lo, his heart hungers for food.
Or perhaps he thinks of wine, until he tastes every kind.

It may be one thinks of wealth, and of how much he is owed.
He thinks how he might be paid, and his eyes are filled with greed.
Truly, we do not see him. We only his shadow see.

One may cause another's need; he himself in need of prayer.
Or another may be here, but his gaze is wickedness.
Or one whose own heart is lost; lo, we only see his face.

One may steal another's goods, but his silence marvels us.
While his gaze is all impure, he sits with the honored ones.
What bitter destruction waits, when a man sins in this house!

Here, a sin considered small, weighs more than a mountain range,
For a single ruined part, causes the whole flesh to rot,
And one limb that has been lamed, lames the whole people of God.

If the human race was lamed, through the sin of only one,
How will our frail gathering, be victorious with such sin?

Monday of *Ba'utha*

Come, let us denounce our sins, and, through them, the evil one.
He is the helper of sin, and deserves our rejection.
Lo, the wrath of God has come: penitents, engage yourselves!

Let us come and take our plows, and bear fruit a hundredfold;
Let us labor in our prayer, and become a well-trimmed vine;
Let us build, within our souls, temples fit to house our God.

If a great man visits you, he brings honor to your door;
How great will your door become, if the Lord of all enters!

Be for him temple and priest, in your heart serve him in faith;
As he became, for your sake, Altar, Priest, and Offering.

When a temple is your soul, do not let it become stained;
Do not let the house of God, contain things against your God;
Ornament the house of God, with the things befitting God.

And if wrath is found in it, evil will dwell there as well;
And if there is jealousy, then the smoke of sin as well;
Rather, fill your soul with love, incense of a pleasing scent.

Sweep away all filth from it, and habits of wickedness.
Plant within it graceful speech, like a blossom and a rose,
And, like flowers of all kinds, ornament it with your prayers.

First Madrasha

- Come, let us repent now, while we have time,
lest we repent then, without benefit.

* Who can speak of your patience with us?
If we sin, we become filled with wickedness,
if we do good, we become filled with pride;
and toward each other, we are cruel, merciless:
we envy one's success, we despise one who falls.
And though life is short, our list of sins is long.

Monday of *Ba'utha*

* You marked out our lifespan to seventy years,
but with these seventy, we sinned seventy over.
You cut down our life that our sins not be lengthened.
I marvel at your Grace, which overcame your Justice:
even an impure man despises one like himself,
and yet you, who are holy, have not despised us.

* I am humbled by your Justice which still loves us,
as well as by your Grace, patient in teaching us,
and how you dawn your sun on those who reject you.
You give without limit; we lose without measure.
You taught us your order; we act against your love.
We have put on mere names, and stripped off our good works.

Second *Qiryana*/Reading

God, have pity on us all, who call you in penitence;
See that, though we have sinned much, we have thanked you even more;
It fits not your Fatherhood, to close up your door in wrath.

A man comforts his own friend; may your friendship comfort us.
Thus, be reconciled to us, for you are our highest hope.
We know of no other door; only yours, O Lord of all.

Where could we go to be safe, if our Lord would let us go?
Who compares to our Maker, who could take the place of God?
Who is gracious as you are, who could wipe away our sins?

Give us time, in your mercy, that we may correct ourselves.
Give us time, in your great grace, that we may punish our sins.
Give us time, O Judge of all, that we may condemn our faults.

Give us time, O Reckoner, to erase our sins with tears.
Give us time, O great High Priest, to be found in purity.
Hear our pleading as we pray, and in mercy, grant our needs.

Prayer is the only key, that opens the door of grace.
Kind One who does not delay: send your salvation quickly.
We confess that we have sinned: may your grace deny us not.

Monday of *Ba'utha*

This suffices for our guilt: against you, Kind One, we sinned.
To one with an open mind, guilt is worse than punishment.
To one who knows his own sin, it is worse than any stick.

A free man is more ashamed, knowing the sins he has done;
To one with intelligence, guilt hurts worse than punishment.

He who fears his punishment, will fear for a time, then cease.
He who fears his guiltiness, is protected by his fear.

He who is shamed before men, still may sin when all alone,
He who is shamed before God, may not sin even alone;
There is no place he may sin, for God is in every place.

You do not punish the good; when he sins, he does himself.
He is wise enough alone, to justly punish himself.
His own guilt is pain enough, to keep him from sinning more.

All our guilt is shame enough: we have sinned against our God.
On our face, our penitence; this, the sign of our regret.
Our regret is shame enough; for our crimes against your Grace.

For our sins, it is enough, to be called wretched servants.
All creation, justly so, upbraids us before our eyes:
Though we hid all of our sins, tribulations unveiled them.

When no prophet can upbraid, tribulations fall on us.
As the Spirit has allowed, we have fed on empty wind.
When there is none to upbraid, famine comes to upbraid us.

When none can call out, instruct, our instructor is a storm.
When none strike us with a stick, earthquakes shake us into fear.
Hurricanes of wind that come; chastise us when none instruct.

If we think ourselves something, we become as non-beings;
If we think ourselves as men, beasts understand more than we.
All creatures have turned away, for we turned away our God.

Monday of *Ba'utha*

The sun in the sky has veiled, for our vice has scarred the earth.
In embarrassment it hid; turned, in shame, from vicious men.
And the moon, the lamp of night; hid its face behind the clouds.

It was honored like Moses, that our shame be all the more.
When there was a just man's prayer, it would beat a warrior.
Righteous men had raised the dead; Death tends us like a shepherd.

Houses were blessed by the just; by our sins, our houses fall.
Wind and rain and rivers beat; these enough to silence us.
Fearful things that frighten us, to the just were naught but dreams.

They, awake, were not afraid; we, while dreaming, quake with fear.
Daniel in the lion's den; Hananiah in the fire;
We, a small fear in our rooms; bad dreams as we lay in bed.

These suffice us for our shame, that we fear a shaking leaf.
These suffice us to be sure, that we have no innocence.

Second *Madrasha*/Meditation

- Plead, O pleaders, do not cease while there is time for pleading,
before God who gives shuts the door, and closes up his treasure.

* Were you to call in groaning, he would answer you sweetly,
and were you to ask in faith, you would receive openly.
The Rich and Merciful One does not become poor giving:
his treasure is of mercy, a chasm filled with pity.

* Approach now, you penitent, ask for mercies while there's time.
Let each one leave bitterness, ask for mercies and pity.
Let us heal and so be healed, that we may be fit for work.
This is the time to repent! Let us work hard in pleading!

* Wrath now runs upon the earth: cut his course, O penitent!
Let us sow seeds in fasting, that our seed bring hundredfold.
Let us be workers in prayer, for it is a great comfort.
Let us be builders of hearts, that they be temples of God.

Monday of *Ba'utha*

Blessings

O Gracious One who showed his love in creating man:
>   ***En, Mar.*** [kneel]

Pacify the world so troubled by the sins of man.
>   ***Amen.*** [stand]

Lover of man, sow your peace among the sons of men,
that one man may not be troubled by another.

O King of kings, who gives kings power upon man,
soften their hearts in regard to all the sons of men.

Abolish wars and end all conflicts between men,
that those who hate men may not dare to disturb them.

Uphold your Church, which knocks on the door of mercy,
that she may not be defeated by the rebel.

Bind all her sons together in perfect harmony,
uproot envy, lies and hatred from among them.

Guard her shepherd, and increase peace in all his days,
that he be an intercessor of your mercies.

Aid and sustain bishops, who stand as our shepherds,
that they may care for all mankind with great gladness.

Shelter this church, in which your name is glorified,
from the rebel, the hater of all the sons of men.

O God of all, whose love flows upon all mankind,
guard our pastor, give him strength to stand as leader.

Adorn the priests, that they be pure in body and soul,
and accept the Sacrifices that they offer.

Monday of *Ba'utha*

Bless the deacons who serve you within your temple,
that they may be found without fault or defilement.

Perfect teachers in their learning and intentions,
and instruct those who learn in their meditation.

Bless the faithful, sealed and signed in your holy sign,
let your holy name be hallowed in all nations.

Visit the choirs who cry out to you every day;
in your mercy, do not leave them to the evil one.

Encourage all the weak, uphold all the weary,
give victory and confidence to the oppressed.

Show your way to all the lost on a wicked path,
the way that leads unto life that lasts forever.

Grant passage safe to all travelers on land and sea,
rescue them from all straying and all weariness.

Hear, in mercies, this our prayer offered before you,
and accept, in love, this pleading we bring to you.

May your great power be a fortress for this gathering,
that our mouth may praise your name, now and at all times.

Response:
Lord, have mercy on us,
Lord, accept our supplication,
Lord, be pleased with your servants.

'unaya:
Maran, ithraḥam 'layn,
Maran, qabbil ba'uthan.
Maran, ith-ra'a l-'awdayk.

TUESDAY OF BA'UTHA

Opening Hymn
In pain and tears and fervent prayer,
we cry to you, good Lord above!

> Be our healer and our wise guide:
> deep are our wounds; bitter our pain.

We have no right to plead to you:
our faults abound, our malice soars.

> The sea and land, and all therein
> have quaked and raged due to our sin.

In our own time, as Scripture says,
the end of days has come upon us.

> In mercy, save us from distress,
> for height and depth have been confused.

O Good Shepherd, come tend your flock,
for whose sake you endured the cross.

> Make peace for us in Church and world,
> that we may live a tranquil life.

May we be yours, as is your will:
Father, and Son, and Holy Ghost.
From age to age, amen, amen.

Response:	'unaya:
Lord, have mercy on us,	Maran, ithraḥam 'layn,
Lord, accept our supplication,	Maran, qabbil ba'uthan.
Lord, be pleased with your servants.	Maran, ith-ra'a l-'awdayk.

Tuesday of *Ba'utha*

Petitions

* Let us all stand composed, in contrition and diligence, let us implore and say: Lord, have mercy on us.

    Lord, have mercy on us.

* Eternal God, who through his Word made all creatures, both visible and invisible, we implore you: **Lord, have mercy on us.**

* God, Lord of all, with whom heaven and earth are filled, and who provides for all creatures, we implore you: **Lord, have mercy on us.**

* O Merciful and Compassionate One, who cares for our humanity, renews our nature and provides for all good things, we implore you: **Lord, have mercy on us.**

* He who created us from the beginning in his grace and redeemed us in the last times through his Christ, we implore you: **Lord, have mercy on us.**

* He who brings joy to all visible and invisible creatures, we implore you: **Lord, have mercy on us.**

* O Patient and Powerful One, whose judgment is just and whose wisdom is great, we implore you: **Lord, have mercy on us.**

* He who gave us this world for our instruction, and who keeps the world to come as a reward for the just and the punishment of the unjust, we implore you: **Lord, have mercy on us.**

* For those who are troubled and persecuted because of their true faith, we implore you: **Lord, have mercy on us.**

* For those who have been wronged and hurt, for those suffering and prisoners of evil, we implore you: **Lord, have mercy on us.**

* For travelers and for those lost on their path, we implore you: **Lord, have mercy on us.**

* For the healing of the sick, the peace of the suffering, the happiness of those in distress, and the consolation of the depressed, we implore you: **Lord, have mercy on us.**

* Hear our pleading; have mercy on us.

    (kneel) **Hear our pleading; have mercy on us.**

* O Good Father, have mercy on us:

    (stand) **Hear our pleading; have mercy on us.**

* Son Eternal, have mercy on us:

    (kneel) **Hear our pleading; have mercy on us.**

Tuesday of Ba'utha

* Holy Spirit, have mercy on us:
    (stand) **Hear our pleading; have mercy on us.**
* Hidden in his Life, have mercy on us:
    (kneel) **Hear our pleading; have mercy on us.**
* Incomprehensible, have mercy on us:
    (stand) **Hear our pleading; have mercy on us.**
* Wonder Worker, have mercy on us:
    (kneel) **Hear our pleading; have mercy on us.**
* Our Great Helper, have mercy on us:
    (stand) **Hear our pleading; have mercy on us.**
* O Giver of Life, have mercy on us:
    (kneel) **Hear our pleading; have mercy on us.**
* Our Great Refuge, have mercy on us:
    (stand) **Hear our pleading; have mercy on us.**
* Hear our cry and have mercy on us. **Lord, have mercy on us.**

* For the sake of the churches and the world, and the peaceful life you provide, we implore you: **Lord, have mercy on us.**
* For our country and for all countries, and all the faithful who live there, we implore you: **Lord, have mercy on us.**
* For the health of our holy fathers... we implore you: **Lord, have mercy on us.**
* For the priests, deacons, every rank of the church and all those who believe in the Christ, we implore you: **Lord, have mercy on us.**
* For those who take their example from the life of the angels, the just whom the world does not accept, we implore you: **Lord, have mercy on us.**
* O Merciful God, who guides all in his mercy, we implore you: **Lord, have mercy on us.**
* He who is glorified in heaven and worshiped on earth, we implore you: **Lord, have mercy on us.**
* Save us all, O Christ our Lord, in your grace, increase your peace and tranquility within us and have mercy on us: **Lord, have mercy on us.**
* Let us pray, peace be with us, and let us bend our knee.
(kneel)
* Arise in the power of God
(stand) **Glory to the power of God.**

Tuesday of *Ba'utha*

Mawtwa

Response:	*'unaya:*
Lord, have mercy on us,	*Maran, ithraḥam 'layn,*
Lord, accept our supplication,	*Maran, qabbil ba'uthan.*
Lord, be pleased with your servants.	*Maran, ith-ra'a l-'awdayk.*

Hpakhatha

May we labor for your pay, Master who gives servants strength.
May we proclaim your Gospel, may it ring to all the earth.
Good Shepherd, gather your sheep, for they beg for sustenance.

Grant us, O Lord, unveiled face, that we may ask for mercy.
We cannot speak before you; our sins have multiplied so.
May our prayer be a key, that opens up your doorway.

Grant us, O Lord, forgiveness, that we may come to your door.
Kind One, accept our pleading, now, as is your own custom.
Lord, who loves the penitent: open the door to our prayer.

Your mercy daily overcomes, the sins we do before you.
Your grace is overflowing, to sinners who call to you.
In your kindness, Merciful One: may your aid come to save us.

You have begun in your grace; in your mercy, complete us.
In grace was the beginning; in it be the completion.
Begin and end in your grace: that in both we may thank you.

First Qiryana

Jonah preached in Nineveh, Jew among a gentile race,
He approached a citadel, and they were stunned by his cries.
The gentiles were made to mourn, by this prophet Hebrew born,
And like the sea they were tossed, by him who came from the sea.

Words struck through them violently, like the ocean with its waves,
Jonah had shaken the sea, and made the land quake with fear.
The sea shook when he had run; the land quaked when he proclaimed,
The sea calmed once he had prayed; and the land when they atoned.

Tuesday of *Ba'utha*

He prayed when within the whale, Nineveh within its walls.
Prayer saved Jonah who ran, and Nineveh, its remorse.
Jonah once had run from God; the Ninevites from purity,
So Justice imprisoned them, both together, as guilty.

Both of them together prayed; they repented, and were saved.
Jonah was saved in the sea, the Ninevites, on the land.
And thus, Jonah learned to know; that those who repent are saved;
Grace used his own life to show to sinners a parable.

As he was dragged from the sea, he would drag a city drowned,
Nineveh, tossed like sea, by him who came from the sea.
When Jonah proclaimed his words, Nineveh heard in penitence;
One preacher of Hebrew blood shook the city to its core.

He had cried out, "Woe is you!" There he distributed death.
This weak preacher stood up then, in a city of great men.
His voice terrified the king: "Your city will overturn."
Thus, with a voice of despair, he gave them the cup of wrath.

The king heard and fell to earth, bent his head, took off his crown.
Nobles heard and they were stunned; they changed to sackcloth from silk.
The old wise men heard as well, they covered their head in ash.
The rich heard and opened up all their treasures to the poor.

Those who were owed money heard, and they let their debtors free.
Those who owed them money heard, and they paid back all their debt.
Debtors, paying back their debt, and creditors letting free.
Each one, from his part, made best; to bring all to righteousness.

There was not a single one, who attempted to deceive.
To the fight of justice came, each one, to win his own soul.
The thieves heard the prophet's words, returned all their stolen goods,
And those robbed forgave the thieves; they let pass the crime to them.

Each of them judged just himself; and on others had mercy.
No one judged his fellow man, each one judged only himself.

Tuesday of *Ba'utha*

No one chastised someone else; God's wrath would fall on them all.
They all partners had become in the verdict placed on them.

Murderers admitted, too, their own unnatural crime,
Judges heard, and understood, that their judgment is no more.
They could not judge them harshly, lest they too be judged harshly.
Each one seeds of mercy sowed, hoped to harvest salvation.

Sinners all heard Jonah's voice; they confessed all of their sins.
That whole vicious city heard, and took off all of her vice.
All those who owned slaves heard him, and they gave their slaves freedom.
Servants heard him righteously, and they served more faithfully.

Free men, when they heard his voice, put on sackcloth like the poor.
Truly did they all repent, and lowered their arrogance.
Compared to their penitence, our own is more like a dream.
Compared to their petition, ours is but a shadow here.

Compared to that humbling, ours is not a distant shape.
Few were those who had allowed a bitter thought in their mind.
The Ninevites poured out their hearts; let us end our jealousy.
Nineveh freed all of its slaves; you, have mercy on the free.

When Jonah was sent to them, to that city filled with sin,
Justice armed him, kept him safe, with words both fearful and bold.
For wounds, Justice gave to him, the bitterest medicine.
A doctor of terror sent, to the city filled with sin.

He showed them their medicines, those with sharp and bitter taste.
And his cries were thundering, and cut through hearts like a sword.
So God's grace, for this purpose, had sent the prophet to them:
Not to overturn their land, but rather to heal their wounds.

But the preacher did not tell Ninevites they should repent.
Thus he showed to all who mourn, that they should go aid themselves.
He locked the door in their face, to show how hard they should knock.
The judgment that Jonah made, had the opposite effect.

Tuesday of *Ba'utha*

Thus he showed how penitence, has the power to save all.
And how much the penitent, can gain mercy with boldness. *Repeat.*

First Madrasha

- Our Creator from nothing, reject us not, like nothing;
for if our faults are many, your grace is overflowing.

* To your mercy do we beg: open the door to our pray'r
which knocks at the door of grace. Hold back Justice, Gracious One,
lest you be enraged by sin. Let your Will's Love pacify.

* May you not seek all our faults, nor search us in judgment.
Because our pleading is short, and cannot reach your great throne,
extend us your Mercy's hand and through it grant forgiveness.

* As enormous is our sin, it is small to your mercy,
and though it has no equal, it is a shadow to you.
Therefore do not shut your door, that our hearts may turn to you.

Second Qiryana

Such things the Ninevites said, to their friends and relatives;
When they would be comforted, they prophesied about peace;
Now that they were penitent, they prophesied like the just:
Honest was their penitence; thus their prophecy was true.

And, despite this comforting, they did not forget their grief:
Their fasting strengthened by fear, their prayer by their terror.
They saw it with true wisdom, that if even just men fail,
How much more must sinners plead, with death standing at the door.

The people beheld their king, saw his sackcloth, and they wept.
He cast down his kingly robes; his fear of God humbled him.
The king, seeing his city in pain, he wept openly.
The king wept before the crowd, wearing sackcloth, crowned with ash.

Tuesday of *Ba'utha*

All the people wept as one; and the very stones would weep.
Who on earth has prayed like this? Who on earth implored like this?
Who else has humbled himself? Who else has bowed down so low?
Who else has stripped off his vice, that outside and that within?

Who has cut off and thrown down pleasures like a body part?
Who heard but a single voice, and tore his heart in penance?
Who heard but a single word, and was tortured in his thoughts?
Who, hearing a simple man, felt the whole terror of death?

Who, once having pictured God, fell to earth in penitence?
Who has seen a righteous man who has removed his scepter?
Who has seen enormous crowds, begging and weeping as one?
Who was able to withstand, children wailing with their cries?

Who was able to withstand, children wailing with their cries?
Those who looked forward to life heard that their years were cut short.
Who was able to withstand the groaning of the old men?
The gravediggers and the graves heard their city would upturn.

Who was able to withstand the great weeping of the young?
Those awaiting marriage beds, instead were called to their graves.
Who was able to withstand the wailing of brides-to-be?
Those seeking to build a home were called to the tombs instead.

Who could hear and not lament of the king when he would weep?
In place of his palaces, he was invited to Sheol.
He, the king of the living, would be dust among the dead!
In place of his chariot, he would be in his casket.

In place of all his delights, he heard death would swallow him.
In place of his couch and bed, a great abyss of distress.
The living called unto death; the king and the crowd as one.
The king called his warriors, and they wept, one for the next.

The king counted before them all the wars they fought and won,
Then the king reminded them how many armies they beat.

Tuesday of Ba'utha

He shrunk, then, put down his head; no army can aid them now.
He started to say to them: "This fight is not like the rest.

Then, we went to battlefields, and were victors, every time.
Even warriors would quake; at the name 'Assyria.'
We have conquered many men, and one Hebrew conquers us.
Our voice shook the hearts of kings, and we tremble at his voice.

We destroyed the citadels; in our home, he panics us.
'Nineveh, mother of the great;' she fears a lone, simple man.
The lioness in her own den, was shamed by a Hebrew man.
Assyria roared in the world; Jonah roars within her walls.

How has all this come to be? Nimrod's seed has fallen low."
The king told his warriors, his mighty men, and his knights:
"My dear ones, I now advise, in this battle, still to fight.
Let us fight like mighty men, lest we die like weakly ones.

Where is he who once was brave? Let him take heart now and win.
If he dies, a mighty one; if he lives, victory-crowned.
In death, there is a good name; in life, he wins victory.
In both, he at least would gain, and be noble in his fight.

In the same way, there are two wounds to gain if we give up.
Death filled with all shame and guilt, or life with an evil name.
Be armed, therefore, and assault; be warriors again and win.
And if we lose everything, we will gain a glorious name.

We have heard from long ago, in the books of men of old,
That there is a righteous God, but he, too, is merciful.
In justice, he disciplines; in mercy, he pities us.
Let us justice satisfy, and honor mercifulness.

For if justice is content, mercy will come to our aid.
But if justice is upset, there is no harm in pleading.
And if it is not content, there is no harm in begging.
Between justice and mercy, penitence will never lose.

Tuesday of *Ba'utha*
Second Madrasha

- Accept our pleading, Kind One, our imploring, Son of God.
We implore in pain and tears – do not turn your eyes from us.

* Hear the pleading of your sons, O Kind One who grants his grace;
accept the fruits of our lips, we offer to your Greatness.
Send us, from your treasury, pity, mercies, salvation
to be unto forgiveness, lest we be condemned justly.

* To you do our souls cry out, Kind One who loves penitence.
Open the door of mercies, for we knock, Pitying One!
Have mercy, correct, regain, leave us not to destruction,
you are our hope and glory; turn not away from our pleas.

* If our malice testifies, forgive us for your Image.
Let not your work be ruined, because of your great mercies.
you established us in being by your good and kind command;
may you now appease yourself, we cannot stand face unveiled.

Blessings

O you who hold height and depth in the palm of his hand,
> *En, Mar.* [*kneel*]

look upon your own creation, and have mercy.
> *Amen.* [*stand*]

O Spring of Life, from whom life flows unto mankind,
aid the world troubled by its sins by your mercies.

Bless now, O Lord, protect, O Lord, and uphold, O Lord,
the great shepherd, the Patriarch, head of our Church.

His prayer be like fine incense to your Godhead,
Hear all his prayers and intentions as you promised.

Tuesday of *Ba'utha*

Bless now, O Lord, the crown of the year in your grace,
let all kings be peaceful in their earthly duties.

Bless now, O Lord, this our country with all blessings,
And keep all of its citizens under your wings.

And let them all be successful in their labors,
and grant them all that they may ask of your Greatness.

Protect us all in this life and at every time,
Let us all together enjoy earthly blessings.

Bless now, O Lord, those who hold power in leadership,
Strengthen their hearts, give them virtue, let them lead well.

Bless now, O Lord, all religious men and women,
and grant them reward for their works in your kingdom.

Bless now, O Lord, all our priests and all our deacons,
and elect them, when they stand before your altar.

Bless now, O Lord, all the elderly and sickly,
Keep them sustained in their old age and eternity.

Grant to the young great advancement to maturity,
and to children, give many years in your good grace.

Command that clouds may give rain to crops and dry land,
and let our fields bear fruit through the dew of mercies.

Bless now, O Lord, seeds and vineyards, fruits of the earth,
feed your servants through your goodness; let them praise you.

Bless now, O Lord, orphans and provide for widows,
for you are the Father of orphans and widows.

Tuesday of *Ba'utha*

Grant now, O Lord, in the mercies that sent you to us,
that we never become strangers to your kingdom.

Grant us, O Lord, to sing praise to you at your right hand,
and love you along with the just who befriend you.

When the horn sounds on the day of resurrection,
make us worthy to see you in that blest Kingdom.

May your mercies intercede for us before you,
may our sins never estrange us from you, O Lord.

The day you come, when the world will see your splendor,
make us worthy to dwell in light with all your saints.

May the weak one who lovingly said these blessings
be granted your mercies and not be judged harshly.

Defend him, Lord, who was crucified for our sake,
and let him not be sent to the outer darkness.

Let us lift praise to him who raises his servants,
may his mercies be upon us from age to age.

Response:	*'unaya:*
Lord, have mercy on us,	*Maran, ithraham 'layn,*
Lord, accept our supplication,	*Maran, qabbil ba'uthan.*
Lord, be pleased with your servants.	*Maran, ith-ra'a l-'awdayk.*

WEDNESDAY OF BA'UTHA

Opening Hymn
In pain and tears and fervent prayer,
we cry to you, good Lord above!

> Be our healer and our wise guide:
> deep are our wounds; bitter our pain.

We have no right to plead to you:
our faults abound, our malice soars.

> The sea and land, and all therein
> have quaked and raged due to our sin.

In our own time, as Scripture says,
the end of days has come upon us.

> In mercy, save us from distress,
> for height and depth have been confused.

O Good Shepherd, come tend your flock,
for whose sake you endured the cross.

> Make peace for us in Church and world,
> that we may live a tranquil life.

May we be yours, as is your will:
Father, and Son, and Holy Ghost.
From age to age, amen, amen.

Response:
Lord, have mercy on us,
Lord, accept our supplication,
Lord, be pleased with your servants.

'unaya:
Maran, ithraḥam 'layn,
Maran, qabbil ba'uthan.
Maran, ith-ra'a l-'awdayk.

Wednesday of *Ba'utha*
Petitions

* Let us all stand composed, in contrition and diligence, let us implore and say: Lord, have mercy on us.

Lord, have mercy on us.

* O Being from the Beginning, O Gracious God who sent his beloved Son in his great mercy, and saved us from our error, we implore you: **Lord, have mercy on us.**

* He, who in the virgin bosom was born of the pious and holy mother, and who gives joy to the angels and mankind as they give new glory to the redeeming Lord, we implore you: **Lord, have mercy on us.**

* He who enlightened us with the light of his revelation in the rays of the existence of his glorious Trinity, and in whose baptism united us to the treasury of the sons through that symbolic death, we implore you: **Lord, have mercy on us.**

* He who by his fasting has paid our ransom and gained victory over Satan, who gave triumph to our weak race and taught us that with fasting we can conquer the evil one, and by prayer we can remove his wiles, we implore you: **Lord, have mercy on us.**

* He who processed upon the donkey and whom the people glorified with olive branches, and to whom children cried Hosanna, we implore you: **Lord, have mercy on us.**

* He who revealed the depth of humility by washing the feet of his disciples, broke his Body shared for the forgiveness of sins, and mixed his Blood as a drink for our forgiveness, we implore you: **Lord, have mercy on us.**

* He who was mocked out of love for us, whose face was spat upon for our sake, whose hands and feet were pierced, and who handed over his pure soul on Golgotha to the Father who sent him, we implore you: **Lord, have mercy on us.**

* He who descended to Sheol, triumphed over death, and was raised on the third day, and who raised many who offered new thanks to the one who resurrected their bodies with him, we implore you: **Lord, have mercy on us.**

* He who showed Thomas the wounds in his hands and the place of the spear in his side, and who, before the eyes of his disciples, ate and drank to confirm that he rose and gives hope in his resurrection, we implore you: **Lord, have mercy on us.**

Wednesday of *Ba'utha*

* Hear our pleading; have mercy on us.
    (kneel) **Hear our pleading; have mercy on us.**
* Adorable Father, have mercy on us:
    (stand) **Hear our pleading; have mercy on us.**
* Eternal Son, have mercy on us:
    (kneel) **Hear our pleading; have mercy on us.**
* Holy Spirit, have mercy on us:
    (stand) **Hear our pleading; have mercy on us.**
* Hope of our Life, have mercy on us:
    (kneel) **Hear our pleading; have mercy on us.**
* O Christ our King, have mercy on us:
    (stand) **Hear our pleading; have mercy on us.**
* O hear our cry, and have mercy on us:
    (kneel) **Hear our pleading; have mercy on us.**
* Forgive our sins, and have mercy on us:
    (stand) **Hear our pleading; have mercy on us.**
* O Merciful One, have mercy on us:
    (kneel) **Hear our pleading; have mercy on us.**
* You rejoice when we are saved, have mercy on us:
    (stand) **Hear our pleading; have mercy on us.**
* O Lover of Mankind, have mercy on us:
    (kneel) **Hear our pleading; have mercy on us.**
* Hear our cry and have mercy on us.
    (stand) **Lord, have mercy on us.**

* For peace in the world and serenity in all nations, for the establishment of the Catholic Church and the protection of her children, and for the salvation of all the oppressed, we implore you: **Lord, have mercy on us.**
* For the health of our holy fathers…, and for all those in the same priestly service, we implore you: **Lord, have mercy on us.**
* For priests, kings and authorities to be established on the hope of the true faith, your own wisdom, and fear of you, that they may lead in mercy, love and harmony, we implore you: **Lord, have mercy on us.**
* For all hermits, those of whom the world is not worthy, and for all monks and nuns who have dedicated themselves to you, we implore you: **Lord, have mercy on us.**

Wednesday of *Ba'utha*

* For all those traveling on sea and land, for the imprisoned, weary and oppressed, and also for our enemies and those who hate us, we implore you: **Lord, have mercy on us.**
* For the sick and depressed to be healed by your will, for all the suffering to take comfort in your hope, and for the weak and poor to be aided by the right hand of your Majesty, we implore you: **Lord, have mercy on us.**
* O Compassionate God, who guides all creatures, and in overflowing kindness pours forth his benefits upon the evil and the good, we implore you: **Lord, have mercy on us.**
* O One whose Honor the Cherubim bless in heaven, whom the Seraphim hallow thricely, whom the spiritual glorify, and whose holy name the angels adore, we implore you: **Lord, have mercy on us.**
* O Gracious, Kind and Compassionate One in his Nature, who created us from nothing: heal our sicknesses in your compassion and salve our wounds with the medicine of your pity, we implore you: **Lord, have mercy on us.**
* Save us all, O Christ our Lord, by your cross, establish your peace in your Church, bought by your victorious Blood, O Christ who withstood the passion on Golgotha for our sake, and have mercy on us: **Lord, have mercy on us.**

* Let us pray, peace be with us, and let us bend our knee.
(kneel)
* Arise in the power of God
(stand) **Glory to the power of God.**

Mawtwa

Response:	*'unaya:*
Lord, have mercy on us,	Maran, ithraḥam 'layn,
Lord, accept our supplication,	Maran, qabbil ba'uthan.
Lord, be pleased with your servants.	Maran, ith-ra'a l-'awdayk.

Wednesday of *Ba'utha*

First Madrasha

- O God Divine, let our pleading come before you;
in your mercies, answer the needs of all our souls.

* O Overflowing in his mercies, show your love,
lest the hater of all men mock your handiwork.
Richer than all, open your treasure unto us,
lest we be poor and sell ourselves to the devil.
Mighty of ages, keep your order by your power,
lo, it is shaken by evil demons and pains.

* O Being of whose Essence heav'n and earth are filled,
may your Will fill us, and in us your name be blest.
O Hidden One: unveil your power within us,
and show in us the riches of your Graciousness.
O Fashioner of all, who made all from nothing,
pity your work, lest it decay because of sins.

* O Free Sustainer, who gives life to beasts and man,
extend your hand and fill us all with your great Gift.
O Fullest One, of whose Fullness the world is filled,
open the door of your Will to our neediness,
O Perfect One, whose constancy has no ending,
perfect in deed the promise of your words to us.

First Qiryana

O Painter of the world in paint which does not dull,
cleanse all the filth of error from our mind and heart.
O Maker of body, Breather of the soul,
tighten us well, lest we be slack in temptation.

O Honorer of man above all in his love,
pity your Honor's image, lest it be ashamed.
Your simple name you gave to our composition,
may your great name not be made dull by our dullness.

Wednesday of *Ba'utha*

In us you have shown your great love toward your works;
show not in us a sign of wrath against your work.
In us you have brought to fullness all creation;
in us you have bound up earthly and heavenly.

In us you composed height and depth as in one flesh:
mute in our body, rational in soul and mind.
Unravel not this construction you have fashioned,
and may the bind that you have bound not be undone.

At this marvelous composition my mind gazed,
and sought to journey through the path bound within it.
In this great bind my own meager mind was bound up,
and wondered at the skillful craft that bound it all.

Through this structure did my short thoughts go wandering,
to seek for words to tell the tale to listeners.
In this hope did my own mind seek understanding,
that I may go, bring good tidings to your creatures.

With this contract among your Scriptures I journeyed,
to tell to men the great tale of your workmanship.
my mind, this way, painted with the pen of my tongue,
that I might paint, for everyone, your own image.

I saw that man, whom you composed, was made wisely,
and wished to show his beauty unto all the world.
In the image of our image I saw tied the whole creation,
and I called all to come and see all within us.

Our nature drags me to seek out all that within,
and how indeed this frail thing contained everything!
I saw your name dwell within him as a temple;
wonder seized me: how can man fit the Hidden One?

Wretched indeed, yet you love him without measure,
and who would not marvel at chosen wretchedness?

Wednesday of *Ba'utha*

If your Love has chosen him from all and named him,
we can be sure that you will not look down on him.

And if you made him lord above all things on earth,
who would not hold onto the yoke of his life's work?
If you have called him to an exalted stature,
who could not know his place is true, his power great?

If you reveal yourself to us in him unveiled,
who would not focus all his gaze to his making?
If you have shown in him both the Son and Spirit,
who would not seek the mysteries found in his name?

If that Word begotten of you unites with him,
who would not call him emperor of height and depth?
If in him you showed your sweetness to the angels,
who would not take refuge in his Body and Blood?

If in him you have brought to rest your providence,
who would not labor for him without weariness?
If through him you judge the earth when time has ended,
who would not fear the trial that is in his hands?

If in him you reward the good and scourge the bad,
who would not beg him to be advocate for him?
If he has strength over this world and that to come,
who would not know he is alone the Son of God?

Second Madrasha

- Your servants knock upon your door, who wills our life,
open to us, let us receive alms like the poor.

* Poor and lacking is our weak race of all good things:
sustain this thing with a small crumb of your great Gift.
He is too weak to gather his daily succor,
he cannot work the land in strength without your Strength.

Wednesday of *Ba'utha*

* His work is filled with great fear, as much as he works,
and there is no security for sustenance.
Suffering and grief meet his toil summer and winter,
all perils are constant for him, and for his own.

* Much is his work, and little that returned to him;
great is his weariness, and weak, his sustenance.
He plants so much, but he harvests little of it
beaten and crushed, before he breathes, death swallows him.

Second Qiryana

In fear he plants, and in alarm gathers his crops,
his heart does not rely on plant or gathering.
He casts his wheat, that it may return and feed him;
he is distressed, lest he perish and lose his life.

He works his land and thinks it may fail to produce;
he walks the path, and Death sits and awaits for him.
As mothers wait, so he waits until his harvest,
the whips of Death strike at his mind at every hour.

He fights a fight of sufferings at every hour,
there is no end to the assault of his desires.
A great assault is posed at all times against him,
and if he sleeps, temptations come and plunder him.

This wretched one is cast before two sad ordeals:
the scourgings of desire and his sustenance.
As leather cords, he is beaten by his passions,
there is no place in him not filled with temptation.

He suffers for his life and for his laboring,
there is no time when he does not rest bitterly.
If the sun burns, his mind burns in desperate worry,
if the rain stops, his thoughts dry up, wilt with his plants.

Wednesday of *Ba'utha*

If heat has gained the upper hand, he dies of thirst;
if cold attacks, he is consumed by frost and snow.
If he is poor, he is sad, begets complaining;
if he is rich, he puts on pride and arrogance.

If he is good, he looks down on the human race;
and if he sins, he is made weak and gives up hope.
If he is wise, he forgets the clay within him;
and if he prides, he is a beast without a mind.

In great and small, his sufferings increase and grow,
and what can he do, where escape, with a brief life?
He is between neediness and bad excesses,
how can it be for him to keep his life in peace?

So difficult it is for mankind to live well,
and righteousness is not made easy for the flesh.
Flesh – he is flesh, much as he desires spirit,
though that desire is not his, but an Other One's.

An Other dwells in him, as in temple of clay,
though in his life, he blossoms quickly, then decays.
He is all death, though he has a portion of life,
and even this life is so small, weighed with his pains.

So if the living that is in him so small,
how can he live a life without his corruption?

Third Madrasha

- May your mercies come to the aid of our weak race,
for its life's strength is burned away in suffering.

* Stretch out your hand to the athlete of desperate heart,
for he admits that he cannot enter the match.
Cry out and save, give heart to the mortal soldier,
for his hands are too weak alone to hit the mark.

Wednesday of *Ba'utha*

* Command the beings of spirit to come help him,
for his hand falls short of grasping a straw of truth.
Call forth the heavenly legions to assist him,
before he falls and becomes a joke to his foes.

* Write and send him a letter of your name above,
that he may be strengthened to carry through his pain.
Lift up your hand and write of his life's salvation,
and sufferings and demons will not look at him.

Third Qiryana

Rebuke the ranks of warriors who threaten him,
and lo, they will fall in dismay by your command.
Send one to watch, like the time of the Assyrian,
and lo, the pow'rs who threaten him will fall away.

Send your command, as Isaiah to Ezekiel,
instead of figs, let it place mercy on our wounds.
Let us all hear what was heard unto the prophet:
"Instead of life, behold, I grant you forgiveness."

Yes, Lord, return us to health of body and soul,
lest we be torn apart by wounds of our disgrace.
Come search for us, like the parable you told us;
let us enter into the flock of spiritual life.

Brighten your Face, seek our straying in mercy,
lest our beauty, stamped in your name, may decompose.
Rejoice in us, like the young son you told us of,
explain to us, the voice of hope in his story.

With the deceitful one, we worked and lost our pay,
and have lived wickedly on swine-pods of desire.
We angered you (though, in fact, you are not angered);
we are unfit to call ourselves sons of your name.

Let us become as hired hands to serve your house;
let us receive the crumbs that fall from your table.
If possible, fulfill now the story's meaning,
and bring to light the symbol you wrote for our sake.

Tell us, your sons, "From death, you have returned to life,
and from the depths of ignorance, have turned to me."
Let your pity clothe us with a robe of glory,
and place a pledge of life on our hand, like a ring.

Prepare for us the Sacrifice of Christ your Son,
in eating it, let us ban death from our bodies.
And if there is one who envies our repentance,
you pacify his bitterness with your sweetness.

Call those above and gladden them when we repent,
that those once saddened by our sins might now rejoice.
Please those who were angered because of our malice,
and turn them to the service of the needs of man.

Fourth Madrasha

- Do not, O Lord, turn from the pleading of our race,
lest our hope in you be weakened by our despair.

* Do not, O Lord, turn your face from us in your wrath,
lest demons who rebel mock us, as is their way.
Do not, O Lord, cast us from you, like the devil,
lest the devil be lifted up in our decay.

* Be not, O Lord, unmerciful, you are Mercy,
(forgive me, Lord! You cannot be unmerciful.)
Let not the name of your Greatness be hurt by us,
(it never can, were we to sin a million times!)

* Be not, O Lord, lacking in help and treasury,
(oh, what I said of your Essence is such a lie!)
Be not, O Lord, a sojourner in creation,
nor like a guest who walks among what is not his.

Wednesday of *Ba'utha*
Fourth Qiryana

Be not, O Lord, like sons of men, for you are God,
and not like man, who cannot save, for you save us.
And if our sins have prevailed more than all ages,
may you forgive due to your name on which we call.

If our vices have made the air an ugly hue,
may you not show an angry face unfit for you.
If our evil has withheld us in our malice,
change not, O Lord, your gracious name, which changes not.

You are all Good, you are all Just, and hate evil;
neither can your Goodness nor your Justice be weighed.
No one can know how to call your name with fairness;
all names are small before the greatness of your name.

If we say "Kind," your Justice thunders on the earth;
If we say "Just," heaven and earth fill with mercies.
If "Hidden," then your works are unveiled before us;
but if "Unveiled," none among us can see your Face.

If we say "Hearing," you hear us before we call,
"Forgiving One," your Love precedes us and our sins.
We cannot know how to pray nor how to praise you;
we fear to speak words that may be unfit for you.

How can we pray to one who has no need of us?
And how can we praise him who is eternally?
If he is praised, does he then increase in glory?
And if he does, is he made perfect by our praise?

If one blasphemes, does this detract from his glory?
If he is hallowed, does he gain it through our mouths?
If angered, was the shame of man hidden from him?
And if appeased, did we show him how to forgive?

Wednesday of *Ba'utha*

If he sees something in remorse after a time,
did time stop him from knowing what he did not know?
If he did not know (blasphemy to even say it),
how could he gain knowledge of his own handiwork?

No, earthly ones, do not think as with earthly things;
there is nothing in Existence lacking in him.
All creatures' name is a preaching of his Essence,
and as he is, his knowledge is all within him.

He is before all else, and he is what he is,
and there is nothing lacking him, in all of time.
Thus should all creatures think of their gracious Creator;
thus is it right for all mankind to repay him:

We owe a debt of love to him who made us all,
come, let us try to pay a small part of so much.
He does not need our repayment, like one needy,
he makes pretexts that we may be enriched by him.

He has a treasure, life unending, in himself;
he longs to give of it to his adopted sons.
He called us sons through the inheritance of Jesus,
because of this, he disciplines us lovingly.

Let us therefore endure the chastisements of God,
and never become weary of hunger and pain.
If the name "sons" truly does apply unto us,
let us be sure our discipline is for our good.

Let us accept our pains without discouragement,
and let us face life's struggles without murmuring.
For this alone do we ask of him when troubled:
do not, O Lord, repay according to our deeds.

Like Jesse's son, let us plead for our wickedness,
and like him, move to the promise of penitence.

Wednesday of *Ba'utha*
Fifth Madrasha

- Yes, Lord, tell us that word you told unto David,
and let us turn to penitence, the way he did.

* Yes, Lord, let pass the faults of your servants, like his,
and let us hear the voice of forgiveness, like him.
David was just, but the evil one entrapped him;
but he turned back and blotted out sin from his heart.

* So if confession blots out evil and writes good,
then there is hope for the evil to become good.
You who forgave both adultery and murder,
forgive our crimes, great as they are, as you see fit.

* It was you who forgave David that lawless crime:
forgive now also all our sins against your Love.
It was you who loosed the judgment fit for murder,
stop now also the tortures fit for our evils.

Fifth Qiryana

You always mixed mercy with wrath in every age,
and gave no room for those who look down and despise.
You are the One who parceled your Love to just ones;
made them worthy to plead, although you need it not.

In your Love, you forgave our faults from the beginning,
and gave reward to all the just in graciousness.
Due to the just, you forgave our fathers' malice,
lo, you forgave before they spoke and turned to you.

You cast out Justice, that mankind may plead to you,
that when they plead, they may know that sin can be fought.
When Moses prayed, you forgave the sin of the calf,
and told him, 'Lo, I have forgiven as you asked.'

Wednesday of *Ba'utha*

Joshua prayed, and you stopped both the sun and moon,
and wrote in the Scriptures that 'Their course was forestalled.'
Samuel prayed, and you answered him in thunder,
and you replied to him through all the rain that came.

King David prayed; he saw the angel would destroy;
the angel stood in awe of him, as if of you.
Elijah called, and you bid the winds to rain down,
and you awoke the people whom his words had bound.

Elisha called, and by his hands you raised the dead,
and you counted his prophecy defeat of death.
Ezekiel called, and you took down the Assyrians,
and as this was, he would defeat the angel's wrath.

And by your strength, Daniel also showed hidden things,
and Babylon wove him a crown of praise for it.
In every age, the just prayed and you responded;
in our age that has no just one, persuade yourself.

Your Kindness can persuade you more than all the just,
your mercy cannot be compared to that on earth.
Your own Love called all the just ones to persuade you,
now, without them, send us your Love without the just.

Yours are persuasion and the words of those who plead,
whom would you load with your own grace to your own sons?
May Goodness be yours entirely (it indeed is),
so grant us all that you gave us when time began.

Who asked you to create the world when it was not?
And who advised you to bind all things within man?
Who was the one who told you to name your image?
And who showed you how to complete your work in us?

So if in all existence, you needed no help,
what help need you regarding sin, a lousy gnat?

Wednesday of *Ba'utha*

Our wickedness is a gnat before your Greatness;
it is a cup if placed beside your Mercy's sea.

Your Mercy is a sea, and greater than a sea,
and height and depth are small compared to its greatness.
'Your Pity is great:' thus do cry both earth and heaven;
when they were not, you spoke and they both came to be.

You made all things from nothing for the sake of man;
how could you turn away from us in times of wrath?
And, what is best, beyond measure by all creatures:
you clothed us all in your own love, and raised us up.

Our own Body, in glory, sits at your right hand,
and may it not be put to shame by wickedness.
Be it hallowed at your right hand in all honor,
for you have raised it to the name, Divinity.

Sixth Madrasha

- O Lord, open the door to all of our pleading
which we offer to you in pray'r, and have mercy.

* Our prayer be a thurible of penitence,
in which your love may be pleased and be made content.
May our pleading come before you, Friend of mankind,
answer the pleas of your servants in your mercies.

* O Lover of mankind, who loves the life of men,
visit creation with the sign of graciousness.
Forgiver of the faults of all the penitent,
forgive our sins, erase our debts, and have mercy.

* O Pitying One, pity us, as is your way,
erase the list of all our sins, before it grows.
Scour all our filth, bandage all our scars, and heal us,
let us fulfill the law of Love, and have mercy.

Wednesday of *Ba'utha*

Blessings

By your prayer, may the Lord grant over all the earth,
>*En, Mar!* [kneel]

tranquil peace and calm serenity, by your prayer.
>*Amen.* [stand]

By your prayer, may kings in all lands and places,
live in love and in unity, by your prayer.

By your prayer, may the Church saved by your living Blood,
raise her head above all danger, by your prayer.

By your prayer, may the Patriarch, our shepherd,
tend his flock with great diligence, by your prayer.

By your prayer, may the Lord support our bishop,
Mar _____, our good father, by your prayer.

By your prayer, may the shepherds in every land
be adorned with every charism, by your prayer.

By your prayer, may the priests who serve the Mysteries
have every blessing and favor, by your prayer.

By your prayer, may deacons who serve the altar
have every aid granted to them, by your prayer.

By your prayer, may the Lord instruct religious,
by the study of the Scriptures, by your prayer.

By your prayer, may this parish be protected
from all harm and all wickedness, by your prayer.

By your prayer, may the Lord help all our leaders,
our pastors and all our elders, by your prayer.

Wednesday of *Ba'utha*

By your prayer, may the Lord help all the faithful,
that they may live in righteousness, by your prayer.

By your prayer, may the Lord grant every blessing
to all husbands and wives greatly, by your prayer.

By your prayer, may he bless orphans and widows,
and provide for and enrich them, by your prayer.

By your prayer, may the Lord comfort the mourning,
and have pity on the needy, by your prayer.

By your prayer, may the Lord instruct and discipline
children, that in him they be saved, by your prayer.

By your prayer, may the Lord save all the tempted,
and free them from the yoke of sin, by your prayer.

By your prayer, may there be rescue for captives,
and release for all in prison, by your prayer.

By your prayer, may those who bear pain and suffering
be inspired by the Lord's cross, by your prayer.

By your prayer, may those who travel on earth and sea
be guided to the path of peace, by your prayer.

By your prayer, the Lord's right hand rest upon you,
and the mercies of Lord Jesus, by your prayer.

By your prayer, be glory to the Lord Jesus,
and thanks to the Power who sent him, by your prayer.

By your prayer, may the one who says these blessings,
and its author be made worthy, by your prayer.

By your prayer, may the Lord make all his blessings flow,
and cast his mercies upon us, by your prayer.

By your prayer, may we all repent and sing praise,
to the Father, Son and Holy Spirit, forever.

Response:
Lord, have mercy on us,
Lord, accept our supplication,
Lord, be pleased with your servants.

'unaya:
Maran, ithraham 'layn,
Maran, qabbil ba'uthan.
Maran, ith-ra'a l-'awdayk.

Epiphany

The Commemoration of the Syrian [and Roman] Teachers
[Ephrem, Narsai, Abraham, Lolian, John]

Basilica Hymn
- They are more precious than gold and fine jewels.
- Which are planted in the house of the Lord.
The feasts of the saints are like radiant light shining in the churches, and they thunder with hymns of thanksgiving to Jesus our Savior, the crown of his true ones, and the assemblies above glorify him in all their ranks. Grant us, O Lord, in your mercy, to be worthy to repay thanksgiving with them, to your holy name, on the commemoration of the priests.

Sixth Week of Epiphany

Evening Psalmody (from Psalm 103)
His angels bless the *Lord*,
    Halleluiah, halleluiah, hal*le*luiah.
His angels bless the *Lord*,
    who have power and accomplish *his* commands.
All his hosts bless the *Lord*,
    his servants who *do* his will.
All his works bless the *Lord*,
    for his authority is over *all* the earth.
Glory to the Father, to the Son and to the Holy Spi**rit.**
    From age to age, a*men*, amen.
Halleluiah, halle*lu*iah, hal*le*luiah.

Basilica Hymn
- And they will glorify your name forever.
- They will glorify you forever.
- Crying out, one to the other, saying.
Above in the heights, all the legions of angels glorify you, and with you, your Father. On earth also, the whole race of mortals kneels before you and adores. For through the Jordan and the water in it, you sanctified all springs: you were baptized in it, while above sin, and showed us, in your mercy, the path of life's salvation. Thus were you pleased to free the whole race of mortals. O Lord, glory to you!

Vigil Hymn
- I will exalt you, O Lord my King.
- You have shown your might among the nations.
- The Spirit of God was flying over the face of the waters.

When you were baptized in the Jordan, you sanctified springs, and when you were lifted up from it, you raised our fall. Even the messenger was filled with joy, and indeed the angels descended in haste to lift up praise to you. From every side, all cried out: "Holy, holy, holy is the King who has come and saved us by his baptism, and promised us the Kingdom – glory to him!"

Madrasha
- Blessed he who was baptized to baptize you, that you may be forgiven of your faults.

* The Spirit stirred above, and sanctified waters in her compassion – the baptism of John. She left all and dwelt upon One – thus now she descends and dwells upon all who are born of water.

* Of all whom John baptized, the Spirit dwelt in only One. But now, she flies and descends to dwell within many, and from the first to the last one who is baptized, she loves and dwells upon him.

* Wonder that the One who purifies all descended to water and was baptized! The seas give blessing to the river in which you were baptized, and even the waters in the heavens are envious, that they were not worthy to wash you.

Morning Hymn – *abbun d-bashmayya*
Heir of the Father, Lord of all that is:
gladden your Church, by your holy dawn.

Daniel Verse
Blessed is Christ our Savior,
Heir of all, from his Father,
who has shared his glory and his power
with the heirs of his kingdom.

Sanctuary Hymn - *sahde brykhe*
- You gave your adorers a sign.

How great is your gift
unto the mortal race,
O merciful God!

Epiphany

Water clothes us in Spirit;
bread feeds us with your Body;
your living Blood hallows us;
mixing us with the angels,
bringing us from earth to heaven above.

MEMORIAL OF THE PATRON SAINT
[KNOWN TO BE OF MAR ABBA, CATHOLICOS]

Basilica Hymn
- **Precious in the eyes of the Lord is the death of his faithful.**
- **Regarding the Lord and regarding his Christ.**
- **Beloved before God and in the eyes of men.**

Precious in the eyes of the Lord our God is the death of his revered one, and the passing away of his saint, the splendid ____, he who competed in spiritual battle in all excellence and left the divine arena in victory, leaving us a choice trophy, one excellent and spotless: his revered and honorable body. And lo, his soul processes with the angels, and offers prayers on behalf of our souls.

SEVENTH WEEK OF EPIPHANY

Evening Psalmody (from Psalm 144)
The Lord is *good*,
    Halleluiah, halleluiah, hal*le*luiah.
The Lord is *good*,
    and his mercies are up*on* his servants.
Your servants will thank you, O *Lord*,
    and your righ*teous* will praise you,
and tell of the glory of your *king*dom,
    and speak *of* your might;
to show mankind your p*ow*er
    and the glory *of* your kingdom.
Your kingdom is a kingdom for*ever*,
    and your authority *in* every age.
Glory to the Father, to the Son and to the Holy *Spir*it.
    From age to age, a*men*, amen.
Halleluiah, hal*lelu*iah, hal*le*luiah.

Epiphany

Basilica Hymn
- **I will exult you, O Lord, my King.**
- **He who was before the ages. They stand forever and ever.**
- **Lo, the Lord our God has shown us his glory and his greatness; he is the living God and he stands forever; and the Three are One.**

The three Individuals of Existence were shown to us in the baptism of the Principal who is from us: the Mystery that had been hidden, in the Lord who was baptized, the Holy Spirit like the flesh of a dove which descended and rested upon the head of that Image from the house of David, and the Father who cried out and was shown to the onlookers: the amazing and wonderful approval. Blessed is he who, in his love, became a man, saved us, absolved us, and sanctified us in his baptism, and washed away our sins in his laver: to him be glory!

Vigil Hymn
- **From the mouths of infants and children.**
- **They will glorify your name forever.**

Glory to you who destroyed the fight with Satan the adversary by your power. For indeed, when you were baptized by water you went out to the wilderness, and overcame and defeated and destroyed the authority of the enemy who wished to defeat you with his evil wiles. You strengthened your servants and said: "Take heart and do not fear, for I am with you in body and soul, and have overcome the world."

Madrasha
- Glory to him who cried out over the river Jordan and said: "This is my beloved Son, in whom I am well-pleased."

* Blessed is he whose mercies clothed him with the vestment of our humanity, and whose eternal dawning shone in our body. Blessed is he who sanctifies all, who opened the fount of his love in the river Jordan for the race of mortals.

* He anointed him priest and prophet with the Holy Spirit in a barren womb, by the Spirit of the Most High. He raised him with visions, and made him stronger than those invited to the banquet. He sent him before his Love in the type of Elijah.

* He established the path of light by his eternal dawning in the land of mortals. Those laying in darkness were provided with forgiveness. He provided the preacher, and in the name of repentance, he granted forgiveness.

Epiphany

Morning Hymn – *byadh shlama*
The Sun that dawned in Judah
was seen by the whole world,
through the preacher of Jesus,
St. John the Baptist,
he who, to those with discerning eye,
revealed Elijah who is to come.
He proclaimed openly to the sinful nations
who were enligh-tened by his preaching.

Daniel Verse
Praise to your revelation,
which the prophets preached in mystery,
and which you have fulfilled now in deed
when you dawned in the Jordan.

Sanctuary Hymn – *lakhu qarenan*
- **I will bless the Lord at all times.**
- **And at all times, his praise in my mouth.**
Blest is he who shared
his great Mysteries
with the mortal race.

MEMORIAL OF THE FORTY MARTYRS

Basilica Hymn
- **I will bless the Lord at all times.**
- **And blessed be his honored name forever.**
Blessed is the hidden power that dwells in the bones of the martyrs: for they are in their graves, but they chase demons out of the world. Through their teaching, they abolished the error of idolaters, and they quietly visit creation, and teach it to worship you, who alone are the Lord.
- **Glory to the Father and to the Son and to the Holy Spirit.**
Glory to you, O good and kind Lord, by whose power your true ones were victorious, and by whose aid scorned the threats of their persecutors, and destroyed the power of the haughty enemy. For he saw that the martyrs did not fall away from their true foundation.

Eighth Week of Epiphany

Evening Psalmody (from Psalm 96)
Give to the Lord, tribes of the *na*tions,
    Hall**eluiah, halleluiah, hal***l***eluiah.**
Give to the Lord, tribes of the *na*tions,
    give to the Lord glory and honor;
        give to the Lord the honor due *to* his name.
Take offerings and enter his *courts*.
    Adore the Lord in his *ho*ly courtyard.
Glory to the Father, to the Son and to the Holy *Spi*rit.
    From age to age, a*men*, amen.
Halleluiah, halle*lu*iah, hal*l*eluiah.

Basilica Hymn
- **Like a day that is filled and passes.**
- **They will pass away, and you will remain.**
- **Nor will its place be known.**

The shadow of the Law has passed by means of the grace that has been revealed: for as the Hebrews were saved from slavery to the Egyptians by a lamb, thus were the Gentiles freed from ignorance by the epiphany of Christ; instead of the pillar of light which shone before the people, the Sun of Justice has risen, and, in place of Moses, Christ has come, and has saved and ransomed all our souls, that we may lift up praise to him, and thanksgiving every day.

Vigil Hymn
- **Light has dawned in the darkness for the upright.**
- **Come let us praise the Lord.**

Through the marvelous and wonderful dawning seen in the land of Judah, angels and men were lifted up from suffering and corruption, and through holy, glorious, and spiritual baptism, he has called us to the banquet of new life, and made the spiritual and the physical one. They glorify his Divinity on his feasts, and exalt his Father and his Spirit with halleluiahs. The legions of the saints exult on the day of his dawning, and we also who are made worthy worship with them and say: our most-merciful God, Lord of all, glory to you!

Madrasha

- Blessed is the Son of the Kind One who sanctified all by his baptism, and erased our debts in the furnace of the water of his baptism.

* The great Sea who washes away sins approached baptism, and opened the doors which had been shut in the face of man. The High Priest went down to the waters and was baptized, and sanctified them, and gave them the power of the Spirit to give life.

* The Holy One approached the weak element of water, and made it a womb giving birth to men spiritually. He descended and drowned in the depths of the Jordan as in a tomb, and he stood and was raised, and gave us life with him mysteriously.

* He ascended from the womb of the new mother, not of nature, and the Spirit descended and anointed with divine power. He anointed him in Spirit, not with the oil of the law, chosen oil, better than others like it.

Morning Hymn – *abbun d-bashmayya*

Blest is he who gave us the saving womb
of our baptism through his Mysteries.

Daniel Verse

"To you glory, Lord of all,"
angels and men are singing,
as they cry out together:
"Blest your dawning which gladdened us."

Sanctuary Hymn - *ḥannana dapthyḥ*

- Come hear this, all you peoples.
- Come see the works of the Lord.

A seraph with a coal
touched the prophet's lips:
he was sanctified;
his sin was absolved.
Come, O nations, now,
through the Mysteries:
purify your sins,
and absolve your faults.

Epiphany

The Friday of the Deceased

Basilica Hymn
- Like a day which is completed and passes away.
- Those pass away, but you are standing.
All the ages pass and fade away, O Lord, power weakens and wealth is impoverished, and even knowledge comes to an end. This alone remains: judgment and righteousness. Teach us to be ready for these, O Lord, and have mercy on us.
- Glory to the Father and to the Son and to the Holy Spirit.
At the fearful judgment of your righteousness, O Lord, all the angels stand in fear, and present the sons of men for your judgment. The Books are also opened before you, deeds are there unveiled, and even thoughts are revealed and categorized. So in what trembling will I stand, I who was conceived in wickedness and born in sin? Who can enlighten me in the darkness, and who can turn off the furnace for me, other than you, O Lord of all? Now, then, turn toward me and have mercy on me, O Friend of Mankind!

Lent

The Week Beginning the Great Fast (Ṣawma/Lent)

Evening Psalmody (from Psalm 74)
Remember your *church*,
    Halleluiah, halleluiah, hal*le*luiah.
Remember your *church*
    which you established from *the* beginning,
and save the tribe of your in*he*ritance.
    This is mount Zion, *where* you dwelt.
Glory to the Father, to the Son and to the Holy *Spi*rit.
    From age to age, a*men*, amen.
Halleluiah, halle*lu*iah, hal*le*luiah.

Basilica Hymn
- O Lord, the God of my salvation.
- We your people and the sheep of your flock. For your grace and your truth.
- Like a glorious Bridegroom and like an adorned bride.

O Lord, behold your Church, saved by your Cross, and your flock bought with your precious Blood, offers a crown of thanksgiving in faith to you, O High Priest of justice who has exalted her by your abasement. And, like a glorious Bride, she rejoices and exults in you, O glorious Bridegroom. In the strength of the Truth, raise the walls of her salvation, and establish priests within her, to be ambassadors of peace on behalf of her children.

Vigil Hymn
- I will exalt you, O Lord my King.
- The great King over all the gods.
- King of kings and Lord of lords.

Christ the King freed creation and saved it from error by his revelation. He eradicated the authority of Satan, who had condemned our race in his envy. He became the glorious and perfecting Head of our faith by his baptism, in whose type we are baptized in the confession of the three Individuals of the Father, Son and Spirit, one Nature, one unlimited Power, he who is from eternity, and adored by all creatures.

Lent

Madrasha
- Blessed is Christ who gave victory to mortals by his fasting, and humbled the power of the rebel before those who watched the contest.
* Satan went up, embarrassed, from the first contest, and instead of a place of battle, the armor of a second war: he awaited with a vain hope, between the fight and the fight, thinking there were many opportunities for him.
* "Through the root of the love of money, which bears the likeness of greed, I shall fight him, for from it sprout evil things. Through the love of money, I will make battle with him." Thus he desired, on the top of the mountain, to show off the beauty of his possessions.
* The Creator gave him his desire, since he knew he wanted to take our Savior up a mountain to struggle against him. Satan was humiliated by our Lord, and his hosts were scattered. The whole left hand sat in mourning over the defeat of the rebel.

Morning Hymn – *abbun d-bashmayya*
May your light, O Lord, push out from your Church,
the demons of doubt, and dark divisions.

Daniel Verse
Brothers, our Lord's own fasting,
has come unto our dwellings.
Let us meet it with gladness,
and accept it in holiness.

Sanctuary Hymn – *sahde brykhe*
- **All you servants of the Lord.**
- **Come, you children, and take heed.**
Let us cleanse our consciences
and scour our minds
from the stain of sin,
and our vices cast away
as we strive for excellence.
May we all discern the truth
of the Flesh and Blood of Christ
who alone forgives all our faults.

Note that no Martyr Hymns are sung during Lent.

Lent

SECOND WEEK OF LENT

Evening Psalmody (from Psalm 95)
Come, let us bless and worship *him*,
    Halleluiah, halleluiah, hal*le*luiah.
Come, let us bless and worship *him*,
    and kneel before the *Lord* who made us.
For he is our God, and we are his *people*,
    and the sheep *of* his flock.
Glory to the Father, to the Son and to the Holy *Spi*rit.
    From age to age, *a***men, amen.**
Halleluiah, halle*lu*iah, hal*le*luiah.

Basilica Hymn
- Come, let us glorify the Lord.
- For his grace has increased upon us.
- To him be glory, honor, and authority, forever and ever.
Come, let us all give thanks and glorify our good God, as much as we are able, for his benefits to our race: honor him for our establishment, from the beginning, in the name of his honorable Image; and, when the enemy envied our honor and cast us out of our glory, the Lord was revealed to us, and spoke to us in his Son, who is the Inheritance and Progenitor of the world to come; in whose birth gathered us from the error of ignorance to the knowledge of his Divinity; who was baptized and gave us a true adoption; who fasted and gave encouragement to our weariness that we might overcome Satan; in whose death conquered the tyrant; and who justified us, lifted us up and raised us with him in glory.

Vigil Hymn
- O God, our mighty stronghold.
- Our help in a time of trouble.
It is the time of mercy and compassion. We plead and beg: have mercy on us, O Lord. There are many signs of coming war, for lo, the sea and the land are filled with quakes. O Christ the King, who was crucified for our sake, as you gave us the knowledge to believe in you when we were lost, and showed us the path of truth. Thus the churches in all lands take refuge in your cross. Grant victory from above in your mercies.

Madrasha

- Behold the free mercies granting forgiveness! You who fast in truth, come and receive help.

* Behold fasting, brethren who fast in truth, which forgives for free: let us love its benefits and rejoice in its medicines. The faster who descended from mount Sinai to the dwelling of evildoers healed them of their wounds; holy fasting supports us in our falling and bandages the grievous fracture of our mind.

* Glory to the Faster who gave victory to fasters, and established fasting as a sign for fasters. May our fasting not be for the pleasure of the evil one; may our fasting be for the appeasement of God. Lo, pure fasting is the enrichment of the soul: let us receive from its treasury and be enriched by its fullness.

* In the beginning, Adam was hired at a loss in the eating from the tree, since he disobeyed the commandment. Holy fasting pays off debts, impoverishes stomachs, fattens up souls. Let us give glory to the First-Born of fasters, who gives the job of fasting to our weakness.

Morning Hymn – *ḥannana da-pthyḥ*

We kneel and adore before you O God,
in the morning now, confessing your grace,
for you dawn your sun on the good and bad,
and provide for all in your great patience.

Daniel Verse

Come, repentant, let us walk
in the path of holy fasting,
with Moses, Elijah, and Daniel,
righteous men who loved fasting.

Sanctuary Hymn – *niṭṭayaw*

- **In you, O Lord I put my trust.**

We trust in your mercies, Lord,
and our trust strengthens us
to ask forgiveness from you;
not that we deserve,
but in your justice, you give for free
to those who knock at your door
in your flowing grace and in your mercies.

Third Week of Lent

Evening Psalmody (from Psalm 143)
Do not enter into judgment with your *ser*vant,
  Halleluiah, halleluiah, hal*le*luiah.
Do not enter into judgment with your *ser*vant,
  for no living thing is just *be*fore you.
For the enemy pursues my *soul*,
  and has lowered my life *to* the ground.
Glory to the Father, to the Son and to the Holy *Spi*rit.
  From age to age, *a*men, amen.
Halleluiah, halle*lu*iah, hal*le*luiah.

Basilica Hymn
- Do not enter into judgment with your servant.
- For you are righteous in your word and just in your judgments.
- For no living thing is just before you.

If you enter into judgment with your servant, O Lord God, what excuse will I find? And where can I beg for forgiveness? For I have rejected and broken all your laws, and have become a dead man in the greatness of my sins. As from Sheol, from the sea of sin draw me out, in your mercy: O Christ the King, have mercy on me!

Vigil Hymn
- Bless the Lord, my soul.
- Return, my soul, to your rest.

Cease now, O my soul, from your many wrongdoings and sins, and consider the last day, which will suddenly steal in and astound you. Remember the fearful judgment kept for you, for there repentance will not help, and tears will gain you nothing. While you have time, plead and beg; return from your evil, O my soul, and live. Cease now from your many sins, and give thanks and say: "O God who forgives sins, forgive and have mercy on me."

Madrasha
- Blessed is he who prepared the diligent through vigil, fasting, and prayer, and made them a vision for those who see in truth.

* Moses, great among those who fast, was armed by means of fasting. He took off the customs of the Egyptians and loved fear of God. He hated and despised milk and honey, with which the daughter of Pharaoh raised him, and he loved fasting and prayer, and thus was brought to perfection.

* Moses, the head of those who fast, despised the bountiful table of Pharaoh. He cast away the pleasure of kingship, and loved fasting on the mountain. He fasted, and his face shone; he prayed, and his reward was celebrated. He ascended with a human appearance, and descended in heavenly splendor.

* He ascended with an earthly appearance, and descended with the glory of the angels. He ascended a man like all others, and descended a faster without equal. This fasting atop the mountain became an April filled with beauties. Moses the shepherd went up and returned, and called upon the Name of God.

Morning Hymn – *sahde brykhe*

Christ, who reconciled all creation with
the One who sent him,
cleanse your Church, saved by your Blood,
from all factions within her,
which come from the evil one,
causing heresies and strife.
Help your priests to preach the one true faith.

Daniel Verse

Blest, him who gave us victory
over Satan by fasting.
He is praised by the angels above,
and below, we adore him.

Sanctuary Hymn – *ḥannana dapthyḥ*

- **He comes to judge the earth.**
- **He comes to us rejoicing.**

The Judge of Justice comes when time will end,
and he will reveal all our words and deeds.
Let us live in awe, not hypocrisy,
for he heals our wounds in wisdom and love.

Lent

Fourth Week of Lent

Evening Psalmody (from Psalm 104)
How many are your works, O *Lord*,
    Halleluiah, halleluiah, hal*le*luiah.
How many are your works, O *Lord*,
    all of them you crea*ted* in wisdom.
The earth is filled with your posses*sions*:
    this is the great sea, an open *space* of hands,
in which are innumerable creeping *things*,
    animals large and small, and on it *boats* go by.
This is Leleuiah, which you created to *laugh* at.
    All of them *wait* for you.
Glory to the Father, to the Son and to the Holy *Spir*it.
    From age to age, a*men*, amen.
Halleluiah, halle*lu*iah, hal*le*luiah.

Basilica Hymn
- The heavens proclaim the glory of God.
- Glorious and exalted are his works.
- Who will make known the wonders of the Lord?
This world, in its construction, daily prepares and awakens rational creatures to the wonder and glory of that wise Creator. The wondrous variations, which oppose one another, harmonize within it: fire, water, earth and vaporous air. But that we may not be led astray and think that, because of their diversity, they have many makers, he took and made, of creation, one body in the forming of man, and in him made known to us that he is the Lord of all.

Vigil Hymn
- Have mercy on me, God, in your grace.
- Have mercy on me, Lord, have mercy.
Have mercy on me, Lord my God, for I have sinned against you. For I do not do the thing I want, but the evil that I hate is what I do. And I love repentance, but my desires fight against me. I rejoice in your commandments, but am defeated by sin. Forgive my soul, O Friend of man, and remove it from the sea of faults that shake me at all times.

Madrasha

- Thanks to him who gave us his holy fast, a mighty weapon against the enemy.

* God, open my mouth that I may sing the story of holy fasting, whose work is filled with blessings: it clarifies the mind; it scours the body; it expels sin from our species. It is the opposer of death and the tricks of the evil one; it overturns the enemy by its mighty power.

* Brethren, put on the armor and the shield of salvation. Let us all diligently labor as much as possible, and prepare our bodies and souls: let us appease God through fasting, tears of remorse, and pure works: visiting the sick and giving to the needy.

* Let us fast together in body and soul: not fasting from bread but causing need in the poor, showing off, making ourselves look righteous, lest we hear the voice that proclaims: "begone from me, you cursed, to the eternal fire prepared for all sinners at the end."

Morning Hymn – ḥannana da-pthyḥ

You send light to the whole world to its ends
through your will, and you let the darkness pass.
We confess you, Lord: do not forget us,
but send us your grace: have mercy on us.

Daniel Verse

Blest, he who made light in his Light,
and has ordered his creatures.
He is praised and adored by them all,
the Creator, wise over all.

Sanctuary Hymn – byadh shlama

- He founded the earth on its base.
- He who was before all time.

He who was before all made the whole creation,
and made it in his grace, that we may learn of him:
a part he made visible to eyes,
another part, of spirit and mind;
he bound them all in mankind,
that it may confess him,
that he is One, who made us in his love.

Lent

Fifth Week of Lent

Evening Psalmody (from Psalm 142)
Answer me quickly, O *Lord*,
  Halleluiah, halleluiah, hal*le*luiah.
Answer me quickly, O *Lord*,
  for my sp*ir*it is finished.
Do not turn your face from *me*,
  lest I be finished with those who go down in*to* the pit.
In the morning, let me hear your *grace*,
  for I *trust* in you.
Show me your path, that I may go upon *it*,
  for I lift my soul to *you*, O Lord.
Glory to the Father, to the Son and to the Holy Sp*ir*it.
  From age to age, a*men*, amen.
Halleluiah, halle*lu*iah, hal*le*luiah.

Basilica Hymn
- For my life is spent in misery.
- And my years in groanings.
The whole span of my life disperses and vanishes vainly in the confusion of the vanities of this world. And because I have not even desired, for a single hour, to prepare myself for tackling work in the spiritual vineyard, I do not expect to receive the wage prepared for the just. But, for the hidden wounds of my sins, I ask forgiveness from you, unworthy though I am. And because of this, before I stand before your frightful judgment-seat and am found guilty of my crimes by your just judgment, say the word, and I will be healed by your mercies: O Friend of mankind, glory to you!

Vigil Hymn
- The son of man is like a vapor.
- My days pass like a shadow.
I believed I will live for a short time in this world, and I have spent this time worthlessly. I have not gained anything useful – would that it were not useful, and at the same time also not harmful! I ran and gathered many sins for myself, as if I were able to bear debts and wounds. From the soles of my feet to my brain are bruises and wounds. In you, O Lord, my bruises are treated, and in your hyssop, my wounds are healed. Have mercy on me, Friend of man!

Madrasha
- Let us love holy fasting, in which the victorious were crowned; let us participate in their contest and be joined to their crowns.

* Daniel longed after fasting as one would thirst for wine; he loved temperance as the greedy love gain. He turned to fasting and grew young: he fasted for three seasons, and his beauty was cleansed of old age. He became lovely because of his fast.

* The angel Gabriel called the man desirable in his old age, who despised delicacies in his youth and was nourished with grains. He fasted for three seasons in his old age as if they were a day, and he carried his riches on his shoulders like a prosperous worker.

* Because he despised love of eating, he was beloved by the heavenly; because he loved fasting and prayer, he was called a man beloved. Brethren, let us also be like Daniel the icon, and shine in his likeness through vigil, fasting, and prayer.

Morning Hymn – *abbun d-bashmayya*
In the morning, all creatures adore
the King who pursued the darkness away.

Daniel Verse
In the morning, all creatures
sing praise with all the nations,
to the King who destroyed ignorance
and enlightened the whole world.

Sanctuary Hymn – *m'yna dṭawatha*
- **O God our mighty stronghold.**
Let us be wakeful,
as we gird ourselves for work,
and trim our lamps with the oil of love,
to see the blessings
that God gives to good servants
when he finds them
wakeful when he comes.

Lent

Sixth Week of Lent

Evening Psalmody (from Psalm 31)
Blessed is the Lord who chose his e*lect*,
  Halleluiah, halleluiah, hal*le*luiah.
Blessed is the Lord who chose his e*lect*
  in the *mi*ghty village.
I said in my *haste*
  that I was lost *from* your eyes.
But you heard the sound of my pleading when I called to *you*.
  Love the Lord, *you* his just.
The Lord protects the *fai*thful,
  and repays the e*vil* their works.
Let your hearts be strengthened and forti*fied*,
  all who hope *in* the Lord.
Glory to the Father, to the Son and to the Holy Sp*ir*it.
  From age to age, a*men*, amen.
Halleluiah, halle*lu*iah, hal*le*luiah.

Basilica Hymn
- My sores have rotted and putrefied.
- From where will come my help?
- Who is like you, O Lord?
 "Who is the doctor who can cleanse my hidden wounds? O, will he be able to heal and to cure them? O who will be able to deliver me from the fire?" thus cried the adulteress. "I will unravel the tangles of sin, and draw near to the Lord and Savior." For indeed, he did not cast the tax-collector away from him, and with his speech, he converted the Samaritan woman. With his word, he gave life to the Canaanite woman, and to the hemorrhaging woman he gave healing with the hem of his cloak. With his merciful word, he freed the adulteress from her sins, and summoned her to the book of life with the holy women. And with these people, my soul says, at all times: Blessed is the Messiah our Savior!

Vigil Hymn
- In the evening there is weeping, and in the morning, joy.
- The Lord examines the just and the wicked.
- Rejoice, O just, and delight in the Lord.

There was joy and sadness among the virgins in their division. The wise ones lit their lamps with the oil of compassion, but the ignorant ones prepared their worthless vessels without compassion. Those who had habits pleasing to the Bridegroom were prepared, and entered the spiritual bridechamber with him. But those who, in the purity of their virginity, did not prepare fruits of justice, were deprived of the Kingdom filled with blessings, and heard the voice denying them, saying: "I do not know you." O Lord, do not reckon us among those who were rejected, but rather count us with those who were accepted, O Savior, for to you alone, O Lord, belongs abundance of grace.

Madrasha

- Through the prayers of the just who pleased you, have pity on sinners who call to you, and send us, from your treasury, pity, mercies, and salvation.

* If our creation is hateful, the blame is with the Creator. If our freedom is evil, the accusation comes to us. If we do not have freedom, why then is our choice put on trial? If not, then he judges it wrongly, but if so, he punishes it rightly.

* Trial accompanies freedom, and law is tied up with both of them: freedom which crosses the line of the Judge is brought to trial. What would the true Creator gain by lying to us, by not giving us freedom, yet writing and giving us the law?

* The truth stands in the middle, to ask and to be questioned: Did our Maker give us freedom or not? Indeed, questions and investigations are born of freedom: Answer and her sister Inquiry are daughters of Freedom.

Morning Hymn – *balmeneh*

All the angels above
glorify you, O Christ.
And we also on earth
lift up praise to you, O Lord.

Daniel Verse

Those in heaven sing glory,
and on earth offer worship,
to the Christ, Savior of all nations,
who has freed all from slavery.

Lent

Sanctuary Hymn – *ḥannana dapthyḥ*
- Let us light our lamps and go.
Make us worthy, Lord,
to preach your Gospel,
and receive the truth
from the treasure of your Word.
With the oil of love
burning in our lamps,
may we be awake
when you come to judge the world.

HOLY WEEK

SEVENTH SUNDAY OF LENT
HOSANNA SUNDAY

Evening Psalmody (from Psalm 8)
O Lord, my Lord, how glorious is your name through all the *earth*,
    Halleluiah, halleluiah, hal*le*luiah.
O Lord, my Lord, how glorious is your name through all the *earth*,
    for you have granted your *glo*ry to heaven.
From the mouth of children and *in*fants,
    you have fa*shion*ed your praise
because of your *en*emies –
    that the enemy taking vengeance *may* be silenced.
For they have seen the heavens, the work of your *fin*gers,
    the moon and the stars *which* you fashioned.
Who is man, that you remember *him*,
    and the son of man, that *you* command him?
You have made him little less than the *an*gels,
    and clothed him with ho*nor* and glory,
and given him authority over the work of your *hands*,
    and placed everything un*der* his feet.
Glory to the Father, to the Son and to the Holy Sp*i*rit.
    From age to age, a*men*, amen.
Halleluiah, halle*lu*iah, hal*le*luiah.

Lent

Basilica Hymn
- O Lord, the God of my salvation.
- Remember your Church, which you acquired from the beginning.
- Like a glorious Bridegroom; like an adorned bride.

O Lord, behold your Church, saved by your cross, and your flock bought with your precious Blood, offers a crown of thanksgiving in faith to you, O High Priest of justice who has exalted her by your abasement. And, like a glorious Bride, she rejoices and exults in you, O glorious Bridegroom. In the strength of the Truth, raise the walls of her salvation, and establish priests within her, to be ambassadors of peace on behalf of her children.

- Glory to the Father, and to the Son, and to the Holy Spirit.

When you were entering Jerusalem, the holy city, O Christ, God and our King, to fulfill all that had been written, young people and children saw you with the enlightened eye of faith and were amazed by you, as they picked up branches and went out to meet you. They threw garments and cloaks on your path, and all cried out the unending praise of the cherubim, as they said: "Hosanna in the highest! Blessed are you who has eternally abounding mercies!" O Lord of all, have mercy on us!

Vigil Hymn
- Bless the Lord, my soul.
- When God stands to judge.
- Pass from evil and do good.

You do not have a lamp of good habits, O my miserable soul; how can you go out to meet the Bridegroom? The wise virgins did not give oil to the foolish ones, those who were rejected by their deeds, and the bridechamber was not opened to them. Abraham did not relieve those who were burning, and a judge does not forgive those who do not repent. Because of this, take refuge in repentance, my soul, and say: "I have sinned before you, Lord. Forgive me and have mercy on me!"

Madrasha 1
- Glory to him who made the Hebrew children wise enough to cry out "Hosanna to the Son of David."
* "Go to the village across from us quietly," our Lord said, "and find a foal tied with an ass standing there, whose back has not been tamed by man, and who

has not been ridden and has grazed in the wilderness from its youth. Untie and bring them to me quickly."
* Zechariah preached and showed the mystery of his bodily humility: "Cry out to Zion and give her the good news: your radiant King comes to you riding on a foal, showing he is gentle and kind in his coming among us." He comforted the preacher in the fulfillment of his prophecy, when children praised him with hosannas.
* Many crowds threw their clothing before the Son of David, for the unspeakable and unlimited wonder and marvel was fulfilled: the wonder saying and the marvel speaking, how the prophet's word is fulfilled, who preached and said: "rejoice greatly and exalt, O daughter of Zion."

Madrasha 2
- Brethren, today let us tell of the glory of Christ, and sing today with hosanna of the greatness of his honor.
* Let us play the strings of the harp, regarding lowly flesh that was exalted, and with the son of Jesse let us sing of him with a ten-stringed harp. Come and rejoice today, O David, in the wedding feast of your Offspring: lift up the sound of your harp, and confess his greatness.
* Come and dance, as is your custom, in the procession of Christ the King, and play even more on your harp, songs of glory to his honor. You exalted before the Ark, and rejoiced among many: rejoice today that the words of your prophecy are fulfilled.
* You brought up the Ark to the holy temple in great procession: come exalt and rejoice today among the many with hosannas. As the daughter of Saul mocked your coming before the Ark, come and mingle today with the heavenly assemblies.

Morning Hymn – *kul nishma*
All living things, and all creatures adore you,
for you are the one true Light, who renews us.

Daniel Verse
Children praised with hosanna,
and exalted with branches,
to the Christ, who has dawned from David,
for all creatures' salvation.

Sanctuary Hymn – *ṭuwwa l-yaludhe*
- **Those on the path without guile are blessed.**
- **All the innocent of heart.**
Our great Savior came
riding on a donkey while
the children waved their branches.
Hosanna on high!
Hosanna to David's Son
who has redeemed our nature!

Monday of Holy Week

Evening Psalmody (Psalm 54): O God, save me by your name; * give me justice by your strength. * O God, hear my prayer; * hearken to the words of my mouth. * For strangers have risen against me, * the wicked seek my life. * They have no regard for you, O God. * But I have God for my help. * The Lord upholds my soul. * Bring evil upon my enemies, * and silence them by your truth; * and I will sacrifice to you in discernment, * and confess that your name, O Lord, is good. * For you have delivered me from all troubles, * and my eyes have seen the fall of my enemies. * **Glory to the Father, to the Son and to the Holy Spirit. * From age to age, amen, amen. * Halleluiah, halleluiah, halleluiah.**

Daily Hymn – *mara dkulla*
- **Hear, O Shepherd of Israel.**
- **Shepherd them and guide them forever.**
O Good Shepherd of our souls,
our help and Savior of all,
guide us according to your will,
under the shade of your right hand.
Accept the fruits of our lips,
which we, in thanks, now offer,
and grant us grace and mercy
from your abundant treasury.

Madrasha

- Blessed is he whom the prophets depicted.
* He has come to us in his love: the Blessed Tree. Wood undone by Wood; fruit cut off by Fruit, the killer by Life.
* In Eden and in the world, the Parable of our Lord; who is able to gather the symbols of his mysteries, that are signified all in one.
* It is written in the Scriptures; it is signed within natures; his truth in the prophets; his forgiveness in the high priests; his crown woven in the kings.

TUESDAY OF HOLY WEEK

Evening Psalmody (Psalm 84): How lovely are your tabernacles, Lord almighty. * My soul yearns for the courts of the Lord. * My heart and my flesh glorify the living God. * Even the bird finds a home and the sparrow a nest. * Fledglings grow near your altar, O Lord almighty. * My King and my God, blessed are they who dwell in your house. * They will glorify you forever. * Blessed is the man who trusts in you, * and who has your paths in his heart. * They will pass through the depth of lamentation and make it a dwelling place. * Even the lawmaker will be clothed with a blessing. * They will go from strength to strength, * and be seen by the God of gods in Zion. * O Lord God almighty, hear my prayer, * and attend, O God of Jacob. * See, O God our help, * and look upon the face of your Anointed One. * For one day in your court is greater than a thousand. * I wished to dwell in the house of God, * more than to dwell in the dwelling of the wicked. * For the Lord God is our nourisher and our help. * The Lord will give mercies and honor, * and not hold back his blessings * from those who walk in innocence. * Lord God almighty, * blessed is the man who hopes in you. * **Glory to the Father, to the Son and to the Holy Spirit. * From age to age, amen, amen. * Halleluiah, halleluiah, halleluiah.**

Daily Hymn – *byadh shlama*

- Come, let us bless and adore him.
Lord Jesus is adored in his passion and death;
Lamb with no stain or blemish,
who in the great strength and majesty of Divinity
is now revealed in humanity,
he is the one who conquered the sin of the world,
the one who raised our whole mortal race.

Lent

- I will exalt you, O Lord, my King.
O Christ, who suffered greatly and faced temptation,
who did not sin, but who knew all of our weakness,
we plead to you, O our Kind Savior,
forgive our sins, in your great mercy;
for you are the true Doctor
who places his balm
upon our wounds, and absolves all our debts.

Madrasha
- Glory to the Son, the Lord of the Mysteries, who fulfilled all Mysteries through his crucifixion.
* Lo, the passover lamb was killed in Egypt, and on Zion, the Lamb of Truth was slain. Let us look at both lambs, brethren, and see whether they are similar or different.
* Balance and compare their victories: that of the lamb of mystery and the Lamb of Truth, and you will see the mystery as a shadow, and the truth as the fulfillment.
* There was, from Egypt, through the passover Lamb, an exodus for the people, and not an entrance; there was, in the Lamb of Truth, an exiting for the people from error, and not an entrance.

WEDNESDAY OF HOLY WEEK

Evening Psalmody (from Psalm 99): O Lord, our God, you answered them. * O God, you were an avenger for them. * Repay them according to their deeds. * Exalt the Lord our God, * and adore at his holy mountain, * for the Lord our God is holy. * Glory to the Father, to the Son and to the Holy Spirit. * From age to age, amen, amen. * Halleluiah, halleluiah, halleluiah.

Daily Hymn – *mara dkulla*
- For the Spring of Life is with you.
- You give them drink from your pleasant valley.
Not from the spring of Jacob,
nor from those very waters
which were sweetened by Moses,
nor from the river Jordan,
which was made holy by your

holy baptism by John,
but from your side, O Jesus,
does the spring of Life gush forth.

Madrasha
- Glory to the Son, who saved us by his Blood, as its symbol saved the sons of Jacob.
* The Lamb of God released, through his Blood, the nations from error as from Egypt. Many lambs were slain, but through one alone was Egypt overcome.
* On feast days, lambs were offered, but one alone overcame error. Samuel brought up a suckling lamb, in which he overcame the warriors and the power of the Philistines.
* Through a lamb, the son of David weakened the mighty evil of Gilead. The priests take the veil from the altar, pure purple, and throw it upon him.

Passover Thursday

Evening Psalmody (from Psalm 42): All your waves and billows passed over me. * In daytime, the Lord commands his mercies, * and at night his praises: * pray with me to the living God. * I said to God, why have you forgotten me, * and why do I walk sadly, * in the distress of my enemies? * My enemies envy me enough to break my bones, * and they said to me every day, Where is your God? * Why are you cast down, my soul, and why do you groan? * Await for God, for again I will thank him, * the Savior of my countenance and my God. * Glory to the Father, to the Son and to the Holy Spirit. * From age to age, amen, amen. * Halleluiah, halleluiah, halleluiah.

Daily Hymn – ṣlywakh amlekh
- The Memorial of your many graces.
- O Lord, your name is forever.
The Memorial of your Passion,
for our salvation perfected,
your Church performs, O Savior:
keep her children from danger.

Lent

Madrasha
- Thanksgiving to Christ, who completed our salvation, and who washed, through his Body, the filth of our sins.
* In the mystery of the Lamb was hidden the mystery of our salvation, and in the blood of beasts was signified the absolution of our malice. If indeed a dumb beast could have absolved the rational, how much more does the Living Blood sanctify us, and wipe away, through his passion, deed of our debts? For we become, through his renewal, men freed from death.
* In the sacrifice of the dumb was signified the image of Life, and in the slaying of the mute, the semblance of the Rational. His Blood is living Blood, freeing all creatures, and like that one, a preacher of all of them. And the Sacrifice of the Rational absolves debts, and clothes mortals with the garment of forgiveness.
* In the path of the mysterious lamb walked the Lamb of Truth, and he arrived at the sacrifice, for the fulfillment of the allegory. He gave the freedom of life to the mortal race, and repaid the debt through his death which his fellows had earned in breaking the commandments, and denying the Creator the keeping of his laws.

PASSION FRIDAY

Evening Psalmody (from Psalm 41): All those who hate me murmured against me together, * and thought evil of me. * They thought with an evil mind: * Henceforth he will be buried and not be able to rise. * Even the man who greeted me, in whom I trusted. * He who ate my bread, in whom I trusted, greatly deceived me. * But you, O Lord, have mercy on me, * and raise me, and repay them. * In this I knew that you delight in me: * that my enemy did not do evil to me. * But you sustained me in my innocence, * and raised me before you forever. * Blessed is the Lord, God of Israel, * from age to age, amen, amen.
* Glory to the Father, to the Son and to the Holy Spirit. * From age to age, amen, amen. * Halleluiah, halleluiah, halleluiah.

Rite of the Washing of the Feet. – *mara d-kulla*
- **Come and hear and I will make known to you.**
On this, most holy of days, let us praise the Messiah
whose Flesh gave us forgiveness, and whose Blood bought salvation.

Lent

He washed the feet of the twelve, with his own holy, pure hands,
and gave us an example, of glorious humility.

- **Who can make known the wonders of the Lord?**

Who understands your graces, O merciful Friend of man,
who gave us holy symbols: holy, glorious mysteries?
The truest humility you taught us in your own deeds,
for you bowed down, a Servant, and washed the feet of the twelve.

- **Hear this, all you peoples.**

Our Lord completed the type, and said to his disciples:
"Behold what I did for you, I, your Lord and your Master:
I washed your feet and cleansed them, and gave you an example;
As I have served before you, so you serve one another."

Madrasha 1

- Awake, O vigilant, and sing praise with your voices: the Lion's Cub is imprisoned; who can go to sleep?

* The Father chose, in his love, to send his Son into the world, and the wicked crucified him; who can go to sleep?

* They judged him and condemned him; they imprisoned him and struck him; they took a reed and beat him; who can go to sleep?

* They drenched his face with spit, and a slave struck him on the jaw, and as he spoke, they condemned him; who can go to sleep?

* Like rabid dogs, they assaulted the Lion to kill him, and he stood silent like a guilty man; who can go to sleep?

* They fastened a crown of thorns, and placed it on the Possessor of Crowns; they inflicted him with all mockeries; who can go to sleep?

* They pushed the all-radiant Sun into darkness, and slammed the doors shut in his face; who can go to sleep?

Madrasha 2

- Awake, O just, and see the suffering that I endure for your salvation; awake!

* Awake, O Abraham, see and rejoice, for the mystery that you signified by the death of Isaac has been fulfilled; awake!

* Awake, O Moses, and see the Son who is brought to suffering due to your people; awake!

* Awake, O David, take your harp and sing before us: "lo, the free man among the dead," awake!

Lent

* Awake, O son of Amos, and come out of your grave, and see Emmanuel on the cross; awake!
* Awake, O Jonah, and come out of the fish; see that the mystery you signified in the depths is fulfilled; awake!
* Awake, O Daniel, come out of the cave, and see that the prophecy you prophesied is fulfilled; awake!

The priest comes out with a Gospel, and two servers with unlit candles, one with an unlit thurible, and they read the Gospel.

- **Let all the people say: Amen, amen.** – *la bhett y-hudha*
On this night, our Lord gave his Flesh and Blood
In the upper room, in great love for us.
    He wished to expose the one who would be
    The one to betray him to be condemned.
The disciples felt sorrow and distress
As each said to him: "Is it I, O Lord?"
    The Lord said to them, "He who dips his hand
    In the dish and eats, he will betray me."
Judas, you betrayed him who was conceived
In the Virgin's womb, as Gabriel said!
    Judas, you betrayed him who was adored
    By the Magi when they came, bearing gifts!
Judas, you betrayed him who was baptized
In river Jordan, by John the Baptist!
    Judas, you betrayed him who made water wine
    Which you drank yourself, at Cana's wedding!
Judas, you betrayed him who was extolled
By children who yelled "hosanna on high!"
    Judas, you betrayed him who washed your feet
    With his sacred hands on this very night!
Judas, you betrayed him who gave his Flesh
And his precious Blood in his Passover!
    Let us all repent of our sinful ways,
    And sing praise to Christ, our merciful King!
Halleluiah, halleluiah!
Glory to you, Lord, our Life and our Hope!

Madrasha 3

- Have pity on me, Pitying One; have pity on me, Merciful One.
    -Ḥunayn, Ḥannana; Ḥunayn, Mle Raḥme.

* Brethren, I look into the Scriptures and I am filled with sadness: when our Savior was suffering, Kepa wept in agony (firstly, because they had crucified his Master, but also because he had denied him), as he cried out in anguish: "My toil has gone in vain, for I have denied my Lord!"

* "Woe is me!" he cried in the foyer of the house of Caiaphas, "for I have become a stranger to the Son whom I denied. He named me Rock, and I have become dust; but he shall not build his Church on dust! I have despised my very self!"

* "He called me 'blessed' when it was revealed by his Father, and I told him 'you are the Christ, the Son of the Blessed One.' To whom can I plead to intercede with his Father? For he will certainly not accept me unless I am with his Son. I am at fault forever!"

HOLY SATURDAY

Evening Psalmody (from Psalm 22): My God, my God, why have you abandoned me? * And have taken away my salvation by my own ignorant words. * My God, I called to you by day and you did not answer me, * and at night, and you did not remain with me. * You are holy, and Israel sits in your glory. * In you my fathers hoped. * They hoped in you, and you delivered them. * They cried to you, and were delivered. * They hoped in you and were not shamed. * I am a worm, and not a son of man; * a reproach of the sons of men and an abomination of the people. * All who see me mock me. * They shoot out their lips and shake their heads. * He trusts that the Lord will deliver him, * and take him out, if he is pleased by him. * For you are my trust from the womb, * and my hope from my mother's breasts. * I was cast upon you from the womb, * and from my mother's belly, my God, you did not leave me. * For distress approached me, and there is none to help. * Many bulls surrounded me, * and the bullocks of Bashan encircle me, * and open their mouths at me, * like a lion that roars and snatches. * I am thrown as into water, * and all my bones are scattered, * and my heart is like wax, * and my recesses melt within me. * My strength dries up like a potsherd, * and my tongue cleaves to my jaw. * You have cast me upon the dust of death. * For dogs have encircled me, * and the assembly of the wicked have surrounded me. * They have pierced my hands and feet, * and weakened all my bones. * They look upon me and see, * and divide my garments among them. * They cast lots for my clothing. * But

Lent

you, O Lord, will not leave me. * **Glory to the Father, to the Son and to the Holy Spirit.** * **From age to age, amen, amen.** * **Halleluiah, halleluiah, halleluiah.**

Verse for *Lakhu Mara*: The free man among the dead, like the murdered buried in their tombs.

They read the two readings from the Old Testament.

Psalmody: Pass from evil and do good; seek peace and pursue it. The eyes of the Lord are upon the just, and his ears hear them. The face of the Lord is against the wicked, that he may wipe their memory from the earth.

They read the Apostle.

Gospel Verse: They have pierced my hands and my feet, and all my bones cry out. They look and see me, and they divide my garments among them.

They read the Gospel.

Petitions

Let us all stand composed, in contrition and diligence, let us implore and say: Lord, have mercy on us.

* O Living One who descended among the dead and preached the Good News to the souls that were held in Sheol, we implore you...

* O One by whose stripes our wounds were healed, and who murdered our murderer through his murder, we implore you...

* O One in whose suffering the lights were darkened, and all creatures wore mourning and sadness, we implore you...

* O One in whose crucifixion the spiritual beings were moved, and whose Father's command held them from destroying his crucifiers, we implore you...

* O One in whose death the tombs were torn, and the dead rose in reproof of his crucifiers, we implore you...

* O One who mingled his Blood with our blood, and who repaid our debts through the sacrifice of himself upon Golgotha, we implore you...

* O One who drank vinegar for the salvation of our race, we implore you...

* For the health of our holy fathers: ... and for all those in the same priestly service, we implore you...

* O Compassionate God, who guides all in his mercy, we implore you...

* O One whom the angels of light glorify in his death in heaven, and in whose killing the earth is saddened and in whose rising is gladdened, we implore you...

* O Shepherd who gave himself for his sheep and saved them by his Blood: redeem our lives from the evil one, O Lord, and have mercy on us...

Lent

Basilica Hymn – *talmydhaw*
- **The whole earth trembled and shook.**
- **The foundations of the earth trembled.**

When you hung on the cross, O Christ our Lord,
The creation saw you naked and the whole world shook;
The lamp of the sun turned into dark,
And the temple tore its veil,
And the dead rose up from their graves,
Giving praise to you, Resurrecting Lord!
- **The dead came forth from their tombs.**

In our Lord's passion was true suffering,
Awe and wonder seized the angels and the sons of men:
The dead who were buried left their tombs,
Singing "glory to the Son,
Who came down and was crucified,
Who cried with his voice, shaking heaven and earth!"
Wake, O Adam from of old: See the Sole-Begotten Son,
Suffering like a sinful one at the hands of sinful men!
    Wake, O cheated Abel just, murdered by brother unjust,
    see the Savior of the world dies for the life of the world!
Wake, O innocent Noah, God's replacement for the world,
see the Son of God Most High, who hangs upon wood today!
    Wake, O sons of blessings both, Shem and honorable Japheth,
    who covered the nakedness of their father as he slept:
Come and see the sun above, and the moon, the lamp of night,
Turn themselves to dark and gloom, lest their Lord be seen disgraced!
    Wake, high priest Melchezidech, who offered his sacrifice:
    come today and see the Son who has offered bread and wine!
Wake, O Father Abraham, see the Son revealed to you:
he hangs upon wood today, as did the ram shown to you.
    Wake, O blessed Isaac, saved by a ram caught in a tree,
    see that true great mystery fulfilled by your Lord today!
Wake, O Joseph, righteous one, by his brethren spat upon,
see the Savior Jesus Christ spit upon now by their sons!
    Wake, O Moses, prophet great, see the Lord of prophecy,
    suff'ring for the prophets' sons, as foretold by prophecy!

Lent

Wake, heroic Joshua, who stopped the sun and the moon:
see, they wear darkness and gloom, due to the death of the Son!
    Wake, O Psalmist, David King, come out of the grave today;
    take up harp and lyre again, and, preaching, sing us a Psalm:
"They divided his clothing, placed their bets upon his robe,
and were like wild dogs around the Lion who answered not."
    Wake, arise, King Solomon, sea of knowledge and wisdom,
    see the Lord of all wisdom who is mocked by ignorance!
Wake, O glorious Isaiah, look and see the Christ and King;
bearing death, a Sacrifice, without his mouth opening!
    Wake, O Jonah, who_for three days was like a man dead in grave,
    and who showed us, his own way, resurrection in three days!
Wake, O Jeremiah, priest, who was thrown into the mud,
see your Lord today asleep, for whom a tomb is a bed!
    Wake, O Zechariah blest, and his son John the Baptist,
    see today your Lord become sacrifice and offering!
Wake, arise, O Patriarchs, who died in hope of new life,
and see, upon Golgotha, the Lord of all that is made!
    Wake, arise, all you deceased, see the dead with the living,
    who preach to all the living, the Lord of dead and living!
Wake, deceased from ages past, see the Son who is of old,
who took your form in his love, in whom Scripture is fulfilled!
    Wake, you who are dead in sin, see the Son who knows not sin,
    who dies with the slaves of sin, that he may kill death and sin!
Wake, deceased, the wonder see: on the cross, the first-born Son,
by whose death has rent the earth by whose death has death destroyed!
    Conqueror, Abandoned One, Judged by servants by his choice:
    let us conquer all our sins in your mercies which made us!
Blest your death, and glorious is your rising from the dead;
pity us; forgive our sins, by your grace which is our hope!
    To you, with your Father be adoration and glory,
    and to the Spirit Holy, forever, from age to age.

Resurrection & Ascension

Resurrection Sunday

Evening Psalmody (from Psalm 45)
Your throne, O God, is forever and *ever*.
 Halleluiah, halleluiah, hal*le*luiah.
Your throne, O God, is forever and *ever*.
  The scepter of your kingdom is a *sim*ple scepter.
You loved justice and hated *evil*,
  and for this, God your God has a*noin*ted you
with the oil of gladness more than your com*pan*ions.
  Myrrh, cassia, and aloes perfume *all* your garments.
Glory to the Father, to the Son and to the Holy *Spi*rit.
  From age to age, a*men*, amen.
Halleluiah, halle*lu*iah, hal*le*luiah.

Basilica Hymn
- Have mercy on me, God, in your grace.
- Turn to me and have mercy on me.
- Like a dry and wearied land that needs water.
Around the tomb, Mary cried "Have pity on me!" for she was remembering you who made her, instead of a dwelling of demons, a dwelling of your love. She had bought spices to perfume your precious Body, by which the scent of our mortal race was perfumed. "By your Resurrection, O Good Lord of the deceased, I beg you, O Tree of Live, who raised Adam who has been passed over, O Fruit that our race did not want to taste, my Savior, may the dew of your mercies sprinkle me!"

Vigil Hymn – *ṭuwwa l-yalodhe*
- Sing a new song to the Lord.
The garden of Joseph
has become like paradise,
for Christ was placed within it.
The cherubim came,
and the ranks of seraphim,
and visited the Lord's tomb.
Glory to you, Lord!
Glory to you, Son of God,
who gladdened us by rising!

The Rite of the Festival of the Peace of the Resurrection

They sing the Easter Hymn by Mar Abba the Great:
* An archangel flew down from heaven above,
    Vested in the glory of angelic kind,
* He rolled away the stone from the tomb, in awe,
    And awoke the guards in fear and trembling.
* To the women, he said, "Do not fear, for Our Lord
    has arisen from the tomb, as he promised,
* and is taken up in glory to the Most High:
    Come and see the place his noble body was,
* And lo, the linens are placed here, witnesses
    of his resurrection, to all the nations."
* He was seen to Magdalene as a gardener,
    and she answered him, according to her thought:
* "Gardener, come, show me the one that I seek,
    for the fire of his love kindles me, and I burn!"
* Our Lord answered and said to her at that time:
    "Mariam, Mariam, I am the Son of the Most High."
* Blessed is the Lord, who was pleased in this deed,
    and completed the mystery of salvation.
* Blessed is he who rose from the dead in power,
    and granted victory to all Adam's race.
* To him praise from every mouth and every tongue,
    And upon us, mercy and pity at all times.

They read this Sermon of Mar Jacob of Sarug (selection):
A blessed joyfulness moves me today, in which I repeat the words of the prophet: "this is the day the Lord has made! Come, let us rejoice and be glad in it!"
This is the day which is unlike any before, and which none after will resemble!
This is the Great Feast; the boast of its kin!
This is the great joy that is given today to the Church!
Welcome, O New Day, on which the power of darkness is undone!
Welcome, O Day unlike any other, which destroys the power of the aged night!
Welcome, O Radiant Day, bringing the beautiful News!

Welcome, O Consoler of the mournful, O Gladdener of the sorrowful, O Gatherer of the lost, O Conveyor of the far, O Renewer of the weary, O Encourager of the fearful, O Planter of good seed in the hearing of the disciples!

Welcome, O Day which has no evening, O Happy Morning which twilight never saddens! Welcome, O Day which death does not overcome, O Rising which meets no fall!

Welcome, O First-Born of Days, with whose gifts both worlds are adorned!

Death is brought down and Life arises; Sheol is shut closed and Baptism opened; the Left Hand is deserted and the Right Hand thunders.

Therefore, let us all cry out and say: O Death, where is your sting? Where is your victory, O Sheol?

Today, the guards accepted a bribe and said: "his disciples took him as we slept."

After this, he was seen by Mary Magdalene and others. With unveiled faces, the Apostles said: "we know that Christ has risen from among the dead, and indeed will not die again – death has no power over him."

Indeed, we have been called to this joy, and invited to this feast: let us embrace each other in love; let us kiss each other in friendship. Let us give peace to one another; peace without deceit; peace without hypocrisy; peace from an undivided mind; that peace that our Savior sent to the assembly of Apostles in the upper room. Peace be with you all, for peace is the undoing of old enmity, and to peace we have been called; for peace we have gathered, as we do every year.

May the Resurrection be upon you! And life in Christ! Our Lord has freed us from death, and made mortals into immortals. Instead of quarrelsome, we are now peaceful; instead of wrathful, gentle; instead of savage, merciful; instead of guilty, innocent; instead of arrogant, humble; instead of sinful, righteous; instead of wicked, just; instead of evil, good.

Let us love one another with all our heart, because to this peace have we been called, my beloved: clap your hands together, glorify greatly, exult majestically, give praise spiritually, to him who this day has arisen from among the dead, and in his Resurrection has raised us all, amen.

And, just as he promised the thief, one of our kind, that "today you will be with me in Paradise," may he make us worthy to accept his heavenly revelation, and share in his heavenly kingdom amen.

Resurrection & Ascension

The servers cry out in one voice, three times: Brethren, give peace to each other in the love of Christ.
The people give the sign of peace to each other, saying: Rising, life and renewal to you!

Morning Hymn – *talmydhaw*
- **He sent salvation to his people.**
- **The Lord shows forth his salvation.**
Great salvation has come to all the world,
for the Lord Messiah
has now risen from the dead.
In thanksgiving and with Psalms,
the nations sing praise to him.
They see their idols casted down,
and the one true faith
preached in all the world.

Daniel Verse
By your rising, O Savior,
the nations gained salvation,
sin unraveled from our race,
death was swallowed by victory.

Sanctuary Hymn – *mara d-kulla*
- **The Lord is King, let earth rejoice.**
- **Rejoice, sing and praise his Name.**
Rejoice, take heart O mortals:
the reign of Death is ended!
Christ crushed it by his passion;
made life reign by his rising!
Earth and heaven rejoice now,
and angels sing together:
praise him who, by his rising,
raised up our race which was lost.

Monday of the Week of Weeks
Memorial of the Disciples of Emmaus

Basilica Hymn
- **The earth was shaken and trembled.**
- **The foundations of the mountains trembled and were shaken.**

In the hour that the wood of your cross was fastened, you shook the foundations of death, O Lord. And those whom Sheol had swallowed in their sins, it released while trembling – your command quickened them, O Lord. Because of this, we also glorify you, O Christ the King: Have mercy on us!

Tuesday of the Week of Weeks

Basilica Hymn
- **Come, let us bless and adore him.**
- **His holy name forever and ever.**

We adore the Memorial of your honorable Passion, O Savior, and also your Cross, which prepared a joyful feast for us. In it, we all accept the forgiveness of debts and sins, and new life apart from Sheol dawns for us, as well as the reproof of unbelievers, the boast of your faithful Church, and the glory of your victorious unending power!

Wednesday of the Week of Weeks

Basilica Hymn
- **Where can I go from your Spirit?**
- **And where can I hide from you?**

In the hour when, in the midst of silence, the trumpet of your coming sounds in great terror, and the awesome legions of the angels fly down in turbulence, and when all men arise from the graves, trembling in their inquisition, the heavenly hosts will shake from the vehemence of the judgment of the earthly, when the cherubim carrying you extol you, O Just Judge, indeed, in that fearful judgment when the actions of each man are repaid, have mercy on me, O Friend of mankind!

Thursday of the Week of Weeks

Basilica Hymn
- I will exalt you, O Lord my King.
- He lifts me up from the doors of death.

Your death, Lord Jesus, became the beginning of new life for us. And through baptism into you, we receive the token of life to come, which is your resurrection from among the dead. And so, in feasting and joy, we glorify your name, O Lord, because you abolished error and took away the sin of the world. And the one on whose head was placed the decree of Adam's condemnation, you returned to life everlasting.

Friday of the Confessors

Basilica Hymn
- I will bless the Lord at all times.
- And blessed be his honored name forever.

Blessed is the hidden power that dwells in the bones of the martyrs: for they are situated in their graves, and they chase demons out of the world. Through their teaching, they abolished the error of idolaters, and they quietly visit creation, and teach it to worship you, who alone are the Lord.
- Glory to the Father and to the Son and to the Holy Spirit.

Glory to you, O good and kind Lord, in whose power your true ones were victorious, and in whose aid scorned the threats of their persecutors, and destroyed the power of the haughty enemy. For he saw that the martyrs did not fall away from their true foundation.

Second Week of the Resurrection
"New Sunday"

Evening Psalmody (from Psalm 97)
Because you are the exalted Lord over all the *earth*,
   Halleluiah, halleluiah, hal*le*luiah.
Because you are the exalted Lord over all the *earth*,
   you are greatly exalted *ov*er all gods.
The friends of the Lord hate *ev*il,
   and he protects the souls *of* his just.
He delivers them from the hand of the *wic*ked.
   Light dawns upon the just, and joy to the up*right* of heart.
Rejoice, O just, in the *Lord*,
   and confess the memory of his *ho*liness.
Glory to the Father, to the Son and to the Holy *Spir*it.
   From age to age, *a*men, amen.
Halleluiah, halle*lu*iah, hal*le*luiah.

Basilica Hymn
- I will exalt you, O Lord, my King.
- He was the head of the building.

Your Resurrection, O Savior, adorned our race with heavenly gifts: it gave us, immediately, a true new life in the spiritual birth of baptism, in which we are baptized in the model of your Death and Resurrection; it also established, for us, teachers and priests in the churches, through whose agency we are brought near to the glorious Mysteries of the knowledge of your Divinity. O Friend of mankind, glory to you!

Vigil Hymn
- I will exalt you, O Lord my King.
- You forgave the sin of your people.
- You undid my bonds.

By your resurrection, you left behind death which had made us dead through the bonds of darkness, and you left your tomb, though shut with seals, from the depths of Sheol, like a bridegroom leaving his chamber, though the wounds were on your body, the nails and spear which were fastened upon you, so that through them Adam and Eve who had fallen could rise from the fall.

You stepped on Sheol like a warrior, and unbound the breaking of the command in your mercy. O Christ our Savior, Friend of man, glory to you!

Morning Hymn – *sahde brykhe*

All creatures adore you,
and the legions of angels confess you,
and we ask you to forgive
us the sins that we have done.
For you have brought us into
this world by your choice, O Lord,
that together we may confess you.

Daniel Verse

All your creatures adore you,
asking pity and mercy.
Lord of all, keep and protect them all,
that they praise you together.

Sanctuary Hymn – *mara d-kulla*

- He, the capstone of the house.

Your resurrection, O Lord, has saved our race which was lost;
we died and rose in your grace, by the power of the cross.
We rejected our idols which led us into error,
and now adore the one God, who saved the world through his Son.

Presentation Hymn (attributed to Mar Shim'un Bar Sabba'e)

- Be mighty and let your heart be strengthened.
- Be careful and do not sin.
- Do not fear those who kill the body, but cannot kill the soul.

Though you may take off your outer garments, you will never take off your inner vestment, O baptized. For if you are clothed with this hidden armor, the storms of many temptations will not defeat you. You know which words you have heard, and you know which living Sacrifice you have eaten. Beware of the evil one, lest he make you stumble, the way he did to Adam, and make you strangers to that glorious Kingdom. For he estranged him from Paradise, and wishes also to estrange you. For this, cry out with us to Christ, that he may strengthen all our souls by his Holy Spirit.

Third Week of the Resurrection

Evening Psalmody (from Psalm 96)
Give to the Lord, tribes of the *na*tions,
    Halleluiah, halleluiah, hal*le*luiah.
Give to the Lord, tribes of the *na*tions,
        give to the Lord glory and honor;
            give to the Lord the honor due *to* his name.
Take offerings and enter his *courts*.
        Adore the Lord in his *ho*ly courtyard.
Glory to the Father, to the Son and to the Holy Sp*i*rit.
        From age to age, a*men*, amen.
Halleluiah, halle*lu*iah, hal*le*luiah.

Basilica Hymn
- I will exalt you, O Lord my King.
- Ignorant and unwise people.
After your glorious Resurrection, evil and deceitful people made centurions stand to guard your tomb. Woe to unbelieving people! If they killed and buried you, why were they standing guard? And if they were terrified of you, how did they dare crucify you? Indeed, your Resurrection on the third day has shamed your crucifiers, and gladdened your Church. Glory to you!

Vigil Hymn
- I will exalt you, O Lord my King.
- You gave him authority over the work of your hands.
- Simon Peter said to them: "I am going fishing." And Simon Peter went up and dragged the net to land.
After your glorious resurrection, Peter went fishing, and you spoke to him, O Savior: "Tend the sheep of my flock; tend my sheep and my ewes. For their sake I stood before Pilate, and for their sake spit was cast upon me. For their sake I endured the shameful cross, and was in a tomb of the dead for three days; I who am the Savior and the Friend of man."

Morning Hymn – *abbun d-bashmayya*
Death now laments and Satan now mourns;
the Church is in joy, in the risen Son.

Daniel Verse
Blest is Christ, by whose death has
murdered the murderer, death,
and who rose, raising our human race,
and gave us life unending.

Sanctuary Hymn – *lakhu qarenan*
- I will bless the Lord at all times.
- And at all times, his praise in my mouth.
Blest is he who died
and who gave courage
to the mortal race.

FOURTH WEEK OF THE RESURRECTION

Evening Psalmody (from Psalm 144)
Age to age shall proclaim your *works*,
    Halleluiah, halleluiah, hal*le*luiah.
Age to age shall proclaim your *works*,
    shall de*clare* your might,
shall speak of your fearful *strength*,
    tell the tale of your won*der*ful works,
shall recount your *great*ness,
    and recall your *ma*ny graces.
Glory to the Father, to the Son and to the Holy *Spi*rit.
    From age to age, a*men*, amen.
Halleluiah, halle*lu*iah, hal*le*luiah.

Basilica Hymn
- Hear this, all you peoples.
- In the gates of daughter Zion. For Jerusalem stumbled and Judah fell.
- For it cannot be that a prophet be lost outside of Jerusalem.

The cross was established in Jerusalem, and all creatures were gladdened; greedy death was unraveled in it, and the power of demons was taken; it chased the Jews away to the four corners of the earth, and it gathered the nations together, and brought them into the Kingdom, that Paradise of Heaven, which Adam lost when he disobeyed, the Second Adam conquered in

Judah, returning its land to the Kingdom. He seized power in heaven and on earth, for behold, the assemblies of the angels worship before him, and they all cry out in one voice: thanksgiving to the Son of the Lord of all!

Vigil Hymn
- **The earth trembled and shook.**
- **The foundations of the mountains trembled and shook.**
- **There was darkness over all the land, the earth shook and rocks were split.**

On the day of your crucifixion, Lord Jesus, all creatures stood in trepidation when they saw that you were mocked by rebellious servants, and in their transformation, they cried out to the rational who were muted: "This is your Lord whom you crucified!" The sun by its darkness; the earth by its quake; the rocks by their splitting, rebuked the lost. And as in confirmation of your glorious resurrection, the bodies of the saints who had been buried rose and went out, as they lifted up glory to your great power, O Lord.

Morning Hymn – *m'yna d-ṭawatha*
On that great morning,
when you come to judge the world
and all who dwell here, you test with fire:
your grace defend us
when our hidden deeds are shown
in that fearful judgment of your Truth.

Daniel Verse
Blest is he, by whose passion
defeated death and Satan,
who has risen and renewed
all creation in glory.

Sanctuary Hymn – *sahde brykhe*
- **I will exalt you, O Lord my King.**

The Messiah's cross has extinguished sin
which had killed our race.
The assemblies up above looked in wonder at the cross,
which defeated both our foes: Satan, who leads us to sin,
and the death that de-cays our life.

Resurrection & Ascension

Fifth Week of the Resurrection
Memorial of Mar Addai the Apostle

Evening Psalmody (from Psalm 66)
Say to God: "How awesome are your *works*!"
    Halleluiah, halleluiah, hal*le*luiah.
Say to God: "How awesome are your *works*!"
    Because of your great strength, your enemies *are* convicted.
Through all the earth they shall adore and sing to *you*,
    and glorify your *name* forever.
Glory to the Father, to the Son and to the Holy *Spi*rit.
    From age to age, a*men*, amen.
Halleluiah, halle*lu*iah, hal*le*luiah.

Basilica Hymn
- Praise the Lord from the heavens.
- He turned the heavens and descended.
A servant descended from heaven, and shook the foundations of the earth; he made those who guarded you like dead men; and he strengthened the women who came to your tomb, and said: "Why do you weep, and why do you seek the one crucified by men, and buried like a man? He has risen above nature! Come and see the place where he was placed; he who has abounding mercies!"
- Precious in the eyes of the Lord is the death of his faithful.
- Beloved before God and in the eyes of men.
Precious in the eyes of the Lord our God is the death of his revered one, and the passing away of his saint, the splendid apostle who competed in spiritual battle and left the divine arena in victory in all excellence, leaving us a choice trophy, one excellent and spotless: his revered and honorable body. And lo, his soul processes with the angels, and offers prayers on behalf of our souls.

Vigil Hymn
- Hear this, all you peoples.
- Those who sow in tears will reap in joy.
- In the evening there is weeping, but in the morning, joy.
- Fear and trembling seized them, and they came to the tomb when the sun had dawned.

The women who had come to see the tomb were seized by awe and wonder when they had seen Christ who had been placed in the tomb, and the guards protecting the tomb, and were comforted to see angels descend and move the rock from the tomb, and the guards clothed with shock and darkness. They were weeping, for they did not know what this was, but Jesus met them, and resembled a gardener. "Lord, if you have taken him, tell me where so I can go and take him." But we plead to you: forgive us.

Morning Hymn – *ḥannana da-pthyḥ*
On that morning when
you will judge the world,
and reveal the works
of each one of us,
do not let us, Lord,
be condemned in sin,
rather, have pity
and mercy on us.

Daniel Verse
Blest is he who broke the doors of Sheol
and defeated sin and death,
who released those imprisoned
through his rising from the dead.

Sanctuary Hymn – *mara d-kulla*
- **Because they did not keep God's covenant.**
The race of men was guilty,
was bound for death and accursed,
but Christ was nailed to the cross,
to free us all from the curse.
The Ocean of mercies
gave himself to his captors;
he tasted death for a time,
to conquer death and the curse.

Resurrection & Ascension

SIXTH WEEK OF THE RESURRECTION

Evening Psalmody (from Psalm 72)
May his name be for*ever*;
    Halleluiah, halleluiah, hal*l*eluiah.
May his name be for*ever*;
    and before the sun *is* his name.
May all the nations be blessed in *him*,
    and all of them glo*ri*fy him.
Blessed is the Lord, the God of *Is*rael,
    who has worked great won*ders* alone.
And blessed be his honored name for*ever*.
    May all the earth be filled with his honor, a*men*, amen.
Glory to the Father, to the Son and to the Holy *Spi*rit.
    From age to age, a*men*, amen.
Halleluiah, halle*lu*iah, hal*l*eluiah.

Basilica Hymn
- All who call upon his name will boast.
- In the Lord is the boast of my soul.
We have gained an unending boast against death in the cross of Christ, and in his resurrection from among the dead. For by his suffering, he uprooted the sentence upon us. In great, unending glory, then, we all cry out and say: Only-Begotten God the Word, who assumed our mortal body, have pity, O Lord, on your servants, who confess your Cross!

Vigil Hymn
- I will exalt you, O Lord my King.
- In him our heart is glad.
- There will be one flock and one Shepherd.
By your holy cross, O Savior, angels and men became one flock, and the heavenly and the earthly one holy Church. Lo, all creatures rejoice and cry out: O Lord of all, glory to you!

Morning Hymn – *istepanos urḥa drash*
In the morning we all rise, and come adore the Father;
we lift up glory to the Son, and thank the Holy Spirit.

Daniel Verse

Let us thank, worship, and praise,
exalt, honor, and esteem,
Father, Son, Holy Spirit,
three Qnome in one Nature.

Sanctuary Hymn – *mara d-kulla*
- He, the capstone of the house.

Your resurrection, O Lord,
has saved our race which was lost;
we died and rose in your grace,
by the power of the cross.
We rejected our idols
which led us into error,
and now adore the one God,
who saved the world through his Son.

THE HOLY FEAST OF THE ASCENSION OF OUR LORD

Evening Psalmody (Psalm 24)

The Lord's is the earth and its fullness, * **Halleluiah, halleluiah, halleluiah.** The Lord's is the earth and its fullness, * the world and all its peoples. * For he set its foundations on the seas; * on the rivers he made it firm. * Who shall climb the mountain of the Lord? * Who shall stand on his holy mountain? * The man with clean hands and pure heart, * who has not sworn deceit in his soul. * He shall receive a blessing from the Lord * and justice from God our Savior. * This is the age which seeks and hopes, * for the countenance of your face, O God of Jacob. * Lift up your heads, O doors, * be opened, doors from of old, * that the King of honors may enter. * Who is this King of honors? * The mighty and powerful Lord. * The Lord is a mighty warrior. * Lift up your heads, O doors, * be opened, doors from of old, * that the King of honors may enter. * Who is this King of honors? * The almighty Lord. * He is the honored King forever. * **Glory to the Father, to the Son and to the Holy Spirit. * From age to age, amen, amen. *** Halleluiah, halleluiah, halleluiah.

Basilica Hymn
- O Lord, the God of my salvation.
- You have arrayed him in honor and glory.
- For he is the Image and Glory of God.
- For you have made us a glorious name.

O Lord, in your love, you had honored our nature: in the beginning, in your living image and in your likeness. And, because the backbiter cast us out of our glory in his envy, you sent your Son. By his birth, he turned our race back from ignorance; by his revered baptism, he promised us adoption; by his suffering and death, he saved us from slavery to sin; by his resurrection, he justified us, and by his ascension, he lifted us up to his right hand.

Vigil Hymn
- What is man that you remember him?
- You have saved us from those who hate us.
- Death was destroyed, which had been victorious from the ages.
- Yours is victory, O Lord.

Through the great suffering of the cross, you defeated death, O Christ our Lifegiver, and became the resurrection and the principle of the rising of the dead. You ascended in glory, and cherubim and seraphim extol you upon the seat of glory. So with the angels, we also glorify you, O Lord, and say: everything that is in heaven and on earth blesses and adores you, O Christ our Savior!

Madrasha
- Thanksgiving to the Victor who won and made all victorious, and ascended in glory to heaven.

* One high Priest was taken from among mortals to the altar of peace, and he entered for priestly service in the divine dwelling on behalf of his flock. He was made worthy to enter into the Holy of Holies higher than the earthly sanctuary; by his own Blood he entered and was seen by the Hidden One, and won salvation forever.

* By his own Blood he absolved the hateful wickedness of the sons of his race, and by his purity he purified mortality, which was filled with sufferings. Like a vestment, he washed them and made them pure vessels; in his Body, he wore them, like a priest his vestment, and entered the great sanctuary of heaven.

Morning Hymn – *sahde brykhe*
On the day our Head
ascended above to
heavenly glory,
clouds of light accepted him,
the disciples stood in awe,
and the angels gave them hope:
"This Jesus who has gone up,
he will come again in great glory."

Daniel Verse
On the day Christ ascended,
the disciples stood in awe,
and the angels above sang to him,
the great King who ascended.

Sanctuary Hymn – *l-ḥayye w-ṭuwwe*
- Your throne, O God, is forever.
Cherubim stand in fear and awe
before your throne, O Mighty One;
they hide their faces with their wings,
lest they behold that fearful sight:
lest their eyes see your Divinity,
the Fire that burns bright unceasingly!
And yet you, so glorious,
choose to dwell among mankind,
not that you may burn,
but that you may shine.
Great, O Lord, is your compassion,
and your grace,
for you have visited our race!

Week after the Ascension

Evening Psalmody (from Psalm 45)
Your throne, O God, is forever and *ever*.
  Halleluiah, halleluiah, hal*l*eluiah.
Your throne, O God, is forever and *ever*.
    The scepter of your kingdom is a *sim*ple scepter.
You loved justice and hated *evil*,
    and for this, God your God has a*noin*ted you
with the oil of *glad*ness
    more than *your* companions.
Myrrh, cassia, and aloes perfume all your *gar*ments.
    Your joy is from the noble temple and *from* myself.
Glory to the Father, to the Son and to the Holy *Spi*rit.
    From age to age, a*men*, amen.
Halleluiah, halle*lu*iah, hal*l*eluiah.

Basilica Hymn
- He who was before the ages.
- And before the sun is his name.
- He who is the Likeness of the invisible God.
- He is the Radiance of his Glory and the Image of his Being.
God the Word, who, in his perfect Existence has increased his mercy toward our lowliness, has assumed our nature and united it to the Individual of his Divinity and bore the suffering of the Cross, that in his death he may give life to our race, and ascended and taken his seat in heaven, above the princes and powers. Thus, as in the first Adam we had been condemned, in the second Adam we have conquered: and who can tell of his glorious age! Thus we glorify, and in knowledge believe, and in wonder confess, as he taught us in truth; nor indeed if even an angel from above were to come and tell us, and alter his Gospel before us, beyond what has been preached to us, we will not deny his humanity, nor will we forget his Divinity.

Vigil Hymn
- You ascended above and made a dwelling. The gates of heaven opened.
- God ascends in glory, the Lord with the sound of trumpet.
- Lo, heaven and the heavens of heaven cannot contain you.

Resurrection & Ascension

O Lord, when you ascended into heaven in glory to your Father, the legions above asked the angels in great awe: "Where has this great honorable King come from?" They saw you in the Head from our race, and marveled in you, our Savior and Life-Giver. They were stunned with fear, trembling, and wonder, and much conversation happened among them regarding your ascension, and your descent that is beyond explanation. Not that you discarded yourself, or were changed, or distanced from your Father, nor that when you received a Body from the Virgin, you made an addition to the Trinity. Great indeed is the mystery of your mercies, O Lord of all. Glory to you!

Morning Hymn – *abbun d-bashmayya*
Blest, the King who rose, and has gladdened all,
by his ascension, to the life above.

Daniel Verse
Blest, the King, Son of David,
who ascended in glory,
who, ascending, has gladdened
us below and those above.

Sanctuary Hymn – *sahde brykhe*
- **The Lord reigns, let earth rejoice.**
Our Lord Jesus Christ
reigns in greatest honor:
let the earth rejoice.
The miserable Adam's race
is now hallowed by angels.
Our weak race rejoices now,
in our Son who now is King,
and who reigns in hea-ven above.

PENTECOST & APOSTLES

PENTECOST SUNDAY

Evening Psalmody (Psalm 99)
The Lord reigns; let the nations tremble. * Halleluiah, halleluiah, halleluiah. * The Lord reigns; let the nations tremble. * He sits upon the cherubim, let earth shake. * The Lord is great in Zion, * and exalted over all the nations. * They confess your great and fearful name which is holy. * The might of the king loves judgment. * You established uprightness and judgment, * and you accomplished justice in Jacob. * Exalt the Lord our God, * and bow down before his footstool. * Holy among his priests were Moses and Aaron, * and Samuel among those who called his name. * They called the Lord and he answered them; * he spoke to them in the pillar of cloud. * They kept his witness, and the covenant he gave them; * O Lord, our God, you answered them. * O God, you were an avenger for them. * Repay them according to their deeds. * Exalt the Lord our God, * and adore at his holy mountain, * for the Lord our God is holy. * Glory to the Father, to the Son and to the Holy Spirit. * From age to age, amen, amen. * Halleluiah, halleluiah, halleluiah.

Basilica Hymn
- The Lord will send his grace and his truth.
- Before the Lord God, the Lord of all the earth.
- The Holy Spirit, whom God gives to those who believe in him.
- And they were all filled with the Holy Spirit.

The Holy Spirit who was sent from God, the Father of Truth, to the assembly of Apostles strengthened them by a graceful gift, encouraged their minds in his Gospel, and made their simplicity wise by his teaching, through a multiplicity of tongues, that they may henceforth become ambassadors among all peoples, proclaimers of the kingdom of heaven, evangelists, and preachers of the Trinity.

Vigil Hymn – *sahde brykhe*
- From the mouths of infants and children.
- They cry out from the mountain tops.

Glory to the One who came down to earth in the latter days,
who took on our Principal, and ascended to the heights,
sending down the Spirit to the Apostles as a flame,
that they burn away the chaff of sin.

Madrasha

- Glory to him who raised and gave victory to his apostles, who preached his confession in the four corners.

* The cunning and innocent; the simple and wise: cunning for good things, simple at evil, they labored for they knew the rebellious envied them. They worked, that they may be found skillful in action, for they had seen the wise foolish in deed.

* The victorious reached out to the truth in their manners: works of splendor, words of modesty. They interpreted the Scriptures, and taught what was written; they did what was commanded by their Lord. They balanced what was needed in proportion to the time; they measured rewards against their afflictions.

* Appropriate fruits they increased in each place. Faithful in action, true in their words: their mouth and their conscience. The blessed opened up a door to the poor and the needy. They made provisions, and filled up their treasures, and each one found rest for his will.

Morning Hymn – *sahde brykhe*

The Gift of the Spirit came upon the twelve
as in tongues of fire.
It accomplished miracles and they preached to all the world.
It dwelt in the holy martyrs, and they conquered fire and flame,
and the mighty sword of their foes.

Daniel Verse

We confess your Spirit, Lord,
whose descent has enriched us.
With the hosts of heaven in the Church,
we lift praise to your Lordship.

Sanctuary Hymn – *sahde qaddyshe*

- **Come, let us praise the Lord.**
Let us together sing glo-ry
to the one Creator all-powerful,
who has revealed three Qnome:
Father, Son, and Holy Spirit.

Pentecost & Apostles

GOLDEN FRIDAY

Basilica Hymn
- I will bless the Lord at all times.
- And blessed be his honorable name forever.
Blessed be Christ who came to suffer and die for us, who righted the fall of our race by the rising of his holy body. And after his resurrection, he ascended to heaven, to his Sender, and sits with him, to his right, and made his glory known to us through the gift of the Holy Spirit.

SECOND WEEK OF THE APOSTLES

Evening Psalmody (from Psalm 134)
The Lord does all he *wills*,
    Halleluiah, halleluiah, hal*le*luiah.
The Lord does all he *wills*,
    in heaven and earth, in the sea and all *the* abysses.
He brings up clouds from the ends of the *earth*,
    and makes light*ning* for rain.
He brought out *winds*
    from *the* storehouses.
Glory to the Father, to the Son and to the Holy Sp*i*rit.
    From age to age, a*men*, amen.
Halleluiah, halle*lu*iah, hal*le*luiah.

Basilica Hymn
- The Lord does whatever he wills.
- Our God is in heaven, and he does whatever he wills.
- Not by the hand of the one who wants, or the one who runs, but by the hand of the compassionate God.
- For all is from him and all is in him and all is by his hand.
The Holy Spirit, by his power, effects and does all things through his gifts: indeed, he supplies prophecy, perfects priests in his grace, is able to bring wisdom to the simple (for to fishermen did he reveal the Individuals of Divinity), and in his power, he presides over the awesome liturgies of the Church. O Kin of the Glorious Nature! O Kin of the Adorable Inhabitance of the Father and the Only-Begotten Son! O Holy Spirit, glory to you!

Vigil Hymn
- He who was before all time. They stand forever and ever.
- This is my God; I will praise him. This is the true and living God forever.
- The Three of them are One. And his Kingdom will have no end.

Father, Son, and Holy Spirit are in one Kingdom, for they enriched fishermen and simple men from the teaching of the treasures of their wisdom, as to all the nations and tribes, in their various languages, they taught the knowledge of the truth through the tongues of fire they received. Lord of all, Holy Spirit, may your power protect your holy Church from all dangers.

Morning Hymn – *sahde brykhe*
All the ranks of angels
come before your throne
at the time of dawn.
They rejoice in you, O Lord,
for you lead them in your grace,
and grant us, with them, to know
the pure wisdom of your Mind.
Lord, grant us the grace to see your Face!

Daniel Verse
Blest is he who filled apostles
with his Spirit, and sent them
to bring light to the world, and uproot
falsehood from all the nations.

Sanctuary Hymn – *balmeneh*
- Bring them to the harbor they desire.

Let us all take refuge
in the fortress of Christ;
we find peace and harmony
within the Holy Spirit.

The Feast of the Body of Christ

Daily Hymns – *l-ḥayye w-ṭuwwe*
- Your throne, O God, is forever.
- I will magnify him and honor him.
Cherubim stand in fear and awe
before your throne, O Mighty One,
they hide their faces with their wings,
lest they behold that fearful sight:
lest their eyes see your Divinity,
the Fire that burns bright unceasingly!
And yet you, so glorious,
choose to dwell among mankind,
not that you may burn,
but that you may shine.
Great, O Lord, is your compassion,
and your grace, for you have visited our race!
- Glory to the Father, to the Son and to the Holy Spirit.
Church, O betrothed of Jesus Christ
who saved you by his precious Blood;
gave you his Body (living Food
which wicked men had sacrificed),
who placed in your hands
his redeeming Cup
(his most precious Blood
that flowed from his side
when they stabbed him by the spear):
listen to the Bridegroom's voice:
repent, leave behind
vain wandering and sin.
Cry out to your Savior
with hymns of thanksgiving: "Glory to you!"

Pentecost & Apostles

Third Week of the Apostles

Evening Psalmody (from Psalm 131)
Your priests will be clothed with *justice*,
    Halleluiah, halleluiah, hal*le*luiah.
Your priests will be clothed with *justice*,
    and your just *ones* with glory.
Because of David your *ser*vant,
    do not turn away the face of *your* anointed.
The Lord vowed to David in *truth*,
    and will not turn *a*way from it,
that from the fruits of your *loin*
    I will make one sit up*on* your throne.
Glory to the Father, to the Son and to the Holy *Spi*rit.
    From age to age, a*men*, amen.
Halleluiah, halle*lu*iah, hal*le*luiah.

Basilica Hymn
- Your priests shall be clothed with justice, your just ones with glory.
- I will clothe the high priests with salvation, and the just with glory.
- These serve an image and a shadow of that which is in heaven.
The priesthood of the house of Aaron, in performing the law, represented a mystery, a shadow and an image. But the apostleship of the house of Simon received the embodiment, the perfection, and the truth of the Incarnation. The Heir of the Father loved that apostleship and by it he captured the Earth. Indeed, by the hands of fishermen he returns and captures the whole creation and, behold! it lifts up glory, being baptized in the fullness of Individuals of the Father, Son, and Holy Spirit – Glory to you.

Vigil Hymn
- I will bless the Lord at all times.
- Blessed be his honored name forever. Let us bless the Lord who made us.
- And God made Adam in his image and likeness.
Blessed is the Good One who made Adam in his image and likeness in the beginning, and in the last days, pitied him who had fallen from his glory. He came from heaven for our salvation, and took from our mortal race a Pledge for his honor. He let him become Provider, Head, and Lord over all in heaven

and on earth, and in him renewed all of nature which had corrupted in death, the patient one who had ruled over him in his sins.

Morning Hymn – *sahde brykhe*
Due to the first Adam,
darkness, decadence,
and death were spread forth
onto every race and tribe
of the sons of weakened flesh.
But in Christ, sin is erased,
and all are called to adore
in the place where light and truth are found.

Daniel Verse
Blest is the Son of Adam
who himself has saved Adam.
blest, the Father who sent him,
with the Spirit he gave us.

Sanctuary Hymn – *ḥannana dapthyḥ*
- **He of pure hands and clean heart.**
When the priest enters
the holy altar,
the angels above
stand in fear and awe.
They gaze at the priest
who breaks and divides
the Body of Christ
which forgives our sins.

THE FEAST OF THE SACRED HEART OF JESUS

Daily Hymn
- **God is good to Israel and to the innocent of heart.**
- **And joy to the upright of heart.**
Come, all of us faithful, in joy and gladness, let us hearken to the command of the Son, and take his yoke upon us, and unite with him delightfully, and find rest for our souls. Glory to you, O Lord! Glory to you, O Son of God, who enlightened our minds with your teaching!

Pentecost & Apostles

FOURTH WEEK OF THE APOSTLES

Evening Psalmody (from Psalm 118)
I have opened my mouth, taken a *breath*,
 Halleluiah, halleluiah, hal*le*luiah.
I have opened my mouth, taken a *breath*,
 and awaited *your* salvation.
Turn to me and have mercy on *me*,
 for I have *loved* your name.
Fashion my steps on your *paths*,
 and let the wicked not rule *o*ver me.
Save me from those who oppress the son of *man*,
 that I may keep *your* commands.
Brighten your face upon your *ser*vant,
 and teach *me* your law.
Glory to the Father, to the Son and to the Holy *Spi*rit.
 From age to age, a*men*, amen.
Halleluiah, halle*lu*iah, hal*le*luiah.

Basilica Hymn
- **The Lord is King, let the peoples tremble.**
- **From a merciless people. There they feared greatly.**
- **The doors shut where the disciples were.**
- **And the glory of the Lord shone upon them.**
O Lord, when the assembly of apostles was hidden, on account of fear and trembling from the Jews, from heaven the gift of the Holy Spirit descended upon them together. And in the four corners, they became preachers of your divinity and your humanity, and converted the whole creation from error, by the great power of the Paraclete; and we also, who take refuge in your grace, glorify you!

Vigil Hymn – *mara dkulla*
- **I stand on rock and guide my steps.**
Apostles, rock unshaken, built up a solid household
empowered by their Master - beat godlessness and built the Church!
O disciples of Truth, who built up and completed
the temples of the Spirit, the souls of all the faithful!

Pentecost & Apostles

Morning Hymn – *m'yna d-ṭawatha*
At dawn of morning, we lift glory to your Name,
for you have saved us and all the world.
Grant us in your grace
that our day be filled with peace,
and we beg you to forgive our sins.

Daniel Verse
In the most joyful morning,
let us sing to the glory
of the Christ, who freed us from our sins,
and made us his pure temples.

Sanctuary Hymn – *balmeneh*
- **They will praise your Name forever.**
- **They will praise you forever.**
Praise to you who gave us
your Body and your Blood,
and brought salvation and hope
when you came down among us.

FIFTH WEEK OF THE APOSTLES

Evening Psalmody (from Psalm 34)
The dwelling of the angels of the *Lord*
    Halleluiah, halleluiah, hal*le*luiah.
The dwelling of the angels of the *Lord*
    surrounds those who fear him and de*li*vers them.
Taste and see that the Lord is *good*.
    Blessed are all who *trust* in him.
Glory to the Father, to the Son and to the Holy Sp*i*rit.
    From age to age, a*men*, amen.
Halleluiah, halle*lu*iah, hal*le*luiah.

Basilica Hymn
- **The Lord will send his grace and his truth.**
- **He will send from heaven and save us.**

Pentecost & Apostles

- Do not take your Holy Spirit from me.
- The Spirit of truth, whom the world cannot accept.
- The Spirit of wisdom and understanding.

The Holy Spirit who was sent from above enlightened, instructed, and perfected the apostles; those who became, all of them, sewers of peace in creation, who drew open the shroud of gloom from the whole creation, and who preached heavenly renewal to peoples and nations. And while they endured constant scourgings from persecutors, that same Spirit strengthened them, and they prevailed and conquered every evil, and healed different diseases by his word. And while our Savior was with them as he promised from the beginning, they were exulting every day, wearing the sword of the Holy Spirit, and warring against the hordes of the tyrant, preaching true life.

Vigil Hymn
- Hear, O Shepherd of Israel.
- Be their Shepherd and guide them forever.
- The good Shepherd lays down his life for his sheep.
- And there will be one flock and one Shepherd.

The heavenly Shepherd who bowed down saved his flock, for he saw that it was scattered by the error of idolatry. He chose from our race twelve diligent workers, and filled them with the wisdom of power sent from above. He taught them to accomplish wondrous and marvelous deeds. When they endured tribulations from those who persecute the truth, they did not neglect to gather the flock saved by the pure Blood which they had drunk as wine, which was squeezed by a spear. For it is the precious Blood by which our debts were forgiven and our wounds were healed. O killed ones who considered their dwelling to be in the mighty fortress of their faith, which cannot be destroyed by the deceit of the rebel!

Morning Hymn – *m'yna d-ṭawatha*

At dawn of morning, we give thanks and praise to him
who came in love, and took on our flesh,
and saved us from death,
who ascended to the heights,
and is adored by the hosts above!

Daniel Verse
We adore him who loved us
and made known his three Qnome,
who exist always, e-ternally:
Father, Son, Holy Spirit.

Sanctuary Hymn – *lakhu qarenan*
- **I will bless the Lord at all times.**
Blest is he who let
us hallow his Name
with the hosts above.

SIXTH WEEK OF THE APOSTLES

Evening Psalmody (from Psalm 89)
I vowed one thing in my *truth*,
    Halleluiah, halleluiah, hal*le*luiah.
I vowed one thing in my *truth*
    to David, and *will* not lie:
that his seed will be for*ever*,
    and his throne like the *sun* before me,
and will be established forever like the *moon*.
    The witness in the *sky* is faithful.
Glory to the Father, to the Son and to the Holy *Spi*rit.
    From age to age, a*men*, amen.
Halleluiah, halle*lu*iah, hal*le*luiah.

Basilica Hymn
- **I will exalt you, O Lord my King.**
- **The Lord is faithful in his words. His word is complete unto the ages.**
- **Let us receive the promise of the Father, the Holy Spirit.**
- **This is the promise which was promised us: life eternal.**
O Lord Jesus Christ, you completed and verified the promise of the Father, promised by means of your holy apostles. They accepted the gift of the Holy Spirit; they went out, made disciples of and baptized peoples and nations, by means of varying tongues and turned them to the knowledge of God.

Pentecost & Apostles

Vigil Hymn
- You are righteous, O Lord, and your judgments are just.
- Let the heart of those who seek the Lord rejoice.
- May joy be upon your heads forever.

Justly, Lord, did you reward joyfulness to the holy apostles who believed in you. To one of them you gave authority over the keys of the Kingdom. His companion, you took up to the third heaven. Another, you let rest on your chest, O Lord. Now, they delight in glory in your holy Church, that by their prayers you may forgive and have mercy on us.

Morning Hymn – *abbun d-bashmayya*
In the morning, we give thanks and praise,
to the true Light, the Lord of the Dawn.

Daniel Verse
By your strength, the apostles
conquered death in their trial.
By their prayers, may your Church be kept safe,
and lift praise to your Lordship.

Sanctuary Hymn – *lakhu qarenan*
- I will bless the Lord at all times.

Blest, the Son of God,
by whose Sacrifice
our whole race was freed.

SEVENTH WEEK OF THE APOSTLES

Evening Psalmody (from Psalm 34)
The just cry out and the *Lord,*
    Halleluiah, halleluiah, hal*le*luiah.
The just cry out and the *Lord*
    hears them and de*liv*ers them.
The Lord is close to the broken *hea*rted,
    and saves the hum*ble* in spirit.
Many are the troubles of the *just* man,
    and the Lord delivers him from *all* of them.

Glory to the Father, to the Son and to the Holy *Spi*rit.
    From age to age, a*men*, amen.
Halleluiah, halle*lu*iah, hal*le*luiah.

Basilica Hymn
- God will send his grace and his truth.
- He will send from heaven and save us.
- He will show his people power in his works.
- The Spirit of truth, who proceeds from the Father.
- For he is the Power of God.

The Spirit, the Paraclete, is the Power that is from the Father and the Son, who dwelt in the Apostles, the friends of the one who gives life to all, and made them the salt which seasons the taste of the dull. They enlightened the world through their teaching, and gained clarity. They believed and confessed in the Father, and the Son, and the Holy Spirit. And while Satan marshaled his armies for battle, they did not tremble from afflictions, nor were they weakened by torments; for by the suffering and death of the Son were they saved, and because of this, they gave their flesh over to accept every torture, that they may resemble their Lord. For they saw that by his suffering he saved his Church, and by his death he gave life to all creatures, that they may become, for him, heirs of the Kingdom.

Vigil Hymn
- He chose them in the innocence of his heart.
- He gave them what they had asked.
- He called those whom he wanted, and chose twelve from them.

O Christ, who chose his apostles and clothed them with the power of the Spirit, that they may be preachers in the world and reveal his glory and Divinity in creation through the mighty works of their hands: gladden your churches with peace and harmony, and lift up the head of the preachers of your name and the keepers of your commandments. With your right hand, O Lord, may our salvation be guarded, and may they preach your righteousness in the peace that comes from you.

Morning Hymn – *abbun d-bashmayya*
In the morning, praise is due to you,
for you give your light to all of the earth.

Daniel Verse
We confess and adore you,
Christ our King, and Life-Giver.
Your strength clothed the apostles
with invincible armor.

Sanctuary Hymn – *balmeneh*
- Holy and awesome is his name.
Holy One who is pleased
with the saints and angels:
Lord, forgive the faults and sins
of your servants, in mercy.

THE FINAL FRIDAY OF THE SEASON OF THE APOSTLES
MEMORIAL OF THE 72 DISCIPLES

Basilica Hymn
- Their Gospel goes out to all the earth.
- They walked from nation to nation.
O holy apostles, who preached and taught the new Gospel in the four corners, and uprooted the thorns that the evil one planted through his weeds, and planted good seed by means of their teaching, and fulfilled and completed the charge they accepted, and transmitted this to the teachers and priests: O victorious athletes, O true pillars, supplicate and plead to Christ for peace!

OPTIONAL HYMNS FOR THE SEASON OF THE APOSTLES
- From the mouths of infants and children. – *sahde brykhe*
Glory to the One who came down to earth in the latter days,
who took on our Principal, and ascended to the heights,
sending down the Spirit to the Apostles as a flame,
that they burn away the chaff of sin.

- Come and see the works of the Lord. – *byadh shlama*
Our Savior chose apostles, who were twelve doctors,
sent out to the four corners, and he adjured them:
"Heal all the sick, raise all those who fall,
and grant forgiveness to all who repent.
Freely you have received, therefore give as freely:
do not hold back the gift you have received."

Summer/Repentance

First Week of the Season of Summer/Repentance
Memorial of the Twelve Apostles; Also Called Nawros-d-El

Evening Psalmody (from Psalm 144)
The Lord is *good*,
    Halleluiah, halleluiah, hal*le*luiah.
The Lord is *good*,
    and his mercies are up*on* his servants.
Your servants will thank you, O *Lord*,
    and your righ*teous* will praise you,
and tell of the glory of your *king*dom,
    and speak *of* your might;
to show mankind your *pow*er
    and the glory *of* your kingdom.
Glory to the Father, to the Son and to the Holy *Spi*rit.
    From age to age, a*men*, amen.
Halleluiah, halle*lu*iah, hal*le*luiah.

Basilica Hymn
- **Their gospel went out to all the earth.**
- **And their words to the ends of the world.**
- **They kept his witness and the covenant he gave them.**
- **Then they went out and preached in every place.**
The holy apostles taught one perfect confession in the Holy Spirit, and uprooted and abolished from the earth the thorns and weeds that the evil one planted in the world. They planted, instead of them, the seed of their teaching. With the light of their words, they quenched and destroyed the darkness of error that had seized the world. They preached the true faith in all the inhabited world, in the adorable name of the Father, the Son, and the Holy Spirit, the Nature that is incomprehensible!

Vigil Hymn
- **Let the righteous praise the Lord.**
- **Let the heart of those who seek the Lord rejoice.**
O apostles of Christ the King, who reconcile those thrown into wars, and give rest to those engaged in battles, and became a great refuge for the afflicted: angels and men are filled with joy today on your memorial, O blessed ones. Plead for all of us, that by your begging, we may receive forgiveness.

Morning Hymn – *sahde qaddyshe lwyshay nuhra*
Holy apostles were clothed with light,
when they went out to preach to all the earth,
the majestic Trinity: Father, Son, and Holy Spirit.

Daniel Verse
Lo, your feast is established,
O apostles who preached Truth,
And your faith will remain on the earth,
to the end of the ages.

Sanctuary Hymn – *sahde brykhe*
- Their Gospel goes through all the earth.
The holy apostles went out to the world
to proclaim the Truth.
They brought all the nations to
knowledge of the one true faith.
All the world accepted it,
and became true witnesses
of the Resurrection of Christ.

SECOND WEEK OF SUMMER/REPENTANCE

Evening Psalmody (from Psalm 25)
Remember your mercies, O *Lord*,
    Halleluiah, halleluiah, hal*le*luiah.
Remember your mercies, O *Lord*,
    which are eternal, *and* your graces.
Remember not the sins of my *youth*,
    but remember me in your *ma*ny mercies,
because of your grace, O *God*.
    God is *good* and righteous.
Glory to the Father, to the Son and to the Holy *Spi*rit.
    From age to age, a*men*, amen.
Halleluiah, halle*lu*iah, hal*le*luiah.

Summer/Repentance

Basilica Hymn
- O Lord, do not reproach me in your wrath.
- I became like a wasted vessel. My life reached Sheol.
- Why was light given to the toiling, and life to the bitter of soul?

O Lord, it is not from this present life that I profit in the greatness of my sins, nor is it from that which is eternal, due to the faults that overcome me. In shamefacedness do I stand on the day of judgment, as I tremble and groan forever, without escape. I call your mercies to come to my aid, O Lord, that on the day of your coming, you may forgive my sins, and have mercy on me.

Vigil Hymn
- O Lord, the God of my salvation.
- All the days of my life, I say but I do not do.

Lord, every day I promise you that I will repent from my sins, and I show my repentance with tear-filled eyes, but then I return to my deeds. Now I beg you, my Savior: do not remember my faults or my many debts, but rather extend your merciful hand to me, as your grace always does. O Good Doctor of all wounds: have mercy on me.

Morning Hymn – *kul nishma*
At the time when
darkness comes, have mercy,
and renew us in daylight
to praise your Name.

Daniel Verse
When the dark overcomes us,
may your Light raise our nature:
grant us, Lord, in your mercy
to give thanks to your Kindness.

Sanctuary Hymn – *lakhu qarenan*
- I will bless the Lord at all times.
- Bless the Lord who made us all.

Blest is God who sent his Beloved Son,
and redeemed our race.

Summer/Repentance

Third Week of Summer/Repentance

Evening Psalmody (from Psalm 69)
Answer me, O Lord, for your grace is *good*,
    Halleluiah, halleluiah, hal*le***luiah.**
Answer me, O Lord, for your grace is *good*,
    and turn to me in *your* great mercies.
Do not turn your face from your *servant*,
    for I am greatly troubled; answer me.
        Bring my soul to *your* salvation.
Glory to the Father, to the Son and to the Holy *Spi*rit.
    From age to age, a*men*, **amen.**
Halleluiah, halle*lu***iah, hal***le***luiah.**

Basilica Hymn
- Bless the Lord, my soul.
- My legs were standing within your gates, O Jerusalem.
- Hope in God and do good. And my life reached Sheol.
- The great door was opened to me, filled with deeds.

You stand at the doorway of the end of your life, O my miserable soul! Indeed, here you have occasion to beg for forgiveness, but there, tears will profit, nor will repentance aid – when the Bridegroom enters, and all his guests enter with him, and he closes the doors, and the veil is drawn. Who, therefore, is my hope, aside from you, O Lord? O Friend of mankind, O God, forgive me!

Vigil Hymn
- O Lord, God of my salvation.
- I have become like a lost vessel.

O Lord, I have drowned in my many faults and sins, and become a lost vessel. I have no forgiveness or unveiled face, for my days pass in vices, and my life is wasted in wretched things. Time is cut short and death hurries, and your revelation will surprise me. I shed tears before you, and beg your grace, that you may rejoice in my repentance, and I be healed by your mercies, and live in your grace.

Summer/Repentance

Morning Hymn – *kul nishma*
Lo, upon earth,
and in heaven, you are Lord,
and you rule in every place:
grant us new life.

Daniel Verse
To you call all the weary,
O Kind One who has mercy:
may your door open up to our prayer,
who confess your salvation.

Sanctuary Hymn – *lakhu qarenan*
- Offer him a sacrifice of praise.
- To you I offer a sacrifice of praise.
Living Sacrifice,
Bread come from above:
we thank you forever.

FOURTH WEEK OF SUMMER/REPENTANCE

Evening Psalmody (from Psalm 51)
Sprinkle me with hyssop, and I shall be *clean*;
    Hal*l*eluiah, halleluiah, hal*l*eluiah.
Sprinkle me with hyssop, and I shall be *clean*;
    wash me with it, I shall be whi*ter* than snow.
May your delight and gladness sustain *me*,
    and my humble bones *will* rejoice.
Turn your face from my *sins*,
    and blot out all of *my* misdeeds.
Glory to the Father, to the Son and to the Holy *Spi*rit.
    From age to age, a*men*, amen.
Hal*l*eluiah, halle*lu*iah, hal*l*eluiah.

Basilica Hymn
- Turn to me and have mercy on me. For I pray to you, O Lord.
- Turn to the prayer of your servant, and to his pleading, O Lord my God.

Have pity on me, O Lord, as you did with the tax-collector: I cry out to you, O Lord: have mercy on me! O Answerer of the pleadings of those who ask him; O Opener of his door to those who knock on it: open to me, O Lord, the door of your mercy, and grant me forgiveness for my faults, for their memory terrifies me. Indeed I know and remember my iniquities, and I am unable to be purified without your mercies. May you grant me cleansing, in your grace, from the foulness of the sins that have defiled me. O compassionate Savior, O Lord of all, glory to you!

Vigil Hymn
- **O Lord, hear my prayer!**
- **I desired to draw near to God.**
- **I desired to do the will of God.**

I wished to scour the filth of my debts with tears, prayers, and supplication, O Lord God, and to please you during the rest of the days and years of my life through the penance I offer you. But my enemy does not leave me, and fights against my soul at all times. I beg you, before I am lost forever: save me, and have mercy on me.

Morning Hymn – *kul nishma*
Blessed are those
who know you and your Light;
when you come again
they will not be condemned.

Daniel Verse
Blest are all the enlightened
by the friendship of our Lord:
who do not turn their eyes to the world,
but have hope in his coming.

Sanctuary Hymn – *balmeneh*
- **For you are a priest forever.**
- **He forgives his land and his people.**

O High Priest of our Faith,
Jesus, King of Glory,
by whose Flesh has saved our souls,
by whose Blood has absolved us.

Summer/Repentance

FIFTH WEEK OF SUMMER/REPENTANCE

Evening Psalmody (from Psalm 104)
He made the moon for *time*,
  Halleluiah, halleluiah, hal*le*luiah.
He made the moon for *time*,
  and knew the time of *the* sun's courses.
He made darkness, and there was *night*,
  and all the beasts of the field pass by *du*ring it.
The lions roar to des*troy*,
  and seek their *food* from God.
When the sun dawns, they are gathered *in*,
  and lie down *in* their dens.
Man goes out to his *work*,
  and for his labor *un*til evening.
Glory to the Father, to the Son and to the Holy *Spi*rit.
  From age to age, a*men*, amen.
Halleluiah, halle*lu*iah, hal*le*luiah.

Basilica Hymn
- O Lord, your servants will confess you.
- Regarding your grace and your truth.
Rational mouths confess you, O Good One who ordered creatures, and who placed a boundary for the day, and whose word does not pass away. For when the day's work is completed, and it has fulfilled its operation it rests in its weariness, in a temporal sleep, and binds for us, in its dusk, a figure of death and burial. And in its dawn, it awakens the sleeping from their sleep, as it preaches to us about our resurrection and renewal.

Vigil Hymn
- I will exalt you, O Lord my King.
- Light has dawned in the darkness for the upright.
O Christ the King, whose light dawned in the four corners, may you forgive your Church in your many mercies, for the backbiter seeks to destroy her children. May the apostles who sowed good seed in the souls of the sons of men be ambassadors on our behalf, and plead to you for your servants. O Kind Lord, have mercy on us.

Summer/Repentance

Morning Hymn – *kul nishma*
The sons of men
and the angels stand in you,
for you are their glorious Light
who gives them life.

Daniel Verse
In you, Lord, stand the angels,
and in you lives humanity,
for you are the true un-ending Light,
Creator and Renewer.

Sanctuary Hymn – *lakhu qarenan*
- Praise the Lord from his holy place.
- They will praise your name forever.
Glory to the Pow'r
preached as Trinity,
adored gloriously.

SIXTH WEEK OF SUMMER/REPENTANCE

Evening Psalmody (from Psalm 103)
The grace of the Lord is et*er*nal,
    Halleluiah, halleluiah, hal*le*luiah.
The grace of the Lord is et*er*nal,
    and is unto the ages over *those* who fear him.
His justice is for the sons of their *sons*,
    for those who *keep* his covenant,
and remember his com*mand*ments
    and *act* on them.
Glory to the Father, to the Son and to the Holy Sp*i*rit.
    From age to age, *a*men, amen.
Halleluiah, halle*lu*iah, hal*le*luiah.

Summer/Repentance

Basilica Hymn
- O Lord, you are a dwelling-place for us unto the ages.
- Fruit-bearing trees and all cedars.
- He set the earth on its might. Man is not comforted by his honor.
- He will be a father to many nations. A land flowing with milk and honey.

A delightful dwelling was given to Adam, the father of all, but he left it through his weakness. And in the breaking of the commandment, the evil one guided him and handed him and his children over to insatiable death. But when the Creator saw that his creature had been corrupted by both of them, he sent his Son and saved him from them, and, instead of the inheritance of the tree, he gave him a dwelling in heaven, and treaded a path for Adam and his sons from lowly Sheol to that land upon which the angels do not dare to gaze out of fear. For this, let us cry out and say: Glory to your mercies, O Lord of all!

Vigil Hymn
- O Lord, the God of my salvation.
- O Lord, I am your servant, the son of your handmaid.
- I have sinned against heaven and before you, and am not worthy to be called your son.

O Lord, you called me son in your grace, while I am not worthy to be a servant. You promised me the inheritance of heaven, and I have scorned all these things, and wasted my days in worthless evils. I therefore have no excuse before you, O Lord. You are a merciful God: save me and have mercy on me!

Morning Hymn – *btylutheh*
At dawn, when the night
turns from dark to light,
let us bend our knees in pray'r.

Daniel Verse
At the dawn, when the darkness
turns to day in its brightness,
let us plead unto Christ by our pray'r
that he may show us mercy.

Summer/Repentance

Sanctuary Hymn – *lakhu qarenan*
- **Clothe your priests in righteousness.**
- **Be wary and do not sin.**
O you holy priests:
cleanse your consciences
from the grime of sin.

SEVENTH WEEK OF SUMMER/REPENTANCE

Evening Psalmody (from Psalm 143)
Do not enter into judgment with your *ser*vant,
    Halleluiah, halleluiah, hal*le*luiah.
Do not enter into judgment with your *ser*vant,
    for no living thing is just *be*fore you.
For the enemy pursues my *soul*,
    and has lowered my life *to* the ground.
He has made me sit in the *dark*
    like *the* dead forever.
My spirit smites me and my heart shakes within *me*.
    I remember you, O Lord, *from* of old.
Glory to the Father, to the Son and to the Holy *Spi*rit.
    From age to age, a*men*, amen.
Halleluiah, halle*lu*iah, hal*le*luiah.

Basilica Hymn
- **Bless the Lord, my soul.**
- **Return, my soul, to your rest. Turn from evil and do good.**
Cease henceforth, O vicious one, and do not be a trap for others. Remember that condemnation is prepared for the wicked, and for those who commit adultery and speak impiously. O you whose soul is defiled with evils: consider that tortuous world that does not pass away, to which you are inviting your soul and your body, that they may go and inherit darkness, whose fire never fades. Repent and plead from the One who is abounding in mercies, that he may forgive your wrongdoings, and you will be saved from the violence of torture; and implore God, that he may take away the weakness of your thoughts, and have mercy on you.

Summer/Repentance

Vigil Hymn
- **Bless the Lord, my soul.**
- **It is the time and hour to awake from our sleep.**

O my miserable soul, awake – why do you sleep? The end is coming, and you are going to be judged. Cry out to him and beg him to forgive you – he who does all according to his will. O Lord, forgive me!

Morning Hymn – *btylutheh*
O Son who came down
and freed us from death:
brighten us with your true Light.

Seasonal Verse
Son of God, who descended
and saved us from our errors:
in your grace, erase all of our sins,
for our souls hope in your love.

Sanctuary Hymn – *balmeneh*
- **Let us praise him forever.**

Let us all praise the Christ
by whose Body and Blood
has made all of us worthy
of his great Gift to our race.

THE FEAST OF ST. THOMAS, APOSTLE

Basilica Hymn
- **Chosen silver that is tried in the earth.**
- **More beautiful in his sight than the sons of men.**

A portion of the heavenly treasure, which is desired by the angels, and by the prophets and apostles, and by the honored martyrs, Christ gave, in his grace, to the faithful Church: Thomas the apostle, he who was stabbed with a spear for the sake of the law of the love of God. Come, all you peoples, in awe and love, and in songs of the Holy Spirit, let us honor the day of his commemoration. He is indeed an unassailable rampart for our people.

- **Glory to the Father, to the Son and to the Holy Spirit.**
A treasure was found in India, beloved of merchants, kings, judges and leaders, O beloved. Our Lord, in his will, gave his believing Church the apostle St. Thomas, he who was pierced with a spear for the sake of religious doctrine. Come, let us all together, with the fervent excitement of love, and with Psalms and glorifications, pay recompense to his honor. He is, indeed, in our corner, an undefeatable power.

- **From age to age, amen, amen.**
The apostle, the friend of Christ, the preacher of Jesus our Savior, carried the cross in his hands like a plough, and weeded and worked, in the Faith, the land that was wasted through the error of idols, and planted the Word of life in it. Let us all honor his feast!

The Holy Feast of the Transfiguration of Our Lord on Mount Tabor

Basilica Hymn
- **O Lord, the God of my salvation.**
- **They have seen your paths, O God.**
O Lord, when you desired, in your love, to show your kingship and the great glory of your coming to Simon, James and John, the chosen apostles, you took them up with you to Mount Tabor, and their faces were lit up and your clothes were like lightning with the radiance of your flesh, the spring of life; your Father cried out and confirmed your Sonship, and made your authority known. Therefore, make us worthy to delight in that same glory, and rejoice and be glad in you, as you spread over us the light of your Countenance!

- **Glory to the Father, to the Son, and to the Holy Spirit.**
O One who is marvelous in his works, and whose mysteries are revealed through his power, in all times and places, to glorious and chosen men, to the living and the dead together, prophets as well as apostles, those worthy of the mysteries of the faithful, until he comes in the open and shines, that each man may be perceived openly in those things which were done hiddenly. Glory to that Power which was pleased and revealed his Mystery to his friends!

Summer/Repentance

OPTIONAL SEASONAL HYMNS FOR SUMMER/REPENTANCE

- **Wash me with it, I shall be whiter than snow.** – *sahde brykhe*
- **Wash me thoroughly from my guilt.**

With tears of repentance
purify me, Lord,
and grant me in grace
and in mercy, to be found
worthy of your saving love;
by my humble tears, absolve
all my trespasses and faults;
O Redeemer, wash away my sins!

- **He will heal the broken hearted & bind up all their wounds.** – *talmydhaw*
- **Turn to me and have mercy.**

The balm of penitence
Lord Jesus gave
to the skilled physicians
who are the priests of the Church.
Let all whom satan has harmed
come and show their wounds to them,
students of our all-Wise Doctor,
and they will heal them
with spiritual balm.

Cross (with Elijah & Moses)

The Feast of the Adorable Cross

Basilica Hymn – ṣlywakh amlekh
- The Lord rules over the nations.
- The Lord rules forever.

May your cross rule in heaven, and may your cross rule on earth,
and may your cross crown the crowds who give thanks unto your cross.
- In heaven and on earth.

May the cross seen in heaven, and revealed to the earthly,
exalt our miserable race, and enter us into heaven.
- Your adornment and your glory; your glory is victorious.

The cross was victorious, the cross is victorious,
the cross defeated Satan, and gladdened all its adorers.
- Its rays lighten the world.

The cross of light that was shown to Constantine in the heavens
went to war like a soldier at the head of his armies.
- From a people without mercy.

May your cross, O Lord, which was hidden from all the wicked
let its rays fly over the world and bring light to creation.
- It will abolish wars from the ends of the earth.

May the cross which reigns above bring peace unto the lowly;
for the heights do not need peace: pacify the sons of men.
- That he may show his greatness.

The cross gave us victory, the cross raised our poverty;
the cross lifted our lowliness, and brought us into heaven.
- The world and all its inhabitants.

By your cross, all are reconciled, by your cross all are renewed;
by your cross, O Lord, guard us from the wiles of the devil.
- May your blessing be upon your people.

Through your cross, O Lord, may priests and kings be brought together,
by your cross may your Church rejoice: you brought her up from lowliness.
- We your people and the sheep of your flock.

By your cross, Lord, may the world which is now shaken by wars
be pacified, and may the sword which slays us be abolished.

Cross

- **The Lord will show his salvation.**
In your cross was salvation for the nations who believed;
by your cross was condemnation for all those who denied you.
- **It will be like the tree that was planted by a stream of water.**
The cross resembles the spring that overflowed in Eden,
the wise drink from it and the ignorant gain clarity.
- **Its branches are as great as a handsome brightness.**
The cross resembles the tree of life within the Church,
whose Fruits are good for eating, and whose leaves are for healing.
- **Glory to the Father, to the Son, and to the Holy Spirit.**
May your cross rule in heaven, and may your cross rule on earth,
and may your cross crown the crowds who give thanks unto your cross.
- **From age to age, amen, amen.**
Holy One, Holy Mighty One, Holy Immortal One: have mercy on us.

First Week of Elijah

Evening Psalmody (from Psalm 97)
All who make idols are *shamed*,
    Halleluiah, halleluiah, hal*le*luiah.
All who make idols are *shamed*,
    those who *pride* in carvings.
All his angels adore *him*.
    Zion hears *and* is glad,
and the daughters of Judah re*joice*.
    Because of your judg*ments*, O Lord,
because you are the exalted Lord over all the *earth*.
    You are greatly exalted o*ver* all gods.
Glory to the Father, to the Son and to the Holy Sp*i*rit.
    From age to age, a*men*, amen.
Halleluiah, halle*lu*iah, hal*le*luiah.

Basilica Hymn
- The Lord will arise and all his enemies will be scattered.
- For the wicked rots away, conceives falsehood and gives birth to deceit.
- Because of this we know that it is the end time. Therefore the evil man will be revealed, he whom the Lord will destroy with the breath of his mouth.

Cross

The Enemy looks forward to the evil hardship of the end times, to casting his net to ensnare the sons of men, and, with the traps he set for Adam from the beginning he schemes against his sons in the end. He will attract the world under the guise of peace, and, if possible, he will even lead the elect astray. But not only will his desire not be fulfilled, his reign will also end. Before the eyes of all creatures he will be judged with a frightful sentence by you, O Lord, who was called the Second Adam, and all those who have followed in the footsteps of the deceiver will be confused and exposed. And even now, you condemn all those who blaspheme you. O Lord of all, glory to you!

Vigil Hymn
- **Bless the Lord, my soul.**
- **Ask your father and he will show you.**

Consider, my soul, and understand how many evil things the enemy has done to you in his impudence: for he estranged you from paradise and brought you out of it, and now also presses on and fights against you without ceasing, to unbind you vainly from many mercies. For this, turn away from his evil traps, and do good deeds, as you cry out to Christ: "Protect me under the shadow of the wings of your grace, and have mercy on me."

Morning Hymn – *nawde w-nisgodh*
Christ, who renews all:
bring light to our hearts;
let us praise the Trinity.

Daniel Verse
Elijah called upon you,
Ezekiel from the chariot,
Daniel from Babylon proclaimed you:
Praise to you who raised his servants.

Sanctuary Hymn – *lakhu qarenan*
- **Bless the Lord, all his angels.**
- **They will praise your name forever.**

The angels above
unceasingly praise
the adored Nature.

Cross

Second Week of Elijah

Evening Psalmody (from Psalm 38)
My friends and companions stand against my *wound*,
  Halleluiah, halleluiah, hal*le*luiah.
My friends and companions stand against my *wound*,
  and my neighbors stand far a*way* from me.
Those who seek my soul seize me and wish evil upon *me*.
  They speak evil *and* deceit.
Glory to the Father, to the Son and to the Holy *Spi*rit.
  From age to age, a*men*, amen.
Halleluiah, halle*lu*iah, hal*le*luiah.

Basilica Hymn
- From the depths I called to you, O Lord, and you heard my voice.
- I meditated and my spirit was shaken.
I have been considering your tribunal, O Christ, and all my limbs have been shaking in fear. Who will be my help before your judgment seat who is from my race - from humanity? All my friends and dear ones will stand and look upon me from far away. O Just Judge, according to the greatness of your mercy, have pity on me, O Compassionate One, and not, O Lord, according to the many debts I have incurred.

Vigil Hymn
- When God stands to judge.
- There is no phrase or words.
When the Judge is seated, and the angels stand before him, horn and trumpet will sound, and living fire will burn. What will you do, my soul, for they are bringing you to court? Then your evil deeds will stand before you, and your vices will rebuke you before the Judge. And so to whom will you go and take refuge? So while you have time, confess and repent of your sins, and beg, plead and supplicate God to forgive you.

Madrasha (if the Feast of the Cross has been celebrated)
- Blessed is he who raised our fall and gave us victory over death by his cross.

Cross

* I saw wood and wood written in the divine verses: the wood of Life and the wood of death, a great wonder, one against the other. The great Power which fashioned all is revealed in their actions: their natures are similar, but their actions are different. Glory to him who gave us life through the Son of our race.
* The wood in the beginning expelled our fathers in shame; the Wood now lifted shamefacedness from us, and clothed us with glory. The wood there sold the house of Adam into slavery to the evil one, and the Wood of Christ undid the authority of death, and made it a mockery for all ages.
* The evil one saw the wood of old, and by its beauty, led the young of heart astray. The Wood now, the angels saw our Lord carry on his shoulders. The Cyrenian, the blessed friend, took it from the start while trembling. Now its depiction is passed down in every icon, and it is adored by all in every corner.

Morning Hymn – *kul nishma*
Let us hallow that morning, best of all;
lo, it comes to raise us and will not delay.

Daniel Verse
Let us hallow that morning
that will come, with the angels;
lo, it will raise the buried,
and will re-ward the working.

Sanctuary Hymn – *lakhu qarenan*
- **They will praise your Name forever.**
- **How good and sweet it is.**

Praise the renewed life
that our Savior gave
to the mortal race.

THIRD WEEK OF ELIJAH

Evening Psalmody (from Psalm 39)
Hear, O Lord, my prayer and my petition, and attend to my *tears*.
　　Halleluiah, halleluiah, hal*le*luiah.
Hear, O Lord, my prayer and my petition, and attend to my *tears*.
　　Do not be silent with me, for I *dwell* with you,

and am a sojourner like all my *fore*fathers.
    Save me, and *I* will rest.
Glory to the Father, to the Son and to the Holy Sp*i*rit.
    From age to age, a*men*, amen.
Halleluiah, halle*lu*iah, hal*le*luiah.

Basilica Hymn
- I said "I will guard my path and not sin with my lips."
- I am a beast with no understanding.

The desires of the passing world have separated me from you, and through them the rebel sets traps for me and ensnares me that I may not please you, O Lord. And while I earned little, and the world and its enticements passed away, regrets and sufferings have overcome me. For I see that the hope of my life is has passed away, and I now have no refuge besides you, O Lord. In the greatness of your mercies, turn to me, and in your grace, have pity on me; rescue me from my sins, as is your way, O Friend of mankind! Lord, forgive me!

Vigil Hymn
- How long, O Lord, will you forget me forever?
- For they are a vapor.

How long will you be enslaved to the desires of this passing world, my soul? How long will you be held by carelessness, all the days of your life? Look down on and despise the things here which do not remain, for you do not know when the thief will come. Thus before he comes and finds you unprepared, plead to Christ your Savior: "O Lord, forgive all my faults and sins, and have mercy on me."

Madrasha (if the Feast of the Cross has been celebrated)
- May our praise please you, O Lord, on the feast of the cross.

* Glory to you, O Lord Jesus, from the lofty and the lowly, for you saved our race by your cross from death and the backbiter. You humiliated insolent death, which had enslaved every age, and by the cross you crushed the head of the serpent, Satan, the murderer of man.

* The staff of Moses had opened up the sea, and evildoers passed through. Your cross, O Lord, opened the gates of Paradise. By the staff of Moses, Egypt and all its magicians were condemned; your cross, O Lord, condemned the whole camp of insolent demons.

Morning Hymn – *btylutheh*
Christ, who frees us all: enlighten our minds,
with your bright, unending light.

Daniel Verse
Blest be Christ, in whose coming
freed us from the yoke of slavery,
and enlightened us all in the Light
of the mind of the Godhead.

Sanctuary Hymn – *lakhu qarenan*
- Sprinkle me with hyssop and I shall be clean.
- Wash me, I shall be whiter than snow.
May the calming dew
of your great mercies
come now to our aid.

FIRST WEEK OF THE CROSS/FOURTH OF ELIJAH

Evening Psalmody (from Psalm 98)
Sing to the Lord with harps and with the sound of *singing*,
    Halleluiah, halleluiah, hal*le*luiah.
Sing to the Lord with harps and with the sound of *singing*,
    and glorify before the King, the *Lord*, with lyre.
The sea trembles in its *fullness*,
    the world and all who *dwell* in it.
The rivers clap their hands to*gether*,
    and the mountains glorify be*fore* the Lord.
For he comes to judge the *earth*.
    He judges the world in truth, and the nations *in* uprightness.
Glory to the Father, to the Son and to the Holy S*pi*rit.
    From age to age, a*men*, amen.
Halleluiah, halle*lu*iah, hal*le*luiah.

Basilica Hymn
- I will exalt you, O Lord my King.
- Who walked in darkness.

Cross

Before your crucifixion, O Savior, the deceit of Satan troubled the whole creation, and until then the race of men had been enslaved under the yoke of death, the murderer of our race. But the wood of the cross killed death and undid sin, and made our race rise from the dead. The exalted beings marveled at our race which had been raised and brought above all sufferings. Because of this, we cry out unceasingly and say: glory to you who raised up our race!
- **Glory to the Father, to the Son, and to the Holy Spirit.**
In the hour the wood of the cross was set up, you shook the foundations of death, O Lord. And those whom Sheol had swallowed up in their sins and left shaking in terror, your command restored to life, O Lord. Because of this, we also glorify you: O Christ the King, have mercy on us!

Vigil Hymn
- **The earth trembled and shook.**
- **The nations shake and the kingdoms tremble.**
When our Savior went up on the cross to free us, all creatures shook and were stunned, for they saw his disgrace. The sun, bright in its rays, darkened its light and hid its radiance, for it saw its Lord hanging on wood and suffering because of the insolent. The moon was changed to blood, to chastise the ignorant people who dared to kill their Lord. Who is this for whom the sanctuary ripped open, and by whose voice even the dead were raised, and the thief was promised the Kingdom? Could it be that this is the Christ, the Life-giver of our mortality? Come, brethren, let us run to adore him who tasted death on behalf of our entire nature, and cry out to him together without ceasing: O Lord of all, glory to you!

Madrasha
- Blessed is he who reconciled all creatures by his cross.
* The cross shines on earth, and the power of error is erased. The race of Adam's house found life again in Adam. Glory to him who returned the nations to his pasture.
* The Crucified One saw death, and returned its deposit: the imprisoned were set free in the death of the Son of our race. Glory to him who undid and erased the decree of our debts.
* Brethren, who has ever seen the marvelous sight: a Body hanging on wood enlightening creatures? In his light those sitting in darkness saw light.

Morning Hymn – *m'yna d-ṭawatha*
The great archangel, Gabriel, extolls the sign
of Jesus Christ, when the morning comes,
and with the trumpet, and the sounding of the horn
he comes in glory before the Prince.

Daniel Verse
Blessed is he who saved us
by his cross, and returned us;
lo, the Church cries out to him:
praise to you, Savior of all.

Sanctuary Hymn – *ṣlywakh amlekh*
- Praise the Lord in the heights.
May the cross which reigns above
bring peace unto the lowly,
for the heights do not need peace:
pacify the sons of men.

SECOND WEEK OF THE CROSS/FIFTH OF ELIJAH

Evening Psalmody (from Psalm 95)
Come, let us bless and worship *him*,
    Halleluiah, halleluiah, hal*le*luiah.
Come, let us bless and worship *him*,
    and kneel before the *Lord* who made us.
For he is our God, and we are his *people*,
    and the sheep *of* his flock.
Glory to the Father, to the Son and to the Holy Sp*i*rit.
    From age to age, a*men*, amen.
Halleluiah, halle*lu*iah, hal*le*luiah.

Basilica Hymn
- The heavens will make known the glory of God.
- O the depth of the richness, and the wisdom of the knowledge of God!

Cross

The mouth of creatures is unable to explain the greatness of your Wisdom, O Great Unlimited Sea, for the things of heaven and earth, with their adornments, are unable to teach us of your greatness. But, through our wretched nature, you have brought us near to your knowledge, and through the shame and contempt of the Cross, you have made creation into a true Body without corruption for yourself, who are the Head who pours forth blessings and new life in the kingdom of heaven. Therefore, we all cry out and say: thanksgiving be to the mercies that had pity on our nature!

- **Glory to the Father, to the Son, and to the Holy Spirit.**

We revere the memory of your adorable passion, O Savior, and also your Cross, whose joyful feast is prepared for us in love, and in which we all receive forgiveness of sins and faults, and in which new life apart from Sheol rises, to the debt of the Jews, and the boast of your faithful Church, and to the glory of your victorious unlimited Power.

Vigil Hymn

- **All my will is in them.**
- **For they are in conflict with me.**

Desire for passing riches and love of the glory of the world divide me in my will from the beautiful work of your just commandments, and I fear lest the fate of the fig tree without fruit be given me. For this, I plead to you who gain and establish me in the branches of the cross: let the repentance of my soul sprout and bear fruit in me, through hope, faith, and perfect love, and have mercy on me.

Madrasha

- O Son who reconciled the worlds by his coming, protect your adorers by your cross.
* My friends, gather around Christ, attend and hear the story of the cross. May the cross be our refuge, and by its power may we speak its story.
* The cross is the treasure of all good things; come, let us receive help from it. The light of the cross has dawned upon all, and destroyed darkness.

Morning Hymn – *kul nishma*

Every morning, let us come adore him:
Jesus Christ who raised our fall and saved our lives.

Daniel Verse
Not a mouth among all creatures
can relate of your wisdom,
for you made, of the shame of the cross,
the fount of life eternal.

Sanctuary Hymn – *lakhu qarenan*
- They will praise your name forever.
- From the mouths of infants and children.
Praise him who has saved,
by his sacrifice,
the whole human race.

THIRD WEEK OF THE CROSS/SIXTH OF ELIJAH

Evening Psalmody (from Psalm 51)
Sprinkle me with hyssop, and I shall be *clean*;
    Halleluiah, halleluiah, hal*le*luiah.
Sprinkle me with hyssop, and I shall be *clean*;
    wash me with it, I shall be whi*ter* than snow.
May your delight and gladness sustain *me*,
    and my humble bones *will* rejoice.
Turn your face from my *sins*,
    and blot out all of *my* misdeeds.
Glory to the Father, to the Son and to the Holy *Spi*rit.
    From age to age, a*men*, amen.
Halleluiah, halle*lu*iah, hal*le*luiah.

Basilica Hymn
- Bless the Lord, my soul.
- Turn, O my soul, to your rest.
O my miserable soul, when you take up your lamp, await and listen for the glorious Bridegroom and, with the wise virgins, prepare and stay awake with them, and with your eyes not hanging in sleep shout the praises of the Lord, and beg him, saying: "O God, forgive me and have mercy on me, O Friend of mankind."

Cross

- Glory to the Father, to the Son, and to the Holy Spirit.
The cross was established in Jerusalem, and all creatures were gladdened; greedy death was unraveled in it, and the power of demons was taken; it chased the Jews away to the four corners of the earth, and it gathered the nations together, and brought them into the Kingdom, that Paradise of Heaven, which Adam lost when he disobeyed, the Second Adam conquered in Judah, returning its land to the Kingdom. He seized power in heaven and on earth, for behold, the assemblies of the angels worship before him, and they all cry out in one voice: thanksgiving to the Son of the Lord of All!

Vigil Hymn
- Bless the Lord, my soul.
- For they are vapor.
O my soul, the beauty and vision of buildings will not remain forever; do you not wish to build and establish yourself in repentance, before fearful death, which takes no bribes, overcomes you? The commandment is spread over all flesh, in which the mind shakes and the thoughts all tremble. Man is unable to plead for everything he has done. Cry out, my soul, and say: forgive me, O Pitying One, on the fearful day of your coming. O Savior, have mercy on me!

Madrasha
- Blessed is he who reconciled height and depth by his cross, and gladdened men and angels by its finding.

* Light dawned in Jerusalem of Judah: the cross of the Life-giver of all who was revealed for our salvation. The wood had been buried in the earth for ages, and justice cried to the king and his faithful mother. They ran to the wood, and placed it in churches, for healing.

* This is not from men, nor through men, nor has it ever entered the mind of men. This is of God, and God provided it. His finger drew it and showed to the true king and his faithful mother. They went out to seek the sign of the Life-giver of all.

Morning Hymn – *m'yna d-ṭawatha*
At dawn of morning, Dani-el rose from the den,
and was not harmed in flesh by the beasts;
Lord, may the devil
not harm us who worship you,
bought by your Blood, and saved by your cross.

Daniel Verse
May the Power that protected
Dani-el in the lions' den
be the guardian of our souls,
from the pains of desire.

Sanctuary Hymn – *lakhu qarenan*
- He spoke parables from the beginning.
- The just and upright one.
The mystery shown
by Jonah in_the whale
has become fulfilled.

FOURTH WEEK OF THE CROSS/SEVENTH OF ELIJAH

Evening Psalmody (from Psalm 72)
May his name be for*ever*;
    Halleluiah, halleluiah, hal*le*luiah.
May his name be for*ever*;
    and before the sun *is* his name.
May all the nations be blessed in *him*,
    and all of them glo*ri*fy him.
Blessed is the Lord, the God of *Is*rael,
    who has worked great won*ders* alone.
And blessed be his honored name for*ever*.
    May all the earth be filled with his honor, a*men*, amen.
Glory to the Father, to the Son and to the Holy *Spi*rit.
    From age to age, a*men*, amen.
Halleluiah, halle*lu*iah, hal*le*luiah.

Basilica Hymn
- May our first sins not be recalled against us.
- For the dwellings of the earth are filled with darkness and sin.
Who does not grieve that our faults have multiplied and our iniquities increased, and that all men have drowned in the sleep of desires as in a sea? The truth has dimmed and injustice has shone in the thorn bush of our malice,

and Justice has become zealous in calling us to account in the war, famine, carnage, and earthquakes that have happened. All the signs that the Lord pointed out have been fulfilled in our days, for by our sins the end of the world reaches us. Let us shed mournful tears as we say: O Lord, who created us in his grace, absolve our souls and have mercy on us!
- **Glory to the Father, to the Son, and to the Holy Spirit.**
We have gained an unending boast against death in the Cross of Christ, and in his Resurrection from among the dead. For by his suffering, he uprooted the sentence upon us. In great, unending glory, then, we all cry out and say: Only-Begotten God the Word, who assumed our mortal body, have pity, O Lord, on your servants, who confess your Cross!

Vigil Hymn
- **O God, have mercy on us.**
- **Turn to me and have mercy on me.**
O Pitying One whose door is opened to the sinners who take shelter in him: have mercy on us. O Help and Deliverer of those who fulfill his will, and their Protector from all dangers: protect our souls in your pity, and deliver us from the evil one, the enemy, who plunders us at every hour. Answer our requests in your mercies, O Knower of all, and pity your servants who call to you at all times. Help and save us from the hand of the evil one, and deliver us from the adversary. O compassionate Savior, Lord of all, glory to you!

Madrasha
- Blessed is the cross which enlightened the nations who were in darkness.
* The cross has made the entire world like a pillar, and all the ends of the earth and all lands are supported by it. All creation hangs upon it and the hidden signal guides them.
* Great Moses showed the cross in extending his hands on top of the mountain, and when he shone, his great light overcame the people, and the sons of warriors of the enemy shrank before him.

Morning Hymn – *btylutheh*
On this morning blest, Son of the Living One,
Lord, forgive our many sins.

Daniel Verse

O God whose love created us,
and called us to his household:
by your strength, may we all live for you,
and lift praise to your Lordship.

Sanctuary Hymn – *lakhu qarenan*

- For your mercies are greater than life.
- Lord, your mercies are forever.

In your mercy's grace,
free our souls and bodies
from greedy death.

FIRST WEEK OF MOSES

Evening Psalmody (from Psalm 129)

If you keep count of sins, O Lord, who would be able to *stand*?
    Halleluiah, halleluiah, hal*le*luiah.
If you keep count of sins, O Lord, who would be able to *stand*?
    For forgiveness *is* from you;
I have hoped in the *Lord*
    and my soul awai*ted* his word.
It awaited the Lord from the morning *watch*
    until the *mor*ning watch.
Let Israel await for the *Lord*,
    for mercies are from him, and salvation *even* more.
Glory to the Father, to the Son and to the Holy Sp*ir*it.
    From age to age, a*men*, amen.
Halleluiah, halle*lu*iah, hal*le*luiah.

Basilica Hymn

- That are written with a pen of iron and with a diamond stylus.
- That which is written in me at the beginning of the Scriptures.

Like an image engraved on a tablet, I am searched, O Lord, in my debts and sins which are written upon my skin and inscribed, and at all times shamefacedness hides my soul. O my Savior, be the absolver of my guilt, and have mercy on me.

- Glory to the Father, to the Son, and to the Holy Spirit.
You have abolished and loosened, through your holy cross, O Christ the King, all the error of idols, and you have exalted and honored all those who believe in you. For lo, the splendid Service of your hidden and holy Mysteries is extolled like a bride in honoring the martyrs who were killed for your sake. The priests who sing, and we also who glorify you, say: O Lord, may the true faith be guarded until eternity!

Vigil Hymn
- O God, save me by your name.
- Extend your hand and save me.
The years of my life are wasted in the waves of thoughts and the storms of temptations; my days are spent in misery, my years in groaning, and I have been useless. O Lord, who silenced the weeping of the sinful woman and changed it to joy: in your mercies, reconcile my convulsing passions, and give rest to the tribulation by which my temptations shake me, for they come against me because of my weakness.

Madrasha
- Blessed is he who reconciled all creatures by his cross, and sowed his teaching in every corner.
* The skillful writer wished to preach the story of the cross of light, and in his mercy, he called and awoke me as from sleep: "Awake, sleeper, and shake off the heaviness of your sin; preach and say: 'the cross is victorious above; the cross is victorious in the depths; the cross gives victory to mortals.'"
* All natures witness the victory of the cross of light, and they teach and preach that the living cross is triumphant in all things. Lo, crosses are fastened on doors and on the garments of kings, and if your gaze moves to the height of heaven, its sign is drawn there among the stars.

Morning Hymn – *m'yna d-ṭawatha*
At dawn of morning, all the hosts above extol
the One Existence, adored by all;
and we, the earthly, glorify Divinity:
forgive our sins, O Friend of mankind.

Daniel Verse
Blest, the lowness of the cross,
which exalts those who bless it;
be the pride of the one, chosen Church,
and the guard of the faithful.

Sanctuary Hymn – *lakhu qarenan*
- From the beginning unto the end.
- The world and all those who live.
May all creatures praise
your holy Nature,
O Eternal One.

SECOND WEEK OF MOSES

Evening Psalmody (from Psalm 98)
Sing to the Lord with harps and with the sound of *singing*,
    Halleluiah, halleluiah, hal*le*luiah.
Sing to the Lord with harps and with the sound of *singing*,
    and glorify before the King, the *Lord*, with lyre.
The sea trembles in its *fullness*,
    the world and all who *dwell* in it.
The rivers clap their hands to*gether*,
    and the mountains glorify be*fore* the Lord.
For he comes to judge the *earth*.
    He judges the world in truth, and the nations *in* uprightness.
Glory to the Father, to the Son and to the Holy Sp*ir*it.
    From age to age, a*men*, amen.
Halleluiah, halle*lu*iah, hal*le*luiah.

Basilica Hymn
- Lord, rebuke me not in your wrath.
- May there not be grief upon grief for me.
Lord, to you do I cry, O true Doctor: heal the wounds of my sins, for they crush me! If your grace does not stand before me, I would be destroyed from eternity in so many evils. Cleanse my faults through mournful tears, and forgive my defilements in the mercies of your grace. O Christ, who has pity on all, pity me

and have mercy on me, and turn me toward yourself in your compassion. O Lord who loves his servants, have mercy on me!
- Glory to the Father, to the Son, and to the Holy Spirit.
In the hour that the wood of your cross was fastened, You shook the foundations of death, O Lord. And those whom Sheol had swallowed in their sins, it released while trembling – your command quickened them, O Lord. Because of this, we also glorify you, O Christ the King: Have mercy on us!

Vigil Hymn
- O Lord, open my lips.
- Set, O Lord, a guard over my mouth and a guard over my lips.
When I open my lips and sing glory to you, O Lord, I see the accuser of my conscience fighting against me every day, and like him, I have works that do not fulfill the words of my lips. And so, enlighten and instruct my thoughts through my tongue, that I may sing to you: halleluiah!

Madrasha
- Blessed is he who reconciled creatures by his cross, and brought all the nations to adore him.
* O cross which is a tower that bows down and brings men to the heights: bring down your great height also for me in your mercies, that I may reach it for you and in you, that my mind may rise and I see the Son at the right hand of the Lord of the heights, and there sing praise to him.
* By the cross, indeed, stand all creatures. The cross gushing forth in garments, a great indescribable wonder; and because the pagan wished to erase the cross, the cross was seen to all in garments. The cross on kings, the cross on their statues, the cross on their precious signets.

Morning Hymn – *abbun d-bashmayya*
Be, O Lord, a great rampart for your Church,
and grant to it all, your unfailing truth.

Daniel Verse
Lo, the watchers adore you,
and the great rank of holy ones;
they cry out all together:
Blest is he who has saved us.

Sanctuary Hymn – *lakhu qarenan*
- **I will bless the Lord at all times.**
- **And all times, his praises in my mouth.**

Our Savior is blest
who redeemed our race
from envious death.

Third Week of Moses

Evening Psalmody (from Psalm 95)
Come, let us bless and worship *him*,
    Halleluiah, halleluiah, hal*le*luiah.
Come, let us bless and worship *him*,
    and kneel before the *Lord* who made us.
For he is our God, and we are his *people*,
    and the sheep *of* his flock.
Glory to the Father, to the Son and to the Holy *Spi*rit.
    From age to age, a*men*, amen.
Halleluiah, halle*lu*iah, hal*le*luiah.

Basilica Hymn
- **I will adore in your holy temple and give thanks to your name.**
- **And I, O Lord, hope in you.**

While I adore you and confess that you are my Lord and God, the enemy fights with me, and I am buffeted by his battles. And when I cast him away by the power of the Cross, he awakens my thoughts against me, and through them he disturbs me. And when he entices my mind, and draws it away from you, he lays traps for me and ensnares me, and with them he binds me. And even when I run and take refuge in you, O Lord, he runs and hinders me by the opposite path, and confuses me with his guiles. Therefore, an earthly being is unable to defeat a spirit without you. In you, O Lord, do I take refuge, that in you I may win and he be defeated. No one calls to you and is deprived of the aid of your grace. O Lord of all: glory to you!

- **Glory to the Father, to the Son, and to the Holy Spirit.**

Through the great suffering of the cross, you defeated death, O Christ our life-giver, and became the resurrection and the principle of the rising of the dead. You ascended in glory, and cherubim and seraphim extol you upon the seat of glory. So with the angels, we also glorify you, O Lord, and say: everything that is in heaven and on earth blesses and adores you, O Christ our Savior!

Vigil Hymn
- I cry out during the day and night before you.
- I will not fear during the day, for I trust in you.

During the day, the deeds I do and my sinfulness bring me to stumble, and during the quiet night, the evil one causes me to sin with empty visions in my thoughts. All the days of my life, I anger you with foolish things, and because of this I beg you: wake my sleepiness through repentance, return me to yourself, and have mercy on me.

Madrasha
- Blessed is Christ, for by his cross he gave victory to our race. Glory to him and the One who sent him, for his gift to us.

* O lambs saved from error and signed in the sign of the cross: bless and adore Christ, who came and saved us by his cross. The cross revealed his power on earth to Constantine in heaven, for Christ is the one by whose power our race receives victory.

* His light dawned in the height above, and the king saw it on earth, like a general goes forth at the head of his army to war. The cross of Christ the King was a general on the side of the Romans, and it strengthened them, by its power, to defeat the side of the barbarians.

Morning Hymn – *kul nishma*
Every morning, every day, she thanks you:
the Church, whom you made your bride in great glory.

Daniel Verse
Blest is he who saved the Church
from error, and returned her;
lo, she lifts up all glory
to the King who exalted her.

Sanctuary Hymn – *ṣlywakh amlekh*
- O God, our mighty stronghold.

We who adore you, O Lord, take refuge in your stronghold,
to receive your Mysteries which forgive all of our sins.

Cross

FOURTH WEEK OF MOSES

Evening Psalmody (from Psalm 69)
Answer me, O Lord, for your grace is *good*,
    Halleluiah, halleluiah, hal*le*luiah.
Answer me, O Lord, for your grace is *good*,
    and turn to me in *your* great mercies.
Do not turn your face from your *ser*vant,
    for I am greatly troubled; *an*swer me.
        Bring my soul to *your* salvation.
Glory to the Father, to the Son and to the Holy *Spi*rit.
    From age to age, a*men*, amen.
Halleluiah, halle*lu*iah, hal*le*luiah.

Basilica Hymn
- **The light of my eyes was not with me.**
Due to the weight of the roof of my offenses, the eyes of my mind have darkened from clarity, and I have strayed from the path of your commandments, which perpetuates life. I have made my journey on the way of destruction, along the path of the many, who inherit darkness and unquenching fire. Return me in your compassion, O Christ our Savior, forgive, in your grace, my offenses and my sins, and have mercy on me!
- **Glory to the Father, to the Son, and to the Holy Spirit.**
The Cross of Christ became a spring for us, from which all our benefits pour forth: in it are demons defeated, and in it Satan falls; the power of error is abolished, sin is uprooted, deviation passes away, the boast of death, which had conquered our nature, fades, we accept, in it a spiritual birth, we dwell in immortal life, inherit the kingdom of heaven in his love, and take the appointment of sons of his glory. For Christ the King has taken the victory through his Cross, and made peace above and below. To him, with his Father and the Holy Spirit, do men and angels sing praise!

Vigil Hymn
- **Bless the Lord, my soul.**
- **Many say to my soul.**

O my soul, awake and throw off the sleep of carelessness, and through the oil of love for the poor, prepare and light your lamp, for the glorious Bridegroom of the holy Church is going to come. Hasten, lest the open door of repentance shuts before you, that you may be made worthy to enter with the Bridegroom, as we say: "O Lord, do not deny us the banquet of your holy Mysteries." O Friend of mankind: glory to you!

Madrasha
- O cross, grant us to glorify you as befits your honor, and protect us under your shadow from the enemies of the truth.
* On this day, the Lord gladdened the people and the nations together, for on it their backs were humbled under the chariot of the cross. The four corners of the world gained renewal in the cross; the rivers of paradise divided the mystery of its powers.
* The warrior who bound his back: the cross established in Jerusalem. The sharpened arrows against the people: the judgment against Pilate. The throne established from eternity: the Divinity of Christ. The anointing and the oil together: the witnesses of his humanity.

Morning Hymn – *btylutheh*
O Unending Light: you are Christ the King;
blest are those who have your Light.

Daniel Verse
Blessed are you, O true Light,
who enlightened the whole Church;
we adore you at all times,
and sing praise to you in her.

Sanctuary Hymn – *byadh shlama*
- **And faith has vanished from the earth.**
The faith has vanished from among all the faithful,
and they show their intentions with empty phrases:
"O Lord, O Lord," they cry with their lips,
but in their hearts, strife and jealousy.
One day, their death will come and will take them captive.
Remember, friends, that judgment waits for us.

Cross

OPTIONAL HYMNS FOR THE SEASON OF THE CROSS

- The Lord has shown forth his salvation. – *lakhu qarenan*
- We hope in his holy name.
Praise the renewed life
that our Savior gave
to the mortal race.
- For your mercies are greater than life.
In your Mercy's grace,
free our souls and bodies
from greedy Death.

- For you are a priest forever. – *balmeneh*
- He forgives his land and his people.
O High Priest of our Faith,
Jesus, King of Glory,
by whose Flesh has saved our souls,
by whose Blood has absolved us.
- Save your people, and the sheep of your flock.
Glorified over all,
and exalted of all:
in your mercy guard your Church,
and save her sons by your cross.

First Week of the Sanctification of the Church
Which is Called "The Renewal"

They enter the church in procession singing: – *mara d-kulla*
- Let us enter his dwelling and adore at his footstool.
- Enter his gates with thanksgiving and his courts with praise.
We enter with thanksgiving, and sing praise in your temple.
Our mouths cry out as we say: "Blest is the honor of the Lord!"
Heaven is filled with your glory, and angels there adore you;
in the Church you have chosen, the nations sing praise to you!
- I have brought her peace and enriched her.
Your Church carries a treasure, and a great wealth, O Savior;
she has received your symbols and mysteries in great hope:
the great book of your Gospel, the wood of your adored Cross,
the icon of your manhood: the symbols of salvation!
- The princess stands in glory.
O Church, betrothed of Jesus, who saved you from your error,
and promised you, by rising, life blessed and unending:
come adorn yourself with care, and repay all thanksgiving:
confession undivided, profession of the true faith.

Evening Psalmody (from Psalm 45)
All the glory of the princess is from with*in*,
    Halleluiah, halleluiah, hal*le*luiah.
All the glory of the princess is from with*in*,
    and her clothing is adorned *with* fine gold.
She goes to the king with *of*ferings,
    and she brings her virgin com*pan*ions with her.
With joy and gladness they go a*long*,
    and they enter the palace *of* the king.
Glory to the Father, to the Son and to the Holy *Spi*rit.
    From age to age, a*men*, amen.
Halleluiah, halle*lu*iah, hal*le*luiah.

Basilica Hymn
- O Lord, God of my salvation.
- You give her peace and greatly enrich her.

Church

O Lord, behold your Church, saved by your Cross, and your flock bought with your precious Blood, offers a crown of thanksgiving in faith to you, O High Priest of justice who has exalted her by your abasement. And, like a glorious Bride, she rejoices and exults in you, O glorious Bridegroom. In the strength of the Truth, raise the walls of her salvation, and establish priests within her, to be ambassadors of peace on behalf of her children.

Vigil Hymn
- **Remember your Church which you gained from of old.**
- **On this rock I will build my Church.**

O Christ, protect your Church from all dangers, and make all of those called to her worthy to become stronger in all the perfection of the true faith, in the patience of peace and serenity, which come from you alone who are the Lord.

Madrasha
- Blessed is Christ who betrothed you to himself through the waters of baptism.
* O betrothed of Christ, seek not another betrothed, for he is the true Bridegroom who is from eternity and will be forever. He gave you his Body as a pledge, and the faith which is his truth. Do not trade it for another, lest he become your adversary.
* No one has ever given his body and blood to his betrothed, nor of old has there ever been a banquet where all hidden things are revealed. This is the true Bridegroom who has done new things for you. Blessed is anyone who has not left behind any of the Great One's commands.

Morning Hymn – ḥannana da-pthyḥ
Holiness is fi-tting unto your house,
for you built it u-pon the rock of faith,
it is a refuge for all those who hope
in your great mercy, and who trust in you.

Daniel Verse
Blest is he who built his Church
on earth, reaching to heaven;
lo the heavenly and earthly ones
in her praise him together.

Sanctuary Hymn – *ha shwan*
- **You made it your holy dwelling.**
Lord, on earth, you made a harbor
which is your Church,
like your Dwelling in heaven.
Though you sit at God's right hand, you fill the earth
with your Presence and Glory.
All the angels sing you "holy"
the day the Church is sanctified.
Its foundation was laid down
by the Father who sent you to us,
you built and formed it,
the Holy Spirit hallowed it.
We beg you to keep it strong,
and guard its peace forever in your mercy.

SECOND WEEK OF THE SANCTIFICATION OF THE CHURCH

Evening Psalmody (from Psalm 74)
Remember your *church,*
    Halleluiah, halleluiah, hal*le*luiah.
Remember your *church*
    which you established from *the* beginning,
and save the tribe of your in*her*itance.
    This is mount Zion, *where* you dwelt.
Glory to the Father, to the Son and to the Holy Sp*i*rit.
    From age to age, a*men*, amen.
Halleluiah, halle*lu*iah, hal*le*luiah.

Basilica Hymn
- **Remember your Church, whom you chose from the beginning.**
- **Indeed, I speak regarding Christ and his Church.**
To your Church, O Savior, who has followed you perfectly by love and the faith which comes from baptism, you first showed the Individuals of glorious Divinity; and by her, the perfect teaching of the mystery of the Trinity was revealed to the spiritual assemblies. By your grace, O Lord, may the creed that has been delivered to her by you in your Gospel be preserved without stain.

Vigil Hymn
- I stand on rock and guide my steps.
- You will not shake forever and ever.

Lord, you built your Church on the foundation of the faith of Simon Peter, and because of your promises to him, the waves and storms of idolatry have not shaken her. And because Satan saw that even with his angels he could not overcome the catholic one, his students withdrew to the ends of the earth to kill each other with the arrows of envy. Erase those without glory from her, those who envy and fight each other, and let your peace reign among her children.

Madrasha
- Blessed is he who brought peace to the desolate one, and filled her with the holiness of his honor.

* "God has called me to his wedding feast," the Church says to the guests. "I will enter with him to his bridal chamber: O nations, rejoice with me, for I have been saved. I have gone up from the market of idols, and have been baptized with living water. By fire and Spirit I have been scoured, and have been joined to the glorious Bridegroom."

* "I was abandoned and beaten, and the King's Son saved me in his love. He bandaged me with oil and water; I covered my shame with his garments: the smoke of the heavens. He refined me and I became sweet-smelling, he filled me with his sweet scent, and now his saints are embracing me."

* "With his fragrant oil, he anointed my head; with his living cup, he intoxicated my heart. His mercies, which are better than wine are an honest life which he desired for me. Jesus: he is mine, and I am his. He desired me, he wore me, and I wore him. He kissed me with the kisses of his mouth, and brought me to the bridal chamber above."

Morning Hymn – *kul nishma*
Every morning, every day, rejoices
the Church, whom you made your bride in great glory.

Daniel Verse
Blest are you, O holy Church;
Blest, the Bride of the Most High;
Blest, Betrothed and Exalted,
Blest, whose joy is in heaven.

Church

Sanctuary Hymn – *ḥadhu ḥayla*
- O God, our great refuge.
- Both rich and poor alike.
All those who adore you, Lord,
take refuge within your Church.
May your holy Mysteries
cleanse their sins and heal their wounds.

Third Week of the Sanctification of the Church

Evening Psalmody (from Psalm 103)
His angels bless the *Lord*,
    Halleluiah, halleluiah, hal*le*luiah.
His angels bless the *Lord*,
    who have power and accomplish *his* commands.
All his hosts bless the *Lord*,
    his servants who *do* his will.
All his works bless the *Lord*,
    for his authority is over *all* the earth.
Glory to the Father, to the Son and to the Holy *Spi*rit.
    From age to age, a*men*, amen.
Halleluiah, halle*lu*iah, hal*le*luiah.

Basilica Hymn
- How lovely is your dwelling place, Lord God almighty!
- That which God, not man, has established.
How glorious is your dwelling place, and beautiful your altar, and great your magnificence, O Being who dwells in the heights! The angels testify, who cry out and shout: holy, holy, holy is the Lord who dwells in Light! The angels proclaim the Trinity with their hallowings, as they say: glory at once to the Father and to the Son and to the Holy Spirit! Grant us to thank you along with them, and cry out to you with hosannas: Great, O Lord, is the grace that you have effected for the whole mortal race; O Lord, glory to you!

Vigil Hymn
- Glorify the Lord in the heights.
- You have placed your dwelling in the heights.

O Lord, you are above in the heights, in the holy of holies, at the right hand of your Father, and down on earth, the saved assemblies of those who glorify you build glorious temples to you. In them they plead and ask for mercies and forgiveness of debts at all times, that you may keep your Church from the evil one and the sheep of your flock from demons. O Christ, who saved the holy Church from error by his Blood: be a mighty fortress for her, shame the evil one in her exaltation, and let your peace reign in her.

Madrasha

- Blessed is he who built the holy Church on the rock of faith, and placed apostles, prophets, and teachers who know the truth within her.

* O Church, gather your children, for you have been a fisherwoman from the beginning. Now that your children have multiplied, stand and knock the dust off you. Virgin, betrothed to the apostles, bride which John preached: the lonely and abandoned one now has kings as foster-fathers. Take the veil off from your face, rejoice in your young sons, and be exalted in your virgins who sing glory within you every day.

* You are the seed of Abraham, protected by the Spirit and the prophets. The apostles gave birth to you by the Gospel, and the angels above rejoice in you. Rejoice, O Church, in all your leaders, splendid and sweet cedars. Lo, young men and virgins are planted and dwell within you. Your blessings are indivisible; reach out to those without forgiveness, as you awake those who enter you, and clothe them with vestments.

Morning Hymn – *abbun d-bashmayya*

Voices thundering in the holy Church;
in her we lift praise to the Creator.

Daniel Verse

At your wedding, holy Church,
those in heaven sing glory
to the Christ, by whose cross saved your sons
and dwells in you in splendor.

Sanctuary Hymn – *l-ḥayye w-ṭuwwe*

- **Lord, who may dwell in your temple?**

Father who made his dwelling on mount Sinai, and filled it
with the holiness of his honor: fill this temple with your praise.
May your wedding feast be a time of love;
may this temple be refuge for the weak.
May your name be glorified,
with your Son and your Spirit.
May all those on earth, and all in heaven,
give you glory at all times
until the end of ages, amen, amen.

FOURTH WEEK OF THE SANCTIFICATION OF THE CHURCH

Evening Psalmody (from Psalm 45)
Listen, O daughter, and see, and incline your *ear*,
   Halleluiah, halleluiah, hal*le*luiah.
Listen, O daughter, and see, and incline your *ear*,
   and forget your people and the house *of* your father,
for the king desires your *beauty*.
   Because he is your *Lord*, adore him,
and the daughter of Tyre will adore *him*.
   The wealthy among the people will seek your *face* with offerings.
Glory to the Father, to the Son and to the Holy Sp*i*rit.
   From age to age, a*men*, amen.
Halleluiah, halle*lu*iah, hal*le*luiah.

Basilica Hymn
- **For he is our God.**
- **Listen, O my daughter, and see, and turn your ear.**
Give thanks, O Church, O Queen, to the Prince who has espoused you; and brought you into his summer home; and given you the dowry of blood that flowed from his side for you; and clothed you with the robe of splendid unending light; and placed upon your head the adorned and illustrious crown of glory; and, as with a pure thurible, has perfumed your scent before all; and, like a flower, blossoms and the buds of spring has increased your radiance; and freed you, on Golgotha, from slavery to idols. Therefore, adore his Cross, on which he suffered for you and exalted your lowliness, honor the priests who extol you with their works, and cry out to him: glory to you!

Vigil Hymn
- Your hand is strengthened and your right hand exalted.
- Yours is the strength and yours is the might.

By the strength and might of your right hand, you were revealed and saved us, O Christ our Savior. Uphold your Church in your mercy, and reconcile, in your compassion, all those who are baptized in her. Grant your great power to all the churches, and let the priests in her serve in awe as they thank you. Grant us to confess you in perfect love, and cry out: have mercy on us!

Madrasha
- Blessed is he who granted that the priesthood be a rank that raises up to heaven.

* O exalted priesthood, show me the treasure of your richness, that I may fill the treasury of my thoughts with your new gifts. O exalted one which was brought low, and given to the earthly, O vision that was poured forth upon the ages of mankind. For that nation was the horn of oil; for us, the priesthood of Christ.

* The Exalted One descended on mount Sinai, and rested his hand upon Moses. Moses placed it upon Aaron, and it extended to John. For that reason, our Lord said to him: "It is righteousness that I be baptized by you," so that this order not be lost. Our Lord handed it on to the apostles, and lo, its tradition is in the Church. Blessed is he who handed his orders over to us.

* It was passed down from Adam to Noah, and extended from Noah to Abraham, and from Abraham to Moses, and from Moses to David, and from David to the exile, and from Babylon to our Savior. The people were scattered and cut off, and all its orders were erased. But the hand passed it on to the apostles. Blessed is the Lord of their traditions.

Morning Hymn – *sahde brykhe*
Christ, who reconciled all creation with
the One who sent him,
cleanse your Church, saved by your Blood,
from all factions within her,
which come from the evil one,
causing heresies and strife.
Help your priests to preach the one true faith.

Daniel Verse
Blest are you, O Holy Church;
Blest, O Bride decorated;
Blest, O Sea of all wisdom;
Blest, O Dwelling of Glory.

Sanctuary Hymn – *sahde brykhe*
- Remember your Church, yours from the beginning.
Lord, protect your Church
which you chose from the
beginning of time.
Keep all conflicts far away;
bind her children peacefully.
May her priests serve faithfully,
and her shepherd guide us as
he asks you to keep her safe from harm.

OPTIONAL HYMN FOR THE SEASON OF THE CHURCH
- The princess stands in beauty. – *l-ḥayye w-ṭuwwe*
Church, O betrothed of Jesus Christ who saved you by his precious Blood;
gave you his Body (living Food which wicked men had sacrificed),
who placed in your hands his redeeming Cup
(his most precious Blood that flowed from his side
when they stabbed him by the spear): listen to the Bridegroom's voice:
repent, leave behind vain wandering and sin.
Cry out to your Savior with hymns of thanksgiving: "Glory to you!"

- Glory to the Father, to the Son, and to the Holy Spirit.
The Son of God held a great wedding feast for his Church betrothed, and set up her bridal bed on Mount Sinai through the son of Amram with great magnificence. He invited the prophets and called the apostles, and the teachers and shepherds, to the day of her banquet. The watchers on high were waiters, and they served manna, flesh, and quail as the food for her dinner. He betrothed her through Moses, and set her dowry through John in the river Jordan; King David served her banquet by composing hymns and songs. Indeed, all the glory of the princess is from within, but she is also adorned with fine gold. Give thanks, O Church, and adore the Lord our Lord who perfected your beauty, cry out to him with your children and say: glory to you.

Holy Qurbana/Eucharist

Eucharistic Adoration

Introduction

Holy, holy, holy are you, pure and spotless Lamb! Seraphim of light and angels above extoll this beloved Sacrifice. How can we stained sinners be worthy of the Body and Blood? Blessed are you from every mouth, and glory and exaltation to you. Amen.	*Qaddysh qaddysh qaddyshat, Pa-ra dakhya, wa-dla muma. Srapay nuhra, w-'yray rawma mzayḥyn l-hana diwḥa rhyma. Ḥnan ḥaṭṭaye, malyay kuthma aykan nispaq l-Paghrha wa-Dma. Brykhat Marya min kul puma. Lakh tishbuḥta, 'am rumrama. Amen.*

Meditation

- There, I feared greatly.
The heavenly and earthly assemblies stand in fear and joy when the Sacrifice is offered for the life of the world: with their wings extended over their eyes, lest they observe that fearful, incomprehensible Sight; and with their voices extolling, and their tongues crying out and saying: Holy, Holy, Holy are you, O Lord, because of this fearful Gift you have given us, in which we are absolved of our sins. Grant us, O Lord, in your mercy, and make us worthy in your grace, to give thanks to you for it, and to say: Glory to you!

- Tamman d-ḥil diḥiltha.
B-diḥiltha wab-ḥadhu-tha qaymyn kinshe kulhon da-shmayyane wdar'anaye ma dmith-qaraw diwḥa da-ḥlap ḥay-yaw d-'alma, w-kadh gip-payhon prysyn qdham 'ay-nayhon d-la nithba-qon b-ḥizwa dḥyla d-la midrekh, wab-qalayhon m-yab-wyn w-lisha-nayhon qa'en w-amryn: qaddysh, qaddysh, qadyshat Marya, 'al apay Maw-hawtha hadhe dḥylta d-yawt lan, d-nith-ḥase bah min ḥawbayn. Haw lan Mar, ba-ḥna-nakh, w-ashwa lan b-ṭaybuthakh, d-nawde lakh 'al appeh w-nemar shuḥa (heyya) lakh.

Silent Adoration

Qurbana/Eucharist

Ending

Priest: You have given them Bread from heaven.
People: Having all sweetness within it.

- Your throne, God, is forever.	*- Kursyakh Alaha l'alam 'almyn.*
Cherubim stand in fear and awe	L-kurs-ya d-ḥyla d-rabbuthakh
before your throne,	kruwwe kry-khyn leh Marya
O Mighty One,	wab di-ḥil-tha byadh gip-pay-hon
they hide their faces	b-zaw-'a m-kas-sen
with their wings,	par-ṣo-pay-hon. bad-la
lest they behold that fearful sight:	mish-k-ḥyn l-mit-la 'ay-nay-hon,
lest their eyes see your Divinity,	wal-miḥ-za nura,
the Fire that burns	hay d-Alahu-thakh,
bright unceasingly!	w-at d-hakhan-na shwyḥ-at,
And yet you, so glorious,	'amar at baw-nay-na-sha,
choose to dwell among mankind,	la l-maw-qa-dhu,
not that you may burn,	illa l-man-ha-ru,
but that you may shine.	rab-bay Mar mraḥ-ma-nuthakh
Great, O Lord, is your compassion,	w-ṭay-bu-thakh,
and your grace,	da-s'ert ṣedh ginsan,
for you have visited our race!	shuḥa lakh!

Benediction

Concluding Hymn

He who quakes the blazing angels	Haw d-nurane zay-'yn min-neh
with his countenance:	dan-ḥurun beh,
he is seen as Bread and Wine	b-laḥma w-ḥamra lehu ḥazet
upon the altar.	'al pa-tho-ra.
Lightning-vested angels burn	'ṭy-pay barqe, in ḥa-zen leh,
in glancing at him;	yaq-dhyn min-neh,
wretched dust is bold, unveiled,	w-'apra shy-ṭa gal-yan ap-paw
as it consumes him.	kadh a-khel leh.

Hymns for the Holy Qurbana/Eucharist

Let us, who have been called to delight
in the glorious and divine Mysteries,
give thanks and adore, in awe and love, the Lord of all,
and, in friendship and faith,
receive the Body of Christ the Son
who was sacrificed for our lives and absolved our sins,
and reconciled the Father to us
through the shedding of his Blood.
For he is extolled on the altar,
and on the right hand of the Father who sent him,
while still one and undivided, above and in the Church,
where daily he is sacrificed for our sins without suffering.
Come, let us approach in purity
the Sacrifice of the Body of him who makes all holy,
and cry out to him together and say: Glory to you!

✳✳✳

The heavenly and earthly assemblies stand in fear and joy
when the Sacrifice is offered for the life of the world:
with their wings extended over their eyes,
lest they observe that fearful, incomprehensible Sight;
and with their voices extolling,
and their tongues crying out and saying:
Holy, Holy, Holy are you, O Lord,
because of this fearful Gift you have given us,
in which we are absolved of our sins.
Grant us, O Lord, in your mercy,
and make us worthy in your grace,
to give thanks to you for it, and to say: Glory to you!

Qurbana/Eucharist

HAW D-NURANE
Attributed to Narsai

He who quakes the blazing angels with his countenance:
he is seen as Bread and Wine upon the altar.
Lightning-vested angels burn in glancing at him;
wretched dust is bold, unveiled, as it consumes him.

The Mysteries of Christ the Son are Fire in heaven,
and so Isaiah testifies who once beheld them.
The Mysteries which are and had been in the Godhead,
for Adam's sons are now divided on the paten.

The earthly altar here is like the throne of angels,
and all the ranks and hosts of heaven come surround it.
The Body of the Son of God is on the altar,
and Adam's sons come in procession now to hold it.

And here the priest is standing like a man in linen,
while giving pearls and gems of beauty to the needy.
If ever there was envy known among the angels,
the cherubim may envy men who take Communion.

Where once the Wood of crucifixion stood in Zion,
there now has grown the Tree producing Fruit Eternal.
Where once the nails were fastened in the hands of Jesus,
there too the binding ropes of Isaac who was offered.

O welcome now, O priest instructed by the Spirit,
who carries in his hand the keys to God's own dwelling!
O welcome now, O priest absolving man below here,
while God above himself absolves him! Halleluiah!

- **The princess stands in beauty.** – *l-ḥayye w-ṭuwwe*
Church, O betrothed of Jesus Christ
who saved you by his precious Blood;
gave you his Body (living Food
which wicked men had sacrificed),
who placed in your hands
his redeeming Cup
(his most precious Blood
that flowed from his side
when they stabbed him by the spear):
listen to the Bridegroom's voice:
repent, leave behind
vain wandering and sin.
Cry out to your Savior
with hymns of thanksgiving:
"Glory to you!"

- **The Memorial of your many graces.** – *ṣlywakh amlekh*
The Memorial of your Passion,
for our salvation perfected,
your Church performs, O Savior:
keep her children from danger.

- **Praise him in his holy place.** – *ha mzamnyton*
Look now at the holy of holies:
see the priest with bread and wine upon the altar.
He calls above, the Spirit comes.
He transforms the bread and wine to Life's Medicine.
Mortals come sinful and receive
forgiveness that destroys their sin,
and cry out: holy, holy, holy Giver of Life!

BLESSED VIRGIN MARY

- **Holy is the dwelling-place of the Most High.** – *baṣlotha dambarakhta*
By the blessed woman's pray'r,
may peace rule in all the world;
by the Virgin's petition,
the children of the Church be kept.
* The Power that came from above,
sanctified her for himself,
and she bore the one true Light,
Hope and Life for all the world,
be among us and in us,
all the days of all our lives;
heal the weary and the sick,
and those in temptation,
turn back all those who are lost
in far paths and journeys,
to the peace of their own homes,
lest they be harmed by evil.
* May those who pass through the sea
be protected from all storms;
may those who journey on land
be kept from dangerous men.
May those who are held captive
be freed from their bonds and chains;
may those who are led by force
be comforted by your grace.
May those who lead by evil
be rebuked by your great strength;
may those who walk in their sins
be forgiven by your grace.
May those who offer you Gifts
be the temples of your Life.
May those buried in your hope
be raised again by your grace.
* Let us, who take refuge in
the prayers of the Virgin,

Marian Hymns

Mary, blessed mother of
Jesus Christ the Savior,
be kept from the evil one
and cast down all of his schemes.
* On that great day when you come
to parse all the good from bad,
may we all rejoice with her
in your banquet up above:
and sing glory to your Love:
Father and Son and Spirit!

- **I will seek your graciousness.** – *ha mzamnyton*
Virgin mother of Christ, surround our paths:
waves and tempests circle us upon every side.
In the great trust you have with Christ,
plead, entreat him to deal with your sons in mercy:
may he grant healing to the sick, comfort to all of the weary,
quick return to those astray, to us, forgiveness.

- **Holy is the dwelling-place of the Most High.** – *bra miltha*
The Son-Word, the Virgin bore with great glory in her womb,
and was mother and handmaid to Jesus Christ, the Savior.
For this, all who dwell on earth celebrate her holy day
and call us to the feast of Light,
to joy which is unending. Thus every generation
gives her blessing constantly, and glory to the One
who chose her as his dwelling.

- **The mountains are covered by her wings.** – *kulnishma*
Mary, who bore Life's Balm for the sons of Adam:
by your prayer may we find mercy when he comes.

- **They say this among the nations.** – *mara dkulla*
Blest are you, holy virgin, blest are you, Christ's own mother,
blest are you, whom all ages and generations call blest!
Blest, you who pleased the Father, Blest, you who housed the Savior,
Blest, you whose name the Spirit made conquer in creation.

WAY OF THE CROSS
Containing Scripture Selections, Spiritual Reflections and Church of the East Liturgical Hymns

OPENING PRAYER

To you, O Awakener of the sleeping, O Raiser of the fallen, O Encourager of the weary, O Absolver of the sinful, O Great Refuge of the repentant, we entreat and plead: awaken, O Lord, our sleepiness in your mercy, shake off the heaviness of our sunkenness in your strength, and grant us, and make us worthy, to stand and serve before you purely and honorably, wakefully and diligently, O Wakeful One whom the wakeful serve with their halleluiahs, and the seraphim with their hallowings, the lowly with their hymns and the nations with their adorations, O Lord of all, Father, Son and Holy Spirit forever.
–From Night Prayer of the First Monday of Lent

FIRST STATION: JESUS IS CONDEMNED TO DEATH

Leader: We adore you, O Christ, and we praise you.
People: For by your holy Cross you have saved the world.

Scripture:
Pilate went out again, and said to them, "See, I am bringing him out to you, that you may know that I find no crime in him." So Jesus came out, wearing the crown of thorns and the purple robe. Pilate said to them, "Behold the man!" When the chief priests and the officers saw him, they cried out, "Crucify him, crucify him!"
–John 19:4–6

Reflection:
The sentence of death was the just punishment of Adam for his disobedience, O Lord, and it is what we deserve for all our sins. And yet, even when we were sinners you took our condemnation and punishment upon yourself. For this, may we thank you forever.

Liturgical Hymn:
The human race was condemned to the judgment of death and the curse, but Christ accepted and was crucified in his love, to free all from the curse; the Immeasurable Sea of Mercies gave himself over to his captors, his body tasted a temporal death, and he destroyed both death and the curse.

–From Evening Prayer of Passion Friday

Our Father...
Hail Mary...
Glory...

SECOND STATION: JESUS CARRIES HIS CROSS

Leader: We adore you, O Christ, and we praise you.
People: For by your holy Cross you have saved the world.

Scripture:
So they took Jesus, and he went out, bearing his own cross, to the place called the place of a skull, which is called in Hebrew Golgotha.

–John 19:17

Reflection:
Your Cross, O Lord, which was a stumbling-block to the Jews and a scandal to the Gentiles, is our greatest glory. To them it shows your weakness, but to us who watch you carry your Cross as you carry us, it shows your immense power and patience. For this, may we thank you forever.

Liturgical Hymn:
The rays of your Cross, O Lord, which were hidden from the malice of your crucifiers, have soared through all creation – to the ends of the world! Indeed, the priests you have chosen to honor you extol it in the Church, and it is made a sign for the faithful, to save them from the curse.

–From Evening Prayer of Passion Friday

Our Father...
Hail Mary...
Glory...

Third Station: Jesus Falls the First Time

Leader: We adore you, O Christ, and we praise you.
People: For by your holy Cross you have saved the world.

Scripture:
Though he was in the form of God, Jesus did not count equality with God a thing to be grasped, but emptied himself, taking the form of a servant, being born in the likeness of men. And being found in human form he humbled himself and became obedient unto death, even death on a cross.
—Philippians 2:6–8

Reflection:
While the world fights for ambition and honor, O Lord, you chose to leave your glory in heaven and take the form of a servant. As you bowed down in inconceivable humility to wash the feet of your disciples, you fell to the earth under the weight of our sins to wash our souls from all evil. For this, may we thank you forever.

Liturgical Hymn:
Who is able to tell of your grace, O Lover of Mankind, who pities all? For you have given us spiritual figures in your glorious and holy Mysteries: you taught us true humility in your works, for you lowered yourself like a servant, and washed the feet of your disciples.
—From Evening Prayer of Passion Friday

Our Father...
Hail Mary...
Glory...

Fourth Station: Jesus Meets His Suffering Mother

Leader: We adore you, O Christ, and we praise you.
People: For by your holy Cross you have saved the world.

Scripture:
Is it nothing to you, all you who pass by? Look and see if there is any sorrow like my sorrow which was brought upon me.
–Lamentations 1:12

Reflection:
As we face loss and hardship in our lives, O Lord, let us always remember the example of your Virgin Mother as she beheld you, her life, suffering so deeply, and had to let you go, in acceptance of God's will. As you gave her the beloved disciple as his mother, give her also to us, that we may face our troubles with grace and acceptance through her prayers. For her, may we thank you forever.

Liturgical Hymn:
O Virgin Mother of Christ, surround our thoughts, for waves and storms surround us from every side. In the confidence you have before Christ, plead and implore him, that he may accomplish his mercies toward us. May he bestow health upon the sick, refreshment upon the weary, return upon those who are distant, and upon us, the forgiveness of sins.
–Marian Hymn traditionally said after Evening Prayer

Our Father...
Hail Mary...
Glory...

Way of the Cross
FIFTH STATION: SIMON HELPS JESUS CARRY HIS CROSS

Leader: We adore you, O Christ, and we praise you.
People: For by your holy Cross you have saved the world.

Scripture:
And they compelled a passer-by, Simon of Cyrene, who was coming in from the country, the father of Alexander and Rufus, to carry his cross.
—Mark 15:21

Reflection:
Unbelievers describe a meaningless, uncaring universe, where even human joys are empty at their root, and sufferings are entirely pointless. You have shown us, O Lord, that everything in creation is, to the eyes of faith, saturated with meaning, even our suffering, when we unite it to yours. Grant us grace to carry our crosses, and see them as your instruments of our sanctification. For this, may we thank you forever.

Liturgical Hymn:
O Good Shepherd who gave himself for his flock and saved it by his Blood: make us worthy to share in your suffering, and accept you in your kingdom.
—From the Third *Mawtwa* of Passion Friday

Our Father...
Hail Mary...
Glory...

Way of the Cross

Sixth Station: Veronica Wipes the Face of Jesus

Leader: We adore you, O Christ, and we praise you.
People: For by your holy Cross you have saved the world.

Scripture:
He was despised and rejected by men; a man of sorrows, and acquainted with grief; and as one from whom men hide their faces he was despised, and we esteemed him not. Surely he has borne our griefs and carried our sorrows;
—Isaiah 53:3–4

Reflection:
God created Adam in his image, to reflect his providential care throughout the whole world. But through sin, Adam's brightness was darkened and his face, modeled after the Creator himself, was corrupted. Your Face, O Savior, which was wiped clean by Veronica, replaced and renewed the damaged face of Adam, when you became the new Head of the renewed human race. For this, may we thank you forever.

Liturgical Hymn:
O Christ the Son who came for our salvation, to renew the image of Adam that had been corrupted, who took on our body, and through it saved our race, giving resilience for the resurrection of the dead: forgive your servants in your grace on the day of your coming!
—From Sunday Evening Prayer

Our Father...
Hail Mary...
Glory...

Way of the Cross

SEVENTH STATION: JESUS FALLS A SECOND TIME

Leader: We adore you, O Christ, and we praise you.
People: For by your holy Cross you have saved the world.

Scripture:
Surely he has borne our griefs and carried our sorrows; yet we esteemed him stricken, smitten by God, and afflicted. But he was wounded for our transgressions, he was bruised for our iniquities; upon him was the chastisement that made us whole, and with his stripes we are healed.

–Isaiah 53:4–5

Reflection:
How patient you are, O Lord, though you deserve nothing of what you endured, and how impatient are we, who deserve so much more than your mercy allows to touch us! Teach us to patiently endure our sufferings, the imperfections of others in our lives, and even ourselves. Let us never give up hope, though we fall a thousand times. For this, may we thank you forever.

Liturgical Hymn:
Who is patient enough to speak of your patience with our sins? If we sin, we become filled with wickedness, if we do good, we become filled with pride; and toward one another, we are cruel and merciless: we are jealous of one who succeeds, we rejoice over one who falls. And though our life is short, the list of our sins is long.

–From Monday of *Ba'utha*

Our Father...
Hail Mary...
Glory...

Way of the Cross
Eighth Station: Jesus Speaks to the Women

Leader: We adore you, O Christ, and we praise you.
People: For by your holy Cross you have saved the world.

Scripture:
And there followed him a great multitude of the people, and of women who bewailed and lamented him. But Jesus turning to them said, "Daughters of Jerusalem, do not weep for me, but weep for yourselves and for your children.
–Luke 23:27–28

Reflection:
We are insulted when those who have hurt us are not sorry enough, O Lord, for we expect their repentance to be from the heart; and yet how easy it is for us to presume upon your kindness and feel so little sorrow for our sins! What a meager repentance after such a weighty offence! Teach us to weep tears of true repentance in your grace, that through their sincerity we may be washed and see the joy of heaven. For this, may we thank you forever.

Liturgical Hymn:
Who will give me a fountain of many tears and modest thoughts, that I may erase my sins and faults through repentance? I am in need of your mercies, O Good and Kind One, but because you love the repentant, I do not give up hope in my life, O Lord.
–From Night Prayer of the First Monday of Lent

<blockquote>
Our Father...
Hail Mary...
Glory...
</blockquote>

NINTH STATION: JESUS FALLS THE THIRD TIME

Leader: We adore you, O Christ, and we praise you.
People: For by your holy Cross you have saved the world.

Scripture:
Upon him was the chastisement that made us whole, and with his stripes we are healed. All we like sheep have gone astray; we have turned every one to his own way; and the Lord has laid on him the iniquity of us all.

–Isaiah 53:5–6

Reflection:
O Kind Doctor who was wounded in order to heal us, save us from our pride, in which we convince ourselves that we need no Healer. As you fell the third time, you showed us the depths of the weakness of the human race, and so remind us also to turn to you in our lowest moments for healing, after every one of our falls. For this, may we thank you forever.

Liturgical Hymn:
Our wretched race is weak, and oppressed by wounds and sicknesses; and if the medicine of your mercy does not heal our wounds, our life would immediately vanish and pass away from the earth. Be, O Lord, a Doctor for our wounds.

–From *Shuḥlapa* 5 of *Qala* 20

Our Father…
Hail Mary…
Glory…

Way of the Cross

Tenth Station: Jesus is Stripped of His Garments

Leader: We adore you, O Christ, and we praise you.
People: For by your holy Cross you have saved the world.

Scripture:
When the soldiers had crucified Jesus they took his garments and made four parts, one for each soldier; also his tunic. But the tunic was without seam, woven from top to bottom; so they said to one another, "Let us not tear it, but cast lots for it to see whose it shall be." This was to fulfill the scripture, "They parted my garments among them, and for my clothing they cast lots."

–John 19:23–24

Reflection:
You were humiliated, O Lord, in order to make up for Adam who was ashamed before his Creator. Help us to be ashamed of our sins, but humble enough to stand before God with unveiled faces. For this, may we thank you forever.

Liturgical Hymn:
When you were hanging on the Cross, O Christ, creation saw you naked and trembled: heaven darkened the light of the glorious lamp of the sun, the temple showed its lamentation in the torn veil, and earth quaked as well, for it saw the insolence of the crucifiers. Even the sleeping, in a great marvel, were awakened and arose from their graves, lifting up praise to your great power, O Lord!

–From Evening Prayer of Holy Saturday

Our Father...
Hail Mary...
Glory...

Eleventh Station: Jesus is Nailed to the Cross

Leader: We adore you, O Christ, and we praise you.
People: For by your holy Cross you have saved the world.

Scripture:
And they crucified him, and divided his garments among them, casting lots for them, to decide what each should take. And it was the third hour, when they crucified him.
—Mark 15:24–25

Reflection:
Because Adam disobeyed, he was found unworthy to eat the fruit of the tree of life in Paradise. Through your sacrifice, O Lord, your Cross became the true Tree of Life, and you the Fruit which one eats and never dies. By the obedience of Faith, let us be made worthy to receive you into our hearts and lives, and live in you eternally. For this, may we thank you forever.

Liturgical Hymn:
The holy cross is like the Tree of Life in the Church, whose fruits are good for eating, and whose leaves are fit for healing.
—From Evening Prayer of the Feast of the Holy Cross

Our Father...
Hail Mary...
Glory...

Twelfth Station: Jesus Dies on the Cross

Leader: We adore you, O Christ, and we praise you.
People: For by your holy Cross you have saved the world.

Scripture:
And Jesus cried again with a loud voice and yielded up his spirit.
—Matthew 27:50

Reflection:
In the nature you have created, O Lord, there is nothing more precious to a creature than his life. And yet this is exactly what you gave up for us. You accepted death – mankind's most terrifying threat – and in doing so you gave mankind life, and life to the fullest. Make every moment of our lives full of meaning and grace by uniting them at all times to the power of your death. For this, may we thank you forever.

Liturgical Hymn:
In your love, O Lord, you were brought low, and became a sacrifice on behalf of our race: your Body tasted a temporal death and your flock was bought with your Blood. Heaven and earth, who saw your disgrace, wore garments of mourning, for you were mocked with the thieves. Blessed is he whose death has given life to all!
—From Night Prayer of Passion Friday

Our Father...
Hail Mary...
Glory...

Way of the Cross

THIRTEENTH STATION: JESUS IS TAKEN DOWN FROM THE CROSS

Leader: We adore you, O Christ, and we praise you.
People: For by your holy Cross you have saved the world.

Scripture:
Joseph of Arimathea went to Pilate and asked for the body of Jesus. Then he took it down and wrapped it in a linen shroud, and laid him in a rock-hewn tomb, where no one had ever yet been laid.

–Luke 24:52–53

Reflection:
The care, O Lord, with which your Body was taken down from the Cross shows us the reverence due to your sacramental Body, the holy Eucharist. Let us always remember the power of your Presence among us, and reverence your Body and Blood at all times. For this, may we thank you forever.

Liturgical Hymn:
Come, let us give thanks to Christ, whose revelation has freed us from error and who has reconciled us to his Father by the oblation of his body, who pacified the exalted beings who were angered because of our sin. To him be glory with his Sender!

–From Night Prayer of the First Monday of Lent

Our Father...
Hail Mary...
Glory...

Fourteenth Station: Jesus is Laid in the Tomb

Leader: We adore you, O Christ, and we praise you.
People: For by your holy Cross you have saved the world.

Scripture:
Joseph of Arimathea bought a linen shroud, and taking him down, wrapped him in the linen shroud, and laid him in a tomb which had been hewn out of the rock; and he rolled a stone against the door of the tomb.

–Mark 15:46

Reflection:
You taught us, O Lord, that unless a seed falls to the ground and dies, it will never become a living plant. This is the price you paid in order to open the gates of heaven for mankind. Grant us the grace to die to ourselves and rise in you. For this, may we thank you forever.

Liturgical Hymn:
The garden of Joseph of Arimathea has become Paradise, for Christ was placed in it. The spiritual descended, and the legions of the watchers and seraphim, to visit the tomb of our Lord. Glory to you, O Lord! Glory to you, O Son of God! Blessed is he who has gladdened us by his resurrection!

–From Night Prayer of Easter

Our Father...
Hail Mary...
Glory...

Closing Prayer

Blessed is he who saved Adam from death by his passion and cross, who fulfilled all the symbols that prepared the way for him by his sacrifice: the lamb sacrificed in Egypt which saved the people and the serpent that Moses lifted up that saved Israel from the poison of the deadly snakes. How much more does the power of the Cross destroy the poison of the deceiver and save the Church from slavery to sin and death. To Jesus, who saved us by his death, be glory and blessing, forever and ever. Amen.

–From Night Prayer of Holy Saturday

ORDERING OF THE MONTH OR YEAR

mara d-kulla
* Order the month and bless the crown of the year in your grace,
and grant a bless-ed future of joyfulness and mercy.
May our pleading come to you, O Lord of months and of years:
our prayer, your creation's key, unlocks the door of mercy.

* May you bless this year, O Lord; harmoniously crown it;
protect it from all terror, and all fear and disturbance.
May the next year come gladly, and go to you as off'ring,
like Elijah and Moses, whose prayer is our fortress.

* You are Mercy Eternal, and Compassion of Ages;
what is creation's malice before your flowing graces?
Sprinkle the dew of mercy upon the face of our race;
redeem us from the evil one and from the weeds of sinners.

* May Adam and all the just, and Moses with the prophets,
Peter and the apostles, Stephen and all the martyrs,
Ephrem and all the teachers, Anthony and the hermits,
plead unto you, Lord Jesus, to grant mercy to the world.

* May the deceased clothed in you, in the water of bap-tism,
be cleansed in soul and body from all the stains of their sins.
May the dead who received you in your Body and your Blood
all be recalled in the land in which the just are dwelling.

NOVENA
of prayers attributed to Mar Abba the Great
Patriarch of the Church of the East, 540–52 AD

Opening Prayer – Every Day of Novena
Hearken, Lord, to the words of our prayers, incline your ear to the sound of our supplication, and do not turn your face from the voice of our pleading; grant us *(state your intentions)*, O Kind One upon whom our confidence rests at all times and ages, Lord of all, Father, Son and Holy Spirit forever.

Day 1 – For Wisdom
Sow, O Lord, the good seed of your teaching within our heart, and let drops of your grace rain upon us, that we may grow according to your will, and bear fruits pleasing to your Majesty all the days of our lives, Lord of all, Father, Son and Holy Spirit forever.

Day 2 – For Hope
Establish your hope, O Lord, within us, fill our souls with your assistance, let your grace absolve our sins, and may the eternal mercies of your glorious Trinity come to the aid of your adorers who call and plead to you at all times and ages, Lord of all, Father, Son and Holy Spirit forever.

Day 3 – For Confidence
To you our Hope and Confidence, our Helper and Upholder, O great Fortress to our weakness, we plead: turn to us, O Lord, pardon us and have mercy on us, as you always do, Lord of all, Father, Son and Holy Spirit forever.

Day 4 – For Piety
To you, O Rich in his love, Overflowing in his pity, Kind in his grace, Indescribable in his radiance; O great King of glory, O Being who exists from eternity, do we give thanks, adore and glorify at all times, Lord of all, Father, Son and Holy Spirit forever.

Day 5 – For Forgiveness
Have mercy on us, O Lord our God, and absolve, wipe away and remove our faults through the overflowing mercies of your grace, O Compassionate One and Forgiver of debts and sins, Lord of all, Father, Son and Holy Spirit forever.

Day 6 – For Protection against Satan

Deliver us, O Lord our God, from the deceits and wiles of the enemy, the rebel, with your great and mighty power and your exalted and invincible arm, O Kind One upon whom our confidence rests at all times and ages, Lord of all, Father, Son and Holy Spirit forever.

Day 7 – For Fear of God

To you who sit upon a chariot of cherubim, is extolled by legions of angels, whose order shakes the land and whose command terrifies the earth, it is our duty to confess, adore and glorify at all times, Lord of all, Father, Son and Holy Spirit forever.

Day 8 – For Strength

O Pitier of the faults of sinners in his great patience, pity, O Lord our God, the feebleness, the corruption and the concupiscence of our miserable race, O Compassionate One and Forgiver of debts and sins, Lord of all, Father, Son and Holy Spirit forever.

Day 9 – For Wonder

O Being without beginning or end, Hidden and Incomprehensible Nature, Eternal One without limitation, Creator, Maker and Provider for all, it is our duty to thank, adore and glorify you at all times, Lord of all, Father, Son and Holy Spirit forever.

Qaddysha Alaha – Every Day of Novena

Holy God, Holy Mighty One, Holy Immortal One: Have mercy on us.

Final Prayer – Every Day of Novena

We hope in you, O Lord, are confident in your mercies and plead to your grace: be an Aid in our weakness, a Fortress in our tribulation, a Sustainer in our neediness, a Gatherer in our dispersion, a Savior in our misery, an Absolver in our sinfulness, and do not turn your face away from the sound of our pleading, O Kind One in whom our confidence rests at all times and ages, Lord of all, Father, Son and Holy Spirit forever.

Various Blessings

House Blessings

* By your great grace, bless and protect, O merciful Lord,
this place and those who live here from demons and evil men.
Grant increase in all good things, love, and peace, and harmony,
and good health of body and soul.
* Cast Satan out, the enemy of all righteousness,
from the houses where we live; let him never enter them.
Firmly place their foundation on the rock of faithfulness,
and grant life eternal to us.

* May this house be blessed by the Trinity, in which the righteous faithful and the fathers of old were blessed, and may it remain blessed, now and forever. Protect, O Lord, those who live in it from all perils and distresses. May it overflow with blessings like the house of Abraham, and increase and abound in benefits like the house of Job the just. May it be upheld through the prayers of the holy virgin Mary, now and forever.

Meal Blessings

Before the Meal:
May the meal of your adorers be blessed by the right hand of your majesty and the word of your grace: Father, Son, and Holy Spirit.

Another:
Extend, O Lord our God, the right hand of your compassion from your holy heaven, and bless this meal of your adorers. Let it abound with benefits and blessings through the adorable name of your glorious Trinity: Father, Son and Holy Spirit, forever.

After the Meal:
You have fed us, O Lord, by your grace, and filled us by your compassion, that we may lift up an unceasing perpetual praise to your glorious Trinity. Glory to him who feeds all in his grace and mercies, forever!

Various Blessings

Prayers for Study

Before: Sow, O Lord, the good seed of your teaching within our heart and let drops of your grace rain upon us, that we may grow according to your will and bear fruits pleasing to your Majesty all the days of our lives, Lord of all, Father, Son and Holy Spirit forever.

After: It is the duty, O Lord, of heaven, earth and all therein to thank, adore and glorify you for all of your benefits and graces whose greatness cannot be repaid, O Lord of all, Father, Son and Holy Spirit, forever.

Prayers for Safe Travel

* Your grace protect us on our path, as so to David, the young man, from Saul. Grant what we need for our sojourn, that we may arrive in peace, as you will.

- Protect us from the malice of the evil one.
Under the wings of your prayers, Virgin Mary, we take shelter. May they guard us now and at all times, in them may we find pity on judgment day.

- They walked from land unto land.
You may move from land to land, but you will not leave your Lord: you bring the Treasure of Life to each land you enter in.

Prayers for Protection

* Arm us, O Lord our God, with a mighty and invincible armor, by the prayers of your blessed mother, the blessed St. Mary, and grant us part and portion with her in the heavenly banquet, Lord of all, forever.

* Be a guardian that never sleeps and a surrounding wall in which your flock may dwell, that they may not be harmed by the wolves that thirst for the blood of your sheep, for you are the sea that never fails, O Lord of all, Father, Son and Holy Spirit, forever.

* Protect us, O Lord, with your right hand, and shelter us under your wings, and let your aid accompany us, all the days of our life, O Lord of all, Father, Son and Holy Spirit, forever.

Various Blessings

Prayers for Healing

* Hear, O Lord our God, the prayer of your servants in your mercy; accept the supplication of your adorers in your compassion, and pity our sinfulness in your grace and mercies, O Healer of our bodies and Good Hope of our souls at all times O Lord of all, Father, Son and Holy Spirit, forever.

* O Giver of Life in his mercy, Upholder of all by his will, O Banisher of all wounds and diseases in his compassion: heal this servant of yours, O Lord, in your mercy, and rouse him from his illness in the greatness of your grace, that he may give thanks to you for your salvation, now, at all times, and forever and ever.

* In your name, O Good Father, in the name of the Only-Begotten, our Lord Jesus Christ, and in the name of the holy and living Holy Spirit, I banish the fever from your servant *(name)*, child of *(mother's name)*. And I cut you off, O stubborn fever, by that Power that called out to Simon's mother in law who was seized with a fever and who arose, was healed, and began serving our Lord. Even now, Lord God almighty, strengthen the knees of this servant of yours *(name)*, child of *(mother's name)*, and let him arise and be healed of this malady, by your Power. O God of gods and Lord of lords, heal and restore this servant of yours, by the prayer of the Blessed Virgin Mary, the mother of Light, and all the saints of the Lord, now, at all times, and forever and ever.

* O Healer of all diseases and Binder of all wounds: heal, O Lord, this servant of yours from the attack of the enemy. As your grace banished Legion from the man who lived among the tombs, and cast him out into the sea, giving your servant relief, so now, O Lord, may your Power banish him and your Will uproot him from this servant of yours, that he may be a dwelling-place for you, be signed with the living sign of the cross, take up your delightful yoke, and be joined to your flock, O merciful Maker: Father, Son and Holy Spirit, forever.

Various Blessings

OTHER BLESSINGS

* May your servants be blessed through your blessing, O Lord our God, may your adorers be protected through the providence of your will, and may the constant serenity of your Divinity, O Lord, and the persistent peace of your Majesty rule among your people and your Church, all the days of the age, O Lord of all, Father, Son and Holy Spirit, forever.

* May the blessing of the One who blesses all, the peace of the One who gives peace to all, and the protection of our adorable God be with us, among us and around us, and protect us from the evil one and his hosts, at all times and ages, O Lord of all, Father, Son and Holy Spirit, forever.

* Through your blessing, O Lord our God, may we be blessed, and in your providence may we be protected. May your power come to our assistance, and your aid accompany us. May your right hand rest upon us and your peace rule among us. May your cross be a great fortress and stronghold for us, and under its wings may we be sheltered from the evil one and his hosts, at all times and ages, O Lord of all, Father, Son and Holy Spirit, forever.

* Blessed, O Lord, are the mercies of your Grace, and adorable are the promises of your Majesty, which teach us to look to you at all times and glory in you. May our hope in you not be cut off, all the days of our life, O Lord of all, Father, Son and Holy Spirit, forever.

* May your blessing, O Lord our God, rest upon your people, and may your mercy be upon us weak sinners constantly, our Good Hope and our Refuge full of mercies, and the Absolver of our sins and faults, O Lord of all, Father, Son and Holy Spirit, forever.

* May the peace of the Father be with us, the love of the Son be among us, and may the Holy Spirit guide us according to his will. Upon us be his mercies and compassion at all times and ages, O Lord of all, Father, Son and Holy Spirit, forever.

* May your peace, O Lord, dwell within us, your serenity rule among us, and your love increase between us, all the days of our life, O Lord of all, Father, Son and Holy Spirit, forever.

Devotional Prayers

When Venerating a Cross:
May the power hidden in the cross grant me strength and courage against the devil, the enemy, by the mercies of our kind God.

When Venerating the Gospel:
May the power hidden in the Gospel, which is filled with life and grace, fill my mind with wisdom to know the meaning of the Word.

When Venerating the Shrine of a Saint:
May our Lord and God let us share in your excellence, O holy patron, and make us worthy for mercies and pity by your prayers.

A Prayer for Comfort:
O Comforter of the mourning, Gladdener of the sorrowful, Encourager of the weary by his true and undeceiving hope, we plead to you: let the sorrow of your servants pass in your pity, and dry the tears from their faces in your grace and mercies, O Lord of all: Father, Son and Holy Spirit, forever.

An Act of Humility:
You know best, O Lord, how I should call to you, for I am a beast and know nothing, and you brought me to the summit of this life. Save me because of your mercies; I am your servant and the child of your handmaid. O Lord, give me life by your Will.

An Act of Trust:
O Lord, what you know, what you wish, what you please, whatever will help my deficiency, my feebleness, and my misery, send to me, for yours are mercies, pity and grace, forever.

FUNERAL RITE HYMNS

Entrance Hymns – *talmydhaw*

- Give thanks to him and bless his Name.
Give thanks, O mortals, to the Son who saved
us from slavery to death,
which had strangled us in sin,
for he went down into Sheol
and raised the dead from the grave.
Who can repay the grace of God
granted to the race of all mortal men?
- My mouth will wisdom speak.
Take refuge in repentance, sinful ones,
for the time is so short:
this world blooms and dies away!
There will be, for the repentant, joy,
death for the unjustified.
For if you judged justly, O Lord,
who on earth would be without any fault?
- Do not depend on power or mankind.
Do not de-pend on riches or on strength,
for they do not save you
from death or eternal fire.
Place your trust upon our God,
in whose hands are death and life,
and he will save you from the dark
which awaits all those who do evil deeds.
- A brother does not save.
Do not pursue the pleasures of this life,
for they flee like shadows,
and you lose eternal life.
What would any of us gain,
if he were to gain the world,
but lose his soul in Gehanna,
whose fire never fades,
and which never ends.

- They leave what they have to others.
As long as we are in this passing world,
the door of repentance
and forgiveness is open.
Let us pacify Justice
by transforming all our sins,
and escape from the just judgment,
whose measure is sharp,
and whose pain is harsh.
- Rich and poor together.
Let us please Christ the King through our good works,
who sees our intentions,
and brings all our thoughts to light,
lest he see us drowned by the
weakness of our temptations,
and say that "I do not know you;
go, depart from me, workers of evil."
- Save your people, and the sheep of your flock.
We implore you, O Christ the King of kings,
that you may forget the
faults of all who have received
your Flesh and your Blood, and may you stand
for them on the day they rise,
that they be saved from Gehenna
and meet you in praise, with the hosts above!

Funeral Rite Hymns

Recessional Hymns – *push bashlama*

- **From now *and* unto an age.**
Farewell to my temporal dwelling,
which cannot save those within it.
I go to the land of glory,
where the faithful and the just live.
- **May the blessing of *the* Lord be upon you.**
Farewell, my friends and relations,
may the Lord repay your kindness.
When you stand before the altar,
please remember me in prayer.
- **Which does *not* have salvation.**
Farewell to the world which passes,
whose wealth ends, and whose glory fades.
I go to the city of kings,
the Jerusalem in heaven.
- **I will bless *the* Lord at all times.**
Blest your day, Son of the Mighty,
which tears open the womb of Sheol!
Glorious is your day of raising,
which all ages await with longing.
- **They will pass, *but* you will remain.**
Lo, this world is passing quickly,
and its pleasures are all empty!
Blest is he who made provision
for the world that lasts forever.
- **I sought, *but* I did not find.**
Lo, I see this world is drowning
in the evils that surround it.
May your living cross protect me,
and bring me to peaceful harbor.
- **The hope of all *the* ends of the earth.**
No hope do we have to boast in
save your cross, O our Absolver,

for it is our mighty fortress,
and it saves us from all peril.
- **In the morning,** *let* **me hear your voice.**
Lord, in mercy, let your servants
hear your voice which gave them comfort.
Say to them the word that you spoke:
"O sinners, your debts are absolved."
- **How good** *and* **lovely it is.**
May we all now hear the word which
comes unto us from the Preacher:
"O sons of men, rise, awaken:
may you repent of all your sins."
- **Praise him** *with* **the sound of trumpet.**
With the sound of horn and trumpet,
all the dead and buried will rise,
and give praise to Father and Son,
and the Holy Spirit, one God.
- **He lifts his** *voice* **and shakes the earth.**
Like the voice which called Lazarus,
and awakened him from the tomb,
may your voice eradicate death,
and raise us up from our decay.
- **Brightness** *and* **glory before him.**
On the day you come, Lord Jesus,
you will raise the dead in glory.
All the just will stand before you;
we pray that we may be with them.

A Biblical Form for Confession

Begin by praying:

> My heavenly Father,
> I have sinned before you,
> and am no longer worthy
> to be called your child.

Say to the priest:

> And to you, my spiritual guide,
> I confess my sins...

Say your sins. The priest will counsel you and give you a penance.

Pray an Act of Contrition:

> O God, have mercy on me, a sinner.

The priest will absolve you in the name of the Father, Son and Holy Spirit.

Various Acts of Contrition

* O God, have mercy on me, a sinner.

* Like the prodigal son I implore you, O Lord: I have sinned against heaven and before you, and I am not worthy to be called your child. Pity me in your grace, and have mercy on me.

* I confess my sins, and the offences I have done before you, my God, and I beg to be made worthy for forgiveness, and to be able to awaken with the strength to do all you command, lest death surprise me like a thief and find me in the deep sleep of carelessness.

* Mary of Bethany appeased you by her tears, and you forgave her sins. Look upon my tears, O Savior, and in your grace, have mercy on my wretched soul.